LAW, LIFE, AND THE TEACHING OF LEGAL HISTORY

Blaine Baker. Photo by Claudio Calligaris.

Law, Life, and the Teaching of Legal History

Essays in Honour of G. Blaine Baker

EDITED BY IAN C. PILARCZYK,
ANGELA FERNANDEZ, AND BRIAN YOUNG

McGill-Queen's University Press
Montreal & Kingston • London • Chicago

ISBN 978-0-2280-1206-1 (cloth)
ISBN 978-0-2280-1207-8 (paper)
ISBN 978-0-2280-1225-2 (ePDF)
ISBN 978-0-2280-1226-9 (ePUB)

Legal deposit third quarter 2022
Bibliothèque nationale du Québec

Printed in Canada on acid-free paper that is 100% ancient forest free (100% post-consumer recycled), processed chlorine free

This book has been published with the help of a grant from the Canadian Federation for the Humanities and Social Sciences, through the Awards to Scholarly Publications Program, using funds provided by the Social Sciences and Humanities Research Council of Canada. Funding was also received from the Fern Gertrude Kennedy Fund and the Law '63 Fund of the Faculty of Law, McGill University.

Funded by the Government of Canada | Financé par le gouvernement du Canada | Canada

Canada Council for the Arts | Conseil des arts du Canada

We acknowledge the support of the Canada Council for the Arts.
Nous remercions le Conseil des arts du Canada de son soutien.

Library and Archives Canada Cataloguing in Publication

Title: Law, life, and the teaching of legal history : essays in honour of G. Blaine Baker / edited by Ian C. Pilarczyk, Angela Fernandez, and Brian Young.
Names: Pilarczyk, Ian C., 1969– editor. | Fernandez, Angela, 1973– editor. | Young, Brian J., 1940– editor. | Baker, G. Blaine, honouree.
Description: Includes bibliographical references and index.
Identifiers: Canadiana (print) 20220179530 | Canadiana (ebook) 20220179778 | ISBN 9780228012061 (hardcover) | ISBN 9780228012078 (softcover) | ISBN 9780228012252 (PDF) | ISBN 9780228012269 (ePUB)
Subjects: LCSH: Baker, G. Blaine. | LCSH: Law—History—Study and teaching Canada. | LCSH: Law—Canada—History. | LCGFT: Festschriften.
Classification: LCC KE290.L39 2022 | LCC KF273.L39 2022 kfmod | DDC 340.071/0971—dc23

This book was typeset in 10.5/13 Sabon.

Contents

Tables and Figures

TABLES

FIGURES

Figure 0.1 | Blaine Baker in his office, ca. 1990.

FOREWORD

Blaine Baker's Quebec

Nicholas Kasirer

Others in this volume have written compellingly about the rich tracings and occasionally tangled strands – that elegant web – of Blaine Baker's own history as a teacher and scholar of Canadian law. As a sometime student and colleague of Professor Baker, and as one of the many held in his thrall over the years, I would like to record a theme in his intellectual life that, I think, runs through many of the essays in this fine book and yet one that is not always as plainly feted as it should be.

While his embrace of this province might have seemed, from a distance, to be a hesitant one, Blaine Baker was a Quebec law teacher for over thirty years. His identity as a Quebec academic figure rested on twin pillars: a deep attachment to McGill University's Faculty of Law which, it must be said, returned that favour; and a sense that some of his own values were reflected in a proper understanding of nineteenth-century Quebec legal history. All this grounded a place for Professor Baker in Quebec law teaching and scholarship, even if many of those working elsewhere in the province on law and history may have been unaware of the extent of his contributions. By way of modest thanks to him and to the editors for the privilege of writing this foreword, I would like to recall an underestimated but not inconsequential aspect of Blaine Baker's intellectual and social life in the law by pointing to these twin Quebec pillars and the measure of stability they brought to his work.

MCGILL AS A HOME FOR BLAINE BAKER'S "PRINCIPLED ECLECTICISM" IN LAW

We know that Blaine Baker was hired at McGill in 1981, a seemingly surprising endpoint on a winding road that led from Muskoka and Mississauga, past Western Ontario, through Columbia and University of Chicago law schools, to Montreal. He was recruited by Dean John Brierley – anxious to shore up the Faculty's common law curriculum – ostensibly to teach Contracts. Soon Professor Baker would add what he called "The Administrative Process," as well as a humanities offering in Canadian legal history, with a course outline slowly crafted and carefully shopped around the country.

Blaine Baker's early teaching would prove to be profoundly uncharacteristic for Old McGill. In Blaine's hands, Contracts became participative or facilitative law – his main concern in the classroom was not the finery of offer and acceptance, much less the *Draft Civil Code of Québec* that dominated teaching in Obligations elsewhere in New Chancellor Day Hall, but fixed instead on the choices made by those in power to let ordinary people craft legal relations for themselves.[1] Far from the local État providence, he taught administrative law at arm's length from judicial review of administrative action that, in an ancient tradition, had been the mainstay of McGill public law since Maurice Duplessis.[2] Canadian Legal History was concerned as much with historiography and Hurst as with the heroics of hometown judges and lawmakers or with the nagging question whether Quebec civil law was, from the perspective of its formal sources, a mixed legal system.[3] In the early days, no doubt to satisfy institutional need, he taught other subjects, including a free-wheeling course in Jurisprudence. For a time, he offered an innovative version of Intellectual Property that was designed to show the state's tolerance of human creativity more than present a guide for students through the opaque statutory schemes of the day.

Generally, his tenured colleagues expressed a mix of genteel surprise and studied disinterest at all of this. The originality of what Professor Baker undertook in the classroom seemed out of step with the concerns of the expatriate common law teachers who had elected McGill and Quebec as a juridical home. For the civilians, with the possible exceptions of the dean and the energetic associate dean Rod Macdonald who would later succeed him, Baker's sociological jurisprudence appeared largely irrelevant to Quebec law. With this apparently dissonant approach to teaching and scant attention to local knowledge, what explained Professor Baker's immediate taking to McGill and McGill's taking to him?

Baker's arrival in Montreal coincided with a low ebb in the fortunes of the Faculty of Law. Quebec's economy was weakened through the 1970s; the referendum of 1980 had made McGill a less obvious destination to study law, even for English-speaking Quebeckers. Organizationally committed to teaching the common law and the civil law in two separate streams, McGill continued to bet the house on its flagship National Programme, even if many out-of-province students came with little French, little curiosity for the civil law, and very often left town with just one degree.[4] The manner and form of the common law taught at McGill in the early 1980s had no hint of the Peel Street location; it mirrored, almost to the case, the commonwealth curriculum received and digested by the Ontario courts and taught in lockstep, with the same materials, in many law schools in Canada. A sizeable number of Quebec students saw McGill's double degree as little more than a delayed ticket to practise on Bay Street or similarly secure points further west. Intellectually, the flagship seemed rudderless at times as the curriculum provided no coordinated teaching of the common law and the civil law and showed no inclination to acknowledge, let alone explore, other legal traditions. Staff recruitment at McGill was condemned – or at least that was the conventional institutional wisdom – to hiring law teachers separately from the two academic solitudes to teach the massive number of required and semi-required courses needed to support the LLB and BCL degrees. The Faculty continued to have particular trouble in finding full-time academics with a scholarly bent to teach the basic common law courses upon which the financial and intellectual value of McGill law project was dependent. Rightly or wrongly, Montreal was sometimes perceived as a juridical exile for an ambitious young person anxious to make a mark in the emergent Anglo-American community of full-time law teachers.[5]

That said, Professor Baker earned an immediate place in the sun at the Faculty. This came from public and private flashes of brilliance and erudition, whether in the classroom, at Faculty Council or the Faculty Club. It resulted from hours of commitment he generously contributed, in formal and informal roles, to institutional governance. It reflected, too, the rewards that came of mentoring the segment of the student body he felt to be his own. McGill quietly made room for Baker's intellectual project, grounded ethically, if not theologically, in teaching all manner of legal subjects as a sort of public virtue. His classes voiced an understanding of law resting on civic responsibility rather than individual rights, and gave expression to his sense that all teaching was an exercise in "character-building" for students, and even for fellow faculty members and university officers with whom he engaged outside the classroom.[6] There was plainly a constituency at McGill for this and Baker's presence and method emboldened a more adventurous approach to law teaching among those hired after him. But above all things, Professor Baker's early and later successes at McGill came from the response of students whose names he learned by heart and on whom he lavished off-hour devotions, especially those in Montreal who were away from home.[7] They began to form a small and loyal army that would follow Baker for years, back and forth from Toronto, and well beyond his formal retirement from teaching at the Faculty.

More fundamentally, McGill's Faculty of Law offered a home to how Blaine Baker saw the law, founded on an ideal comparable to the Faculty's aspirations tied to pluralism and diversity in legal studies. In a brilliant essay on Quebec legal history written by David Howes, one of Blaine Baker's earliest students, the connection between "polyjurality" at McGill and Baker's intellectual self was explained.[8] Drawing on scholarship in history and on the writing of anthropologist Clifford Geertz, Howes observed that in the late nineteenth and early twentieth century Quebec legal thought had not been simply characterized by the formal coexistence of the common law and the civil law as distinct spheres of legal knowledge. Howes showed, using venerable legal sources, that the comparative endeavour held a broader promise reflecting in an approach to diversity that needed to be recalled: "what is meant by the term 'polyjurality,'" wrote David Howes, "is a tendency to regard other legal traditions (or cultures) as presenting 'alternatives for us,' as opposed to 'alternatives to us.'" Howes went on to connect this idea directly to Blaine Baker's work: "[t]he opposition polyjurality/monojurality corresponds to the distinction between the 'principled eclecticism' of the nineteenth century law and the 'ungrounded, inarticulate conceptualism' of today [described by] Baker."[9]

In the years that followed, "polyjurality" became what Blaine Baker might have styled a watchword for describing the Faculty of Law's self-understanding of its mission, rooted in legal pluralism and the comparative turn. McGill's polyjurality was an open door for Baker's own idea of difference that he recognized as an inherent aspect of the law he wanted to teach. Polyjurality was a way to link legal pluralism to the social history of law that helped Baker make sense of his place at McGill. It signaled an aspiration to tolerance and a diversity of sorts that he held dear. It echoed the way in which he imagined legal cultures had engaged in informal exchanges of ideas in nineteenth-century Canada and the habit of mind for law that he knew best.

David Howes' paper has proved to be one of the most influential forces on intellectual life at McGill of the last generation. In rereading it, one hears much of the principled eclecticism that, when he was at the height of his powers, Professor Baker infused into his sparkling lectures and his spirited interventions in Faculty Council. "Polyjurality" in this broad sense was embraced, or re-embraced, by the Faculty in the 1980s and 1990s. It was incorporated, as Rod Macdonald explained, in the "universalist, polyjural" themes alluded to by the Faculty in public expressions its professors gave to its vocation.[10] By the 1990s, polyjurality took hold of the Faculty. The open attitude to interdisciplinarity and the brand of legal pluralism it championed plainly coincided with the principled eclecticism Blaine saw at the core of his work in and out of the classroom.[11] Law teaching at McGill was less instrumental, more speculative, and more nomadic in ways that transcended the common law and civil law divide, all in a way that suited colleagues working in a mode similar to Baker. This included, in the mid-1990s, a major reform of the Faculty's curriculum and primary mission anchored in polyjurality that, significantly, Professor Baker supported notwithstanding the limits of his own comfort in teaching the modern civil law.[12] As long as McGill resisted a dogmatic turn to a more formalistic understanding of the relationship between legal cultures, this polyjural orientation would remain a welcome place for all manner of scholars who shared Baker's commitment to principled eclecticism in law teaching.

NINETEENTH-CENTURY QUEBEC AS A SITE FOR BLAINE BAKER'S "COSMOPOLITANISM" IN LAW

For a common law professor working at McGill, the province of Quebec could be, oddly enough, a distant place. Several McGill teachers from afar did cultivate Quebec scholarly profiles in this period – notably Patrick Glenn and Rod Macdonald – but that was not the norm. Rarer still were younger professors appointed to teach in the common law stream who learned Quebec law in order to integrate into McGill's main project. David Stevens, who arrived from Western Ontario at about the same time as Blaine, and who trained as a notary after teaching common law property at McGill, fell into that exceptional category.

Blaine Baker might have been expected to content himself with deepening his scholarly interests in Upper Canadian legal culture when he took up a full-time Canadian appointment at the McGill outpost. Further, his instincts and taste for the social history of law meant that Baker probably felt no real common cause with Quebec historians in the law faculties, including most of the historically-minded law teachers at McGill preoccupied with the untangling of the mixed legal sources that Quebec legal historians favoured most.[13] Added to this was what might be fairly called Blaine's modest interest in Quebec law in its modern guise and his shyness to engage in French with colleagues in other Quebec universities. He might well have left Quebec to one side in pursuit of other scholarly ambitions in legal history.

This did not happen. Baker sought out and found primary materials in local archives to support his view that nineteenth-century Quebec law reflected, as was the case in Ontario, the "cosmopolitan, eclectic quality of British North American legal culture."[14] In an award-winning paper published in his early years at McGill, Baker saw the Quebec materials to which he was newly sensitized in nineteenth-century Ontario sources as evidence of a "cross-pollination [that] represents a form of cosmopolitanism in law that is radically different from the liberal, legal universalism of the twentieth century fostered in common law Canada."[15] He had no ear or taste for the regionalism, and less still for the cultural nationalism at work in some of the legal scholarship in Quebec.[16] But his Quebec exertions would be more than highlighting the smattering of Romanist learning unearthed in nineteenth-century Ontario case reports or the discovery of annotations in some English law books in one or another Quebec advocate's library. In archives he began to explore in those early years, Baker worked hard to identify primary Quebec materials that appeared to confirm his own values of cosmopolitanism in law and tolerance for difference in the nineteenth-century Quebec legal culture – more principled eclecticism, now unearthed in Quebec.

Central to Blaine Baker's emerging status as a Quebec legal scholar was a four-year collaborative project he undertook, starting in 1983, to catalogue late eighteenth- and nineteenth- century sources of Quebec law in the collection of the McGill Law Library.[17] As part of a group of like-minded Montreal historians and jurists, Blaine Baker scoured the shelves of the McGill collection over three years, identifying books with Quebec use or provenance between 1760 and 1890 in an effort to "reconstruct" part of Canadian legal culture.[18] Regrettably, this highly stimulating and scholarly book that followed was privately published and distributed almost confidentially such that it is less known than it should be as a working tool for legal historians. It includes an ambitious survey of Quebec historiography that, say the authors, sought to transcend a technical account of the "internal structure of the law" but rather to see Quebec legal history as a field that concerned the "organic relation between law and society."[19] The materials are considered and ordered epistemically, at a distance from modern legal categories, based on a fine sense of the varied character of nineteenth-century sources but also one that draws on historiographical trends in Canada, the United States, England, and France. The manner in which the work was presented reflects a sophisticated understanding of Quebec law and was organized on an intellectual grid that includes and transcends local scholarly themes. Baker's Quebec project was not to provide an account of the law in force but to champion, through the far-flung materials recorded in learned footnotes, a nineteenth-century "nomadic" cast of mind that reflected this cosmopolitanism for Canadian law that he so readily embraced.[20]

Through this project, and no doubt under the guidance of historian Brian Young, Baker learned both aspects of the Quebec legal system and of the manner in which its history had been told in Quebec that would serve him over his whole career. The influence of Young on this moment of Blaine Baker's acculturation cannot be overstated. Thanks to his engagement with primary documents and the material culture of Quebec law, Professor Young's scholarship enjoyed influence and profound credibility in Quebec law faculties where his work on elites, social hierarchy, and ethnicity in nineteenth-century Quebec has been relied upon to round out even the finest histories of law undertaken by academic lawyers.[21] For years, Young and his colleagues in the Montreal Business History Group served as Blaine

Baker's interpreters of Quebec legal history who, literally and figuratively, spoke Baker's language.

Professor Baker gave full expression to his brand of cosmopolitanism for nineteenth- century "British North American legal culture" in the Quebec topics he chose to examine.[22] He fixed the compass of his research, and indeed what he would record as the source of legal cosmopolitism, according to his own interests in Quebec and a Red Tory worldview that he would freely acknowledge. But it was no less tied to his espoused views that resisted formalism and uniformity in law.[23] In this endeavour, and in his effort to explore how these scholarly values could be introduced into a view of nineteenth-century Quebec legal history and historiography, there were some deep affinities between Baker's thinking and historical work done by colleagues in other Quebec law faculties at the time, but these connections were not fully exploited.[24] While his reach into Quebec universities might not have been as effective as it should have been, Blaine Baker did receive critical support for this work from outside Quebec from his colleagues at the Osgoode Society, including Jim Phillips and Philip Girard. A late expression of Baker's views can be found in his essay on how Quebec materials fit into the wider Canadian landscape in the collection he co-edited with Donald Fyson.[25]

Importantly, Blaine Baker's connections to Quebec legal history were explored, and steadied, by many of his best students in the McGill Law Faculty. There were a number of students who, at his behest and with their own happy versions of the Baker method, took on archival work that he might have loved to do. By way only of example, I note his influence on Angela Fernandez, and her influence on him. A legal historian at the University of Toronto, Professor Fernandez has realized in her accomplished teaching and scholarship many of Blaine Baker's own ambitions for himself.[26] Tom Johnson,[27] Ian C. Pilarczyk,[28] and Kathleen E. Fisher[29] also contributed in different ways that helped orient Baker in Quebec historical sources, alongside countless graduate and undergraduate students who undertook original work on aspects of Quebec legal history that not only bore the Baker imprint of cosmopolitanism, but also serve to school and anchor Professor Baker in Quebec law and in the Quebec legal academy.[30]

* * *

Blaine Baker was, by his own account, sometimes rootless in Montreal, changing apartments in the student quarter regularly and, for some protracted periods of intense teaching and research at McGill, contenting himself with a friend's couch or a room in a hostel during term. The overnight train from Toronto, long summers in the country north of Toronto, repeated teaching leaves hunkered down at home in Mimico, Ontario, and an intellectual circle that meant long-distance calls from his office in Old Chancellor Day Hall, all suggest a sort of transience to his Montreal existence. Even when in Montreal, he never strayed far from the Roddick Gates. His early departure from Quebec lends itself too easily to the conclusion that his open heart and open mind as a law teacher were properly situated elsewhere.

The truth of the matter is that Professor Baker found, for a time at least, a congenial intellectual home at McGill and, by extension, saw a place for himself in the Quebec legal academy where he could pursue his work. Whether McGill and Quebec made room for him or he made room for McGill and Quebec is, ultimately, not the important matter to reflect upon. Over thirty-some years, the Faculty of Law and Quebec legal culture were not just outposts or assignments for him. His engagement with the sources and ideas relevant to nineteenth-century Canadian legal history suggest that Blaine Baker's Quebec was a real place for him and that McGill was an anchor for his identity as a law teacher.

NOTES

1 For an early expression of this theme that lingered in his work, see G. Blaine Baker, "Government Involvement in Nineteenth-Century Economic Growth: The Transition from Promotion to Regulation in Upper Canada," (unpublished LLM thesis, 1979, Columbia University Law School). Baker would have shared the idea of his former student, David Sandomierski, that teaching contracts was also a mode of training law students to be "citizens" in various settings, as "problem solver, activist, advocate, counsellor, policy thinker, and architect of social structures.": David Sandomierski, *Aspiration and Reality in Legal Education* (Toronto: University of Toronto Press, 2020), 5. See his essay in this volume.

2 An influence was John Willis. See G. Blaine Baker, "Willis on Cultured Public Authorities," *University of Toronto Law Journal* 55 (2005):

335–60. Professor Baker would discover, thanks to Rod Macdonald and Richard Janda among others, that many of his instincts for what he called the "worm's eye view" of the administrative state echoed in the work of Quebec scholars in the school of René Dussault and Louis Borgeat, *Traité de droit administratif*, t. I-III (Quebec City: Pr. Univerité Laval, 1984–89).

3 For its method and as a sign of how his early course was imagined, see G. Blaine Baker, "The Reconstitution of Upper Canadian Legal Thought in the Late-Victorian Empire," *Law and History Review* 3 (1985): 219–92.

4 Roderick A. Macdonald, "The National Programme at McGill: Origins, Establishment, Prospects," *Dalhousie Law Journal* 13 (1990): 211–363, 328 *et seq.*

5 Some of these travails are alluded to by John E.C. Brierley in a paper published soon after Blaine arrived at McGill: "Developments in Legal Education at McGill, 1970–1980," *Dalhousie Law Journal* 7 (1983): 364–74.

6 These themes are very apparent in the tribute he wrote to his former colleague Roderick A. Macdonald: G. Blaine Baker, "Character-Building at Multiple Sites of Justice: Administration and Teaching as Texts, Scholarship as Ethical and Political Action," in *The Unbounded Level of the Mind: Rod Macdonald's Legal Imagination*, edited by Richard Janda, Rosalie Jukier, and Daniel Jutras (Montreal; Kingston: McGill-Queen's University Press, 2015), 214–22.

7 I think it fair to say that Professor Baker saw the Faculty as replete with informal sites for learning: see, for its evocations, an essay co-written by Desmond Manderson, one of his former students and later a professor at the Faculty: Desmond Manderson and Sarah Turner, "Coffee House: *Habitus* and Performance among Law Students," *Law & Social Inquiry* 31 (2006): 649–76.

8 David Howes, "From Polyjurality to Monojurality: The Transformation of Quebec Law, 1875–1929," *McGill Law Journal* 32 (1987): 523–58. Professor Howes acknowledged his "intellectual debt" to Blaine Baker in the first footnote (523).

9 Ibid., 525, citing to Baker, "Reconstitution."

10 Macdonald, "The National Programme at McGill," 345. Baker's mark on Macdonald's soaring history of the Faculty, is acknowledged by the author in the first footnote.

11 See the repeated references to Howes' conception of polyjurality in the academic literature on McGill's transsystemic teaching across legal traditions in the undergraduate programme in Shauna Van Praagh,

"Preface: Navigating the Transsystemic: A Course Syllabus," *McGill Law Journal* 50 (2005): 701–6. These connections to an anti-formalist, interdisciplinary, and pluralist approach to law teaching – one that made room for teachers like Baker – ensured against an essentialist understanding of the common law and the civil law that some outside observers of the programme warned against: see Harry Arthurs, "Madly Off in One Direction: McGill's New, Integrated, Polyjural, Transsystemic Law Programme," *McGill Law Journal* 50 (2005): 707–20.

12 See Richard Janda's essay in Part I of the book.

13 But see, for an especially accomplished example of this method, infused with concerns for social history that Baker found relevant to his teaching, Jean-Maurice Brisson, *La formation d'un droit mixte: l'évolution de la procédure civile de 1774 à 1867* (Montréal: Éditions Thémis, 1986).

14 Baker, "Reconstitution," 239.

15 Ibid., 247.

16 See J.E.C. Brierley, "Quebec Legal Education since 1945: Cultural Paradoxes and Traditional Ambiguities," *Dalhousie Law Journal* 10 (1986-7): 5–44, 17–19, 29.

17 G. Blaine Baker, Kathleen E. Fisher, Vince Masciotra, and Brian Young, *Sources in the Law Library of McGill University for a Reconstruction of the Legal Culture of Quebec, 1760–1890* (Montreal: McGill University Faculty of Law and Montreal Business History Project, 1987).

18 In addition to the preface, ibid.,1–6, a partial description of the process by which the work was compiled is given in G. Blaine Baker, "Bibliographic Reconstruction of Canadian Legal Culture, Quebec, 1760–1890," *Bulletin of the Bibliographical Society of Canada* 25 (1985): 11–20. The method was congenial to Baker but by no means of his invention: see, for example, the understanding of method for historical research in law alluded to by co-author Brian Young at the time in "Law 'in the Round,'" *Acadiensis* 16, no. 1 (1986): 155–65.

19 Ibid., note 17, 19, with references to the American, English, and French historical literature this approach drew upon. See Vince Masciotra, "Quebec Legal Historiography, 1760–1900," *McGill Law Journal* 32 (1987): 712–32.

20 Here again David Howes pointed to a "nomadic" jurisprudence that characterized the nineteenth century Quebec legal thought that was associated with Baker's own thinking: ibid., note 8, 530.

21 Examples of Young's work appearing in this period that Professor Baker and historically-minded members of the McGill law faculty would have encountered included the work that explained the social significance of

law reform to Baker and the Faculty, *The Politics of Codification: The Lower Canadian Civil Code of 1866* (Montreal/Kingston: Osgoode Society/McGill-Queen's University Press, 1994).

22 Consider the wide-ranging sources, and scope of activities that he saw fitting into an elite legal practice, in G. Blaine Baker, "Law Practice and Statecraft in Mid-Nineteenth-Century Montreal: The Torrance-Morris Firm, 1848–1868," in *Beyond the Law: Lawyers and Business in Canada 1830 to 1930*, edited by Carol Wilton (Toronto: The Osgoode Society, 1990): 45–91.

23 See, e.g., with its emphasis on the professional gentry in Quebec law, G. Blaine Baker, "Public Frivolity and Patrician Confidence: Lower Canada's 'Brothers in Law,' 1827–1833," in *Mélanges offerts par ses collègues de McGill à Paul-André Crépeau/Mélanges presented by McGill colleagues to Paul-André Crépeau*, edited by J.E.C. Brierley et al. (Cowansville, Quebec: Y. Blais, 1997): 47–73.

24 Some of his contemporaries in other faculties used the theme of "legal acculturation" to explain how disparate sources of law took root in Quebec legal thought, and did so in a manner that mirrored some of Baker's cosmopolitanism: see, e.g., André Morel, "La langue et l'acculturation juridique au Québec depuis 1760," *Revue juridiques Thémis* 24 (1990): 99–108; Sylvio Normand, "La culture juridiques et l'acculturation du droit: Le Québec," ISAIDAT *Law Review* 1 (2011): Art. 23, 1–47.

25 See G. Blaine Baker, "Introduction: Quebec and the Canadas, 1760 to 1867: A Legal Historiography," in *Essays in the History of Canadian Law: Volume XI – Quebec and the Canadas*, edited by G. Blaine Baker and Donald Fyson (Toronto: University of Toronto Press/ The Osgoode Society, 2013): 3–45.

26 Her superb essay, written as a student, is an early published sign of a longstanding dialogue with Baker: Angela Fernandez, "Albert Mayrand's Private Law Library: An Investigation of the Person, the Law of Persons, and 'Legal Personality' in a Collection of Law Books," *University of Toronto Law Journal* 53 (2003): 37–64.

27 "'In a Manner of Speaking': Towards a Reconstitution of Property in Mid-Nineteenth- Century Quebec," *McGill Law Journal* 32 (1986-87): 636–72.

28 "'Too Well Used by His Master': Judicial Enforcement of Servants' Rights in Montreal, 1830–1845," *McGill Law Journal* 46 (2000–01): 491–529; "The Law of Servants and the Servants of Law: Enforcing Masters' Rights in Montreal, 1830–1845," *McGill Law Journal* 46 (2000–01): 779–836. While Professor Baker was not an active participant in the Association des

professeurs de droit du Québec, Pilarczyk won the APDQ Prize for best LLM dissertation in law in Quebec in 1997.

29 "After First Meeting Percy Corbett" (1983), reprinted in Ian C. Pilarczyk, ed., *"A Noble Roster": One Hundred and Fifty Years of Law at McGill* (Montreal: McGill University, 1999), 68. Blaine Baker served on the editorial board of this McGill historical album.

30 His encouragement of student work in legal history at and around the McGill Law Journal was notable. See e.g., Mario Nigro and Claire Mauro, "The Jewish Immigrant Experience and the Practice of Law in Montreal, 1830 to 1990," *McGill Law Journal* 44 (1998–99): 999–1046.

Acknowledgments

I would like to acknowledge the invaluable insistence of our McGill Law research assistant, Genevieve Westgate, BA '18, BCL/JD '21, and thank Angela and Brian for the precious gift of collaboration that they provided. It has been a pleasure and a privilege working with you both. I also wish to thank Robert Leckey for his support and that of the Faculty of Law; Daniel Boyer for his insightful comments; and Nicholas Kasirer and Richard Janda for their encouragement and participation. I also wish to thank Osler, Hoskin & Harcourt LLP, Douglas Francis Roche, and Gary Lawrence, whose financial support made this publication possible.

I dedicate this book to my twin daughters, Emma and Samantha, who are largely unaware of its existence yet have delightfully hindered it in innumerable ways over the past two years – and I would not have it any other way.

Ian C. Pilarczyk

* * *

Meditation teacher La Sarmiento says they start each day with the following prayer: "May I be given the appropriate difficulties and sufferings in life so that my heart may be truly awakened and my practice of liberation and universal compassion be truly fulfilled. May we *all* be given the appropriate difficulties and sufferings in life so that our hearts may be truly awakened and our practice of liberation and universal compassion be truly fulfilled." Participation in the production of this book has been a challenging but heart-awakening and opening experience, from interacting with the authors in the collection, sharing memories of and experiences with Blaine Baker, many very moving, witnessing their own stretchings and reckonings, to the conceptualization and execution of the vision Ian, Brian, and I shared for the book. It has been an honour and a privilege to work with them both. I dedicate my efforts here to my child, Isabel, the light of my life. May they experience the awakening effects of their difficulties and sufferings in life that will result in them feeling free, safe, happy, healthy, and living a life filled with joy and ease.

Angela Fernandez

* * *

I join in thanking Genevieve Westgate for her innovative work as research assistant. Hunkered down, thinking about Blaine Baker's intellectual contribution, and participating in the editing process of this work in the surreal circumstances of a pandemic, has been an experience hugely enriched by the collaboration of Angela Fernandez and Ian C. Pilarczyk. During preparation of this volume, another McGill historian, much younger than Blaine, died. Student and then generous colleague in the History Department and in the Montreal History Group, Jarrett Rudy (1970–2020) would have appreciated, I think, the provocative legal history proposed here. I miss his friendship and counsel.

Brian Young

PART ONE

Blaine Baker, His Life and Work

footnotes margins minutes

for Blaine

Kathy Fisher

Now they are going, and I stand again on new frontiers.
... I wish you goodbye and good housing.

– F.R. Scott, "On Saying Goodbye to My Room
at Old Chancellor Day Hall."[1]

it is my second year when you arrive —law school comes alive
you in tweed and handknit woolen vests   huge hands
huge laugh   know all our names   in stellar Contracts class

still young   yet old (just like Prince Charles)   old-fashioned
ways   progressive mind   you understand the student
body   collegial ears   you listen hear   behind the scenes   you work discretely
for decades incite   change   still   you never change   your residence
to Montreal   *la belle province*   your touchstones —cottage Scout camp
in Muskoka   brick house   in Toronto

your passions   teaching history   delving into primary sources   old books
and deeds   hand-written wills   contracts admin and chains of title
marginalia scratched on yellowed pages   in tomes from Rare Book Room
where we smoke in then-law library   you enlighten   study influences
catalogue ideas and thinkers   organize from metal shelves   collections
gathering dust   rescue countless spines   remaindered   tossed
in grey metal garbage bins

we shelf-check every volume   note   collections owned by lawyers' clerks
what did they read?   lawmakers   judges?   up until the 20th century
1890 is the cut-off point   clues for legal context of drafters of   the Civil
Code of Lower Canada   and colonial nation's Fathers
of Confederation   backstory to the 1980s   Crépeau's dark-blue covered
three-tomed draft —the DCC[2]   fermenting in your McGill residency

with you —the past blows open wide   springs alive   expansive
your brilliance spreads   wild   contagion   still   you stagger
on the cusp   of computer revolution   you   analogue   reluctant user   resist
keyboard and mouse   pen in cursive longhand   neat script on yellow
legal notepads   legible insightful comments   you mentor encourage   think
traditionally   in blue ballpoint ink

for over thirty years   you teach commute —*VIA Rail's most frequent traveller?*
you ride the rails through bordered space   Lower to Upper Canada
your restless constant pilgrimage   when something foments from inside
you start to destabilize   wobble at your core   your genius never vanishes
but moods echo autumn's falling leaves   as darkness buries you
you struggle as its grip grows strong   you chase it   drink red wine and beer
write essays   make phone calls —depression grabs you by the throat
you teeter stumble fall   while allies   colleagues seek to get you
well

and at the end   your voice still strong —body more aged than your years
we hear an upbeat cheerful voice   familiar   from your landline   you ask
How may I help you?   your tone masks sorrow demons wounds   we never
know the source of them   you slip away   one summer's day   three
days 'til you are found   that takes a toll on we who love you —*how did we miss*
such obvious clues?   your inexorable march from living   leaves us gutted
in your wake

and you —who lived for contracts   bylaws   English and notarial wills
leave no testamentary disposition   no words to guide your grievers
friends and colleagues   students allies   final wishes   distribution falls
to your estranged sister   you —enigma while you lived   die just
the same —a mystery   nothing explicit in your name   yet leave
a trail behind you all the same   concealed in mainstream scholarly texts
and deep in tangential pockets   buried in footnotes   letters   references
and now this book   collection of the kinds of essays you'd adore

light shining here on darker corners   you'd never have illuminated
but we must   and so inspired   reclaim you —beautiful and broken man
whose huge mind held such vision   kindness   huge hands   loved
to sand antiques   and raise a glass or cigarette   we write you back
from loss regret   and so your lifelong gift's returned   light   transforms black
burns darkness transmutes flaws   we feel you whole and human

we picture you   red-faced and bashful   humble yet delighted
recognition that you'd never seek —professor's final lesson   your intellect
and lineages   reclaimed through remembrance celebration   our hearts   revived
embrace this resurrection —your legacy perfected now   voiced
through collegial expression   you   found   and lost   and found
again   with truths released   from footnotes margins minutes   your spirit
breathes   and springs alive   in *Gedenkschrift*
immortalized

NOTES

1 Frank Reginald Scott, "On Saying Goodbye to My Room at Chancellor Day Hall," *The Dance is One* (Toronto: McClelland & Stewart, 1973), 9.
2 Draft *Civil Code* which final version was adopted in 1991 as the *Civil Code of Quebec*.

I

Blaine Baker, a Tribute

Ian C. Pilarczyk

This volume of fourteen essays – nearly a baker's dozen – represents the efforts of friends and colleagues to both situate and salute Blaine Baker's life and work. All our contributors were touched by Blaine in some way significant to them: inspired by his teaching, influenced by his scholarship, and stimulated by his generous collegiality. We are grateful that we were all able to meet, in person and virtually, at the University of Toronto in December 2019 – a luxury that was soon to seem foreign as the global pandemic burned its way through all of our lives. If the pandemic has taught us anything it is surely the importance of valuing our relationships. Blaine stirred something resonant in all of us, as this volume demonstrates.

I have no more insight into Blaine, the person or the professor, than others in his circle. Through the vicissitudes of life, I am but one person attempting to delineate who Blaine was. That there is at least a hint of futility to this scarcely needs to be mentioned, as Blaine was a consummate study in contrasts united by his ability to be an enigma to everyone who thought they knew him – because if one thing stands out from the conversations and interviews we had about Blaine, no one really did. It was entirely at Blaine's design that he was to everyone the same, and to everyone different. As one old friend succinctly put it at his memorial in Muskoka:

> [i]t occurred to me that many of us have probably built, in our own minds, slightly different, maybe markedly different composites of Blaine – each with its own validity yet somehow incomplete. It is like the old task of trying to describe an elephant by grabbing its leg – you're going to be partially correct, but not entirely.[1]

This metaphor strikes me as an apt one indeed, not only because I struggled about whether to allude to the elephant in the room in discussing his life (more on that later). Candidly, I admit to unease about whether Blaine would have welcomed the attempt, even while I am equally sure that Blaine would have been supremely gratified by this *Gedenkschrift*.

I first met Blaine a year after my entrance into the Institute of Comparative Law at McGill in 1995, fresh (or rather exhausted) from having completed my JD and passing the Massachusetts bar exam. Blaine was on leave that year, but I understood from my supervisor Professor Shauna Van Praagh that Blaine was aware of my project and would be delighted to be involved upon his return. The archival research was mind-numbing, desolate, and wonderful – hour after hour entombed in the windowless room that then housed the archives for the Judicial District of Montreal, pouring over moldy documents and reconstructing and analyzing the results. It was the type of solitary and diligent undertaking that Blaine appreciated, and he took an equal delight in my unexpected discoveries as I did. Blaine proved to be a rigorous surrogate supervisor, reading everything with great diligence, providing potential secondary sources, and scribbling liberally in red pen, so much so that at times I quite lost sight of the underlying text. Occasionally he would add an encouraging statement such as "you should explore this more" or "this seems to be an important point" but it was clear that he did not impress easily. Once completed, however, he urged me to publish the thesis, which I did while conducting my DCL studies under his supervision from January 1998 to June 2003 with a one year interregnum in 2001–2002.[2]

If it was my place to remonstrate with Blaine about his unannounced absence (at least to me) during a sensitive time in my dissertation process, it did not occur to me; and like other events in his life it was never discussed. Blaine disappeared and reappeared without a word, and Nicholas Kasirer filled in during his absence. My relationship with Blaine shifted for reasons I never fully understood, even as I recall vividly the moment it did. After the defence was concluded, but I had not yet moved away from Montreal, Blaine called one evening. When I addressed him in the usual manner, he said, "You can call me Blaine – it's a perfectly acceptable Christian name" – which was as unambiguous as it was awkward. I gather, in hindsight, that Blaine had decided that now that I had entered the Academy we were friends. As others have pointed out, you did not choose Blaine as a friend; he chose you.

Blaine and I stayed in touch regularly and we shared discussions of politics, academia, and the vagaries of life (the latter nearly entirely on my end). Even though I knew there had been some parallels in a few areas of our lives, and Blaine had every opportunity over the years to mention how his experiences had been similar, he never really did, nor did I ever press him. It was always clear with Blaine that the personal was off-limits. He seemed to particularly enjoy speaking while I was in the Adirondacks and he was in Muskoka, as it gave him the opportunity to compare our respective cabin-country experiences. In the main, however, I spent twenty years anticipating a reciprocity which, except for a handful of guarded moments, never really happened. This reserve did not make me admire or like him any less, to which I am sure many of his friends can relate. His droll sense of humour and trenchant observations on politics and seemingly any topic made him an engaging conversationalist, and to amuse him resulted in a very gratifying, explosive guffaw. Conversations focused at least in part on academic projects I was pursuing, and he was unfailingly generous with time and thought on sources to consult, avenues to explore, and appropriate journals in which to publish. It bears mentioning that he wrote and commented on drafts, often multiple drafts, of every piece I published from 2001 onwards (sadly, with the exception of this one). They all benefitted immensely from his discerning eye, and for that I am grateful.

I do not really know what Blaine gained from my friendship, or what it was that he needed. Only once do I recall feeling pity for Blaine when I saw him at his most vulnerable, albeit at a distance. I knew then, as I do now, that he would have found that sentiment most unwelcome. Phoning him while he was homebound in Toronto following hospitalization from a heart attack, his voice sounded wispy, his enunciation fuzzy. By happenstance it came out that he was subsisting on canned pineapple and other miscellany in his cupboard. The only thing I could think to do was to hire a meal-delivery service. Blaine called me soon after the meals began arriving and discussed at unusual length and in laudatory terms the efficiency of the delivery service as well as the variety of the meals. He was clearly very thankful, and also nonplussed. At one point he asked, "but why did you do this?" I replied "that's what friends do." He was silent for an unnaturally long time, and then said something to the effect of "well, thank you for this. You are very kind" before segueing to another topic. He mentioned the nurse who came on a regular basis to take blood samples but otherwise had no visitors. In short order a circle of friends, including a fellow editor of this volume, took turns ordering meals for him until Blaine had recovered. In this foreshadowing of the Covid pandemic and our sense of collective isolation also resides an allegory that illustrates several disparate aspects of Blaine's life and personality: the emotional and physical seclusion, the averseness to being vulnerable, the outsider-looking-in aspect of much of his life, and yet also the abiding warmth that he engendered in so many. Blaine could not ask for help even had it occurred to him; but he was sometimes much in need of it, and all of us would have helped him more if we could. For all his generosity of spirit, his omnipresent concern for others and inexhaustible desire to be helpful, he asked for nothing in return.

The main purpose of this introduction is not to provide a comprehensive biography of Blaine, even were that possible. Rather, it is to trace some of the contours of his academic life, using our essays as lodestones. Let us begin with his obituary:

> PROFESSOR EMERITUS GEORGE BLAINE BAKER
> JUNE 9, 1952–JULY 11, 2018
>
> Blaine passed away at 66 years. Predeceased by his father, George Grant Baker QC, his mother, Muriel Isabel Baker, and his brother, Eric William Baker. He is survived by his sister, Jill Elizabeth Baker. A private family service is being held. Blaine was a professor of law at McGill University for 28 years. During his time there, he served as Associate Dean (academic) from 1999 to 2001, and Associate Dean (graduate studies) from 1997 to 1999. A beloved teacher, Blaine received several teaching awards. His scholarship as an accomplished legal historian earned him encomiums from various learned academic institutions. Blaine wrote many leading and influential articles and book chapters on Canadian legal history. Professor Baker also taught at the University of Toronto and Osgoode Hall law schools. He was also an accomplished adjudicator with the Ontario License Appeal Tribunal. A commemorative ceremony is planned for Professor Baker on Friday, September 7, 2018 at 2 p.m., Birks Heritage Chapel, McGill University, 3520 University St, Montreal. Contributions to the Professor Blaine Baker Scholarship Fund may be made through McGill University.[3]

Blaine was a brilliant student from an early age. He completed Springfield Elementary and then Erindale Secondary School in Mississauga, Ontario. He was elected president of the student council in his senior year, following a campaign replete with pun-filled slogans such as "Baker Takes the Cake" and "Baker: One Smart Cookie."[4] Described as a "bit of an odd duck" even then, his sartorial style was already established, and even as his classmates embraced bell-bottoms he gravitated to corduroys and sweater vests.[5] He went on to earn his BA from Huron College in London, Ontario in 1974, where he studied philosophy and appeared on the dean's honour list. He completed an LLB from the University of Western Ontario in 1978, concentrating in commercial law and non-constitutional public law. He again excelled in his studies, and in his 1L year was awarded the Harold G. Fox Education Fund Award for "exceptional promise in law," and graduated with various other honours including the Dean Ivan Rand Award for "meritorious academic standing over three years together with outstanding contributions to extra-curricular activities." In 1978 he entered Columbia University's LLM program and specialized in administrative law and Anglo-American legal history. His academic career began by serving as a Bigelow Fellow at the University of Chicago Law School in 1981, with his graduate work providing the foundation for some of his work that followed. In the fall of 1981 he joined McGill University's Faculty of Law which was to prove his academic home for most of his career.

To state that Blaine was a superlative educator hardly does him justice. He taught all subjects with zeal and unfettered enthusiasm, although socio-legal history remained his true passion. He was an assistant professor from 1981–1987, associate professor from 1987–1994, and full professor from 1994–2009, and multiple recipient of the Faculty's teaching award. For nearly thirty years, Blaine's students valued him for his intellectual honesty, encyclopedic depth of knowledge, luminous intellect, kindness, self-effacing humour, generosity, irreverence, and explosive exuberance (and laugh). They recalled fondly his tendency to memorize the names of students by the first day of class, and with significant frequency graduates remembered him as the single best professor they ever had. Notably (even proudly) unconventional he was aptly described by one former student as "both a mad scientist and a favorite uncle."[6] Some representative examples of student evaluations are immortalized on ratemyprofessors.com, of which three will suffice to evidence the depth of respect he was accorded:

> I've earned four McGill degrees spanning nineteen long years, and throughout it all, I feel blessed for encountering G. Blaine Baker, the most outstanding professor imaginable. I cannot thank you enough, Professor Baker, your class was far and away the most magnificent and thrilling experience throughout my entire journey at McGill.
>
> Absolutely the finest and (I dare say) most intelligent professor I came across in the faculty. Makes the material clear, coherent, and interesting. Witty, too. Shows more respect for the students than most. A genuine man with a genuine interest in teaching
>
> Amazing breadth of intellect which he is able to dispense with magnanimity and insight.[7]

His classroom delivery was unique, and consequently as difficult to describe as it was recognizable to generations of McGill law students. Jason Mogg, tasked with playing Blaine in Skit Night ca. 1987, thus described imitating him:

> Dressing as Blaine: brown corduroy pants, white collared shirt (a little rumpled was ok), prep-school tie – not fully tightened up, grey pullover sweater-vest, and, larger than strictly necessary Sorel winter boots (in which one had to shuffle or waddle in a certain very specific manner when moving around). The last two, boots and sweater-vest being particularly important to the zeitgeist, and particularly Blaine [...]. I remember the physical part of the imitation too. In order to imitate Blaine one had to a) stand pigeon-toed in the big boots, right hand in pants pocket […] b) alternate, in a spasmodic, jerky fashion between staring bashfully at the floor in front of one's feet and pointing the head up as if staring at the ceiling directly overhead; c) the instant before a portion of the upward head jerks, smack one's forehead with the open palm of the left hand; d) when the head is in a 'normal' position and immediately before said jerking head motion, roll one's eyes upward so that only whites of eyes are visible; e) stutter and utter a series of rapid staccato "uh, uh, uh,uh's" and "ah, ah, ah, ah's" followed immediately, and breathlessly, by a few sentences or even paragraphs […] full of four and five syllable words

> strung together in a grammatically correct way, the content of which, once one had taken the time to digest and understand (if you could), was nothing short of remarkable, even stunning.[8]

These moments of dense monologue typically sent students into a paroxysm of frantic scribbling or typing, although some preferred just to listen. It would be fair to say that Blaine's eclectic teaching manner was not for everyone. Some found his oratory opaque and convoluted, the lateral thinking he venerated requiring too many intellectual leaps or simply too much patience to easily follow, his teaching too wedded to the theoretical and conceptual rather than the practical – a not-infrequent criticism of law professors in general, bien sûr. But, in the main, students thought highly of him indeed; and years later practitioners still recalled things they learned from him; as one posted on Blaine's tribute page, he was "[o]ne of those professors whose classroom teachings come back to you in day-to-day practice, whistling through the decades, providing the spark for a new angle or approach or research point."[9] Blaine won the Faculty of Law's John W. Durnford Award for Teaching three times, as well as the student-voted version the year before the award was established officially. He was a central figure in the life of the faculty, and even students who had not taken his courses generally knew him, or at least knew of him. His memory of students, eclecticism, engagement in admissions, investment in student learning, and seeming ubiquity at social events gave him a profile that few other professors achieved.

Unsurprisingly, therefore, he was a frequent focus of inclusion in the Faculty's fabled annual "Skit Nite." Found amongst his papers were the lyrics of one such occasion, immortalized in Skit Nite ca. 1990 – "the very model of a legal academian."[10] Years after the fact, alumni recounted his references to "peppercorn consideration" (immortalized in one performance during my LLM studies as "the dance of the peppercorn"), the "camel's nose in the tent," and evocative sayings like "the six most expensive words in the English language: 'it's the principle of the thing.'" His students were routinely struck by his seemingly boundless knowledge, witty banter and bon mots, and ability to conjure legal citations and obscure bibliographical references after just a few second's recall.[11] Blaine was also preternaturally accessible and unfailingly generous with his time and attention to students and colleagues alike. Students knew he had an extremely liberal open door policy; and that his office

Figure 1.1 | Plaque with recipients of the John W. Durnford Award for Teaching Excellence.

hours were, to put it mildly, expansive (recalled by Dean Robert Leckey as being in the region of 10 a.m.–10 p.m. on most days) and included weekends.[12] He was frequently found at Thomson House (headquarters of the Postgraduate Students' Society), where he repaired after lunches at the Faculty Club; and he was a fixture at the Faculty of Law's Coffee House (which served copious amounts of alcohol but never coffee) rather more than he perhaps should have been.[13] He released a booming " A HA!" or "BRAVO!" when he was amused, gratified by an intellectual epiphany, or felt accolades were deserved. He dispensed advice liberally but never uninvited.

Blaine's pedagogical contributions included over 150 independent study papers he had supervised, numerous theses he oversaw officially and unofficially, and students he encouraged to publish: thirty-three such papers he had fastidiously tracked in his curriculum vitae as of 2008. His intellectual influence shaped and supported many scholars along the way. Blaine pushed students to excel and agonized over his grading – he read each paper or exam several times, and (at least in the absence of grade curves) only awarded one A grade. To be awarded that elusive A or A- from Blaine necessitated not only technical proficiency in the subject, but some level of risk-taking and personal investment in the subject above and beyond topic mastery.[14]

Several of the contributors in this volume were supervised by Blaine or cite him as a mentor. His influence was also manifested in less evident ways; his tenure as Scholar in Residence at the firm of Borden Ladner Gervais (2001–2002), for example, is recalled in the acknowledgments section by the author of *Accountants' Liability in Canada* (2002).[15] He gave freely of his time and talents, serving as a director or editorial board member of, inter alia, the *Canadian Guide to Uniform Legal Citation*, the Canadian Law and Society Association, *Histoire sociale/Social History*, the James McGill Society, the Montreal Bar, and the Wellington (Guelph) Law Association. He was an avid supporter of student activities: the *McGill Law Journal*, surely (for which he served both as official and unofficial faculty supervisor); but also the law school's newspaper *Quid Novi* and other initiatives. He was also supervisor and coach in the 1980s and 90s for the Corporate Securities, Gale, Jessup, Laskin, and Wilson moot court teams and took pride in their numerous successes which he carefully documented in his CV.[16]

While there were areas that were closer to his intellectual heart, his immersion in socio-legal historiography was vast: he was a voracious consumer of scholarship centred in the UK, the Canadas, and the US; and seemingly no work by any former students could go published without his notice. His provision of bibliographical information to colleagues and graduate students is all the more remarkable when one contemplates that he appears to have done little or none of it through electronic research: he would comb through the table of contents of issues of journals as they came in and the *Index to Canadian Legal Periodical Literature*, delving into articles that interested him, and seemingly committing much of their content to memory. This unquenchable appetite, coupled with a polymath's range of interests, made Blaine a uniquely gifted editor, graduate adviser, and colleague.

Blaine was much committed to academic renewal, to reimagining curricula so as to best capture what he thought was the true complexity of subjects and the nuances and nexuses that frequently went unexplored in traditional classes. He was deeply interested in the formation of legal thought, education, practice, codification, and the related phenomena of formation of legal culture and professionalism. He, along with Rod Macdonald, pushed and pulled boundaries in teaching administrative law and legal process.[17] Blaine's contribution, in the main, was to rethink administrative law as a study of how decision-making power was centralized and applied, from the state and state enterprises all the way down, with human interactions as a locus point for the application of state power. Contracts, then, were a private extension of this, a "government-in-miniature" as he termed it.[18] He was an innovator in teaching Canadian legal history, assuredly; and while he published no scholarship in contracts, he was also a gifted teacher of that field and more widely in the law of obligations (which included extracontractual or what are called in the common law torts, as well as contractual relations). The breadth of his interests can be gleaned by noting that other courses he taught at McGill included: Radical Lawyering; Foundations of Canadian Law; Comparative Modern Legal History; Intellectual and Industrial Property; and Legal Research and Writing. And again, he taught them with great facility. This continued unabated even in his last years; by way of example, he parlayed his experience in arbitration into a course on Ethical Issues in Alternative Dispute Resolution, which he offered at the University of Toronto in 2016. This latter course was, in his words, "a study of the reconciliation of professional ethics and standards with 'normative and institutional pluralism,' and with the 'pluralized subjects' of those diverse rules and informal sites of justice."[19]

Blaine was also an enthusiastic biographer of others, contributing fourteen biographies to the *Biographical Dictionary of the Common Law* and two to the *Dictionary of Canadian Biography*; and his last work completed was as co-editor and contributor to a collective work on Justice Gerald Le Dain.[20] He co-edited three volumes for the Osgoode Society for Canadian Legal History, and wrote chapters for a half-dozen more; the bibliography we have appended to this volume also details nearly three dozen articles, essays, and reviews. Along the way, he earned many accolades, including publishing awards from the American Society for Legal History, the Canadian Historical Association, the Canadian Law and Society Association, and the Canadian Association of Law Libraries.

One of the oddities of his career is that Blaine showed no affinity for producing book-length monographs, as Brian Young notes.[21] Perhaps writing a book, even a scholarly one, was too transparent and intimate an undertaking for Blaine's comfort. His colleague at the Faculty of Law, Richard Janda, recalled his disdain for writing books, summarized in Blaine's pithy-yet-controvertible statement that "you really only have one book in you." What if anything Blaine thought that book might be in his case remains an enthralling point of conjecture.[22] Young notes in his essay the fittingness that Blaine's last work, with Janda, focused on Gerald LeDain; he was very sympathetic about LeDain's accomplishments and struggles, and wrestled during the project with how (and to what extent) to reference LeDain's mental health issues. I had several conversations with him on that topic and he ultimately was of the view that referencing those issues was essential to an understanding of LeDain's life and career, but he did not reach that conclusion easily. Similarly, our grappling with the question of what to pass over in silence, and what to include in order to contextualize Blaine's life, struck us from the inception of this project.

Notwithstanding his lack of a monograph, Blaine left behind a rich and intriguing historiography that positioned him in the top echelon of Canadian legal historians. His scholarship was not as prolific as some of his colleagues, but his work was of the highest caliber: meticulously researched; posing and answering intriguing questions;

and weaving "so elegant a web" in the threads and connections that he constructed and uncovered.[23] He was an ardent and somewhat infamous devotee of voluminous footnotes, seemingly conveying an article's worth of content through that epistemological vehicle alone.[24] They remain a treasure trove for orienting oneself in the secondary sources on many topics. Perhaps unsurprisingly, he was intellectually most interested in the mid-to-late-nineteenth century, excavating the periods when Ontario lawyers still embraced cosmopolitan legal thinking that included engagement with American, English, and Quebec legal influences and traditions.[25]

Beyond his teaching and scholarship, Blaine also served as law-school administrator. Whether Blaine enjoyed these responsibilities is not obvious, but his dedication to McGill's students and zeal for the institution is unquestioned. The list of committees at the university and faculty level on which he served is too lengthy to mention; but those he chaired is sufficient to give a sample of the breadth of his contributions: University Copyright Committee (1993–1995); Faculty Graduate Studies Committee (1997–1999); Faculty Library Committee (three non-consecutive terms as chair); Faculty Promotion and Tenure Committee (ditto), and others. He had innumerable other roles in addition to these and others already cited, but Blaine's service on numerous admissions committees especially deserves to be highlighted, prized as he was for his ability to recognize characteristics and talents not always reflected in the dry metrics of grades and test scores.[26] He became invested in students even before their matriculation, and numerous alumni commented that he remembered biographical details about them years later, even if they were not students in his classes.

When his office was cleared following his death, the files full of notes and copies of letters of recommendation he had written for students – many of whom went on to become partners, jurists, deans, and government ministers – reflected not mere rote comments on students' aptitude, but carefully crafted and personalized works of art. It is significant that Blaine could say in writing what he would never have dreamed of saying in person; and his fondness for, and understanding of, his students is richly demonstrated in these files. They remain touching tributes to how invested he was in the students he taught over the years. When thanked, his usual response was to simply ask the recipient to "pay it forward" for others in the future.

As mentioned, Blaine was a friend to many, but an open book to none. Nicholas Kasirer, long-time colleague, dean of the Faculty from 2003–2009, and author of the foreword of this volume described him as: "Brilliant. Modest. Alone. A height of charm when he wanted to be. A height of isolation when he didn't feel like interacting with the world. A great teacher."[27] Another former student pronounced him "an absolutely singular individual."[28] Blaine was a man for all seasons but unfailingly reticent about his areas of aptitude, which included hobbies and interests as diverse as antique motorboats and semi-antique cars (always manual), caning chairs, gardening, and rebuilding stone walls and docks, disparate interests put to good use by him in Muskoka.

It has been noted by many that his students were a type of surrogate family, for which he showed a real respect and regard while still keeping all at a distance. To spend time with Blaine was to feel there was some hollow place, a pool of unspoken sadness and longing that tinted his life. Unmarried, a weekly denizen of Via Rail's sleeper train to Toronto, he was social yet remained consummately on the periphery. While in residence in Toronto or Muskoka, and to a lesser extent in Montreal, he had an active phone tree, with a list of friends whom he called on a regular basis, inevitably by opening the conversation with "Blaine Baker … what am I disturbing?" This was, perhaps, both a way of feeding his insatiable curiosity about those around him as well as his self-conscious way of ensuring that he was not intruding. His calls ended equally invariably with "is there anything I can do for you?" This valediction was a testament to his unceasing desire to be helpful, but there was also a hint of pathos to that question – underlining as it did Blaine's deep need for support and to be needed – even as he was incapable of admitting as much. His openings and closings were as genuine as they were immutable, another sign of the social awkwardness he displayed even to those with whom he was most at ease: for Blaine could never be said to truly be at ease.

Indeed, Blaine was to remain forever on the penumbra of the lives of people around him, estranged from close members of his family, sometimes discomfited by others, and often isolated. Whether this was by choice, or whether he simply could not find his place, is unclear. That he was commonly at his most garrulous and charming at events that involved the consumption of alcohol bore witness to his need for social lubricant. Informal meetings with students at

Thomson House, in a haze of cigarette smoke and beer, were a treasured memory for many law students. But drinking could and did exacerbate his contradictions, bringing to the forefront the mercurial, melancholic, and misanthropic side of Blaine. Over the years, old friends receded or withdrew, troubled by the behavior that was painful for them to witness, for while Blaine was notoriously guarded, his fragilities and issues were apparent to those around him. He was, as Brian Young aptly termed, a type of "private open book."[29] What wellspring drove Blaine's demons, however, was never clear.

Some of the ways in which Blaine supported people he cared about also speaks to the whims and eccentricities that he appeared to cultivate. As Angela Fernandez likewise recalls, one of his hallmarks was providing bibliographic information he deemed might be of interest, appearing in one's mailbox unannounced on scraps of legal paper embellished with his distinctive cursive in red ink. Some of Blaine's last batch of suggested sources were to find their way into my essay, sent via post in a plain white envelope that appeared unannounced but inevitably marked across the flap with a ≠ or similar symbol – to ward off tampering? – an archaic and wholly superfluous ritual that I only knew Blaine to do.[30] Despite his pedagogical innovation, he was nonetheless a walking archaism, a vestige from an earlier era. I had often felt that meeting him was as if one's late-Victorian great-grandfather had materialized unexpectedly through a wormhole. Blaine was prototypically formal and oddly old-fashioned, including an almost Luddite discomfort with email until the last few years of his career and historically reliant on faculty assistants to type his manuscripts. Social media was entirely foreign to him, and popular culture eluded him except as the occasional item of curiosity (viewed as an entomologist might view a peculiar beetle). Blaine conducted his life largely reactive to modernity, and in many ways appeared to be a nineteenth-century gentleman trapped in a twentieth-century body. Blaine was not just passionate about history, he seemed to live it and live in it.

His eccentricities aside, Blaine was never dull and enjoyed a reputation as an engaging conversationalist. Blaine was, as Jim Phillips remarked, "sort of a full-time professor," and more at ease talking to small groups or large audiences than he sometimes was with individuals.[31] He was regarded as at least nominally conservative, and while he may have been slow to embrace cultural and social trends and evolutions, he was fundamentally egalitarian towards those around him. Notoriously introspective, Blaine was the unofficial chronicler of his family history, and proudly traced his roots back to Virginia Loyalists who fled the American colonies for British North America.[32] Described by one long-time colleague as a sort of "patrician, family-compact Upper Canadian," Blaine had shades of elitism but his was generally of an intellectual variety rather than snobbery based on class or background.[33] He researched family homesteads, and made regular pilgrimages to place flowers and tend family plots in Orillia.[34] He saw himself as steward of his family's patrimony and property, which included a large tract on Long Bay in Lake Muskoka. Tellingly, he was more comfortable discussing long-deceased relatives than he was living members of his family. While Blaine was in many ways the archetypical anglophone within Quebec sociohistorical circles, somewhat predictably supporting the St Andrew's Society and similar groups, he lived in Montreal's student ghetto for years. Despite it being his main residence, he did not immerse himself in cultural life outside of McGill's Roddick Gates. He read French fluently but was never heard to speak it. To the armchair psychologists among us, it may have betrayed his unwillingness to be vulnerable in the face of not being as erudite a speaker in French as he wished.[35]

While not his alma mater, Blaine was a fervent ambassador of McGill which he saw as a quintessentially Canadian yet global institution. He was most gratified when he saw its Faculty of Law reach for international prominence. He was an enthusiastic proponent of the chronicling of the Faculty of Law's history and contributions to legal education. At the forefront of efforts to mark the Faculty's sesquicentennial, it was at his behest, along with then-dean Stephen Toope and Nicholas Kasirer, that a volume on the history of the Faculty was undertaken and with my nomination as author.[36] Of particular interest to Blaine were the stories I unearthed of all-but-forgotten visionaries such as Robert Warden Lee who became dean in 1915 until his departure for Oxford in 1921. Blaine was resolute that Lee should be recognized for his progressive views on legal instruction, which included introducing the LLB degree in addition to the BCL, a forerunner of McGill's renowned dual degree National Programme by some fifty years. This was not to last, as the LLB experiment met with opposition from the Quebec bar and was discontinued in 1924.

While it may be tempting to see Blaine as the archetypal common law professor, wedded as he was to that world, this would fail to appreciate his embrace of the reform and reimagining of legal education. It is not a coincidence that Daniel Boyer, Wainwright Librarian at McGill, remembers having first met Blaine during an exchange between students and faculty of both common law and civil law held in Sherbrooke in 1994.[37] Boyer vividly remembers Blaine's exposition of his speculative yet ambitious theory of legal development whereby the topology of the Saint Lawrence watershed informed the joint development of the law in Lower and Upper Canada. When the two became colleagues at McGill a few years later, they repeatedly worked together, notably on the Faculty's Legal Research and Writing program as Blaine strongly supported this often overlooked course. They also collaborated on reintroducing the teaching of Roman Law at the Faculty. Furthermore, Boyer recalled Blaine's strong connection with the late Brian Simpson and how together they tracked down the location of a few well-known Canadian private law cases. Like Simpson, Blaine was acutely interested in situating cases in their socio-historical context.

Blaine's fascination with McGill's abortive experiments in comparative legal education in the 1920s lay in how the succeeding decades would eventually culminate in the launching of the National Programme in 1968 during Maxwell Cohen's deanship. Blaine's interest was not merely that of a chronicler but as an avid proponent of the desirability of a more intertwined comparativist teaching of the two main Western legal traditions (common law and civil law, both part of Quebec's legal system). This process was to begin around 1992, and gained traction under Dean Stephen Toope in the fall of 1995. Blaine did not play a formal part in the various committees tasked with curricular reform, although he supported the gestational proposal to integrate the BCL and LLB streams, and had been a steadfast proponent through his intellectual commitment to pluralism, as noted by colleagues such as then-dean Kasirer and Janda.[38] Blaine, ever the historian, saw McGill's reimagining of its curriculum as the natural continuation of an evolutionary arc that ran from its initial attempt at bijuridical education in the 1920s to the National Programme, and beyond.

That he did is the more striking when one contemplates that Blaine must have known that this process, if successful, would ultimately marginalize him given his traditional areas of expertise, and with it his sway on the Faculty itself. But to Blaine the process itself was invaluable, involving as it did collective introspection as an epistemic tool to till and replenish the intellectual soil of the Faculty. He shared at least aspects of this with Rod Macdonald. As Blaine wrote of him, Macdonald stated that "thoughtful curricular debate is a law school's primary heuristic or autodidactic device and that the process of collective self-reflection and renewal that underlie curricular reform are therefore more important than reforms' results (however divisive that debate may be)."[39] Blaine valued the intellectual exercise as precisely that: an intellectual exercise that was innately salutary, which could also happily result in a reimagining of curriculum, culture, and character. Fall 1999 marked the launching of McGill's "transsystemic" program, a holistic and integrated curriculum that was the culmination of the efforts begun in 1995. The result was a poly-juridical and comparative program that studies law "through the lens of the common law and the civil law; with Indigenous legal traditions and perspectives from legal traditions the world over incorporated into our pluralistic approach to teaching law."[40] Blaine's satisfaction in seeing it launch was tinged with some sense of disappointment and wistfulness in no longer being as comfortably embedded within the fabric of the Faculty, and a hint that the comparative nature of the curriculum had extended beyond his reach. Whatever his misgivings may have been about his eventual place at the reimagined table of McGill's curriculum, Blaine was amongst the intrepid pioneers ushering in the new integrated first year comparative courses, teaching Contractual Obligations in 1999–2001, and again in 2004–2006.

Truthfully, it was not Blaine's wish to seek emeritus status in 2009. Blaine's issues had ebbed and waned, but the last few years found him increasingly unmoored from his academic home. Over the decades Blaine had of course taken sabbaticals, but also leaves of absence planned and unplanned. Gone, however, were the days when Blaine could merely slip back into teaching his traditional courses. His expertise did not lend itself easily to this comparative paradigm that continued to evolve over this period, heightened by his being less present in Montreal. Blaine became self-evidently more peripheral to the Faculty in the last few years, and his health issues also made his peripatetic ways untenable.

In Blaine's last phase of his career he bristled at the suggestion he had retired from McGill, and indeed he remained involved in a variety of professional activities there and elsewhere. An initiative to celebrate his legacy culminated in the endowment of the Blaine Baker Entrance Scholarship Fund, a project that he was both involved with and found supremely gratifying.[41] The annual Baker scholarship was first offered in 2013.[42] During that time Blaine continued to maintain an office at McGill, and he co-supervised a graduate student in 2015, informally mentored and supervised others, and taught a legal history seminar in the fall of 2016 – an academic year which coincided with the introduction of further curricular changes including two one-week integration periods in addition to other innovations.[43]

Following his naming as professor emeritus, Blaine's accustomed overnight train rides between Montreal and Toronto gave way to activities closer to home, as he served as visiting professor at the University of Toronto Faculty of Law (2011–2016),[44] director of the Wellington County Law Association History Project, a per diem Superior Court mandatory mediator for the attorney general of Ontario, and License Appeal Tribunal member and adjudicator. He continued to travel frequently to his beloved Muskoka, although in later years not to the family lake house but to a former Boy Scout campground with several ramshackle cabins. It was in Muskoka that Blaine seemed at his most serene. A series of heart attacks never sidelined him permanently but resulted in an inexorable deterioration in his overall health, exacerbated by his inability or unwillingness to heed medical advice. His death was tragic yet not surprising; and he passed away at his George Street home in July 2018.

* * *

Onto the work-at-hand: Part One contains four essays that focus on Blaine's life and work, with contributions by all three co-editors and a long-term McGill colleague. The poem that prefaces this section was written for this volume by Kathy Fisher, a former law student of Blaine's, who is a multidisciplinary artist, writer, documentarian, performer, legal researcher, filmmaker, biographer, and oral historian. Her poem, "footnotes margins minutes" contains many of the same threads that we explore in these essays, and her presence is also eminently fitting as she is a prime example of the varied backgrounds and talents that Blaine valued in his role on admissions committees. Angela Fernandez, member of the University of Toronto Faculty of Law, co-editor, and likewise a former student of Blaine's, depicts Blaine's beauty and fragility (the "butterfly," borrowing from an analogy made by Nicholas Kasirer), against the backdrop of the historic reluctance to recognize issues of mental health, addiction, and the like within the legal academy. Using her own experiences with Blaine as a mentor and colleague, she reminds us that as adept and willing as he always was to assist others, he could not admit he needed support himself. Brian Young, professor emeritus of history at McGill and long-time colleague and friend of Blaine, offers a longitudinal perspective on Blaine's intellectual and scholarly positioning. As Young notes, scholars may debate Blaine's precise place in Canadian historiography as he did not neatly fit within conventional definitions and parameters. This essay provides insight into Blaine's complex and sometimes shadowy persona, someone Young described as "original, enigmatic, inspirational, and yet somehow anachronistic in both his personage and in his search for a coherent, conservative Canadian legal past."[45] Richard Janda offers a capstone to Part One by examining Blaine's "present absence" in the Faculty's curriculum reform in the 1990s, also using one of Blaine's works on marginalia as an inspiration for examining his effect in ways both explicit and discrete. He shows us that much of Blaine's contribution to the reimagining of legal teaching at McGill was not overt or well-documented, but nonetheless significant, tangible, and enduring.

By design the essays in Part Two are grouped alphabetically by author rather than by topic, to mirror the structure of a work that Blaine had co-edited.[46] There are elements of commonality to them: each author presents a facing page that discusses their relationship with Blaine and his influence on the field of legal history. While at first glance the essays are disparate, covering both pre- and post-Confederation Canada and a wide array of topics, nonetheless each channels Blaine in some manner, be it in terms of methodology, time period, topic, or the like. It can even be said (as was suggested by one of our anonymous reviewers) that there are shared threads amongst many of them and Blaine himself – such as cross and undercurrents and things unspoken. While it is ultimately up to the readers to discern this for themselves, those elements could be said to include trans-identity, race, and subterfuge (Backhouse); nation building through trade protectionism (Fernandez); transnational conversations-to-be in judicial biography (Girard); legislation that foreshadowed constitutional division of powers (Phillips and Collins); criminal acts against children (Pilarczyk); promoting national identity vis-à-vis government protection of intellectual property (Piper); clandestine acts and crime as female survival strategies (Poutanen); subverting the hegemony of the Catholic church (Reiter); resistance in legal education to non-adjudicative process (Sandomierski); and liberalism in the provincial- rights movements and opposition to the formation of the welfare state (Verbauwhede).

Blaine, ever the consummate historian, admired deep dives into archives although he typically focused on more circumscribed sources to produce his scholarship.[47] Archival research is therefore well-represented here, as are micro-histories, biography, and legal education. It is fitting that Constance Backhouse opens our collection with a piece of modern legal history. She recounts the story of an enigmatic American fraudster operating in early twentieth-century prairie Canada. Beginning with a serendipitous find within the Saskatchewan archives thirty years ago and culminating in this essay, it intersects with themes of gender, suffrage, race, and women's criminality, all against the backdrop of a motoring (and possibly gender-fluid) huckster in the early days of the Roaring 1920s. It is also an embedded narrative, used as a vehicle by Backhouse to discuss how more recent methods of historical inquiry including critical race theory and feminist legal history offer tools for an altogether different, more robust and more inclusive analysis.[48] It bears further mention that Backhouse and Blaine were briefly junior faculty together at Western, Ontario.[49]

Angela Fernandez was a former law student inspired and mentored by Blaine. His participation in recreating private libraries within the rare books of the McGill law library was an inspiring resource, and she credits Blaine as introducing her to myriad canons of legal inquiry and legal scholarship, which in turn helped inform her work detailing the history of the quirky, yet seminal, American property case *Pierson v. Post*. Fernandez's contribution examines an under-appreciated Supreme Court of Canada case on fishing rights from the waning years of the nineteenth century.[50] Building on her 2018 book on *Pierson* published by Cambridge University Press, this piece has much to say about national identity, and draws hitherto-unnoted parallels between the two cases.[51] It also uses a 1985 article by Blaine on legal thought as an aid in analysis.[52] Similarly to Backhouse, Fernandez invites us to consider how perspectives and analysis of the *Gerring*'s legal issues might have shifted over time.

Philip Girard enjoyed a career path in direct juxtaposition from Blaine's: he graduated from McGill and went to teach at Western. Girard pays homage to Blaine's interest in "juristic biography," among other subjects, as well as "his interest in the migration of legal personnel, law books, and legal ideas."[53] That there is also tie-in to Blaine's last published work (on Justice LeDain, as noted earlier) is all the more fitting. Here Girard explores the new dynamics of the international judiciary, and why juristic biography now needs to be considered as both more global as well as comparative.

Jim Phillips is another long-time colleague of Blaine's. With Phillips, Blaine edited two volumes for the Osgoode Society for Canadian Legal History, including the aforementioned tribute volume to R.C.B. Risk.[54] Phillips and Tom Collins offer here a story that would have captured Blaine's imagination: in their words, the "continuity of legal and political ideas between the Canadas of the pre-1867 world and the Canada forged by Confederation." To do so, their works present a methodical comparison of the consolidations and sections 91–93 of *the British North America Act* with that of section 91 of the *Consolidated Statutes of Canada*, and sections 92–93 of the *Consolidated Statutes of Lower Canada*.[55]

My contribution bears Blaine's fingerprints in no small measure. Culled from research intended for my doctoral thesis under his tutelage, it was at Blaine's prodding that I began work on this piece several years ago. It utilizes the judicial archives and newspapers from the first half of the nineteenth century to examine sexual assault against female children.[56] The type of legal archaeology prized by Blaine, he encouraged me to consider the multi-faceted consequences that a patriarchal and gendered legal system would have on victims who were both females and minors, and I was grateful for his comments on an early draft.

In some ways my piece and that of Mary-Ann Poutanen are companions; hers likewise is legal archeology that delves into Montreal's judicial archives. Poutanan examines the records of the court of general criminal jurisdiction to examine female larcenists in her contribution to our collection. It offers a study of the dynamics of female criminality from a feminist perspective, and its underlying causes, the actors, and intersection with criminal justice.[57] Poutanen, along with Brian Young, are instrumental members of the Montreal History Group.[58] Blaine admired Poutanen's and Backhouse's work even as they often challenged his conservative leanings. While not an area of his own inquiry, he was intrigued by the theme of female agency in nineteenth-century society and the interplay between historically-marginalized groups and the legal system, themes that resonate throughout Poutanen's work.

Tina Piper commenced her career at McGill just as Blaine was concluding his; and it bears noting that she now teaches the Canadian Legal History course pioneered by Blaine (which, as further examples of baton passing-and-sharing, was also taught along the way by myself, and more recently by fellow contributor Cory Verbauwhede).[59] She offers us an example of modern legal history recounting the formation of the first technology transfer office with multiple themes that interested Blaine, including intellectual property, nation-building, and national identity, all set against the backdrop of Canadian railways and two world wars.[60] Eric Reiter, a former law student of Blaine, offers a case study of a "theologizing blacksmith" named Damase Richer, who in 1870 initiated a libel action against a local *curé* in a rural Quebec parish. While Richer's legal quest was ultimately unsuccessful, Reiter's piece provides us with an account of the courts' grappling with issues involving the religious freedoms and the possible boundaries of clerical immunity.[61] In it we see the themes of secular and religious forces, law and society, and liberalism and conservatism battling for supremacy within two loci of power in Quebec: the courts and the Church.

David Sandomierski presents an essay that traces curricular rejuvenation at the University of Toronto Faculty of Law. Sandomierski was a former student and frequent interlocutor with Blaine whilst completing his SJD at the University of Toronto.[62] There are more than mere shades of Blaine here given, inter alia, the legacy of his inventive Administrative Process course at McGill and his unfinished reimagining of his Legal Process course at Toronto. Echoing Richard Janda's story of Blaine's absence or presence in the curricular debate around McGill's turn to the transsystemic program, Sandomierski examines the history of initiatives to include more public law and awareness of law as process in the first year curriculum at the University of Toronto. Sandomierski appends a copy of the syllabus Blaine intended to use for the course but sadly did not live to teach, found at the end of the volume.

Rounding out our tribute, both alphabetically as well as topically, is a piece that reflects and incorporates Blaine's legacy. Cory Verbauwhede uses Blaine's thoughts, published and unpublished, as a roadmap for exploring the implementation of the modern Canadian welfare state.[63] In so doing, he cites a favorite phrase of Blaine's: "the camel's nose in the tent," also referenced in a cartoon reproduced in one of Blaine's legal history examinations as a prompt to discuss Red Toryism as an impetus for the Canadian welfare state.

If we have struck the correct balance in this tribute volume, if we have managed to do justice to the illuminating, implausible, inscrutable Blaine, then we will also have succeeded in showing the depths of our affection and admiration for him. As Blaine was wont to say after he elicited an interesting opinion that met with his approval, "I think that's about right." That is the most we can aspire to here.

August 2021
Boston, MA

NOTES

I am indebted and grateful to Angela Fernandez and Brian Young for their editorial comments on this essay, and for the privilege of having worked with them on this volume. I have also greatly benefitted from the support and suggestions of Nicholas Kasirer and Daniel Boyer.

1 Bill Thompson, memorial speech emailed to Kathy Fisher, 11 August 2018.

2 Ian C. Pilarczyk, "'Justice in the Premises': Family Violence and the Law in Montreal, 1825–1850" (DCL thesis, McGill University Institute of Comparative Law, 2003); Ian C. Pilarczyk, "'Too Well Used by His Master': Judicial Enforcement of Servants' Rights in Montreal, 1830–1845," *McGill Law Journal* 46 (2001): 491–529; Ian C. Pilarczyk, "The Law of Servants and the Servants of Law: Enforcing Masters' Rights in Montreal, 1830–1845," *McGill Law Journal* 46 (2001): 779–836.

3 *Globe and Mail*, 18 August 2018.

4 Rick Levick, email message to Genevieve Westgate, 18 October 2019. He apparently began his campaign speech by plucking pieces of paper out of a paper bag and reading first lines from famous historical speeches before discarding them, which the student body found very amusing. He won handily.

5 Chris Wallace, interview by Genevieve Westgate, 13 September 2019 (all interviews herein conducted by Genevieve Westgate unless otherwise noted).

6 Tribute page, comment of Dean Taylor, BCL/ LLB '01, https://www.mcgill.ca/law/community/memoriam/baker-blaine/tributes-blaine-baker.

7 See "Rate my Professor: Rating of Blaine Baker," https://www.ratemyprofessors.com/ShowRatings.jsp?tid=101562.

8 Jason Mogg, BCL/LLB '99, email message to Richard Janda, Ian C. Pilarczyk, Cory Verbauwhede, and Robert Leckey, 27 May 2019.

9 Tribute page, comment of Michael J. Doyle, BCL/ LLB '88, 2018, https://www.mcgill.ca/law/community/memoriam/baker-blaine/tributes-blaine-baker.

10 See "The Very Model of a Legal Academian," *infra*, 119–20.

11 By way of example, in his *Ethics in Alternative Dispute Resolution* syllabus at the University of Toronto, under the unit "Bad Faith and Unconscionable Behaviour," Blaine included the following suggested supplementary reading: D.J. Trump, *Trump: The Art of the Deal* (New York: Random House, 1988). See comment on Tribute Page by Jeremy Greenberg, https://www.mcgill.ca/law/community/memoriam/baker-blaine/tributes-blaine-baker.

12 Interview with Robert Leckey, 10 June 2019. This availability continued until the last; his syllabus for Canadian Legal History offered at the University of Toronto (LAW 354 H1S) in January 2018 likewise noted that his office hours generally included "Sunday afternoons." His syllabus for Ethical Issues in Dispute Resolution (LAW 521 H1S), a course offered on Wednesdays in Winter 2016, mentioned that he "will put time aside after each of the appointed class sessions for informal, small group, or one-on-one conversations," and noted that with respect to office hours he "would generally be there much of the day on Tuesdays and Wednesdays" and in a rather droll manner that "otherwise I will be there by chance, but the chances of presence are good." His planned syllabus for what was meant to be his Legal Process (LAW 100 H1S) course at the University of Toronto in the winter term of 2019 stated with respect to office hours that "I will generally be there on Tuesdays, Thursdays, and Saturdays in the winter term of the 2018–19 academic year (otherwise, I will be there by chance)." David Sandiomerski, "The Limits of Adjudication in the First-Year Curriculum: The Recurring History of Legal Process at the University of Toronto Faculty of Law," Appendix, Instructor Contact.

13 Interview with Robert Leckey, 10 June 2019.

14 Aptly captured in ibid.

15 R. Foerster, ed., *Accountants' Liability in Canada* (Toronto: Carswell, 2002), page iii:

> I owe a huge debt of gratitude to Professor Blaine Baker of the McGill Law School. By fortunate coincidence, Blaine arrived at the firm in which I am a partner, Borden Ladner Gervais, for a term as Scholar in Residence just as the book was evolving from rough draft to gainful product. He spent a good deal of time while he was at the firm working on the book. His role is best described as an editor of the work,

but he also served as an invaluable sounding board and generously gave me the benefit of his many years of legal scholarship.

16 His CV lists first, second, and third place finishes (by year and competition) for ten teams he coached between 1982–1995.

17 His contributions to the re-conception of administrative law at McGill was a common theme in interviews with colleagues and former students. See, e.g., Armand De Mestral interview, 3 June 2019; Robert Leckey, 10 June 2019; Cory Verbauwhede, 17 June 2019. Macdonald was of course a towering figure in the intellectual life of the Faculty until his passing in 2014. His memorial page may be found at https://www.mcgill.ca/law/community/memoriam/macdonald-roderick.

18 Interview with Cory Vanbauwhede, 17 June 2019.

19 G. Blaine Baker, syllabus for Ethical Issues in Alternative Dispute Resolution (LAW 532 H1S), Winter 2016.

20 G. Blaine Baker and Richard Janda, *Tracings of Gerald Le Dain's Life in the Law* (Montreal: McGill-Queen's University Press, 2019).

21 Brian Young, "It Was a Man's World: Blaine Baker and the Writing of Canadian Legal History, 1981–2018," *infra*, 49–82.

22 Richard Janda, comments on the author's draft on 3 June 2019.

23 G. Blaine Baker, "'So Elegant a Web': Providential Order and the Rule of Secular Law in Early-Nineteenth-Century Upper Canada," *University of Toronto Law Journal* 38, no. 2 (1988): 184–205. For a complete list of Blaine's works, see the bibliography at the end of the volume.

24 This extraneous endnote is therefore dedicated to Blaine and as a reward to the perceptive reader. Blaine might have uttered a hearty guffaw at this despite the seriousness with which he viewed citations.

25 See, e.g., G. Blaine Baker, "The Reconstitution of Upper Canadian Legal Thought in the Late-Victorian Empire," *Law and History Review* 3, no. 2 (1985): 219–92.

26 See, e.g., Bonnie Brown's remarks at Blaine Baker's memorial service at McGill University, 7 September 2018:

> [h]e put together a fascinating group of students, an eclectic and diverse group which he believed could learn a lot from each other, and that our experience, and the profession itself, would be richer for it … Those of us in the common law class of 95–96 had a strong sense that we were actually Blaine's class. That he cared about each of us, and he expected us to work hard. He impressed on us what a privilege it was to be at McGill Law, and to take our education seriously.

27 Interview with Nicholas Kasirer, 26 June 2019.

28 Interview with Bonnie Brown, 17 July 2019.

29 Interview with Brian Young, 26 June 2019.

30 Robert Leckey likewise noted the "needlessly old-fashioned" manner in which he would do things, including formally addressing envelopes and adding "by internal mail" for routine items he would leave in faculty mailboxes. Interview with Robert Leckey, 10 June 2019. I was always a little surprised he did not take it a step further and secure every envelope with a signet ring and sealing wax.

31 Interview with Jim Phillips, 21 June 2019.

32 On a few occasions I recall Blaine speaking about this; he always seemed slightly embittered that his family's properties had been confiscated during the American Revolution. I admit my American sensitivities were not overly sympathetic.

33 Interview with Nicholas Kasirer, 26 June 2019.

34 Interview with Chris Wallace, 13 September 2019.

35 See, e.g., interview with Nicholas Kasirer, 26 June 2019. He did appear much more comfortable engaging in the written word; and on the few occasions I found myself travelling on the same Via Rail train I noted he enjoyed completing crosswords in French as well as English.

36 Ian C. Pilarczyk, *A Noble Roster: One Hundred and Fifty Years of Law at McGill* (McGill University, Montreal, 1999).

37 Interview with Daniel Boyer, 4 June 2019.

38 Interview with Nicholas Kasirer, 26 June 2019. For discussion, see Richard Janda, "Traces of Blaine Baker Upon McGill's Faculty of Law," *infra*, 83–115.

39 G. Blaine Baker, "Character-Building at Multiple Sites of Justice: Administration and Teaching as Texts, Scholarship as Ethical and Political Action," in *The Unbounded Level of the Mind: Rod Macdonald's Legal Imagination*, edited by Richard Janda, Rosalie Jukier, and Daniel Jutras (McGill-Queen's Press, Montreal & Kingston, 2015), 216. See also Roderick Macdonald, "Curricular Development," *Journal of Legal Education* 32 (1982): 569.

40 "McGill's Unique BCL/JD Program," https://www.mcgill.ca/law/bcl-jd/program-description. Since November 2019 the joint degree program awards a BCL/JD rather than the BCL/LLB.

41 From the Faculty of Law's newsletter, *Focus* (Fall 2013):

> Upon being made Emeritus Professor in 2009, donors created the Blaine Baker Entrance Fund. The Blaine Baker Entrance Scholarship Fund will be awarded on the basis of academic merit to a student with graduate studies experience entering a full-time undergraduate Law program. The Scholarship was created by friends, colleagues,

> family, and former students of Blaine Baker, Professor Emeritus, who taught administrative law, legal history, and contract law at the Faculty. "Through his teaching, guidance, and research, Blaine formed the foundations for legal education for every student he had taught," said Ian Pilarczyk (LLM'97, DCL'03), who co-chaired the committee to help establish the fund, along with Mario Nigro (BCL'00, LLB'00). From this year forward, the Blaine Baker Entrance Scholarship will be a fitting way to honour Professor Baker's career at McGill. "Professor Baker clearly had a big impact on his former students," remarked [Associate Director of Development Ester] Driham. "We heard time and time again how he always had time to help guide them. There was such a strong emotional response – we've never seen anything like it."

42 From *Focus* (Fall 2018):

> The Blaine Baker Entrance Scholarship was established in the Faculty of Law in 2013 by former students, friends, family, and colleagues of Blaine's in recognition of his 30 years of service. It is awarded to one or more outstanding students entering the BCL/LLB program on the basis of high academic standing, with a preference for students having pursued prior graduate studies."

See also "Tuition and Financial Support," https://www.mcgill.ca/law/bcl-llb/tuition-and-financial-support.

43 "The next phase of legal education," updated June 2015, https://publications.mcgill.ca/droit/2015/06/01/curriculum-renewal/.

44 He also served as such from 1988–89, 1995–96, and 2006–07. He was visiting professor at Osgoode Hall Law School from 1987–88 and 1994–95.

45 Brian Young, "It Was a Man's World: Blaine Baker and the Writing of Canadian Legal History, 1981–2018," *infra*, 49–82.

46 G. Blaine Baker and Jim Phillips, eds., *Essays in the History of Canadian Law, Volume VIII: In Honour of R.C.B. Risk* (Toronto: University of Toronto Press, 1999).

47 See, e.g., G. Blaine Baker, "Musings and Silences of Chief Justice William Osgoode: Digest Marginalia about the Reception of Imperial Law," *Osgoode Hall Law Journal* 54, no. 3 (2017); G. Blaine Baker, "Testamentary Archeology in Late-Victorian Ontario: William Martin's Little, Posthumous Legal System," *Canadian Journal of Law and Society* 30, no. 3 (2015): 345–64; G. Blaine Baker, "Law Practice and Statecraft in Mid-Nineteenth-Century Montreal: The Torrance-Morris Firm, 1848 to 1868," in *Beyond the Law: Lawyers and Business in Canada 1830 to 1930*, edited by (Toronto: Butterworth, 1990): 45–91; G. Blaine Baker,

"The Juvenile Advocate Society, 1821 to 1826: Self-Proclaimed Schoolroom for Upper Canada's Governing Class," *Historical Papers of the Canadian Historical Association* 20 (1985): 74–101.

48 Constance Backhouse, "The Historical Exploits of Stella March: Reflecting on Feminist Legal History," 121–47.

49 For further discussion, see Young, "'It Was a Man's World,'" *infra*, 49–82; see also Constance Backhouse's facing page of her essay, *infra*, 121.

50 Angela Fernandez, "The Case of the *Frederick Gerring Jr*: Fish, Colony, and Nation," *infra*, 148–91.

51 *Pierson v. Post, The Hunt for the Fox: Law and Professionalization in American Legal Culture* (Cambridge: Cambridge University Press, 2018).

52 See, e.g., G. Blaine Baker, *Sources in the Law Library of McGill University for a Reconstruction of the Legal Culture of Quebec, 1760–1890*, with K.E. Fisher, V. Masciotra, and B. Young, eds. (Montreal: McGill University and Montreal History Project, 1987); Supra 27: 219–92; G. Blaine Baker, "Bibliographic Reconstruction of Canadian Legal Culture," *Bull. Bibliographical Soc. Can.* 25 (1985): 11–20.

53 Philip Girard, "New Directions in Judicial Biography: More Humane, More Transnational, More Comparative," *infra*, 192–210.

54 G. Blaine Baker and Jim Phillips, eds., *A History of Canadian Legal Thought: Collected Essays of R.C.B. Risk* (Toronto: The Osgoode Society and University of Toronto Press, 2006); Ibid., *Essays in the History of Canadian Law, Volume VIII: In Honour of R.C.B. Risk*.

55 Jim Phillips and Tom Collins, "The Colonial Origins of the Division of Powers in the British North America Act," *infra*, 211–48.

56 Ian C. Pilarczyk, "'A most atrocious crime': Sex Crimes Against the Woman-Child in Early Nineteenth-Century Montreal," *infra*, 249–96.

57 Mary-Ann Poutanen, "Theft in the City: Women and Everyday Justice in the Montreal Archives, 1768–1841," 337–80.

58 An offshoot of the Montreal History Group was the project both Brian Young and Blaine were involved with, *Sources in the Law Library of McGill University for a Reconstruction of the Legal Culture of Quebec, 1760–1890* – with K.E. Fisher, V. Masciotra, and B. Young.

59 I was asked to take over the teaching of Canadian Legal History rather precipitously before the start of the semester in the academic year 2001–2002. My experience here echoed Tina's comments on the facing page of her essay – the course was so intrinsically and idiosyncratically wedded to Blaine's unique teaching style and his encyclopedic knowledge of legal history that I was unable to teach it with his materials and jettisoned

many of them in favour of my own. If I appreciated his inimitable teaching method before, I appreciated it even more afterwards.

60 Tina Piper, "The Making of Canada's First Technology Transfer Office (1916–1939)," *infra*, 297–336.

61 Eric Reiter, "The Case of the Theologizing Blacksmith: Liberalism, Ultramontanism, and Defamation in Quebec," 381–412.

62 David Sandomierski, "The Limits of Adjudication in the First-Year Curriculum: The Recurring History of Legal Process at the University of Toronto Faculty of Law," *infra*, 413–53.

63 Cory Verbauwhede, "The Camel's Nose in the Constitutional Tent: Extrapolating from G. Blaine Baker's Thoughts on Late-Nineteenth-Century Legal Liberalism and Elite Lawyer Resistance to the Canadian Welfare State," *infra*, 454–92.

2

Blaine Baker, a Butterfly

Angela Fernandez

When I started as a law student at McGill in 1996, I had the good fortune to be in Blaine's year-long Contracts course in my first year. In the upper-year program, I took Blaine's Canadian Legal History course and learned about what he called the "worm's eye view" of administrative agencies in his Administrative Law class.[1] I also wrote a directed research paper co-supervised by Blaine and Nicholas Kasirer that became my first published article.[2] I have been teaching Contracts very much in the historically-informed approach Blaine introduced me to since I came to the University of Toronto in 2004. I even used a version of the same supplement (created by Robert W. Gordon) that Blaine starting to employ at McGill and in Toronto in the 1980s.[3] Before developing my own course, Legal Archaeology: Studies in Cases in Context, I taught versions of Blaine's legal history course, and he and I both taught the introduction to civil process and procedure course at the University of Toronto Faculty of Law, and Legal Process (the history of which David Sandomierski writes about in his essay in this volume) in the years closely preceding his death (see Appendix for the last version of Blaine's syllabus for that course). The last sustained professional contact Blaine and I had was around the fine piece he contributed to a collection I was co-editing, published in 2012.[4] The last positive personal memory I have of seeing him looking really well was at my fortieth birthday party in 2013, where he brought me some dusty old books he knew I would like.

The first paper I wrote in law school in my Foundations class at McGill focused on issues that still preoccupy me and which Blaine played a key role in directing. The assignment, given by Daniel Jutras, was to choose a case that we had encountered to date in one of our first-year courses and to write a short paper about it. I selected a mistake case, *Raffles v. Wichelhaus*, which Blaine had flagged in my Contracts class as a curious case that stood for a proposition of law found nowhere in the reported decision, yet had been appropriated and recreated by treatise writers keen to find a case to stand for the meeting-of-the-minds or *consensus ad idem* principle in contract law. In discussing the case, Blaine relied on legal archaeological work on the case by Brian Simpson, which had been published in his *Leading Cases in the Common Law* the previous year, 1995.[5] Blaine knew Simpson, having crossed paths with him (I believe in the 1980s). Blaine liked to say that Simpson referred to studies like the ones in *Leading Cases* as his "party pieces."[6] They were certainly more engaging and easier to read than the tome Simpson wrote on the doctrine of assumpsit.[7] Even Simpson's "short simple book" on English land law would hardly be thought a page-turner.[8] I am not sure if "party piece" was meant to be a criticism. Blaine was not above the occasional caustic comment of this kind. However, I did not view the point as negative, given what I took to be the implication that it was a topic people would be interested in speaking to you about, say at a party, as opposed to a subject it would be difficult to discuss with pretty much anyone anywhere. I took that lesson to heart in terms of deciding to focus on a famous, indeed infamous, property law case, *Pierson v. Post* in my later work.[9] I did, however, also experiment with a lesser known local mistake case, *Leaf v. International Galleries*, telling the story of how it came to be included in the 1963 University of Toronto Contracts casebook edited by J.B. Milner.[10]

It would be difficult for me to overstate the influence Blaine has had on my teaching and research trajectory at the Faculty of Law at the University of Toronto, where I am now (in what seems to be a blink of an eye) a full professor. It has been twenty-five years since I raised my hand in one of our first Contracts class. "Yes, Ms Fernandez," he said when he saw my hand. "How did he know you?" my classmates asked me afterwards, not aware that he had our photos and was the kind of teacher to take the time to try and memorize his students' names and faces. I always looked for him to talk to at the weekly "Coffee House." I remember the conversation on the front lawn of McGill's Old Chancellor Day Hall where he explained to me that he was not really a contracts scholar but a legal historian. Really? Was that a thing one could be? I was intrigued. I did not fully commit to the field of legal history until after I finished my clerkship and entered into the graduate program at Yale Law School, where I was lucky to study with Bob Gordon, not realizing at the time I had already worked through some of his thinking about legal history through Blaine's supplementary contract materials.[11] I was explicitly introduced to Gordon's work in Blaine's Canadian Legal History course, not, interestingly enough, by reading Gordon's famous "Critical Legal Histories" but through a book review on a book about the nineteenth-century American codification movement assigned by Blaine, a topic I was very interested in, studying law in a "mixed" codified legal culture in Quebec.[12]

It might seem strange for a Festschrift, which one of my fellow editors, Ian C. Pilarczyk, teaches us is technically a *gedenkschrift* (as it is being presented posthumously), to stray into personal matters that are not uniformly positive. It is unusual for biographies of important legal figures to deviate from the story of a great man (it is usually a man), his wonderful family life (or at least passingly functional), and his illustrious career at the bar and on the bench. The goes-without-saying is that the negative (e.g., depression, alcoholism, marital affairs) are not to be spoken about or only in the most circumscript terms. Probably in most cases, this is the correct call, especially where there are surviving family members who would be hurt by public discussion of that kind of personal information. However, in Blaine's case, he had no spouse or children and is survived only by a sister from whom he was estranged.[13] Also, the many problems that entered into and interfered with his personal and professional relationships cannot really be ignored in any kind of tribute that aims to be authentic.

As Ian points out, Blaine thought it was important in the collection he organized (and co-edited with Richard Janda) for Gerald Le Dain to include reference to Le Dain's mental health challenges. Discussing the "nervous exhaustion" or "depression" that led to Le Dain's premature departure from the Supreme Court of Canada, Blaine wrote: "A different result might have followed today, almost thirty years later, since treatment regimens and especially public understanding of mental illness have changed considerably."[14] The author of the Preface to the collection, Bernard Hibbits, put the point in even sharper terms:

> Canadian society in general and the Canadian legal profession in particular have made great strides over the last thirty years in the consideration, diagnosis, and treatment of mental illness. We are no longer as frightened or dismissive of it. We know it is [a] disease, like cancer, that can strike any one of us at any time. We therefore accord its sufferers more attention and respect.[15]

If Le Dain had been given more time, he "might have become the first Canadian high court judge to have publicly overcome a depression diagnosis. What a role model that would have made him! What an impact he might have had on the interpretation of Canadian mental illness laws and on the *Charter* rights of those suffering from mental disability!"[16] The book also contains a powerful statement by Le Dain's daughter, Caroline Burgess, who recounted in a CBC radio documentary "One Judge Down" that when her mother went to the Chief Justice to ask for more time for her husband before he was asked to resign, Dickson spoke about Le Dain, and specifically his mind, in the past tense:

> It was – he had a brilliant mind. As if somehow mental illness is associated with some kind of brain damage […] there was no question, from the reception my mother got […] that there was going to be any support. There wasn't an enlightened kind of sense of […] this is treatable. He will recover. He can come back. There was just that sense of […] it's done.[17]

As Philip Girard notes in his essay in this collection, there is a need to address "[t]he mental strain imposed by the demands of judicial office" for both contemporary and historical judicial figures, from the recent resignation of Supreme Court of Canada judge Clémont Gascon, due to his long-suffering depression and anxiety, to chief justices from the nineteenth century who also suffered from depression.[18] Justice Gascon's situation was handled in a much more progressive and humane way than Le Dain's was, demonstrating, in the opinion of one lawyer, that there has been "progress over time."[19]

Yet, as Ian also recounts, Blaine was extremely reticent opening up about his personal life and likely would not welcome that in any kind of public forum. As my other fellow editor, Brian Young, discusses in his excellent biographical essay in this part of the volume, Blaine chose not to discuss at any length his own personal connection to the Martin family, the subject of one of his historical studies.[20] Yes, Blaine was very much part of the "law and life" movement inspired by Rod Macdonald's style of legal pluralism at McGill in the 1990s; but that did not necessarily mean putting his own life under the microscope. That kind of consistency might just be too much to expect of any individual. As Blaine would often say to a student expressing frustration in class at a situation in which two cases yielded inconsistent results: "Why would you expect things to be consistent? Where did you get the idea that things [in law or in life] would be consistent?" This was a point he also liked to make by teaching a book review David Sugarman wrote in 1983 of a biography of Albert Venn Dicey, which concluded with the following words: "To end on a paradox should not surprise. Dicey, like most people, was not internally consistent."[21] It is just such an inconsistency to know that while Blaine felt it was important to air the mental health issues around Le Dain, his own struggles would remain intensely private, as if he did not quite believe that all that much had changed in thirty years, specifically how such struggles would be perceived by a (still very) conservative legal profession.

The Gordon and Sugarman book reviews remind me that it was Blaine who taught me the utility of book reviews as a vehicle for promoting legal history, a lesson I carry forward and find motivating in the book review editor role for the Americas I currently occupy for the journal *Law and History Review*. Blaine's use of those reviews in his Canadian Legal History course also taught me the value of book reviews as a teaching tool. Blaine would say that they are a good length to realistically expect students to read and will often contain a very good overview of the topic or field, although the field overview seems a little too much to ask reviewers to provide, especially in the number of words allotted to a standard review.[22] Blaine also taught me the importance of being a generous and available referee for junior scholars coming up in the field. I recall apologizing to him for asking him for so many reference letters, especially leading up to my graduate school years, and he explained to me that the work goes into the creation of the original letter. The subsequent ones are easy, a point that I now know well but I had little appreciation of at the time. Both of these lessons are of the garden-variety professional development kind, but are not to be sniffed at in a world where practical mentorship, especially vis-à-vis pedagogy and the day-to-day role of a law professor, can be thin on the ground. Yet Blaine had a way of making you feel like he had all the time in the world for whatever you needed.

Probably most importantly, Blaine taught me to meet law students where they are as human beings in their lives. I felt he encouraged me to keep connected to the person I was before I came to law school, not to feel I had to check myself, the person I was, at the door, in terms of personal interests such as reading choices but also with respect to the work I did at a graduate level in philosophy. He did that for me at crucial moments in my first year when I thought perhaps I should quit the program, as the legal profession was not a place I could see myself in, much less in which to occupy the role of a professor. There was something about Blaine's own fragility and self-doubt that made him able to see it in others and he had the instinct to reach out and try to help. Returning the favour was difficult. Yes, a nomination for the teaching award he won in 1999, or help starting the scholarship Ian Pilarczyk refers to, and the meals-on-wheels intervention that Ian organized when Blaine's health was very poor. Like many people who give a lot and who are very private, Blaine was not as adept at being open to receiving help. The expectation was that he was the one who would help you (the "What can *I* do for *you*?" Ian explains that Blaine would add at the end of a phone call). What he wanted and what many of us were able to give him over the years, I think, was the human contact (I recall that he would also often add at the end of the call "I appreciate the contact" or "I am grateful for the contact"). This was true even if many of us, like myself, found it increasingly difficult to sustain that contact in the last years of his life.

I really cannot count all of the things that Blaine taught me. Some of these lessons were sadly, by way of negative example. The importance of travelling to conferences and extending one's network of professional contacts and acquaintances. How crucial it was to avoid becoming isolated, frustrated, and bitter. The imperative of refusing to get stuck in negative thinking and habits that are self-sabotaging. To reach out for professional help when one's mental well-being is shaken by traumatic life events such as divorce, deaths, especially by suicide, which took Blaine's own brother, Eric. Nicholas Kasirer once described Blaine to me as a butterfly. I cannot remember when that was. I think I might have been a student, and I am sure I did not understand at the time what Nicholas meant, as it took me a long time to see any crack in a person who was really like a hero to me in terms of his generosity, patience, and the genuine interest he took in my life. The first intimation I had that there was something seriously wrong was when a former classmate called me in Connecticut to say she heard he had not come to the class he was teaching at McGill. That incident occurred in what Ian describes as the "interregnum" year in his doctoral supervision (2001–2002), when I was in the LLM program at Yale Law School. A similar incident occurred at the University of Toronto shortly after I began teaching there, I believe it was the fall of 2005. In the wake of that failure to appear to teach the first-year Contracts course, I told him, when he later asked, that I would not co-teach the Contracts class with him unless he undertook to get some professional help for the mental health issues relating to alcoholism. I did not want to be left not knowing if he would or would not show up for the class we were supposed to be co-teaching; or find myself leaving increasingly distressed messages on the answering machines (home and cottage) to find out where he was and if he was okay; or driving to his house in Mimico, in the southwest end of Toronto, to see for myself how bad the situation was this time. He was stubborn in his refusals to seek any professional help. This was much more serious than anything I could have imagined when I was a student, blissfully unaware, as yet untouched by the ravages of my own divorce and traumatic family deaths.[23] Another bout re-surfaced in 2014, likely triggered by the celebration for Rod Macdonald in February of that year. I think he might have felt that, like Le Dain, he had been prematurely retired (he was made an professor emeritus at McGill in 2009 when he was just fifty-seven) and was smarting with that rejection. I am sure that his colleagues at McGill would point out that he had been given a long time to deal with his issues. Blaine was not a person to whom "dealing with your issues" would have made a lot of sense. He was not someone who felt comfortable talking about psychological interiority, which put him at a distinct disadvantage in terms of being able to do this very difficult task. Plus, unlike Le Dain, he had no spouse or other family support to assist him in the demon-facing process. Or, as Ian Pilarczyk pointed out reading a draft of these pages, it might have been the demons that prevented him from having those things. At any rate, it was a vicious cycle.

I separated from my husband in the fall of 2014, and I had little extra emotional bandwidth when issues around Blaine not showing up to teach and being out-of-touch again became a problem. Richard Janda reached out to ask me to intervene to try and help, which I did by working with an understanding associate dean in my faculty, Ian Lee. The mental health issues that plague the legal profession are underdiscussed. We have an opportunity here, as Blaine (and Richard) did with Le Dain, to acknowledge them and to try to model for each other as well as for younger people in the profession more positive ways of coping. This is especially needed around substance abuse, depression, or reacting to a suicide, sadly such a regular occurrence, not just in post-secondary institutions but in society at large.[24] We must all struggle with the different challenges life throws at us; the skillfulness or unskillfulness is in how we react to them.[25] Do we bury them or deal with them? In this, Blaine taught me that if you want to come out the other end in one piece, you must deal with them.

I have come to see the analogy Nicholas made to Blaine as a butterfly as extremely apt, as he was very special, beautiful in his uniqueness and eccentricity, but also very fragile. His wings were brushed (and outright bumped and torn) by life's circumstances to a point where he was no longer able to fly. Our tribute to him should capture his fragility, as well as authentically honour him as an important Canadian intellectual, legal historian, colleague, teacher, and mentor. Funerals are, as they say, for the living; insofar as there are lessons to learn from Blaine's struggles, we ought to step forward to embrace them, as tempting as it is to sweep them under the "southern Ontario Gothic" rug (to echo Philip Girard invoking Margaret Atwood's descriptor in his essay in this volume). Dying alone as Blaine did, at the age of just sixty-six, is tragic. There is a lot to learn in the juxtaposition of Blaine's difficult personal life and what he was nonetheless able to accomplish in terms of his scholarship, his teaching and the way he was able to be so inspiring to his students, and his contribution to the legal historical thinking of those, like the contributors to this collection, whom he touched by way of inimitable personal professional connection. As Richard Janda wrote in relationship to Le Dain: "I think he would have acknowledged himself, significant fragility. But people with significant fragility can be absolutely remarkable contributors."[26] Being pulled under by fragility, as Caroline Burgess put it powerfully in relationship to her father: "I wish it would happen to nobody."[27] Yet, as any death reminds us, that fragility is all around us.

NOTES

I dedicate this essay to the memory of my student Meruba Sivaselvachandran (1997–2021), whose untimely and tragic death gave me the courage to write this piece as it needed to be written. I would like to thank Ian C. Pilarczyk for his leadership in bringing forward the idea of doing this collection, gathering together our editorial team, and shepherding the work through all the stages from mere flicker through to production, including playing the role of conduit to the first-class editorial support provided by Jonathan Crago at Queen's University Press. Once it became clear that this book would not be an ordinary (and wholly celebratory) tribute to its subject, the Osgoode Society for Canadian Legal History decided to remove its support for and involvement in the project. Personalized facing pages, essays weaving references to Blaine Baker, and not editing out negative aspects of his personal and professional life proved to be too much of a deviation from standard *Festschrift* form. However, these were important aspects of the collection as Ian, Brian, and I conceptualized it, which we were not prepared to compromise. I learned so much in this process from Brian Young, not just about history, of which he is a master practitioner, but also about speaking from the heart, finding and staying true to one's authorial and editorial vision and voice. I feel very privileged to have worked with both of my co-editors on this very special project, which has shown, I think, that one does not need to stay inside the box in order to produce original and important work. My hope is that it will encourage others to push at the boundaries of narrow and conservative understandings of history and the range of permissible speech, especially when writing about the legal profession.

1 See G. Blaine Baker, "Character-Building," in *The Unbounded Level of the Mind: Macdonald's Legal Imagination,* edited by Richard Janda, Rosalie Jukier, and Daniel Jutras (Montreal; Kingston: McGill-Queen's University Press, 2015), 214–22, 217.

2 See Angela Fernandez, "Albert Mayrand's Private Law Library: An Investigation of the Person, the Law of Persons, and 'Legal Personality' in a Collection of Law Books," *University of Toronto Law Journal* 53 (2003): 37–64.

3 See Robert W. Gordon, *The Rise and Fall of Classical Individualism in Anglo-American Legal Thought* (1983), located at the Nahum Gelber Law Library in their mimeographed casebook collection. Blaine was an assistant professor at that time, having started teaching at McGill in 1981. This work is listed under the same title in the York University library

catalogue, under just Bob's name in 1983 and again under Bob and Blaine's names in 1988, presumably in conjunction with Blaine's visit to Osgoode Hall Law School in 1987–88. It also appears in the University of Toronto catalogue under the same title under both names, also in 1988, presumably in conjunction with Blaine's visit to the Faculty of Law in 1988–89. When I realized the provenance of the book, I asked Bob for permission to also use it in my course, and I added to it and took things out over the next fifteen years.

4 See G. Blaine Baker, "Story'd Paradigms for the Nineteenth-Century Display of Anglo-American Legal Doctrine," in *Law Books in Action: Essays on the Anglo-American Legal Treatise*, edited by Angela Fernandez and Markus D. Dubber (Oxford: Hart Publishing, 2012), 82–107.

5 See A.W.B. Simpson, "The Beauty of Obscurity: *Raffles v. Wichelhaus and Busch* (1864)," in *Leading Cases in the Common Law*, edited by A.W.B. Simpson (Oxford: Oxford University Press, 1995), 135–62. I sometimes assign this piece to my Contracts students. I also use the following review of the collection in my Legal Archaeology course: Robert W. Gordon, "Simpson's Leading Cases," *Michigan Law Review* 95 (1996–7): 2044–54.

6 Simpson also produced book-length studies such as *Cannibalism and the Common Law: The Story of the Tragic Last Voyage of the Mignonette and the Strange Legal Proceedings to which it gave Rise* (Chicago: University of Chicago Press, 1984).

7 See A.W.B. Simpson, *A History of the Common Law of Contract: The Rise of the Action of Assumpsit* (Oxford: Clarendon Press, 1987), which I attempted (unsuccessfully) to get through in my first year teaching Contracts at the University of Toronto in 2004–2005. Stephen Waddams reassured me that this was just fine.

8 A.W.B. Simpson, preface to *A History of the Law*, 2nd ed. (Oxford: Clarendon Press, 1986). It was originally published in 1961.

9 Angela Fernandez, *Pierson v. Post, The Hunt for the Fox: Law and Professionalization in American Legal Culture* (Cambridge: Cambridge University Press, 2018).

10 See Angela Fernandez, "An Object Lesson in Speculation: Multiple Views of the Cathedral in *Leaf v. International Galleries*," *University of Toronto Law Journal* 58 (2008): 481, 503–14. The work in there on Milner has been helpful to David Sandomierski. See, e.g., David Sandomierski, "Catalytic Agents? Lon Fuller, James Milner, and the Lawyer as Social Architect, 1950–1969," *University of Toronto Law Journal* 71, no. 1 (2021): 91–125. One of the research questions from this "internal" perspective is to examine how casebooks change over time, explored in

relationship to *Pierson* in relation to American property law casebooks, see ibid., 274–86, and in Contracts casebooks in Canada, see David Sandomierski, *Aspiration and Reality in Legal Education* (Toronto: University of Toronto Press, 2020).

11 Blaine taught Contracts the year that I took it from the Angela (then John) Swan and Barry Reiter, 4th ed., *Contracts: Cases, Notes and Materials* (Toronto: Butterworths, Emond Montgomery, 1991). See Sandomierski, *Aspiration and Reality in Legal Education*, 79 n. 208 (listing the different editions of Swan and Reiter, from the first edition in 1978 to the ninth edition in 2015). I took a Remedies course with Swan in my second year. It was a course that focused mostly on contractual remedies and in which I learned many of the key practical points I find myself communicating to my students in my Contracts and Legal Process courses (e.g., in litigation, even when you win you lose, because of the way that costs work and usually only partially indemnify). Bob Gordon's American Legal History course was one of the highlights of my LLM year at Yale Law School (2001–2002).

12 Robert W. Gordon, "Critical Legal Histories," *Stanford Law Review* 36 (1984): 57–125; Robert W. Gordon, [Book Review of Charles M. Cook, *The American Codification Movement, A Study of Antebellum Legal Reform* (Westport, Conn.: Greenwood Press, 1981)] *Vanderbilt Law Review* 36 (1983): 431–58. For a sense of the influence of the famous 1984 work, see the Symposium on Gordon's "Critical Legal Histories," *Law and Social Inquiry* 37 (2012): 147–215. Blaine published a "reading list for his students" in 1984 that included Gordon's earlier work "Historicism in Legal Scholarship," *Yale Law Journal* 90 (1980–81): 1017–56, located in the section entitled "Thinking and Writing About Legal History." See G. Blaine Baker, "A Course in Canadian Legal History," *Now and Then* 2 (1984): 56–62, 56. The idea that this list could be covered in one course is fantastical. It is as jam-packed as Blaine's footnotes. It seems more like a list for a graduate student than a JD or LLB/BCL student.

13 See "George Blaine Baker," *Globe and Mail* (18 August 2018), obituary available at https://www.legacy.com/obituaries/theglobeandmail/obituary.aspx?n=george-blaine-baker&pid=190128496.

14 G. Blaine Baker, "Juristic Biographies, Homage Volumes, and 'Tracings of Gerald Le Dain's Life in the Law,'" in *Tracings of Gerald Le Dain's Life in the Law*, edited by G. Blaine Baker and Richard Janda (Montreal: McGill-Queen's University Press, 2019), 3–48, 13.

15 Bernard J. Hibbits, preface to *Tracings of Gerald Le Dain's Life in the Law*, edited by G. Blaine Baker and Richard Janda (Montreal: McGill-Queen's University Press, 2019), vii–xi, ix.

16 Ibid., x.

17 *The Sunday Edition*, CBC Radio One (14 January 2018), produced by Bonnie Brown. See "One Judge Down," in *Tracings of Gerald Le Dain's Life in the Law*, edited by G. Blaine Baker and Richard Janda (Montreal: McGill-Queen's University Press, 2019), 406–16, 414.

18 See Philip Girard, "New Directions in Judicial Biography: More Humane, More Transnational, More Comparative," *infra*, 193–210.

19 See Elizabeth Raymer, "Gascon's Treatment by SCC Lauded as Compared to Le Dain's," *Canadian Lawyer*, 17 May 2019 (quoting criminal litigator David Butt), available at https://www.canadianlawyermag.com/news/general/gascons-treatment-by-scc-lauded-as-compared-to-le-dains/276141.

20 G. Blaine Baker, "Testamentary Archeology in Late-Victorian Ontario: William Martin's Little, Posthumous Legal System," *Canadian Journal of Law and Society* 30, no. 3 (2015): 345–63, for which he was awarded the Canadian Law and Society Association Article Prize in 2016 for the best article published in the journal in the preceding year. See https://www.acds-clsa.org/?q=en/prizes. See Brian Young, "It Was a Man's World: Blaine Baker and the Writing of Canadian Legal History, 1981–2018," *infra*, 49–82.

21 See David Sugarman, "The Legal Boundaries of Liberty: Dicey, Liberalism and Legal Science," [Review of Richard A. Cosgrove, *The Rule of Law: Albert Venn Dicey, Victorian Jurist* (London: Macmillan, 1980)] *Modern Law Review* 46, no. 1 (1983): 102–11, 111. Blaine included the following work by Sugarman in the 1984 *Now and Then* reading list: Gerry R. Rubin and D. Sugarman eds., *Law, Economy and Society, 1750–1914: Essays in the History of English Law* (Abingdon, Oxon: Professional Books, 1984). See Baker, "A Course in Canadian Legal History," 58.

22 My experience has also been that more senior colleagues, who would be best positioned to provide that kind of overview, say in a review essay format with a longer word count, are not as keen to take on the task of reviewing. I have found that it is easier to enlist more junior entrants, who perhaps are reading new books more avidly and are more keen for a publication that senior colleagues do not need at a late stage in their career.

23 My father died on 25 October 2017 and my mother about three and a half months later on 13 February 2018. When Blaine died in July of the same year, I could hardly believe how fast it had all happened, how they

could all be there smiling and singing "Happy Birthday" one minute and gone in what seemed like the next, although it was in reality more like a four-year period. See obituaries available at http://www.inmemoriam.ca/view-announcement-2290742-dr-peter-fernandez.html; https://www.carnells.com/?obituaries=dr-dzintra-fernandez-nee-parums.

24 See https://www.canada.ca/en/public-health/services/suicide-prevention/suicide-canada.html#a1 (in 2019, the average rate of death by suicide was more than ten Canadians a day).

25 I take here as a model the memoir recently published by former Supreme Court of Canada judge Michel Bastarache, who I clerked for in 2000–2001, in which he discusses, and indeed addresses his book to, his two deceased children, lost so very painfully to a rare genetic condition. See Michel Bastarache and Antoine Trépanier, *Ce que je voudrais dire à mes enfants* (Ottawa: Université d'Ottawa, 2019). Justice Bastarache's wife Yolande used to say to us clerks that we were to him like the children that did not make it to adulthood. She sadly passed away in December 2019. See her obituary in the *Ottawa Citizen* (14 December 2019), available at https://ottawacitizen.remembering.ca/obituary/yolande-bastarache-1078001355

26 "One Judge Down," 416.

27 Ibid.

I met Blaine in 1982 shortly after he joined McGill's Faculty of Law. Hearing of my interest in judicial archives and Quebec legal history, he looked me up among the historians in McGill's Leacock Building. His erudition in everything concerning Law, his evident vulnerability, and his particular form of Red Toryism, attracted me. We joined in a project to inventory rare books on the open shelves of McGill's Law Library. Working together, exchanging readings, commenting on each other's work, and chatting about gardens, his solitary summer life in Muskoka, and 'must' books, we shared much over 35 years.

When I retired and left McGill and as his health and will broke down, we kept in touch mainly by phone. I last saw Blaine in the summer of 2017. Coming off the train from Toronto, he was laboring up Peel Street to the Law Faculty. Stooped now with a cane and cloudy eyes, his ruddiness had become a startling red. There, on the corner of Sherbrooke Street, we chatted for the last time. He seemed uncomfortable, in a hurry, and didn't want to talk about our plans to share an office near the Rare Books Room in the Law Library. A year later, in July, I received a phone call from Toronto. Blaine was dead.

Brian Young

3

It Was a Man's World: Blaine Baker and the Writing of Canadian Legal History, 1981–2018

Brian Young

Somewhere, Proust commented that an author's true self is revealed only in his writing. This truism is particularly apt as a means of exploring Blaine Baker's legal culture and his contribution to Canadian legal history, a field that evolved hugely over the some four decades of his career, 1981–2018. A complicated, curmudgeonly, and very private individual, Baker cut a visible intellectual swath with his publications, his reputation for remarkable teaching and mentoring, and his eccentricities. Many of his peers are comfortable naming him a critical member of "the founding generation" of Canadian legal history or, more, "the leading legal historian" of his generation in Canada. Others question this rank, citing his failure to produce a notable monograph, his deteriorating health from alcoholism and depression, and his inability to make the intellectual turn imposed by social, colonial, and feminist historians.[1]

Fascinated by historiography and historical research, by law as a profession, and by the process of legal change, Baker published his first article in 1981 and his last posthumously in 2018. We have the course of study for his last course in legal history, given just months before his death in July 2018, as well as the course in Legal Process he planned to teach in the winter term of 2019 at the University of Toronto. Born in 1952, Baker can be situated squarely in the centre of what has been called "the pivot generation" of historians.[2] His career, and the pages below, reflect the historical profession's larger adjustment to changing methodologies in the social sciences, to the mushrooming of universities and academic positions, to the entry of significant numbers of women into the profession, to cultural, social, and sexual upheaval, and to the technological revolution in communication and information. Of particular importance in Baker's Ontario was the Americanization of graduate work in history in the face of the declining influence of British graduate schools. In the specific field of the history of Canadian law, the thirty-seven years of his career were marked by fundamental shifts in its parameters: dramatic changes in the construction of "rights" and the role of the courts following the *Canadian Charter of Rights and Freedoms* (1982); the rise to prominence of Indigenous law alongside dominant European-based legal traditions; and the new importance of social and cultural history, and of feminist influences in teaching and writing.[3]

INSIDER AND OUTSIDER

Born to the robe as the son of a Toronto law practitioner, Baker was educated in philosophy, history, and law, at the University of Western Ontario, Columbia University, and the University of Chicago.[4] At first glance, his career is that of an academic insider. From 1981, he taught Contracts, Administrative Law, and Canadian Legal History in the prestigious Faculty of Law at McGill University in Montreal. His works won prizes from the American Society for Legal History and the Canadian Historical Association. He was a prominent editor and author in multiple volumes published by the Osgoode Society for Canadian Legal History. The principal organ for the promotion of legal history in Canada, the Osgoode Society initiated a series in the history of Canadian law in 1981: Baker edited three volumes in the series (1999, 2006, 2013) and wrote five articles or introductions. Across the major academic journals, he wrote a series of research articles, biographies, institutional studies, historiographical essays, and reviews. He was invited professor at both the University of Toronto Faculty of Law and at Osgoode Hall Law School. At McGill University, his ubiquitous presence and evident eccentricity ensured that he was noticed by both deans and students. As a former student remarked: it was as if "he was from the eighteenth century. It's like he walked out from another set, some stage set."[5] He was the first and a four-time winner of the Law Faculty's John W. Durnford Award for Teaching Excellence (see plaque, p. 14 and Richard Janda's observation, p.106). In the first two decades of his career, he was a regular at the law faculty's lunch table in the Faculty Club or, later in the day, at the graduate students' bar in Thomson House. Across his career, making himself available to students was a sacrament. In his last course of study, students were told that his office hours included Sunday afternoon and that they were always welcome without appointment. In the faculty's front offices, he served as Associate Dean of Graduate Studies (1997–99) and then as Associate Dean, Academic (1999–2001).

But, in the academic worlds of both Montreal and Toronto, Baker the insider, was paradoxically, a flagrant outsider: his distinctive intellectual approach, his loneliness, his fondness for alcohol and tobacco, were apparent to all. Most of his university colleagues had nuclear family lives and nine-to-five office schedules that meshed not at all with Baker's hours. McGill's law faculty stars jetted to second careers as advisers in the developing world, as media talking heads, and as distinguished advocates before the Supreme Court of Canada. His generation at McGill overlapped with seniors such as F.R. Scott, Paul-André Crépeau, and John E.C. Brierley, giants of constitution and codification, and men at ease in the star chambers of public policy. Baker in contrast, had no profile in the corporate law offices, courts, and TV newsrooms of the city below the hill. An old-fashioned "bachelor," as one interviewee put it, he fought in a neoliberal university for apparently minor causes like the place of legal history in the curriculum of a presentist law school and the preservation of rare books in a digitalizing university. This marginality had parallel in his publications where he could be dismissed as a "rabbit-hole" historian who devoted precious energy to editing the works of others and to the writing of *Festschrifts* and obscure local narratives. His belief in the detailed footnote as a major epistemological device dumbfounded speed readers and students looking for a quick quote: colleagues joked that he wrote his footnotes first, constructing the body of his article from the bottom up.[6] To the end, he wrote up his research by hand and his comfort level with technology never progressed beyond the landline telephone and penned reference letters. In 1983, as a young academic in an ambitious law faculty that encouraged the public profile of its professoriate, he signaled his belief in other intellectual values, reporting that his most important contribution to the university had been the "shelf read" he had supervised of rare books held in the McGill law library.[7]

Conservative by instinct, Baker was shaken by the sea changes of democratization, feminism, and neoliberalism that buffeted his university world. In his very bailiwick of research, progressive and feminist legal historians brought to the fore deep historical veins of race, class, sexuality, and patriarchy: new discourses in Canadian legal history such as "Whores and Worthies: Feminism and Prostitution" left Baker visibly gasping for oxygen and anchor.[8] At the same time, and speaking to his complexity, he included readings such as Mary Anne Poutanen's work on prostitution in his Canadian Legal History course syllabus.

Baker was well aware of his isolation and contradictions. In a handwritten diary-like note penned circa 1989 and tucked into his archives, he mused about his intellectual life, his writing, and his future. Concerned by his slow academic production, he noted that his "thesis was gathering dust" and that he must "return to it." Pointing to his limited production of just four articles and several reviews published over the last five to six years, he commented that it "has to be said, it's early." He continued: "Why did I do it? How did I do it? What did I learn? How does it sit in a literature? What next?"[9]

CANADIAN LEGAL HISTORY AS A MÉTIER

Baker attended Toronto's elite Upper Canada College and then Erindale Secondary School in the affluent suburb of Mississauga.[10] His ability and suburban social class made the University of Western Ontario, in nearby London Ontario, an evident option. In 1972, Baker entered Huron College, Western's prestigious liberal arts college. Graduating with a major in philosophy, he entered Western's Faculty of Law in 1975 with the "Dean Ivan Rand Scholarship." Although he listed his law school concentration as "Commercial Law and Non-Constitutional Public Law," he had in fact been hooked by David Flaherty's seminar in legal history. A colonial historian and member of the History Department, Flaherty was an indefatigable promoter of Canadian legal history. He remembers Baker as a "standout student" and "prodigious intellectual and reader."[11] For his part, Baker recalled Flaherty's insistence on the "close alignment" of legal history with cultural, social, political, and economic history.[12] Graduating on the dean's honour list with a bachelor of laws in 1978, Baker left for New York and graduate work at Columbia University, perhaps not coincidentally, David Flaherty's *alma mater*. Awarded a Donner

Foundation scholarship in Canadian Studies, Baker spent two years in Columbia's master of law program specializing in Commonwealth history. His master's thesis, "Government Involvement in Economic Growth: Promotion to Regulation in Upper Canada, 1791–1875" was directed by economic historian Stuart W. Bruchey.[13] Baker always pointed to Bruchey's influence in helping him understand history as a discipline and in opening the fundamental relationship of the law to the state, administrative authority, and local economic development.[14] With its emphasis on market relations, the "Wisconsin School" and in particular, Willard Hurst's *Law and Economic Growth: A Legal History of the Lumber Industry in Wisconsin, 1836–1915* (1964) had evident influence on Baker's thesis. And, it was at Columbia that he sharpened his interest in historiography, particularly the larger themes of Anglo-American legal history.

Baker remained in American academia after Columbia attending the University of Chicago with a Harry A. Bigelow Teaching Fellowship in Law.[15] Designed to prepare graduate students for teaching careers in law, the Bigelow fellowship gave Baker the academic year, 1980–81, to read Anglo-American legal historiography and to undertake research in what his curriculum vitae described as "Legal Education and Professional Discipline in Upper Canada."[16] Brian Simpson, a major and continuing influence on Baker's thinking, was visiting professor at the University of Chicago Law School in 1980.[17]

Baker's development as a young legal historian coincided with the rise of the Critical Legal Studies movement. Peers and friends like Robert W. Gordon, David Sugarman, and Douglas Hay introduced him to a socially-engaged legal history and to Marxian and Gramscian principles of the hegemonic role of law in capitalist society.[18] Critical Legal Studies had a direct pipeline into the nascent field of Canadian legal history through the University of Western Ontario's summer Seminar in Legal History for Law Teachers organized in the mid-1980s by David Flaherty. Baker himself was on the faculty for several summers and "Flaherty's camp" welcomed an international Critical Legal Studies contingent that included Gordon, Sugarman, Morton Horwitz, and Michael Grossberg.[19] As Sugarman and Gordon put it: "it was if this renaissance in Anglo-North American legal history was actually taking place in the seminar halls of [the University of] Western Ontario."[20]

Baker was an enthusiastic participant in these intellectual rounds of international academic sociability and it was not happenstance that, in 1987, he used the term "Legal Culture" in a publication title.[21] But, whatever the vitality of this link to an engaged and presentist legal history, Baker was too much a red tory and too anti-ideological to be drawn into the orthodoxy of a "school" or Critical Legal Studies' modes of social didactic and class conflict. "Assuming that all postures in the world are, in some measure, self-interested," he remained skeptical of utopianism or socialism.[22]

In any case, his life, both personal and academic, was shifting. In 1981, Baker had been appointed to teach Administrative Law at McGill University in Montreal. However, the suicide of his brother, Eric, and the decline and death of his father kept his focus on Toronto. Whatever his growing responsibilities at McGill, he in fact remained a Torontonian sharing an apartment in Montreal's student ghetto and returning to Toronto on weekends. With a leave from McGill, he taught at the Osgoode Hall School, 1987–88, and at the University of Toronto law school, 1988–89. Frustrated in attempts to obtain a permanent law-faculty post in Toronto, in 1989, aged thirty-seven, he enrolled in graduate work at the University of Toronto. Significantly, he chose to specialize in Canadian history passing over for example, study with John Beattie, senior professor at the University of Toronto and a distinguished historian of British crime and policing. The University of Toronto's PhD program in history had a mandatory first year of three courses. For the area of Historiography and Historical Methods, he joined some fifteen students in William Dray's Theory of History. For courses in the Canadian area, he chose Carl Berger's History of Canada and Ian Radforth's, Canadian Social History.[23] As Canada's preeminent intellectual historian, Berger was a natural fit with Baker's interest in historiography. A labour historian, Radforth taught the "new social history" with its broad approach to the social sciences and its concerns with "real" people and human experience. Baker wrote essays and apparently completed the course work but did not do his comprehensive examinations nor undertake a thesis. In 1991 and after a two-year absence, he returned to teaching at McGill and full immersion in the teaching and writing of Canadian legal history.

CANADIAN LEGAL HISTORY AS AN EMERGING FIELD

Named to teach Administrative Law, Baker took a year, 1981–82, to plan and introduce his course in Canadian Legal History.[24] This was a critical period in the teaching of legal history in North American universities. Like their American counterparts, law faculties in universities such as Dalhousie University and the University of British Columbia had been dropping or marginalizing their traditional legal history offerings, courses based on the English legal histories of F.W. Maitland, W.S. Holdsworth, S.F.C. Milson, or J.H. Baker.[25] Despite the expanding study of Canada across the social sciences and the rise of Canadian Studies as an interdisciplinary field, the expansion of Canadian legal history into law faculties across Canada remained a tough sell.[26] R.C.B. Risk for example, had introduced an elective course in Canadian legal history in the University of Toronto's law faculty in 1962. Discouraged by the field's sterility and its lack of penetration into law faculty curricula, he complained a decade later that the intellectual component of legal history should not be "the monopoly of lawyers."[27] In 1975, the Symons' Report, a broad examination of academic research on Canada, pointed to Canadian legal history as a "particularly neglected field."[28] In 1981, in the Osgoode Society's first volume in the history of Canadian law, David Flaherty described Canadian legal history as being at the "fledgling stage" with historians in the field "groping in the dark" because of the lack of research.[29] Université de Montréal legal historian André Morel described an intellectual dark ages in Quebec before its Quiet Revolution: "the legal historian [of Quebec] of the 1960s almost had to start anew ... our knowledge remains very incomplete and, in some cases, quite wrong."[30] Most damning was *Law and Learning/ Le Droit et le Savoir (1983)*, a report commissioned for the Social Sciences and Humanities Research Council. Chaired by Harry Arthurs of Osgoode Hall Law School, this study was devastating in its conclusion that neither legal education nor legal research in Canada "adequately treats scholarly or intellectual themes."[31]

In his proposition to the law faculty's curriculum committee, Baker echoed these criticisms noting the "lack of scholarship in this field and the lack of sensitivity among members of the Canadian legal community to the history of our legal institutions."[32] He also drew aim at the failure of Canadian universities "to participate in the international renaissance of modern legal history"; in 1984, he named seven Canadian law schools that lacked a legal history specialist.[33] This strong condemnation of what he saw as an endemic ahistoricism in law faculties persisted across his career. Evaluating a submission to the *McGill Law Journal* in 1994, Baker criticized it as "doctrinal scholarship" based on "derivative and dated epistemologies." Continuing, he dismissed this form of legal scholarship as the work of "beachcombers who pick up legal artifacts randomly from common law sands, take them home, collect and hoard them, and reassemble or disassemble them repetitiously."[34] In 2005, he took aim again attacking what he called "a century of mainstream legal commentary that ostracized [substantive issues] to faculties of arts and social sciences."[35] As example, he used William Proudfoot, professor of Roman law and English legal history at the University of Toronto, emphasizing Proudfoot's unsuccessful efforts in the 1880s to prioritize academic education over practical training.[36] This was in fact, part of Baker's larger criticism of the Ontario law profession's early twentieth-century drift to insularity, its diminishing intercourse with neighbouring American and Quebec legal traditions, and its hunkering down into a closed common law silo that he characterized as "oligarchic," an "Empire," and a "Tory posture." He pointed out with irony that English Canada's first academic law teacher, William Hume Blake, worked from American, rather than English materials.[37]

Not surprisingly, Baker's Canadian Legal History seminar reached broadly into the humanities to treat "cultural subjects" and "citizenship skills."[38] Nor did he teach notions of law in the conventional law school form of the case study or Socratic method. Instead, his seminar encouraged the acquisition of legal knowledge around historical themes and interdisciplinary historiographies. He assigned lengthy readings and students wrote research papers in which primary sources, historical analysis, and effective writing were principal criteria. This resulted in a cadre of devoted students, many of whom went on to graduate degrees in Canadian legal history.

"LIBRARIES WITH WALLS"

Assessment of Baker's contribution to research in Canadian legal history must begin with his passion for books as raw physical objects and his insistence on the "literature of the law" as a "key component of legal culture." Rather than collecting books himself, he relished

McGill's Chancellor Day law building, prowling its library, indefatigable in protecting its archival and rare-book collections, and conducting what he called "institutional prosopography."[39] While fellow historian of the book, Roger Chartier, writing in 1993, anticipated the significance of digitalization and of "Libraries Without Walls," Baker doubled down on the written, on the physicality of the book, on the sanctity of the rare book, and on the law library as a particular institutional form of ordering knowledge.[40] Cloistering himself in a world of traditional print culture, he was in the last generation that could ignore the digital revolution. For his part, McGill's chief law librarian admired Baker's vision of the library describing it as a "total part" of a law faculty's "pedagogical" and "research" function.[41]

This profound attachment to a book world and to the university law library reached back to Baker's education as a legal historian. As a law student in the 1970s, Baker came to know Margaret Banks (1928–2010), the University of Western Ontario's legendary law librarian, legal historian, and author of *Using a Law Library: a Guide for Students and Lawyers in the Common Law Provinces of Canada* (1971).[42] As a graduate student at Columbia University and later at the University of Chicago, Baker rummaged their libraries for Canadian law collections – what he called "heirlooms" – that had "migrated" into the libraries of American law schools.[43] Once at McGill, he was co-author and the driving force of *Sources in the Law Library for a Reconstruction of the Legal Culture of Quebec, 1760–1890* (1987). With a view to isolating works of Quebec provenance or of use in Quebec before 1890, this "shelf read" of the McGill law library's five floors resulted in a bibliography of some three thousand entries of monographs, treatises, pamphlets, and institutional works.[44] The study gave a vital snapshot of law books acquired by McGill and subsequently used in the teaching of law since the founding of its law school in 1848. Baker also showed the presence of fifteen substantial private law libraries that had been integrated into the McGill collection as well as the remnants of forty to fifty smaller private law libraries.[45]

Baker was fascinated, not only by the origins, size, content, and migration of these private law libraries, but by the significance for the construction of Canadian legal culture of the marginalia in individual books, in their annotations, and in the insertion of newspaper clippings and pamphlets.[46] He published first on the subject in 1985 and then, three decades later and conscious of a hugely expanded historiography, he came back to the study of book annotations as case studies in legal anthropology.[47] Writing in 2016, he paused over the hand-written marginalia or "scribblings" in the five folio volumes of Chief Justice William Osgoode, a collection first held by the Literary and Historical Society of Quebec and which found final home in McGill's law library.[48] Linking the annotations in Osgoode's law books to the organization of knowledge in commonplace books, Baker emphasized that Osgoode's use of wide margins for his musings and scholarship represented superb primary evidence for the construction of Canadian legal culture. Following the Chief Justice's "Canadian trail" and "his shadowy historiographic presence," Baker speculated on how Osgoode's collection might serve to understand the "colonial reception of imperial law." He also mused over the significance of silences and, citing Sherlock Holmes and instances "when the dog didn't bark," argued that "Osgoode's marginal silences seem as important as his marginal musings."[49] Commonplace books kept by legal professionals, and he found five in the rare books collection of McGill's law library, were another source of research delight for Baker. Seeing them as much more than meandering scrapbooks, he insisted that commonplace books represented distinct and highly personal forms of ordering knowledge by subjects: scientific, literary, religious, or legal.[50] He used commonplace books to situate the larger culture of Montreal legal practitioners into an enlightenment context, writing that "there is an important and closely-related study of science in law waiting to be written about Lower-Canadian legal codifiers like [William] Badgley and [Alexander] Morris who were compulsive 'botanizers' and 'natural historians' in their leisure hours."[51] Baker effectively used Badgley's seven hundred-page commonplace book to contextualize his project to codify Canadian criminal law.[52]

RESEARCHING EVERYDAY LAW

Baker's greatest strength as a researcher was undoubtedly in the micro and the biographical. Instead of the imperial, constitutional, or national legal regimes that attracted a majority of his peers, he was most comfortable in the local, in the quotidian, and in projects such as linking the social warrens of law school, law society, law office, and drinking clubs. Dismissive of dry "lawyerly readings of reception statutes," he pointed instead to the "material vehicles and human relations of transmission," to legal change over time, and to what he called "historical contingent character."[53]

In his study of the archives of five Montreal-based law firms, Baker, as he put it, tried to get "as close to the ground of law practice and business ordering as possible."[54] This goal, modest in appearance, allowed him to demonstrate how narratives of the daily working relationships of lawyers contribute to larger understandings of the construction of Canada's different legal cultures. Mid-nineteenth-century Montreal, he reminded his readers, was a turbulent capitalist and multicultural city, hub to banks, manufactures, dioceses of both the Church of Rome and the Church of England, and an English-speaking university that hosted Quebec's first law faculty. Canal and rail networks and the strategic Victoria Bridge ensured Montreal a central position in the exchange of both goods and ideas from the Atlantic, the American Midwest, and the emerging pan-Canadian state. These commercial law firms also understood the implications of the fact that, resident in Quebec, they operated under the jurisdiction of that province's French-based civil law with its codes and distinct laws of contract, land tenure, and family: their very law offices were located on the seigneurial land of a Catholic religious community. Finally, Montreal law firms also had to contend with the fundamental mid-century reform of local legal structures: professionalization of the bar and legal education, institution of a registry system, deconstruction of the seigneurial system, codification of both civil and procedural law, restructuring of the court system, and integration of Quebec's judicial system into a federal structure.

Reveling in this complexity, Baker demonstrated that, whatever their role as international mediators, the major law firms remained "small and disorganized" entities who operated "on the hoof."[55] There was no contradiction, he argued, between their double rootedness, first in a broad North Atlantic "legal pantheism" and then in a distinctly Montreal legal culture that involved neighbourhood, office location, and the role of apprentices, clerks, and office boys as informers, copiers, and runners. Using two firms as case studies, he showed the artisanal methods of "Frederick Griffin" and "Torrance and Morris" in "generating, ordering, storing, and applying legal knowledge" through "scratch books," "lecture books," "authorities books" and indexed commonplace books.[56]

His "contextualizing" of the will of William Martin (1816–87) represents another example of his ability to draw larger historical significance from what he termed affectionately as "little legal systems." Borrowing Brian Simpson's methodology of "testamentary archaeology," he used Martin's will to assess "the everyday impact of a private legal instrument on family members." Baker described it as a method of "reclaiming the parties' understanding of the episode in issue and to contrast that vision with the meaning or identity the event acquired in law when sprung loose from the social setting that gave rise to it."[57]

William Martin arrived in Canada in 1848, head of a typical Scot immigrant family undistinguished by either poverty or wealth. After several moves, the family acquired "Chestnut Haven," a farm on the market-garden flats along Lake Ontario west of Toronto's Humber River. Decades later, the property attracted real-estate developers who saw its potential as part of what would become the industrial suburb of Mimico. For their part, the Martins led unremarkable lives with William's eldest son James remaining at home, even after marriage. Baker uses photos, family correspondence, Anglican church records, and obituaries to trace these banal, small-town lives and their crises of early death, economic misfortune, and migration north to a cramped cottage at Lake Simcoe on Shingle Bay near the town of Orillia. In his 1886 will, William Martin bequeathed his landed property to the children of his son James. A decade later, William died, victim of a home accident: "Family lore suggests that he was installing boards on the inside, low-sloping portion of a back kitchen when he was fatally injured in a fall from a ladder."[58]

What Baker savours most in this Martin narrative was its "unpredictability," its "indeterminacy," and "its shifting government in miniature." Brushing aside "the law in book" and "the law in action" as well as structuralism, social histories of the family, and theories of male hegemony, Baker argues that the will can only be understood as a "notional blank statement" resulting from the "English common law world's most permissive regime of facilitative law." In the end, William Martin's intentions came to naught, thwarted by a collapse of the Mimico real-estate boom, lethargic courts, and the incompetence of his heirs. For its part, Baker's conclusion rang with cynicism as to the utility of formal law: "the entropy of human relations effectively defeated ideologically-grounded and carefully-crafted legal formalism."[59]

There is an odd, and perhaps revealing, reserve in his history of the Martin family. Except for the careful footnote sleuth, Baker does not reveal that he is in fact doing genealogical history and that William Martin, through his mother, was his great-great grandfather.[60] It is ironic that, despite the emphasis across his work on the role of the human and biographical in explaining how law and legal culture interact over time, he was evidently not comfortable writing himself into the text of the Martin family story. Or, perhaps with a wink, he wanted to give the diligent reader a payback for the effort of combing his footnotes.[61]

WRITING BIOGRAPHY

Baker recognized biography as a staple of legal history scholarship, writing multiple biographies himself as well as an important qualitative and quantitative assessment of jurist biographies in Canada.[62] Although an insistent supporter of the *Dictionary of Canadian Biography,* its vigorous academic editorship, and its inclusion of 320 biographies of Canadian legal professionals, he himself, somewhat surprisingly, authored only two biographies for the *Dictionary*.[63] Early in his career, he contributed fourteen biographies, including that of two women, to the *Biographical Dictionary of the Common Law*.[64] He compared these scholastic biographies to the unfortunate predominance in Canadian legal history of "vanity press" works that were one-dimensional, anecdotal, and limited in primary research.[65] Writing biography is an important revelation of self: the choice of subject of course as well as in the treatment of class, gender, period, family condition, and social relations. Baker's vitae lists eighteen biographical articles and he contributed in a major way to seven homage volumes in Canadian legal history. Across the 1980s and into the 1990s, Baker published a series of juristic biographies of notables in Upper Canadian law. In his last work, published posthumously in 2019, he turned to a biography of Supreme Court Justice Gerald Le Dain. Several of these biographies allow us to reach behind Baker's normally guarded personal curtain. In September 2004, he participated in a conference organized by the University of Toronto and Osgoode Hall in honour of John Willis (1907–97), long-time professor of public law in the University of Toronto law school. Willis' importance in the early writing of Canadian legal history had been long recognized.[66] Publishing his paper, the usually discreet Baker was outspoken in his admiration for Willis: "I spoke with Willis once and the statement he made in that conversation that made the greatest impression on me was that one does not need to believe in anything but oneself to engage the market contractually." Continuing and surely reflecting his own pessimism with the rank individualism and capitalism that characterized Canadian society, Baker described the curious comment of Willis as a "near-mystical statement."[67] He also drew on Willis' faith in education to assert his own conservative views of training in the law. "Cultural learning," Baker wrote, "is civilized, refined, mannerly education."[68] Continuing, he insisted that legal education must involve "training in decency and fair-mindedness" and, in striking language for him, was "effected on a class-by-class basis by inviting students to look in the mirror of Lear raging against the elements of nature or Vesuvius erupting with legal lava."[69] This belief in the law as a discipline demanding a broad legal culture was reflected in his letters of recommendation, themselves superb case studies of his values. Recommending one of his research assistants for graduate work at the University of Victoria, he wrote of her as "a person of letters in the nineteenth-century sense."[70] Writing to the Chief Justice of Canada in support of one student's application for a clerkship, Baker used the terms "gracious, modest, and conscientious"; "a mature young person with a balanced lifestyle."[71]

THE STUDY OF QUEBEC AND FRENCH CANADA

Although a quintessential Ontarian, Baker spent his career at McGill University, one of North America's oldest law faculties and home in Quebec to a "National Programme" that prepared students for both a bachelor of civil law (BCL) and a bachelor of common law (LLB). Within the faculty, Baker was a persistent and strong supporter of this integrated program.[72] He was outspoken in his insistence that McGill law students should "never be indifferent to French Canada" and, part of an Ontario generation profoundly influenced by the politics of Pierre Elliott Trudeau, he noted that "since biculturalism and bilingualism are Canadian legal facts," bilingualism at McGill "is nothing more than what one might expect."[73] At the same time and perhaps not in contradiction, Baker was somewhat typical of a certain professoriat of his generation at McGill. He read French easily but, although French had been declared the official language of Quebec in 1976, he seems never to have conversed in French with Quebecois students or colleagues: he never published significantly in French.[74] Despite his research and his solid understanding of Quebec legal literature, he steered away from French-speaking events, a choice that ghettoized him from Quebecois academic life and major influence on francophone historians of Canadian legal history.

As his career progressed, Baker increasingly straddled the legal cultures of his native Toronto and that of his Montreal workplace. With a first degree in philosophy and a graduate thesis in economic history, he emphasized a balance between the disciplines of history and law and, across his publications, his frequent use of terms such as "transnational" give a strong sense of the centrality he gave to poly-jurality. In one of his last works, Baker summarized the importance he gave to comparison in Quebec and Ontario of "the diversities of language and culture, low, high and informal law."[75]

His increasing hostility to what he saw as the drift in Ontario to "formalism," to "imperialism," to "rampant forgetfulness," to "ahistoricism," and to the suppression of the "richness and diversity" which European law had brought to North American legal traditions has already been noted.[76] Describing these Ontario common law lawyers as "formalistic and Anglican in outlook," he decried their disinterest in "cross-pollination" with the Quebec legal tradition and regretted the gradual collapse of professional intercourse between Canada's common and civil law communities.[77] This indifference, he suggested, had contributed to the early twentieth-century anger of Quebec legal intellectuals at English Canada's "contempt" for Quebec law, their increasing reliance on codes as a means of self-preservation, and the deepening association by nationalists of "the province's law with Québécois culture."[78] Baker was also on the lookout for works that purported to be Canadian but which ignored the country's fundamental Quebec constituency. Commenting on a manuscript that covered the transformation of Canadian constitutional law, Baker noted that "the biggest gap in your text is French Canada and that will be a hard hole to fill."[79] Baker also strongly resisted francophobe attitudes that he perceived in certain of his McGill colleagues. Baker's career overlapped with the last years of renowned constitutionalist F.R. Scott, and he benefitted from many conversations with Scott. Whatever Scott's reputation as a civil libertarian, Baker described Scott as a "bundle of contradictions" and as "oligarchic and bigoted."[80]

Baker had a profound understanding of Quebec legal history, of the significance of codification, and of Quebec's distinct approach to individual rights. He gave particular place to the interpretations of John Brierley and Robert Yalden as to the centrality of polyjurality.[81] Baker situated the *Civil Code* of 1866 at the core of Quebec legal history presenting it as a tipping point between an "aristocratic, pre-liberal regime" and a modernizing Quebec.[82] In tandem with seigneurialism, he argued, codification has to be interpreted as part of the historic "transition" from feudalism to capitalism. The primary concern of the draftsmen of the *Civil Code*, he told a Duke University audience, was "to create legal infrastructures facilitative of a movement from pre-capitalist (feudal, Georgian-Tory) and formative capitalist (mercantilism) modes of production to an industrial and ultimately corporate capitalism."[83] The *Code* incarnated a form of "human rights" confirming liberal values of freedom of contract, the inviolability of the person, freedom of land ownership, and freedom of willing. Baker pointed to the *Code* as "one big definition section" concerning property and civil rights that originated in *The Quebec Act*. Expressed in the form of a code, these rights served to define "the constitutional boundary between federal and provincial spheres of power."

Baker, as we have seen, took it as a mission to present Quebec's legal history as an integral element in the North American legal experience. Writing for example, in 1993 in the *Encyclopedia of the North American Colonies*, he offered a precise comparative description of "French civil law" and the "legal professions" in Louisiana as well as New France and British North America.[84] One of his persistent projects was to introduce English Canadian readers to Quebec legal history. In 1990, he proposed a potential manuscript, "Political Ideology and Law Reform in Pre-Confederation Quebec," for the Osgoode Society's series, *Essays in the History of Canadian Law*. With contributions from major English and French legal historians, this work would range across civil, criminal, procedural, and administrative legal history. Unlike many Quebec academic works that were bilingual with authors publishing in their own language, Baker proposed the translation of French articles into English.[85] Although this work never materialized, Baker, despite his increasing health incapacity, kept gnawing at the bone. With Quebec legal historian Donald Fyson as co-editor, *Essays in the History of Canadian Law: Quebec and the Canadas* (2013) can be seen as a superb bookend to his insistence on a comparative Canadian legal history.

Baker's incorporation of Quebec's legal experience into the larger Canadian legal tradition is also clear from the courses of study for his Canadian Legal History seminar.[86] He was adamant in never cornering Quebec into a continental-European, civil law straightjacket or as a box somehow foreign and peripheral to Canada's dominant English common law tradition. His course systematically included Quebec readings, most in French: for example, of forty-four readings in his 1995 course outline for Canadian Legal History, twelve treated Quebec subjects. Included in the first week's readings were J.G. Belley's "La nouvelle histoire du droit" and in the second seminar, Engaging Canadian History, he juxtaposed Ronald Rudin's revisionist analysis of Quebecois nationalist historians with Carl Berger's study of English Canadian historical writing.[87] For the seminar on self-governance, he included André Vachon's *Histoire du notariat* and, for the class on Legal Culture, Sylvio Normand's "La sauvegarde de l'intégrité du droit civil." And, alongside readings on charivaris and other forms of popular resistance, his students read Nicholas Kasirer's study of Montreal feminist and teacher of law to women, Marie Lacoste Gérin-Lajoie.[88]

Finally, it is easy to dismiss his journeyman labours in editing a bibliography of legal works produced or used in Quebec before 1890. Admittedly a co-editor with Baker, I would insist that *Sources in the Law Library of McGill University for a Reconstruction of the Legal Culture of Quebec, 1760–1890* represents a unique inventory of legal scholarship in Quebec before 1890.[89] This work brought attention to the richness of writing in Quebec legal history and prompted transfer of multiple unique works in Canadian legal history from the law library's general stacks into the safety of McGill's Rare Book Collection.

Besides this bibliographical, historiographical, editing, and teaching commitment, Baker also made an important contribution to primary research in Quebec legal history. His study of Montrealer William Badgley's failed promotion of a criminal code led to important observations on Lower Canadian land, succession, and registration law. Badgley had served as attorney general and as the first dean of the McGill law school. Using Badgley's draft code, commonplace book, and account books, Baker separated Lower Canadian codifiers from their continental European counterparts linking them instead to American codifiers like David Field and Edward Livingston.[90] He perceptively showed the osmosis of this

Anglo-American legal ideology through Louisiana and the border states of Maine and New York. He also emphasized codification in Quebec – criminal, procedural, or civil – as a process with few ambitions for doctrinal creativity and one oriented rather to the consolidation, standardization, and uniformization of law.

MASCULINITY AND GENDER

As historians at McGill University in the early 1980s, we came to know Baker in the then-normative professorial context of masculine collegiality. He was our go-to historian for Canadian legal history, an innovative researcher of the nineteenth-century legal profession, and a generous mine of historiographical nuggets. Sitting with Baker and a second beer in the cool red leather of the McGill University Faculty Club, we recognized that the masculine legal culture, so effectively described by him for the 1820s, had in fact persisted largely intact for a century and a half, through the Bay Street practice of his father in Toronto, his own Southern Ontario legal training in the 1970s, and into our professorial world in a major Canadian university. As one observer at McGill put it in 1983: "While feminism has directed attention towards the history of women and their present legal condition, there has been inadequate research on the historical roots of the present legal situation of Quebec women."[91]

In fact, Baker's mindset and his interpretative position in the formative field of Canadian legal history were coming under scrutiny just as he was settling into publishing his several studies of the Ontario legal profession. In 1981, in the first volume of the Osgoode Society's *Essays in the History of Canadian Law,* Jennifer Stoddart, a recent McGill University law graduate, published "The Dorion Commission, 1929–1931: Quebec's Legal Elites Look at Women's Rights."[92] A year later, Stoddart merged this feminist analysis into the Collective Clio's *Quebec Women: A History.* This work was just the most visible of a series of second-wave feminist studies in the 1980s and 1990s that challenged traditional interpretations of Quebec legal history by proposing new frames of historical periodization, by positioning patriarchal authority in family and public life as fundamental legal vectors, and by demonstrating the legal elite's endemic discrimination in blocking female access to public space, to the franchise, and to entry into higher education and the legal professions.[93]

These were the pivotal years in Baker's writing on the history of the legal profession in Ontario. In 1983, in the second volume of *Essays in the History of Canadian Law*, he published "Legal Education in Upper Canada, 1785 to 1889," an important study of old boys, old families, and old connections – and a work already striking in its unguarded gender polity. His contribution stood alongside Constance Backhouse's chapter, "Nineteenth-Century Rape Law, 1800–92": within the same volume, the sharply contrasting use of discourse and of the treatment of gender, class, race, and social injustice was unmistakeable. Continuing, Backhouse published "Gender and Race in the Construction of Legal Professionalism," a paper which challenged the tenets of masculine professionalism, collegiality, and civility. Utilizing many of the same archival sources as Baker, particularly those of the Law Society of Upper Canada in the 1820s (but without citing or criticizing his work), Backhouse pointed to the legal profession's intolerance, its "discrimination," its whiteness, its "tightly knit community," and its "shared culture" that by definition excluded entry to female or Indigenous candidates.[94] These fundamental interpretative revisions in Canadian legal history from feminists trained in law schools found echo among a broad front of social historians who brought new research perspectives to criminal justice, registry law, widowhood, prostitution, and racially-mixed marriages.[95]

It is important to differentiate between Baker's teaching and mentoring and his own primary research. Baker read, acknowledged, and assigned readings drawn from this feminist legal history. His teaching and bibliographies drew attention to married women's property acts, married women as "sole traders," and Lower Canadian-registry acts.[96] "Family relations" were emphasized as a major legal category in both his teaching and publications. Several of his graduate students were female, including Angela Fernandez, an editor of this volume, and they almost universally pay tribute to his generosity and kindness and to his skills as a graduate director.[97]

But this recognition of feminist scholarship and of the history of women did not penetrate his research questions nor his writing from primary sources. He continued for example, to give centrality to masculine expressions of popular agency such as charivaris. While he drew attention to the historiographical importance of the writing of feminist legal historians like Bettina Bradbury, her work dating from the 1980s on female agency, on the legal implications of widowhood, and on the use of the law by elite women, was never brought forward into his own social analysis.[98] Indeed, as the assured masculinity of his generation of law professoriate evaporated, he persevered in writing about the gendered experience of the nineteenth-century law profession: men in law offices, men in law school, men in the courts, men in drinking clubs, and men collecting books. In multiple works, Baker gave recurrent attention to the daily life of legal professionals and to what he called "workaday processes."[99]

Based on club minutes held in the archives of the McCord Museum of Canadian History, his study of the Montreal lawyers' drinking club, the Brothers-in-Law, is perhaps his most effective expression of elite masculine culture. Limited to fifteen members, the club met for long tavern lunches on significant dates in the legal calendar. The club had a constitution, minutes, and a brotherhood bond exemplified in their name, a nomenclature that put male fraternity on the same plateau as family and marriage bloodlines. Drawn from the English-speaking legal elite and what Baker calls "second or third generation, socio-economic entrenchment," its members included the solicitor general, the sheriff, and Baker's irrepressible subject, William Badgley.[100] More than shared professional interests in law, the club's glue was a male sociability around drinking, conversation, toasts, fines, declarations of fraternal and class solidarity, and thinly veiled suggestions of elite violence associated with swords and dueling.

In this excellent primary research and very skillful bridging of law and male society, he essentially ignored domesticity, wives, children, widowhood, and the societal implications of the masculine world he described in such technicolor. He seems to have intentionally skated around occasions when he might have included these issues. In his excellent case study of willing in Ontario for example, he did circulate a version in which "Widower Martin" was in his title but this reference to gender with its implied attention to the male life cycle and wills as a reflection of masculinity were absent in the published version. Writing, as noted above, about the "posthumous legal system" of his mother's family, it is curious that he gave little attention to the experience of Martin women in this collapse of family wealth.[101]

Several individuals interviewed for this volume, including female students and colleagues, remarked on a certain edginess as Baker moved to incorporate feminism, race, aboriginal relations, and antisemitism into his courses. For example, Canada's preeminent feminist legal historian, Constance Backhouse, was a contemporary of Baker and their paths crossed often. They were briefly in the same department at the University of Western Ontario and she may have been offered a tenure track position over him. Both were profoundly influenced by their experience in American graduate schools and both wrote Canadian legal history from the perspective of intensely gendered human narratives. Although simplistic, parallels in their research interests are instructive. While Baker concentrated on the male legal culture of Upper Canada and Ontario, Backhouse, early in her career, wrote a biography of Clara Brett Martin, Canada's first female lawyer. Later and significantly, both turned to biographies of Supreme Court judges: Baker on Gerald Le Dain (2019) and Backhouse on Claire L'Heureux-Dubé (2017). Whatever Baker's social awkwardness, Backhouse insisted in an interview that he was always "generous and sharing."[102] For his part and describing them as "pioneering essays," Baker systematically assigned readings from Backhouse in his legal history course and publications.[103]

* * *

Baker's career straddled well into the twenty-first century and his life was caught up in profound changes that altered both the academy and the cardinal directions of Canadian legal history. If, by way of conclusion, we circle back to Proust's adage about writing as revelatory of the persona, it is perhaps in his biographies and homages, particularly of William Badgley, John Willis, R.C.B. Risk, and Gerald Le Dain, that Blaine Baker lets us close in. In these nineteenth- and twentieth-century narratives of male intellectuals grappling with codification, professionalization, and the teaching of law, his profound attachment to Canadian legal history as a field of knowledge comes through strongest. It might be said that, as a perceptive historian, he succeeded above all in putting Canada's pervasive male legal culture on the dissecting table, its organs, ideology, and forms of authority, exposed to historian pathologists. A second major contribution, this one pedagogical as well as intellectual, is surely his defence of print, of law books as physical objects, and of the law library, with its bedfellow the university archives, as principal wells of legal history. Much, much more than antiquarianism, his publications on library collections, both private and university, on marginalia, and on commonplace books, speak forcefully to his emphasis on epistemology and to his insistence on the law student's understanding of the historical organization and transmission of legal knowledge. Further, his series of micro studies on professionalization and legal education drive home the primacy of class, elite schooling, and Anglicanism in the history of the law profession in Upper Canada and Ontario. From yet another perspective, he towers in his generation in his determination to open Canadian legal history to larger American and Atlantic historiographies. He positioned these historiographies as exercises in the "fence-posting" of Canadian legal history, that is, in establishing the field's terrain and boundaries, in giving it a certain solidity, coherence, and definition, and in forcefully opening its gates to transnational and interdisciplinary literatures.[104] Perhaps above all, and over the long haul of a career, he fought passionately for what he saw as the essential link between construction of the law student's legal culture and the study of Canadian legal history. The discipline of history, he insisted, contributes in a fundamental way to the "comprehensive understanding of law in context."[105]

But there was a dark, trapping side to Baker's humanity and intellect. At the end, and like his cardigans and handwritten manuscripts, he seems somehow to have stopped in time. Despite enormous reading, erudition, and recognition of the insights of economic, social, and cultural history, he was unable to open his own superb research on lawyers "at work" to an effective dimension of gender in private law, to lawyers "at home" or lawyers "in society." Fearful of women, but respectful, he kept his distance in both scholarship and personal relations. His unease with terms like feminism, race, and postcolonialism as leitmotivs of history forms part of his complex generational, gender, and individual positioning as an intellectual. For, whatever his learned footnotes and broad course syllabi, there remains a serious gap between his research and the discourse of "Women in the Law"; "Race and the Law"; and "Indigenous Legal Traditions," that characterize recent publications in Canadian legal history.[106] Baker strongly supported McGill's National Programme of teaching Canada's dual system of common and civil law and encouraged comparative studies of the legal traditions of Quebec and Ontario. His research and his teaching hammered at the distinctiveness of Quebec's legal culture and what he called "legal pantheism" as core realities of the Canadian experience.[107] These represent major contributions to the field of Canadian legal history.

But here too, in the end, he remained awkward, isolated by language and character, unable to connect in intimate exchanges with francophone academics. Nor, despite a professional lifetime in the Montreal university community, would he ever define himself as an English Montrealer nor as a Montrealer tout court. Rooted and yet uprooted in a mid-twentieth century, Ontario-based, intellectual comfort zone, he could do no better than to identify himself as "a recycled Ontarian."[108] His alienation was accentuated by a profound sense of failure in maintaining the place won in the 1980s for Canadian legal history in the curricula of Canadian law schools. This was particularly pointed at McGill where his Canadian Legal History course remained in limbo from his last offering in 2016 until his death.[109] In this life mission of encouraging the penetration of history as an essential discipline in the teaching of law, his conclusion was bitter. Of the some one thousand references to secondary historical works in his major legal historiography of Quebec and Ontario (2013), not a single one, he wrote, appeared in the readings of the University of Western Ontario's mandatory law course, "Foundations in Canadian Law" in the period 2005–2010, nor, across the same period, in McGill's required law-faculty courses, "Legal Traditions," or "Foundations in Canadian Law."[110] Baker died in July 2018. Published posthumously, his edited volume and article on Gerald Le Dain spoke to his empathy with the Supreme Court justice as "a man of knowledge" and yet a legal intellectual whose end of career was a "tragedy."[111] Le Dain's isolation, depression, hospitalization, and forced retirement at aged sixty-four under pressure from the Chief Justice, resonated strongly with how Baker interpreted his own end of career, his declining health and intellectual influence, and his sense of McGill University's institutional indifference to his contribution. Around Blaine, and with dismay and impotence, we all recognized his profound solitude, his devastating addiction and depression, his sense of academic futility, and his misplaced anger with his dean and with the university which had served so long as his surrogate home. Baker concluded his Le Dain biography by emphasizing the Justice's "passion, courage, perseverance, flexibility, empathy, and conciliatory spirit," qualities he would surely appreciate having attributed to himself.[112]

At the end, Blaine Baker's strength was in observing and in listening, in fastidious mentoring, and in reminding law students enveloped in the digital world of the rich intellectual traditions built on Canada's distinct written, printed, and oral legal circuits. With a fine research hand and a mastery of historiography he made a broad and original contribution to our understanding of the legal space of nineteenth-century Upper Canada, a period and political space that he cherished. Certainly, his historiographies and teaching recognized violence, resistance, patriarchy, race, and class struggle, as elements in Canadian history. However, past the classroom and course outlines, his publications circled back to a somehow ideal time and to an ordered, cultured, tolerant, and pluralist legal community. Did his reticence with the forceful legal and social themes of his era represent conservative wisdom, an instinctive resistance to political correctness, and a steady compass for what he saw as the essential issues of legal history? Or, does the key to his writing lie in the fact that he was a wounded man in life, his intellectual production limited by self-inflicted glass ceilings that ultimately left a disenchanted and alienated academic? Gone, Blaine Baker remains a powerful figure in the writing of Canadian legal history: original, enigmatic, inspirational, and yet somehow anachronistic in both his personage and in his search for a coherent, conservative Canadian legal past.

NOTES

Many colleagues, students of Blaine, McGill staff who worked with Blaine, and various university archivists contributed to this piece. Special thanks to Tom Johnson and Constance Backhouse for thoughtful interviews, to Sean Mills who dug out University of Toronto records, to Richard Janda who facilitated access to Blaine's archives at McGill, and to Cory Verbauwhede for his enthusiastic help. Genevieve Westgate was an innovative research assistant for the volume. David Flaherty, David Howes, Rande Kostal, Jim Phillips, and Jonathan Swainger all made thoughtful contributions. Useful comments on a draft of this contribution were received from Contance Backhouse, Kathy Fisher, Philip Girard, Tom Johnson, Nicholas Kasirer, Eric Reiter, Cory Verbauwhede, and Nancy Ward, as well as fellow editors, Angela Fernandez and Ian C. Pilarczyk, and participants in the Toronto workshop, 7 December 2019.

1 For assessments of his rank, Jonathan Swainger to author, 2 June 2019, and in French, Yves-Marie Morissette, "Une Epistemologie du Droit. L'État Providence de François Ewald. Note," *Cahiers de Droit*, 28 (1987): 409. At the Toronto conference held to discuss the articles in this volume, there was sharp debate about his place in Canadian legal history as well as

over the inclusion in the volume of references to his health or gender attitudes. Interviews conducted by Genevieve Westgate for this volume support the claim that his legacy in the Canadian legal history community was a mixed one.

2 Jean-François Sirinelli, "Historiennes et historiens baby-boomers: une génération pivot?" in Yann Potin and Jean-François Sirinelli, *Générations historiennes XIXe-XXI siécle* (Paris: CNRS Éditions, 2019), 235.

3 For one example of the transformation in the teaching and writing of Canadian legal history see Janet Ajzenstat, "The Law Class," *Discovering Confederation: A Canadian's Story* (Montreal & Kingston: McGill-Queen's University Press, 2014), 74–80.

4 Baker was the son of Grant Baker QC (1921–1990), a lawyer in the Bay Street firm of Woolley, Dale, and Dingwall, and Muriel Isobel (Martin) Baker (1923–2011), a special education teacher before her marriage. In 2018, the University of Western Ontario officially became Western University.

5 Westgate interview with Kathy Fisher, 18 July 2019.

6 Comments in Toronto workshop, 7 December 2019.

7 Baker Archives, Baker to R.C.B. Risk, 16 August 1983.

8 Janice Dickin McGinnis in *Canadian Journal of Law and Society* 9, 1 (Spring 1994): 105–22.

9 McGill University Faculty of Law, Blaine Baker Archives [Baker Archives], handwritten diary-like note, "Studying central-Canada's nineteenth-century legal professions," nd [c.1989].

10 The family lived in a large suburban home on Robin Drive, backing onto a stream and "Sherwood Forest," Mississauga.

11 David Flaherty email to author, 11 June 2019. In 1980, and inviting Baker to present a paper, Flaherty convened the Osgoode Society's first academic conference on the theme of the state of scholarship in Canadian legal history. G. Blaine Baker, "R.C.B. Risk's Canadian Legal History," in *Essays in the History of Canadian Law, Volume VIII: In Honour of R.C.B. Risk*, edited by G. Blaine Baker and Jim Phillips (Toronto: University of Toronto Press, 1999), 17. For an example of Flaherty's work in colonial legal history, see "Law and the Enforcement of Morals in Early America," in *American Law and the Constitutional Order* edited by Lawrence M. Friedman (Cambridge, Mass.: Harvard University Press, 1988).

12 Baker and Phillips, eds., "Introduction," *Essays in the History of Canadian Law, Volume VIII: In Honour of R.C.B. Risk*, 4.

13 Columbia University, 1980.

14 Baker Archives, handwritten note, "Studying central-Canada's nineteenth-century legal professions," nd [c.1989].

15 Established in 1947, the Bigelow Teaching Fellowship in Law gave six recent law graduates a one-year scholarship with a view to their preparation for academic careers through a combination of research, attendance at seminars, and interaction with faculty. Bigelow fellows were expected to give tutorial instruction to first year law students.

16 Baker listed his supervisors as Lea Brilmayer, the only tenured female member of the University of Chicago law faculty, James White, author of *The Legal Imagination* (1973), and Geoffrey Stone.

17 For Simpson's work, see for example, https://www.researchgate.net/publication/262945112_Brian_Simpson's_Reflections_on_'The_Concept_of_Law'_An_Introduction_to_the_Symposium.

18 Juhana Salojarvi, "A Counter-Culture of Law: Jurisprudential Change and the Intellectual Origins of the Critical Legal Studies Movement," *American Journal of Legal History* 59:4 (December 2019); Robert W. Gordon, "Critical Legal Histories," *Stanford Law Review* 36 (1984): 57–125; David Sugarman and G.R. Rubin, "Towards a New History of Law and Material Society in England, 1750–1914," in *Law, Society and Economy, 1750–1914*, edited by Sugarman and Rubin (Abingdon: Professional Books, 1984); Michael Grossberg, "Social History Update: 'Fighting my Faiths' and the Challenges of Legal History," *Journal of Social History* 25 no.1 (1991): 191–201. Classics of this genre include E.P. Thompson, *Whigs and Hunters: the Origin of the Black Act* (Harmondsworth: Penguin, 1977) and Douglas Hay, Peter Linebaugh, John Rule, E.P. Thompson, and Cal Winslow, *Albions's Fatal Tree: Crime and Society in Eighteenth-Century England* (London: Penguin, 1977).

19 Three decades later, Gordon reminisced about the vitality of these seminars in the construction of Canadian legal history and in his exchanges with a generation of legal historians that included Baker, Constance Backhouse, Paul Craven, Hamar Foster, Philip Girard, William Kaplan, John McLaren, Jim Phillips, Wesley Pue, Paul Romney, Jonathan Swainger, Mariana Valverde, and Rob Vipond. Robert W. Gordon, *Essays on Law in History and History in Law* (Cambridge: Cambridge University Press, 2017), introduction, np.

20 David Sugarman and Robert Gordon, "Richard C.B. Risk: a Tribute," in *Essays in the History of Canadian Law, Volume VIII: In Honour of R.C.B. Risk*, edited by Baker and Phillips, 6.

21 G. Blaine Baker, Kathleen Fisher, Vincent Masciotra, Brian Young, eds., *Sources in the Law Library of McGill University for the Reconstruction of the Legal Culture of Quebec, 1760-1890* (Montreal: McGill University and Montreal Business History Project, 1987).

22 G. Blaine Baker, '"So Elegant a Web': Providential Order and the Rule of Secular Law in Early-Nineteeth-Century Upper Canada," *University of Toronto Law Journal* 38, no. 2 (1988): 187.

23 *Calendar*, 1990–91 University of Toronto School of Graduate Studies. Sean Mills to author, 22 May 2019; Ian Radforth to author, 23 May 2019; Jim Phillips to author, 24 May 2019.

24 After 1985, he complemented this course with a periodic offering in Comparative Modern Legal History. Baker's teaching and research were well-recognized at McGill. He was promoted to associate professor in 1987 and to a full professorship in 1994. He was named emeritus in 2009, a status that grated since it did not permit him to supervise graduate students.

25 Michael Lobban, "The Varieties of Legal History," *Clio@Themis Revue électronique d'histoire du droit*, 5 (June 2012); referring to the 1970s, Robert Gordon noted that American law faculties might offer one course in legal history, usually what he described as the "Development of Legal Institutions" with heavy emphasis on the English background of American law. A solid bibliography in American legal history, he continued, could be contained in two pages. Robert W. Gordon, *Essays on Law in History and History in Law*, introduction, np.

26 See R.C.B. Risk, "A Prospectus for Canadian Legal History," *Dalhousie Law Journal* 1 (1973): 227 and Graham Parker, "The Masochism of the Legal Historian," *University of Toronto Law Journal* 24 (1974): 279; and for Quebec, Vince Masciotra, "Quebec Legal Historiography, 1760–1900," *McGill Law Journal* 32, no. 3 (1986–87): 712; André Morel, "Canadian Legal History – Retrospect and Prospect," *Osgoode Hall Law Journal* 21 (1983): 159.

27 Risk, "A Prospectus for Canadian Legal History," 229.

28 T.H.B Symons, *To Know Ourselves: the Report of the Commission on Canadian Studies* (Ottawa: Association of Universities and Colleges of Canada, 1975): 214, cited in Girard, "Who's Afraid of Canadian Legal History," *University of Toronto Law Journal* 57 (2007): 741. All subsequent references in the text and in the notes will refer to this as the Symons' Report.

29 David Flaherty, "Writing Canadian Legal History: An Introduction," in *Essays in the History of Canadian Law*, edited by David Flaherty (Toronto: University of Toronto Press, 1981), vol 1: 4, 33.

30 André Morel, "Canadian Legal History – Retrospect and Prospect," *Osgoode Hall Law Journal* 21 (1983): 161, 163.

31 Ian Fletcher, *Law and Learning/Le Droit et le Savoir* [the Arthurs' Report], report to the Social Sciences and Humanities Research Council of Canada (Ottawa: Minister of Supply and Services Canada, 1983): 156.

32 Baker Archives, "Course Proposal in Canadian Legal History," Faculty of Law curriculum committee, 29 September 1981.

33 Baker Archives, Baker to Jeremy Webber, 24 September 1984. He named the University of Alberta, the University of Saskatchewan, the University of Windsor, Queen's University, the University of Ottawa, the University of New Brunswick, and Dalhousie University.

34 Baker Archives, Baker to Ed Vandenberg, *McGill Law Journal*, 24 March 1994.

35 Willis, "'Cultured' Public Authorities," *University of Toronto Law Journal* 55 (2005): 357; for similar remarks in (2013) see G. Blaine Baker and Donald Fyson, eds., "Quebec and the Canadas, 1760–1867," in *Essays in the History of Canadian Law: Quebec and the Canadas* (Toronto: University of Toronto Press, 2013), 95; see also "The Reconstitution of Upper Canadian Legal Thought in the Late-Victorian Empire," 219.

36 G. Blaine Baker, "William Proudfoot," *Dictionary of Canadian Biography*, http://www.biographi.ca/en/bio/proudfoot_william_1823_1903_13E.html

37 G. Blaine Baker, "The Migration of Upper Canadian Law Libraries," *Gazette* (Law Society of Upper Canada), vol. 14 (1980): 364.

38 Willis, "'Cultured' Public Authorities," 349.

39 G. Blaine Baker, "Ordering the Urban Canadian Law Office and its Entrepreneurial Hinterland, 1825 to 1875," *University of Toronto Law Journal* 48, no. 2 (1998): 175. Baker did not have a large personal collection of books at McGill and libraries at his Toronto home and in Muskoka were apparently quite modest.

40 Roger Chartier, "Libraries Without Walls," *Representations* no.42 (Spring 1993): 48.

41 Daniel Boyer interview, 4 June 2019.

42 Philip Girard pointed out the pedagogical importance of this work that went through several editions until at least 1994. Girard to author, 25 November 2019.

43 G. Blaine Baker, "The Migration of Upper Canadian Law Libraries," *Gazette* (Law Society of Upper Canada), vol. 14 (1980): 362–5.

44 For the influence of Baker's method of using cards to catalogue law libraries see Angela Fernandez, "Albert Maynard's Private Library: An Investigation of the Person, the Law of Persons, and 'Legal Personality' in a Collection of Law Books," *University of Toronto Law Journal* 53, no. 1 (2003): 37.

45 Baker Archives, Baker to R.C.B. Risk, 16 August 1983.

46 G. Blaine Baker, "The Reconstitution of Upper Canadian Legal Thought in the Late-Victorian Empire," *Law and History Review* 3, no. 2 (1985): 289.

47 H.J. Jackson, *Marginalia: Readers Writing in Books* (New Haven: Yale University Press, 2001); see also, Eric H. Reiter, "Imported Books, Imported Ideas: Reading European Jurisprudence in Mid-Nineteenth-Century Quebec," *Law and History Review* 22, no. 4 (2004); Peter F. McNally and Christina M. Boyle, "Judge Robert Mackay's 1882 Catalogue of Books," *Fonantus* vol. 10 (1998); Nicholas Kasirer, "Apostolat juridique: Teaching Everyday Law in the Life of Marie Lacoste Gérin-Lajoie (1867–1945)," *Osgoode Hall Law Journal* 30, no. 2 (1992); Angela Fernandez, "Albert Mayrand's Private Library: An Investigation of the Person, the Law of Persons, and 'Legal Personality'": 37–64.

48 Baker, "Musing and Silences of Chief Justice William Osgoode. Digest Marginalia about the Reception of Imperial Law."

49 Ibid., 762, 772, 767.

50 On this subject, see Mary Poovey, *A History of the Modern Fact: Problems of Knowledge in the Sciences of Wealth and Society* (Chicago: University of Chicago Press, 1998), 325.

51 Baker, "Ordering the Urban Canadian Law Office and its Entrepreneurial Hinterland, 1825 to 1875"; for another example of his emphasis on the link between the legal profession and Victorian sciences see "Quebec and the Canadas, 1760–1867," 36–7; for larger connections see Ann Laura Stoler, "Colonial Archives and the Art of Governance," *Archival Science* 2 (1–2) (March 2002): 87–91.

52 Other commonplace books belonged to Andrew Stuart, George Okill Stuart, Eugene Lafleur, and Gustavus G. Stuart. "The Reconstitution of Upper Canadian Legal Thought in the Late-Victorian Empire," 243. Elsewhere, Baker noted the presence in Montreal of several dozen commonplace books; "Ordering the Urban Canadian Law Office and its Entrepreneurial Hinterland, 1825 to 1875," 210.

53 Baker, "Silences of Chief Justice William Osgoode. Digest Marginalia about the Reception of Imperial Law," unpublished paper prepared for the *Osgoode Hall Law Journal, Festschrift* for Douglas Hay, 30 August 2016: np.

54 Baker, "Ordering the Urban Canadian Law Office and its Entrepreneurial Hinterland, 1825 to 1875," 175.

55 Ibid., 248.

56 Ibid.

57 Baker, "Quebec and the Canadas, 1760–1867," 24; for Simpson's career at the Universities of Chicago and Michigan, see https://www.researchgate.net/publication/262945112_Brian_Simpson's_Reflections_on_'The_Concept_of_Law'_An_Introduction_to_the_Symposium; Baker's

attraction to "Simpson-izing" is clear from the Westgate interview with Daniel Boyer, 4 June 2019.

58 Baker, "Testamentary Archaeology in Late-Victorian Ontario: William Martin's Little Posthumous Legal System."

59 Ibid.

60 Baker's connection to William Martin becomes evident from reading what he calls a "companion" "genealogical" "account" sourced in his footnote 27.

61 Baker did not neglect the relationship between public and private in explaining the work of others. Commenting on law professor F.R. Scott's intellectual development, Baker insisted that important place be given to Scott's origins as "a son of the manse" and to the larger cultural influence of his wife, Marian Scott, "an artist in her own right." Baker Archives, McGill University, Baker to Eric Adams, nd (c. August–September 2009).

62 Baker, "Juristic Biographies, Homage Volumes, and 'Tracings of Gerald Le Dain's Life in the Law,'" 5.

63 William Proudfoot and William Albert Reeve.

64 Emily Cowan Murphy and Helen Emma MacGill.

65 Baker, "Juristic Biographies, Homage Volumes, and 'Tracings of Gerald Le Dain's Life in the Law,"' 35.

66 R.C.B. Risk, "John Willis: a Tribute," *Dalhousie Law Journal*, 9 (1984–85): 521–54.

67 G. Blaine Baker, 'Willis, "'Cultured' Public Authorities," *University of Toronto Law Journal* 55, no. 3 (2005): 336–60.

68 Ibid., 349, 355.

69 Ibid., 356.

70 Baker Archives, letter of recommendation for XX, 19 March 1993.

71 Baker Archives, Baker to Chief Justice on behalf of A.W.C., 11 January 1999; in a recommendation to the McCarthy Tétrault law firm, Baker described XX, as a "person of good sense" and "suitable ambition." Baker Archives, Baker to Robert Forbes, 7 April 1994.

72 Westgate interview with Daniel Boyer, 4 June 2019.

73 Baker Archives, Baker to R.C.B. Risk, 4 February 1986.

74 His *Dictionary of Canadian Biography* articles appeared in French translation.

75 Baker, "Quebec and the Canadas, 1760–1867."

76 Baker, "The Reconstitution of Upper Canadian Legal Thought in the Late-Victorian Empire," 219.

77 Philip Girard points out that Baker may have underestimated the counter-trends in Ontario legal culture which led, for example, to creation of the

Canadian Bar Association in 1914, a venue where common law and civil law lawyers could meet. Girard to author, 25 November 2019.

78 Baker, "The Reconstitution of Upper Canadian Legal Thought in the Late-Victorian Empire," 234, 243, 263.

79 Baker Archives, Baker to Eric Adams, nd (c. August–September 2009).

80 Baker to Eric Adams, nd.

81 J.E.C. Brierley, "Quebec's Civil Law Codification: Viewed and Reviewed," *McGill Law Journal* 14 (1968): 520; Yalden, "Unité et différence: The Structure of Legal Thought in Late Nineteenth-Century Quebec," *University of Toronto Law Review* 46, no. 2 (1988).

82 Baker to Eric Adams, nd.

83 Baker Archives, "Notes for Duke University seminar," 22 February 1983.

84 In J.E. Cooke, ed., *Encyclopedia of the North American Colonies*, vol. 1 (New York: Charles Scribner 1993), 430–2, 443–5.

85 Baker Archives, Baker to Peter Oliver, editor-in-chief, Osgoode Society, 13 December 1990; Baker to Sylvio Normand, 22 April 1991. Baker's proposed authors represented a who's who of Quebec legal history: John Brierley, Jean-Maurice Brisson, John Dickinson, Jean-Marie Fecteau, Donald Fyson, Iain Gow, Murray Greenwood, René Hardy, David Howes, Nicolas Kasirer, Evelyn Kolish, James Lambert, André Lachance, André Morel, Sylvio Normand, and Christine Veilleux.

86 Baker Archives, "Course of Study, Canadian Legal History Seminar, January 1995"; "Quebec and the Canadas, 1760–1867: A Legal Historiography."

87 Belley, "La Nouvelle histoire de droit," *Cahiers de droit* 27 (1986): 371–80; Rudin, "Revisionism and the Search for a Normal Society: A Critique of Recent Quebec Historical Writing," *Canadian Historical Review* 73 (1992): 30–61.

88 Vachon, *Histoire du notariat, 1621–1960* (Québec: Les Presses de l'Université Laval, 1962); Normand, "Un thème dominant de la pensée juridique traditionelle au Québec. La sauvegarde de l'intégrité du droit civil," *McGill Law Journal*, 32 (1987): 559–601; Kasirer, "Apostolat Juridique: Teaching Everyday Law in the Life of Marie Lacoste Gérin-Lajoie," 427–70.

89 Baker, Fisher, Masciotra, Young, *Sources in the Law Library of McGill.*

90 Baker, "Strategic Benthamism: Rehabilitating United Canada's Bar through Criminal Law Codification, 1847 to 1852," in *Essays in the History of Canadian Law: A Tribute to Peter N. Oliver*, edited by J. Phillips, R.R. McMurtry, and J.T. Saywell (Toronto: University of Toronto Press, 2008), 257–319.

91 Vince Masciotra, "Quebec Legal Historiography, 1760–1900," *McGill Law Journal* 32, no. 3 (1986–87): 729.

92 David Flaherty, ed., *Essays in the History of Canadian Law, Volume I*: 323–57.

93 Clio Collective, *Quebec Women: A History* (Toronto: Women's Press, 1992); for entry into the larger context of gender history see Joan Scott, "Gender: a Useful Category of Historical Analysis," *American Historical Review* 91:5 (1986).

94 Constance Backhouse, "Gender and Race in the Construction of Legal Professionalism: Historical Perspectives," https://papers.ssrn.com/sol3/papers.cfm?abstract_id=2273323. Paper delivered to colloquia on legal professionalism (October, 2003).

95 See, among multiple examples, Mary Anne Poutanen, "Regulating Public Space in Early Nineteenth-Century Montreal: Vagrancy Laws and Gender in a Colonial Context," *Histoire social/Social History* 35, no. 69 (2002): 35–58; Bettina Bradbury, *Wife to Widow: Class, Culture, Family and the Law in Nineteenth-Century Montreal* (Vancouver and Toronto: UBC Press 2011); Josette Brun, *Vie et mort du couple en Nouvelle-France. Québec et Louisbourg au XVIIIe siècle* (Montréal: McGill-Queen's University Press, 2006); for race, see Backhouse, *Petticoats and Prejudice: Woman and Law in Nineteenth-Century Canada* (Toronto: Women's Press, 1991).

96 Baker Archives, Course of Study, Canadian Legal History. Seminar, January 1985.

97 For another example, see the Westgate interview with Kathy Fisher, 18 July 2019.

98 For Bradbury's early works on women and the law see "Surviving as a Widow in Nineteeth-Century Montreal," *Urban History Review* 17 (1989): 148–61 and *Wife to Widow: Class, Culture, Family, and the Law in Nineteenth-Century Quebec* (Programme d'études sur le Québec de l'Université McGill 1997).

99 Baker, "Quebec and the Canadas, 1760–1867," 6.

100 Baker, "Public Frivolity and Patrician Confidence: Lower Canada's 'Brothers-in-Law' 1827 to 1833."

101 Baker, "Testamentary Archaeology in Late-Victorian Ontario."

102 Interview with Constance Backhouse, Montreal, 6 May 2019. Pointing to what she saw as Baker's persistent support for her work, Backhouse gave him the backhanded compliment of describing him as less sexist than a group of her former colleagues at the University of Western Ontario law school who "hated feminists." Cited in Diane Peters, "Courting Conflict," *University Affairs/Affaires universitaires*, 10 October 2012; see also

Backhouse, "Gender and Race in the Construction of 'Legal Professionalism,'" paper delivered to a conference on legal professionalism, October 2003: https://papers.ssrn.com/sol3/papers.cfm?abstract_id=2273323.

103 See, for example, Baker, "Quebec and the Canadas, 1760–1867," 74.

104 He attributed the term "fence-posts" to a conversation with Brian Simpson. Ibid., 42.

105 Ibid., 21.

106 See Philip Girard, Jim Phillips, and R. Blake Brown, *A History of Law in Canada, Volume One: Beginnings to 1866* (Toronto: Osgoode Society for Canadian Legal History, 2018); for an overview of the significance of gender in the field of legal history see Sebastian Vandenbogaerde et al., *(Wo)Men in Legal History* (Lille: Centre d'Histoire Judiciaire, 2016).

107 Baker Archives, Baker to Prof. Bernard J. Hibbitts, 18 March 1998.

108 Baker Archives, Baker to R.C.B. Risk, 4 February 1986.

109 In 2016, he co-taught the Canadian Legal History course with Cory Verbauwhede.

110 Baker, "Quebec and the Canadas, 1760–1867," 95.

111 Baker, "Juristic Biographies, Homage Volumes, and 'Tracings of Gerald Le Dain's Life in the Law,"' 22.

112 Ibid.

Blaine and I showed up on the McGill campus almost simultaneously – he as a freshly minted professor, and I as an incoming student. From the very first, I found that he had a compelling, idiosyncratic persona, astonishingly glittering insight, and an explosively hilarious sense of humour. His care and concern for students was unmatched. When I was editor of *Quid Novi*, the student newspaper, he would always wander by for late night gab sessions in the dean's office while I tried to do formatting with the clunky word-processors the dean allowed us to use. Only years later did I discover that these encounters with Blaine were not quite as innocent as they appeared. He had solemnly promised the dean to monitor the newspaper's activities so as to ensure that the precious machines, or any other objects in the office for that matter, were not being vandalized. Little did we know that *Quid Novi* would not have appeared but for Blaine's undertaking.

Blaine and I became friends and colleagues. It is perhaps a shared characteristic of most contributors to this volume that we were among those to whom Blaine reached out for periodic – and memorable – telephone cross-examinations. I regret that Blaine did not see the results of a project upon which we collaborated and discussed at length: an essay collection entitled *Tracings of Gerald Le Dain's Life in the Law*. We had both found compelling the idea that a brilliant career cut short – that of soldier, lawyer, professor, dean, and ultimately Supreme Court Justice Gerald Le Dain – nevertheless left certain indelible traces. I could not resist therefore pursuing that line of thought in connection with Blaine himself. In my paper I have only managed to explore one extended episode in Blaine's academic life. But I hope my effort is true to his spirit, and console myself that if nothing else, he would recognize himself in this piece and perhaps even have a good laugh.

Richard Janda

4

Traces of Blaine Baker upon McGill's Faculty of Law

Richard Janda

I have been trying to trace what remains present of Blaine Baker in his absence from the Faculty of Law of McGill University.[1] I felt the need to engage with this task by looking into archival materials of his that fell into my hands after he passed away, because Blaine, the historian, himself sought to find traces of the continued presence of the past in this way. I am inspired in significant degree by Blaine's study of the digest marginalia of Chief Justice William Osgoode in which he made as much of the silences in the margins as he did of Osgoode's formal annotations.[2] What I seek to show, paraphrasing his account of Osgoode, is that Blaine's "activity and inactivity and his marginal musings and silences help to highlight the historically contingent character of" contributions to the legal academy and to an educational institution.[3]

Blaine was the most accomplished teacher and arguably the most powerful intellect of his generation at McGill.[4] Yet it is difficult to detect his trace upon the "transsystemic program," the signature pedagogical project of the faculty which was implemented during his time as a faculty member. In his own personal materials kept in his office, with the exception of an extensive collection of reference letters written for students, Blaine did not preserve a record of the files he managed while Associate Dean, Graduate Studies (1997–1999) or Associate Dean, Academic (1999–2001). However, he kept quite a complete record of materials related to the adoption of the transsystemic program, which was designed to produce integrated study of the common law and civil law traditions.[5] A number of these materials contain his annotations on the documents produced in advance of or during Faculty Council meetings. There are occasionally caustic jottings about the quality of presentations being made, apparently as documents were passed back and forth with other colleagues (I recognize Roderick Macdonald's handwriting on one of them).[6] But as with Chief Justice William Osgoode's copy of John Comyn's *Digest of the Laws of England*, the silences are as revealing as the annotations.

I will begin by setting the scene briefly for the reform of McGill's program in the period 1992–1999. I will then seek to assemble what can be learned from Blaine's comments and observations in order to demonstrate that he did leave an important trace upon the most significant curricular reform undertaken by the faculty. Finally, I will reflect briefly on what can be learned from the challenge of detecting his trace upon an institution for which he cared deeply despite his disappointment that his legacy remained unfulfilled.[7] Notwithstanding, Blaine's aversion to buried themes in articles, I have deliberately left it to the reader to pay attention to the leitmotif concerning administrative process – the successful conduct of which Blaine understood to be the task of the citizen-jurist.[8]

THE REFORM OF MCGILL'S NATIONAL PROGRAMME

Political Context

The story of McGill's transsystemic program has been told and re-told many times.[9] A reacquaintance with the background materials, even for someone like me who was present through the entire debate, makes clear that the faculty went through an astonishing and divisive saga. Until and past 30 October 1995, we lived the *Sturm und Drang* of the second Quebec referendum, for which over 93 per cent of eligible voters turned out to vote and the "Non" option won by a mere 54,000 votes: a 0.58 per cent margin of victory.[10] It is far from a coincidence that Dean Stephen Toope created the Ad Hoc Curriculum Review Committee in September, 1995 and indeed had begun the review process earlier mindful of the evolving Quebec context.[11] As of the date of the referendum, McGill offered what was called the "National Law Programme" which allowed students to complete a BCL degree in civil law and an LLB degree in common law, but to do so sequentially in four years.[12] Students could enter either in

Figure 4.1 | Blaine Baker receiving the John W. Durnford Award for Teaching Excellence, 2005.

civil law (approximately one hundred students of each year's cohort were in that stream) or common law (approximately fifty students of each year's cohort were in that stream).[13] In practice this meant that the majority of students entering in common law only graduated with an LLB and sought to practice outside Quebec, whereas the majority of students entering in civil law ended up graduating with both degrees, keeping open their options for practice outside Quebec. Quebec's political circumstances were having an impact on the viability of this structure. Fewer students from outside Quebec were applying to the common law program and even students from inside Quebec, notably anglophones, were applying in lower numbers to the civil law program. A 1995 memorandum from then-assistant dean (admissions) Robin Geller to Shauna Van Praagh, chair of the Ad Hoc Curriculum Review Committee, conveys some of the urgency that was being felt at the time but not always uttered out in the open:

> [I]n 1991 we received 1007 LLB applications and 540 BCL applications. This year, we have received about 630 LLB applications and 443 BCL applications. Thus, even if the size of our *potential* applicant pool remains constant, we would still be likely to see a continuing decrease in applications.
>
> It is also important to recognize that the decrease in the number of applicants has a direct effect on the total number of admissible applicants. That is, we are receiving fewer of both strong and weak applications. Finally, it is important to note that raw numbers of applicants doesn't tell the whole story. In addition to the number of applications, we must look carefully at our yield rate. It has been fairly steadily in the 50 per cent range until last year when it dipped to 39 per cent. If last year's trend were to continue, we will soon see an overall decrease in the quality of the students attending the Faculty of Law.
>
> […]
>
> We are in a Faculty of Law, with a French component, and an anglophone university in a francophone province. The number of applications to faculties of law is decreasing, our traditional constituent bases are diminishing, and the interest in what we do and how we do it is also on the wane. If we do not redefine ourselves in a meaningful way in order to broaden our constituency and offer something that is truly attractive to potential

applicants, we will slowly become an irrelevant player in the world of legal education. We need to carve out a space that is ours alone and that we can do better than anyone else. Then we need to go out and tell the world that is what we are doing.[14]

Already in April 1992, the faculty's standing curriculum committee had issued a report entitled "A Three-Year National Programme" which reflected the committee's assessment of "two, unrelated types of argument as to whether a three-year option was desirable": instrumental and pedagogical. As to the former, the committee noted:

In the first group are instrumental arguments related to the current state of our admissions pool, and our competitiveness with respect to other faculties. From that point of view, a three-year National Programme might be desirable because it might make our faculty more attractive to students who do not wish to spend four years in law school, and because it might enable us to move to a single admissions pool. Some have argued, on the other hand, that establishing a three-year programme in the place of our current four-year programme might have the opposite effect: applicants might have doubts about the marketability of the compressed, diluted degrees and consequently prefer a single degree from another institution. They might also be frightened by the intense nature of a three-year compressed program, and by the potential reduction in the number of electives that it would require. At this stage, those claims are difficult to evaluate, as is the impact of a move to a single admissions pool on the proportion of Quebec students, and in particular Francophone Quebec students in the faculty. At the very least, and without saying more about the desirability of a three-year programme, the committee thinks that further studies are required to determine whether such a programme would indeed have a positive effect on the applicant pool, and increase the Faculty's profile in the student market.[15]

I am here deliberately over-emphasizing the instrumental goals over the pedagogical ones that were pursued, because as the discourse around the program has settled, understandably the pedagogical side of the equation is almost uniquely discussed.[16] As we will see, Blaine covertly attended to instrumental goals by paying attention notably to how students perceived the desirability of the program while maintaining what proved to be a somewhat iconoclastic view concerning what was meant by "transsystemic legal education." In the end, after years of deliberation, the new program of integrated studies, which was built around courses drawing upon and comparing civil law and common law perspectives on legal problems, was eventually implemented in 1999.[17] Exactly how that outcome unfolded is worth documenting and will eventually shed light on Blaine Baker's own particular mode of engagement with debate in the faculty.

Toward Curriculum Reform

The Ad Hoc Curriculum Review Committee chaired by Shauna Van Praagh finished its work in April 1996 issuing a twenty-four-page report. That report explicitly considered but rejected creating what it called "bisystemic, integrated courses" as of the first year. It recommended the creation of an integrated McGill program with a single application pool while opting to maintain separate streaming through common law and civil law within that combined program. It also recommended the creation of the Ad Hoc Curriculum Implementation Committee to move from general reform principles to specific reform proposals.[18]

The Ad Hoc Curriculum Implementation Committee was indeed struck with Patrick Glenn as chair. That committee issued its report in March 1997 and made a short set of curriculum-reform proposals. In particular, Glenn's committee (of which Shauna Van Praagh was a member) explicitly recommended abolishing the tradition-specific courses as of the first year and creating a single new eight credit Obligations course to cover contracts and extracontractual responsibility. This represented a significant departure from the report of the Review Committee, which, as mentioned, had not yet taken the leap toward transsytemic teaching.

Upon initial debate in Faculty Council in March 1997, the Implementation Committee's specific proposals were deemed premature. A motion was adopted requesting that the Implementation Committee instead articulate and present underlying "Principles and Corollaries" informing its report, and to present those to Faculty Council in April. The Implementation Committee came back with a two-page document, the first principle of which was that: "The faculty is committed to a single, unified program, within which the civil law and common law can continue to coexist in a sustained and vital equilibrium, while respecting the integrity of each." The third corollary to that principle was: "the first year programme shall include comparative and transsystemic teaching in the law of obligations." This was the first time the word "transsystemic" was used in a document approved by Faculty Council.[19] The Curriculum Reform Principles were adopted but with amendments and significant dissent.[20]

Immediately thereafter Dean Toope struck a steering committee, chaired by Jeremy Webber, and three working groups: Private Law Foundations chaired by Rod Macdonald and subsequently by Daniel Jutras, Year-by-Year Progression chaired by David Stevens, and Enhancing Public Law and Comparative Law Offerings chaired by Patrick Glenn. That intensive work led to the formal proposal of an integrated BCL/LLB program that eventually reduced total credit load to 105 credits from 125 and could be completed in three, three and a half, or four years. The preliminary vote on the basic elements of the reform took place on 28 November 1997 and passed by the slim margin of eighteen to fourteen (with four abstentions).[21] A subsequent vote to adopt the overall reform took place on 4 March 1998, and passed by a similarly slim margin of nineteen to fourteen with no recorded abstentions.

These were rare, recorded votes in the faculty's history. In fact, five members of council were not at the meeting, had left, or abstained from voting on 4 March 1998.[22] But for the eight students on Faculty Council, who voted unanimously in favour, the reform would not have been adopted. Except for an extensive summary of the remarks by Dean Stephen Toope on 28 November 1997, the minutes of Faculty Council are laconic, simply listing the eighteen other speakers who addressed the motion and noting that "a debate ensued." The 4 March 1998 Minutes are even more compressed.

In his 28 November remarks, the dean anticipated the deep divisions within the faculty, noting that he "had pressed the process, despite the discomfort it caused, because of its fundamental importance" and emphasizing that "complacent institutions prepared their own decline." At the time, many colleagues believed that combining civil and common law teaching was untested and infeasible; they could not picture themselves doing it and feared that it would leave students disoriented and insufficiently grounded in either legal tradition. A substantial number of civilian colleagues feared that an integrated program would by default emphasize the common law. Some common law colleagues, including Peter Benson who departed from the faculty soon after the vote, thought the proposal lacked rigour and sufficient resource planning. He was also concerned that the new integrated courses would constrain academic freedom in teaching.[23]

BLAINE BAKER'S COMMENTS, OBSERVATIONS, AND INFLUENCE

There is no formal trace of Blaine on the process of curricular reform in the 1992–99 period. He was not on the 1995–96 Ad Hoc Curriculum Review Committee, the 1996–97 Ad Hoc Curriculum Implementation Committee, or on the 1997–98 Steering Committee or working groups. In the critical period of January–May 1997, he was secretary to Faculty Council and thus did not speak. Even after he was replaced by Stephen Scott and Geneviève Saumier as secretary, there is only one indirect record of him addressing Faculty Council during any of the many meetings at which curriculum reform was addressed.

Yet there are many traces of him and his deep reflection on the issues at stake in the files that he kept as well as in one file kept by Prof. Van Praagh. Before reviewing that evidence, a general observation about the unfolding of the collegial process of deliberation is in order.

Collegiality and Managerialism

A return to the 1992–99 record of debate in the faculty has led me to acknowledge that by going back not so far in time, I am already losing the ability to construct a proper record. This is not simply because I have had to re-familiarize myself with committee structures, reports, and minutes, and assemble elements of an archive.[24] Nor is it entirely because I have had to confront my own susceptibility to false memory syndrome, since based on my years of conversation with Blaine, I had come to believe that he was the author of a report that was an important part of the curricular process although he was not even on the working group that produced it.[25] Rather, it is because the kinds of administrative processes within which I now find myself embedded in the faculty differ so significantly from those that existed in that period that I tended to read the record with what Blaine would have called "presentism" informing my expectations. I have come to expect a managerial rather than collegial process. I have come to expect that decisions emanate from those who are formally assigned delegated authority. Thus, for example, if someone within the university is charged with producing a report, that person is thought to be the author on behalf of the institution. Our Faculty Council today receives reports of the outcome of delegated authority; it rarely conceives itself as the locus of collective decision-making. Thus, since I cannot find any formal delegation of authority to Blaine or see a record of his participation in the minutes of meetings, I could conclude, from today's vantage point, that he was not involved. This is not to say that managerial rather than collegial processes lack informal as well as formal use of authority. However, it arises differently within them. Within a managerial process, the delegate may be called upon to consult and draw on networks of what we now call stakeholders rather than colleagues. In the reports ultimately deposited, typically there would be allusion to information meetings often scantly attended and to calls for comment that went largely unheeded. One might observe, too formulaically perhaps, that in a managerial process there is often a formal mandate to consult and informal deference to the determinations of the delegate. By contrast, within a collegial process, the requirement to consult will tend to be implicit rather than formal, and the delegate will often give formal deference to the ultimate collective decision. Thus, in the 1992–99 period, characterized by a collegial process, the various committees were conceived as instruments to engage with the faculty, staff, and students to enable collective decisions. For example, Shauna Van Praagh kept a record of all the documents gathered by the committee she chaired. It is an impressive compilation not only of her work but also of the efforts almost all colleagues were making to engage with her process. Indeed, the formal mandate she received, and that the other relevant committees subsequently received from the dean, was to contribute to the faculty's decision-making process.

Given the context of the times, I have to take seriously the notion that Blaine was one of the quiet, even formally silent, decision-makers participating in a collegial process. The story I am seeking to tell could be told in parallel for all the members of the faculty of the period. I single him out not only because of the occasion of this essay, not only because his contributions to the faculty are largely unsung and clouded by the context of his departure when he was suffering from alcoholism, but also because, false memory and all, I wish to record his partly fulfilled and partly unfulfilled contributions to deepening the pedagogical and intellectual project of the McGill Faculty of Law. He was there, even if it is difficult to see from the written record, and he had views that he mostly conveyed privately rather than around the table at Faculty Council. Blaine had a predilection for working in the interstices of administrative processes and for viewing and imagining the roles of agents as parts of an organic whole. Thus, for example, his 8½" x 14" yellow pages of class notes for the administrative law class that he gave at the University of Toronto in 2013 had interspersed a sheet from his Administrative Process class taught at McGill in 1993 where one finds a list of some of his favorite themes:

1. Governments in miniature:
   - lots [of them]
   - large strain on public purse
   - largesse as "new property"
2. Choice of governing instrument
3. Accountability
4. Rule of law

He thought of Faculty Council as a governing instrument formalizing the process of decision-making for the faculty community through its government in miniature, which was subject always to forms of inter-personal, collegial accountability that taken together generated a kind of rule of law. For Blaine, the citizen-jurist generally had responsibility to undertake the proper design of administrative processes and assure the internal aspirations informing them. The faculty, in its own governance, had to model what it sought to teach.

Blaine's Response to the 1996 Ad Hoc Curriculum Review Committee

I turn then to the archival traces of Blaine. The earliest example I have found is from 3 April 1996. It is a fax from Blaine to Shauna Van Praagh that she kept in her extensive committee binder.[26] Blaine was at the time a visiting professor at the University of

Toronto and the fax therefore comes from Falconer Hall. It is a marked-up copy of the four-page preliminary report of the Ad Hoc Curriculum Review Committee and looks very much like the kind of commentary he would put on student papers. Unlike other colleagues who wrote memorandums, Blaine chose to respond to the committee by annotation. Mostly the annotations read with a range of approval from "✓" (three times) to "OK" (four times) to "good" (once) to "yes" (twice) to "agree" (once) to "agree strongly" (seven times) to "yes yes yes" (once). That last emphatic annotation relates to the most controversial element that ended up in the final curriculum reform proposal adopted by the faculty. The committee's earlier interim report had put out the trial balloon that "we might consider teaching one of the areas of private law in the form of an integrated and comparative course (e.g., Personal Liability – Torts and Extra-Contractual Obligations)."[27] Blaine sought to rally the troops in that direction.[28] This annotation also helps clarify a longer marginal note that was cut off by the fax machine. It relates to possible models of curricular reform: 1) integrated and comparative from the first year; 2) starting all students in civil law and switching to common law; and 3) streaming cohorts as in the National Programme. Blaine's note reads: "options # [1] and # 3 are accept[able] – option # [2] is not good." I have filled in the blanks. Thus, Blaine's goal in the process was to aim toward an integrated first year curriculum, to resist the possibility that a single sequential program starting in civil law be adopted, and to have a three-year version of the National Programme with two entry streams as a fall-back position. The single sequential program, in his view, would have been a step backwards because it would mark all students as initially the product of a single tradition, civil law, and thus forego even the modest hydridization that took place among the existing National Programme first-year cohort. In the existing program, students who started in common law interacted with students who started in civil law.

It may be surprising to note that Blaine "strongly agreed" that more courses should be offered in French – his own comprehension of French was much stronger than his refusal to speak it made out. He also agreed that comparative approaches should be extended to Indigenous law. He strongly agreed with the idea of an honours designation for students who could choose an area of concentration and complete a senior thesis-like essay. He underscored his support for small group teaching opportunities and multiple forms of evaluation. On the other hand, he crossed out the term "Human Rights" and substituted the words "Administrative Process" in the discussion of where students might be given opportunity to write in first year.[29] His preoccupation with the importance of the Administrative Process course and the relative weight accorded to it comes through clearly in his response to the following passage of the report:

> Given the fact that McGill is understood to excel in international law and international human rights, the interests and perspectives of the students who come here are understandably varied and diverse. Both the stated commitment of the faculty and the associated concerns of today's students should be more effectively reflected in the programme. A Human Rights or Civil Liberties course (comparative in nature i.e., provincial human rights legislation, state constitutional instruments, introduction to international human rights) should be offered in the first or second year, and could be seen as the second part of Constitutional Law, Federalism being the first. Public International Law could become mandatory.

In the margin, Blaine wrote, with some bitterness: "'Administrative Process' was designed to be a compulsory first-year course, but Faculty Council of 1982 balked."[30]

There is more that can be gleaned from his annotations to the preliminary report. Blaine's longest annotation addresses the one allusion to instrumental concerns made explicit: "the Committee is aware of the significant connections between admissions and the program. It is also aware of possible political ramifications and considerations." Blaine offered the following perspective: "I don't think there is any statistically reliable way of determining impact on student/'markets.' Impressionistically, my guess is that the change proposed would have a little impact on best applicants."[31] Blaine did not believe that instrumental concerns could guide overall curricular design. He did not deny the political challenges facing McGill in Quebec or even that curricular reform might perhaps have an impact upon student perceptions of the program and on the ability to attract strong candidates. However, he simply did not see evidence that we had the tools to assess candidate perceptions and believed that, in any event, the principal goal of deliberations was to build the most challenging and compelling intellectual project for pedagogy.[32] Nonetheless, Blaine was prepared to

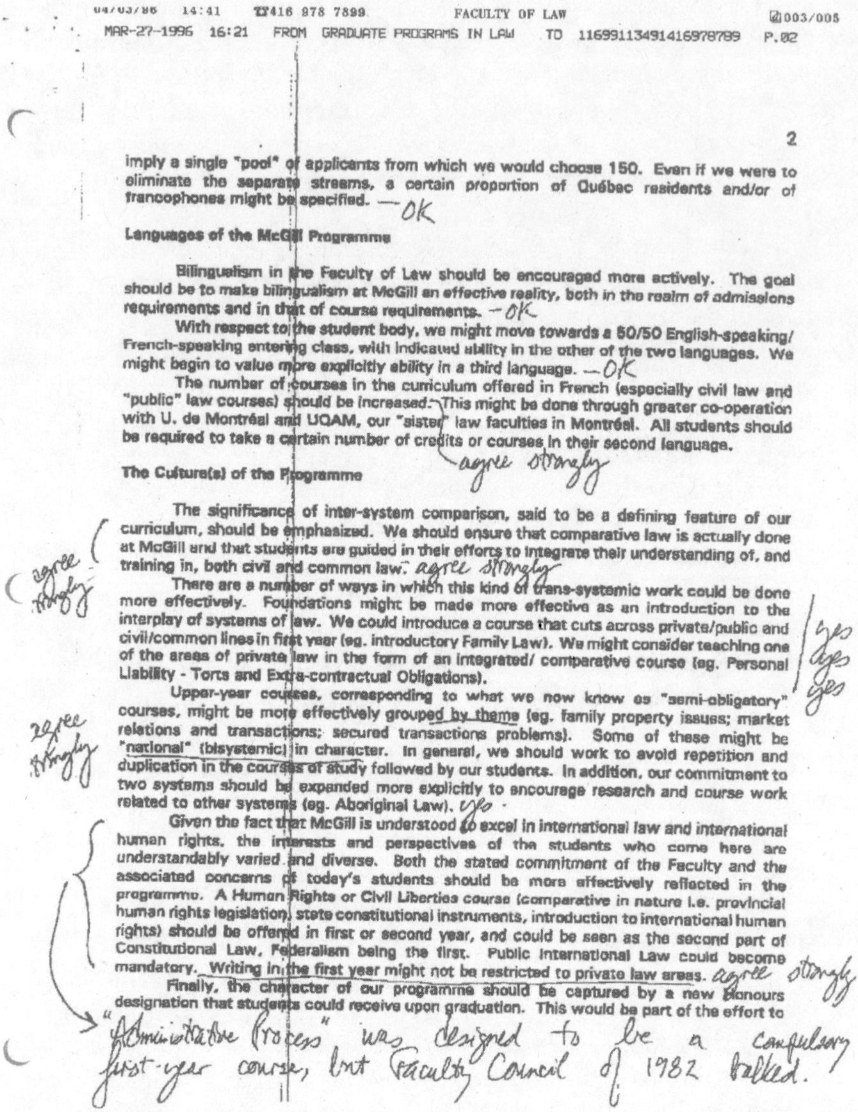
04/03/96 14:41 ☎416 978 7899 FACULTY OF LAW 003/005
MAR-27-1996 16:21 FROM GRADUATE PROGRAMS IN LAW TO 11699113491416978789 P.02

2

imply a single "pool" of applicants from which we would choose 150. Even if we were to eliminate the separate streams, a certain proportion of Québec residents and/or of francophones might be specified. — OK

Languages of the McGill Programme

Bilingualism in the Faculty of Law should be encouraged more actively. The goal should be to make bilingualism at McGill an effective reality, both in the realm of admissions requirements and in that of course requirements. — OK

With respect to the student body, we might move towards a 50/50 English-speaking/French-speaking entering class, with indicated ability in the other of the two languages. We might begin to value more explicitly ability in a third language. — OK

The number of courses in the curriculum offered in French (especially civil law and "public" law courses) should be increased. This might be done through greater co-operation with U. de Montréal and UQAM, our "sister" law faculties in Montréal. All students should be required to take a certain number of credits or courses in their second language. agree strongly

The Culture(s) of the Programme

The significance of inter-system comparison, said to be a defining feature of our curriculum, should be emphasized. We should ensure that comparative law is actually done at McGill and that students are guided in their efforts to integrate their understanding of, and training in, both civil and common law. agree strongly

There are a number of ways in which this kind of trans-systemic work could be done more effectively. Foundations might be made more effective as an introduction to the interplay of systems of law. We could introduce a course that cuts across private/public and civil/common lines in first year (eg. introductory Family Law). We might consider teaching one of the areas of private law in the form of an integrated/ comparative course (eg. Personal Liability - Torts and Extra-contractual Obligations). yes yes yes

Upper-year courses, corresponding to what we now know as "semi-obligatory" courses, might be more effectively grouped by theme (eg. family property issues; market relations and transactions; secured transactions problems). Some of these might be "national" (bisystemic) in character. In general, we should work to avoid repetition and duplication in the courses of study followed by our students. In addition, our commitment to two systems should be expanded more explicitly to encourage research and course work related to other systems (eg. Aboriginal Law). yes

Given the fact that McGill is understood to excel in international law and international human rights, the interests and perspectives of the students who come here are understandably varied and diverse. Both the stated commitment of the Faculty and the associated concerns of today's students should be more effectively reflected in the programme. A Human Rights or Civil Liberties course (comparative in nature i.e. provincial human rights legislation, state constitutional instruments, introduction to international human rights) should be offered in first or second year, and could be seen as the second part of Constitutional Law, Federalism being the first. Public International Law could become mandatory. Writing in the first year might not be restricted to private law areas. agree strongly

Finally, the character of our programme should be captured by a new Honours designation that students could receive upon graduation. This would be part of the effort to

"Administrative Process" was designed to be a compulsory first-year course, but Faculty Council of 1982 balked.

Figure 4.2 | Blaine Baker's fax with his annotations on the Preliminary Report of the Ad Hoc Review Committee, 1996.

consider an empirical investigation of student perceptions, as another of the documents in his file attests: a survey conducted by students themselves, which Blaine helped to conceive.

Blaine's Involvement in the National Programme Student Survey

The Law Students Association of the period had its own active committees participating in curriculum reform proposals. However, it too faced the challenge of collegial consultation. A group of students took it upon themselves to create the National Programme Student Survey Committee to canvass student opinion about possible curricular reform. That committee produced a spiral-bound version of its report, dated 24 March 1997, prepared for Faculty Council, with a title page stating that it had been "Presented to: Professor G. Blaine Baker."[33] A student member of the committee, Gregory MacKenzie, wrote: "Professor Baker, Thanks for your tip-off 2 weeks ago at Coffee House. Cheers."

In separate correspondence, I was able to learn from Gregory MacKenzie what the "tip-off" had been:

> Professor Baker let us know that the faculty was in the final stages of mandating the National Programme for future McGill law classes, without having had any substantive consultation with students. Being from Ontario (as was Professor Baker), I was particularly concerned about the impact of turning the National Programme from being optional to obligatory. Would this affect the desirability or viability of McGill law for out-of-province students, and the standing/ranking of McGill law? These were, I thought, questions worth asking, so I subsequently organized a working group to conduct a student survey over the next few weeks of 1997.[34]

He also provided some insight into how the students understood Blaine's contribution:

> I had the sense that Blaine was hoping for students to raise concerns which he could use to persuade his colleagues on Faculty Council to moderate some aspects of the changes that were coming. His approach to me (at Coffee House) seemed quite directed at stirring

> things up which succeeded: us students whipping together a working committee which produced the wildcat survey and its quite telling results while Professor Baker watched from a distance.[35]

This attests to Blaine's mode of interaction. He engaged personally with the students about their own involvement with the process and was anxious to ensure that they were active participants influencing the broader collegial outcome. It also shows his respect for and use of the power of informal over formal ordering.[36]

In essence, the results of the survey showed that by a wide margin, students favoured curricular changes characterized as follows:

- Stronger civil law and common law comparative perspective
- Elimination of separate BCL and LLB streams
- Integration of some first-year courses (i.e., Torts, Contracts, Obligations)
- Greater flexibility in upper year course selection.

However, by a similarly wide margin, they said they would not support the changes if they resulted in the elimination of the option to do a single degree and the adoption of a mandatory four-year program. This led to the hunt for a compromise to gain student support. Indeed, at the meeting of 16 April 1997, after the survey was issued, student members of Faculty Council secured a friendly amendment to the "Principles and Corollaries" document, discussed earlier.[37] This amendment established that in considering the proposed duration of the new McGill program, including a possible three-year option, "the duration should take account of the opinion of members of this community including that of students expressed in surveys."[38]

Since Blaine did favour a single integrated curriculum of study and a single admissions pool, his ultimate gambit became to work behind the scenes to ensure that students could graduate from the program after three years. I well recall strategizing with Blaine about securing an amendment to the proposals brought by the Ad Hoc Curriculum Review Committee on 7 November 1997 so as to ensure that total program credits were reduced to 105 and thus within the range perceived by students to be manageable for those who wanted to finish studies in three years.[39] This amendment assured student support for the entire reform package. In short, Blaine worked quietly and pragmatically to help guarantee that the final vote would pass. I do not think it is an exaggeration to say that but for this work, the curriculum reform would not have been adopted, since unanimous support of the students proved to be the difference between adoption and defeat.

Blaine's Influence on the Year-by-Year Progression Report

In the years following the curricular reform, and over the course of discussions with me and others, Blaine took a certain pride of ownership in the 4 June 1997 report of the year-by-year progression working group. It will be recalled that that working group was one of three set up by Dean Toope to elaborate the details of the curricular reform. I have already alluded to my false memory syndrome about Blaine's authorship of that working group's report. So it was with some surprise that I discovered, in Blaine's document collection, that he had not even been named to that group.[40] However, David Stevens, a close colleague of his, chaired that working group and I was also a member.[41] David, Blaine, and I certainly had lively exchanges among us before the report was issued. It was thus perhaps legitimate for Blaine to take some ownership of the proposals on year-by-year progression, and his expressed personal stake in the report reveals something further about how he imagined collegial process.[42]

Whereas the report made several specific curricular proposals that were eventually folded into the comprehensive curricular reform emanating from the Ad Hoc Curriculum Review Committee, the main feature of the report, reflected in the name of the working group, in essence was not acted upon. This became a source of constant grousing by Blaine.[43]

In effect, the first key task handed to the working group in its mandate was an "articulation of a year-by-year progression in pedagogical goals and styles of learning."[44] In its report, the committee distinguished among skill sets and knowledge sets, dividing the former into communication skills, reading skills, research skills, and team-work skills.

In his annotations to the report, Blaine focused on the pages discussing skill sets and knowledge sets. He was very keen on seeing:

- Interpersonal coordination of knowledge delivery
- Coordinated delivery [he wrote and then crossed out the word "development"] of skill sets – challenge a class
- Efficient, course-related legal writing.

What attracted Blaine to this part of curricular reform was the notion that learning outcomes would be mapped for the curriculum as a whole and that individual courses would be conceived as part of an unfolding intensification of the acquisition of skills and knowledge. Students should find themselves increasingly intellectually challenged through their studies. He was of the view that the main problem was to ensure that in upper years, students were not simply accumulating additional content through pedagogical methods they had already encountered many times before (notably reading and summarizing cases). Thus, for example, Blaine highlighted the report's conclusion that in upper years (at 7–8):

> Skill Sets
> (i) Communication Skills
> Students should be able to analyze complex legal problems, draft comprehensive legal memorandums, design project programs, and write appellate court factums. They should be able to convey their ideas clearly and persuasively in writing and orally to senior members of the legal profession.
> (ii) Reading Skills
> Students should be able to read and understand any text relevant to the practice of law, including texts written for non-legal audiences by specialists in collateral disciplines.
> (iii) Research Skills
> Students should be confident that they can conduct legal and social scientific research in any Canadian or American library.
> (iv) Team Work Skills
> Students should be able to collaborate effectively with other lawyers and professionals on complex and lengthy projects.

Consequential proposals included the creation of certain courses to be available only in the graduating year, including courses on complex transactions, a six-credit senior essay, and tutorial leader positions. For Blaine, there had to be a rhythm to pedagogy. He explained to me once that when he planned his classes, he divided them up into approximately ten-minute sequences with the purpose being to convey to students a narrative arc and overall direction to their learning. That same principle applied to the course as a whole and ought by extension to apply to the entire curriculum.[45] The final year should feel like a synthesis of everything that had been learned and ideally lead to a culminating experience. Indeed, the faculty ultimately did adopt an optional six-credit senior essay which is now called the Capstone Project.[46]

Blaine's One Speech

On the back of the 8 January 1998 memorandum from the Ad Hoc Curriculum Review Committee entitled "Proposed Amendments," Blaine left notes for a speech he must have made to Faculty Council presumably at the momentous meeting of 4 March 1998 where the entire curricular reform was formally adopted.[47] Blaine spoke specifically in favour of the "centrepiece" of curricular reform, which was the "merger of transystemic [sic] teaching." He began his notes for the remarks with the exclamation that he was "very keen" to see the reform proceed. This statement was of significant symbolic significance for the faculty as a whole. Blaine, whose teaching award had come in significant measure because of his Common Law Contracts course, was expressing himself as enthusiastically in favour of the wholesale revision of that course. His colleague Peter Benson taught the other section of Common Law Contracts, had also won the teaching award, and spoke emphatically against the curricular reform. Blaine embraced the idea that transsytemic teaching was "not a merger of 2 existing things" – rather it was an "entirely new course & subject matter." In like vein he noted that the reform was "not merely about teaching k [contracts] and obs [obligations]" – it should be viewed as "providing [a] cornerstone for [an] entirely new curricular orientation." He predicted that "70 per cent of the reform task = in implementation," adding that I "promise to do my best, if asked."[48]

His final note was more enigmatic: "the whole curriculum ≠ transystemic – only 1 course with this novel subject matter." If he was referring to the new Contractual Obligations course, the note is perplexing since there was at least one other formally transsytemic course, which came to be known as Extra-Contractual Obligations/ Torts. Since Blaine knew the details of the reform inside out, I offer a slightly tendentious interpretation informed by another remark in his notes as well as my recollection of conversations with him: he was referring to the Administrative Process course. I conclude this because after he had praised the merger involved in transsytemic teaching as producing entirely new subject matter, his next bullet point was "not unlike unprecedented courses like Administrative

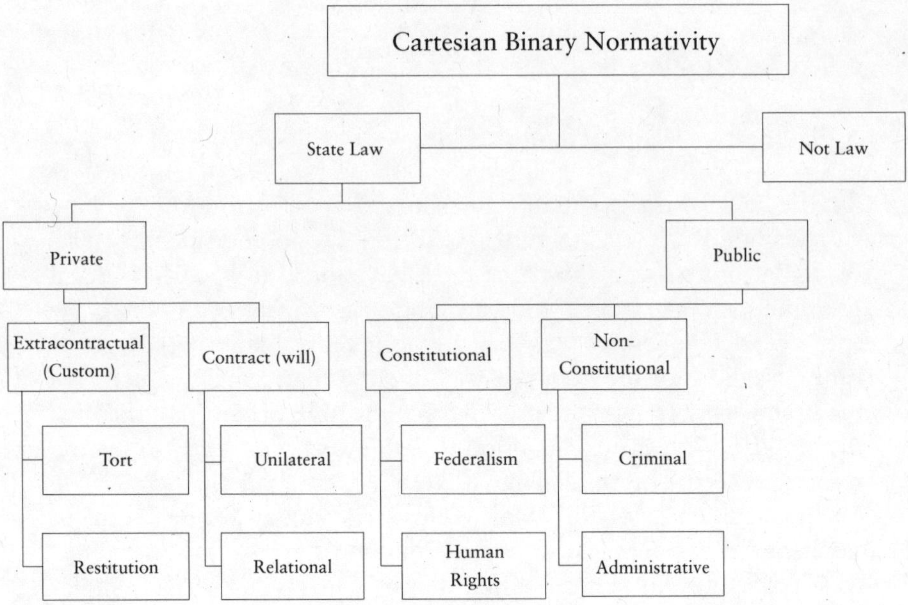

Figure 4.3 | Blaine Baker's breakdown of Cartesian binary normativity based on his teaching notes.

Process." I noted earlier that Blaine had a bee in his bonnet about how Administrative Process was an unacknowledged model for curricular reform. I will argue that he was obliquely implying that that course, which he had designed together with Rod Macdonald, was the one existing transsystemic course.

What was transsytemic about Administrative Process? I will try to marshal the archival evidence to make this out. One hint comes from a checkmark he placed on his copy of the final report of the working group on private law foundations, issued 16 June 1997 with Rod Macdonald as chair. That report begins by trying to define the term "transsytemic," noting (at 4) that "the term 'system' in the expression 'transsytemic' is not a word with a single meaning," concluding that "transsytemic teaching would require teaching that sought to transcend the instantiation of concepts in both of the Civil law

DISTRIBUTIVE JUSTICE	CORRECTIVE JUSTICE
Politics	Law
Bureaucracy	Market
Discretion	Rules
Legislatures	Courts
Changeable	Timeless
Capricious	Principled
Public	Private

SOCIAL GOODS	DISTRIBUTIVE UNITS
Education	Contract
Professional School Places	Merit
Medical Services	Love
Ability to Grow Crops	Chance
Capacity to Broadcast	Clanship
Human Rights	I.Q.
Religious Office	Ethnicity
Marriage	Age
Lottery Price	Gender
	Friendship
	Piety

Figure 4.4 | Blaine Baker's analysis of legal taxonomy related to "governments in miniature," based on his teaching notes.

and Common law traditions." Administrative Process, as conceived by Blaine, corresponds to that latter aspiration. Several of Blaine's teaching preparation notes for Administrative Process underscore how he conceived the problem of transcending instantiations of legal concepts. One page tackles, critically, "Cartesian binary normativity" and its division between "state law" and "not law," the latter including "religion, ethics, custom" (he crossed out "politics, morality, politeness"). He then drew a series of binaries.

In Blaine's view, such binaries led to the ascendancy of courts over agencies and the pigeon-holing of administrative law as the judicial review of administrative action. They also led to a sharp division between common law and civil law, reinforcing the notion that there were broad, fixed legal categories rather than local contexts to everyday law that shifted over time.[49]

By contrast with a binary declension of law, and inspired in significant degree by John Willis, Blaine proposed the study of "governments in miniature."[50] Any government in miniature seeking to organize a community – whether that be through a formally constituted administrative agency or through a long-term relational contract – would draw upon a pluralistic taxonomy of distributive justice claims, corrective justice claims, social goods, and "distributive units," which another set of teaching notes listed as Figure 4.4 demonstrates.

One observes that the Cartesian dichotomies are here reorganized to produce "an entirely new course and subject matter" seeking to integrate and cross-reference stale legal binaries, which Blaine took to be the legacy of a certain late nineteenth-century positivism cast upon the law. He sought, by contrast, to instill an organic and transversal understanding of the connections between public and private, distributive and corrective, which he believed was critical to the frame of mind required of citizen-jurists.[51] He would later characterize his Administrative Process course as emphasizing the "interactive relations of bureaucrats with each other and with their regulatees, the range of hard, soft and implicit forms in which administrative norms can be expressed, and especially inter- and trans-systemic comparisons among delegated governments-in-miniature or sites of bureaucratic justice."[52] That was Blaine's conception of transsystemic education, which only Administrative Process truly instantiated.

CONCLUSION: THE TRACE BLAINE HAS LEFT

Reflecting in 2002 on the trace he would himself leave, Jacques Derrida observed (my translation):

> I can die at any moment, the trace remains there. The cut-off point is there. It's a part of me that is excised from me and therefore a-part of me in both senses of the term: it proceeds, it emanates from me but at the same time does so by separating, by cutting, by breaking away from me. And so this part of me parting from me, I gain narcissistically, but lose at the same time.[53]

Blaine may not have gained narcissistically all that he hoped his trace might leave. We do not associate the aspirations for McGill's current academic and curricular project with his legacy. The terms of his departure, in illness, have tended to repress and bury his contribution. Yet if a trace can involve a celebrated absent presence – such as that of Rod Macdonald or Patrick Glenn – it can also involve a present absence – such as that of Blaine whose mark on the program remains, if largely unacknowledged. The main trace I continue to feel is in the waning sense, best articulated and instantiated by Blaine, that the transformation of the curriculum is the community's binding intellectual project to enable citizen-jurists. Indeed, the very idea of a scholarly community that shares a common civic project now feels oddly quaint, as if it could only be conjured in the imagination of a novelist.[54] What Brian Young has called Blaine's "anachronistic... personage" did sometimes seek to summon the spectres of a bygone McGill, gathered in the Faculty Club to preside over the Dominion.[55] Yet there was always and remains also something of critical significance in Blaine's way of being a colleague, teacher and citizen of the university: critical in all senses of the word. Blaine's expectations as to what was required of an academic community stood and stand in critique of habituation to managerial processes that erode community. Blaine's willingness to work informally, largely without recognition, proved critical to the success of what has become the hallmark of McGill's Faculty of Law. And when he was at his finest, his presence and example, with that of others, sustained for a time the critical mass of a remarkably active collegium.

But I have written enough; now I must go off and prepare to teach Administrative Process.

NOTES

I am grateful to Angela Fernandez, Mireille Fournier, Ian C. Pilarczyk, Brian Young, and Shauna Van Praagh for their assistance with this article.

1 Blaine would have been annoyed at the reference in this text to Jacques Derrida, *Of Grammatology* (Baltimore: John Hopkins University Press, 1997), chapter 2, "Linguistics and Grammatology, The Outside ~~Is~~ the Inside," 47: "The absence of *another* here-and-now, of another transcendental present, of *another* origin of the world appearing as such, presenting itself as irreducible absence within the presence of the trace,

is not a metaphysical formula substituted for a scientific concept of writing."

2 G. Blaine Baker, "Musings and Silences of Chief Justice William Osgoode: Digest Marginalia about the Reception of Imperial Law," *Osgoode Hall Law Journal* 54, no.3 (2017): 746: "Indeed, there is a sense in which this article is all about John Lange's seminal historical 'silences' or [Sherlock] Holmes' quiet dogs insofar as significant parts of it describe what Osgoode appears not to have done during his Canadian career." See also Brian Young, "It Was a Man's World: Blaine Baker and the Writing of Canadian Legal History, 1981–2018," *infra*, 49–82.

3 Baker, "Musings," 777.

4 Blaine won the faculty's teaching award, for which students make nominations to the Law Students Association, four times, more than any other McGill professor. Although he is listed three times on Honour Roll displayed in the faculty, he also received it once in 1993 after the prize had been created by the Law Students Association but not yet formally adopted by the faculty or approved by university authorities (see memorandum of Dean Yves-Marie Morissette, "LSA Teaching Excellence Award," 16 February 1994, referring to the 1993 award but not mentioning Blaine's name). Blaine did become the first recipient at convocation in 1994. The prize became officially designated in 1997 as the John W. Durnford Award for Teaching Excellence.

There was no shortage of bright lights at the time: Rod Macdonald, Patrick Glenn, about both of whom I have written (Richard Janda, "The Governance of Human Communities," in *The Unbounded Level of the Mind: Rod Macdonald's Legal Imagination*, edited by Richard Janda, Rosalie Jukier, and Daniel Jutras (Montreal: McGill-Queen's Press, 2015), 184, and "Cosmopolitan Normative Information: Patrick Glenn's Legal Theory," *Inter Gentes* (2016): 6 April 2016, http://intergentes.com/cosmopolitan-normative-information-patrick-glenns-legal-theory/, as well as Margo Somerville, Jeremy Webber, and Nicholas Kasirer come quickly to mind. This paper touches a more general theme, which is that Blaine's erudition and depth of reflection, aspects of which surely emerge in the relatively compact record of his crystalline writing, were as much evinced in conversation and in the classroom as they were in the formal record. There are such people.

5 The neologism "transsytemic" was sometimes written "trans-systemic" or "transystemic" (the latter being the spelling favoured by Blaine in his notes). I adopt "transsytemic" since it has become the official version: see, e.g., https://www.mcgill.ca/law/bcl-jd/program-description.

6 Notes written on the back of minutes of the closed session of 16 January 1992: Rod Macdonald: "What is the gain in forcing a vote"; "wow, what is David thinking of by casting this as 'us negotiating with the students.'" Blaine: "Obviously, not thinking enough." Rod: "support this agreement!" This clearly refers to a discussion that took place at the next Faculty Council meeting of 13 February 1992 at which the minutes for 16 January would have arisen for approval. The minutes to the 13 February meeting record that then-Associate Dean David Stevens had presented a proposal to have certain classes rescheduled on days other than Fridays in response to student requests. They also state that "Prof. Macdonald objected to the characterization of the issue as a matter of individual choice." Blaine did not speak to the subject. The motion was withdrawn. Given what will be discussed below concerning Blaine's informal involvement in bringing student views to bear on curricular reform, this exchange with Rod Macdonald may seem surprising. However, for Blaine, and for Rod, there was a world of difference between coming to informal accommodations and undertaking a practice of explicit, formal negotiation.

7 I permit myself the latter remark because I was a steady interlocutor of his over the years and know that the questions touched upon here remained of concern to him until he left us. I am also strengthened on my conviction that the themes I raise were of great importance to Blaine after having spoken to David Sandomierski.

8 In his contribution to Janda, *Unbounded Level,* entitled "Character-Building at Multiple Sites of Justice: Administration and Teaching as Texts, Scholarship as Ethical and Political Action," Blaine playfully described his partially vain efforts to edit Rod Macdonald's texts, crediting himself nonetheless because "buried themes have normally been reduced in number from double to a single digit," 214.

9 See Julie Bédard, "Transsystemic Teaching of Law at McGill: 'Radical Changes, Old and New Hats,'" *Queen's Law Journal* 27 (2001): 237; Yves-Marie Morissette, "McGill's Integrated Civil and Common Law Program," *Journal of Legal Education* 152 (2002): 4; Roderick A. Macdonald and Jason MacLean, "No Toilets in Park," *McGill Law Journal* 50 (2005): 721; and Helge Dedek and Armand de Mestral, "Born to be Wild: The 'Trans-systemic' Programme at McGill and the De-Nationalization of Legal Education," *German Law Journal* 10, no. 7 (2009): 889. A more recent article by Jeremy Webber, Val Napoleon, Mireille Fournier, and John Borrows, "Sally Engle Merry, Legal Pluralism, and the Radicalization of Comparative Law," *Law and Society Review* 54, no. 4 (2020): 850–3, touches on this reform. Unlike those accounts, which

are largely prospective and celebratory, inspired by Blaine I will try to do some more work on the historical context and archival record of the reform.

10 For the official results, see Élections Québec, Référendums au Québec, https://www.electionsquebec.qc.ca/francais/tableaux/referendums-quebec-8484.php.

11 The committee was chaired by Prof. Shauna Van Praagh with the membership of Profs Cantin Cumyn, Cotler, Jutras, and Klinck as well as a student representative, Ms Williams. I have been fortunate to get access to Shauna Van Praagh's own compilation of memorandums and background documents. In his article about the McGill's intergrated program, Yves-Marie Morissette, also a former dean, acknowledges the political context as a factor explaining how it came into existence: Morissette, "Integrated," 17: "For years, and possibly since the very early days of the Faculty of Law, a fluctuating proportion of students originally from Quebec chose to leave the province upon graduation. After the mid-1970s the risk that Quebec might secede from Canada became a genuine concern for some graduates and an added reason to look for work outside the province. The National Programme opened the possibility of finding employment in a common law jurisdiction. But conversely, and this is the other facet of the question, unless McGill's law programme was made especially attractive to out-of-province students, persuading them to come to the Faculty for their legal education would become more difficult in light of political events." Indeed, this was explicit in the memorandum from Dean Stephen Toope dated 25 March 1996, entitled "The Task Ahead" sent to the members of the Ad Hoc Curriculum Review Committee after it had completed its preliminary report. He wrote: "the current state of political uncertainty surrounding constitutional arrangements between Quebec and Canada has forced many people – faculty members, students, alumni(ae), and prospective applicants – to focus their attentions once again upon McGill's place in Montreal, Quebec, Canadian, and world societies. Evaluations of the dynamism and appropriateness of our curriculum will be affected by the attitudes which emerge in our current situation of political uncertainty."

12 See Roderick Macdonald, "The National Law Programme at McGill: Origins, Establishment, Prospects," *Dalhousie Law Journal* 13 (1990): 211.

13 See McGill University, Faculty of Law, Admissions Annual Report 1998–99 (the last year of the National Programme, with its separate BCL and LLB streams). In that year there were ninety-six students admitted into the BCL stream and fifty-one into the LLB stream.

14 In our current combined application pool, we have had between 1,200 and 1,500 applications over the past ten years with a total yield ratio of 68–80 per cent over that period. Entering classes are now slightly larger than they were in the 1990s, at between 174 and 186 over the past ten years. The proportion of Quebec students in the entering class was between 58 per cent and 64 per cent over that period, with students reporting French as their first language accounting for between 23 per cent and 36 per cent of the class. See Andra Syvänen, Assistant Dean (Admissions & Recruitment) 2021 report to Faculty Council of BCL/JD Admissions 2 February 2022.

15 McGill Faculty of Law Curriculum Committee, report, "A Three-Year National Programme" (April 1992): 1–2. The report proposed several options for achieving a three-year program, including increasing the number of credits per semester, adding an additional semester, creating a compressed double-degree opt-in after first year, restructuring the curriculum into largely obligatory mostly four credit blocks, and redesigning the curriculum to have civil law and common law blocks in the first year and comparative law courses in third year. A transsytemic first year was not envisaged.

16 See for example the Faculty's public description of the program: https://www.mcgill.ca/law/bcl-jd/program-description. It should be said that although Dean Stephen Toope was quite explicit in emphasizing instrumental concerns, the various committees studying curricular reform remained rather oblique in their references to them.

17 There were originally obligatory second year courses in Advanced Civil Law Obligations and Advanced Common Law Obligations, and Property Law was at first taught as two separate civil law and common law courses. The advanced courses are no longer mandatory and Property was recently turned into a single integrated course. An obligatory course in Indigenous Legal Traditions is now taught in the first semester of first year.

18 See minutes of the meeting of Faculty Council of the Faculty of Law, 11 April 1996, at 2–3, where this report was considered. Ronald Sklar's Minutes note (at 3) that Dean Toope "reviewed the reasons the project was undertaken, including the need for the Faculty to remain exciting and energetic, current University fiscal realities, and the current state of political uncertainty."

19 The first use of the term I have found in Faculty reports is in the preliminary report of the Ad Hoc Curriculum Review Committee of 7 March 1996 which had a heading entitled "The Culture(s) of the Programme": "the significance of inter-system comparison, said to be a defining feature of our curriculum, should be emphasized. We should ensure that comparative

law is actually done at McGill and that students are guided in their efforts to integrate their understanding of, and training in, both civil and common law. There are a number of ways in which this kind of trans-systemic work could be done more effectively." An undated memorandum from Margaret Somerville to Shauna van Praagh had emphasized the shift from inter-disciplinarity to trans-disciplinarity and favoured "trans everything." See also Margaret Somerville and David Rapport, *Transdisciplinarity: ReCreating Integrated Knowledge* (Montreal: McGill-Queen's University Press, 2002) in which Faculty of Law colleagues Rod Macdonald and Desmond Manderson also participated.

20 See minutes of Faculty Council of 13, 21, 27 March and 16 April 1997, 10–12. These were largely a series of committee of the whole discussions, culminating in the adoption of the "Curriculum-reform Principles and Corollaries" and grouped together in one long set of minutes taken by Blaine Baker. The vote tallies were not recorded.

21 The Steering Committee chaired by Jeremy Webber continued to work through 1998. In 1998–1999 enough of the new program had been adopted to permit the standing Curriculum Committee to take up its usual task of proposing curricular changes. Blaine Baker was on the Curriculum Committee *ex officio* as Associate Dean (Graduate Studies and Research).

22 See Webber, "Merry," 850.

23 See minutes of Faculty Council of 13, 21, 27 March and 16 April 1997, 8.

24 I am struck that none of the reports or other documents relating to the curricular reform are in our dean's office. Everything related to the period has been sent to the McGill Archives for storage. This means that for current curricular purposes, the documents leading to the reform are conceived to be of historical rather than administrative concern. They are no longer touchstones for planning, deliberation, or even pedagogy. Nor have they been put into an electronic archive.

25 See below, "Blaine's Influence on the Year-by-Year Progression Report."

26 I am grateful to Prof. Van Praagh for having received access to her materials.

27 This was the course that Prof. Van Praagh ultimately played a leading role in designing and teaching.

28 Blaine was ultimately in the initial group of professors teaching the integrated course in Contracts.

29 See David Sandomierski, "The Limits of Adjudication in the First-Year Curriculum: The Recurring History of Legal Process at the University of Toronto Faculty of Law" in this volume.

30 Fax to Shauna Van Praagh, 3 April 1996, 3.

31 Ibid., 5.

32 I acknowledge that my gloss on Blaine's comment is informed by discussions that I had with him. At the time, I was among those who were perhaps too attuned to the political dynamics facing the faculty. I recall being pushed by Blaine to suspend instrumental concerns in favour of pedagogical priorities.

33 Blaine also had in his files a memorandum drafted 21 March 1997 by Fred Headon, then a student, to Dean Toope and Prof. H.P. Glenn, the chair of the Ad Hoc Curriculum Implementation Committee. That memorandum contained the annotation: "Prof. Baker – more ramblings. – talk to you soon. Fred." His files also contained a subsequent memorandum drafted by students Vincent de Grandpré, M.J. Fernandes, and Fred Headon. These memorandums were not circulated to the faculty as a whole, and their presence in his files demonstrates that students thought of Blaine as an important and sympathetic interlocutor.

34 Email correspondence between Richard Janda and Gregory MacKenzie, 9 December 2019.

35 Email correspondence between Richard Janda and Gregory MacKenzie, 17 December 2019.

36 In Baker, "Character-Building," 219, Blaine characterized as "strategic, provocative, and even outrageous" Rod Macdonald's articles "Office Politics," *University of Toronto Law Journal* 40 (1990): 419 and "Understanding Regulation by Regulations," in Ivan Bernier and Andrée Lajoie, eds., *Regulations, Crown Corporations and Administrative Tribunals* 9 (Toronto: University of Toronto Press, 1985), 81, in which the theme of formal and informal ordering was prominent.

37 I gather this from Blaine Baker's notes to the meeting, for which he was serving as secretary as well as from the minutes of Faculty Council of 13, 21, 27 March and 16 April 1997, 11, which he prepared.

38 I do not mean to suggest that students were exclusively concerned about the length and overall credit-weight of the program. For example, one student representative, David Outerbridge, on 25 March 1997 circulated a twenty-five-page memorandum to Faculty Council canvassing in detail the entire range of proposals under discussion. Blaine Baker's minutes record Martha-Marie Kleinhans, then a student representative, urging the faculty to take a "wholistic and thematic, rather than partial, view of its goals for the curriculum" and recommending "explicit discussion of equity and diversity issues, which she hoped would lead to debate about pedagogy and skills-based curriculum." See minutes of Faculty Council of 13, 21, 27 March and 16 April 1997, 7.

39 The 7 November 1997 consultation document issued by the Ad Hoc Curriculum Review Committee had proposed a 110-credit integrated double-degree programme as "Option B" – the option that was to be addressed by Faculty Council first to see if it attracted adequate support. At the 19 February 1998 meeting of Faculty Council, "Option B" was amended on a motion by Richard Janda seconded by student member Doron Goldstein so as to reduce the total required credits to 105. The alternative proposal, "Option A," would have been a 120-credit double-degree allowing students to leave after three years with one degree. Option A would have maintained streaming of civil law and common law students in respect to property law in the first year.

40 It must be said that in a parallel attempt to introduce upper-year learning progression into the programme, Blaine, as an associate dean and a member of the Curriculum Committee that produced a "Report on Upper-Year Curriculum Reform Implementation" on 16 March 1999, poured himself into the now all-but defunct honours and majors options, as well as minors options (which are more frequently used).

41 Other members were colleagues William Foster and Shauna Van Praagh as well as then student Charles (CJ) Prober.

42 Commenting on Rod Macdonald's influence "on others working in university committee rooms, in classrooms, and at academic writing desks," Blaine could not resist underscoring his favorite theme (supra note 8 at 216):

> "[I]t bears recollection that, when McGill's Faculty of Law set out twenty years ago to restructure its private-law curriculum, there was significant professorial opinion to the effect that the teaching and learning of skills (including the skill or state of mind called citizenship) should be as prominent in the new program as that of legal information. That meant that there should be planned, course-to-course, and year-to-year 'skills progression' and that the teaching of doctrinal topics as platforms for the acquisition of skills and the pursuit of virtue should be justified not on the basis of the volume of library space occupied by that doctrine but on the grounds that particular topics were especially suitable springboards for engagement with skills and for introspection."

43 The Curriculum Reform Principles and Corollaries adopted on 16 April 1997 included as Principle 5: "The Faculty is committed to a programme that moves us to the forefront of pedagogical innovation." Corollary to the principle was: "The Faculty shall establish a pedagogical outline of the McGill Programme, with specific indications of objective for each year.

In addition, the final year of the programme shall be structured in such a way as to offer significant opportunities for advanced research and writing (eg. a senior essay), intensive practical engagement in law reform, clinical work, exchange programmes and clerkships."

44 This was set out in an 8 May 1997 memorandum from Dean Stephen Toope entitled "Next Phase of Curriculum Review," 3.

45 On several occasions, Blaine noted that he had been influenced by having taken the Legal Education seminar led by Walter Gellhorn at the Columbia Law School, notable in his recollection for having involved an experiential learning exercise: walking in the middle of Amsterdam Avenue and staring down traffic. This apparently helped develop the requisite presence to dominate a classroom.

46 In the notes to the speech he gave on 4 March 1998, discussed below, Blaine, who was then Associate Dean, Graduate Studies and Research, noted, with skepticism (perhaps passing a note to someone else): "LLM thesis = 29 credits = 100-150 pp. Sr. essay = 6 credits = 120 pp. ?!?" Blaine clearly saw the incongruity of the requirements placed side-by-side, suggesting either that further credits should be allocated to the senior essay or that its length should be reduced.

47 See minutes of the 4 March 1998 Faculty Council meeting at 2. Stephen Scott had taken over as secretary so Blaine was in a position to speak. Prof. Scott's minutes did not record individual interventions. I have excluded the possibility that this speech was made at the intervening 19 February 1998 meeting because none of the motions at that meeting pertained to the merger of the Contracts and Obligations courses. I assume that Blaine brought all relevant documents along with him to the 4 March meeting, including the document on which he wrote his notes, which contained supplementary motions to the 25 November 1997 document from the Ad Hoc Curriculum Review Committee entitled "Curricular Reform Proposal – Motions." Both documents had been discussed at the 19 February 1998 meeting and formed the basis for the "General motion on 'Option B'. Adoption of programme revision as a whole." That motion was the single substantive item for discussion on 4 March. It was a solemn occasion on which many members spoke, and I have no reason to believe that Blaine prepared notes for an address and then did not make it.

48 Blaine did follow through on that promise. He was among the first cohort to teach the new transsytemic Contractual Obligations course and became associate dean presiding over the implementation of the new program. He sought, unsuccessfully, to produce a common set of materials for the

Contractual Obligations course. While there were transitional headaches, it is notable that the programme was implemented successfully, in no small measure due to Blaine's ability to put out fires given the confidence students placed in him.

49 It is striking that one of the sharpest and most significant critics of the intellectual pedigree of transsytemic legal education, Pierre Legrand, who insists on the singularity of national law and resists any effort to produce an overarching metalaw, shares with Blaine an aversion for Cartesian binaries and an insistence upon local knowledge: see Pierre Legrand, "On the Singularity of Law," *Harvard International Law Journal* 47 (2006): 522 and 524. Unlike Legrand, however, Blaine believed that one could seek to study the plurality of ways in which local knowledge manifested itself over time to become sensitive, as a citizen-jurist, to the array of contexts in which one will be called upon to exercise judgment. As he wrote of himself: "contingency, human agency and 'everyday law' have a place in my scholarship primarily because I write history" (Baker, "Character-Building," 217). Furthermore, for Legrand to insist on an irreducible singularity to every manifestation of legality under the banner: "Only in *deferring* to the nonidentical can the claim to *justice* be redeemed" (Legrand, ibid., 530), is to offer a metalegal insight. Legrand is the metajurist claiming to critique metalaw. Nor is it at all obvious, taking up Blaine and John Willis' worm's eye view of the law, that law's singularity can be captured at a national scale, a point that Legrand acknowledges but then resorts (526) to "the cultural/traditional embeddedness of the discourse" to provide a common, non-singular, frame allowing him to speak of "French Law" or "Turkish Law."

50 G. Blaine Baker, "Willis on 'Cultured' Public Authorities," 42, where he writes: "*Canadian Boards at Work* was a milestone in local scholarship on normative pluralism because of Willis's insights as editor: that each of his sample administrative agencies was a 'government in miniature' or a little legal system in its own right, and that worm's-eye views of the administrative process were more revealing than the bird's-eye views of those processes provided by pathological cases of things gone wrong reviewed by courts."

51 This becomes clear in the essay Baker, "Character-Building," 215–6, where he sought to characterize legal education: "[V]irtue, wisdom, decency, citizenship and character can be said to be matters of pervasive and critical presence in legal education, largely due to the social and economic privilege that follows that training's completion in many North American jurisdictions and to the self-regulating character of most local bars."

52 Ibid., 217.

53 Dialogue with Jacques Derrida, *Trace et archive, image et art*, Collège iconique, (25 June 2002), https://www.google.com/search?q=Trace+et+archive%2C+image+et+art+Jacques+Derrida+Dialogue.+Coll%C3%A8ge+iconique.+INA.+25%2F06%2F2002&rlz=1C5CHFA_enCA-877CA877&oq=Trace+et+archive%2C+image+et+art+Jacques+-Derrida+Dialogue.+Coll%C3%A8ge+iconique.+INA.+25%2F06%2F2002&aqs=chrome..69i57.169j0j9&sourceid=chrome&ie=UTF-8 at 21: "Moi je peux mourir à chaque instant, la trace reste là. La coupure est là. C'est une part de moi qui est coupée de moi et qui donc part de moi aux deux sens du terme : elle procède, elle émane de moi mais en même temps en se séparant, en se coupant, en se détachant de moi. Et donc cette part de moi, je la gagne, je la retrouve narcissiquement, mais je la perds en même temps."

54 See Hermann Hesse, *The Glass Bead Game (Magister Ludi)*, trans. Richard and Clara Winston (New York: Holt, Rinehart and Winston, 1969).

55 See Brian Young, "It Was a Man's World: Blaine Baker and the Writing of Canadian Legal History, 1981–2018," *infra*, 49–82.

PART TWO

Blaine Baker and the Field of Legal History

Model of a Legal Academian

G. Blaine Baker

(sung to the tune of "Model of a Modern Major General")[1]

I am the very model of a legal academian;
I will display my knowledge from the front of the proscenium.
I frequently bombard you all with interjections factual,
which I will intersperce [sic] with maximizing tortions and contractuals.

On everything you want to know of contract law I'll fill you in;
administrative law as well, both Anglo and civilian;
I'm a stevedore of knowledge – that's why I am on the faculty,
Unloading the box of K – things, yes that is my ontology.[2]

Chorus: Unloading the box of K – things, yes that is my ontology
(Repeat three times)

Although you may believe that what I say is just mere puffery,
Considering it thusly won't alleviate your suffering;
In short despite the muddle that you frequently will see me in,
I am the very model of a legal academian.

Chorus: In short despite the muddle that you frequently will see me in,
I am the very model of a legal academian.
(Repeat three times)

I'm a notionally equal rights and duty bearing individual,
Engaging in the dance of Ks manifesting my free will;
I will do the easy part then you can do the difficult,
From paradigm to paradigm our nimble minds will catapult.

Chorus: From paradigm to paradigm our nimble minds will catapult.
(Repeat three times)

Some say that Coke's the real thing but that is their proclivity;
For me it's Ks that's the king – how's that for normativity?
You may think my font of verbiage is totally inscrutable,
Too bad, so sad, I will keep using words like hermencutical.[3]

Chorus: You may think my font of verbiage is totally inscrutable,
Too bad, so sad, I will keep using worlds like hermencutical.
(Repeat three times)

My ties, my vest, I do my best but if the colours make you ill,
Too bad for you, *tant pis pour vous*, that's how they dress up at McGill;
In short despite the muddle that you frequently will see me in,
I am the very model of a legal academian.

NOTES

1 This work, found amongst Blaine's personal effects in his office, was written for Skit Night ca. 1990 and is based on William Schwenck Gilbert and Arthur Sullivan's comic opera *Pirates of Penzance* (1879). The editors were unable to determine authorship of this piece.

2 "K" referring to contracts.

3 This misspelling of the word hermeneutical was either a mistake in transcription or, as one editor has posited, an intentional play on words as homage to Blaine's use of complicated terminology that was sometimes misheard or misinterpreted by students. The editors enjoy the ambiguity ("hermeneutical" for "hermetical," as in "hermetically sealed" – see Fernandez, "The Case of the *Frederick Gerring Jr*: Fish, Colony, and Nation," *infra*, 178n12). "Too bad, so sad" was a favorite Blaine-ism.

I met Blaine Baker in 1979, when I started teaching at the University of Western Ontario law school. He had graduated from UWO law the year before, where his stellar performance impressed Jay McLeod, an eccentric but much beloved professor, enough to incorporate Blaine as the co-author of the 1979 Butterworth's text *Contracts in the Family Law*.[1] Jay McLeod's and Blaine Baker's co-authorship continued through 1981, when they completed Carswell's *Reports of Family Law Reprint Series (1824–1970)*.[2] It was unusual then for professors to co-author with law students, even former law students, and it symbolized Jay McLeod's high esteem for Blaine. Truth be told, I think Blaine's unusual teaching style was modelled in part upon Jay McLeod, and on Bruce Welling, two UWO professors with famously non-mainstream pedagogical methods. In turn, Blaine regarded UWO law as his formative home, and he published his first article, a review essay on Joseph Vining's work on "Legal Identity" in UWO's law journal in 1981.[3]

My imperfect memory suggests that Blaine also taught a course or two at Western in those early years, but since he does not list this in his CV, perhaps the long hours he spent around the law school just made him feel like a young colleague. He left for graduate studies shortly after but returned to participate in David Flaherty's summer camp for legal historians, where all of us marvelled at his encyclopedic knowledge of Upper Canadian legal thought and education.

Blaine was absent from the annual luncheon of the American Society for Legal History when its president announced that his 1985 article, "The Reconstitution of Upper Canadian Legal Thought in the Late-Victorian Empire" had won the Surrency Prize that year, a distinction that no Canadian legal historian had achieved before. I was one of the few Canadians there, and could not restrain myself from jumping up and shouting in triumph. It felt as if the whole country had arrived to a new threshold of recognition. That was Blaine, the person who carried off the noteworthy honour, whose legendary modesty meant that he did not show up to receive it. He contributed so much. Canadian legal history is the stronger for it.

Constance Backhouse

5

The Historical Exploits of Stella March: Reflecting on Feminist Legal History

Constance Backhouse

I began researching Canadian legal history in the late 1970s, when the field emerged as a distinct genre within socio-legal studies. In an era when the feminist movement was making inroads within academia, I turned to gender as a defining framework for my own work, and watched with interest as legal history and women's studies grew in range, depth, and strength over the next decades. My writing has often taken the form of narrative, using micro-analysis of a specific case to illustrate broader themes. Here I will follow this pattern by focusing on the exploits of Stella March, a captivating and elusive female fraudster, to demonstrate how legal history has expanded over time to more fully encompass the categories of race and gender. The Stella March narrative illustrates how legal history research that began with a feminist analysis of Canadian criminal fraud law could stretch to incorporate an intersectional critical race focus, and then expand to produce questions regarding "trans"[4] sexual identities, topics receiving increased attention by the 2020s.

I first came across the saga of Stella March in the summer of 1992. I was teaching at the University of Saskatchewan, where I spent every afternoon reading old newspapers on microfilm in the provincial archives then housed on campus. This was long before digitization enabled fine-tuned probes with the marvelous tools of word search. One simply turned on the microfilm reader, threaded strips of dark plastic into the bobbin, adjusted the blurry image with a button, and turned the rotary handle to display the daily newspapers page by page. It was a cumbersome process, guaranteed to induce headaches if pursued for long. But it could also transport a late twentieth-century reader back to a slower-paced time, to become immersed in the lives of Saskatchewan farmers, townsfolk, urban elites, and police courts.

As all who labour in the archives will explain, there is magic mixed with the drudgery of primary historical research. And so there was that summer. While searching for news on issues that mattered most to women – family disputes, sexual assault trials, prostitution raids, paid labour force opportunities, the activities of women's organizations – I stumbled upon a set of articles published in the *Regina Leader* in the fall of 1922. Featured between advertisements for eczema ointments and corn plasters was a detailed exposé about a woman of many aliases who was operating under the name "Stella March."[5] There was no byline to the articles, but all appear to have been penned by the same unnamed staff reporter. His curious tale would do much to enshrine Stella March as one of the more remarkable fraudsters to grace the prairies.

My research agenda in the early 1990s prevented me from doing more than simply photocopying those news clippings. But I was as captivated with Stella March as the reporter had been back in 1922. I stored the faint photocopies in a bright pink folder, labelled it "Stella," and carted it from office to office, university to university, city to city, for over two decades, always hoping to work more on the file. Over time I searched for court documents relating to her escapades. Although I was unable to determine her real name or unearth further relevant records, it was clear that the story contained a goldmine of rich historical material. I will describe the story that emerged from the Regina press coverage, and then try to explain how my understanding of the events deepened with widening intersectional analysis over the succeeding years.

STELLA MARCH, THE WOMAN BEHIND THE SCAM

Stella March was a woman who made a grand entrance, even at the outset of a decade that would come to be known as the Roaring Twenties. As she drove through southern Saskatchewan in the fall of 1922, her arrival invariably attracted attention. The *Regina Leader* depicted her as a "nervy woman," who "radiated energy and self-reliance" and had "set all Saskatchewan agog." It described her as about forty-five years old, blonde, blue-eyed, tall, a bit portly, American by birth, and probably Norwegian or Swedish by heritage. Standing at five foot seven inches, she weighed around 180 pounds. The consensus, according to the press, was that Stella March's beauty was somewhat faded: "Her features revealed that in her younger days she possessed that beauty, of flamboyant type, which dies with the approach of middle age." No one would have mistaken her for a classic beauty, added the reporter, but she could "unquestionably be classed as attractive." She initially gave her name as Mrs Cora McLeod but later said that her real name was Mrs Stella Blanche March. Her only luggage was a "good-sized black leather club-bag."[6]

The press dwelled in detail upon her attire. She wore a plain but well-cut suit of brownish tweed, with a crushed velour hat of smart "citified" appearance, which gave her something of a "flair" when motoring. The "lone chauffeuse" wore "driving gloves" and a pair of "driving goggles that magnified vision," apparel that she displayed to general astonishment in an era when motor vehicles were still something of a luxury. Henry Ford had begun producing the Model T in 1908, but automobile ownership remained the prerogative of the wealthy until well into the 1920s, particularly in rural areas. Stella March's arrival was emblematic of a glamourous new car culture, accentuated by her gender and her American origins. She arrived in a "borrowed" Chevrolet but was known for switching cars frequently and was soon sighted at the wheel of a McLaughlin Six roadster tearing up and down the country backroads at all hours of the day and night.[7]

When she removed her gloves, passersby gasped at the "glittering array of diamonds." The press noted that "her hands were covered with diamond rings" and she wore "a diamond-studded comb" and "jewelled hatpin." Said one observer:

> The sparkle of diamonds fairly dazzled me. I'll guarantee that she was carrying not one cent less than $5000 on her hands. She wore a plain gold wedding ring on the third finger of the left hand, but on the other fingers there were several big cluster rings, diamonds and sapphires. On her left wrist she wore a big bracelet, thickly encrusted with precious stones.[8]

The jeweled finery set off controversy, with some remarking that the ornate rings were of a "rather cheap pattern." When Stella March nonchalantly offered some of her jewellery as gifts to people she befriended, one suspicious resident took it to a jeweler for valuation. Lyon Findlater had a diamond stickpin set in onyx evaluated by a Glenside jeweller, who indicated that it was one and three-quarters carat in weight, "undoubtedly genuine."[9]

The townsfolk "fell" for Mrs March due to her personality, which captivated women and men alike. She was a welcome addition to the meetings of the Ladies' Aid and other social activities. The men swooned. "This woman knew human nature as an open book," advised the reporter. "She entertained; she flattered; she skilfully ministered to men's comforts."[10] A local bank manager, F.P. Boyce of the Canadian Bank of Commerce, who "puffed away at a cigar" during his interview with the *Leader* was quoted as saying:

> She had one of the most interesting personalities with which I have ever come into contact. [H]er presence was positively magnetic. She was astoundingly clever. Her memory was wonderful. She could grasp the details of even the most intricate business transaction without difficulty. In sum, he concluded, "there was nothing small about this woman."[11]

THE TOWN AND PROVINCE IN WHICH SHE DISEMBARKED

The press coverage emerged first in Broderick, a typical prairie town, 145 miles south of Saskatoon and twenty-five miles northeast of Moose Jaw on the Canadian Pacific Railway line. In the fall of 1922, its claim to fame was having twice shipped a million bushels of wheat in a single season.[12] As the reporter would discover, Broderick was just one in a chain of Saskatchewan towns that embraced the charms of Stella March. Her exploits could also be traced to Arcola, Glenside, Gilroy, Outlook, Mossbank, Strongfield, Avonlea, Craik, and Clouston, as well as the larger cities of Moose Jaw and Prince Albert.[13] Even the capital Regina, which boasted itself as the "Queen City of the Plains" and was counted the fifteenth largest city in Canada by 1921, was not immune.[14]

Saskatchewan joined the Canadian federation in 1905, and for the next six years, it registered three out of every five new homesteads filed across the prairies. By 1911, its population doubled to almost half a million, making it larger than the neighbouring provinces of Alberta and Manitoba. During the Great War, Saskatchewan harvests fed the Allied armies' "seemingly insatiable demand for wheat." War's end brought a steep economic downturn and the price of wheat dropped by 75 per cent between 1919 and 1923. Between 1921 and 1926, mounting farm debt spawned an "agrarian revolt" that focused blame on "big money interests." As one of western Canada's most illustrious historians Bill Waiser explains, farmers protested governments controlled by banks, railways, and manufacturers, while extolling the virtues associated with rural life: "energy, thrift, efficiency, sobriety, equality, and independence." Reality occasionally trumped idealism. Although prohibition was still in force in 1923, police estimated that "Saskatchewan had more home brew stills than all other provinces combined."[15]

What drew Stella March to Saskatchewan? She portrayed herself as fabulously wealthy, a widow who owned large sums and vast properties, ranches with purebred horses and cattle in South Dakota. Yet she said that she wished to start a new life north of the border. As she told the people of Broderick, she desired to escape the "false glitter of the social whirl" of South Dakota, and saw rural Saskatchewan as an "antidote for ennui." Her "sole objective" was "to forget the boredom of society and revel in an out-of-doors which did not constantly remind her of those stupendous sums of money."[16] For those who were familiar with the Arctic winds that swept across the Saskatchewan plains for as much as nine months of the year, the fascination with nature romps seems a bit of a stretch. But Stella March's praise of the homespun pleasures of small-town Saskatchewan may have soothed any self-doubts they fostered about their own lifestyles in the face of mounting postwar challenges. Manipulating the vanities of rural farm folk, the well-heeled American rendered them particularly susceptible to her charms.

THE "CONFIDENCE GAME" OF A "PRINCESS OF LIARS"[17]

With great attention to detail, the press covered the "confidence game" Stella March was accused of playing. Apparently, she travelled up and down country roads advertising herself as a "housekeeper for hire." She encountered scant difficulty finding positions with widower and bachelor, farmers and ranchers. Men outnumbered women in 1920s Saskatchewan, roughly three to two, with two-thirds of those single and under the age of forty-five.[18] Many of them were desperate for companionship to break their solitude and for the essential labour women performed in western farm households.[19]

Those who hired Stella March described her as a "clean and economical" household manager, a "willing worker" who could cook for farm hands, hitch teams to wagons, and haul bags of coal and barrels of soft water. She asked little in the way of wages, insisting that money was no object, that she was only seeking "a home and friends." Occasionally, she purchased groceries, coal, and gasoline with her own cash. Her employers were entranced by her "ladylike manner," her "sparkling conversation" and "unfailing store of anecdotes." Once she gained their trust, she convinced the men to loan her money or cars, and then vanished without a trace. Some she tried to persuade to cash out their worldly goods with promises that they could travel with her to see the sights of New York, Florida, and California. Eventually, she might suggest, they could return to settle on her South Dakota ranches. The objective was simply to get her hands on the cash.[20]

No one knew for sure how many she had bilked, for as the press speculated, she "wisely chose for her victims those who would be likely to shun publicity, ashamed to own that a woman's wits had made fools of them."[21] Lyon Findlater was one of the few men willing to talk, probably because he had eluded Stella March's scam. The press identified him as a "solitary rancher" about forty years old, "powerfully built" and about five foot eleven inches and 185 pounds. A man with "bright grey eyes and humorous mouth" he was known for his "industry, honesty, and generosity." He ran one of the "best-kept farms in the district," with a freshly painted house, lawn and flowerbeds, red barn with modern hay hoists, and a powered pumphouse in the yard.[22] Findlater had hired Stella as his housekeeper when the autumn harvest was underway, the threshing season approaching, and there were numerous farm hands to feed. Within three weeks, he fell for her when she told him that he was the "second man" other than her husband with whom she had ever been in love. As evidence of her bona fides, she instructed Broderick's bank manager to draw up a will bequeathing her estate, purportedly worth $750,000, to Findlater.[23] Then she suggested that Findlater sell his Broderick property, valued at $25,000, and his stock and "hit the trail" with her. She proposed that they blend their finances, and move back to her horse ranch in Draper, South Dakota, where

Findlater would become the manager. But first they would take in the "night life of New York" and the "riot of bloom in the Florida orange groves." A cautious Findlater requested that she first deposit $10,000 to his credit in the Broderick bank. Stella March drafted a letter to her South Dakota bankers asking them to transfer the sum immediately. She never posted the letter.[24]

A "shrewd" and "canny Scotchman," Findlater explained that he began to suspect something when his elderly black spaniel took a dislike to Stella March. His new housekeeper had never shown affection for his beloved pet, and when the dog took sick with symptoms of poisoning, he wondered if she was the instigator. He confronted her and although she denied it, he confided that, "[t]he incident didn't help to increase the friendship, which I must admit, had grown up between this strange woman and myself." In fact, the dog survived to be featured in the photograph of him that accompanied the *Regina Leader* story. Soon after, Stella March told Findlater that she had been called back to South Dakota to deal directly with her bank. That was the last he saw of her. "I guess you've got to publish this," he said to the reporter, "but my conscience is clear. Don't make me appear too much of a sucker. I miss the old girl around here. She was handy to do the running around, and you don't get a housekeeper every day who pays the grocery bills."[25]

OTHER MEN IN STELLA MARCH'S SIGHTS

F.P. Boyce, Broderick's bank manager, another object of Stella March's attention, was also proud to have escaped a sting. Three days before she vanished, she brought him $257,000 in cheques drawn on the Draper State Bank in Dakota and the Wautoma First National Bank in Wisconsin. She said the money was from her husband's estate and her father's large timber limits. Boyce told the *Leader* that "her hand never trembled and she showed not the slightest sign of nervousness when signing those cheques," although he confessed that he was "shaking a bit myself when I took them. I couldn't see any object for the transaction unless it was a bona fide one and – well, it was quite a chunk of money." He prided himself on giving her "the most courteous treatment" while at the same time "exercising every possible safeguard to prevent fraud." The chunk of money, it turned out, was illusory. The American banks had no accounts and no knowledge of "any such party."[26]

Mysterious Woman Under Suspicion as the "Brains" Of Recent Bank Robberies

SCENES MENTIONED IN "MYSTERY" WOMAN CASE

The left upper picture shows the Canadian Bank of Commerce branch at Broderick, Sask. The "mystery woman" made several unsuccessful attempts to inspect the vaults of the bank. Below is seen the Findlater home near Broderick where the woman worked as housekeeper; disappearing on dates coincident with bank robberies. At the reader's right is seen Lyond Findlater, the dog "Nig," which plays a part in the story, and the McLaughlin car in which the woman investigated the roads and trails near Broderick.

Figure 5.1 | *Regina Leader* photos, 21 November 1922, p.1. Caption reads: "The left upper picture shows the Canadian Bank of Commerce Branch at Broderick, Sask. The "mystery woman" made several unsuccessful attempts to inspect the vaults of the bank. Below is seen the Findlater home near Broderick where the woman worked as housekeeper: disappearing on dates coincident with bank robberies. At the reader's right is seen Lyon Findlater, the dog "Nig," which plays a part in the story, and the McLaughlin car in which the woman investigated the roads and trails near Broderick."

Stella March also tried to swindle money from two Regina car dealers, spinning a vivid tale of her connections with the Franklin Automobile Company.[27] She professed to own two hundred shares of the motor vehicle company valued at $1,000,000, and advised that she intended to open branch sales offices in Regina and Edmonton. Her understanding of the mechanics of the luxury air-cooled car and the operations of the business astonished the men. "Her knowledge of the company and dealers was uncanny. She knew more about Franklin automobiles than 90 per cent of the dealers," said one. "Enthralled" by the story she told them of her past, the men confessed that they were almost convinced until one wrote to the Franklin head office, and received notification that Stella March was unknown to anyone there.[28]

The *Regina Leader* tracked down several others whom Stella March had duped. Lambert Lennox, a widowed storekeeper, hired her to be his housekeeper in Craik. After she had worked three weeks, she asked for leave to go to Regina on the premise that she needed to pick up a new car. Lennox gave her a full month's wages, only to discover she had vanished, but not before charging $100 in merchandise to his account. He paid the bill. Henry Schleuter, a Clouston farmer, discussed marriage with Stella March before she made off with $50 in advanced wages and a suitcase full of his silverware, linen, cut glass, fountain pen, and a three-stone diamond ring.[29]

LINKS TO BANK HEISTS

Stella March's notoriety grew as the reporter disclosed suspicions that she was tied to a string of bank robberies across rural Saskatchewan and Manitoba in the autumn of 1922. The gang struck "in the dead of the night" and then vanished, leaving "peace-loving" communities "shocked" and "scared." Was Stella March a "lone hand" swindler or a member of a "desperate strong arm" gang of criminals? Could she be "the bandit queen," queried the *Regina Leader*?[30] Residents speculated that she must be in league with the robbers, working as a "spy or agent," using her position as housekeeper to scout out banks and then retreat from view to the safety of rural farmhouses. Her pattern of disappearing for several days before and after a robbery exacerbated the suspicion. Some wondered whether she was the getaway driver for the gang. The press added, "Springfield and Broderick residents speak of her strange habit of going for long automobile rides

Figure 5.2 | The Franklin Car, advertisement directed to wealthy men, 1916. Part of the advertising copy which appeared below this image reads: "The typical Franklin owner is a successful man who thinks for himself: and who owes his place in the world to his habit of *getting the facts* and using his *own judgment*."

in the country, her enquiries concerning roads and trails, her interest in bank and post office methods in the villages, and her questions directed to operators at rural telephone exchanges." Bank manager Boyce mentioned her persistent efforts to get inside the bank vault to inspect the safety deposit boxes, ostensibly to ensure the safety of her valuable securities from the depredations of burglars. He bragged that his cautionary instincts had thwarted all of her insistent pleas.[31] Her expertise as a driver and car mechanic was deemed further proof of her accomplice status. Local car repairmen were dazzled over her knowledge of multiple cars, the Chevrolet, McLaughlin Six, and the classic Franklin touring car – the latter reputed to be immensely powerful and practically silent – a perfect getaway vehicle. "I can see her yet," said S. Taylor, an office employee at Regina Motors Garage on South Railway Street, "as she stood across the street laying down the law to the man who had worked on her car." She may have given peremptory orders to mechanics about spark plugs, rear axles, and timers, but she also charmed the men who worked there, describing her fabulously rich South Dakota properties, and chatting them up to see if any would leave their job to hire on as her chauffeur for her next trip to California. None took her up on the offer, but at least one, to whom she had not presented the offer, wished she had invited him along. "She didn't ask me or you bet I wouldn't have been here today," N. Fraser told the *Regina Leader*. Ever the gentleman, he added, "she didn't talk much to me and I don't like to give my impressions of any woman. I've seen apparent angels turn out the opposite and apparent sinners turn out to be angels. So I don't want to tell my impression of the Mystery Woman." The mechanics delivered her car to Stella March at Champ's Hotel, where she had stayed overnight. "The bill was paid and with club bag in hand, she stepped in the automobile, threw the gears into mesh and with a farewell wave, steered her way through the traffic leaving the mechanics on the sidewalk to take a last look at Mrs Stella B. March, the woman of diamonds and steam cars."[32]

A CLEAN GETAWAY

Funds were advanced by hapless prairie farmers. Cheques worth hundreds of thousands of dollars bounced. Banks were robbed. Yet the law offered little solace. Efforts by the *Regina Leader* to question the police about their tracking of Stella March brought no elucidation. "If the owner of fictitious lands, bonds and automobiles is known to the Saskatchewan provincial police, they won't admit it. On the other hand, they don't deny it. They say nothing," recounted the reporter.[33] Was there perhaps a sense that the men who fell for Stella March's ploys were foolish and undeserving of a more fulsome police investigation? A letter to the editor pointed out that Stella March's automobile had been repaired "within 75 yards of the Provincial Police headquarters," and wondered sarcastically whether she had chosen the repair shop "by coincidence or sheer bravado." The writer concluded: "[T]here were no doubt several officers who would have liked very much to have made her acquaintance – in a professional way."[34] Did the letter writer mean to suggest, in a backhanded way, that even the police officers might have fallen under Stella's spell?

Several of her victims tried to bring her to justice without success. Lambert Lennox, the Craig widower who was out the housekeeper's wages he had advanced along with $100 for Stella's purchases on credit, complained to the police that she had obtained money under false pretences. The police responded that they were unable to locate Mrs March, and the case went no further.[35] Henry Schleuter, the Clouston farmer who was also out the wages he had advanced and a suitcase full of valuables, laid charges of theft against her in Prince Albert in the spring of 1922. The Saskatchewan Provincial Police were more successful this time, and they caught up with Stella March on 31 March 1922 at the Western Hotel in Saskatoon. After placing her under arrest, they escorted her to Prince Albert.[36] Despite extensive archival searching, no judicial files have yet been located on this case or others involving Stella March, but the *Leader* summarized what ensued when she appeared for trial at the Prince Albert District Court on 5 May 1922. Testifying before Judge A. E. Doak, Stella March swore that the goods were gifts from Schleuter. The judge said that he believed "there was more to the case than what appeared on the surface," but nonetheless acquitted her.[37] The lawyer who had defended her held her trunk and clothing as sureties for his professional fee. He was never paid for his services.[38]

The police force was left smarting over the growing public sentiment that its officers were inept in tracking down the fraudster. Responding to the sarcastic letter to the editor about the automobile repairs Stella March had obtained seventy-five yards from police headquarters, Saskatchewan Provincial Police Commissioner

Charles Augustus Mahoney delivered the following statement to the *Leader* on 25 November 1922: "I would say we have no reason to want to locate the present whereabouts of Mrs McLeod [Mrs. Stella March] as we have no charge pending against her."[39] The last trace of her was a short newspaper account on 2 December of her stopover in Mossbank on the way to Avonlea. Stella March departed unscathed, shaking the "dust of Broderick from her feet" and vanished into "thin air."[40] The pièce de resistance was the community's puzzled response to the remarkable Stella March. How to make sense of this extraordinary thief? How to account for her business and financial acumen, her ability to master the intricacies of southern Saskatchewan's thick geography of back roads and lanes, her furious driving skills and expert grasp of car mechanics? The reporter revealed that in the wake of her departure, some Broderick residents insisted that Stella March must have been "a man masquerading in woman's attire."[41] It was as if the men she duped could not handle the thought that a woman got the better of them.

EXPANDING FRAMEWORKS: FROM CRIMINAL AND FEMINIST LEGAL HISTORY TO CRITICAL RACE AND TRANS PERSPECTIVES

The saga of Stella March is perplexing to describe, but even more complex to analyze. In attempting to understand how our academic perspectives have shifted over time, it is helpful to trace my evolving assessment of this case. When I first began to think about the significance of Stella March's exploits in the early 1990s, the initial conclusion I drew related to the futility of law. Although it is uncertain whether she was part of a bank-robbing ring, her fraudulent activities seem clear-cut. Yet the police, prosecutors, and courts seemed unable to reckon with the likes of such a determined fraudster. This case suggested that historical research might unearth important information about the failure of law to respond to these tangled types of property theft, where goods or cash might be freely "given" but under profoundly false pretenses. The task of the traditional legal historian would have been to expand the search to examine relevant legislation, more court records, and additional judicial decisions to try to make sense of how society was trying to regulate these problematic human interactions through law.

The analysis was deepened because Stella March's situation offered an opportunity for feminist analysis. Drawing upon the strengths of the second-wave women's movement in the later decades of the twentieth century, I had begun to define myself as a feminist legal historian. Women's legal history proved to be a rich field, with women emerging from the criminal law records as practitioners of prostitution, infanticide, and abortion, as well as victims of sexual and domestic assault.[42] They were far less visible as perpetrators of fraud. Stella March stood out as a historical anomaly worthy of special attention. Stella March cut her swath through Saskatchewan when voting rights had only just been (reluctantly) ceded to women.[43] Most women were still denied ownership of property and barred from well-paid, high-status "men's jobs."[44] Stella March, a woman who could match wits with a bank manager, navigate roads like an accomplished chauffeur, and joust with auto mechanics over the intricacies of motor vehicle repair, was toiling away as a housekeeper. She may have chosen such positions opportunistically, as promising platforms for her fraudulent schemes, but the gender-segregated business world and labour market left her scant hope of financial success except through male largesse. Lonely farmers seeking sexual consort and companionship offered favourable prospects for fraudulent exploitation.[45]

Witnessing a woman "outsmart" the men around her turned the gender norms upside down. It was what captivated the *Regina Leader* reporter and his prairie readers. And that was precisely what drove the residents of Broderick to speculate that Stella March must be "a man masquerading in women's attire." To the historian's gaze, it lays bare the rigidity of sex roles on the Canadian prairies in the 1920s. As the newspaper admitted, a good rural Saskatchewan housekeeper could handle horses, hitch up wagons, haul water, and heave bags of coal. It was not a question of dividing jobs by strength or stamina. Yet the capacity for mastering newfangled machines, managing other people's money, plotting scams, and carrying out intricate bank heists was understood to rest with the male of the species. Whether in brain, body, or both, a woman was perceived as biologically and socially unfit for such tasks and incapable of performing them. Any woman who did must be a man.

The sexist assumptions at play underlay Stella March's successes, and they also suggest why her feats were so startling. To make sense of it all, observers were driven to wager that the brain and body that had pulled off scams must be male underneath it all. If it was inconceivable to topple the gender hierarchy by admitting that women had the same capacities for scheming as men did, then one way out of the unthinkable was to topple the gender of Stella March herself. Here is where I would have stopped in the early 1990s, satisfied that a feminist appraisal of rigid and sexist gender roles could elicit all we needed to learn from Stella March.

By the late 1990s, it would have become (belatedly) evident that this was insufficient. Feminist theory was expanding to encompass critical race analysis. A theoretical framework that uses critical analysis to examine society through intersecting categorizations of race, law, and power, this perspective can add entirely new elements to this case.[46] Although initially I might have concluded that there were no race dimensions in Stella March's story, I would eventually learn that race underlies virtually all Canadian legal history. Occasionally, the race dimensions can surface in telling absences. The 1920s was a time of pioneering settlement on the prairies, yet there were apparently no Indigenous people present in this story.This was no accident. Homesteaders had stampeded into Saskatchewan in search of cheap land, doubling the province's population in the first decade of the twentieth century. But they were not peopling an empty land as settlement myths suggested. The homesteaders first had to remove the original Cree, Assiniboine, Dene, Gros Ventre, Saulteaux, and Blackfoot Indigenous inhabitants, whose ancestors had resided there for more than three hundred generations. Despite their spirited and persistent resistance, Indigenous people had been forced onto isolated reserves through extortionate treaties, starvation, communicable diseases, the coercion of law, and where law ran out, by force. They had their children imprisoned in residential schools, their languages rooted out, and their cultures outlawed. The appalling treatment of Indigenous communities had been a sine qua non, their absence a prerequisite to the presence of the farmers and businessmen upon whom Stella March preyed.[47] Nor ought the critical race analysis to stop there. Current debates about racism in Canada make ongoing inquiries increasingly urgent.[48] Questions might be asked about the racial and ethnic identification of Stella March and the farmers and townsfolk she sought to defraud. Canadians tend to view our history as largely "raceless," and the "whiteness" of dominant historical actors so evident as not to need acknowledgment.[49] And so it was here. The racial and ethnic identities of the reporter, banker, car dealers and mechanics, farmers and ranchers, police officer, lawyer, and judge who tangled with Stella March were invisible in the historical record. White European-descent heritage was normalized into invisibility.[50] Despite the hypocrisy of a society in which everyone but the Indigenous peoples were outsiders, race was viewed as something that only marked outsiders who were tarred as subordinate. If any of these Saskatchewan residents had been of African or Asian heritage, for example, this would almost certainly have been noted, highlighting and reinforcing the whiteness of the dominant race.[51] Bruce Shepard has studied the racist efforts of Saskatchewan citizens to deter migration from African-American communities fleeing arson and slaughter in Oklahoma in the first two decades of the twentieth century.[52] Racist head taxes and immigration restrictions of the late nineteenth century would culminate in the blanket exclusion of Chinese immigrants from 1923 to 1947.[53] Yet closer examination shows that "race-less-ness" was another myth. The immigrants in the new settler society were jockeying among themselves all the time over racial classifications and hierarchy. The very category of "whiteness" – so often unnamed – was contested. No one doubted that English and Scottish settlers, indisputably "white," ruled the top echelon. The reporter may have stereotyped Lyon Findlater as a "shrewd" and "canny Scotchman," but the adjectives were meant as positive. The complicated reality of other European immigrants was partly unmasked by a racist Saskatchewan statute enacted in 1912. The *White Women's Labour Law* made it a crime for men of Asian heritage to hire white female employees. One of the only laws to specifically name "whiteness" set off a legal and cultural debate over whether two Saskatoon female waitresses – a Russian and a German – should be classified as "white" and removed from the reach of Asian employers. After lengthy deliberation, the court's answer came back "yes," that white women were to be defined as females of "any of the civilized European nations."[54] Vis-à-vis Asian men, the two were permitted to join the category of "white," but the matter was not beyond dispute. And no one suggested that they had achieved parity with Anglo-Canadians.

Some of the participants in this story had surnames that also suggested non-British heritage. That their ethnicities were not identified in the newspaper accounts provides some indication that their communities were beginning to blend into the white population of settlers. But neither they, nor the Saskatoon waitresses, would yet be accepted as full equals within political, economic, and social life. Anglo-Canadian immigrants continued to hold their position at the top of the ladder, the rungs of which they had designed.[55] Stella March was in a category of her own in this story. She alone was identified by ethnicity in the newspaper. The reporter gauged her to be Norwegian or Swedish, probably based upon her physical description: blonde, blue-eyed, and tall. Scandinavians were "preferred" immigrants in Saskatchewan, the fourth largest group of newcomers in the early twentieth century, many of whom arrived from the United States.[56] Their northern European Scandinavian heritage would have qualified as "civilized" without much dispute, and Stella March's ethnicity would have given her a leg up among the Ladies Aid, and as a preferred applicant for the job of housekeeper or even marriage partner.

Stella March's American status is more complicated. This was a period of great fluidity between the United States and Canada, with nearly 600,000 Americans migrating to Saskatchewan and Alberta between 1896 and 1914, a third of them from the north-central states and originally from Sweden, Norway, and Germany.[57] The response to Stella March may have reflected the entangled relations that Canadians often experience with our southern neighbours. The stereotypes of American ambition and know-how may have contributed to the fascination that Stella March inspired. At the same time, that attention appears to have been tinged with some degree of envy and resentment.[58] The consternation over her roadster antics was accentuated in an era when some Canadians, particularly rural residents, were inclined to scapegoat American drivers for reckless driving.[59] That Stella March's Scandinavian and American ethnicity found its way into the newspaper coverage was a signal of just how much curiosity she aroused. A focus on race and ethnicity – absences as well as presences – enriches our understanding of Canadian legal history.

A further dimension of intersectionality has opened up with the blossoming concept of "trans" identity.[60] By the decade of the 2010s, I realized that my initial assessment of the speculation that Stella March was "masquerading as a woman" needed additional thought. I had considered this a stubborn sexist refusal to concede that women could accomplish what she had done. I had not given much thought to the potential truth of the accusation. Nor had I considered the possibility that Stella March might have crossed gender boundaries not as a ruse to aid in the fraudulent schemes but as a manifestation of divergent, gendered behaviour, self-presentation, and identity that had a life of its own.[61]

As historians expand their frameworks of analysis, we are often met with claims that the application of modern ideas to earlier eras is ahistorical or "present-ist," wrongful and unfair.[62] The better response is that historians should not assume that trans identities did not exist in the past until we have searched more widely and diligently for evidence of them. While surgical and pharmaceutical intervention to change human gender appears to be a recent phenomenon, illustrations of gender switching and disruption are evident in historical records. At the very least, we know there were women and men who cross-dressed through history, assuming temporary or permanent identities of another gender.[63] Their histories and those of other trans people remain largely unresearched and constitute an important field for future development.

While it is impossible to know how the elusive Stella March would have self-identified, and how she would have thought about gender fluidity, the newspaper was filled with conjecture about her masculine features that testifies to an anxiety the reporter felt about the "confidence" man or woman, whose gender might be part of the "con." The troubled reporter depicted her as an individual with "very wide shoulders," with a "thick but not overly full chest," and "large hands and feet." He suggested that her energy and self-reliance gave her "that masculine tinge, remarked by all who knew her."[64] He left his readers with the sex-indeterminate image of a "skilled intrepid driver (man or woman?)" at the wheel of a "big, silent" roadster.[65] Mrs George Findlater, sister-in-law of Lyon the rancher, was certain that Stella March was a man. "Her skin was a bit coarse," she explained, "and her voice husky." Furthermore, she insisted that the "pseudo female capitalist wore a wig," something the members of the Broderick Ladies Aid Society could confirm. Broderick bank manager F.P. Boyce agreed that "she had a tinge of coarseness in her manner and the timbre of her voice was slightly husky."[66] Others were of the opposite view. The mechanics who fixed her car laughed at the "supposition that she was a man attired in women's clothing." The Champs Hotel manager pointed out that Stella March's entry on the register was written "in smooth, rounded strokes, apparently the handwriting of a woman."[67] Lyon Findlater scoffed at his sister-in-law's suspicions and rejected the notion that

Stella March wore a wig, explaining that he had watched her wash her hair in his kitchen. But then he offered a last anecdote about his former housekeeper that would leave everyone guessing: "I do know that she needed to shave her neck. She used to say that it was easier to cut the short, straggling hairs off than to do them up. In her opinion, it looked neater. Once she cut my hair and several times she shaved me. Apparently, she was completely familiar with both processes. I have had many a barber who was not nearly as expert."[68]

The attributes of gender were divided here on the basis of physique, psychological affect, mannerisms, skin texture, voice register, handwriting, hair, and shaving techniques. It is a stark reminder of the irrationality of gender binaries. The tasks of housekeepers on the rural prairies required "the weaker sex" to hitch wagons, haul bags of coal, and hoist barrels of water, heavy labour that strict gender-binary-keepers might relegate to men. Yet when women demonstrated competence over such chores day in and out, it did nothing to shift the strict separations. Contradictions might thread their way through socially conditioned beliefs about gender, but never dismantled them.The intricacies of high finance and the complex plotting of bank robbers were understood as fitted to male cranial capacities. The newfangled roadsters that were appearing in prairie towns might have provided uncharted territory, yet Saskatchewan townsfolk were quick to assign car driving, sales, and repairs to men. It meant that for some observers, because Stella March could do things coded "male," she must not be female. And in this case, perhaps they were correct, underscoring the importance of historical frameworks encompassing trans analysis to enrich our understandings of the past and present.

This research also underscores the importance of historical analysis to socio-legal studies. Studying the past has the potential to bring clarity to modern-day debates and to permit observations and questions that challenge many of our current assumptions and perspectives. It can help us understand the roots of inequality, and the patterns of hierarchy based on gender, gender identities, and race. It can retrieve from the depths of the past stories of individuals who embraced inequalities and those who resisted. It can remind us of how much times have changed, and how little.

The story of Stella March reveals important information about the wider histories of immigration, transportation, work, romance, sex, gender perspectives, male solitude, and economic survival on the prairies. The swath Stella March cut through Saskatchewan in the early 1920s can be viewed through many lenses: traditional criminal legal history, feminist legal history, critical race analysis, and trans frameworks. The widening of our inquiry has the potential to improve historical research in parallel with the growing recognition of diversity within our society and the academy. This is a welcome development, and holds the promise of more to come. And makes me glad I did not write this up in the 1990s.

NOTES

1 J.G. McLeod and B. Baker, *Contracts in the Family Law* (Toronto: Butterworths, 1979).

2 J.G. McLeod, B. Baker, G.P. Rodrigues, eds., *Reports of Family Law Reprint Series (1824–1970)* (Toronto: Carswell, 1979–81).

3 G. Blaine Baker, "Legal Identity: From Maine and Durkheim to Graveson, Tribe, and Vining: An Essay on Legal Identity: The Coming of Age of Public Law, by Joseph Vining," *University of Western Ontario Law Review* 19 (1981): 307–41.

4 I have chosen to use the term "trans" as broader than transsexual or transgender to describe multiple forms of gender non-conformity, an "umbrella term for anyone who does not fit the norms of gender." Krista Scott-Dixon, ed., *Trans/Forming Feminisms: Trans-Feminist Voices Speak Out* (Toronto: Sumach, 2006), 12–16; Joshua Goldberg and Caroline White, "Anti-Violence Work in Transition," in Scott-Dixon, ed., *Trans/ Forming Feminisms*, 224.

5 "Mysterious Woman under Suspicion as the 'Brain' of Recent Bank Robberies," *Regina Leader*, 21 November 1922, 1 and 10.

6 Ibid.; "Saskatchewan's Mysterious Woman Believed Implicated in Daring St Paul Banditry," *Regina Leader*, 24 November 1922, 1 and 14; "Stella Still an Enigma to Her Victims," *Regina* Leader, 25 November 1922, 1 and 13. The reporter also characterized her as "the fair and fat type." The observer quoted was Broderick's bank manager, F.P. Boyce of the Canadian Bank of Commerce. Previous aliases apparently included Mrs Cora Moon and Miss Irwin.

7 "Mysterious Woman under Suspicion as the 'Brain' of Recent Bank Robberies"; "Saskatchewan's Mysterious Woman Believed Implicated in Daring St Paul Banditry." The press account describes the Chevrolet as "borrowed," but the exact circumstances were not revealed, and based on later incidents, the car may have been taken without permission. The

McLaughlin Six was presumably purchased in Canada, since the McLaughlin Motor Company, a Canadian automobile manufacturer incorporated in 1907, was based in Oshawa. Heather Robertson, *Driving Force, The McLaughlin Family and the Age of the Car* (Toronto: McClelland & Stewart, 1995). See Christopher Los, "A Danger and a Nuisance: Regulating the Automobile in Ontario, 1903–1912," *Ontario History* 106, no. 2 (Autumn 2014): 143–5; Gerald T. Bloomfield, "Motorisation on the New Frontier: The Case of Saskatchewan, Canada, 1906–1914," in *The Economic and Social Effects of the Spread of Motor Vehicles*, edited by Theo Barker (London: Macmillan, 1987), 165.

8 "Mysterious Woman under Suspicion as the 'Brain' of Recent Bank Robberies"; "Saskatchewan's Mysterious Woman Believed Implicated in Daring St Paul Banditry."

9 Ibid.

10 Ibid.; "Stella Still an Enigma to Her Victims."

11 "Mysterious Woman under Suspicion as the 'Brain' of Recent Bank Robberies."

12 Ibid. The long-term fortunes of the town did not bode well. By 2016, the population would register just eighty-five, only a 20 per cent increase over the 2011 count of seventy-one. Broderick, Saskatchewan https://en.wikipedia.org/wiki/Broderick,_Saskatchewan.

13 "Mysterious Woman under Suspicion as the 'Brain' of Recent Bank Robberies"; "The Banks of Arcola Were Given a 'Once Over' from Mysterious Mrs McLeod," *Regina Leader*, 22 November 1922, 1; "Saskatchewan's Mysterious Woman Believed Implicated in Daring St Paul Banditry"; "Stella Still an Enigma to Her Victims"; "Mysterious Woman Visits Mossbank," *Regina Leader*, 2 December 1922, 28.

14 "Stella Still an Enigma to Her Victims." On Regina, see Constance Backhouse, *Colour-Coded: A Legal History of Racism in Canada, 1900–1950* (Toronto: University of Toronto Press, 1999), 132–3.

15 Bill Waiser, *Saskatchewan: A New History* (Calgary: Fifth House, 2005), 59, 207–10, 236, 239–40, 256. See also Reginald G. Smart and Alan C. Ogborne, *Northern Spirits: A Social History of Alcohol in Canada* (Toronto: Addiction Research Foundation, 1986).

16 "Mysterious Woman under Suspicion as the 'Brain' of Recent Bank Robberies."

17 "Stella Still an Enigma to Her Victims," 1.

18 Waiser, *Saskatchewan*, 64.

19 Sandra Rollings-Magnusson, *The Homesteaders* (Regina: University of Regina Press, 2018); Sandra Rollings-Magnusson, "Canada's Most

Wanted: Women on the Western Prairies," *Canadian Review of Sociology* 37, no. 2 (May 2000): 223; Veronica Strong-Boag, "Pulling in Double Harness or Hauling a Double Load: Women, Work and Feminism on the Canadian Prairie," *Journal of Canadian Studies*, 21, no. 3 (1986): 32–52. Marjorie Griffin Cohen, *Women's Work, Markets, and Economic Development in Nineteenth-Century Ontario* (Toronto: University of Toronto Press, 1988) examines how significant women's labour was to agricultural export, subsistence production, and the household economy.

20 "Mysterious Woman under Suspicion as the 'Brain' of Recent Bank Robberies"; "Stella Still an Enigma to Her Victims."

21 "Stella Still an Enigma to Her Victims."

22 "Mysterious Woman under Suspicion as the 'Brain' of Recent Bank Robberies."

23 A codicil specified payment of $5,000 each to two Dakota girls, Althia and Myrtle Piper. Although the will left no indication of the relationship of the pair, it may have furnished a clue to Stella's real identity. She signed the document "in her clear and flourishing chirography." Ibid.

24 Ibid.

25 Ibid.

26 Ibid. "The Banks of Arcola Were Given a 'Once Over' from Mysterious Mrs McLeod," 1. In today's dollars, $257,000 US dollars paid in 1922 equals US $3.9 million in 2020. www.carinsurancedata.org/calculators/inflation.

27 The H.H. Franklin Manufacturing Company produced luxury air-cooled automobiles noted for their lightness and responsiveness, from 1902 to 1934 in Syracuse, New York. Sinclair Powell, *The Franklin Automobile Company* (Warrendale, PA: Society of Automotive Engineers, 1999).

28 "Stella Still an Enigma to Her Victims," 1.

29 Ibid., 13.

30 "Mysterious Woman under Suspicion as the 'Brain' of Recent Bank Robberies," 1; "Stella Still an Enigma to Her Victims," 1.

31 "Mysterious Woman under Suspicion as the 'Brain' of Recent Bank Robberies."

32 Ibid.; "Saskatchewan's Mysterious Woman Believed Implicated in Daring St Paul Banditry."

33 "The Banks of Arcola Were Given a 'Once Over' from Mysterious Mrs McLeod."

34 "Stella Still an Enigma to Her Victims," 13.

35 Ibid.

36 Ibid.

37 Ibid., 1 and 13; "Mysterious Woman under Suspicion as the 'Brain' of Recent Bank Robberies."

38 "Mysterious Woman under Suspicion as the 'Brain' of Recent Bank Robberies."

39 Ibid., 13.

40 "Mysterious Woman under Suspicion as the 'Brain' of Recent Bank Robberies." Further searching of newspaper and legal records elicited no subsequent reference to Mrs McLeod or Mrs Stella March. Perhaps she changed her name again; perhaps she moved on to parts unknown; perhaps she quit.

41 Ibid.

42 The complexity of criminal law history reveals women as both victims and perpetrators of crime. Constance Backhouse, *Petticoats and Prejudice: Women and Law in Nineteenth-Century Canada* (Toronto: Women's Press, 1991), 2nd ed. republished by Canadian Scholar's Press/Women's Press (2015); Constance Backhouse, *Carnal Crimes: Sexual Assault Law in Canada, 1900–1975* (Toronto: Irwin Law, 2008); Kirsten Kramar, *Unwilling Mothers, Unwanted Babies: Infanticide in Canada* (Montreal: UBC Press, 2006); Ian C. Pilarczyk, "So Foul a Deed: Infanticide in Montreal, 1825–1850," *Law and History Review* 30 (2012): 575–634; Angus McLaren and Arlene Tigar McLaren, *The Bedroom and the State: The Changing Practices and Politics of Contraception and Abortion in Canada, 1880–1997* (Toronto: Oxford University Press, 1997); Elizabeth Pleck, *Domestic Tyranny: The Making of Social Policy Against Family Violence from Colonial Times to the Present* (New York: Oxford University Press, 1987); John P.S. McLaren, "Chasing the Social Evil: Moral Fervour and the Evolution of Canada's Prostitution Laws, 1867–1917," *Canadian Journal of Law and Society* 1 (1986): 125–65; Judy Bedford, "Prostitution in Calgary 1905-1914," *Alberta History* 29 (1981): 1–11; Constance Backhouse, "Nineteenth-Century Canadian Prostitution Law: Reflection of a Discriminatory Society," *Social History/Histoire sociale* 18, no. 36 (1985): 387–423; Constance Backhouse, "Involuntary Motherhood: Abortion, Birth Control and the Law in Nineteenth-Century Canada," *Windsor Yearbook of Access to Justice* 3 (1983): 61–130.

43 Joan Sangster, *One Hundred Years of Struggle: The History of Women and the Vote in Canada* (Vancouver: UBC Press, 2018). The franchise extension was limited, and some women remained excluded by virtue of ethnicity, race, and Indigeneity.

44 Backhouse, *Petticoats and Prejudice*, chapters 6, 9, and 10; Lori Chambers, *Married Women and Property Law in Victorian Ontario* (Toronto: University of Toronto Press, 1997).

45 William Kuby, *Conjugal Misconduct: Defying Marriage in the Twentieth-Century United States* (Cambridge: Cambridge University Press, 2018), chapter 1 examines matrimonial advertisements and matchmaking bureaus for lonely farmers in areas with few eligible women, noting that some women used fraudulent advertisements as a platform for robbery as well.

46 Kimberlé Williams Crenshaw, *Critical Race Theory: The Key Writings that Formed the Movement* (New York: New Press, 1995).

47 Bill Waiser, *A World We Have Lost: Saskatchewan Before 1905* (Markham ON: Fifth House, 2016), 53, 69; Waiser, *Saskatchewan*, chapters 1 and 2, 211–12, 242–3; Backhouse, *Colour-Coded*, chapters 2–4. For a more detailed description of earlier dispossession, primarily focused upon other geographic regions, see Philip Girard, Jim Phillips, R. Blake Brown, *A History of Law in Canada, Volume One: Beginnings to 1866* (Toronto: University of Toronto Press, 2018), 542 and 608, and chapters 2, 8, 17, 24, 27, and 30. See also Myra Rutherdale et al., eds., *Roots of Entanglement: Essays in the History of Native-Newcomer Relations* (Toronto: University of Toronto Press, 2018); Olive P. Dickason, *Canada's First Nations: A History of Founding Peoples from Earliest Times* (Don Mills, ON: Oxford University Press, 2002); Janna Promislow, "'I smoothed him up with fair words': Intersocietal Law, from Fur Trade to Treaty" (PhD diss., York University, 2013); J.R. Miller, *Skyscrapers Hide the Heavens: A History of Indian-White Relations in Canada* (Toronto: University of Toronto Press, 1989); Christopher Tomlins, *Freedom Bound: Law, Labor, and Civic Identity in Colonizing English America, 1580–1865* (Cambridge: Cambridge University Press, 2012); Stuart Banner, *Possessing the Pacific: Land, Settlers, and Indigenous People from Australia to Alaska* (Cambridge: Harvard University Press, 2007).

48 Truth and Reconciliation Commission, *Final Report of the Truth and Reconciliation Commission* (Winnipeg, TRC, 2015); Desmond Cole, *The Skin We're In: A Year of Black Resistance and Power* (Toronto: Doubleday Canada, 2020).

49 Backhouse, *Colour-Coded*, 3.

50 Edward W. Said, *Orientalism* (NY: Vintage, 1979).

51 Backhouse, *Colour-Coded*; R. Bruce Shepard, *Deemed Unsuitable* (Toronto: Umbrella Press, 1997).

52 Shepard, *Deemed Unsuitable*.

53 Backhouse, *Colour-Coded*.

54 *An Act to Prevent the Employment of Female Labour in Certain Capacities*, S.S. 1912, c. 17. See Backhouse, *Colour-Coded*; Constance Backhouse, "White Women's Labor Laws: Anti-Chinese Racism in Early Twentieth-Century Canada," *Law and History Review* 14, no. 2 (Fall 1996): 315, 359, footnote 144. Although the Saskatoon judge's decision was unreported, the case was covered in the press and subsequent letters to the editor weighed in on the proper categorization of "white." See also Megan Ross, "Morality Police: Sexuality Governance at the League of Nations" (SJD Thesis, Faculty of Law and Bonham Centre of Sexual Diversity Studies, University of Toronto, 2020).

55 Waiser, *Saskatchewan*, 248.

56 Ibid., 67.

57 Ibid., 69.

58 Thomas Chandler Haliburton, *The Clockmaker, or the Sayings and Doings of Samuel Slick of Slicksville* (London: Routledge, 1884), first serialized in 1835, provides an early example of an American caricature written by a Nova Scotia judge, offering a fictional illustration of the sly wit of a Yankee.

59 Los, "A Danger and a Nuisance," 145, 160.

60 For discussion about the choice of the word "trans," see note 1 above.

61 Some writers describe trans to include cross-dressing, gender fluidity (moving back and forth from one role to the other in equal mixture), and crossing permanently due to a belief that born gender and felt gender are irreconcilable. Lesley Carter, "Female by Surgery," in Scott-Dixon, ed., *Trans/Forming Feminisms*, 53. Because biological sex is on a spectrum rather than firmly divided into two categories, trans can also encompass intersex individuals whose gender classification is complicated due to variable genetic, hormonal, and physiological developments.

62 This was a critique often applied to early historical research on racism. See Backhouse, *Colour-Coded*, chapter 1.

63 Although I am not aware of Canadian statutes that made it unlawful to cross-dress in itself, police often arrested cross-dressing individuals and charged them with violation of public decency, vagrancy, and other offences. See the flurry of Montreal newspaper articles on Antoinette Arsenault, who married Mimi Ouellette in 1942 under the name of André Arsenault. Both were co-workers at the Bouchard munitions plant in St Therese, Quebec, where Arsenault had presented herself as a male for two years. The couple married after a short courtship, but Ouellette later

insisted she was misled and turned Arsenault over to the authorities. After the suspect was arrested, medical experts pronounced Arsenault a woman. Arsenault claimed she had difficulty earning a living as a woman and so posed as a man. The court entered a conviction for falsifying birth and marriage documents and having a national registration card under a false name. Arsenault was sentenced to twenty-three months in prison. The RCMP advised the press that "other cases of changed identity, if not of impersonation, must certainly exist."; "Two-Year Pose as Male Revealed When Girl Worker 'Weds' Girl," *Montreal Gazette*, 13 March 1942, 13–14; *Standard*, 14 March 1942, 4; *La Patrie*, 13 March 1942, 3, 26 and 16 March 1942, 3, 26; *Le Soleil*, 13 March 1942, 17 and 14 March 1942, 3 and 16 March 1942, 16 and 18 March 1942, 11; *La Presse*, 13 March 1942, 3, 37 and 18 March 1942, page not recorded. I am indebted to Line Chamberland for advising me of this case and these references.

64 "Mysterious Woman under Suspicion as the 'Brain' of Recent Bank Robberies"; "Saskatchewan's Mysterious Woman Believed Implicated in Daring St Paul Banditry."

65 "Mysterious Woman under Suspicion as the 'Brain' of Recent Bank Robberies," 1.

66 Ibid., 1 and 10. It is unclear whether Mrs Findlater's reference to "pseudo" was meant to modify "female," "capitalist," or both.

67 "Saskatchewan's Mysterious Woman Believed Implicated in Daring St Paul Banditry."

68 "Mysterious Woman under Suspicion as the 'Brain' of Recent Bank Robberies."

Blaine was a very important teacher to me in the years I attended the National Programme at McGill University's Faculty of Law (1996–2000). I took all the courses I could with him and then relied on his counsel and assistance in pursuing what has now been a near twenty-year long career as a legal academic and legal historian at the University of Toronto. I am not sure how Blaine would have reacted to the shift in my work and thinking towards nonhuman animals, specifically historical and theoretical questions about their legal status and inadequate protection under the law. Blaine tended to shy away from external social or political considerations in his own work and something tells me he would have been suspect. I think however that Blaine would have been very interested in the environmental aspects of the *Gerring* case. At any rate, the chapter begins with a very Blaine-like internal archaeological investigation of the case as a literary fragment "sprung loose," as he would have put it, and moves towards more external issues that relate to conservation and animal use. In that respect, it makes for an apt follow-on to Constance Backhouse's piece about how the passage of time injects differing perspectives on the potential meanings of cases.

Angela Fernandez

6

The Case of the *Frederick Gerring Jr*: Fish, Colony, and Nation

Angela Fernandez

INTRODUCTION

This essay is part of a larger legal archaeological study of an over-fishing case from the Supreme Court of Canada in 1897 about an apprehended vessel, the *Frederick Gerring Jr.*[1] The *Gerring* case can be seen as Canada's *Pierson v. Post* for at least two reasons. First, one of the three judges who wrote for the majority, Désiré Girouard, a francophone judge from Quebec, actually reproduced large swaths of the *Pierson* majority decision, almost three quarters of the text, in his (English-language) concurrence.[2] Second, all three judges adopted the *Pierson* capture rule for wild animals, but here fish rather than foxes.

The *Gerring* is a leading case on the definition of "fishing" under the Federal *Fisheries Act*, with all three judges in the majority adopting the definition put to them by the lawyer for the government, W.B.A. Ritchie, of fishing as a "continuous act."[3] This principle is usually cited to the decision written by one of the anglophone judges, former deputy minister of Justice and then sitting Supreme Court of Canada judge, Robert Sedgewick. Justice Girouard's explicit endorsement of *Pierson* and arguably the adoption of the capture rule by the other two judges in the majority, and the incorporation of *Pierson* into Canadian law, went unnoted, quite a significant oversight given how famous *Pierson* is, at least in the United States but also in Canada, where it is regularly taught in property law classrooms.[4] As one nineteenth-century New York lawyer and commentator on the

Pierson case put it, "[q]uestions arising out of conflicting claims concerning the whale industry, game laws, fish law, whale law, all bow to the decision in *Pierson v. Post*."[5] This deference was very much on display in the decision of Justice Girouard in the *Gerring* case, triangulated as it was by the leading British case setting out the capture rule for the possession of fish, *Young v. Hitchens*, and a bevy of Roman and natural law writers and thinkers supporting the capture rule, the listing and discussion of which far outstrips *Pierson* itself.[6]

This essay is a tribute to Blaine Baker insofar as I use his very rich article, "The Reconstitution of Upper Canadian Legal Thought in the Late-Victorian Empire," to see if it can help explain (at least in part) why the incorporation of *Pierson* in the *Gerring* decision has gone uncommented on until I wrote about it in my book on *Pierson*.[7] It will proceed in three stages. First, I will first provide some background on the *Gerring* case and explain the important role Ritchie played in framing the question as one turning on the definition of fishing as a "continuous act." Second, I will explore each of the three majority-judge's decisions, with particular attention to the ways in which each echoed *Pierson v. Post* (directly or indirectly). For Justice Girouard's decision, this will mean focusing on the majority decision in *Pierson*, its cosmopolitan learning, and intensification of those features in his hands. In the case of Justice Sedgewick, I will delve into the ways in which his turn to ordinary language to understand what "fishing" meant and use of a range of literary references can be understood in terms of the witticisms of Brockholst Livingston's dissent in *Pierson*. Third, I will build on the insight Blaine's "Reconstitution" gave us in terms of understanding why Justice Sedgewick's decision became the aspect of the case that gave it its leading case status, while the incorporation of *Pierson* in Justice Girouard's decision went unacknowledged and unclaimed.

The two dissenting judges in the *Gerring* case, Chief Justice Sir Henry Strong and Justice Edward Gwynne (with Justice Gwynne writing the decision in which Chief Justice Strong simply concurred) were both Ontario appointments to the Supreme Court of Canada. Coming from Ontario, they were, I suggest, much less invested in protecting the east coast fisheries than the maritime judges and lawyers involved such as Justice Sedgewick (Nova Scotia), Justice King (New Brunswick), and the lawyer for the government, W.B.A. Ritchie (Nova Scotia). Quebec also had a strong interest in warding off the predations of American fisherman in and around the Gulf of St Lawrence, a fact that helps explain Justice Girouard's inclusion in the majority. Geography and regional interests do not tell us everything about why the judges saw the legal question in the way that they did; it is however suggestive of the political dimensions that underlay the legal analysis, lying, figuratively speaking, just below the surface of the water.[8]

Fishermen living along the east coast of the United States coming from places like Gloucester, Boston, and Wellfleet in Massachusetts had been fishing in the waters of Nova Scotia, New Brunswick, Prince Edward Island, Newfoundland, and the Gulf of St Lawrence for hundreds of years. When Great Britain objected to Americans using what Americans considered to be their historic fishing grounds after the War of 1812, Americans pushed back. The three-mile limit was established in the Treaty of 1818 but conflicts and tensions arose given the mutual habit both sides had of ignoring the treaty.[9] This strategy of having a treaty but not abiding by it worked in the sense of preventing another war between the United States and Britain, but it was less successful at avoiding a series of skirmishes or fish wars with Americans that persisted for a century.[10]

The conflicts over Americans fishing in Canadian waters were especially charged in the 1880s and 1890s. The cosmopolitan learning of Justice Girouard completely obscured this context. Justice Sedgewick brought in some of the politics, as did Edward King, the third judge in the majority. However, Ritchie's strategy, marching all of the judges towards the definition of fishing, specifically holding them to the question whether or not fishing was "a continuous act," was key to keeping this a legal rather than political affair. This was an uphill though largely successful battle even if the post-Supreme Court of Canada life of the case continued rather dramatically for decades.[11] To put the thesis in what one might call Blainesque terms, Ritchie's strategy to "hermetically seal" the larger politics relating to protectionism from the narrow definitional question was largely a successful one even if the cracks (and downright fissures) become evident upon closer historical examination.[12] And cracks of course are how the light gets in.[13]

The capture rule established in *Pierson*, where a wild animal is qualified property until it is finally taken, was supported by a number of exotic Roman, and later, civil and natural law authorities Justice Girouard used to bolster his position in the *Gerring* case.

Pierson (in)famously included those authorities, which law students often do not understand given the practice in many law school casebooks of not translating the quotations in this judgment that are in Latin.[14] Yet the decision of Justice Girouard in the *Gerring* case invokes these authorities in an even more intense way. In addition to Justinian, Barbeyrac, Grotius, Puffendorf, Fleta, and Bracton relied on by the majority in *Pierson*, Justice Girouard added discussion of Trebatius, Domat, Savigny, Heinneccius, Pothier, and Cujas.[15] Unlike the meteoric rise to fame *Pierson* experienced and the ways in which it became iconic in discussions of American property law and more generally American law school experience, the Canadian over-fishing case created a much narrower splash.[16] Yes it was, and is, the leading case of the definition of fishing under the *Fisheries Act*; however, it is not well or widely known in anything like the way *Pierson* is, despite having incorporated the (in)famous fox case, both in swaths of the text of its majority judgment and its adoption of the capture rule for wild animals.

Blaine's "Reconstitution" helps us see why Justice Girouard's decision would have landed with a thud, at least in common law Ontario in the 1900s. As Blaine explained, by the 1920s and 1930s, Ontario had taken an "arch-formalist" turn, as evidenced in such things as the express statutory requirement to follow English law, aggressive British law book publishers epitomized by the popularity of and near mandatory use of *Halsbury's Laws of England*, and the Judicial Committee of the Privy Council playing a larger role in Canadian legal life than it had in the nineteenth century.[17] Gone were the days when the library of the Supreme Court of Canada and the Great Library at Osgoode Hall were interested in acquiring extensive American materials.[18] The focus was on England in what Blaine (and many other Canadian legal scholars in the twentieth century) saw as a regression in the story of Canada's march from colony to nation.[19]

Blaine was deeply interested in the "cross-pollination" and "transplantation" of American, Roman, and civil or natural law books and references that created a "legal pantheism" in Victorian Upper Canada.[20] In "Reconstitution," he told us that this cosmopolitan orientation was coming to an end by about 1890.[21] This is an excellent starting point in terms of helping us understand why Justice Girouard's decision (and its incorporation of *Pierson v. Post*) would not have resonated with a very anglicized twentieth-century Ontario legal community. The essay will explain that it was not until the 1960s or 1970s that *Pierson* came to stand out from a wide range of sources typically discussed when referring to possession of a wild animal. Hence, legal scholars in Canada would have little reason to pay it, or its reproduction and incorporation in the *Gerring* case, as worthy of any special attention. That situation would, however, have changed in the 1980s. By that time legal scholars, frustrated with the focus on England were eager to pay more attention to domestic Canadian sources.[22] *Pierson v. Post*, an American case, did not fit with or further that new agenda.

"Reconstitution" was very much about the way in which legal "literary fragments" moved across jurisdictions and time periods, changing as they went.[23] Blaine explored this idea, for instance, in the context of migrating law books and libraries.[24] He said of the scattered libraries of Upper Canada (many of which ended up in the United States in the nineteenth century) that their eclecticism "suggests a well-developed and subtle supranationalism, or at least pan-Americanism at work."[25] Pan-Americanism is evident in the story I tell here, dealing as it does with the travelling and changing meanings of an 1805 foxhunting case from New York, as it made its way into an 1897 Supreme Court of Canada overfishing case. The ship itself, the *Frederick Gerring Jr*, was from Massachusetts but was caught fishing in waters off the coast of Nova Scotia. Its conviction was secured using a brief of a lawyer for the government who relied, not on a British or "Canadian" text, but on a cheap (nearly bootlegged) edition of James Kent's *Commentaries on American Law*.[26] Ritchie's was an excellent (if ultimately unsuccessful) attempt to depoliticize what had long been a very sensitive topic between either Canada or Great Britain, or both, and the United States over mutually desired and hotly contested fishing grounds. Supranationalism or pan-Americanism (perhaps predictably) broke down when three of the Supreme Court of Canada judges, from regions with fishing areas to protect, sided with a definition of fishing that created a protectionist result, upholding the actions of the Dominion cruiser, which seized the American ship. In other words, the cosmopolitanism turned out to be acting in service of vested regionalism within Canada.

Was the Supreme Court of Canada decision colonial? Yes, in the sense of protecting those jealously guarded fishing waters from Americans, as was Britain's desire since American independence and the War of 1812. Yet, the decision was anything but servile in the

Figure 6.1 | "Mackerel Purse Seine Boat and Dory" reproduced from "Fishing Relics and Curios: Monstrous Sea Turtle and Hideous Serpent of the Deep Exhibited at T Wharf – Hookers of a Vanished Type and Devices of the Codders' Calling."

sense that it resulted in the British and Canadian governments taking a strong stance towards the United States in their defence of the Supreme Court of Canada's jurisdiction to decide the matter and the subsequent refusal to compensate Mr Gerring for the loss of his ship to the high sum that the American politicians representing his interests were demanding.[27] However, the openness to *Pierson* shows that late nineteenth-century Canadian legal identity was not uniformly anti-American, even if, when push came to shove, a majority of the Canadian judges wanted, perhaps unsurprisingly, to protect Canadian, especially specifically regional, interests.

W.B.A. RITCHIE – DEFINITION OF FISHING AS A "CONTINUOUS ACT"

The *Frederick Gerring Jr* was a wooden fishing schooner owned by Edward Morris of Gloucester, Massachusetts. It was apprehended by a Dominion cruiser in May 1896 off the coast of Nova Scotia for fishing inside the three-mile limit in violation of the Treaty of 1818 between the United States and Great Britain.[28] The key legal question was whether the crew were indeed "fishing" at the time of the arrest, as the fish were netted in permissible waters with a large purse seine net and while the men were bailing them, the ship drifted inside the three-mile limit. At the time, such a net would have been set by men in dories who would row out to the school of fish and encircle the school by dropping the net with weights attached. The sides of the net would fall a long distance with the top staying suspended on the water by a line of corks. The net was then pursed or cinched at the bottom to make something resembling a large floating bowl or pudding bag in which the fish were contained (see Figure 6.1).[29]

The Dominion government, arguing that the *Frederick Gerring Jr* had been rightfully arrested for drifting (however inadvertently) into Canadian waters, was ably represented by W.B.A. Ritchie, a "member of [...] Nova Scotia's best-known legal dynasty."[30] His uncle, Sir William Johnstone Ritchie, was one of the first six Supreme Court of Canada judges appointed in 1875 and was chief justice from 1879–1892.[31] His son, Roland Almon Ritchie, Oxford educated, would go on to sit on the Supreme Court of Canada from 1959–1984. W.B.A. Ritchie attended Harvard Law School in 1881–82 and returned to Nova Scotia where he was called to the bar in June 1882.[32] In 1889, future Canadian prime minister, Robert Borden, asked W.B.A. Ritchie to join his law firm and they practised together in Halifax until Borden left to pursue his political career in earnest in 1905. Ritchie himself left Nova Scotia to become chief counsel for the immigration branch of the Department of the Interior in Vancouver in 1911, a position Borden likely assisted in arranging. Philip Girard described Ritchie as "an exemplar of the maritime lawyers who in the 1890–1910 period migrated to the Western provinces, where they soon rose to positions of power and influence."[33] Indeed, Girard wrote, "he and Borden were two of the most sought-after counsel in Nova Scotia appeals before the Supreme Court of Canada in the years 1890–1905."[34] The *Gerring* case in 1897 falls squarely in this period.

Ritchie was the solicitor on record for the respondent, the Dominion government.[35] He wrote the factum for the government's position.[36] In this factum, Ritchie proposed a definition of fishing as a "continuous act."[37] The *Fisheries Act* did not define "fishing" (nor did the treaty specify what "taking" fish meant) and Ritchie relied on a criminal-law treatise by Joel Prentiss Bishop and British criminal cases to urge the Supreme Court of Canada to adopt a "continuous act" understanding of the crime, here fishing in violation of the treaty.[38] Indeed, Ritchie used the term "continuous act" no less than four times in two consecutive paragraphs in his factum, just to make sure the judges would not miss the theory he wanted them to adopt.[39] Ritchie wrote: "Fishing is a continuous act and is going on from the time when a man begins to lure fish until he finally secures them in his basket or boat."[40] In putting forward this definition, Ritchie drew upon a criminal-law idea that when distinct acts undertaken by different individuals together constitute a crime (e.g., forgery of bank notes where different individuals did different parts of the work), guilt goes not just to the party who performs the last action (e.g., the one providing the signature of the forged instrument). It is all a "continuous act." Even one who is not present when the last act is performed is guilty (as was found in the English case of *R. v. Bingley* as described in Joel Prentiss Bishop's treatise on criminal law).[41]

In making his "continuous act" argument, Ritchie also relied on the passage in *Kent's Commentaries* on the *Pierson v. Post* capture rule for wild animals (at page 348), along with a passage in *Blackstone's Commentaries* on the "qualified" nature of property in a wild animal (the 15th edition at page 403). Ritchie wrote:

> It is submitted that fish caught in a net on the high seas and still in the water are not in the possession in any sense of the fisherman; but assuming that they are to be so regarded, and that property in them is thereby vested in the fisherman his title is qualified, a special interest liable to be divested before they are killed by the escape of the fish.

If the fish were in possession, title in them was "qualified" as they might still escape. Calling this qualified right "special and very precarious," Ritchie wrote that according to "the ordinary use of language" the act of fishing is not complete because "something more remains to be done before the fishing is completed and the fish finally taken."[42] He pointed out, relying on Vattel, that "we ought not to deviate from the common use of the language" when interpreting treaties.[43]

THE SUPREME COURT OF CANADA JUDGES

The Dissenting Judges – Chief Justice Strong and Justice Gwynne (Ontario)

The chief justice at the time of the *Gerring* case, Sir Henry Strong, along with Justice Gwynne dissented from the other three judges, holding that the seizure was illegitimate because, as Justice Gwynne wrote, the *Frederick Gerring Jr* "by force of the winds or currents was driven or drifted into Canadian waters" and this was after the fish had been "taken in the seine," which "was hauled up and pursed, as it is called, and attached to the vessel."[44] Justice Gwynne, the author of the opinion (Chief Justice Strong wrote only that he agreed with Justice Gwynne), explained that the owners of the ship were "in possession" of the fish insofar as they would have "an action of trespass against any one who should bring a vessel alongside of the seine" and either take the fish or cut the seine so that the fish escaped.[45] The use of "taking" in the treaty did not necessarily mean the "finally taken" that the wide range of property-law sources on first possession in wild animals had long debated.

Justice Sedgewick (Nova Scotia)

Justice Sedgewick wrote the first of the three concurrences in the majority decision upholding seizure of the vessel. He noted that setting the seine and pursing it up would have taken between ten and twelve minutes, whereas the bailing of the fish would take hours, at least two.[46] He enthusiastically adopted the "continuous act" theory Ritchie proposed, writing:

> The act of fishing is a pursuit consisting, not of a single but of many acts […]. It is not the isolated act alone either of surrounding the fish by the net, or by taking them out of the water and obtaining manual custody of them. It is *a continuous process* beginning from the time when the preliminary preparations are being made for the taking of the fish and extending down to the moment when they are finally reduced to actual and certain possession. That, at least, is the idea of what 'fishing,' according to the ordinary acceptation of the word, means, and that, I think, is the meaning which we must give to the word in the statutes and treaty.[47]

If the fish were not "finally reduced to actual and certain possession" until they were taken from the purse seine net, then the bailing or scooping them out of the net inside the three-mile limit was "taking" the fish (under the treaty) or "fishing" (as per the *Fisheries Act*). The Dominion authorities had been correct then to apprehend the ship. It is this part of the *Gerring* that is most often cited in subsequent Canadian cases on the question of what constitutes fishing and has given the *Gerring* its status as a leading case.[48] As the Prince Edward Island Court of Appeal put it in 2006, the *Gerring* is "the seminal case clarifying what constitutes 'fishing' within the meaning of s. 2 of the *Fisheries Act*."[49]

Justice Sedgewick was impressed by the fact that the fish "are still alive in their native element" while they are in the net, "possibly with few but still some chances of escape."[50] He wrote: "They are never *all* taken; numbers escape."[51] And there were many things that might result in a substantial escape such as "the seine breaking, or the fish falling from the dip net between the seine and the vessel, or of a storm arising and the vessel breaking away from the seine altogether [...]. The 'fishing' is not over [...] until *as a fact they are secured*."[52] Where the dissent saw enough of a "taking" in the original pursed up netting of the fish, Justice Sedgewick wrote "[t]rue, they were encompassed by the net; true, there was, I admit, almost a certainty that they would ultimately be secured, but they were not yet 'taken.'"[53]

Justice Sedgewick did not refer to the large body of Roman, civil, and natural-law jurisprudence that existed on the question of how one acquired possession in or occupation of a wild animal, or to any specific thinker in any of these traditions, the most relevant of which would have been the laws established under the Roman Emperor Justinian. The two important texts on those laws, the *Institutes* and the *Digest*, emphasized the importance of the possibility that the wild animal might escape and regain their "natural liberty."[54] Even in the context of wounding, many things might happen to prevent an "actual capture."[55] If the animal's liberty was regained, then the qualified property of the pursuer disappeared and the animal returned to their previously unowned state. *Pierson* was understood by legal luminaries such as Oliver Wendell Holmes Jr and Frederick Pollock as having adopted a capture rule understood in terms of impossible escape even if this is not how the case or Kent originally framed the question.[56]

The reasoning relating to the hunted fox in *Pierson* could (and was) applied to fish as well as land animals. In a British case in 1844, *Young v. Hitchens*, the understanding of possession as requiring a final taking of the wild animal (i.e., one from which escape was not possible) was applied to fish in a net intercepted by another; the court held the fish could not have been stolen because they had not been reduced to possession by the first person who netted them and another could come into the net and scoop them away, as they had not been finally secured.[57] As "uncourteous or unkind" as this behaviour might be – on par with Jesse Pierson's depiction as the "saucy intruder" swooping in to take the fox Lodowick Post had already declared his intention to take – it did not interfere with a possessory right.[58] A qualified property, that is, one in which additional steps were required, was the only property right held by the one who originally set the net or pursued the fox. This was a concept Blackstone, Kent, and *Pierson* lifted straight from Roman and natural or civil law, and Ritchie put it into play relying explicitly on the first two of these sources, with the passages in Kent's *Commentaries* relying heavily on *Pierson*.

Justice Sedgewick did not cite or discuss Kent, *Pierson*, *Young v. Hitchens* or any of the other older Roman, natural, or civil law authorities on acquiring possession of a wild animal such as fish or any other. He rested his interpretation, as Ritchie urged him to do, on "the ordinary use of language" or "the common use of the language."[59] And indeed Justice Sedgewick expressed some impatience with the fine question of how possession in a wild animal was established, writing: "It is not necessary to determine at what particular point of time, or at the conclusion of what particular operation, did the fish became the property of the catchers."[60] What was more important, in his view, was that the work was ongoing and it was happening in Canadian waters at the time the vessel was arrested. There was still more that needed to happen before there was a "final taking" and on that score, we will see, all three judges in the majority opinion were in agreement.

It is tempting to contrast the common sense practical approach of Justice Sedgewick, with his emphasis on common or ordinary language and disinterest in older scholarly sources on the question of wild animals and possession, against the far-ranging, learned, elaborate posture assumed by the academically-oriented judge from the civilian jurisdiction of Quebec, Justice Girouard. At the risk of relying on a cliché, there would seem to be something in the (practical) common law v. (theoretical) civil law juxtaposition in terms of the judges' respective backgrounds. Justice Sedgewick was a Nova Scotian son of a Presbyterian reverend from Scotland.[61] His strengths lay in the practical policy work he did as a pioneer of legal education at Dalhousie and as a gifted and talented civil servant working on projects such as the codification of Canadian criminal law.[62] Hence, we see him happily following Ritchie's lead, keeping his nose pointed down to the ground rather than gazing up into the stars, as the caricature of judges operating in the two legal systems goes.[63]

Yet the absence of cosmopolitan legal learning did not prevent Justice Sedgewick from participating in his own form of elaborateness. His judgment in the *Gerring* case contains some strikingly gratuitous and flowery material that must be noted. For instance, Justice Sedgewick referred to "the hardy fisherman along our multitudinous coast waters and tidal rivers."[64] If fishing was not understood as a continuous act, he argued, those men would be fishing when they set their nets in the evening but not when they hauled them in in the morning, a proposition that made little sense.[65] Weaving himself into the narrative, Justice Sedgewick wrote it cannot be that "I *am* 'fishing' while I am whipping the water with my line, 'fishing' also when the salmon rises and takes the fly, but, having hooked him, I am *not* 'fishing' when for minutes, or perhaps hours, I play him in the water, weaken him before the final tragedy, and at last land him dead upon the sward [i.e., grassy land]."[66] Referring next to a work of English intellectual and imperial apologist James A. Froude, *The English Way in the West Indies* (1888), Justice Sedgewick wrote, it was similarly incongruous that "[t]he Negro boys" who "were 'fishing' when they were placing the net in the water and surrounding the fish with their improvised contrivance, but when the cord was drawn and the net closed, they were *not* 'fishing' while they were hoisting them into the boat and carrying them ashore."[67] He continued in this vein, using an example of Jesus's apostles fishing "on the waters of the Gallilean Sea" and their "multitude of fishes."[68] He also referred to the city of Troy and the way that it was under siege but did not fall for ten years in order to demonstrate that even when a taking might be almost certain, it has not truly occurred until it has been secured.[69] He presented this bundling of references to classicism, Christianity, and romanticized colonial racism through a lens that was decidedly masculine and "Aryan," writing that to give fishing a strict interpretation would be "to emasculate language, to filch from that word – a word which, with recognized variations, appears to be common to all the Aryan races – all but a fraction of its meaning."[70] To emasculate both language and fishing would be to render both manly fishing and manly legal interpretation as problematically feminine, a double sin.[71]

It was probably Ritchie's call to turn to common or ordinary language that suggested to Justice Sedgewick it would be appropriate to go beyond *Webster's* in a different way and draw on everyday life and his non-law books (Froude, the Bible, and Homer's *Odyssey*). Ritchie, perhaps even knowing Justice Sedgewick was a fly fisher, reminded the judges what all fishermen know: hooking a fish is only ever a *maybe* in terms of whether or not there will be a successful landing of the fish. As Ritchie wrote in his factum, finding that "a fish would be caught as soon as is hooked … would, I think, be found to be contrary to experience."[72] Industry purse sein fishing, involving as it did here "one hundred and thirty barrels (more or less) of mackerel," was no one's weekend diversion.[73] Nevertheless, it was a good way to connect and relate, namely, to get the judges thinking about their own experiences with "the one that got away." Rather than grounding his romp in a bevy of Roman and civil law texts, which were second nature to someone like Justice Girouard, Justice Sedgewick, with some prompting from Ritchie, turned to what was comfortable and familiar to him: his books, his "mother tongue," his culture (Christian, white, male, humanistic, imperial-identified).[74]

Was Justice Sedgewick suggesting that Justice Girouard, whose "mother tongue" was French and whose culture was Quebecois, did not quite get it? Such disparagement would be consistent with the other glimpses of xenophobia, racialization, and othering in Justice Sedgewick's decision (e.g., references to "[t]he Negro boys" and "the Aryan races").[75] There is a decidedly anglophone inflection in his call to avoid doing "violence to the mother tongue" in a way that would "shock the intelligence of the ordinary English student," that one senses he perhaps felt Justice Girouard was not well positioned to appreciate.[76] "We must not do violence to ordinary language," Justice Sedgewick wrote, "we must not take from plain words their ordinary and universal meanings."[77] When Ritchie wrote in his factum that "we ought not to deviate from the common use of *the* language" it is clear that "*the* language" to him and Justice

Sedgewick was English.[78] It was unusual for Sedgewick to engage in this kind of legal literary play. As Philip Girard, the author of Sedgewick's entry in the *Dictionary of Canadian Biography*, puts it, "this kind of language was not common in Sedgewick J.'s decisions. His judgments tend much more to the quantitative and policy oriented (as befitted a former federal deputy minister of Justice) and not at all to the literary."[79]

When Justice Livingston wrote his dissent in the *Pierson* case, he used a lot of witty language. There is his characterization of Jesse Pierson as a "saucy intruder, who had not shared in the honors or labours of the chase," the fox as a "pirate," whose "depredations on farmers and on barn-yards, have not been forgotten" and who had been "so cunning and ruthless in his career" he should be put to death wherever found, and the hunter as a "gentleman, [who] at the sound of the horn, and at peep of day, would mount his steed, and for hours [...] pursue the windings of this wily quadruped."[80] I argued in my book on *Pierson* that this dissent should be understood as a literary text, at least in part, and that it fits into a tradition of literary lawyerly writing I call "legal solemn foolery," examples of which often involve nonhuman animals.[81] Indeed, sport fishing should probably be its own subcategory.[82] Something about the perceived moral and economic insignificance of nonhuman animals, especially hunted ones, seems to translate to the idea that it is permissible to use humour in the resolution of legal disputes about torturing and trying to kill them. I argue that something importantly ideological is going on in such situations, with its (implicit) reinforcement of the view that human beings are superior to all other animals, standing outside and above nature, so superior that they are entitled to use the violent deaths of nonhuman animals as an opportunity for fun and wit. As such, it seems it is perfectly acceptable to have fun with the fox, a morally and economically insignificant animal, a pest even, a premise shared by everyone involved in *Pierson* and almost everyone in the over two hundred years of treatise writers, readers, and, in the last one hundred and twenty-five years, law-school casebook compilers, and law-review authors.

Girard wrote that he would go beyond my suggestion that Sedgewick's style is "somewhat like Livingston's solemn foolery in *Pierson*" and says further than that "Sedgewick J felt that Justice Henry Livingston's opinion gave him permission to engage in this kind of literary embellishment."[83] It was so unlike the way in which

Sedgewick usually expressed himself, Girard thinks that his decision was evidence of what "has often been the case. Canadian judges [who] seem to require permission from a metropolitan authority, whether British or American, to colour outside the lines."[84] It is noteworthy that Sedgewick did this in a majority decision rather than a dissent. It is sometimes suggested that Livingston gave himself permission to engage in a literary romp in *Pierson* given the fact that a dissent would not matter in terms of the authoritative statement of the law, which as one very witty slogan on *Pierson* "merch" (or merchandise) puts it: "*Pierson v. Post*, 3 Cai. R. 175 (1805). Held: Slow hunters get outfoxed."[85] In other words, Livingston was flippant in a situation "where his dissent could do no harm" and its "refined drollery" was therefore forgivable in exchange for "an opinion such as Charles Lamb [an English essayist and popularizer of Shakespeare] might have prepared for hypothetical delivery [...] unhampered by any judicial responsibility."[86] Interestingly, the literary embellishment might have assisted Justice Sedgewick insofar as it was his formulation of the continuous act definition of fishing that was adopted by subsequent cases rather than the one provided in the more plain-spoken concurrence written by his colleague Justice King.[87] While subsequent cases do not mention any of the literary references, it certainly seems possible that their inclusion made Justice Sedgewick's decision more readable and attractive than Justice King's.[88] It also was placed in the report physically before Justice King's and so was the first of the three majority opinions a reader would encounter, a not insignificant factor given the overall length of the decision, which clocks in at thirty-seven pages.[89]

Perhaps the most explicit echo of Livingston's dissent in Justice Sedgewick's decision is his personification of the *Frederick Gerring Jr*, emphasizing its legal personhood or "personality," even its "moral consciousness," and its legal status as an offender deserving punishment, a criminal in effect.[90] We might recall that this was a criminal-law case and Ritchie developed the "continuous act" idea from criminal-law sources. As noted above, Justice Livingston described the fox in *Pierson* as a very particular kind of criminal, "a pirate '*hostem humani generis*'" who deserves to be punished.[91] Like the ship's "forfeiture in the event of transgression," Justice Livingston wrote that "to put him [the fox] to death, wherever found, is allowed to be meritorious, and of public benefit."[92] This is a very old personification of the fox as outlaw, grounded in and popularized by tales like "the old medieval beast epic" *Reynard the Fox*, which Livingston explicitly invokes when he refers to the fox in *Pierson* as "poor Reynard."[93] Wolves were painted in even worse terms than foxes.[94] For example, a man who was an outlaw was called "a wolf" in order to emphasize that he was not merely "friendless," he was deplorable with "no status in society and likely could be treated as a reviled animal, and perhaps even killed on sight without consequence."[95] The "lone wolf" stands outside the bonds of society.[96] The status of foxes and wolves as "beasts of prey" created a justification for a declared open season or permanent state of warfare against them, grounded in texts of international law such as Hugo Grotius' *On the Law of War and Peace* (1625).[97] Foxes became the targets of sport hunting starting in the eighteenth century, the cruelty of which was acknowledged by English-style fox hunters even if they overrode it with a stock set of anthropomorphizing justifications, peddled also to children in the form of fox-hunting stories in order to anesthetize them against that cruelty.[98]

In addition to personifying the fox as a pirate or criminal, deserving punishment, perhaps the most memorable phrase in Justice Livingston's dissent is his description of Pierson as "a saucy intruder" for interfering in Post's hunt with his hounds.[99] That famous line has a particularly troubling dimension in terms of its relationship to one of Shakespeare's most violent plays, *Titus Andronicus*, and sexual uses of this phrase.[100] The fox in *Pierson* was a "him," not a "her."[101] However, "he" was reduced to the status of a contested object in much the same way that the raped and mutilated Lavinia was in Shakespeare's play. Ships of course were often gendered female and one thinks of this in relationship to the *Frederick Gerring Jr*, seized by one government in what was perceived by the other to be an unjustified show of (legal) force, becoming an object of argument for decades amongst the male lawyers, judges, and, later, politicians. Arenas of male forensic argument and display such as courts of law, Courts of Dover (that often mocked or imitated courts of law in the way of "solemn foolery"), social clubs, and non-legal fraternities engaging in legal rituals, were of course male preserves in the nineteenth century.[102] Legal discourse inflected with ribaldry often traded in gendered stereotypes.[103]

Indeed, there is a strikingly male clubby tone to a situation in which Justice Sedgewick so keenly adopts the theory that Ritchie presented in his factum and was argued before the Supreme Court of Canada by

Justice Sedgewick's successor as deputy minister of Justice and deputy attorney general, Edmund Leslie Newcombe.[104] Justice Sedgewick was occupying one of the Maritime seats on the Supreme Court of Canada that W.B.A. Ritchie's uncle held.[105] Newcombe, an avid hunter, also from Nova Scotia (and someone who would presumably know about Sedgewick's fly fishing interests) would go on to take his own seat on that Court in 1924.[106] Ritchie was smart then to phrase his argument in terms of "the one that got away," which given the other men's hobbies, they could relate to, a phrase, it must be noted, that is often used as a way of describing an unsuccessful amorous pursuit.[107] Fishing interests aside, it is difficult to imagine Justice Sedgewick not being sympathetic to the government's position in this case, having been in Newcombe's shoes as recently as 1893. These men formed the very definition of an old boys' club, for which a hunting and fishing club might well have stood instead.

Justice King (New Brunswick)

Justice King wrote the second concurrence in the judgment. In it he also endorsed and adopted Ritchie's "continuous act" language.[108] Like Justice Sedgewick, he was impressed by the fact that the hauling and emptying of the net would take much longer than the setting and drawing in or pursing up of the seine.[109] He discussed the concept of qualified property, introduced by Ritchie using Blackstone and Kent's *Commentaries*.[110] And he emphasized the way in which that precarious title might be defeated – "by the state of the weather, or by the fouling of the seine [i.e., its ripping or destruction], or the breaking of it with the weight and pressure of the fish, or by a variety of causes."[111] He cited to Kent's *Commentaries* at the spot Ritchie specified, referred to *Young v. Hitchens*, as well as Frederick Pollock's work on possession, which adopted the capture rule in its strongest form.[112] Justice King agreed that there was probably enough control and dominion for a qualified property but, like Sedgewick (and the Justinian texts), he was bothered by the possibility of escape – "an operation at sea of taking several hundred, or one hundred barrels (as here) of loose and live fish from a bag net, is attended with such obvious chances of some of them at least regaining their natural liberty, that the act of fishing cannot be said to be entirely at an end in a useful sense until the fish are reduced into actual possession."[113]

Justice King recognized the hardship involved in seizure of the vessel in a situation where it had inadvertently drifted into Canadian waters and the harshness of this measure given that the fish were not netted from those waters. Purse seine nets could be "fouled" or destroyed by the ship if the efforts to keep it in one place went astray.[114] Hence, the ship was not anchored, as Justice Sedgewick also recognized when he wrote "[a]t no time during any of these operations is the vessel or seine at anchor; the vessel lays to, and the whole drifts at will with the tide or current."[115] And it was certainly possible to say that the crew of the *Frederick Gerring Jr* were simply taking their catch on board at the time they were arrested. However understandable the drift was, Justice King wrote that "[t]he remedy for cases of hardship lies in the pardoning power of the Crown" rather than a court of law bound to determine the legal question.[116]

Justice King had been appointed the previous year to the Anglo-American Arbitration Commission created to deal with claims for damages that occurred when Americans seized Canadian and British sealing ships in the Bering Sea.[117] This helps explain why he was thinking about the political fallout and restitution and arbitration options for the United States (and the owner of the *Frederick Gerring Jr*) even if the seizure was legally upheld by the Supreme Court of Canada. This is significant, as his vote, added to the Chief Justice and Justice Gwynne's would have made a majority decision overruling the Nova Scotian Admiralty Court which confirmed the legality of the seizure. His sense that a political avenue was preferred probably left his conscience clear to join the other two judges in making a majority finding against the *Frederick Gerring Jr*.

The words of Justice King about the possibility of a pardon form a contrast with the lack of sympathy shown by Justice Sedgewick, who says nothing about the disproportionate loss the inadvertent drift caused the owner of the ship, pointing out (rather unhelpfully it must have seemed to the ship's owner, Mr Morris) that it was not the captain or crew who were being punished by its seizure. Justice Sedgewick wrote: "In the eye of the statute the vessel itself is the offender. The statute gives to it a moral consciousness – a personality – a capacity to act within or without the law, and imposes upon it the liability of forfeiture in the event of transgression."[118] The ship's personhood made it the bearer of culpability. However, it was also the (valuable) property of Mr Morris.[119] The fiction of legal personality would have been of little consolation to him, and he successfully enlisted the assistance of the American government in launching his own decades-long war against the Supreme Court of Canada's decision.[120] The American press was prone to pointing out that the Chief Justice of the Supreme Court of Canada sided with Morris, even though, as noted above, Chief Justice Strong merely concurred in the reasoning of Justice Gwynne, hardly a ringing endorsement from the nation's top jurist, as the Americans wanted to bill him, arguing that a mistake had been made in Mr Morris's case.[121]

Justice Girouard (Quebec)

In the third and final concurrence, Justice Girouard not only referred to James Kent in the context of the discussion in the *Commentaries* of *Pierson*, he reproduced much of the *Pierson* majority decision in the body of his judgment, specifically, almost seven hundred of its one thousand words.[122] Unlike Justice Sedgewick and Justice King, Justice Girouard was very keen to immerse himself in discussion of the capture rule and its elaborate and extensive authorities for and against. These were sources with which he felt comfortable and at home; his books and his authors.

Justice Girouard began by expressing disappointment that lawyers for the ship relied too heavily on a non-legal authority, *Webster's Dictionary*.[123] The question, he wrote, "must be decided according to the principles of law," lacking in the appellant's argument.[124] He quoted from the trial judge in the case, who wrote that "[f]urther labour is required to save the fish from the sea, and reduce the property to useful possession."[125] Justice Girouard then went on to report what he found "[a]fter a careful research in the text books and digests, both English and American."[126] He provided a lengthy discussion of the British case *Young v. Hitchens*, which suggested that the possession of the fish must be complete.[127] Like the other two judges in the majority opinion, he emphasized the fact that "the fish may and do in fact escape from the seine after it is pursed up."[128] He continued: "The seine may break, the fastenings at either end of the vessel might give way, the jibs and sheets might become unmanageable, the fish may jump into the sea or over the floating sides of the seine, or from the dip net, and many other things may happen which would prevent the fishermen from capturing the fish enclosed in the seine."[129] He wrote that the bailing "was necessary to reduce the property to useful possession."[130]

In terms of the legal authorities, Justice Girouard noted that "[t]he soundness of the decision in *Young v. Hitchens* has never been questioned either in England or in the United States," observing that it was favorably quoted in "American text books and digests, and more particularly in the American and English Encyclopedia of Law [...] Addison on Torts, Gould on Waters [and] Angell, Tide Waters."[131] Justice Girouard wrote: "I have no hesitation in following the decision in *Young v. Hitchens*, as I find it based upon the Roman law, which everywhere is considered as *written reason*, and in the absence of other regulations has been accepted as law by all modern civilized nations."[132] He marched through Justinian's *Institutes*, Gaius's *Digest*, which included Trebatius's view, quoting from the 1865 English House of Lords case *Blades v. Higgs* to support the point that there was no difference between the common law and Roman law on "live animals in a wild and unreclaimed state."[133] Moving then to civilian interpreters of Roman law, Justice Girouard noted that Domat (in French, rather than the English translation) emphasized manual seizure by the hands (i.e., manucaption) and a quotation from Savigny stressed actual capture given the possibilities of escape.[134] Puffendorf, Heinneccius, and Grotius were brought in to consider the effect of "snares, nets, traps, weirs, hooks and the like," obviously relevant to the purse seine net.[135] However, these "instruments" only give the possession if they are "entirely under our control," according to Puffendorf.[136] In other words, escape cannot be possible.[137] However, Justice Girouard noted that Barbeyrac disagreed. Pothier too observed that "mere discovery and pursuit, with the intention to capture it" is sufficient in practice in France.[138] Justice Girouard then noted that a Quebec Superior Court decision about a hunted bear, *Charlebois v. Raymond*, supported this position relying on Cujas (and I would add Pothier).[139] This is a longer list of authorities than is contained in *Pierson*, itself so elaborate.[140] After all, a long time had elapsed between the two cases, specifically, ninety-one years in which to dig up further layering on the fine legal point. All of these sources definitively established in the eyes of Justice Girouard that "a wild animal caught in a net or trap is not in the full possession or the absolute property of its owner unless finally seized."[141] He then went on to reproduce the secure seizure understanding of Kent's discussion of *Pierson*, reproducing the text of the four essential paragraphs of the *Pierson* majority decision, along with an excerpt from the other 1822 New York case Kent discussed in his *Commentaries on American Law* about a hunted and wounded deer, *Buster v. Newkirk*.[142]

Justice Girouard was a lawyer from Quebec with academic interests. He attended McGill in 1857, graduated with a BCL in 1860 at the top of his class, practised in Montreal, was a member of Parliament for seventeen years and the mayor of Dorval in 1892.[143] His writings were varied, including highly regarded work on letters of exchange and promissory notes.[144] He helped to found the journal *La Revue critique de législation et de jurisprudence du Canada*. He also wrote a number of works in history and genealogy. In 1882, he sponsored and was ultimately successful in securing the passage of a law permitting a man to marry his deceased wife's sister.[145] He became disillusioned with politics for a number of reasons, including the treatment of Quebec in its relationship with the rest of Canada and the Conservative government's handling of the Louis Riel affair in 1885.[146] He was appointed to the Supreme Court of Canada in 1895.[147]

Justice Girouard's decision was more *Pierson* than *Pierson* in the way that those who were colonized by the British were often said to be more English than the English.[148] In other words, his opinion relied on an even longer lineup of Roman and natural-law authorities than *Pierson* did. Like his fellow Supreme Court of Canada colleague from Quebec, Justice Henri-Elzéar Taschereau, Justice Girouard was anxious to establish that civil law principles were found in some common law rules influenced by Roman law, which also influenced the major legal systems of their day (Germany, the United States, and France).[149] Focusing on Justice Taschereau, David Howes called this polyjural orientation "judicial nomadism" or, following Blaine, "principled eclecticism."[150] Howes included Justice Girouard in this style, which he stated was shared by the early members of the Supreme Court of Canada from Quebec.[151] However, it did not survive in the twentieth century when a new "monojural" orientation dominated the approach taken by Quebec jurists who took on a survivalist posture.[152] Noting that Justice Girouard's reasons for judgment possessed many of the characteristics described by Howes, Michel Morin noted the pleasure that Justice Girouard took in analyzing the state of the *ancien droit* and the great number of different sources he would cite in his reasons, traits that are certainly on display in his concurrence in the *Gerring* case.[153]

WHY NO "UPTAKE" OF THE *GERRING* CASE'S INCORPORATION OF *PIERSON*?

Pierson has never been a widely cited case in the sense of operating as a working precedent.[154] It was really James Kent's presentation of *Pierson* and his (apparent) endorsement of the capture rule that operated as its driving intellectual engine, keeping it on what Blaine would call the "supra-national" legal intellectual radar screen, as edition after edition of Kent's *Commentaries on American Law* appeared for almost three quarters of a century.[155] *Pierson* was included in the *Gerring* case, in other words, because it was in Ritchie's factum. It was in Ritchie's factum, because Kent discussed it and, along with Blackstone's *Commentaries on the Laws of England*, Kent's *Commentaries on American Law*, were a standard touchstone for a well-educated lawyer like Ritchie. As Nova Scotia judge, Alexander Stewart, wrote to Kent himself in 1847, the year Kent died, "[y]our Commentaries are the textbook we put into our students' hands and next to Blackstone ... are our most esteemed works."[156] Kent's set of books remained relevant for a long stretch in the United States, the United Kingdom, Canada, and other Commonwealth nations. When new editions of the *Commentaries* stopped being produced – the last one was the fourteenth edition in 1896 – we can see that this coincides with a drop in citations to *Pierson* in American case law for over a near straight eighty years.[157]

That might well have been it for *Pierson*. However, the case experienced a renaissance in the 1960s and 1970s in the United States when it began to be discussed in some very influential fora owing to the way that legal academics and judges knew about it, not as a working precedent but as a memorable casebook case which they learned when they were law students, part of what is sometimes called "the pedagogical canon."[158] It was standardly (and often prominently) included in American law school property casebooks from 1915 on, often as the first case in the collection, dealing as it did with such fundamental first principles relating to possession, specifically first possession, and how it was acquired when the object in question was not already owned. However, the dissent did not begin to appear in its full form until the 1950s.[159] Two prominent twentieth-century academic legal mandarins writing in the *Yale Law Journal* and *Harvard Law Review* in the 1960s discussed *Pierson* (both of these articles by Charles Reich and Frank Michelman are among the top twenty most-cited law review articles of all time) and *Pierson* was mentioned in a dissent by Justice Rehnquist at the United States Supreme Court in 1977, all of which seemed to foster a resuscitation or revival of interest.[160] This is important because it suggests that any Canadian encountering Justice Girouard's reproduction of *Pierson* in the *Gerring* case before the 1960s or 1970s would have little reason to see it as noteworthy or any more important than the flotilla of other (equally) obscure references on the old-chestnut question of how one establishes possession of a wild animal. In other words, if *Pierson* was not being used as the way to introduce students to the concept of first possession in property in Canada between 1900 and the 1960s or later, then there was no reason for seeing its inclusion in the *Gerring* case as significant. It is more difficult to explain why at least from the 1980s on no one seemed to notice it or give it any attention.

Bruce Ziff, a Canadian property-law scholar interested in the law of capture and wild animals and *Pierson* specifically has not drawn any attention to the *Gerring* case in either his property-law casebook or treatise. The casebook, first published in print in 2004, reproduced passages from *Pierson* and asked for comparisons between it and a series of Newfoundland cases concerning seal hunting, which are useful to excavate questions about what a final taking means when seals are killed but left on ice pans where they can "escape" and be lost to the hunters (although this is not an escape that means anything to the seal).[161] Ziff has cited *Pierson* in his property-law treatise, since its first edition in 1993, for the principle that even hot pursuit is insufficient to confer ownership rights in a wild animal.[162] There are no citations, however, to the *Gerring* case in either the casebook or the treatise, although Ziff appears to have been aware of the *Gerring* case, as it appears in a footnote in his work on the seal-hunting cases.[163]

The *Gerring* is not exactly a property case in the way that *Pierson* is in terms of discussing what minimum level of control is necessary for occupation or first possession, nor does it ask what impact abandonment has on who owns a wild animal as in the Newfoundland cases on seal hunting. Yet the *Gerring* case provides a Supreme Court of Canada decision that relies on the principle of the capture rule from *Pierson* and carries well the question of how the fact of incomplete labour interacts with what is required for legal possession. If there is no legal possession until the work of bailing has finished, then the American ship was "fishing" in violation of the treaty. If legal possession has been attained by the fish just being in the net, then the fact that significant labour remains is neither here nor there and the ship was wrongly arrested and confiscated. It is a fine and delicate question relating to the interaction between legal possession or occupation, and whether a significant amount of labour remains and how essential it is that the labour be complete. As in *Pierson* and the cases about sealing from Newfoundland, escape or the "fugitive" resource slipping away, is central to the analysis. Many of these fish certainly could escape and so, at least a majority of the judges thought, they were not sufficiently controlled in order to be possessed even if many had been netted and would likely be taken or secured. There was, in other words, an inadequate degree of control, a point Justice Sedgewick agreed with even if he wanted to resist saying when was the precise moment of legal possession. The extent of the labour left to be performed showed that the fish while netted were not yet in that finally controlled state.

Justice Sedgewick's opinion was very flowery and positively quirky. Yet, it was his elegant rendition of the "continuous act" theory that subsequent decisions have picked up on rather than Justice King's. The unusual or eccentric nature of the rest of Justice Sedgewick's opinion was ignored, including the literary material. Justice Girouard and his feast of authorities disappeared almost completely.[164] His was the last of three lengthy opinions, which likely did not help its uptake. Moreover, the "principled eclecticism" would no longer resonate inside Quebec, which had largely turned away from the polyjural approach.[165] It would have had a small to non-existent audience in English-speaking common law Canada, especially Ontario in the twentieth century, for the reasons Blaine suggested in "Reconstitution." A heavily anglicized or British-oriented legal culture was not going to embrace the kind of "principled eclecticism" on display in that decision, especially not an American case.[166] Even if an exception in pro-British and anti-American sentiment, or both, would have been made for such a famous American case, it is not obvious that any Canadian encountering *Pierson* in the *Gerring* case would have thought much of it until the revival of interest in *Pierson* starting happening in the 1960s and 1970s and really took off in the 1980s.

Blaine wrote about "literary fragments ... sprung loose from their host political-legal culture for transplantation," which when they did so "acquired a different meaning and identity."[167] Understood in this way, *Pierson* was "sprung loose" from an early nineteenth-century American context to be taken up by Justice Girouard in a late nineteenth-century Supreme Court of Canada decision, where it was just one among many other obscure learned legal authorities on the abstract question of how to acquire first possession in, or occupation of, a wild animal. Canadian legal scholars did not adhere to the dominant twentieth-century American understanding of *Pierson* as an artifact-turned-weapon carrying the broader message about the importance of clear (and allegedly more efficient) legal rules as "bright line" rules such as the capture rule (as opposed to "fuzzy standards" like a hot pursuit rule).[168] This is true even of someone like Ziff who incorporates law and economics perspectives into his work.

Chief Justice Strong and Justice Gwynne were the Ontario appointments to the Supreme Court. While they often disagreed, they did not in the *Gerring* case.[169] Coming from Ontario, neither of these judges probably felt the pull that the other three in the majority would have to protect the east coast fisheries, or at least east coast fishermen. Nova Scotia (Justice Sedgewick), New Brunswick (Justice King), and communities around the mouth of the St Lawrence in Quebec (Justice Girouard) all had important fishing industries that had been locked in a long-standing battle with Americans coming up from the east coast of the United States to fish in what Canadians viewed as their waters, the very sore spot at issue in the case. Ontario (or an earlier Upper Canada) did not play much of a role in these fish wars. Indeed, the *Gerring* case is still not cited in Ontario courts.[170]

Justice Gwynne was certainly totally uninterested in any kind of excavation of the possession or capture issue; taking the fish was all the treaty required, not a final taking as per the first possession of wild animals authorities. Later, even for Wright, Laskin, and their lot, mid-twentieth-century Canadian legal academics, heavily influenced by American models of legal education, the Roman, natural, or civil law orientation around the discussion of *Pierson*, would have been unfamiliar and foreign to them. Such material would have looked like it was only for Quebec judges and lawyers, as the "two solitudes" settled into their respective enclaves.[171] Yet Justice Girouard's second wife came to Montreal from New Orleans with her brother and sister in 1865.[172] It is not surprising then that her husband's cosmopolitanism included something both as American and as civil law orientated as *Pierson v. Post*.[173]

CONCLUSION

Reading the *Gerring* case today, one is most struck by the strikingly prescient language in the judgment of Justice Sedgewick when he wrote: "We Canadians are in a sense the world's trustees. The North American fisheries have been committed to our guardianship, not for ourselves alone, but for posterity, not for Canada alone, but for humanity. They are the most prolific in the world."[174] He described the measure to outlaw purse seine nets as the Canadian Parliament "recogniz[ing] its obligations to preserve [the fisheries] for the benefit of future generations."[175] He continued: "Purse seining is inimical to that policy. It means, not a reasonable use of, or participation in, the deep sea fisheries or their natural annual increment, not their preservation, but their annihilation, their absolute destruction for all time; in familiar words, 'the killing of the goose that lays the golden egg.'"[176] Justice Sedgewick explained that the Federal government banned the use of the purse seine net in 1891 precisely because it caused so much destruction of fish stocks on the United States Atlantic seaboard that the Americans were also considering a ban on it.[177] Hence, the idea that an American-owned boat from Massachusetts would come to fish in Nova Scotian waters with such a net, when Canadian fishermen could not do so, was evidently particularly riling to Sedgewick. That was unfair competition. Also there was a sense of outrage that the Americans, having destroyed their own industry, felt they could come and risk the destruction of the Canadians' also. These were injustices to which the Nova Scotians (i.e., Ritchie, Newcombe,, and Justice Sedgewick) involved in this affair would have been particularly sensitive.

Justice Sedgewick was actually deputy minister of Justice and deputy attorney general when the ban on the purse seine net was adopted in 1891. Hence, he would have known that key to the bill's passage was the fact that the ban applied only to use of the purse-seine net for inshore fishing. However, it is a net that must float suspended in deep water so there was little use of it in the inshore fishery, where it would be damaged by rocks in shallow waters if it came into contact with the bottom of the ocean floor. Americans viewed the right to fish inshore as worthless precisely because they were using these deep water nets.[178] Moreover, Canadians were also using the net outside the three-mile limit in deeper waters where it was better suited to catch a mid-water fish like mackerel, competing alongside the

Americans for the same fish. A report from Halifax from the day the *Frederick Gerring Jr* was seized, 25 May 1896, stated that "[t]he entire coast ... was swarming with mackerel yesterday and today, and local fishermen have made rich hauls."[179] Two of the hauls by local fishermen were identified as having been obtained by small schooners using purse seines.[180] In the debate in the House of Commons on the bill to ban use of the purse seine net, the question was raised whether Maritime fishermen were using these nets and it was noted that, yes indeed, one of the sitting members of Parliament, absent that day, had "two large vessels fitted with purse seines."[181] Another member of Parliament, representing "one of the largest fishing establishments in Nova Scotia," was reported to have said that he would support the Bill only if it did not apply to the kind of purse seines in use in his county.[182] Hence, Justice Sedgewick's warning words about "the goose that lays the golden egg" and the perniciousness of the purse seine net must be taken with large grains of salt. This was much more about protectionism than proto-environmentalism. The purse seine ban was a perfect example of what is sometimes called a paper tiger statute, that is, a piece of legislation that sounds fierce but really poses an empty threat, an unfortunate feature of much animal and environmental protection law.[183]

The *Gerring* case was about nation in quite a strong sense. First, the nation with borders that could not be traversed with impunity by Americans "fishing" in Canadian waters, which the majority of the Supreme Court of Canada judges were keen to defend. And second, a nation with a resource it wanted to exploit with as little foreign competition as possible, an industry based on the lives of entities whom were not to be thought of as within the nation or circle of moral or legal consideration. The fish were food for the nation and for export. As such, those dragged into Canadian waters were only for Canadians to use and exploit. The Supreme Court of Canada was clearly asserting Canada's territorial sovereignty against the Americans in furtherance of domestic fish industry use in the *Gerring* case, or at least that would have been on the minds of the three judges from the eastern parts of the country where this industry mattered. It is difficult, however, to pass over the disingenuousness in the concern Justice Sedgewick expressed over the sustainability of the fisheries, which future politicians would continue to repeat. This often took the form of a call to protect the species and the resource, not to leave them in peace but to eliminate foreign competition in the race to exploit them to the point of collapse, a story that we now know played itself out with disastrous consequences for the cod fish of the Grand Banks off the coast of Newfoundland and small communities in that province.[184] Protection for the sake of future exploitation, rather than protecting as an end in itself has a long history in the nation after 1885 and the creation of Banff National Park.[185] Indeed, the very idea of sustainability presupposes that it is justifiable to find just the right amount of pressure that the resource in question can sustain without falling into collapse, a dangerous and morally questionable way of proceeding.

The words of Justice Sedgewick sound very different today than they would have in 1985 when Blaine wrote "Reconstitution." In addition to contentious issues like the French and English divisions and the differing common law and civil law influences on the Supreme Court of Canada and how national that institution could ever be, Canadians now want to understand where Indigenous perspectives and knowledges fit in national understandings and their institutional mouthpieces.[186] The legacies of violence and the formal and legal government policies that fueled and continue to perpetuate systemic social inequalities have yet to be reckoned with in any kind of meaningful way. Powerlessness is nowhere more evident than in the situation of the vast majority of nonhuman animals such as fish (wild-caught and farmed) and other food animals who are reduced to the status of resource or economic unit.[187] Issues relating to the large-scale industry use of nonhuman animals and a liveable environment have risen to the surface with renewed urgency, as a matter of self-interest if nothing else, given that the failure to prioritize these areas puts the survival of our species at risk in such dramatic ways. The *Gerring* case then takes on a very different aspect today than it would have in the 1980s, when, at least to some people, the time to tackle scarcity still seemed to be in abundance and many people continued to behave as if we had all the time in the world.

NOTES

1 *Frederick Gerring Jr (The) v. R.* (1897) 27 SCR 271.

2 See ibid., 305–7. See also *Pierson v. Post* (1805) in George Caines, *Caines' Reports* (NY SC), 3:175. This is an 1805 New York Supreme Court case, which established the common law rule in the United States on what was required in order to establish first possession of a wild animal, here a fox,

as between two contenders: the first (Lodowick Post) who was engaged in hot pursuit or the second (Jesse Pierson) who swooped in to intervene and actually took the fox. The judges chose the "saucy intruder" who intervened and the capture rule. Ibid., 181.

3 Focusing on a leading case has been made popular at least since the 1990s by the work of Brian Simpson. See, e.g., A.W.B. Simpson, *Leading Cases in the Common Law* (Oxford: Oxford University Press, 1995). On the legal archaeological approach taken by Simpson and others, see Angela Fernandez, "Legal History as the History of Legal Texts," in *Oxford Handbook of Legal History*, eds. Markus D. Dubber and Christopher Tomlins (Oxford: Oxford University Press, 2018), 243–61.

4 See Angela Fernandez, *Pierson v. Post, The Hunt for the Fox: Law and Professionalization in American Legal Culture* (Cambridge: Cambridge University Press, 2018), 1 (setting out the quote from one casebook stating that "[s]o many students have begun their legal studies with *Pierson v. Post*, it is almost unbelievable that an American-educated lawyer would be unfamiliar with it" and providing the HeinOnline citation count of nearly eight hundred references in law journal articles and other secondary legal sources in 2015). It is less consistently covered in the Canadian property law canon but is still well known and often included. See, e.g., Mary Jane Mossman and Philip Girard, *Property Law: Cases and Commentary*, 4th ed. (Toronto: Emond, 2019), 95–9 (not reproducing the decision itself but discussion of it by Carol Rose and Angela Fernandez). As far as I am aware, all but one Property professor at the University of Toronto (Jim Phillips), teach it in their Property course (Lisa Austin, Larissa Katz, Douglas Sanderson, Abraham Drassinower), or at least they did when I last checked. See Fernandez, *The Hunt for the Fox*, 25, n. 88.

5 H.P. Hedges, "Pierson vs Post," *Sag-Harbor Express* (24 October 1895), frontpage.

6 *Young v. Hitchens* 6 QB 606 (1844), 115 ER 228. See *Gerring*, 299–308.

7 G. Blaine Baker, "The Reconstitution of Upper Canadian Legal Thought in the Late-Victorian Empire," *Law and History Review* 3, no. 2 (1985): 219–92. See Fernandez, *Pierson v. Post, the Hunt for the Fox*, 223 n. 84, 264–8.

8 I often use an iceberg metaphor to explain the approach of legal archaeology in my course, telling students that the legal historical investigation is like the poster of the iceberg and tooth image they might have seen at their dentist's office with the caption "Only Your Dentist Knows What Lies Below," see https://in.pinterest.com/pin/801288958682115815/. The idea to communicate is that the reported case that they see in their casebooks (often itself excerpted) is just the tip of the iceberg.

9 See Phillips E. Myers, *Dissolving Tensions: Rapprochement and Resolution in British-American-Canadian Relations in the Treaty of Washington Era, 1865–1914* (Kent, Ohio: Kent State University Press, 2015). The three-mile limit was based on the distance a cannon could fire from the shore and made sense from a territorial perspective. It means nothing, however, to fish such as mackerel who swim where they please.

10 See Ronald Duea Tallman, "Warships and Mackerel: The North Atlantic Fisheries in Canadian-American Relations, 1867–1877" (unpublished doctoral thesis, Department of History, University of Maine, 1971).

11 The far-reaching afterlife of the case will be explored in the larger co-authored book project under contract with University of British Columbia Press in their Landmark Cases in Canadian Law series. For an overview of the parties and issues involved in what became very complex negotiations between Canada, the US, and Great Britain extending well into the early twentieth century, see Christopher Shorey, "The Last Voyage of the *Frederick Gerring, Jr*," in *Canada's Legal Pasts: Looking Forward, Looking Back*, eds. Lyndsay Campbell, Ted McCoy, and Mélanie Méthot (Calgary: University of Calgary Press, 2020), 51–81.

12 Blaine would often emphasize in his law teaching that doctrinal topics were not hermetically sealed from each other, e.g., the first-year course topics and the boxes between public and private law. He also would speak about the personal and the professional and the way they too did not exist in water-tight compartments, an important component of the law-and-life or "everyday law" philosophy at McGill. See, e.g., Nicholas Kasirer, "Apostolat Juridique: Teaching Everyday Law in the Life of Marie Lacoste Gérin-Lajoie (1867–1945)," *Osgoode Hall Law Journal* 30, no. 2 (1992): 427–70; Roderick A. Macdonald, *Lessons of Everyday Law* (Montreal: McGill-Queen's University Press for the School of Policy Studies, Queen's University and the Law Commission of Canada, 2002).

13 To quote from the Leonard Cohen 1992 song "Anthem": "Ring the bells that still can ring / Forget your perfect offering / There is a crack in everything / That's how the light gets in."

14 See Fernandez, *Pierson v. Post: The Hunt for the Fox*, 281–2.

15 See *Gerring*, 302–5.

16 On the place of *Pierson* in the pedagogical canon, see Stuart Banner, "21st Century Fox: *Pierson v. Post*, Then and Now," *Law and History Review* 27 (2009): 185–8 in the forum organized around my discovery of the record in the case in 2008: "Forum. Pierson v. Post: Capturing New Facts about the Fox," *Law and History Review* 27 (2009): 145–94.

17 See Baker, "Reconstitution," 234; 267–9.

18 Blaine noted in "Reconstitution" that about 50 per cent of the holdings of both libraries were American by the end of the nineteenth century. See ibid., 235. He also recorded that between 1840 and 1880, specifically, the Great Library sought to acquire (and succeeding in acquiring) a near complete American collection, with annual expenditures exceeding funds spent on English and Canadian materials combined. See ibid., 236.

19 Arthur R.M. Lower, *Colony to Nation: A History of Canada* (Toronto, London, New York: Longmans, Green & Co., 1947).

20 See Baker, "Reconstitution," 239 (legal pantheism); 242, 245, 261 (cross-pollination); 256, 260 (transplantation).

21 See ibid., 262–3 (noting that the disruption to the legal pantheism that characterized the nineteenth century occurred between approximately 1890 and 1920).

22 See, e.g., Bora Laskin, *The British Tradition in Canadian Law* (London: Stevens, 1969).

23 Baker, "Reconstitution," 256.

24 See G. Blaine Baker, "Notes on the Migration of Upper Canada's Law Libraries," *Gazette – the Law Society of Upper Canada* 14 (1980): 362–5.

25 Baker, "Reconstitution," 234.

26 See Angela Fernandez, "The Textbook Edition of Kent's *Commentaries* used in the *Gerring*," in *Canada's Legal Pasts: Looking Forward, Looking Back*, eds. Lyndsay Campbell, Ted McCoy, and Mélanie Méthot (Calgary: University of Calgary Press, 2020), 83–100. This is a piece Blaine would have been very interested in, dealing as it does with the migration of this important text to Nova Scotia. I say nearly bootlegged because although the Text Book Series in which this 1889 edition of Kent's *Commentaries* appeared (the series was published by the Blackstone Publishing Company in Philadelphia) were generally not breaching copyright, their cheap reprints (mostly of British treatises) were often referred to by British commentators as pirated. There was no international copyright law to protect the English books and so that charge was a moral one rather than a legal claim. The question of whether new editions of the *Commentaries* specifically, a domestic American publication, were covered by copyright so many years after Kent's death in 1847 is contestable. The notes and additions of new editors might have been but without the underlying text, which remained essentially unchanged, even the notes Oliver Wendell Holmes Jr added to the twelfth edition likely would not have been. However, Holmes and Little, Brown, the publisher of the family's authorized editions of Kent's *Commentaries* from 1858 on,

viewed Kent's heirs and the estate as holders of the copyright. The fact that Kent's heirs responded to the appearance of the Blackstone Publishing edition by offering the Holmes' edition at a good price rather than threatening suit would seem to indicate an awareness that they would not have had a strong case in court. See ibid., 86–90.

27 See Shorey, "The Last Voyage of the *Frederick Gerring, Jr*," 65–71.

28 For more on background of the ship, the man who owned it, and what happened on the day the ship was arrested, see ibid., 51–5.

29 See Joseph Gough, "History of Commercial Fisheries," *The Canadian Encyclopedia* (published 12 August 2013, last edited 25 July 2015) available at https://www.thecanadianencyclopedia.ca/en/article/history-of-commercial-fisheries (floating bowl); "The North American Fisheries and the Halifax Commission," vol. 123, issue 749 *Blackwood's Edinburgh Magazine*, March 1878, 287–304, 302 (pudding bag).

30 Philip Girard, "RITCHIE, WILLIAM BRUCE ALMON," in *Dictionary of Canadian Biography*, vol. 14, University of Toronto/Université Laval, 2003, available at http://www.biographi.ca/en/bio/ritchie_william_bruce_almon_14E.html.

31 Gordon Bale and E. Bruce Mellett, "RITCHIE, Sir WILLIAM JOHNSTON," in *Dictionary of Canadian Biography*, vol. 12, University of Toronto/Université Laval, 2003, available at http://www.biographi.ca/en/bio/ritchie_william_johnston_12E.html. See also Gordon Bale, *Chief Justice William Johnstone Ritchie: Responsible Government and Judicial Review* (Ottawa, Supreme Court of Canada Historical Society, 1991).

32 Girard, "RITCHIE, WILLIAM BRUCE ALMON."

33 See Girard, "RITCHIE, WILLIAM BRUCE ALMON."

34 Ibid.

35 See *Gerring*, 308.

36 See *Great Britain[,]Arbitration of Outstanding Pecuniary Claims Between Great Britain and the United States of America[,] The Frederick Gerring, Jr[,] Answer of His Majesty's Government* (Ottawa: Government Printing Bureau, 1913), appendix, annex 5, "Filed in the Registry of the Supreme Court. Respondents Factum. In the Supreme Court of Canada, 1896," 34 [Ritchie's Factum].

37 See ibid., 25–34.

38 Ritchie cited to and quoted from "Bishop on Criminal Law (7th Edition) Section 650." See Ritchie's Factum, 29. See also Joel Prentiss Bishop, vol. 1, *Commentaries on the Criminal Law*, 7th ed. (Boston: Little, Brown: 1882), 392–3. While in the position with the immigration branch in Vancouver, Ritchie defended Canada's actions in the infamous case of the

Komagata Maru and another "continuous" argument, the "continuous journey" provision, which Canada used to exclude immigrants coming from non-white countries, including British India. See Renisa Mawani, *Across Oceans of Law: The* Komagata Maru *and Jurisdiction in the Time of Empire* (Durham and London: Duke University Press, 2018).

39 See Ritchie's Factum, 30.

40 Ibid., 29.

41 See ibid., 29–30.

42 Ritchie's Factum, 31.

43 Ibid.

44 *Gerring*, 276.

45 Ibid., 273, 276.

46 Ibid., 280.

47 Ibid., 280–1 (emphasis added).

48 See, e.g., *R. v. Frederick W. Saunders* SCC No. 02129 (21 December 1989, unreported); *R. v. Denton* [1991] NSJ no. 148, 105 NSR (2d) 357 (C.A.); *R. v. White* 2006 NLCA 71; *R. v. McKinnell Fishing Ltd.* 2016 BCCA 472, paras 21–2 (setting out the definition of "continuous act" and lodging it in Sedgewick's opinion).

49 *R. v. Dorgan* 2009 PECA 23, quoted in *Mckinnell*, ibid., para. 23.

50 *Gerring*, 281–2, 282.

51 Ibid, 282 (emphasis in the original).

52 Ibid. (emphasis in the original).

53 Ibid., 283.

54 Justinian's *Institutes* (book 2, chapter 1, section 12). The full passage is reproduced from the George Harris 1761 English translation in Fernandez, *Pierson v. Post, the Hunt for the Fox*, 5.

55 Justinian's *Digest* (chapter 41, 1, and 2). The full passage is reproduced in Fernandez, *Pierson v. Post, the Hunt for the Fox*, 6 n. 20. This point about wounding and the "many accidents" that might still happen is also made in the *Institutes*, Book 2, Section 13. See *Gerring*, 303 (for Girouard J.'s reproduction of both sections of the *Institutes*).

56 See Fernandez, *Pierson v. Post, the Hunt for the Fox*, 258–60 (Holmes); 263–4 (Pollock). *Pierson* was taken to stand for a standard of impossible escape despite the fact that the case itself, and Kent's discussion of it in the *Commentaries*, really only established that *mere* pursuit of a wild animal was insufficient and not that escape needed to be made impossible. See Fernandez, *Pierson v. Post, the Hunt for the Fox*, 7–11 (on the case), 14–20 (on Kent's framing).

57 *Young v. Hitchens*, 6 QB 606 (1844), 115 ER 228.

58 *Pierson*, 179, 181. See Fernandez, *Pierson v. Post, the Hunt for the Fox*, 113–24 (on the phrase "saucy intruder").
59 Ritchie's Factum, 31.
60 *Gerring*, 284.
61 Philip Girard, "SEDGEWICK, ROBERT," in *Dictionary of Canadian Biography*, vol. 13, University of Toronto/Université Laval, 2003, available at http://www.biographi.ca/en/bio/sedgewick_robert_13E.html.
62 Ibid.
63 The contrasting image was presented to me, if my memory serves, by Daniel Jutras, in my first-year Foundations class at McGill.
64 *Gerring*, 282.
65 Ibid.
66 Ibid.
67 Ibid.
68 Ibid., 282–3.
69 Ibid., 283.
70 Ibid., 285.
71 Thanks to Reviewer 1 of the collection for pointing out the dual nature of the gendered dynamic at play in the quotation.
72 Ritchie's Factum, 31.
73 *Gerring*, 280.
74 Ibid., 286.
75 Ibid., 282, 285.
76 Ibid., 286.
77 Ibid., 280.
78 Ritchie's Factum, 31 (emphasis added).
79 Philip Girard, "Book Review [of Angela Fernandez, *Pierson v. Post, the Hunt for the Fox: Law and Professionalization in American Legal Culture* (Cambridge, UK: Cambridge University Press, 2018)]," *University of Toronto Law Journal* 70 (2020): 382, 383–4.
80 *Pierson v. Post*, 180–1.
81 See Fernandez, *Pierson v. Post, the Hunt for the Fox*, 45–139. See Jennifer Nadler, "Book Review [of Angela Fernandez, *Pierson v. Post, the Hunt for the Fox: Law and Professionalization in American Legal Culture* (Cambridge, UK: Cambridge University Press, 2018)]," *University of Toronto Law Journal* 70 (2020): 387, 388–91 (digging into the different senses in which the text is or is not "literary").
82 See, e.g., *Dycus v. Sillers* 55 So. 2d 486 (Miss. Sup. Ct., 1990) (a case about "a fishin' hole"). Discussed in Fernandez, *Pierson v. Post, the Hunt for the Fox*, 79–80. Interestingly, the case that was like the *Pierson v. Post*

of McGill when I was there was a property case about a fishing club, though not at all humorous. See *Duchaine v. Matamajaw Salmon Club* (1919) 58 SCR 223; reversed on appeal to the Privy Council, *Duchaine v. Matamajaw Salmon Club* (1921) 2 AC 426 (PC). Thank you to Tina Piper for helping me reconstruct this from my memory of my Civil Law Property course with John E.C. Brierley. She reports that the case survived the transition to the Transsystemic Property course at McGill, i.e., covering both common and civil law property. Email to the author (15 February 2021).

83 Girard, "Book Review," 383.

84 Ibid., 384.

85 The slogan can be ordered on a mug, t-shirt, or tank top. See Pierson v. Post | Held: (creator-spring.com). See also this "saucy intruder" travel mug: "Pierson v. Post - Saucy Intruder" Travel Mug by SAITKEN | Redbubble. Thank you to Douglas A. Kyser for bringing this *Pierson*-related merchandise to my attention.

86 Charles Haven Hunt, *Life of Edward Livingston* (New York: D. Appleton, 1864), 53. The full passage is quoted in Fernandez, *Pierson v. Post, Hunt for the Fox*, 50.

87 See Shorey, "The Last Voyage of the *Frederick Gerring Jr*," 61 (pointing out that of the over sixty decisions that cite to the *Gerring*, only two cite to the King or Girouard JJ.'s concurrence rather than Sedgewick's).

88 For more on the King J. concurrence, see below.

89 See *Gerring*, 271–308.

90 Ibid., 284.

91 *Pierson v. Post*, 180. See Fernandez, *Pierson v. Post, the Hunt for the Fox*, 124–9 (on the pirate and "*hostis humani generis*" language).

92 *Gerring*, 285; *Pierson v. Post*, 180.

93 *Pierson v. Post*, 180. See also Anne Louise Avery, "Introduction: A Fox for all Seasons," in *Reynard the Fox* (Oxford, UK: Bodleian Library, 2020), ix–xxvi, ix. Isengrim the wolf is Reynard's "principal adversary" in the "'great, grim war' between fox and wolf" (xi), also noting that the fox in this tale became "so wildly popular in France that the word for fox eventually changed permanently from the old *goupil* to *renard* (xi). See 147, 166, 253, 255, 259, where the outlaw concept is explicitly invoked. Avery writes that "[t]his Reynard remains our Reynard today: the direct ancestor of Beatrix Potter's dastardly Mr Tod, the charming Fantastic Mr Fox and Disney's devastatingly charismatic Robin Hood," xii. Avery's rendition gives a lot more dimension to the female animal characters, particularly Reynard's wife Hermeline, making her a scholar. Such aspects make

Avery's text a much more interesting read than William Caxton's, which burst on the print publishing scene in 1481, "an immediate bestseller." See xiv–xvi, xvi.

94 See, e.g., Avery, ibid., xxvii, 6–7, 364. Isengrim has none of Reynard's charm and wit and wolves generally do not come in for the (sometimes lovable) "trickster" treatment that foxes do.

95 See Justin Marceau, *Beyond Cages: Animal Law and Criminal Punishment* (Cambridge; New York: Cambridge University Press, 2019), 31 (quoting from several sources, including Pollock and Maitland's *The History of English Law* (1898) and the connection made in other sources between the "wild beast," the outlaw, and the wolf).

96 Thanks to Ian C. Pilarczyk for making the "lone wolf" connection.

97 Stephen C. Neff, *Hugo Grotius on the Law of War and Peace* (Cambridge, UK: Cambridge University Press, 2012).

98 And again thanks to Ian C. Pilarczyk for prompting me to include reference to the sport and its cruelty. See Angela Fernandez, "Fox-Hunting in North America, in Perspective," in *Regulation & Imagination: Legal & Literary Perspectives on Fox-Hunting, Featuring the Autographed Manuscript of Arthur Conan Doyle's "The King of the Foxes,"* edited by Ross E. Davies (Washington, DC: Green Bag Press, 2021), 49–71 (providing a history of the sport, with a focus on North America); Angela Fernandez, "Anthropomorphizing Animals: Foxhunting Stories and the Nature Faker Controversy," (*Animals and Society*, forthcoming) (canvassing justifications for fox hunting in children's stories and the histories of fox hunting enthusiasts, contrasting these against the animal story writers, best practiced by two Canadians credited with creating the genre, Charles G.D. Roberts and Ernest Thompson Seton, who both wrote fox stories and were both publicly criticized for creating overly humanized animal heroes by two prominent Americans, the eminent naturalist John Burroughs and sitting president Theodore Roosevelt).

99 *Pierson v. Post*, 181.

100 See Fernandez, *Pierson v. Post, the Hunt for the Fox*, 113–24 (on *Titus Andronicus* and its use of: "sauciness"; "saucy controller"; and "unmannerly intruder" in an important hunting scene in the play).

101 I changed the fox to a "her" for the feminist experiment re-writing *Pierson* from the perspective of what the fox would say. See Angela Fernandez, "Pierson v. Post, 3 Cai. R. 175 (N.Y. Sup. Ct. 1805) Justice Angela Fernandez, Dissenting" in *Feminist Judgments: Rewritten Property Opinions*, edited by Eloisa C. Rodriguez-Dod and Elena Maria Marty-Nelson (Cambridge, UK: Cambridge University Press, 2022), 98–118.

102 See Fernandez, *Pierson v. Post, the Hunt for the Fox*, 91–6 (on Courts of Dover). Blaine was interested in legal fraternities and other all male spaces. See, e.g., G. Blaine Baker, "The Juvenile Advocate Society, 1821–1826: Self-Proclaimed Schoolroom for Upper Canada's Governing Class," *Historical Papers/Communications historiques* 20, no. 1 (1985): 74–101; G. Blaine Baker, "Public Frivolity and Patrician Confidence: Lower Canada's 'Brothers-in-Law,' 1827 to 1833," in *Mélanges offerts à Paul-André Crépeau par ses collègues de McGill/Mélanges presented by McGill colleagues to Paul-André Crépeau*, edited by J.E.C. Brierley, N. Kasirer, D. Jutras, R.A. Macdonald, and Y.M. Morissette (Cowansville, Quebec: Yvon Blais, 1996), 43–73.

103 See Fernandez, *Pierson v. Post, the Hunt for the Fox*, 310–17 (on *Moby Dick* and the legal case *Gale v. Wilkinson*, in which the contested loose whale was compared to a married woman out of her husband's possession).

104 See Philip Girard, "NEWCOMBE, EDMUND LESLIE," in *Dictionary of Canadian Biography*, vol. 16, University of Toronto/Université Laval, 2003, available at http://www.biographi.ca/en/bio/newcombe_edmund_leslie_16E.html. The case identifies Newcombe as the QC who argued the case before the Supreme Court of Canada. See *Gerring*, 273.

105 Girard, "SEDGEWICK, ROBERT."

106 Girard, "NEWCOMBE, EDMUND LESLIE."

107 Thanks to Ian C. Pilarczyk for making this point.

108 See *Gerring*, 298 (using the term "continuous act" twice).

109 See ibid., 294.

110 See ibid., 297.

111 See ibid.

112 See ibid., 298.

113 Ibid.

114 Ibid., 292, 301 (accomplished by lying with the jibs down and sheets off, i.e., with the foremost triangular sail and its attached lines down).

115 Ibid., 280

116 Ibid., 298.

117 T. W. Acheson, "KING, GEORGE EDWIN," in *Dictionary of Canadian Biography*, vol. 13, University of Toronto/Université Laval, 2003, available at http://www.biographi.ca/en/bio/king_george_edwin_13E.html.

118 *Gerring*, 284–5.

119 For an exploration of the "quasi" property and personhood status of non-human animals, see Angela Fernandez, "Not Quite Property, Not Quite Persons: A 'Quasi' Approach for Nonhuman Animals," *Canadian Journal*

of Comparative and Contemporary Law 5 (2019): 155–232. See also Angela Fernandez, "Animals as Property, Quasi-Property, or Quasi-Person," paper and video in Brooks U Video-Documentary Series on "Animal Law Fundamentals," (December 2021).

120 See Shorey, "The Last Voyage of the *Frederick Gerring Jr*," 65–71.

121 See, e.g., "Case of the Gerring: Chief Justice Strong Was for Liberation of the American Schooner," *Boston Daily Globe* (11 July 1897), 16 (noting that Strong "stood very decidedly for the liberation of the vessel" and that he had been recently appointed to the Privy Council in England "so that great weight is attached to his opinion"). The Americans were not alone in thinking that a mistake had been made, and that Strong C.J. strongly disagreed with what the majority held in the case. Sir Wilfred Laurier's minister of Marine and Fisheries, Sir Louis Henry Davies, reviewing the case shortly after the Supreme Court of Canada's decision, recommended clemency, noting the closeness of the decision (3:2) and a strongly worded dissent by the Chief Justice, when really it was by Justice Gwynne. See the report of Louis Henry Davies (21 June 1897), 6–7. This report is included in the Privy Council minutes, RG2, Privy Council Office, Series A-1-a (vol. 738, Reel c-3656, Access Code 90) 161955, Library and Archives Canada, available at http://www.baclac.gc.ca/eng/CollectionSearch/Pages/record.aspx?app=ordincou&IdNumber=161955&new=-8586327857132766265.

122 See *Gerring*, 305–7.

123 See ibid., 299.

124 Ibid. (the appellants "quote no authority ... except Webster's definition of the word *fishing*" and even the 1896 international edition did not suffice).

125 Ibid., 300.

126 Ibid.

127 Ibid., 300–1.

128 Ibid., 301.

129 Ibid.

130 Ibid., 302.

131 Ibid.

132 Ibid. Emphasis added.

133 Ibid., 302–3.

134 Ibid., 304.

135 Ibid., 304–5.

136 Ibid., 304.

137 Ibid.

138 See ibid., 305.

139 Ibid. See Fernandez, *Pierson v. Post, the Hunt for the Fox*, 8-9 (on Pothier); 27 n. 95, 270 (on *Charlebois v. Raymond*).

140 The *Pierson* authorities were primarily Justinian, Grotius, Puffendorf, and Barbeyrac but the case also mentions Bracton, Fleta, Blackstone, and (for Livingston J. only) John Locke.

141 *Gerring*, 305.

142 See ibid., 305–8. *Buster v. Newkirk* was eminently distinguishable as the deer in that case had been abandoned. See Fernandez, *Pierson v. Post, the Hunt for the Fox*, 18–19

143 Michael Lawrence Smith, "GIROUARD, DÉSIRÉ," in *Dictionary of Canadian Biography*, vol. 14, University of Toronto/Université Laval, 2003, available at http://www.biographi.ca/en/bio/girouard_desire_14E.html.

144 See Désiré Girouard, *Essai sur les lettres de change et les billets promissoires* (Montreal: J. Lovell, 1860); (with son Désiré H. [Henri] Girouard), *The Bills of Exchange Act, 1890: an Act to Codify the Law Relating to Bills of Exchange, Cheques and Promissory Notes, Passed by the Parliament of Canada, 55 Vic., Ch. 33: with Notes and Comments* (Montreal: J. Valois, 1891). His son Désiré Henri helped him with translations from French to English. Another son, Percy became a famous British Imperial Officer. See Michael L. Smith, *Sir Percy Girouard: French-Canadian Proconsul in Africa, 1906–1912* (unpublished MA thesis, Department of History, McGill University, 1989), 8–12 (on father Désiré). Thanks to Brian Young for direction to this source.

145 See Smith, "GIROUARD, DÉSIRÉ." The prohibition on a man marrying his deceased wife's sister was an issue that would have been important in Quebec given large Catholic families and the way that it prevented men left widowed after the death of their wife (e.g., in childbirth) to legitimize (religiously and legally) the de facto marriages that would sometimes arise with a former sister-in-law who came to help take care of those men and the remaining children after the death of her sister. The prohibition is more famous in connection to the Anglican Church given its roots in the creation of the Church of England and the multiple marriages of Henry VIII (who used it to rid himself of Catherine of Aragon in order to marry Anne Boleyn) and long-standing resistance to changing the rule in England; however, these allegedly "incestuous" marriages were also forbidden in the Catholic Church, which shared the interpretation of *Leviticus* upon which the prohibition was based. See Angela Fernandez, "American Treatise Writers and the Nineteenth-Century Debate on

Marriage to a Deceased Wife's Sister in Transatlantic Context," *American Journal of Legal History* 59 (2019): 324–57.

146 See Smith, "GIROUARD, DÉSIRÉ."

147 Ibid.

148 See Baker, "Reconstitution," 268 (giving examples of commentators noting that legal practices in Upper Canada were "more English than the English themselves"). Indeed, the fact that Justice Girouard's son Percy was an important (and, according to Smith, famous) British colonial administrator in Africa, is noteworthy given his French-Canadian roots, and the multiple levels and kinds of colonization in the situation – British over African, British settlers over French ones, and French colonial rule in Africa. See Smith, *Sir Percy Girouard*.

149 Thanks to Reviewer 2 of the collection for making this point.

150 See David Howes, "From Polyjurality to Monojurality: The Transformation of Quebec Law, 1875–1929," *McGill Law Journal* 32 (1986-87): 523–58, 551 ("nomadism"), 542 ("principled eclecticism"), 525 n. 7 (grounding "principled eclecticism" in Baker's "Reconstitution"). Blaine taught this piece in the Canadian Legal History course. Nicholas Kasirer notes its extensive influence on the McGill Faculty of Law's thinking around the shift to its Transsytemic Programme in his foreword to this collection.

151 Ibid., 527.

152 See Howes, "Polyjurality," 551 ("N'oublions pas le cas de la Louisiane," i.e., "do not forget the case of Louisiana," a civil law jurisdiction which came to be largely swallowed up by the common law).

153 Michel Morin, "Des jurists sédentaires? L'influence du droit Anglais et du droit français sur l'interprétation du *Code civil du Bas Canada*," *Revue du barreau* 60 (2000): 247–386, 333, 334, 337.

154 See Fernandez, *Pierson v. Post, the Hunt for the Fox*, 331–5, appendix A, "Citation History" (listing and giving a brief description of the thirty-one cases citing *Pierson* up to 2010 and which ones are animal and not animal related).

155 I will refrain from doing what Blaine would have done in this footnote by listing all of them. Some of the many different editions and shifts in publishers and editors are discussed in Fernandez, "The Textbook Edition of Kent's *Commentaries*," 85.

156 Quoted in Philip Girard, "'Of Institutes and Treatises': Blackstone's *Commentaries*, Kent's *Commentaries* and Murdoch's *Epitome of the Laws of Nova Scotia*," in *Law Books in Action: Essays on the Anglo-American*

Legal Treatise, edited by Angela Fernandez and Markus D. Dubber (Oxford: Hart Publishing, 2012), 43–62, 60.

157 Appendix A, "Citation History," in Fernandez, *Pierson v. Post, the Hunt for the Fox*, 332 (noting the case in 1926 from Massachusetts about a hunted deer that broke the gap). I am indebted to Philip Girard for connecting the dip I tracked in the appendix to the last edition of the *Commentaries*. See Girard, "Book Review," 385.

158 See J.M. Balkin and Sanford Levinson, "Legal Canons: An Introduction," in *Legal Canons*, edited by J.M. Balkin and Sanford Levinson (New York: New York University Press, 2000): 3–44, 7.

159 See Fernandez, *Pierson v. Post, the Hunt for the Fox*, 274–81.

160 See ibid., 286–7.

161 See Bruce Ziff, *A Property Reader: Cases, Questions and Commentary* (Toronto: Thomson Carswell, 2004), 255 n. 6 and n. 9. The second edition in 2008 keeps the same presentation as the first edition, reproduction of lots of *Pierson* but the seal hunting cases multiply.

162 See Bruce Ziff, *Principles of Property Law* (Scarborough, Ont.: Carswell, 1993), 93 n. 10. The first sealing case reference appeared in the second edition in 1996. See Bruce Ziff, *Principles of Property Law*, 2nd ed. (Scarborough, Ont.: Carswell, 1996), 118 n. 11.

163 See Bruce Ziff, "The Law of Capture, Newfoundland Style," *University of Toronto Law Journal* 63 (2013): 53–72, 56 n. 11; first published in Eric Tucker, James Muir, and Bruce Ziff eds., *Property on Trial: Canadian Cases in Context*, (Toronto: Osgoode Society for Canadian Legal History; Irwin Law, 2012), 9–33, 30 n. 15 (where *Young and Hichens* and the *Gerring* are cited as cases where the standard that a trap or net would normally be sufficient to establish capture was not met).

164 But see *Dubeau c. Rule* 1943 CanLII 229 (QC CS), para. 77, available at http://canlii.ca/t/gp1nc (a female moose that escaped from her enclosure was killed by a group of partridge hunters and the judge turned to Girouard J.'s adoption of the Justinian rule for wild animals from the *Gerring* case to support the position that in breaking free the moose had returned to the status of *res nullius* and was part of the common property when she was killed).

165 See Howes, "Polyjurality."

166 Baker, "Reconstitution," 261.

167 Ibid., 256, 260.

168 See Fernandez, *Pierson v. Post, the Hunt for the Fox*, 289–301. See also Angela Fernandez, "Fuzzy Rules & Clear Enough Standards: The Uses and

Abuses of *Pierson v. Post*," *University of Toronto Law Journal* 63 (2013): 97–125, which appeared in the same "Focus" forum, "Foxes, Seals, Whales and the Rule of Capture: Animals in the Law and Legal History," as Ziff's work on the sealing cases cited above. See also Fernandez, "Editor's Note," *University of Toronto Law Journal* 63 (2013): 30–4.

169 The two, who often feuded, were in agreement in the *Gerring*. See Paul Romney, "GWYNNE, JOHN WELLINGTON," in *Dictionary of Canadian Biography*, vol. 13, University of Toronto/Université Laval, 2003, available at http://www.biographi.ca/en/bio/gwynne_john_wellington_13E.html.

170 Of the fifty-four citations to the *Gerring*, none are to judgments from Ontario courts.

171 See Hugh MacLennan, *Two Solitudes* (Toronto: Macmillan, 1945). Baker, "Reconstitution," 264 (the "origins of the two Canadian legal solitudes of the 1980s can be located in the decades surrounding the turn of the twentieth century").

172 See Smith, *Sir Percy Girouard*, 11 n. 10 (Essie Cranwell; brother a trader for the Confederate states in Montreal during the American Civil War). Smith writes that the ten children were increasingly anglicized over the course of the three marriages as the family moved from the east end of Montreal to the west end. See ibid., 10–11.

173 Essie died in 1879, almost twenty years before the decision here. See ibid., 12. His third wife, whom he married in 1881, Edith Bertha Beatty, would not appear to be the sister of either of his two previous wives, in case you were wondering (as I was). See Smith, "GIROUARD, DÉSIRÉ.

174 *Gerring*, 286.

175 Ibid.

176 Ibid.

177 See ibid.

178 See, e.g., "Treaty Rights Violated," *New York Times*, 20 January 1887, 3; "The Fishery Controversy: An Important Statement About In-Shore Fishing by Capt Collins," *Saint Louis Post-Dispatch*, 2 May 1887, 3.

179 "Swarming with Mackerel: Coast of Nova Scotia is Yielding Rich Hauls for Fishermen," *Boston Daily Globe*, 26 May 1896, 2 (from Halifax 25 May).

180 Ibid.

181 *Official Report of Debates, House of Commons*, vol. 32 (Canada Parliament, House of Commons) (30 July 1891): 3157–99, 3163, available at https://books.google.ca/books?id=kiUlAQAAIAAJ&pg=PA3173&lpg=PA3173.

182 Ibid., 3190.

183 See, e.g., Angela Fernandez, "Fish Farms in Canada: Where is the Law?" in *Green Criminology and the Law*, edited by James Gacek and Richard Jochelson (New York: Palgrave Macmillan, 2022), 113–45.

184 See Dean Bavington, *Managed Annihilation: An Unnatural History of the Newfoundland Cod Collapse* (Vancouver: University of British Columbia Press, 2010). I grew up in Newfoundland in the 1980s and so this particular collapse made quite an impression on me, specifically the way that both government and industry ignored the scientific evidence that there was a serious problem with the way the resource was being managed, essentially how it was being mismanaged.

185 See Christopher Armstrong and H.V. Nelles, *Wilderness and Waterpower: How Banff National Park became a Hydroelectric Storage Reservoir* (Calgary: University of Calgary Press, 2013).

186 Blaine used the word "indigenous" to refer to domestic or home-grown Canadian, rather than Indigenous perspectives, a usage that is now, over thirty years later, striking. See Baker, "Reconstitution," 234 ("before about 1890, indigenous, continental, and American legal literature played a more important role in Ontario than it plays today").

187 Fish lives, for instance, are typically weighed in tons rather than counted as individuals.

I knew that Blaine belonged to an intellectual community I wanted to join as soon as I read his contribution on "The Law Society as Educator" in *Essays in the History of Canadian Law, Volume II*. It is a piece I have returned to many times over the years, most recently in preparing to write *A History of Law in Canada, Volume One*. However, we were destined not to live in the same physical community for a long time, not until I moved to Toronto in 2010. We had effectively switched places in the early 1980s: soon after finishing my LLB at McGill I started teaching at the Faculty of Law, University of Western Ontario, while Blaine started teaching at McGill soon after graduating in law from Western. I cannot say I knew Blaine well, but I doubt many would claim that honour. There was always an air of displacement about him: Blaine seemed marooned in the wrong time period, and for much of his adult life in the wrong city. An aura of what Margaret Atwood called "southern Ontario Gothic" hung over him, while in his quirkiness and single-mindedness, his persona was reminiscent of Glenn Gould's. Yet from that singular personality emerged the significant body of legal history scholarship that we honour in this volume.

Philip Girard

7

New Directions in Judicial Biography: More Humane, More Transnational, More Comparative

Philip Girard

Blaine Baker was always interested in the people who made, interpreted, and used the law throughout history. As others in this collection have pointed out, he devoted less attention to those who found themselves subjected to the law; as a result, the people in his scholarly universe were primarily elite WASP males, though he descended the social scale somewhat in his late-career study of the will of farmer William Martin.[1] Blaine both wrote, and wrote about, what he called "juristic biographies" – studies of legal professionals broadly defined – with his posthumously published volume on Gerald Le Dain containing his last words on the subject.[2] This contribution will pair Blaine's devotion to juristic biography with his interest in the migration of legal personnel, law books, and legal ideas.[3] It will also introduce a theme – what is now called "law and emotions" – that featured in Blaine's last work on Le Dain. It does not, however, share Blaine's view that juristic biography exists outside of what he called "mainstream legal history," whatever that might be.[4]

* * *

Some time early in 2007, an American judge wrote to an Australian judge in the following terms:

> Just to say I am thinking about you with cheers for your courage. I have no doubt you will remain steadfast in the pursuit of justice. And if you feel lonely in Canberra, please remember that you have legions of like-minded colleagues and applauders among jurists around the world.[5]

The writer was Justice Ruth Bader Ginsburg of the United States Supreme Court, the recipient, Justice Michael Kirby of the High Court of Australia. They had met nearly twenty years earlier, before either was on their country's highest court, at a judicial gathering in India. The letter came late in Kirby's career, when he was locked into a pattern of seemingly perpetual dissents, a position Ginsburg herself could sympathize with later in her career.

On the surface the letter may seem inconsequential, but it speaks to new realities in judicial appointments and experience in the last few decades. The first, one that has been quickly incorporated into judicial life writing, is simply the opening up of judicial office to a wider applicant pool than the traditional affluent white heterosexual male of Judaeo-Christian background. Both the writer of the letter, the second woman to join the United States Supreme Court, and the recipient, the first openly gay judge to join the top court of a major country, also came, notably, from humble backgrounds. Ginsburg, born Joan Ruth Bader, was the child of Russian Jewish immigrant parents who settled in Brooklyn, where her father made a modest living in the garment business; her mother died when Ginsburg was fourteen. Although her Jewish background was no longer a novelty at the US Supreme Court when she was appointed in 1993, her gender certainly was. Michael Kirby was born to a working-class Catholic father, himself the child of an unwed mother, and a middle-class Protestant mother, albeit one who was obliged to work to help support the family. He came out publicly, if discreetly, soon after his appointment to the High Court of Australia in 1996, but was marginalized by most of his colleagues even as his reputation as a jurist continued to grow with the Australian public and international observers.[6]

Ginsburg and Kirby belong to a small cohort of women and of male judges from less traditional backgrounds who joined their country's highest court in the closing decades of the twentieth century or early in the twenty-first. Others I will discuss include the first three women on the Supreme Court of Canada, Bertha Wilson,

Claire L'Heureux-Dubé, and Beverley McLachlin (appointed in 1982, 1987, and 1989 respectively); Sandra Day O'Connor and Sonia Sotomayor of the Supreme Court of the United States (appointed in 1981 and 2009 respectively); Mary Gaudron, the first woman on the High Court of Australia (appointed in 1987); Thurgood Marshall and Clarence Thomas (appointed in 1967 and 1991 respectively), the first two Black appointees to the United States Supreme Court; and Bora Laskin, the first Jewish appointee to the Supreme Court of Canada (appointed 1970). The personal differences of this cohort from traditional judicial profiles could not help but stand out, making them obvious targets for biography.[7]

The second new reality, however, has been much less noticed by those in the life-writing business. That is the extent to which judges in the late twentieth and early twenty-first century have been on the move, as my introductory epistle indicates. This movement encompasses intellectual and personal exchanges between east and west, between north and south, between national and international legal norms, and among countries with civil law, common law, and mixed legal systems. The reasons behind this mobility will be explored later, but it has grown to such an extent that it is now common to speak of "a global constitutional dialogue, and the corresponding emergence of an international epistemic community of courts and judges."[8] While an epistemic community can exist based purely on the written word, without the personal acquaintance of its members, in noting the factors contributing to this phenomenon scholars have pointed to "the importance of the international professional networks that judges operate in (e.g., [the] judicial urge to join or be associated with an international epistemic community of cosmopolitan jurists)."[9]

This paper will consider the impact of these two factors, the growing personal diversity of the bench in some countries and the growing international contacts of the judiciary, on both the content and the form of judicial biography. It will argue that the time has come for juristic biography, historically a purely national enterprise, to become more international and comparative. Demands for a more diverse and representative bench are now common to many countries, even as the judicial mission, particularly with regard to constitutional interpretation, human rights, and the meaning of equality, becomes more internationalized, and the boundary between national and international law more fluid. Biography permits us to observe the working out of these trends at the level of individual lives, and to see the personal costs imposed on the pioneers of diversity as well as their potential influence through international networks of solidarity.

A MORE DIVERSE BENCH

For centuries, the subjects of judicial biography in the common law tradition were powerful white males. In the nineteenth century, the shape of such works always focused on the pre-judicial career. The emphasis on superlative legal ability and sterling character was meant to demonstrate the worthiness of these men for the bench, but on their judicial contributions themselves the biographers usually fell silent. It would, after all, have been contrary to dominant trends in legal thought to admit that the personality or predilections of a judge should influence their decisions. Law was a science, and all that mattered was demonstrating that judicial candidates were good scientists.[10]

The realist turn in the legal thought of the early twentieth century, whose exponents argued that judges were influenced by their political, social, and moral inclinations more than by legal doctrine, took some time to infiltrate the writing of judicial biography.[11] This shift took place first in the United States, and experienced an uneven uptake elsewhere. However, when judicial appointments themselves took a realist turn, when it was admitted that the bench itself should be broadly reflective in its personal characteristics of the society it served, judicial biography found itself with a new and potentially more controversial mission. It could be summed up in the title of a well-known 1990 article by Canada's first female Supreme Court judge, Bertha Wilson, "Will Women Judges Really Make a Difference?"[12] Substitute Black or Jewish or gay or any other relevant characteristic, and you will have described the orientation of the new wave of judicial biography, or at least a subset of it. Justice Wilson's answer to her own question was, to paraphrase, "maybe women judges will make a difference in some particular areas, such as sexual assault law, but in most areas of the law they will not make a difference."[13]

Judicial biographers have problematized Wilson's minimalist account of the possible influence of gender (and by extension, other identity-based characteristics) on judicial decision-making, in two ways. First, they consider their subjects' entire life experience rather than reducing them to their gender, race, religion, or class background, although these of course remain important elements of their identity. In Wilson's case, for example, her judicial persona reflected not just her gender but the fact that she was a Scottish immigrant, a clerical spouse, and a student of philosophy. Second, they do not confine themselves to interrogating their subjects' influence on particular areas of law, but consider broader dimensions of their possible impact. Bora Laskin, for example, was always concerned about the architecture of the legal order and openly challenged the highly precedent-oriented nature of the judicial reasoning of his generation, while Michael Kirby pushed the relationship between international law and domestic law much further than his colleagues were usually prepared to accept.[14]

What these newer biographies have in common is a sensitivity to their subject's outsider status, a status that may be signalled by a particular characteristic such as gender but is not subsumed by it. Thus, Constance Backhouse highlights Claire L'Heureux-Dubé's French-Canadian cultural traits as well as her gender in analyzing her uneasy reception in the largely anglophone Supreme Court of Canada, while Pamela Burton stresses Mary Gaudron's working-class background and leftish political views in reviewing her role on the High Court of Australia. Perhaps surprisingly, by contrast US Supreme Court Justice Clarence Thomas found his new colleagues to be mostly receptive and welcoming even after the tumultuous and unprecedented confirmation hearings during which he was accused of sexual harassment by law professor Anita Hill.[15]

These biographers have blended the personal and the professional, the public and the private, in ways that bring judicial biography more into the mainstream of life writing in general, rather than confining it to a specialized subgenre. In doing so they have moved closer to the practice of literary biography (i.e., the biography of literary figures), which is arguably the best model for judicial biography. While I may disagree with Richard Posner about many things, I agree with his observation that "judicial biography is a cousin of literary biography."[16] Like literary biographers, judicial biographers are faced with the choice of how to balance the written work with the life. Just as literary biography and literary criticism are two distinct genres, so judicial biography and what is called (in Canada at least) legacy scholarship – the study of a judge's jurisprudential corpus and its influence over time – are, or should be, distinct. When

Quentin Bell's biography of his aunt Virginia Woolf appeared, it was at first criticized for not saying enough about her novels.[17] In my view, such criticism is misplaced. Bell wanted to give the most comprehensive account possible of Woolf's life, one that could be used by critics in exploring the connections between her work and her life.[18] The guiding principle for both judicial and literary biographers should be: "be comprehensive about the life, selective about the work." In other words, draw suggestive parallels, certainly, but do not overdo the analysis of the work itself.

Obviously, one must address a judge's case-law legacy in some way, and the biographers of my cohort of judges have dealt with this in various creative ways. In a thirty-eight-chapter biography, Constance Backhouse chose to devote seven chapters to case studies of her subject's most characteristic and significant decisions, plus one each of a more synthetic nature to L'Heureux-Dubé's judging at the trial and appellate levels before she reached the Supreme Court of Canada.[19] Less than a quarter of Burton's biography of Mary Gaudron is devoted to her case law at the High Court; aside from one chapter devoted to the ground-breaking *Mabo* decision on Indigenous land rights in Australia, the approach is thematic rather than focused on individual cases.[20] A similar approach is taken in my biography of Bora Laskin, with only the *Patriation Reference* of 1981 singled out for special attention.[21] Michael Kirby's biographer A.J. Brown was more interested in what his subject's decisions tell us about Kirby himself and his interactions with his colleagues and the public, than in the decisions themselves.[22]

Another aspect of this cohort of biographies is the privileging of the role of emotion, or what Bernard Hibbitts terms in his preface to the Le Dain volume, the "'humanity of judging,' relating the function and role of the judge to his or her status and standing as a human being."[23] This, in a profession traditionally devoted to the suppression and abstraction of human emotion rather than its embrace, is particularly striking. The central characters in such biographies are living, breathing human beings with all their foibles and complexities, not just stoic generators of judicial prose or individuals who have climbed the greasy pole of professional status to achieve high judicial office. In part this is because the principal subjects are still alive in many instances; either they have given interviews to their biographers or a wide circle of their acquaintances and colleagues have done so. Only the biographers of Laskin and Marshall in my cohort wrote without personal access to their subjects. Personal correspondence between the subject and others, the traditional privileged source of many biographers, is often not as prominent in these works as in the past. And while such correspondence can provide valuable insights into a subject's character, it can also be distancing compared to the immediacy of personal interviews.

This embrace of judicial humanity can be seen especially in the ways these "outsider" judges were treated by their judicial colleagues and in the media. They were often given a chilly reception that was hurtful, if not downright painful. They were often assumed to have been appointed to satisfy a political agenda, which in some cases they were, rather than because of their qualifications (or in addition to their qualifications). Hence an aura of "not being good enough" hung over them in the eyes of their colleagues, was furthered by the media, and in some cases may have affected their own self-confidence. This was particularly the case with the first women judges. Claire L'Heureux-Dubé told her biographer that she "was received like a dog in a china shop" by her colleagues on the Quebec Superior Court when appointed in 1973.[24] When she had tried to register for law school at Laval University in 1948, the university secretary told her "No, it's only for men," and encouraged her to enroll in social work.[25] A few years later, Bertha Wilson, too, was discouraged by Dean Horace Read from enrolling in Dalhousie law school. Even after she graduated near the top of her class, he advised her not to take up a postgraduate scholarship that she had been offered at Harvard: according to Read, there would never be women legal academics in her lifetime.[26] She opted for articling instead.

A generation after these experiences, things had improved for some women. In 1964 Beverley McLachlin, encouraged by her future husband to think about studying law, found an acceptance letter in her mailbox four days after writing Dean Wilbur Bowker of the University of Alberta Faculty of Law merely asking for information about law school. Later, her desire to try her hand at full-time law teaching was supported by her Vancouver law firm. She was hired without controversy on a tenure-track position at the University of British Columbia Faculty of Law in 1974, although she was given "a host of subjects that no one else wanted to teach."[27]

In some instances, the process of a judge's othering was more multifaceted. Judges on the Ontario Court of Appeal were deeply suspicious of their new colleague Bora Laskin when he was appointed in 1965, the first Jew and the first academic appointed to that court. While it may be difficult to disentangle these two sources of discontent with him, the one vocalized by his new colleagues related to his previous career. They felt that academics were too soft and fuzzy-minded and would not be able to stand the pace of work. Like women and minorities in other workplaces, Laskin had to work twice as hard as everyone else to prove himself, which he eventually did.[28]

In other cases, matters did not improve over time. Michael Kirby's general approach to law was considered unsound by most of his colleagues, even though his biographer argues that he was stereotyped as a judicial activist when this was far from his own self-image and from his conservative views on many legal matters. The negative view of him held by his colleagues was probably reinforced by his homosexuality. His rate of dissent reached 48 per cent in 2006, and his judicial colleagues, even if they themselves dissented, virtually never joined in an opinion authored by Kirby.[29] In 2002, when he was wrongfully accused by a senator of using government cars to ferry young men to and from his house for sexual purposes – the documents relied upon were soon shown to be forgeries – only one of his colleagues, Mary Gaudron, supported him and the chief justice did nothing.[30] Similarly, when Claire L'Heureux-Dubé was attacked in a national newspaper by an appeal court judge whose reasons she had criticized in a controversial sexual assault case, Chief Justice Lamer did not come to her aid and she felt a "lack of support from her fellow justices."[31] When Kirby retired in 2009 after twenty-three years on the court, only two of his six judicial colleagues came to the retirement event he himself had organized (the court's tradition was to organize such events only for a retiring chief justice). By contrast, in spite of her semi-outsider status on the Supreme Court of Canada, Claire L'Heureux-Dubé was treated to a "cascade of Claire-fests" on her retirement in 2002, in the words of Chief Justice Beverley McLachlin.[32] Thus, it seems that the members of some apex courts can agree to disagree on important matters but still display mutual respect and some sense of cohesion, while others possess a more individualistic sense of the judicial office.

The commonalities of the life stories of this cohort of judges have suggested a new form of life writing: the joint biography. This form is not entirely new: in *The Warrior and the Priest* John Milton Cooper Jr compared and contrasted the lives of Theodore Roosevelt and

Woodrow Wilson, while more recently Doris Kearns Goodwin used the form to study William Howard Taft and Theodore Roosevelt.[33] Linda Hirshman followed suit in 2015 with *Sisters in Law: How Sandra Day O'Connor and Ruth Bader Ginsburg went to the Supreme Court and Changed the World*.[34] Constance Backhouse employed the same format in her 2019 book, the more modestly titled *Two Firsts: Bertha Wilson and Claire L'Heureux-Dubé at the Supreme Court of Canada*.[35]

Although identical in form, the latter two books are quite different in their focus. Hirshman spends about 40 per cent of the book reviewing the lead-up to her subjects' US Supreme Court appointments, and then about 60 per cent comparing and contrasting their major decisions, mainly in the field of women's rights. Backhouse is much more interested in the lived experience of her subjects and allots only one chapter to each of her judge's decisions while on the Supreme Court of Canada. *Sisters in Law* is principally biography as intellectual legal history, written for an American audience assumed to be familiar with the US Supreme Court's jurisprudence on a variety of topics, while *Two Firsts* has a broader, more socio-cultural focus. Backhouse is more interested in the making of her subjects' careers, in the barriers Wilson and L'Heureux-Dubé faced and how they were overcome, in the evolution of legal and judicial culture, and in the complicated ways in which these two women engaged, or not, with feminism, though *Sisters in Law* also engages with the latter theme to some extent.

These two books only begin to explore the potential of joint judicial biography. There is no reason that the genre should be confined to figures from one country, though it is probably true that it works best with individuals who are contemporaries, broadly speaking. Comparing the lives of judges of different national backgrounds would be a new way to explore comparative legal culture. Take Michael Kirby and Claire L'Heureux-Dubé, for example. Born in 1939 and 1927 respectively, they both enjoyed long judicial careers as trial, appellate and supreme court judges, and were actively involved in law reform, seen as legal iconoclasts, and were very widely known in international legal circles; L'Heureux-Dubé in fact succeeded Kirby as president of the International Commission of Jurists in 1998. A joint biography of them would provide not only a way into comparing Canadian and Australian legal culture, but a way of studying the growing internationalization of the judiciary.

Given the historic links between Jewish and Black lawyers in North America, a joint biography of Thurgood Marshall, named the first Black judge on the US Supreme Court in 1967 and Bora Laskin, named the first Jewish judge on the Supreme Court of Canada in 1970, would be intriguing. Although both were involved with the cause of civil rights, their modes of engagement were almost completely opposite, with Marshall nationally known for his role on the NAACP while Laskin's work on behalf of the Jewish community was almost entirely behind the scenes.

Or, consider the parallels between the lives of Claire L'Heureux-Dubé and Sonia Sotomayor.[36] Both were products of a devout Catholic childhood with most of their education provided by nuns. Moreover, the close-knit communal life experienced by L'Heureux-Dubé in the town of Rimouski was not as different as might be expected from Sotomayor's Puerto Rican neighbourhood in the Bronx, which she described as a village far removed from big-city life in Manhattan.[37] Whereas it was her gender that made L'Heureux-Dubé an outsider on the courts in her home province, however, Sotomayor's Latina heritage, more than her gender, was the main reason many believed she was not up to the job when she was named to the bench.

I have no illusions that a spate of such cross-national judicial biographies will be forthcoming any time soon. National conventions and preoccupations with respect to legal biography are too well entrenched. Yet it is well worth considering what intellectual rewards could be harvested from the writing of such works. This call to action also provides a convenient lead-in to my second theme, which is the growing international dimension to judicial life and work.

A MORE INTERNATIONALLY CONNECTED BENCH

At one time, international gatherings of judges were decorative affairs, usually spurred by some anniversary or important commemoration in the host country, with the presence of foreign judges lending an air of legitimacy and gravitas to the occasion. Thus, when Harvard University celebrated its tercentenary in 1936, the law school held a Conference on the Future of the Common Law at which jurists from Britain, Canada, and the Irish Free State joined their American colleagues for three days of leisurely discussion and lunch al fresco on the Harvard lawns.[38] When the Supreme Court of Canada observed its centenary in 1975, a symposium on "The Role and Functions of Final Appellate Courts" featured just three speakers, the Lord Chancellor of the United Kingdom, the president of the French Cour de cassation, and Associate Justice Byron White of the US Supreme Court.[39] At these gatherings judges typically said something about their home tradition, people applauded politely, and everyone went home after some nice dinners.

Several events in the 1990s made that decade a turning point with regard to such judicial gatherings. The most important was the fall of the Berlin Wall and the consequent dismantling of the Warsaw Pact. All of a sudden, many emerging democracies were putting together new constitutions and trying to establish independent judiciaries. Who better to ask about the latter than judges from countries with well-established independent judiciaries? The end of apartheid in South Africa and its constitutional and judicial reforms also sparked worldwide interest. At the same time the number of women judges around the world reached a critical mass and sparked the creation of the International Association of Women Judges in 1991.[40] This organization engages in judicial and public education on the topic of women's rights around the world; some of its meetings have drawn as many as four thousand members from one hundred nations.[41] The 1990s also saw the beginnings of social context education for judges in Canada and elsewhere, albeit not without controversy. Initially, many judges, including the Chief Justice of Canada, feared that any such education would become "a vehicle for indoctrination."[42] Canada's National Judicial Institute (NJI) began a study of social context education in 1994 but did not begin offering programs until 1998.[43] Ironically, the social context education that got off to such a rocky start in Canada became very popular in the Global South, particularly with regard to issues of gender justice. Naina Kapur, who had been raised in Canada but chose to practise law in India, her parents' home, found that the problem there was not with the law as such but with the discriminatory attitudes of male judges. She went to the Chief Justice of India, Aziz Mushabber Ahmadi, and obtained his support for judicial training. The two of them decided to expand the initiative to neighbouring countries in South Asia, and to invite Michael Kirby of Australia, Albie Sachs of South Africa, and Claire L'Heureux-Dubé and Douglas Campbell of Canada. The inaugural meeting in 1997 assembled twenty-six judges and twelve representatives of feminist NGOs from India, Sri Lanka, Bangladesh, Nepal, and Pakistan, and the program continued for ten years. "The participants visited courts, women's shelters, sexual assault centres, juvenile detention homes, and prisons," providing them with sometimes shattering experiences and causing them to rethink some of their attitudes and assumptions.[44]

Claire L'Heureux-Dubé became a superstar at these meetings, and the range of countries who sought her out in connection with their democratic, legal, or judicial reforms expanded exponentially. By the time of her retirement in 2002 she had delivered 240 speeches in at least thirty countries from Argentina to Zimbabwe. Her presence spread the reputation of the Supreme Court of Canada and particularly its jurisprudence on equality far and wide, as she became one of the best-known participants in the "international epistemic community" of cosmopolitan jurists noted earlier. Although her biographer argues that she was not particularly good on race issues in her Canadian jurisprudence, this did not seem to hamper her reception in cross-cultural settings in the Global South. Observers attributed this to her never standing on ceremony or demanding the privileges of a Supreme Court justice; she would travel in jam-packed Indian trains, visit Palestinian prisons, and accept without complaint whatever accommodation was available. She could instantly develop a rapport with anyone, no matter what their background or station in life. As someone who had been an outsider for so much of her life, even at the Supreme Court, L'Heureux-Dubé had developed the skill of putting people at their ease immediately. This personal rapport went a long way in getting her message on gender equality accepted by those who might have been otherwise unreceptive.[45]

In these international settings, L'Heureux-Dubé was also prepared to go much further in identifying her own experiences with sex discrimination than she had been at home. In Canada she was a highly reluctant feminist icon, always distancing herself from the label. Abroad, in her later years as a judge and in retirement, she was prepared to embrace it. Bertha Wilson, too, in retirement became more overtly involved with gender and Indigenous issues than she had ever been before.

Mary Gaudron too was able to move to the international sphere after her retirement from the High Court of Australia. Just months after her retirement in 2003 she was named to the International

Labour Organization's Administrative Tribunal in Geneva, later serving as its president from 2011 to 2014. The tribunal decides upon complaints from those employed by the ILO itself and by a number of other international organizations that recognize its jurisdiction. She was also appointed by Kofi Annan to a panel tasked with reviewing the dispute resolution system of the United Nations system, which reported in 2006. While not as impactful or high-profile as addressing global chief justices on gender equality, these tasks allowed Gaudron to continue to contribute to her chosen fields, labour law and anti-discrimination law. Her greatest contribution to global jurisprudence, however, will always be the decision she co-wrote with Justice Deane in the *Mabo* case on Indigenous rights in Australia, a case that has joined others in settler societies around the world in attempting to right historic wrongs against Indigenous peoples.[46]

Of all the judges in my cohort, Michael Kirby is the one who most consistently engaged with the international sphere at both the personal and ideational level. By the time he was named to the High Court of Australia in 1996, he had served on committees of the United Nations, the United Nations Educational, Scientific and Cultural Organization, the World Health Organization, and the Organization for Economic Cooperation and Development, he was already "a world figure in the fight against HIV/AIDS," and his international engagements only multiplied thereafter.[47] Kirby often cited the decisions of other national courts but it was, according to his biographer, at the Bangalore Judicial Colloquium of 1988 convened by the former Chief Justice of India, P.N. Bhagwati, that he had his Damascene moment with regard to international law. There he became fully converted to the idea that international human rights law, even when not formally incorporated into domestic law, could be used to interpret and develop national law, including constitutional law. It was in Bangalore, in the course of discussions with senior judges from South Asia and Africa, that Kirby realized they were already taking the law in this direction, and that he had much to learn from them, rather than the other way round.[48] It was on this same occasion that Michael Kirby and Ruth Bader Ginsburg met for the first time, the origin of their decades-long friendship.

In spite of considerable resistance from his colleagues, Kirby began to use the *International Covenant on Civil and Political Rights*, the *European Convention on Human Rights*, and other international instruments liberally in his decisions. His approach finally bore fruit in a 2007 case in which federal Australian legislation depriving all prisoners of the right to vote was challenged. In *Roach v. Electoral Commissioner*, all seven judges referred to the *European Convention on Human Rights* and to Canadian Supreme Court authority in holding the legislation invalid.[49]

CONCLUSION

If there is one factor that characterizes biographies of what we might call the "diversity cohort" of judges, it is the emphasis on their subjects' humanity. This of course should always be at the core of life writing, but in legal biography, and particularly in judicial biography, this has not always been the case. In the common law tradition, the idea that a judge's personal predilections should not influence his or her decision-making remained strong, and tended to drive a wedge between the life and the work instead of uniting them.[50] Indeed, there has been no shortage of voices claiming that diversity candidates had to leave their gender or race at the door when they crossed the judicial threshold – including at the Supreme Court of Canada itself.[51] But the turn to the ideal of a more responsive and representative judiciary undermined that traditional idea. Why appoint a Black judge, for example, if not to bring something of the Black experience into the interpretation and application of the law? How those early appointees navigated their entry into all-male, all-white, all-fill-in-the-blank institutions is a subject of absorbing human interest as well as legal significance.

My second theme, that of "judges on the move," is meant to highlight an underrecognized dimension of judicial life. It is too early to offer any definitive interpretation of its consequences, given the recency of this development, but I offer some suggestions. Judges are expositors of national law, and their biographers have not traditionally been interested in their transnational connections. Given the long resistance to foreign authority in the US Supreme Court, biographers of its judges have been particularly insular in this regard. Yet the evidence culled from the biographies of judges in my cohort demonstrates that personal connections between judges of different countries are on the rise, and that the intellectual consequences of these connections are not just one-way, from jurisdictions of the developed North to those of the Global South, but rather are multidirectional. Those who wish to trace the emergence of global trends in jurisprudence would do well to keep in mind the circulation of persons as well as ideas in the formation of these trends. And in this effort, judicial biography will be a crucial resource.

NOTES

I thank Victoria Barnes of the Max Planck Institute for inviting me to present an earlier version of this paper at a workshop on Legal Biography in Frankfurt in July 2019, and I thank the participants for their comments. I also thank Anisha Nag for her research assistance.

1 G. Blaine Baker, "Testamentary Archeology in Late-Victorian Ontario: William Martin's Little, Posthumous Legal System," *Canadian Journal of Law and Society* 30, no. 3 (2015): 345–64.

2 G. Blaine Baker and Richard Janda, eds., *Tracings of Gerald Le Dain's Life in the Law* (Montreal and Kingston: McGill-Queen's University Press, 2019).

3 E.g., G. Blaine Baker, "Notes on the Migration of Upper Canada's Law Libraries," *Law Society of Upper Canada Gazette* 14 (1980): 362–5.

4 Baker and Janda, *Tracings*, 7. For an argument that legal biography makes an essential contribution to legal historical scholarship, see David Sugarman, "From Legal Biography to Legal Life Writing: Broadening Conceptions of Legal History and Socio-legal Scholarship," *Journal of Law and Society* 42, no. 1 (2015): 7–33.

5 Cited in A.J. Brown, *Michael Kirby: Paradoxes and Principles* (Annandale, NSW: Federation Press, 2011), 397.

6 Biographical information on Kirby is derived from Brown, *Michael Kirby*. For Ginsburg, see Linda Hirshman, *Sisters in Law: How Sandra Day O'Connor and Ruth Bader Ginsburg Went to the Supreme Court and Changed the World* (New York: Harper Collins, 2015).

7 Ellen Anderson, *Bertha Wilson: Law as Large as Life* (Toronto: University of Toronto Press for the Osgoode Society for Canadian Legal History, 2001); Constance Backhouse, *Claire L'Heureux-Dubé: A Life* (Vancouver: UBC Press for the Osgoode Society for Canadian Legal History, 2017); Constance Backhouse, *Two Firsts: Bertha Wilson and Claire L'Heureux-Dubé at the Supreme Court of Canada* (Toronto: Second Story Press, 2019); among several biographies of Sandra Day O'Connor, those referred to here will be Evan Thomas, *First: Sandra Day O'Connor* (New York: Random House, 2019) and Hirshman, *Sisters in Law*; Pamela Burton, *From Moree to Mabo: the Mary Gaudron Story*

(Crawley, W.A.: UWA Publishing, 2010); Michael D. Davis and Hunter R. Clark, *Thurgood Marshall, Warrior at the Bar, Rebel on the Bench* (New York: Carol Publishing, 1994); Juan Williams, *Thurgood Marshall, American Revolutionary* (New York: Times Books, 1998); Ken Foskett, *Judging Thomas: The Life and Times of Clarence Thomas* (New York: Morrow, 2004); Andrew Peyton Thomas, *Clarence Thomas: A Biography* (San Francisco: Encounter Books, 2001); Philip Girard, *Bora Laskin: Bringing Law to Life* (Toronto: University of Toronto Press for the Osgoode Society for Canadian Legal History, 2005). There is no biography of the recently retired Beverley McLachlin, but her memoir *Truth Be Told: My Journey Through Life and the Law* (New York and Toronto: Simon & Schuster, 2019) will be referred to. Sonia Sotomayor has published a memoir, which stops with her appointment to the US Supreme Court: *My Beloved World* (New York: Knopf, 2013); and there are several biographies, including Antonia Felix, *Sonia Sotomayor: The True American Dream* (New York: Berkley Books, 2010), published soon after her appointment to the Court; and Joan Biskupic, *Breaking In: The Rise of Sonia Sotomayor and the Politics of Justice* (New York: Farrar, Straus and Giroux, 2014).

8 Ran Hirschl, *Comparative Matters: The Renaissance of Comparative Constitutional Law* (Oxford: Oxford University Press, 2014), 20. See also Christopher McCrudden, "A Common Law of Human Rights: Transnational Judicial Conversations on Constitutional Rights," *Oxford Journal of Legal Studies* 20, no. 4 (2000): 499–532; I thank David Sugarman for the latter reference.

9 Hirschl, *Comparative Matters*, 21.

10 Philip Girard, "Judging Lives: Judicial Biography from Hale to Holmes," *Australian Journal of Legal History* 7, no. 1 (2003): 87–106. The role of individual judges in civil law and other legal traditions is less prominent than in the common law, such that judicial biography is a less prominent genre in those jurisdictions.

11 For overviews of the development of legal realism, see Laura Kalman, *Legal Realism at Yale, 1927–1960* (Chapel Hill, NC: University of North Carolina Press, 1986); Justin Zaremby, *Legal Realism and American Law* (New York: Bloomsbury Academic, 2014). On its reception in Canada, see R.C.B. Risk, "Canadian Law Teachers in the 1930s: 'When the World Was Turned Upside Down,'" *Dalhousie Law Journal* 27, no. 1 (2004): 1–54.

12 *Osgoode Hall Law Journal* 28, no. 3 (1990): 507–22.

13 Ibid., 515.

14 Girard, *Bora Laskin*, 539–42; on Kirby, see below, text accompanying note 49.
15 Foskett, *Judging Thomas*, 256, 260.
16 Richard Posner, "Judicial Biography," *New York University Law Review* 70, no. 3 (1995): 502, 512.
17 Michael Rosenthal, "The High Priestess of Bloomsbury," *The New York Times Book Review* (5 November 1972): 1.
18 Quentin Bell, *Virginia Woolf: A Biography* (New York: Harcourt Brace Jovanovich, 1972).
19 Backhouse, *Claire L'Heureux-Dubé*, chapters 20, 23, 29–32, 34–5.
20 Burton, *Mary Gaudron Story*.
21 Girard, *Bora Laskin*.
22 Brown, *Michael Kirby*.
23 Baker and Janda, eds., *Tracings*, x. The discussion of Le Dain's humanity is inevitably tied to the diagnosis of clinical depression in 1988 that led to his resignation from the Court. The recent episode in which Justice Clément Gascon of the Supreme Court of Canada went missing briefly and later revealed he had long suffered from depression and anxiety, also highlights the issue of mental health and judging ("Clement Gascon, High Court Justice Who Went Missing, Says He Had a Panic Attack," *National Post*, 14 May 2019). Nor is this a new theme. Chief Justice of Upper Canada John Beverley Robinson (1791–1863) also suffered from depression (Patrick Brode, *John Beverley Robinson: Bone and Sinew of the Compact* (Toronto: Osgoode Society for Canadian Legal History, 1984)), as did Chief Justice Edward Jarvis of Prince Edward Island (1788–1852) (personal information from Anna Jarvis, currently writing a biography of Jarvis). The mental strain imposed by the demands of judicial office is a topic that deserves more research, both contemporary and historical.
24 Backhouse, *Claire L'Heureux-Dubé*, 231.
25 Ibid., 103.
26 Anderson, *Bertha Wilson*, 48. Harvard Law had begun to accept women students only in 1950.
27 McLachlin, *Truth Be Told*, 100, 147. It should be noted that these subjects were not the obviously gendered ones such as family law.
28 Girard, *Bora Laskin*, 339–41.
29 Brown, *Michael Kirby*, 399.
30 Ibid., chap. 15. The senator made his remarks in the legislature, where he was protected from libel actions by parliamentary privilege.
31 Backhouse, *Claire L'Heureux-Dubé*, 491.
32 Ibid., 524.

33 Doris Kearns Goodwin, *The Bully Pulpit: Theodore Roosevelt, William Howard Taft, and the Golden Age of Journalism* (New York: Simon & Schuster, 2013).
34 Hirshman, *Sisters in Law*.
35 Backhouse, *Two Firsts*.
36 I thank Constance Backhouse for making this suggestion.
37 Sotomayor, *My Beloved World*, 11–12, 116.
38 Girard, *Bora Laskin*, 84–5. The papers were published as Roscoe Pound, ed., *The Future of the Common Law* (Cambridge, MA: Harvard University Press, 1937).
39 Girard, *Bora Laskin*, 429–30.
40 www.iawj.org.
41 Backhouse, *Claire L'Heureux-Dubé*, 515.
42 Ibid., 507.
43 Ibid., 507–9. Some provincial courts had moved ahead of the NJI; in British Columbia, training on gender, race, and Indigenous issues had been offered since 1988.
44 Ibid., 511.
45 Ibid., 517–18.
46 Burton, *Mary Gaudron Story*, 275–90.
47 Brown, *Michael Kirby*, 225.
48 Ibid., 223.
49 Ibid., 397–8.
50 For examples, see Girard, "From Hale to Holmes."
51 Various views on whether a racialized judge could or should rely on her own life experience in interpreting the events before her were expressed in the Supreme Court of Canada's decision in *R. v. RDS*, [1997] 3 SCR 484, in which the decision of a Black Nova Scotia judge, Corinne Sparks, had been impugned on the ground of alleged racial (anti-white) bias. The two female justices on the Court at the time, Justices McLachlin and L'Heureux-Dubé, were the most receptive to the idea that Judge Sparks could rely on such experience, while the male judges were split, with some only reluctantly in favour of the idea, and others downright hostile. This issue will be explored more fully in the forthcoming book devoted to the case, by Professor Constance Backhouse.

I was never a student of Blaine Baker's in a formal sense, but like everybody who has read, written about, and taught Canadian legal history, I learned an immense amount about the subject from him over the last thirty-plus years. Blaine's writings were always in equal measure deeply researched, highly imaginative, and beautifully written. As importantly, Blaine was a highly dedicated mentor, always willing to devote large amounts of his time to discussing the work of others and sharing his immense knowledge of all genres of Canadian history and Anglo-American legal history. At times Blaine seemed to know not only what had happened in the past, and why, but also the people, or some current day relative of them, who made the world we live in today. Scholarship and teaching were his life, and he imbued both with his eclectic personality and rambunctious humour. His trademark was perhaps his late evening phone calls, which started with "What am I interrupting?" continued through "What are you doing?" and always ended with "Is there anything I can do for you?" Not getting those phone calls has left a gap in my life, only partly compensated by having his remarkably rich vein of scholarship to read and re-read. I know he would have liked the topic I have chosen for this collection, which stresses the continuity of legal and political ideas between the Canadas of the pre-1867 world and the Canada forged by Confederation. I also know that had he still been with us it would be a better essay for his comments.

Jim Phillips

8

The Colonial Origins of the Division of Powers in the *British North America Act*

Jim Phillips and Tom Collins

INTRODUCTION

The origin of the precise division of powers in sections 91 and 92 of the *British North America Act* (BNA *Act*) is a subject to which historians have paid scant attention. Political historians of Confederation have always been more interested in how and why various colonies decided to unite (or not to unite) in 1867.[1] Lawyers and legal historians have been primarily concerned with what the various heads of legislative power were considered to include in 1867 and, more importantly, with what they came to include in the decades following 1867 as a result of judicial decisions.[2] When the general structure of the BNA *Act*, and the content of sections 91 and 92, has been discussed, the focus has been on the felt need to construct a centralist constitution, one in which residual power was given to the central government. A deliberate choice was made to reject the American model, in which central government powers were specifically enumerated and limited and all residual powers were given to the states.

This paper is a modest contribution to the literature on Confederation, and argues that the choice of which subjects to put into sections 91 and 92 of the BNA *Act* was substantially influenced by a functional division of powers that had emerged in the Province of Canada [hereafter Canada] after the 1840 *Act of Union*. We think Blaine Baker would have been pleased to see an essay about the politics of the Union period, a quarter century of Canadian history which he wrote about on many occasions. While Canada was a legislative union, with one legislative body replacing the two assemblies of Upper and Lower Canada, and in no formal sense a federation, the Canada legislature functioned to some degree to create a de facto federal polity, with the law in some areas being different as between the two sections. From the outset the Canada assembly passed some legislation applicable only to one of the two Canadas, and some legislation applicable to both. This was one aspect of the almost immediate failure of the assimilationist vision that lay behind the *Act of Union* and its consequence, what one historian has labelled administrative "dualism."[3] By the later 1850s, when the Canada assembly embarked on a revision and consolidation of its statutes, this distinction between legislation applicable to just one section and legislation applicable to the whole colony was a sufficiently firmly established feature of how the Union worked that the consolidated statutes were organized and published in three volumes reflecting a distinction between general and sectional legislation. The first consolidation to be completed was *The Public General Statutes Which Apply Exclusively to Upper Canada as Revised by the Commissioners Appointed for That Part of the Province.* The following year this was superseded by *The Consolidated Statutes for Upper Canada* [hereafter CSUC], and *The Consolidated Statutes of Canada Being the Public General Statutes Which Apply to the Whole Province, as Revised and Consolidated by the Commissioners Appointed for That Purpose* [hereafter CS *Canada*]. In 1861 the consolidation process was completed by the publication of *The Consolidated Statutes for Lower Canada, Proclaimed and Published under the Authority of the Act 23 Vict. Cap 56, 1860* [hereafter CSLC].[4]

Close examination of the different subject matters in the various consolidations of 1859 and 1861 reveals that at the very least there was a striking similarity between the allocation of subjects among those consolidations and sections 91 and 92 of the BNA *Act.* This paper therefore supports what David Mills, the one-time minister of Justice, senator, and puisne justice on the Supreme Court of Canada, stated in 1897, that "[t]he experience acquired during the continuance of the Legislative Union [of the Province of Canada] assisted the framers of the present Constitution in drawing the line between matters of provincial and of national concern."[5] This paper is divided into five further sections. In the first, we provide an analysis of Canada's legislation from 1841 onwards, looking at the evolution of the practice of passing some legislation applicable to the colony as a whole and some pertaining to just one of the two sections, Canada East and Canada West, referred to here by the names that most contemporaries used throughout the Union period, Upper and Lower Canada. The second section briefly examines the statutory consolidation process of 1859–1861. In the third section we compare the 1859 CS *Canada* and section 91 to establish the extent of similarity between the two, and also does the same for CSUC and CSLC and section 92. The fourth section offers an explanation of why there were such substantial similarities between the consolidations and sections 91 and 92. The final section examines the major areas where the consolidated statutes differed from the BNA *Act*.

PROVINCE OF CANADA LEGISLATIVE PRACTICE: A FUNCTIONAL DIVISION OF POWERS

From its first legislative session the Province of Canada assembly passed some legislation applicable only to one of the colony's sections. Of the forty-five statutes of 1841 that enacted substantive law or dealt with some aspect of the judicial system, twelve applied only to the former Upper Canada, five to the former Lower Canada, and twenty-eight to the colony as a whole.[6] The last included a general *Naturalisation Act* (c. 7), qualifications to practise medicine (c. 41), currency regulation (c. 93), and six statutes harmonizing the criminal law (c. 17, 24–7, and 69). The Upper Canadian statutes included three on the court system (c. 3, 5, and 8) and others relating to local government (c. 10), school lands (c. 19), and insurance companies (c. 64). Lower Canadian insurance companies had their own legislation (c. 40), and other statutes dealt with roads (c. 30), and the court system (c. 20). The titles of statutes that applied only to one section generally contained the phrase "that part of this province formerly constituting [or "heretofore"] the Province of Upper or Lower Canada," or some such variant.[7] A similar story could be told of every subsequent legislative session to 1848.

From 1849 the practice of legislating differently for each section was formalized in the arrangement of the annual statute book. Henceforth the contents pages no longer simply listed statutes by chapter number, but also grouped them by categories. In 1849 the assembly passed ninety-two "public" statutes. Chapters 1 through 36 were listed as "Public General Acts Extending to the Whole Province," chapters 37 through 62 (26 statutes) were listed under

"Public General Acts Relating to Lower Canada," and chapters 63 to 92 (thirty statutes) were "Public General Acts Relating to Upper Canada."[8] Thus, only a little over a third of the legislation named "Public General Acts" was for the whole colony, a third was for Upper Canada, and the remainder was for Lower Canada. The year 1849 was also significant because the *Interpretation Act* of that year decreed that, henceforth, statutes applicable only to one section would use the pre-Union names of Upper and Lower Canada.[9] Accordingly, chapter 38 was titled *An Act to amend the Laws relative to the Courts of Original Civil Jurisdiction in Lower Canada*, not "that part of this province formerly known as Lower Canada."

This statutory nomenclature was an acknowledgment that the Union was one in which each section effectively had its own laws in relation to particular subject matters. We are not suggesting in any sense that the Union was a federal one, for the two sections of Upper and Lower Canada did not have their own legislatures. The Province of Canada was a legislative union, not a federation, and it was never the case that assembly members from one section only could legislate for that section. We are rather describing a functional, de facto division of powers, not a de jure one. This functional division was also present in the government departments and colonial civil service, for many departments had separate officials for each section, such as the attorney general, the crown lands department, and a number of others.[10]

To demonstrate this point about the statutes we will not review all subject matters, but will content ourselves with highlighting some major areas. Among the subjects legislated for the whole colony, in 1841, was the criminal law applicable to serious offences such as robbery, burglary, rape, and the like. Before the Union the two colonies had different criminal laws. Both had received English criminal law, albeit as of different reception dates, 1760 and 1792 in Lower and Upper Canada respectively. In 1833 Upper Canada's criminal law was made substantially different from the inherited English law. Lower Canada's criminal law, on the other hand, had never been subject to wholesale reform. That the Canadas had slightly different criminal laws before the Union was not remarkable; they differed from each other in this respect just as the criminal law in Nova Scotia differed from that of New Brunswick. In every case the content of a colony's criminal law depended on a combination of the reception date and the content of local legislation. Following this, the Union legislators thought it self-evident that the criminal law prescribing definitions of and punishment for the more serious offences should be the same in both sections, and consequently three major statutes of 1841 consolidated the law relating to offences against the person and property.[11] Conversely, before the Union, Upper and Lower Canada had distinctive court systems and, from the outset, all legislation that pertained to the structure, organisation and procedure in the courts dealt with one section only.[12]

Contemporaries naturally were well aware of how the Union assembly operated. John A. Macdonald, speaking in the assembly in February 1865, noted that:

> We, in Canada, already know something of the advantages and disadvantages of a federal union. Although we have nominally a legislative union in Canada – although we sit in one Parliament, supposed constitutionally to represent the people without regard to sections or localities, yet we know, as a matter of fact, that since the Union in 1841 we have had a federal union; that in matters affecting Upper Canada solely, members from that section claimed and generally exercised the right of exclusive legislation, while members from Lower Canada legislated in matters affecting only their own section. We have had a federal union in fact, though a legislative union in name.[13]

This quotation implies that not only did the Province of Canada assembly often legislate separately for each section, but that when it did so only members from the section affected took part in the debates and votes. Whether Macdonald meant to imply that is unclear, but in fact that was not the case. A sampling of the sectional bills passed by the assembly shows that members from both sections voted, and that there was no particular pattern discernible as to how they voted.[14] In fact one would not have expected otherwise, because of the double-majority convention, a tacit understanding, never a formal rule, that legislation affecting both parts of the colony should have the support of a majority of members from each section.[15] The effective division of powers worked out through the 1840s and 1850s was most manifest when the Province of Canada passed and published comprehensive consolidations of its statute law in 1859 and 1861. It is to those consolidations that we now turn.

THE CONSOLIDATIONS OF 1859 AND 1861

The statutory consolidations of 1859 and 1861 were but one set of many such consolidations enacted in British North America in the pre-Confederation period.[16] The earliest tended to do no more than collect all extant statutes in one volume, and arrange them chronologically by the year in which they were originally passed; later ones tended to organize the statutes thematically. The *Revised Statutes* of Nova Scotia (1851) and of New Brunswick (1854) had, in addition, the larger ambition of reforming the law through codification – altering the content of some statutes, modernising their language, and so on.[17] Canada consolidated its statutes in 1843 (Upper Canada) and 1845 (Lower Canada).[18] The former was a modest exercise, largely designed to produce a useful collection by omitting all repealed statutes or sections of statutes. The latter was more ambitious, organizing the statutes into ten categories, which were called classes, rather than listing them by year of initial passage. But the very fact that the statutes were consolidated by section shows that a de facto federalisation existed.

The next major consolidation of the Canada statutes began in 1856, with two sets of commissioners appointed, one for Upper and one for Lower Canada.[19] The former was initially comprised of six, largely elite, lawyers;[20] the latter also numbered six, somewhat less prominent and successful men.[21] The commissioners devised jointly a plan to first work on the Upper and Lower Canadian consolidations, and then to compile the province-wide consolidation. They defined their task as not being to reform the law, but to "classify and arrange" the statutes in the manner they thought best, generally "retaining the language of the enactments as they now stand." Somewhat inconsistently they also purported to be able to "abbreviate and improve the language," although changes in wording must not "change the law." Substantive reform was something they could only recommend; they were to suggest "such amendments of the law as ... they may find necessary or desirable."[22]

The Upper Canadians worked more quickly that their Lower Canadian counterparts, publishing a consolidation in 1858, which was really only a draft. It comprised 133 statutes, but the statutes themselves were simply numbered consecutively, not divided into categories. An amended consolidation, with five fewer statutes (128) differently arranged and divided into thirteen categories, called Titles, was published in 1859. Also published in 1859 was CS *Canada*, 111 statutes organized into eleven titles. In 1861, the Lower Canadian consolidation was published, with 111 statutes under twelve titles.[23] The reports cited above make it clear that a number of the commissioners for both sections worked on the projects for a fairly short time, and that most of the Lower Canada work was done by Gustavus William Wicksteed, law clerk to the assembly, which may explain why its publication was delayed. Much credit for the CS *Canada* and CSUC consolidations was given by Macaulay to prolific legal author James Gowan, the county court judge for Simcoe County, who may not have been a commissioner but who was drafted by Macaulay to help.[24] The consolidations excited a very limited interest, partly because elite lawyers took the lead for CS *Canada* and CSUC, partly because Lower Canadians were much more interested in the in-progress new *Civil Code* than in CSLC, and partly because they were unambitious undertakings, consolidation not law reform. But whatever their shortcomings, and however little role they would play in any history of codification, they did show what was sectional and what was the preserve of the colonial state, a schema that would in a few years lay the groundwork for what was national and provincial.

SECTIONS 91 AND 92 AND THE CONSOLIDATIONS

The most significant thing about the 1859 and 1861 consolidations was the congruence between them and sections 91 and 92 of the BNA *Act*. That congruence was not complete, but it was very substantial. We begin with comparing section 91 and CS *Canada*, working from twenty-six of the twenty-nine heads of power because three of the section 91 subsections – 1, 13, and 29 – could have had no counterpart in 1859.[25] Of the twenty-six remaining heads of jurisdiction in section 91, twenty-three were also matters listed, to a greater or less extent, in CS *Canada*: see Table 8.1. That is 88 per cent of section 91. If one uses the inverse calculation, the number of statutes in CS *Canada* that fit into what became section 91, the figure is lower but nonetheless impressive – 74 per cent – because some of the CS *Canada* statutes covered matters included in section 92.[26] For some subjects, only part of what ended up in section 91 was in CS *Canada*. Section 91 (17), for example, gives jurisdiction over all weights and measures, but chapter 53 of CS *Canada* included only "weights and measures – grain, pulse, and seeds." The most significant heads of power in section 91 as of 1867 – trade and commerce and the criminal law – were represented by fifty-one of the 111 statutes in CS *Canada*. CS *Canada* also included major areas of later federal jurisdiction like indirect taxation, the militia and defence, navigation and shipping, banking, interest, and the currency, as well as patents and copyright.

The three subject areas which are in section 91 but not in CS *Canada* were 91 (9) "beacons, buoys, lighthouses, and Sable Island," 91 (21), "bankruptcy and insolvency," and 91 (26), "marriage and divorce." One of these, 91 (9), was partially inapplicable in 1859; navigation generally was in the CSUC but Sable Island, as far as we are aware, was where it currently is and thus not part of the Province of Canada. The two major areas, therefore, where there are differences between CS *Canada* and section 91 are bankruptcy and insolvency and marriage and divorce. The former was included in CSUC and CSLC and not in CS *Canada* because creditors' remedies against insolvent debtors were, in their origin, a matter of civil (as in non-criminal) law and thus treated differently by the civil (as opposed to common) law and the common law. Both Upper and Lower Canada passed a number of statutes before the Union modifying their laws in this area, and after 1841 the practice of legislating for just one section of the province in the debtor-creditor area was continued by the Canada assembly. Only for a brief period, between 1843 and 1849, was bankruptcy, but not insolvency, law the same for both sections.[27] Marriage and divorce were not mentioned in CS *Canada*, but marriage was part of both CSUC and CSLC. Divorce was not part of any of the consolidations. It was entirely unavailable in predominantly Catholic Lower Canada and available only by legislative act, not judicially, in Upper Canada. We will return to a discussion of marriage and divorce in the final section of this paper.

Having established that much of section 91 was in CS *Canada*, it is also necessary to note that some of what was in CS *Canada* was not included in section 91. These subjects fall into two categories. First, some of the statutes in CS *Canada* dealt with subjects that ended up in the BNA *Act* as provincial powers, the most obvious example being education, which was included in some of its aspects in CS *Canada* and in other aspects in CSUC and CSLC.[28] After much going back and forth education was given its own section in the BNA *Act*, section 93, and was not part of section 92 despite being a provincial jurisdiction.[29] Also included in this category are the following titles in *CS Canada*: public lands (chapters 22 and 23), public health (chapters 38 and 39), benevolent associations (chapters 71–73), rectories (chapter 74), the professions (chapters 75–77); private rights and remedies (chapters 79–80); and municipal matters (chapters 82–88). Some of these subject areas are one of the specific heads of power listed in section 92 – public lands,[30] municipal institutions, and charitable and other voluntary associations. Others – the professions, private rights and remedies – are included within one of the section 92 catch-alls: property and civil rights (section 92 (13)) and all matters of a merely local or private nature in the Province of Canada (section 92 (16)). We will return later in this paper to the question of why some subjects in *CS Canada* were allocated to section 92 in the *BNA Act*.

Second, some of the subjects in *CS Canada* were included in the *BNA Act* as concurrent powers. Agriculture, part of CS Canada (chapter 32, "Agriculture and Agricultural Societies") is covered in section 95 of the *BNA Act*, where, along with immigration, it is a concurrent power of both federal and provincial legislatures.[31] Public works, chapter 28 of *CS Canada*, is also in effect a concurrent power. It is not specifically mentioned in section 91, but its definition in section 92 places it in both sections by inference. Section 92 (10) refers to local works and undertakings and then lists exceptions of those that are extraprovincial or intraprovincial but of national importance.

A similar comparison, establishing substantial congruence, can be made between sections 92 and 93 of the *BNA Act* and the other two consolidations of 1859 to 1861, *CSUC* and *CSLC*. The comparisons are laid out in Tables 8.2 and 8.3, which demonstrate that both *CSUC* and *CSLC* were substantially similar to section 92. Section 92 has sixteen subsections which allocate substantive areas of jurisdiction to the provincial governments, of which thirteen are applicable to this analysis.[32] Similarly applicable is section 93, dealing with education. All but one of the fourteen section 92 and 93 heads of power were included in *CSLC* (92 per cent) and all but two were included in *CSUC* (85 per cent). Using the same alternative analysis as above we see that ninety-nine of *CSLC*'s 108 statutes (92 per cent) cover areas coming within sections 92 and 93. The equivalent figure for *CSUC* is 86 per cent.

The most important of section 92's subsections were municipal institutions, incorporation of companies with provincial objects, property and civil rights, the administration of justice in the province, and "all matters of a merely local or private nature in the province." Statutes relating to all of these appear in CSLC, and five of the titles in CSLC have very similar wording to section 92 heads of power – municipal and rural matters, private rights personal, real property and rights, joint stock companies, and administration of justice. Education, as mentioned above, is a provincial power under section 93. Between them, these five section 92 and one section 93 heads cover eighty of the 108 statutes in CSLC. The same section 92 and 93 subject areas dominate CSUC. Titles in the latter include administration of justice (twenty-four statutes), municipal institutions (ten statutes), religious and benevolent institutions (six statutes), domestic relations, rights and remedies (eight statutes), and real estate (fourteen statutes) – a total of sixty-five. To this total must be added twenty-eight of the statutes listed under Title 12, criminal law, in CSUC, which are mostly about criminal procedure, and Title 5, the professions (nine statutes), as well as education (four statutes).

THE CONFEDERATION PROCESS, THE CONSOLIDATIONS, AND THE DIVISION OF POWERS

Explaining why there was such a substantial congruence between the consolidations and sections 91, 92, and 93 requires us to advert to one central aspect of the Confederation process as it played out in the 1860s.[33] Confederation was very much driven by Canada rather than by all British North American colonies. By 1864 the chaotic politics of the Union, discussed below, had resulted in most politicians believing that a legislative union could not be sustained, and that some form of federation, be it a federation between Upper and Lower Canada only,[34] or one involving also the other colonies, was the only alternative. Politicians in the maritime colonies may have talked occasionally at various times about maritime union, but the Maritimes were never impelled by political deadlocks to seek new political arrangements as a matter of urgency. Thus it was an assembly committee in Canada that first seriously advocated a "federative system" in June 1864, and it was in Canada that shortly afterwards the unlikely coalition between the George Brown-led reformers, Macdonald's conservatives, and Cartier's bleus (the Lower Canadian conservatives) was formed, with the object of finding a solution to the political impasse.

It is true that the Charlottetown conference of September 1864 began as a conference about maritime union to which the Canadians were invited at the suggestion of Governor General Monck. But it is equally true, and more significant, that Charlottetown was not a negotiation among the colonies but a presentation to the maritime leaders of a set of proposals worked out shortly before by the Canadian cabinet. In a remarkably short time the Canadians went from thinking about how to federalise their own legislative union to thinking about how to construct a broader federation incorporating the eastern colonies. As Confederation historian Peter Waite long ago confidently asserted, "[t]he division of powers between the central government and the local governments had obviously been well thought out even before the [Charlottetown] conference began."[35] At Charlottetown the Canadians' proposals for a division of powers were presented and broadly accepted. A few weeks later those proposals were fleshed out and became resolutions 29 and 43 of the Quebec conference, which in turn became "with very few changes, the substance of the ... British North America Act."[36] In short, the Canadian delegation made the running in the two major conferences, they drafted specific proposals in a short period of time, and those proposals replicated much of the functional division of powers they had lived with for two decades. Robert Vipond has argued that in the 1860s most politicians were vague about how the local should be distinguished from the general; we suggest that the Canadians did not need to articulate that, they knew it from experience.[37]

The influence of the consolidated statutes can also arguably be seen in the few proposals for a division of powers put forward before the formation of the Macdonald-Brown grand coalition in 1864. The earliest detailed proposal for a division of powers appears in an 1858 letter from George-Étienne Cartier and others to Sir Edward Bulwer-Lytton, the Secretary of State for the Colonies. The Canadians hesitated to be specific about details because they were largely concerned with the general question of whether the federal legislature would have a plenary power. However, they did suggest that the federal Parliament would have power over "customs, excise and all trade questions; postal service, militia, banking, currency, weights and measures, and bankruptcy; public works of national character; harbours and lighthouses; fisheries and their protection; criminal justice; public lands, public debt, and government of unincorporated and Indian territories."[38] Nine years later all of these heads of jurisdiction except for public lands appeared in section 91. As importantly for our purposes, all of the aforementioned subject matter heads were in CS *Canada* except for bankruptcy, harbours, and lighthouses. Cartier et al. could obviously not have drawn directly on CS *Canada*, which had yet to be published. But CS *Canada* merely consolidated the existing statutes, which, as we have argued, represented a functional division of powers established long before 1859.

The leading role played by Canada's ideas at Charlottetown is also evidenced by a non-Canadian observer at the conference, New Brunswick's Lieutenant Governor Arthur Hamilton Gordon, who reported to London afterwards that the delegates had "roughly" agreed to empower the federal government to legislate on trade, currency, banking, general taxation, interest and usury, insolvency and bankruptcy, weights and measures, navigation of rivers and lakes, light houses, sea fisheries, patent and copyright laws, telegraphs, naturalization, marriage and divorce, the postal service, militia and defence, criminal law, and intercolonial works. This list of federal powers is remarkably similar to what made it into section 91. More importantly for our purposes, the list bears a striking resemblance to CS *Canada*. Gordon also reported that the delegates had agreed to entrust the local legislatures with education (with the exception of universities), inland fisheries, public lands, immigration, mines and minerals, prisons, hospitals and charities, agriculture, roads and bridges, registration of titles, and municipalities.[39] These local heads of power largely mirrored section 92, apart from the inclusion in Gordon's list of immigration, which is a concurrent power and contained in section 95 of the BNA *Act*, and drew substantially upon CSUC and CSLC. Thus, again, the Canadian delegates to Charlottetown used their experiences with the Union to structure the division of powers.

The Confederation process also explains why there was so much similarity between section 92 and CSUC and CSLC. As is well known, the political impasse in Canada had a number of constituent parts, institutional, political, and cultural. Central to the institutional problems was the fact that the two sections of the colony had an equal number of seats in the assembly, an arrangement that was very difficult to change because the *Act of Union* 1840 stipulated that a two-thirds majority was required to do so. This arrangement – usually termed sectional equality – worked initially to the benefit of Upper Canada, which at the time of the Union had a population of about 460,000 compared to Lower Canada's 650,000. But by the early 1850s the tables had been turned, with Upper Canada at 950,000 and the lower section at 890,000, and the gap continued to grow thereafter, so that by the early 1860s Lower Canada had almost half a million fewer people than the upper section. The problem of it being possible for one section to impose its will on the other was always mitigated by the "double-majority" convention, as mentioned earlier. Despite such attempts to make the system work, by the late 1850s Upper Canadian reformers, which included the radical Clear Grit party whose members had mostly been absorbed into the Reform coalition, became increasingly resentful at always being out of power because of the coalition of the Upper Canadian conservatives and substantial numbers of members of their francophone equivalents, the bleus. Reformers' response was to become increasingly vociferous in their demands for representation by population in the assembly. Lower Canadians strongly resisted, fearing rule by an anti-Catholic majority.

The political and cultural issues fuelling this institutional crisis were, to put it too crudely and simplistically, the pitting of largely Protestant, economically liberal Upper Canada against a more conservative, Catholic, and economically traditionalist Lower Canada.[40] Two nationalisms conflicted – what might be termed an imperialist Upper Canadian nationalism intent on progress and what they called "improvement," and a Lower Canadian nationalism intent on preserving its religion, language, and laws. Lower Canadian politicians wanted to see a division of powers that gave control over the various elements of their distinctive culture – the civil law, the court system, language, education and, perhaps most of all, religion, to a government they could manage. As George-Étienne Cartier's biographer has aptly put it, Cartier "envisaged his duty as that of protecting Quebec's strong conservative … traditions."[41] Many influential Upper Canadians, notably George Brown, did not value what they saw as a backward culture, but even Brown had come to realise that Quebec francophones would never be assimilated, which had been one of the objects of the *Act of Union*, and a compromise had to be made. Brown made this point very clearly in his reflections on the Quebec conference. He conceded that "[i]n thus defining the functions of the general and local government it will, no doubt, be objected that we have committed certain matters of an important character to the local Bodies which the people of Upper Canada would have been well content to have seen left to the general government." But, he went on to say, "we have given nothing to the local bodies which did not necessarily belong to the localities, except education and the rights of property, and the civil law, which we were compelled to leave to the local governments, in order to afford that protection which the Lower Canadians claim for their language and their laws, and their peculiar institutions."[42] Brown's recollections emphasize one point very clearly – that among the powers accepted as necessarily local were those that gave Lower Canada the power to legislate on the cluster of subjects relating to French-Canadian culture, especially the civil law.

A set of legislative arrangements embodying such a compromise was ready made in the 1860s – the 1861 CSLC. The administration of justice, municipalities, personal rights (including marriage), real property, various statutes relating to religion, the professions, and the educational system were all included in CSLC. And we can draw on a variety of statements made by Lower Canadian francophone politicians to highlight contemporary awareness of the link between CSLC and sections 92 and 93. In the later 1850s Antoine-Aimé Dorion, a leading figure in the Lower Canadian rouge party (the radicals), proposed a federation within Canada as an alternative to the increasing demand by Upper Canadian reformers for representation by population. In 1859 he again called for a "small federation," and on both occasions he listed as necessary powers for the local governments education, the administration of justice, the militia, the laws relating to property, and the police.[43] Most of these subjects were in CSUC or CSLC, either explicitly, or, in the case of the police, implicitly.[44] Dorion was allied with Brown in the 1850s, but was a critic of the Confederation proposals of the 1860s. His reasons for taking that stance were complicated, but they included a concern that Lower Canadian interests would be subsumed in a wider federation, one that included the maritime colonies as well as Upper Canada. In an impassioned speech against Confederation in the legislative council he asserted that "the people of Lower Canada are attached to their institutions in a manner that defies any attempt to change them in that way. They will not change their religious institutions, their laws, or their language for any consideration whatever.... [Y]ou will see the whole people of Lower Canada clinging together to resist, by all legal and constitutional means, such an attempt at wresting from them those institutions that they now enjoy."[45]

THE CONSOLIDATIONS, THE QUEBEC RESOLUTIONS, AND THE *BNA ACT*

The previous sections have established the continuity between the consolidations and the BNA *Act*. In doing so they have also noted some areas of discontinuity. In this final section we examine the latter more closely, and include in our account the Quebec Resolutions of 1864, which Peter Russell argues were, "with very few changes, the substance of the ... British North America Act."[46] There were seventy-two Quebec Resolutions, of which the two that matter to us are resolution 29, which has thirty-seven subsections laying out federal powers, and resolution 43, which has eighteen subsections laying out provincial powers (see Table 8.4). For our purposes what matters is not so much Russell's correct forward looking analysis, but one that also looks backward, comparing the consolidations, the resolutions, and the BNA *Act*. That the Quebec Resolutions replicated much of what was in the consolidated statutes is self-evident, given that they bear considerable similarity to the BNA *Act* which itself was substantially based on the consolidations. We nonetheless note that of the eighteen subsections of section 43, fifteen correspond to titles or statutes, or both, in *CSUC* or *CSLC*, or both. Together, those fifteen subsections cover nearly 90 per cent of *CSUC*'s and *CSLC*'s statutes.[47]

The correspondence is made easy to identify because the Quebec Resolutions usually employ similar language to the consolidations. For example, section 43 (11), municipal institutions, has the same title as chapter 54 of *CSUC* and a similar one to chapter 24 of *CSLC*.[48] In some instances the connection is less obvious and direct, but it requires only minimal imagination to make it. For example, section 43 (13) is "local works," a title that does not appear in either sectional consolidation, whereas chapter 28 of CS *Canada* is entitled "public works" and two other CS *Canada* statutes also dealt with public works.[49] Overall in this area there is substantial continuity between the consolidations and the Quebec Resolutions. *CSLC* chapter 24, *An Act respecting Municipalities and Roads in Lower Canada*, is divided into four parts, the second of which concerned "roads, bridges, and other public works."[50] Section 43 (13) was conceived to encompass a similar scope of subjects as the Lower Canadian statute. When reading *CSLC* and CS *Canada* together, and in conjunction with the Quebec Resolution 29 (8–11) and 43 (13), one finds jurisdiction over public works divided in the same way as in the BNA *Act*.[51]

The same point can be made about subsection 29 of the Quebec Resolutions and CS *Canada*. We have already sketched the congruence between CS *Canada* and the BNA *Act*. Suffice it to add here that thirty-two of section 29's thirty-seven subsections, or 86 per cent, have one or more corresponding statutes in CS *Canada*. In addition, two subsections of section 29 were inapplicable in 1859. Subsections 33 and 34 deal respectively with the creation of a general court of appeal – what would be the Supreme Court of Canada – and making uniform the laws relative to property and civil rights in all the potentially federating colonies except Lower Canada. Discounting those two sections, thirty-two of section 29's thirty-five subsections, or 91 per cent, can be traced to CS *Canada*. As with section 43, the correspondence between section 29 and CS *Canada* is usually easy to identify because of the nomenclature used. For example, "aliens, naturalisation of" was CS *Canada* chapter 8, and "naturalization of aliens" was subsection 29 (30) of the Quebec Resolutions. It is true that if we base our count on statutes in CS *Canada* rather than heads of jurisdiction in section 29 the similarity between the two seems less striking – only sixty-one of CS *Canada*'s 111 chapters appear in Quebec Resolution 29. Yet here it must be borne in mind the explanation given earlier in this paper for the discrepancies between section 91 of the BNA *Act* and CS *Canada*. Several of CS *Canada*'s statutes were placed in other parts of the BNA *Act*, and that phenomenon began in the Quebec Resolutions. For example, sections 6 to 28 of the Quebec Resolutions effectively covered the same subject matter as chapters 1 to 7 of CS *Canada* – the institutions of government. The BNA *Act* dealt with those institutions in sections 23 to 52, which discuss the Senate and House of Commons.

We here return to the principal subject of this section – the few areas in which there is discontinuity between the treatment of a subject in the consolidations and its placing in the BNA *Act*.[52] We begin with subjects in CS *Canada* which were allocated to section 92 of the BNA *Act* – public lands, public health, benevolent associations, the professions, and municipal matters. We have already adverted to the importance in the negotiations of the 1860s of the need to protect core values and institutions of French-Canadian national identity, and many contemporaries and historians have seen this as an explanation of why subsections 8 (municipal institutions in the province), 13 (property and civil rights) and 16 (matters of a merely local or private nature) are in section 92.[53] Moreover, while municipal institutions was in CS *Canada*, it also appeared in the other two consolidations, albeit under different names. And the statutes under that title (10) in CS *Canada*, called "municipal matters," actually dealt not with municipal institutions as such, but with, inter alia, public meetings, the municipal loan fund, public works, and fire investigations.[54] Municipalities as such were dealt with in long and detailed statutes in both CSUC and CSLC.[55] Also, CSUC Title 7, municipal institutions, included public health.[56]

Another subject in CS *Canada* that was placed in section 43 of the Quebec Resolutions and section 92 of the BNA *Act*, public lands, had been a matter of contention between the imperial government and all colonies prior to Confederation.[57] It was a particularly touchy issue for the maritime colonies, which had endured a long history of seeing much of their land granted by Britain to absentee owners. That issue was especially acute in Prince Edward Island. Nova Scotia and New Brunswick had also objected to Britain introducing a policy of land sales rather than free grants in the late 1820s, a policy both colonies thought unsuitable for local conditions and that retarded settlement and development. They did not want to substitute a federal government for the imperial one on this issue. Thus it was one of the few issues on which the maritime colonies insisted at Charlottetown. Ex-premier of Prince Edward Island and a delegate to the Charlottetown and Quebec conferences, John Hamilton Gray, put it simply: "The retention of the ungranted Crown lands and of the mines and minerals by the several Provinces, in which they were situated was deemed best, as affording to them severally additional sources of revenue, stimulus for local improvements, and the means of encouraging immigration." It would also remove "causes of conflict and dissension between the Local and General Governments"; indeed "[t]he regulation and management of lands and royalties within a Province by a Government other than that of the Province would only be creating an '*imperium in imperio*,' which would surely become antagonistic."[58] On the public lands issue the maritime leaders were in any event pushing against an open door. Stumpage, licence fees and the like from the lumber industry had long been very important sources of revenue for all governments in the Canadas. Agriculture was another subject which underwent some change in the various allocation of powers schemes. In 1859 it was part of *CS Canada*, but not of CSUC and was only parenthetically dealt with in CSLC.[59] In the Quebec Resolutions it appears by that single word in both sections 29 (36) and 43 (4), and in the BNA *Act*, s. 95, it is one of the few concurrent powers listed. Section 95 also states that any provincial law on either agriculture or immigration, another power listed in s. 95 as concurrent, "shall have effect in and for the province as long and as far only as it is not repugnant to any Act of the Parliament of Canada." Given this paramountcy provision, agriculture and immigration (the latter not mentioned in *CS Canada*) were effectively federal powers. These two subjects also were contentious ones in the 1860s. At the Quebec conference voices were heard for both being a local power and a concurrent one. Charles Tupper observed that immigration was "intimately connected with the Crown Lands," which were within each colony's jurisdiction. At the same time Thomas D'Arcy McGee, then minister for Agriculture in the Canada government, observed that "[t]he General Government may draw attention to this country for settlement. The only permanent attraction we can offer is cheap land." He therefore proposed that the local legislature "should be bound to let immigrants have lands as hitherto. Immigrants should feel that they came to British America as a whole, and that they are free to choose lands as they like."[60] McGee's proposal effectively won the day by virtue of the combination of concurrent power and paramountcy. The federal government controlled immigration, the provinces were largely left to their own devices with agriculture.

Finally, we turn to marriage and divorce. Divorce does not appear in any of the consolidations, for the simple reason that it was entirely unavailable in Lower Canada and obtainable only in Upper Canada through a private act of the legislature; there was no judicial divorce available and thus no need to legislate the grounds on which it could be obtained. Marriage does not appear at all in *CS Canada*, but it is in both CSUC and CSLC. CSUC chapter 72 was *An Act Respecting Marriages in Upper Canada*, and provided that they could be performed by any ordained minister of any denomination, so long as a licence had been obtained and the marriage was registered. In CSLC the only provision respecting marriage disallowed opposition to a marriage based on an actual or alleged breach of promise to marry another.[61] Yet in both the Quebec Resolutions and the BNA *Act* marriage and divorce are central government powers;[62] "the solemnization of marriage in the province" is section 92 (12) of the BNA *Act* and was added very late in the process. It does not appear in the Quebec Resolutions, but was one of the very few changes made at the final, London, conference.[63] The distinction between the federal and provincial powers is that the federal government can legislate on the essential requirements of marriage, and the province on solemnization. Having marriage and divorce as a central power appears counterintuitive, given what has been said above about the felt need to protect French Canada's status as a Catholic community. One would have thought that this made marriage and divorce ideal subject areas for inclusion in section 92, so that no national Protestant majority could legislate in an area so central to francophone culture – marriage is a sacrament in the Catholic faith and divorce unobtainable. Indeed, in a legislative council debate in 1865 Jacques-Olivier Bureau was alarmed by the idea that the federal government would have jurisdiction in these areas: "Our laws which regulate our marriages at present are very important to us, and are based on the Roman law. These are the only laws suitable to Canadians, and the wise provisions characterizing them were the fruit of the experience of several ages. We should not incur the risk of a change in them by a legislature, the majority of whose members do not hold our opinions on this subject."[64] Why then not put divorce under provincial jurisdiction? There were two answers to this question given in an 1870 Commons debate. Hector Langevin, who thought divorce was "destroying the basis of society," also knew that it had to go into one of sections 91 or 92, and as only two provinces at that time, Nova Scotia and New Brunswick, had a divorce court, everybody else would have to get their divorces by private act of the federal Parliament. "It would be more difficult," he correctly stated, "for persons seeking divorces to come to Ottawa than to get them from the Local Legislatures."[65] Second, and rather less expediently, in the same debate Cartier saw it as a way to allow Protestants to obtain divorces while not giving Catholic Quebec a jurisdiction it would detest and which no Catholic would want.

CONCLUSION

This paper had made two distinct, but related, arguments. The first is that while the Province of Canada was undoubtedly a legislative union, with a single legislature replacing the two legislatures of

Upper and Lower Canada that had existed prior to the Union, that single legislature behaved in a quasi-federal manner, legislating from the outset for one part of the colony or the other, or for both, in distinct statutes. This can most obviously be seen in the late 1850s when the assembly brought out the most comprehensive consolidations of its statutes, for the result was three consolidations, one of statutes for the colony as a whole, one of statutes for Canada West (Upper Canada) and one of statutes for Canada East (Lower Canada). We believe this argument is relatively novel; certainly nobody has demonstrated this informal federalization so thoroughly.

The second argument, we believe a more novel one, is that the informal federal arrangements made in 1859 and 1861 for the Province of Canada formed the basis of the division of powers in the *British North America Act*. A comparison between the consolidations and sections 91, 92, and 93 of that Act displays substantial similarity between the *Consolidated Statutes of Canada* and section 91, and between the *Consolidated Statutes of Upper Canada* and the *Consolidated Statutes of Lower Canada* and sections 92 and 93. We have also presented evidence for this being no mere coincidence, for the central Canadian politicians who drove the Confederation process relied on their experience of informal federalization during the Union to largely define the division of powers. There were a few exceptions, powers that were allocated differently in the *British North America Act* than they had been in the consolidations, but the overall similarity suggests where the Confederation arrangements came from.

Table 8.1 | *BNA Act* section 91 and *CS Canada*

BNA Act	Content	*CS Canada* Title
91 (2)	The regulation of trade and commerce.	4 – Trade and commerce. Twenty-two statutes, incl. those relating to navigation, banking, interest, and fishing noted below 5 – Trading companies and corporations. Eight statutes.
91 (3)	The raising of money by any mode or system of taxation.	3 – Public departments, revenue, and property. Five statutes on customs, excise, and various duties.
91 (4)	The borrowing of money on the public credit.	3 – Public departments, revenue, and property. Two statutes.
91 (5)	Postal service.	3 – Public departments, revenue, and property. One statute on "Post Office, Provincial."
91 (6)	The census and statistics.	3 – Public departments, revenue, and property. One statute on "Registration and Statistics," "Census," &c.
91 (7)	Militia, military and naval service, and defence.	3 – Public departments, revenue, and property. Three statutes on the militia and naval defence.
91 (8)	The fixing of and providing for the salaries and allowances of civil and other officers of the Government of Canada.	2 – Executive government and public officers generally. Two statutes on the civil list, the civil service and salaries.
91 (9)	Beacons, buoys, lighthouses, and Sable Island.	Not included in *CS Canada*.
91 (10)	Navigation and shipping.	4 – Trade and commerce. Five statutes on ship registration, seamen, navigation, steamboat inspection and passenger safety.
91 (11)	Quarantine and the establishment and maintenance of marine hospitals.	3 – Public departments, revenue, and property. One statute on "Emigrants and Quarantine."
91 (12)	Sea coast and inland fisheries.	4 – Trade and commerce. One statute on "Fisheries and Fishing."
91 (14)	Currency and coinage.	3 – Public departments, revenue, and property. One statute on "Currency."
91 (15)	Banking, incorporation of banks, and the issue of paper money.	4 – Trade and commerce. Two statutes.

BNA Act	Content	CS Canada Title
91 (16)	Savings banks.	4 – Trade and commerce. One statute on "Savings Banks."
91 (17)	Weights and measures.	4 – Trade and commerce. One statute on "Weights and Measures – Grain, Pulse, and Seeds."
91 (18)	Bills of exchange and promissory notes.	4 – Trade and commerce. One statute on "Promissory Notes and Bills of Exchange."
91 (19)	Interest.	4 – Trade and commerce. One statute on "Interest and Usury."
91 (20)	Legal tender.	3 – Public departments, revenue, and property. One statute on "Currency."
91 (21)	Bankruptcy and insolvency.	Not included in CS *Canada*.
91 (22)	Patents of invention and discovery.	3 – Public departments, revenue, and property. One statute on "Patents for Inventions, Designs," &c.
91 (23)	Copyrights.	9 – Private rights and remedies. One statute on "Copy Rights."
91(24)	Indians, and lands reserved for the Indians.	1 – Constitution and political rights, legislation etc. One statute on "Indians, Civilization, and Enfranchisement of."
91 (25)	Naturalization and aliens.	1 – Constitution and political rights, legislation etc. One statute on "Aliens, Naturalization of."
91 (26)	Marriage and divorce.	Not included in CS *Canada*.
91 (27)	The criminal law, except the constitution of courts of criminal jurisdiction, but including the procedure in criminal matters.	3 – Public departments, revenue, and property. Two statutes on offences on public works. 11 – Criminal law. Nineteen statutes on criminal law and procedure.
91 (28)	The establishment, maintenance, and management of penitentiaries.	11 – Criminal law. One statute on "Penitentiary, Provincial."

Notes: The 111 statutes in CS *Canada* were divided into nine titles. The statutes are numbered consecutively from title to title. The total of seventy-seven statutes listed in the third column is 74 per cent of the 104 statutes, a number which excludes the first seven statutes, dealing with the assembly and legislative council.
Four titles in CS *Canada*, a total of fourteen statutes, had no equivalent in section 91: 6 – benevolent associations etc; (three statutes); 7 – religious matters (one statute); 8 – professions (three statutes); and 10 – municipal matters (seven statutes).
Not included in the list of section 91 powers because they are completely inapplicable are 91 (1), 91 (13), and 91 (29), for which see above, note 23.

Table 8.2 | *BNA Act* sections 92 and 93 and CSLC

BNA Act	Content	*CSLC* Title
92 (2)	Direct taxation within the province in order to the raising of a revenue for provincial purposes.	1 – Legislation and governmental and fiscal affairs. Six statutes dealing with various taxes, four also appear below under 92 (9).
92 (5)	The management and sale of the public lands belonging to the province and the timber and wood thereon.	Not included in CSLC.
92 (6)	The establishment, maintenance, and management of public and reformatory prisons in and for the province.	12 – Administration of justice. Two statutes dealing with gaols and houses of correction.
92 (7)	The establishment, maintenance, and management of hospitals, asylums, charities, and eleemosynary institutions.	8 – Trade and commerce. One statute on "Sick Mariners, Provision of Medical treatment of."
92 (8)	Municipal institutions in the province.	5 – Municipal and rural matters. Ten statutes, one dealing with "Municipalities and Roads generally" and the others with specific regulations. One deals with "Masters and Servants in the Country Parts."
92 (9)	Shop, saloon tavern, auctioneer, and other licences in order to the raising of a revenue for provincial, local, or municipal purposes.	1 – Legislation and governmental and fiscal affairs. See 92 (2) above.
92 (10)	Local works and undertakings.	1 – Legislation and governmental and fiscal affairs. One statute on "Certain Ferries over the St Lawrence."
92 (11)	The incorporation of companies with provincial objects.	9 – Joint stock companies. Three statutes.
92 (12)	The solemnization of marriage in the province.	6 – Private rights – personal. One statute which, inter alia, includes "marriages."

BNA Act	Content	*CSLC* Title
92 (13)	Property and civil rights in the province.	5 – Municipal and rural matters. See above. 6 – Private rights – personal. One statute on "Divers personal rights, viz: Majority, Wills, Marriages – Crim. Con. – Guardians of Foundlings – Jews – Quakers – Inhabitants of Indian Reserves." 7 – Real property and rights. Nineteen statutes. 8 – Trade and commerce. Five statutes dealing inter alia with "Seaman's Wages, recovery of," "Bills of Exchange and Promissory Notes," limitations, and partnerships.
92 (14)	The administration of justice in the province.	12 – Administration of justice. Thirty-five statutes, about court structure and jurisdiction, procedure, court houses, JPs, police, etc.
92 (16)	Generally all matters of a merely local or private nature in the province.	2 – Matters of public order. Two statutes on "Unlawful Associations and Oaths" and "Newspapers and like publications." 4 – Matters connected with religion. Six statutes on inter alia parishes, churches, and of religious congregations, registration of births etc. 10 – Professions. Four statutes on the medical and legal profession. 11 - Territorial divisions for general purposes, one statute.
93	Education.	3 – Public education. Three statutes dealing with normal, common, and fabrique schools, and with McGill College.

Notes: The 111 statutes in *CSLC* were divided into nine titles. The statutes are numbered consecutively from title to title. Not included in this table is Title 1, Legislation, which has three statutes dealing with the *CSLC*, the Civil Code, and the proclamation etc. of acts. Thus, the total of ninety-nine statutes listed in the third column is 92 per cent of the 108 statutes, excluding these three.

Not included in the list of section 92 powers in this table because they could not have an equivalent in *CSLC* are: 92 (1) the amendment from time to time, notwithstanding anything in this act, of the constitution of the province, except as regards the office of lieutenant governor; 92 (3) the borrowing of money on the sole credit of the province; 92 (4) the establishment and tenure of provincial offices and the appointment and payment of provincial officers; and 92 (15), the imposition of punishment by fine, penalty, or imprisonment for enforcing any law of the province made in relation to any matter coming within any of the classes of subjects enumerated in this section.

Table 8.3 | *BNA Act* sections 92 and 93 and CSUC

BNA Act	Content	*CSUC* Title
92 (2)	Direct taxation within the province in order to the raising of a revenue for provincial purposes.	Not in CSUC.
92 (5)	The management and sale of the public lands belonging to the province and the timber and wood thereon.	11 – Real estate. One statute on "Claims to lands for which no Patents have issued."
92 (6)	The establishment, maintenance, and management of public and reformatory prisons in and for the province.	12 – Criminal law. One statute on "Court Houses, Gaols, and Houses of Correction."
92 (7)	The establishment, maintenance, and management of hospitals, asylums, charities, and eleemosynary institutions in and for the province, other than marine hospitals.	7 – Municipal institutions. One statute on public health. 9 – Religious and benevolent institutions. Six statutes.
92 (8)	Municipal institutions in the province.	7 – Municipal institutions. Seven statutes on "Municipal Institutions," property assessment, public highways, fencing, game laws.
92 (9)	Shop, saloon tavern, auctioneer, and other licences in order to the raising of a revenue for provincial, local, or municipal purposes.	Not in CSUC.
92 (10)	Local works and undertakings other than ... following classes.	6 – Trade and commerce. Three statutes on "Ferries," "Rivers and Creeks," and "Mills and Mill Dams."
92 (11)	The incorporation of companies with provincial objects.	6 – Trade and commerce. Three statutes on joint stock companies. 7 – Municipal institutions. Two statutes on mutual insurance companies and building societies.
92 (12)	The solemnization of marriage in the province.	10 – Domestic relations, rights and remedies, one statute on "Marriages."

BNA *Act*	Content	CSUC Title
92 (13)	Property and civil rights in the province.	4 – Administration of Justice. One statute on "Law of England in relation to Property and Civil Rights." 6 – Trade and commerce. Four statutes on bills of exchange and promissory notes, interest, written promises, and chattel mortgages. 10 – Domestic relations, rights and remedies. Seven statutes on "Separate Rights of Married Women," guardianship, master and servant, apprentices and minors, seduction, actions by and against executors, etc., and limitations, of certain actions, and accidents. 11 – Real Estate. Thirteen statutes dealing with real property. Not included is 11, c. 80, listed under 92 (5) above.
92 (14)	The administration of justice in the province, including the constitution, maintenance, and organization of provincial courts, both civil and of criminal jurisdiction, and including procedure in civil matters in those courts.	4 – Administration of justice. Twenty-three statutes on the constitution of various courts, procedure, juries etc. 5 – Professions etc. Four statutes on court reporters, crown attorneys, sheriffs, and commissioners to take affidavits. 12 – Criminal law. Despite its title, twenty-three statutes dealing with criminal procedure and the administration of civil justice. Not included here is 12 (127), "Gaols etc.," see above in 92 (6). 13 – Administration of justice in unorganized tracts. One statute.
92 (16)	Generally all matters of a merely local or private nature in the province.	2 – Territorial divisions of Upper Canada. One statute. 5 – Professions etc. Three statutes on the legal profession and two on the medical profession.
93	Education.	8 – Education. Four statutes on grammar, common and separate schools, and on universities.

Notes: The 128 statutes in CSUC were divided into thirteen titles. The statutes are numbered consecutively from title to title. Not included in this table is Title 1, Preliminary Provisions, dealing in two statutes with CSUC and interpretation; legislation, which has three statutes dealing with the CSLC, the *Civil Code*, and the proclamation etc. of acts. Thus the total of 109 statutes listed in the third column is 86 per cent of the 126 statutes, excluding these two.
Not included in the list of section 92 powers because they could not have had an equivalent in CSUC are the same four heads of section 92 jurisdiction as in Table 8.2.

Table 8.4 | The Quebec Resolutions of 1864

	29 – Federal Powers		43 – Provincial Powers
29.1	The public debt and property.	43.1	Direct taxation and the imposition of duties on the export of timber, logs, masts, spars, deals and sawn lumber, and of coals and other minerals.
29.2	The regulation of trade and commerce.	43.2	Borrowing money on the credit of the province.
29.3	The imposition or regulation of duties of customs on imports and exports, except on exports of timber, logs, masts, spars, deals and sawn lumber from New Brunswick, and of coal and other minerals from Nova Scotia.	43.3	The establishment and tenure of local offices, and the appointment and payment of local officers.
29.4	The imposition or regulation of excise duties.	43.4	Agriculture.
29.5	The raising of money by all or any other modes or systems of taxation.	43.5	Immigration.
29.6	The borrowing of money on the public credit.	43.6	Education; saving the rights and privileges which the Protestant or Catholic minority in both Canadas may possess as to their denominational schools, at the time when the Union goes into operation.
29.7	Postal service.	43.7	The sale and management of public lands, excepting public lands belonging to the general government.
29.8	Lines of steam or other ships, railways, canals and other works, connecting any two or more of the provinces together or extending beyond the limits of any province.	43.8	Sea-coast and inland fisheries.
29.9	Lines of steamships between the federated provinces and countries.	43.9	The establishment, maintenance and management of penitentiaries, and of public and reformatory prisons.

	29 – Federal Powers		43 – Provincial Powers
29.10	Telegraphic communication and the incorporation of telegraph companies.	43.10	The establishment, maintenance and management of hospitals, asylums, charities, and eleemosynary institutions.
29.11	All such works as shall, although lying wholly within any province be specially declared, by the acts authorizing them, to be for the general advantage.	43.11	Municipal institutions.
29.12	The census.	43.12	Shop, saloon, tavern, auctioneer and other licences.
29.13	Militia, military and naval service, and defence.	43.13	Local works.
29.14	Beacons, buoys, and lighthouses.	43.14	The incorporation of private and local companies, except such as relate to matters assigned to the general Parliament.
29.15	Navigation and shipping.	43.15	Property and civil rights, excepting portions thereof assigned to the general Parliament.
29.16	Quarantine.	43.16	Inflicting punishment by fine, penalties, imprisonment or otherwise, for the breach of laws passed in relation to any subject within their jurisdiction.
29.17	Sea-coast and inland fisheries.	43.17	The administration of justice, including the constitution, maintenance and organization of the courts – both of civil and criminal jurisdiction, and including also the procedure in civil matters.
29.18	Ferries between any province and a foreign country, or between any two provinces.	43.18	And generally all matters of a private or local nature, not assigned to the general Parliament.
29.19	Currency and coinage.	29.20	Banking, incorporation of banks, and the issue of paper money.
29.21	Savings banks.	29.22	Weights and measures.

Table 8.4 | The Quebec Resolutions of 1864 (*continued*)

	29 – Federal Powers		43 – Provincial Powers
29.23	Bills of exchange and promissory notes.	29.24	Interest.
29.25	Legal tender.	29.26	Bankruptcy and insolvency
29.27	Patents of innovation and discovery.	29.28	Copyrights.
29.29	Indians, and lands reserved for the Indians.	29.30	Naturalization and aliens.
29.31	Marriage and divorce.	29.32	The criminal law, excepting the constitution of the courts of criminal jurisdiction, but including the procedure in criminal matters.
29.33	Rendering uniform all or any of the laws relative to property and civil rights in Upper Canada, Nova Scotia, New Brunswick, Newfoundland and Prince Edward Island, and rendering uniform the procedure of all or any of the courts in these provinces; but any statute for this purpose shall have no force or authority in any province until sanctioned by the legislature thereof.	29.34	The establishment of a general court of appeal for the federated provinces.
29.35	Immigration.	29.36	Agriculture.
29.37	And general respecting all matters of a general character, not specially and exclusively reserved for the local governments and legislatures.		

NOTES

We thank Don Fyson, Christopher Moore, Iain Wilson, the editors of this volume, and participants in the Osgoode Society Legal History Workshop for their comments on a previous draft.

1 The literature on this is very extensive, though much of it is rather dated. We have principally relied on four recent accounts: Christopher Moore, *Three Weeks in Quebec City: The Meeting that Made Canada* (Toronto: Allen Lane, 2015); Christopher Moore, *1867: How the Fathers Made a Deal* (Toronto: McClelland and Stewart, 1997); Peter Russell, *Canada's Odyssey: A Country Based on Incomplete Conquests* (Toronto: University of Toronto Press, 2017), chapter 7; and Jack Saywell, *The Law Makers: Judicial Power and the Shaping of Canadian Federalism* (Toronto: Osgoode Society for Canadian Legal History and University of Toronto Press, 2002), chapter 1.

2 The leading modern study of this litigation is Saywell, *The Law Makers*.

3 The term is used in William G. Ormsby, *The Emergence of the Federal Concept in Canada, 1839–1845* (Toronto: University of Toronto Press, 1969). Ormsby argues that the roots of federalism lay in the failure of assimilation, which can be traced back to the initial years of the Union. He and others see this as reflected in, inter alia, various ministries, including that of the attorneys general, being split into two. In his epilogue he uses the term we employ here, a quasi-federal system (124), although he elaborates very little on the idea.

4 The first three of these consolidations were published in Toronto by Derbishire and Desbarats in 1858 and 1859, the fourth in Quebec in 1861 by the same publishers.

5 David Mills, "Confederation Law of Canada," a review of Gerald John Wheeler, *Confederation Law of Canada*, in *Review of Historical Publications Relating to Canada* 1 (1897): 96, 101–2. The journal became the *Canadian Historical Review* in 1919.

6 Precisely one hundred statutes were passed in 1841, but we have not included in this analysis private act incorporations, statutes related to particular institutions or localities (examples include the Trinity House of Lower Canada or the town of Woodstock), appropriations acts, naturalisation acts for individuals, and the like. The same is true for the other years mentioned here.

7 See, for example, *An Act to Amend the Militia Law of that Part of this Province Formerly Constituting the Province of Upper Canada*, Statutes of the Province of Canada [SPS] 1841, c. 2.

8 See also for the same point Margaret Banks, "Upper or Lower Canada or Canada West and East, 1841–1867," *Canadian Historical Review* 54, no. 4 (1973): 473–80. The assembly also passed a further 106 statutes, c. 93–199,

which were either "local" acts "not for the personal or private advantage of individuals," or "personal and private acts," including special act incorporations. Both of these categories were also divided into those pertaining to Upper and Lower Canada respectively.

9 SPS 1849, c. 10.

10 See J.E. Hodgetts, *Pioneer Public Service: An Administrative History of the United Canadas, 1841–1867* (Toronto: University of Toronto Press, 1955).

11 *An Act for Consolidating and Amending the Laws in This Province, Relative to Larceny and Other Offences Connected Therewith*, SPS 1841, c. 25; *An Act for Consolidating and Amending the Laws in This Province Relative to Malicious Injuries to Property*, SPS 1841, c.26; *An Act for Consolidating and Amending the Statutes in This Province Relative to Offences Against the Person*, SPS 1841, c. 27. See also *An Act for Improving the Administration of Criminal Justice in This Province*, SPS 1841, c. 24. For an account of criminal law reform in the Canadas, before and after 1841, see Philip Girard, Jim Phillips, and R. Blake Brown, *A History of Law in Canada Volume One: Beginnings to 1866* (Toronto: University of Toronto Press, 2018), ch. 28.

12 See, for example, *An Act to Repeal the Laws Now in Force in That Part of This Province Called Upper Canada, for the Recovery of Small Debts, and to Make Other Provisions for That Purpose*, SPS 1841, c. 3, and *An Act to Provide for the More Easy and Expeditious Administration of Justice in Civil Causes, and Matters Involving Small Pecuniary Value in That Part of This Province Heretofore Lower Canada*, SPS 1841, c. 20. For the court systems in Upper and Lower Canada see Girard, Phillips, and Brown, *History of Law in Canada Volume One*, ch. 22.

13 6 February 1865, cited in *Parliamentary Debates on the Subject of the Confederation of the British North American Provinces* (Quebec: Hunter, Rose & Co., 1865), 30 [hereafter *Parliamentary Debates*].

14 To come to this conclusion, we sampled a number of statutes dealing with the court systems of Upper or Lower Canada. Lists of members who voted when the house divided are rarely given in the *Journals* of the Assembly, but when they are they are revealing. One 1849 vote on receiving the committee of the whole report, second reading, of what became *An Act to Make Further Provision for the Administration of Justice, by the Establishment of an Additional Superior Court of Common Law and also a Court of Error and Appeal, in Upper-Canada*, SPS 1849, c. 63 saw fifteen Upper Canadian members and twenty-three Lower Canadian members voting: *Province of Canada Assembly Journals*, 22 May 1849, 331 [hereafter *PC Assembly Journals*]. The proceedings relating to what became *An Act to Amend the Judicature Acts of Lower Canada*, SPS 1857, c. 44, produced many

amendments and many recorded votes, because of infighting among Lower Canadian members about where courthouses for new judicial districts should be located. One amendment to establish the courthouse for Kamouraska district at Fraserville was defeated 42-31. Fourteen Upper Canadian members were among the forty-two, and thirteen Upper Canadians among the thirty-one: PC *Assembly Journals*, 29 May 1857, 572. Much more research into particular bills would be required to assess why people voted the way they did, and that is beyond the scope of this paper.

15 For the double majority convention see, inter alia, J.M.S. Careless, *The Union of the Canadas: The Growth of Canadian Institutions, 1841–1867* (Toronto: McClelland and Stewart, 1967).

16 Girard, Phillips, and Brown, *History of Law in Canada Volume One*, ch. 23.

17 *Ibid.*, 439–46.

18 *The Statutes of Upper Canada,* 2 vols. (Toronto: Robert Stanton, 1843); *The Revised Acts and Ordinances of Lower Canada* (Montreal: Derbishire & Desbarats, 1845). These two consolidations are discussed in Margaret Banks, "An Annotated Biography of Statutes and Related Publications: Upper Canada, the Province of Canada, and Ontario 1792–1980," in David Flaherty, ed., *Essays in the History of Canadian Law, Volume I* (Toronto: Osgoode Society for Canadian Legal History and University of Toronto Press, 1981), which also lists other collections of statutes brought out during the Union period.

19 The following account is based on Desmond H. Brown, *The Genesis of the Canadian Criminal Code of 1892* (Toronto: Osgoode Society for Canadian Legal History and University of Toronto Press, 1989), 86–91, and on four contemporary reports: "First Report of the Commissioners for the Revision of the Statutes of Upper Canada," 19 April 1858 [hereafter First Report], and "Supplementary Report" of the same commissioners, 1859, both in PC *Assembly Journals*, 1859, appendix 9; "Joint Report of the Commissioners appointed to Revise and Consolidate the Statutes which apply to the Whole Province of Canada," 3 March 1859, published in CS *Canada*; "Report of the Acting Commissioner appointed finally to Revise, Print and Edit the Consolidated Statutes for Lower Canada," 10 April 1860, published in CSLC.

20 A total of eight men, all successful lawyers, served as Upper Canada commissioners because of resignations and replacements. They were David Breakenridge Read, a Tory and legal author; Joseph Morrison, a minister in the Hincks-Morin ministry and later a judge of the Court of Common Pleas and then the Court of Appeal; Oliver Mowat, a leading Chancery lawyer and later vice-chancellor of Ontario and premier of the province; John Hillyard Cameron, a Family Compact Tory; Dr George Skeffington Connor, a

Dublin-trained lawyer, the brother-in-law of William Hume Blake who he succeeded as law professor at King's College, Toronto, and from 1863 he was a judge of the Court of Queen's Bench; Samuel Henry Strong, a leading equity lawyer and, from 1868, a judge of the Court of Queen's Bench, then the Court of Error and Appeal, then the Supreme Court of Canada; Adam Wilson, municipal politician and then assemblyman, who was appointed a judge of the Court of Queen's Bench in 1868; and James B. Macaulay, recently retired chief justice of the Court of Common Pleas. For these men see variously Jamie Benidickson, "Sir Samuel Henry Strong," John D. Blackwell, "John Breakenridge Read," Gordon Dodds, "Sir James Buchanan Macaulay," R. Lynn Ogden, "George Skeffington Connor," Graham Parker, "Sir Adam Wilson," Paul Romney, "Sir Oliver Mowat," Donald Swainson, "John Hillyard Cameron," and Various Authors, "Joseph Curran Morrison," all in *Dictionary of Canadian Biography* online, biographi.ca [hereafter DCB *online*]. For the court system in Upper Canada prior to Confederation see Girard, Phillips, and Brown, *History of Law in Canada Volume One*, ch. 22.

21 Six men were appointed commissioners for Lower Canada, the best known of whom was Thomas-Jean-Jacques Loranger, later a judge of the Superior Court and a prolific legal author, and Andrew Stuart, who was appointed to the Superior Court bench in 1859 and who eventually became chief justice of that court and of Quebec. The others included Robert Mackay, who was later batonnier of the Lower Canada bar and, from 1868, a judge of the Quebec Superior Court; Gustavus William Wicksteed, law clerk to the assembly who did most of the work; Antoine Polette, QC, a former mayor of Trois-Rivieries and the MLA for that city, who was made a superior court judge in 1860; and George de Boucherville, a lawyer and a former radical who went into exile for a few years after 1837 but who was well connected; his father Pierre had been a legislative councillor in the 1840s. For these men see variously Jean-Charles Bonenfant, "Thomas-Jean-Jacques Loranger," Céline Cyr, "Sir Andrew Stuart," André Lemelin, "Pierre-Georges-Prévost Boucher de Boucherville," Louisette Pothier, "Antoine Pollet," all in DCB *online*, and Archival Record for Gustavus William Wicksteed in McGill University Library. For the court system in Upper Canada prior to Confederation see Girard, Phillips, and Brown, *History of Law in Canada Volume One*, ch. 22.

22 First Report, para 6.

23 For the various titles in each consolidation see Tables 8.1–8.4.

24 Although his name does not appear as a commissioner in any of the reports, Gowan's biographer states that he was made a commissioner, and he is listed as such in one compilation of office-holders in the Province of Canada: see Desmond H. Brown, "Sir James Robert Gowan," DCB *online*, and Narcisse

Coté, *Political Appointments and Elections in the Province of Canada, 1841–1865*, 2nd edition, edited by J. A. Coté (Ottawa: G. Desbarats, 1866), 127.

25 See Table 8.1. They were: 91 (1): "The amendment from time to time of the Constitution of Canada"; 91 (13): "Ferries between a Province and any British or Foreign Country or between Two Provinces"; and 91 (29): "Such Classes of Subjects as are expressly excepted in the Enumeration of the Classes of Subjects by this Act assigned exclusively to the Legislatures of the Provinces."

26 For examples see below, discussion of those parts of CS *Canada* later placed in section 92.

27 For the tangled history of bankruptcy law see Girard, Phillips, and Brown, *History of Law in Canada Volume One*, ch. 31.

28 Chapter 26 of CS *Canada* dealt with "School Lands and Fund for Education." Title 3 of *CSLC*, Public Education, comprised three statutes covering all classes of schools. Title 8 of *CSUC* comprised four statutes dealing with schools and universities.

29 As late as December 1866 drafts of the BNA *Act* included education as one of the provincial heads of power in what became section 92. But, through various drafts, the provision became longer and more complicated as the issue of minority education rights was fleshed out. It was far and away the longest section in section 92, and for this simple reason may have been allocated its own section in the final bill.

30 The management of public lands is a head of power in section 92 (5), but also relevant here is section 109 of the BNA *Act*, which vested ownership of lands, mines, and minerals in the provinces.

31 After conferring concurrent power, section 95 goes on to say that provincial laws "shall have effect in and for the Province so long and as far only as it is not repugnant to any Act of the Parliament of Canada."

32 See Tables 8.2 and 8.3. The inapplicable sub-sections of s. 92 are: 92 (1), "the amendment ... of the Constitution of the Province"; (92 (4), "the establishment and tenure ... and payment of provincial officers"; and 92 (15), "the imposition of punishment ... for enforcing any law of the province."

33 The following section is based principally on the sources cited in note 2, above. In what follows we do not discuss the influence of the American counter-example – a decentralized federation and the civil war that resulted in part from that decentralization. It is well established that most participants in the Confederation process wanted the general government to have more powers than the US federal government. But our concern here is not with the general approach but with the specifics of exactly which heads of power would be federal and which would be provincial.

34 See in this respect Paul Romney's assertion that Confederation "originated as an agreement to federalize United Canada": Paul Romney, *Getting It Wrong: How Canadians Forgot Their Past and Imperiled Confederation* (Toronto: University of Toronto Press, 1999), 88. There were indeed suggestions that a federation could be made out of the Union in the late 1850s and 1860s, especially by the short-lived Brown-Dorion ministry of 1858 and by the Reform party in the early 1860s. But these came to nothing, and are beyond the scope this paper. See, in addition to the sources cited above in note 2, the classic study by Careless, *The Union of the Canadas.*

35 P. B. Waite, *The Charlottetown Conference* (Ottawa: The Centennial Commission, 1967), 18.

36 Russell, *Canada's Odyssey,* 137.

37 Robert C. Vipond, "1787 and 1867: The Federal Principle and Canadian Confederation Reconsidered," in Jaqueline D. Krikorian, et al., eds., *Roads to Confederation: The Making of Canada, 1867,* 2 vols. (Toronto: University of Toronto Press, 2017), I: 224.

38 George-Étienne Cartier, John Jones Ross, and Alexander Galt to Sir Edward Bulwer-Lytton, 25 October 1858, in G.P. Browne and Janet Ajzenstat, eds., *Documents on the Confederation of British North America: A Compilation Based on Sir Joseph Pope's Confederation Documents Supplemented by Other Official Material* (Montreal: McGill-Queen's University Press, 2009), 18.

39 Arthur Hamilton Gordon to Edward Cardwell, 26 September 1864, in *ibid.*, 47–8.

40 As the text states, this is a simplistic statement, especially as regards the complicated society and politics of Lower Canada, as demonstrated, inter alia, by the debates over the abolition of seigneurial tenure and the reform of the *Civil Code.* But the characterisation very broadly works in the context dealt with here, a discussion of why certain subjects were given to what became the province of Quebec, and other provinces, in 1867. For the complexities of Lower Canadian thought see, inter alia, Brian Young, *George-Étienne Cartier: Montreal Bourgeois* (Kingston and Montreal: McGill-Queen's University Press, 1981), and *The Politics of Codification: The Lower Canadian Civil Code of 1866* (Toronto and Montreal: Osgoode Society for Canadian Legal History and McGill-Queen's University Press, 1997), and Girard, Phillips, and Brown, *History of Law in Canada Volume One*, 425–39 and 591–6.

41 Young, *George-Etienne Cartier,* 75.

42 Speech delivered 3 November 1864, quoted in Edward Wheland, *The Union of the British Provinces* (Charlottetown: Haszard, 1865), 196–7.

43 Cited in W.P.M. Kennedy, ed., *Statutes, Treaties and Documents of the Canadian Constitution 1713–1929* (Toronto: University of Toronto Press, 1930), 592.

44 "Police," a term with a broader use in the nineteenth century than it now has, encompassing all manner of social regulation, was effectively included within both the administration of justice and municipal affairs.

45 Legislative Assembly debate of 16 February 1865, in *Parliamentary Debates*, 263–4. For Dorion see Jean-Claude Soulard, "Sir Antoine-Aimé Dorion," DCB *online*.

46 Russell, *Canada's Odyssey*, 137.

47 The Quebec Resolutions cover ninety-nine of *CSLC*'s 111 statutes, or 89 per cent. The resolutions cover 110 of *CSUC*'s 128 statutes, or 86 per cent.

48 *An Act Respecting Municipalities and Roads in Lower Canada*, *CSLC*, c. 24.

49 *An Act Respecting the Sale of Intoxicating Liquors Near Public Works*, *CS Canada*, c. 30, and *An Act Respecting Riots Near Public Works*, *CS Canada*, c. 29.

50 *CSLC*, c. 24, preamble.

51 See Table 8.4 for the federal powers on public works in the Quebec Resolutions. Note also that schedule A of chapter 28 of *CS Canada* gave Canada's commissioner of public works authority over ports, intersectional highways (as in those running between Upper and Lower Canada), canals, and other works affecting both regions of the colony.

52 We do not discuss here subjects which went from *CS Canada*, to section 43 of the Quebec Resolutions, to section 91 of the *BNA Act*. That is, subjects which started and ended as central powers but which were provincial or concurrent in the Quebec Resolutions. The prime example is "Sea Coast and Inland Fisheries." It was included in *CS Canada* as c. 62, "Fisheries and Fishing," then became a concurrent power in the Quebec Resolutions, the identical words appearing in both sub-sections 29 (18) and 43 (8), and then reverted to a central power in the *BNA Act*, section 91 (12).

53 This argument was made by the 1956 *Royal Commission of Inquiry on Constitutional Problems* (the Tremblay Commission), which asserted that "Lower Canada only consented to enter the Union on the express condition that it would conserve control over its civil and social organization. That is why sub-heads 8 and 13 of Section 92 reserve legislation on municipal institutions, property, and civil rights to the exclusive jurisdiction of the provinces": *Royal Commission of Inquiry on Constitutional Problems, Nature of Confederation*, in Krikorian, et al., eds., *Roads to Confederation*, I: 316. The Tremblay Commission did not specifically address 92 (16), but it is not difficult to imagine that the same anxieties which compelled the Lower Canadian

delegates to protect French Canada's control over its civil and social organization would have applied to legislative competence over "all Matters of a merely local or private Nature in the Province."

54 CS *Canada*, c. 82–8.

55 *An Act Respecting the Municipal Institutions of Upper Canada*, CSUC, c. 54 (125 pages in the statute book, 428 sections), and *An Act Respecting Municipalities and Roads in Lower Canada,* CSLC, c. 24 (122 pages in the statute book, with many sections divided into numerous sub-sections).

56 CSUC, c. 59.

57 For what follows in this paragraph see Girard, Phillips, and Brown, *A History of Law in Canada Volume One*, 596–607.

58 John Hamilton Gray, *Confederation; or the Political and Parliamentary History of Canada, from the Conference at Quebec in October 1864, to the Admission of British Columbia, in July 1871* (Toronto: Copp Clark, 1872), 62–3.

59 *An Act Respecting the Bureau of Agriculture and Agricultural Societies*, CS *Canada*, c. 32; *An Act Respecting Abuses Prejudicial to Agriculture*, CSLC, c. 26.

60 Debate at the Quebec Conference, 21 October 1864, cited in cited in Browne and Ajzenstat, eds., *Documents on the Confederation*, 119. See also Moore, *Three Weeks in Quebec City*, 142.

61 *An Act Respecting Divers' Personal Rights*, CSLC 1861, c. 34, s. 4.

62 Quebec Resolutions 29 (31) and BNA *Act*, s. 91 (26).

63 Gray, *Confederation*, 386.

64 Debate in Province of Canada Legislative Council, 15 February 1865, cited in *Parliamentary Debates*, 192.

65 *House of Commons Debates*, 23 March 1870, 672. For the complex history of divorce in the post-Confederation period see Jim Phillips, Philip Girard, and R. Blake Brown, *A History of Law in Canada Volume Two: Law for the New Dominion, 1867–1914* (Toronto: Osgoode Society for Canadian Legal History and University of Toronto Press, 2022), ch. 15.

This essay is grounded in research I conducted for my doctoral dissertation from 1998–2003 under Blaine's supervision, although an eventual narrowing of topical focus necessitated discarding that research. Since the time of my LLM studies at McGill, Blaine was an unceasing supporter of my efforts at legal history, and he continued to encourage me to publish my work, which I have done sporadically over the past two decades. It was Blaine who suggested that I should revisit this particular topic for my next project, and I am grateful to have had the benefit of his comments on early drafts. Not long before his passing he sent me an envelope containing a list of potential secondary sources written by hand in red ink on yellow legal note paper, as was his wont from time to time. Neither of us could have foreseen that ultimately this essay would find its place as part of a *gedenkschrift* in his honour. I only wish he could have seen it in its final form; and had I the benefit of further critiques and comments from him, the end result would surely have been still better.

Blaine was an enthusiast of microhistories and appreciated both the difficulties and sacrifices attendant to deep archival research as well as the richness of historical inquiry and interpretation they offered. He had an unbounded ability to help situate one's work within the larger socio-legal historiography, and while Canadian legal history was his primary academic love he had an encyclopedic recall of scholars and their oeuvres across a spectrum of subjects and jurisdictions. He leaves behind a rich and unique legacy.

Ian C. Pilarczyk

9

"A Most Atrocious Crime": Sex Crimes against the Woman-Child in Early Nineteenth-Century Montreal

Ian C. Pilarczyk

> On Thursday last a most atrocious crime was committed in the parish of St Joseph de Chambly. A wretch, named Joseph Mass[é], induced a girl of 7 years of age to drink rum until she was intoxicated; after which he violated her person with circumstances of aggravation too shocking to be detailed. He has been committed to gaol, and a legal investigation of the affair is going on.[1]

This account from 1826 is illustrative of the phenomenon of sexual abuse of female children during the first half of the nineteenth century. Offering scant details, it merely hints at the sordid and violent nature of the crime. More tellingly, it omits mention that the accused was the child's uncle. The language of villainy, the "atrocious crime" committed by a "wretch," reflects the evocation of pollution and disgust common to these crimes of the period. Despite the evidence that was to come out, this case, like so many others, resulted in acquittal within the strictures of a jurisprudential system intersected by patriarchy, racism, classism, and other social constructs.

Sexual violence was a common feature of nineteenth-century life in Montreal, as indeed it would later be in Canada generally.[2] Cases of sexual assault appeared recurrently within the judicial archives and newspapers (even if only in truncated form), and no doubt scores of incidents went undisclosed and unreported. It was a sad reality that, then as now, children were a particularly vulnerable group. In a time prior to widespread social reform movements, child welfare societies, and legislative concern over the safety of children, the notion of children as rights holders was still very much inchoate.[3]

This paper seeks to add to our understanding of the phenomenon of sex crimes against children in an early nineteenth-century jurisdiction, the Judicial District of Montreal. It begins by offering a summary background of the demographics of the city during a time of considerable flux, before situating laws against child sexual violence in the larger framework of sexual assault, and discussing how the twenty cases identified in this study (involving nineteen defendants) were categorized, prosecuted, and concluded. These twenty cases examine sexual crimes against females below the age of majority: unlawful carnal knowledge of a female under ten; unlawful carnal knowledge of a female under twelve; miscellaneous misdemeanour charges related to sexual assault; and abduction of a female under sixteen.[4] The manner in which some of these crimes intersect with the phenomenon of incest will also be explored. This study illustrates how litigants navigated a system involving sexual exploitation of females under age-based statutory regimens, within the confines of a gendered and patriarchal legal system. As shall be discussed, many of the factors that militated against successful prosecution of sexual assault in general were in full play here, in addition to other dynamics such as the nature of the crimes themselves and the impediments imposed by evidentiary requirements.

HISTORIOGRAPHY AND METHODOLOGY

Sexual assault, like many forms of interpersonal violence, was ubiquitous within the criminal annals of many jurisdictions, and the historiography is ample.[5] Canadian historiography is likewise abundant, albeit similarly focusing largely on the late nineteenth century and thereafter.[6] These works focus broadly on sexual violence, and offer valuable insight into these crimes and the social, cultural, and legal responses customary for those periods while sharing the commonality of marginalizing children. This is somewhat surprising, given that, as Constance Backhouse has noted, "child sexual abuse has always been a terrifying reality for Canadian children both male and female."[7] Exceptions to this include focused works by Louise Jackson[8] and Stephen Robertson,[9] and sections of others devoted either to children's or women's issues or sexual assault in general.[10]

In the Canadian context, examples are relatively few and those for Quebec rarer still: Bruce Curtis examined sexual exploitation of children through the lens of public education in Ontario from 1840–1907;[11] more on point is Terry Chapman's work on child sexual assault cases in western Canada at the turn of the twentieth century.[12] Sandy Ramos' study of sexual violence overlaps with the period and jurisdiction but emphasizes adult victims.[13] Several works also discuss incest within the Canadian family.[14] This study, then, adds to our knowledge of how these offences were handled in the first half of the nineteenth century, and in so doing seeks to address the fundamental question of how the dynamics and contours of these cases may have differed from sexual assault cases in general.

A word about methodology: this study depends on microhistories: an examination of individual cases found within period sources. These cases were not captured in published trial reports nor subject to appeal and can be reclaimed only from the judicial archives and contemporary newspapers. All extant relevant records for the Judicial District of Montreal for the years 1825–1850 were examined, a voluminous albeit spotty archive.[15] The sources suffer from obvious lacunae and identifying the true authorial voice in affidavits is complicated as these events were typically transcribed by jurists into formulaic legal language common to the period, with acts molded to fit within narrow legal categories, involving offences deemed too distasteful for discussion. The obstacles are even more acute when the victims were under the age of being able to swear an oath. One should also note that the courts were class driven and – more problematically here given that victims were female – gender driven.[16]

Newspapers are of limited utility in supplementing the sources, as social convention precluded covering these cases except in summary form and through language that was at best oblique; and frequent were references such as "the evidence was of course unfit for publication."[17] This held true in English as well as French language newspapers, just as it did in affidavits. While sexual assaults were frequently included in newspaper's sporadic coverage of criminal trials, they tended to receive less coverage than other crimes such as spousal murder and infanticide.[18] The tendency of editors to evade direct reference to the charge itself also impairs reclamation. For example, one would be forgiven for overlooking a "misdemeanor of a very grave character" in 1847 were it not clear from other sources the charge was for assault of a child under twelve.[19] I have decided on balance to use the names of parties when they are known as they were often mentioned in newspaper articles.[20] Despite their limitations, newspapers allow us to reclaim information on court procedures, witnesses, dispositions of cases, and unconscious testimony about social norms and mores that might otherwise be lost.[21] Ultimately, however, what we are observing is penumbral: an outline of events receded in time and place, found in archives that survived, of complaints that were filed, of allegations of clandestine acts that were made public, and which resulted in some form of legal process. Much was obscured, lost, or never reported along the way, and for all of these reasons sources should be viewed as impressionistic and heuristic rather than as statistically reliable and empirical. One might hazard to say that what is disclosed is a mere fraction of the actual incidence.

Indeed, an obstacle to studying criminality in general is the innate difficulty of reconstructing furtive acts of social pathology.[22] Issues around family were not considered appropriate fodder for public discussion, and the sordidness of these offences militated against detailed publication.[23] Murder cases, in contrast, were often covered extensively, while sex-based crimes (such as infanticide or sexual assault) were sometimes covered if deemed particularly newsworthy but with prurient detail censored. Much more likely was the publication of the bare details of a defendant's name and the charge included in coverage of the most recent session of the criminal court. Child sexual assault, then, shared intersections with crimes such as infanticide, prostitution, and family violence; and in the case of incest, may well have shared commonalities with them all. These acts implicated crimes for which the underlying causes were not discussed; moreover, the victims as minors could not meaningfully act as agents for themselves within a gendered (and in this context one might add agist) legal system in which they were effectively voiceless; and as shall be discussed, many of the norms that were common to nineteenth-century rape prosecutions held true in the area of child sexual assault as well.

MONTREAL: DEMOGRAPHICS AND HISTORY

Montreal and Quebec went through myriad demographic and other changes during the first half of the nineteenth century. Quebec reached a population of 500,000 inhabitants by 1831, and doubled again within the span of two decades.[24] In Montreal itself the changes were perhaps even more acute; a population of roughly 23,000 in 1825 had ballooned to more than 90,000 in the next forty years, making it the largest city in pre-Confederation Canada.[25] In 1825 one-third of Montreal's populace were English speaking, swelling to a short-lived majority.[26] It was also perhaps British North America's preeminent centre of commerce during this period, with an English-speaking elite at its apex.[27] After 1840 Montreal took on a different economic character, becoming a manufacturing, transportation, and commercial centre owing to a proliferation of canal, railroad, and other industrial projects.[28] As noted by Danielle Gavreau, "the city's economic base shifted from commercial capitalism focused on a few products (fur, wheat, wood) to industrial capitalism based on factories and workshops."[29] It remained a port city with a significant military garrison, and a constant flow of seasonal labourers, merchants, immigrants, and seamen. Worthy of note also is the political upheaval that convulsed Lower Canada, culminating in the Rebellions of 1837–38 and the unification of Upper and Lower Canada in 1840 into the Province of Canada.[30] The Rebellions, among their other effects, resulted in the temporary cessation of normal civilian courts, with irregular courts such as the Court of Oyer and Terminer and General Gaol Delivery supplementing regular courts once civilian order was re-established.[31]

Many urban Montrealers lived in crowded, spartan homes clustered around the city core, with everyday life revolving around communal spaces.[32] Children occupied those same spaces, weaving in and out of public arenas in conducting their daily lives, and sharing rooms with extended family and even strangers. Idleness was a luxury that the working classes could neither afford nor abide, reflected by the children caught up within these realities who were accosted while running errands or engaged in household tasks. Their lives played out against this backdrop of significant economic, political, social, and demographic flux.

CHILD SEXUAL ASSAULT LAW IN HISTORICAL CONTEXT

By the seventeenth century the common law settled on a definition of rape as "unlawful carnal knowledge of a woman committed by force against her will."[33] At this time, British North American criminal law generally mirrored English law as it related to sexual assault, as both Upper and Lower Canada adopted English law as it existed on 17 September 1792.[34] The British Parliament passed the *Offences Against the Person Act* in 1828 which sought to clarify an evidentiary standard and facilitate convictions by providing that proof of penetration was sufficient to sustain the offence.[35] A reform statute some five years later abolished the benefit of clergy as a defence for sexual assault and reduced the number of capital felonies, although rape and carnal knowledge of a girl under the age of ten years remained capital.[36] This law was adopted verbatim in 1841 during the consolidation of the criminal laws for the united Province of Canada. Thus, rape remained a capital felony;[37] and proof of penetration was required for conviction.[38] The legislature of the Canadas modified the law in 1842 to include assault with attempt to commit rape, punishable by up to three years' incarceration in the provincial penitentiary or no more than two years in a common gaol or the House of Correction.[39] Only the crimes of assault with intent to commit rape or buggery were subject to this heightened sanction, the penalty for assault with intent to commit a felony being a maximum of two years' imprisonment.[40] In the event that a defendant was found not guilty of rape or assault with intent, he could be charged with misdemeanour assault and battery, punishable by fine and costs not to exceed £5 which could be summarily imposed by a justice of the peace.[41]

The legal regime governing sexual assaults against children shared similarities to the law against rape, but categorized the offence based on the victim's age. Minority, or infancy, was a fluid concept insofar as it was defined differently at varying times and by different legal systems; it was sufficiently complex a topic to justify works such as the *Treatise on the Law Relating to Infants*.[42] As MacPherson noted, in Lower Canada the age of majority was customarily set at twenty-one.[43] This mirrored the French *Civil Code*, which further limited males' right to contract marriage to a minimum of twenty-five years of age, and females to twenty-one.[44] English law likewise set the age of majority at twenty-one.[45] As such, minors were below twenty-one, but the age of consent was historically set at ten years – thus Blackstone could rail against the "abominable wickedness of carnally knowing or abusing any woman child under the age of ten years; in which case the consent or nonconsent is immaterial, as by reason of her tender years she is incapable of judgment and discretion."[46] The phrase "woman child," referring to females below the age of consent, conflates two concepts considered binary in the modern period, capturing the duality of these females being (theoretically) legally protected by virtue of their youth whilst simultaneously being targets for sexual exploitation.

As mentioned, childhood was not yet conceived of as a distinct stage; by our period, a female child was classified as twelve years of age or younger, a threshold that would remain in place for decades.[47] Offences against females were therefore centred on the age of consent: sexual assault of females under ten was capital; while the same act against a female aged ten to twelve was a misdemeanour punishable by a discretionary term of imprisonment.[48] As reflected in Tables 9.1 and 9.2, variants of these offences were found within the archives, often more descriptive than legally accurate, including "unlawful carnal knowledge," "indecent assault," "ravishment," and "criminal intercourse," while usually specifying the victim's age. As also shall be discussed, another age-based offence was abduction, which shared commonalities with sexual assault but also encompassed older victims as well as a wider spectrum of acts. All were predicated on an ethos of patriarchy grounded in a centuries-old concept of the underage child as property of her father or guardian, rather than of the child as an intrinsic rights holder.

This essay focuses on female children, under twelve years of age for crimes of sexual assault, and under sixteen for abduction. However, sexual assault prosecutions in general for this period provides useful background. My provisional analysis of the judicial archives and secondary sources identifies more than 150 cases of sexual assault against adult women for the years 1825–1850; given lacunae in the sources, this number cannot be viewed as more than a heuristic indication of the relative rate of these crimes, but it is clear they were common. These crimes included rape or ravishment, and assault with intent; but also disparate offences such as prostitution, infanticide, buggery, and abduction.[49] The largest category of offences was assault with intent to ravish, comprising just under 50 per cent of the total – but this does not include the cases in which the charge of rape was reduced to a lesser charge during indictment, nor does it generally include indecent assault. This essay adheres to the legal categorization common to the period, such that while females aged twelve or older might have been described as "minors" in period sources they were treated under the legal regime governing sexual assault of adults, and therefore are not included.

CHILD SEXUAL ASSAULT

Late Georgian and early Victorian conceptions of childhood saw the child – the "little innocent" – as inherently pure and virtuous unless sullied by their environment.[50] This construct was itself created by the respectable classes, so environment here could include race, ethnicity, social class, and the like. But this paradigm of the innocent child lived uneasily alongside its darker parallel of the "erotic child." As stated by Louise Jackson, the "concept of sexual innocence, which was elevated in the Victorian 'cult of the little girl,' was clearly dependent on its opposite: the lurking shadow of experience and adult corruption."[51] The construct of childhood therefore encompassed the dichotomy of children both as sexual innocents and as objects of sexual desire, echoes of which can be found in the woman-child duality.

The 1860s to 1870s in the UK and US saw a dawning of public awareness of child sexual abuse, a "product of a coalition of interests between the social purity societies and the burgeoning child welfare movement."[52] By the late Victorian and early Edwardian period, there were well-organized and publicized movements agitating against issues such as child prostitution and sexual abuse, although discussions of incest remained largely taboo, and debate continued over the appropriate age of consent.[53] By the end of the century, the delineation of the female child firmly took on the mantle of being an allegory for purity and goodness, a stylized depiction of the innocent victim of crime appearing in Anglo-Canadian courts, literature, and elsewhere. Of course, Lady Justice herself ironically presided over a male-dominated system.[54]

By the dawning of the twentieth century, sexual abuse was seen as perhaps the most deviant and sinister form of child abuse.[55] The legal system of this period reflected the woman-child dyad, simultaneously creating legal offences to govern harm inflicted against children while also applying evidentiary standards and doctrines that precluded successful prosecution of many such crimes. The first half of the nineteenth century had few laws safeguarding children and no social welfare agencies tasked with their protection, and child victims surfaced relatively rarely in prosecutions. Children had some nascent ability to enforce rights relative to abusive parents or masters, but these protections were circumscribed and ordinarily required adults to activate legal process.[56] Culturally, children were often the subject of sexual predation for myriad reasons; for example, in addition to the "erotic child" motif was the superstition that venereal disease could be cured through sexual congress with child virgins.[57] And if the legal system proved ill-suited to address sexual offences, predicated as it still was on private prosecution, this was even more so for crimes against children. Certainly Quebec society condemned child sexual assault in strident terms; malefactors were depicted as "wretches," "fiends," and "monsters," similarly to other jurisdictions such as late nineteenth-century Ontario.[58] This had the effect of highlighting society's condemnation while simultaneously marginalizing these crimes, permitting that they be "at the same time condemned and dismissed as an aberration."[59] Violence against children, in all its forms, tended to be situated within an "imaginary geography"[60] related to socio-economic class, race, place, and other externalities, rather than perceived as the "oppressive consequence of power and patriarchy" as Joan Sangster has noted.[61] Similarly to rape, there was a pronounced disconnect between what society and the law said about these acts, versus what the legal system actually punished.

SEXUAL ASSAULT OF A FEMALE CHILD UNDER TEN YEARS OF AGE

The most common category of child sexual assault prosecutions identified herein involved children under ten, with eight such cases being found. This is counterintuitive given the evidentiary obstacles impeding such cases, and the fact that capital crimes engendered greater reluctance on the part of juries to convict. Here two of eight cases resulted in conviction, one leading to a sentence of death (respited to a term of imprisonment) and the other to a one-year prison term for a lesser included offence. All others failed at some stage of the legal process or were frustrated by defendants eluding arrest, failing to appear in court, or fleeing.

The 1840 case of James Horn, a Chateauguay schoolmaster, resulted in his conviction for assault with intent (see third entry in Table 9.1). Newspapers revealed solely that the victim was an "interesting child of only six years of age,"[62] and that Horn was between forty and fifty and attended court on crutches.[63] The evidence against him was described as "most conclusive" and "brought the charge home to the prisoner." This assertion is buttressed by the jury returning a guilty verdict without deliberating. Newspapers predictably provided no allusion to the evidence except to note it was highly

Table 9.1 | Disposition of cases of sexual assault of a child under ten

Year/Defendant	Charge	Disposition	Sentence
1825 Jean Baptiste Labelle	Two counts unlawful carnal knowledge under age of five.	Fled jurisdiction.	N/A
1826 Joseph Massé	Rape of child under ten.	Acquitted.	N/A
1839 James Horn	Assault with intent to rape of child under ten.	Convicted.	One year's imprisonment.
1840 John Spooner	Rape/rape of child under nine.	Defendant defaulted.	N/A
1841 William Smout	Rape/assault with intent to carnally know a child under ten.	Acquitted. (Witnesses defaulted.)	N/A
1841 Andre Chevrier dit Lejeunesse	Carnally knowing a female child under ten.	No bill (no indictment).	N/A
1843 Ėtienne Carrier	Rape/violence against female child under ten.	Acquitted.	N/A
1848 Godfroy Céré	Rape/carnally knowing a child under ten.	Convicted.	Death (commuted to fourteen years' imprisonment).

inculpatory.[64] His file, however, consists of the affidavit filed by the girl's parents and extensive (albeit sometimes illegible) documents summarizing evidence, as well as a letter sent by her father to the attorney general with suggestions on how to present the case.[65] The parents alleged he "abuse[d] and assault[ed] their little daughter …

with the intent of committing a Rape" and that he "was caught in the act by the said [parents] or was so taken before he had risen from the floor or had his clothes adjusted."[66] Ultimately Horn was sentenced to one year in prison.[67] It is likely that he was charged with the lesser offence due to penetration not being alleged.[68]

Only one case during this period was found to have resulted in conviction for the full offence: the trial of Godfroy Céré for having "carnally abused" a five-year-old girl (see eighth entry in Table 9.1). Little has survived save for a fragmentary deposition from the prosecutrix who alleged that in November 1847 the victim had entered her house about 6 a.m. and told her that Céré had "laid her in his bed … taking off her clothes.[69] Described by one paper as a man of "about twenty-one or twenty-two years of age … whose appearance was by no means unpossessing," he was convicted in February 1848.[70] As sentence of death was imposed, it was said he "raised his hands in agony, as though the terrible words … had crushed his very soul."[71] The sentence was commuted to fourteen years in the provincial penitentiary, a common occurrence for this period.[72]

The difficulty in obtaining convictions in most cases can be illustrated by the 1843 case of Étienne Carrier.[73] Multiple affidavits including medical testimony outlined the case against him, alleging that he had assaulted the four-and-a-half-year-old granddaughter of a tavern keeper, Ambroise Peloquin. Carrier, a lodger, went downstairs to ask Mrs Peloquin if it was her granddaughter or grandson who would be sharing a room with him, and was told it was the former. If Carrier showed undue interest in the little girl, as it appears from the affidavit, it seemed not to have caused concern. About 3:30 a.m. another lodger heard the girl screaming.[74] Despite the testimony of the child's mother, attending physician, committing magistrate, and city registrar of births at trial, the defendant was acquitted. Newspapers highlighted (not altogether approvingly) the defence counsel's "ability and ingenuity"[75] and "eloquent and pathetic" jury summation.[76]

In contrast, prosecutions for crimes against children aged ten to twelve were fewer, as set out in Table 9.2. Perhaps the ages of the victims worked against them, as they were close enough to the age of consent to be seen as less childlike and parents declined to file complaints, yet they lacked the agency to agitate on their own behalf – the embodiment of the woman-child. The small number of these cases militates against generalizations, but it is worth noting that three of the four resulted in conviction, albeit two for a lesser offence. François

Table 9.2 | Sexual assaults against children between ten to twelve years of age

Year/Defendant	Charge	Disposition	Sentence
1829 François Reaume	Rape of a child under twelve.	Convicted of assault with intent.	One year in prison, and £25 surety for good conduct after release.
1842 Luke Bowen	Rape of a child under twelve.	Acquitted.	N/A
1847 François X. Brunelle	Rape/criminal intercourse with a child under twelve.	Convicted.	Three years' imprisonment.
1847 Michael McCluskey	Rape of a child over ten and under twelve years of age.	Convicted of assault.	Six months' hard labour.

Reaume, tried and convicted before the Court of Oyer and Terminer in August 1829, was sentenced to one year in prison coupled with surety for good behaviour in the amount of £25. He was charged with raping eleven-year-old Henriette Deparoit, but convicted of assault with intent.[77] Two other defendants were indicted on 1 February 1847, in unrelated proceedings: Michael McCluskey, a farm servant, was indicted for a "brutal assault" on an eleven year old;[78] while a true bill of indictment was found against François X. Brunelle.[79]

McCluskey was ultimately convicted of simple assault and sentenced to six months' imprisonment.[80] Brunelle suffered the most severe sentence of anyone convicted in this category, three years' imprisonment. The facts as known are that eleven-year-old Marie Belle had gone to take care of her neighbour's infant. According to her affidavit, Brunelle entered the house and accosted her but was rebuffed. He forced her upon the bed and covered her mouth with his hand before effecting his attack, threatening her life if she reported it. The neighbour returned and found Belle crying, and although initially reluctant to reveal what transpired, Belle swore out a complaint.[81] Charged with "criminal intercourse with a child under twelve years of age," Brunelle was tried a year later and convicted.[82] None of the newspapers relayed details of the evidence presented at trial.[83]

The limitations of rape law vis-à-vis children are readily apparent when one contemplates that rape necessitated an application of force, as was the case with Brunelle. Anything less than an overt attempt fell short of rape or attempted rape, and it was uncertain what offence it could constitute. Acts that now are categorized as sexual molestation, or attempts that were frustrated by a child's youth, fell into a legal no-man's-land. Moreover, it had not yet been established that nonviolent acts were actually offences at all. As Christine Stansell posited, "men's erotic attention to girls ... was not a discrete and pathological phenomenon, but a practice that existed on the fringes of 'normal' male sexuality."[84] The notion of childhood remained in flux, bringing with it the troubling questions of what rights to append to children and the repercussions of so doing. It was not until late in the nineteenth century that a growing conception of childhood began to take hold, involving different stages of physical and other development distinct from adulthood, and with it an understanding that some actions involving children were wrongs even if not involving overt violence.[85] As the century gave way to the twentieth, and legal systems took cognizance of the fact that harms visited upon a child could implicate acts that fell short of rape, offences such as "carnal abuse of a child" were promulgated.[86] Legislation of this type did not yet exist for our period, however, sheltering these acts from prosecution.

Evidence that these acts did occur, and that at least some victims or guardians engaged the legal process (however unsuccessfully) may be found in the handful of easily-overlooked offences that have survived fitfully for the Court of Quarter Sessions, the lower court of general criminal jurisdiction. The fragmentary nature of the records does not allow for significant reconstruction; and some cases involving minors may not have been identified as such. Nonetheless they are illustrative of sexual exploitation of children not fitting cleanly within the aged-based categories of child sexual assault, shoehorned imperfectly under categories such as "assault and battery with intent to ravish" or "indecent assault," as set out in Table 9.3.

Table 9.3 | Misdemeanor sexual assaults against children

Year/Defendant	Charge	Disposition	Sentence
1826 Charles Cooper	Criminal and indecent assault upon a ten-year-old girl.	No record found.	No record found.
1833 Malcolm Fraser	Assault and battery with intent to ravish.	No record found.	No record found.
1840 Thomas Williamson	Assault with intent to ravish a six-year-old girl.	Dismissed.	N/A

One of the rare surviving affidavits by a child falls into this category, wherein Charles Cooper was accused of committing "criminal and indecent assaults" upon ten-year-old Mary Wright.[87] In her affidavit, she alleged that two months earlier, the defendant "threw her down on the ground, then lay down himself, and afterwards got up again, and took her to his house, where being alone, he took her on his knee, unbuttoned his small clothes and put his hands up her petticoats." She continued by saying that three weeks later she was sent by her mother to get apples from Cooper who "again treated her in the same manner until she cried."[88] Her mother's deposition complemented Mary's, alleging that she would not have sent her to Cooper's house had she known of the abuse; and that she understood that on the first occasion "Cooper assaulted and behaved very indecently to her putting his hand up her petticoats and taking down his own small clothes," while on the second he "made a similar indecent assault upon the said child exposing and feeling her private parts and his own and did not let her go until she cried."[89] It is evident these acts did not fit under the definition of sexual assault as it then existed, but equally so that both the victim and her mother viewed this as a violation the law could and should address. The allegations against Malcolm Fraser, for "assault and [b]attery ... with intent to ravish" have survived only as a short defence affidavit by his father that attested to nothing more than his birthday.[90] Nothing further could be gleaned about this case; and the affidavit, while cryptic, likely was prompted by the doctrine that a male under fourteen was legally incapable of committing rape.[91] The inference that Malcolm Fraser was therefore not quite eleven and a half years old would presumably have been clear to jurists. The charge itself implied there was no penetration, another example of the difficulties attendant to prosecuting these cases.

The last of these implicated the defendant in two contemporaneous complaints emanating from the same incident, for assault with intent to ravish, as well as being idle and disorderly. Sworn by Francis C.F. Arnoldi, a justice of the peace himself, he alleged:

> [H]e hath every reason to believe that an individual servant to William Douglas of Montreal merchant whose name is unknown to the Deponent hath committed an assault upon one Fanny Arnoldi, the daughter of the deponent aged six years old with intent to ravish her ... that the said individual hath given his name in presence of the deponent as Thomas Williamson.[92]

The same day Arnoldi also swore out a complaint against Williamson charging him with being a "loose idle and disorderly person" who "hath so acted in openly and indecently exposing his person contrary to the provision of the ordinance in such case made and to the evil example of all others in like case offending." Here at least we know the outcome; the records of the Montreal Gaol reveal the complaint against him was dismissed after he was examined.[93] The absence of information on other cases is frequently indicative that the case did not proceed. In this instance, even a well-connected and respectable person such as Arnoldi, himself a jurist, was not able to move a prosecution forward, as the misogyny embedded in the system apparently triumphed over class.These three cases, fragmentary as they are, all involved parents as active participants in legal process – Cooper and Arnoldi as prosecutors; and Fraser as a parent intervening to forestall further legal proceedings. These cases highlight how singularly ill designed the law was to capture anything other than a narrow range of sexual acts perpetrated against children. Indeed, it is likely that jurists viewed such acts as more akin to assault and battery. As William Oldnall Russell's treatise explicated, in the context of discussing the requirement of emission:

> [W]here the violence has proceeded to the extent of an actual penetration of the unhappy sufferer's body, an injury of the highest kind has been effected. The quick sense of honour, the pride of virtue, which nature, in order to render the sex amiable, has implanted in the female heart, is violated beyond redemption; and the injurious consequences to society are in every respect complete.[94]

This "sense of honour, the pride of virtue," et cetera might have been "violated beyond redemption," as Russell wrote, but none of that helped effect conviction, even less so where the act stopped short of penetration. This ambiguity as to whether these acts were non-sexual or indecent assaults helped doom them. If sexual offences, they did not meet the requisite evidentiary standards for the crime; if not, they likewise did not fit neatly under the rubric of assault and battery. These cases signify some halting attempts to incorporate these within existing categories of the criminal law, albeit in ways more descriptive than legally accurate, such as the 1832 complaint alleging "assault and battery and outrages committed upon the body of a woman." Amidst a sea of assault and battery complaints, this stands out for its reference to gross and illicit behaviour ("outrages") that neither rose to assault with intent, nor was captured within the taxonomy of criminal law. Suggesting both a physical and moral violation, it was ultimately charged as aggravated assault and battery.[95] But "aggravated" it could not be without the use of a weapon or showing of serious physical injury, rendering the charge legally futile.

A period example showing the conundrum posed by such acts occurred in 1850 involving a prosecution for assault with intent to commit a rape. It was alleged the defendant made "insulting propositions" before returning later the same night to fondle the prosecutrix while she was in bed. There was no claim of penetration nor of the attempt. The jury convicted him of simple assault, which the presiding judge took under advisement as "he did not know if the offence could be properly stiled (sic) an assault as … the offence would partake more of the nature of a caress."[96] Acts such as these therefore straddled two categories, but were successful as neither, until the legal system evolved to recognize "indecent assaults" later in the century.[97]

LEGAL PROCESS, DYNAMICS, AND THEMES

Our ability to analyze these trials is limited by the many obstacles posed by the sources and processes themselves, but they suggest some conclusions about child sexual assault trials during this period. The definition of rape – unlawful carnal knowledge committed by force and against the victim's will – accorded jurists wide latitude in interpreting whether an offence had taken place, in this as in other jurisdictions.[98]

While it cannot be stated based on these sources whether there was an ideology of sex and gender specific to Montreal of this period, conviction in rape cases was predicated on a much higher evidentiary threshold than the law required.[99] Since there were widely-accepted standards as to the level of resistance expected, for example, the question of consent took on heightened importance and centred on the victim's credibility.[100] Indeed, victims were responsible for driving the administration of justice, as cases were initiated by a prosecutrix or other individual swearing out complaints and initiating and paying for legal process, which, as noted earlier, was particularly burdensome for children.[101] Embedded in this are three distinct points that must be highlighted with regard to the child victim: firstly, while women were expected to have shown fierce resistance before being overcome, this would have been nonsensical in most cases involving children. Secondly, the issue of credibility was met with legal ambivalence. On the one hand, no evidence was found that children's precociousness was used against them nor were there allegations they had been willing participants in the sexual bartering that surfaced in many defences to allegations of sexual assault. Moreover, consent could not be at issue; in fact, these offences were precursors to the crime of statutory rape.[102] On the other hand, children's credibility was implicitly suspect due to their age, which disqualified many from giving sworn evidence and required corroborative testimony from other witnesses, and there is evidence that the credibility of relatives impacted the outcome as any hint of "ill repute" sabotaged successful prosecution. Lastly, children could not navigate the legal system themselves, even were they aware of it; they required an adult to initiate and finance the filing of a case.

The strong evidentiary hurdles that militated against successful sexual assault prosecutions in general were even more heightened here. If proof of penetration was required – and in its absence even the most egregious violations fell short – what could this have meant for the youngest victims? Their physical immaturity could stymie completion of the assault, rendering it legally a mere attempt no matter how traumatizing or injurious it might have been. Such was the case with François Reaume's eleven-year-old victim.[103] So too with John Spooner, charged with assaulting a nine-year-old girl in 1840. Her father, a house joiner, accused Spooner of "intent to commit a rape and did with force lay hold of her … and her abuse and evilly entreat in a most shameful manner," but "owing to her tender years he could not succeed in having carnal knowledge."[104] Proof of injury neither obviated the need for a showing that the act was completed, nor was sufficiently inculpatory to generally support conviction on the full offence. And, as shown, molestation did not fit within these definitions at all.

With respect to the victims, few left behind written evidence. Period affidavits often reflected the magistrate's transposition of allegations into formulaic legalese, and this could only have been even more probable when child victims were involved.[105] It is unlikely that eleven-year-old Malonie Poutré stated that she had been "violently and feloniously assaulted by the same Luke Bowen … [who] with force and arms against the will of the said Malonie Poutré then and there feloniously did ravish and carnally know"; this reflects a synthesis of her allegations into legal jargon that would have been outside the commonplace usage of a nonjurist, let alone an eleven year old.[106] Contrast this with nine-year-old Julia Dunvar's complaint, which alleged that her assailant had "pulled her down into his lap and pulled out all that he had and put it between her legs … before he began to do it, he took spittle from his mouth with his finger and put it upon her between her legs."[107] Dunvar's affidavit seemingly captured her account verbatim; while Poutré's voice was entirely erased. Also common was opaque verbiage that might (but probably did not) reflect the complainant's words such as "[he] executed his design in spite of all my resistance."[108]

If the complainant was rendered largely mute, forensic medical evidence could be expected to play an important role. Children's allegations required corroboration seldom available from eyewitnesses, and so medical testimony was crucial.[109] While pediatric medicine was yet to emerge as a distinct field, treatises on medical jurisprudence provided information on the evidence useful in prosecuting sexual assault, including that of children.[110] The semiology of children's bodies provides unsettling proof of the physical trauma they endured as well as delineations of the type of evidence offered at trial, such as the four-year-old twins "infected ... with the Venereal disease" in 1825. This case could have been instructive insofar as how this might have been used at trial but the accused unhelpfully fled prior to arrest.[111] Newspapers alluded to such evidence; as delicately noted in one newspaper, "certain parts of the child had been injured by the prisoner."[112] Allegations in affidavits could be more explicit, including appalling disclosures by one mother who found the "parts" of her four-and-a-half-year-old daughter "to be much inflamed the blood flowing abundantly," with her bed and clothes blood soaked.[113] This case file includes affidavits from surgeons attesting to "evident marks of injury," including that she was found "bleeding profusely from the vagina, the perineum was lacerated and the membrane torn, [and] the hymen had also been lacerated."[114] Tried on the "horrible and revolting charge," with several witnesses appearing for the Crown and damning medical evidence, the defendant was nonetheless acquitted.[115] The verdict resulted in a commotion from the audience.[116]

The file for François Reaume has not survived but offers the only pardon application found for such a case. In it evidence of injury was referenced although almost in passing. Reaume's (unsuccessful) petition alleged that he "has a wife of a very sickly constitution and two helpless children which are now totaly (sic) distressed, and Depends only upon your Excellency's Petitioner to Suport (sic) them" and that he "Humbly beg(s) leave to hope as it is the first time he had fell (sic) in the hands of Justice that your Excellency may be most Graciously pleased to take his unfortunate Case into your Excellency's most well known human(e) consideration, and to grant him a Pardon."[117] A letter written by Chief Justice James Reid and Justice George Pyke, to the administrator of the Province of Lower Canada, opposed his request for clemency as the "evidence at his Trial was one of a highly aggravated nature" in which he followed the victim from her father's house "where he had been hospitably received,"and "dragging her with violence into the wood where her youth alone prevented the perpetration of the crime he had meditated, though not without injuring the Child in other respects."[118] The emphasis on Reaume's predatory conduct towards a neighbour, the act of forcibly removing and restraining the victim, and the nature of her injuries were all factors emphasized by the judges in their condemnation of this crime as "highly aggravated," and no doubt had swayed the jury as well. The role of medical evidence in these cases therefore appears to be simultaneously crucially important and yet often legally irrelevant. While it may have offered compelling indicia of force, strictly speaking that was unnecessary as victims were below the age of consent; if inculpatory in demonstrating an assault had taken place, it nevertheless could not corroborate that it had been committed by a specific assailant.[119] The inability of medical testimony to substantiate the complainant's evidence by itself – or to take its place, when the complainant's youth meant they could not be sworn – meant this evidence was routinely presented to, and just as routinely disregarded by, the jurors who heard it. Cases such as Reaume's remained the exception.

Indeed, many of the victims were very young, and these offences clearly pedophilic. Witness the ages of the alleged victims of Jean Baptiste Labelle the younger (both four years old), Ėtienne Carrier (four and a half), Geoffrey Céré (five), and James Horn and Thomas Williamson (six).[120] These cases also indicate similar clustering around the upper limits of the band covered by these offences, such as the cases of John Spooner (nine), Charles Cooper (ten), and François Brunelle, François Reaume, and Michael McCluskey (eleven). This latter group, by virtue of the victims' ages, generally fits within the misdemeanour offence by definition; but is also suggestive that assailants viewed these victims as the woman-child to whom they had the right of sexual access: "[y]ou must lie with me," said Brunelle to eleven-year-old Marie Belle, prior to forcing himself on her.[121]

The victims' youth had many repercussions here. For the younger victims, as noted, it might prevent assailants from consummating the offence at all; but in general, it made children easy prey. As also noted, it meant that victims were frequently disqualified from having their testimony taken down as sworn statements. Little can be said about how children's testimony in these cases was received, except to note that there is no indication their age could do anything other than hamper prosecution.[122] This disability, coupled with the lack of corroborative testimony, would have doomed many cases at the onset. And of course fear or the sexual shame experienced by these children also made some reluctant to disclose the abuse; as Mary Wright attested, "[t]hat being then afraid of the said [defendant] she told her mother of what had happened as indeed [she] should have done from the beginning had she not been ashamed."[123] Threats were sometimes explicit; Marie Belle's attacker vowed that "if I told or disclosed the deed he would cut my guts out with his knife [while] at the same time showing me the knife."[124] The agency shown by some children in swearing out affidavits after the traumatic events they endured, even after threats such as these, is remarkable. Other children, particularly the youngest, would not have understood what had happened to them, or been too scared to confide in their parents.[125]

Cases that survived indictment tended to fail for the usual litany of reasons common to sexual assault cases. These included the failure of parties to appear, such as in an 1842 case for "assault with intent carnally to know and abuse a woman child under ten years of age" in which no Crown witnesses appeared.[126] This was not uncommon, as parties might be expected to appear in court repeatedly, unaware of when their case would actually be heard, or have informally settled the case, among other explanations.[127] As always, some defendants opted to abscond prior to their arrest or defaulted on bail.[128]

Given the attendant difficulties in securing a conviction, one may well wonder why parents pursued legal redress at all. It is possible that some naively felt that justice was surely to be had, but this alone could not account for the number of cases. The involvement of women from the lower classes in the legal system, as litigants, prosecutors (and defendants), renders it unlikely to suppose that the parents in these stories were not aware of the hurdles they faced.[129] Why did they, then, believe it worthwhile to engage with the criminal justice system? Were they motivated by a desire for accountability, with the hope that the public nature of these cases would tar the defendants regardless of the formal outcome? Or did they hope the process itself would restore or preserve the respectability of the child victim and her family? Did they seek vindication, settlement from the defendant, or some form of acknowledgment?[130] While these cases may have tarnished defendants' reputations, given social mores of the period, it seems just as likely that these children would be seen as "damaged goods" regardless of the outcome of such cases. These factors suggest a complex reality underlying the motivations for such cases.

Both Anglo-Canadians and French-Canadians engaged the legal system here. French-Canadian names are well represented and constitute a bare majority of ten out of nineteen defendants, with the rest identified as Anglo-Canadian. None of the parties were identified as Indigenous or Afro-Canadian.[131] What is striking amongst this demographic is that victim-perpetrators fell on clear ethnic lines: Anglo-Canadians preyed on Anglo-Canadian children, and French-Canadians preyed on French-Canadian children. The exception, Luke Bowen's assault in 1842, appeared to be an opportunistic one.[132] This is consistent with the view that adults targeted children within their communities and social circles, which mirrored linguistic and ethnic lines.

Regardless of their ethnicity, the reputation of the complainant was all-important as a determinant.[133] As Philip Girard observed, "Defense counsel ... employed a range of techniques to weaken or gainsay the prosecution evidence ... includ[ing] putting the victim on trial in sexual assault cases."[134] Impugning a victim's reputation remained a stratagem as common as it was effective. For the youngest victims, it was their parents whose reputation was targeted, although older children could be as well. A case involving the rape of a twelve-year-old girl in 1842 was described as "fully made out on the part of the Crown" but failed as defence counsel showed the "complainant was a person of bad character and that her mother and elder sister, who ... were the only essential witnesses, were persons of loose character, and as such could not be believed on oath." The jury returned a not guilty verdict without deliberating.[135]

Indeed, parents and guardians played an outsized role in these cases; no doubt they decided in many instances whether to pursue legal proceedings at all, but they were always central figures. Most typically it was one parent (or both jointly) who swore out a complaint, often supplemented by testimony from an attending physician, as well as other supporting witnesses if available.[136] This likely provides us with the evidentiary contours common to most prosecutions, as illustrated by a rare account detailing a trial in which the solicitor general "called the mother of the child, the physician, committing Magistrate, [and] the Registrar of [B]irths, who deposed to the facts charged in the indictment."[137] We can infer that the mother was called to testify to the circumstances surrounding the assault; the physician to the medical evidence; the committing magistrate to the circumstances and timing with respect to the charges being filed; and the registrar of births to the child's age and parentage. This array of testimony was likely the most robust that a typical case could realistically muster, and it was not often successful.

It is true that defendants could incriminate themselves, and sporadically did – although not at trial as they could not testify – but this rarely had any effect. Judges held an institutionalized mistrust of confessions and excluded those found to have been made in the hope of leniency. This phenomenon was reflected in other criminal cases, including infanticide and spousal murder, and also here.[138] Joseph Massé "[o]on the road to Chambly … after he was arrested, made several confessions, but as they appeared to be extorted by a hope of freedom, the Court did not permit them to go before the Jury."[139] This custom was derided by some contemporary critics. As one editorial posited under the heading of "Suppression of Truth and Exclusion of Evidence," when a prisoner was examined by a magistrate "the first care of his worship is to caution the man to say nothing that may betray him, as if the great business of justice was to keep the truth from too prompt and distinct a discovery." Moreover, police "are looked coldly on or rebuked if they tender any evidence of confession, though not extorted, but yielded in the confusion of guilt or in the despair of concealment. They profit by these lessons, and become the protectors of criminals." The editor went on to reference a recent case:

> A miscreant forcibly violated an infant under five years of age, the child of his mistress. When apprehended he began his confession to the officer, who stopped him short, desiring him to say nothing to commit himself, just as any magistrate would have done. The only evidence for the conviction of the wretch was thus excluded. The horribly injured child was under the age for an oath, and her testimony could therefore not be had, and there was no other, the lips of the criminal having been closed by the servant of justice when about to reveal the particulars of his detestable crime.

As the editor concluded, the suspect "is therefore acquitted, may repeat the same part to-morrow, and others may imitate him, and the police fulfil the office of the criminal's remembrancer.[140] If the child victim could not testify, and there were no other eyewitnesses, even the defendant's own confession would not prove inculpatory.

These cases share the commonality of male predatory conduct against the children of neighbours and friends. Children lived in close proximity to adults, in crowded inner-city tenements, barracks, boarding houses, and homes. They traveled freely to perform errands, were left at home by parents, and were targeted whilst doing the most banal activities, unsupervised, in the most mundane of places in which they lived and worked.[141] These acts encompassed a range of activities, although seemingly not playing.[142] They were assaulted in their homes as parents laboured outside, as George Burhart was alleged to have done.[143] Children fell victim to lodgers in taverns and inns owned by their parents as they slept.[144] They were attacked in neighbour's homes whilst tending infants.[145] Even children living in crowded army barracks were vulnerable, as evidenced by Mary Anne Anderson, the young daughter of a colour serjeant in Her Majesty's Sixty-Seventh Regiment of Foot. Following a forty-five-minute absence on Good Friday, the parents returned to find a private in the regiment lying upon their daughter: her "cloathes (sic) were raised above her knees and she was struggling with him"; as they entered the room the defendant ran past them "in a stooping position." Mary Anne was at first uncooperative in detailing what had occurred until her father threatened to flog her.[146]

If children could be easily preyed upon in cities, this was no less true in the relative privacy afforded by rural locales. Children were waylaid in woods where they gathered berries and flowers, or retrieved cows for milking.[147] There was no evidence that these perpetrators offered gifts or other inducements to lure children, but rather pursued children who were already known to them.[148] This included close relatives, although this appeared much less frequent. A rare example found in print was published under the tagline "PUNISHMENT OF DEATH," recounting how a labourer was sentenced to be hanged "for violating the person of his own daughter, aged ten years and a half." At his sentencing the presiding judge "intimated to the culprit that the circumstances of his crime would render the Executive deaf to any application for a mitigation of his punishment." The editor went on to describe this crime as having "a character of unexampled demoralization. It is one of those, almost unheard of in the annals of humanity."[149] While the tone of abhorrence was unequivocal – to which the incestuous nature of the crime no doubt contributed – power dynamics within families meant that the force used in many cases of incest was more likely psychosocial rather than physical.[150] Daughters were often reluctant to allege, and families equally reluctant to disclose or acknowledge, such abuse.[151] Incest was also an ecclesiastical rather than statutory offence.[152] As such, these cases were even less likely to surface within the records, and realistically were only prosecutable if they could be subsumed under the rubric of sexual assault. Shadow evidence of these acts did emerge, most often in the context of domestic violence or child abuse, but these were uncommon.[153] The sanctity of family privacy, the dynamics of the acts themselves, the revulsion with which they were viewed, and the fact that an overt use of force was required all militated against prosecution; hence it was only rarely these acts were captured within the archives. One such case was found here, the 1826 trial of Joseph Massé for assaulting his niece. Described as a crime of the "most flagrant nature ... attended with circumstances the most shocking by a married man," a newspaper account documented that "the child's mother and the wife of the prisoner went in search of her, and found her lying on the floor of the cellar [of her uncle's house], covered with blood and quite intoxicated."[154]

This theme of intoxication was recurrent. Alcohol was used to make children pliant, as was the case with Joseph Massé; but more often the assailant himself was inebriated, as was François Brunelle. The interplay between alcoholism and violence was legally conflicted, often mitigating the actions of the assailant and enhancing the culpability of the victim. James Horn's file contains a letter from the victim's father to the attorney general which identifies a witness to establish that the "prisoner ... was sensible and not intoxicated," while the magistrate's notes on witness testimony include reference to the defendant as a "dangerous and dissipated person" who was "so drunk he could not get to the door"; and ends with a query: "[given] the characteristic of men never to allow they are drunk; how given it that the schoolmaster admits it?"[155] The implication here was that Horn would only admit to drunkenness if it was exculpatory. It was not always, of course, and a claim of inebriation did not accrue to Reaume's benefit in his 1829 bid for clemency referenced earlier. The judges who had presided over his trial were pointed in their opposition to his petition: "We can readily believe such brutal conduct may have been the effect of Liquor, but we cannot on that account feel justified in recommending the prisoner to the clemency of His Excellency."[156] Alcohol played its part in the sexual assault of children, just as it did in cases of domestic violence and homicides.[157]

THE OFFENCE OF ABDUCTION

However uneasy the fit between child sexual abuse and the legal regime governing it, there were other offences that implicated similar crimes. One such offence, abduction, is a logical adjunct to child sexual assault despite not always implicating rape, and being aimed at females under the age of sixteen rather than under twelve. Abduction was defined as the "unlawful taking or detention of any female for purposes of marriage, concubinage, or prostitution."[158] Included in this was therefore taking or detaining for purposes of ravishment. Russell's treatise discussed abduction in the section immediately following rape, unlawful carnal knowledge of female children, and sodomy.[159] Its relationship to other acts can be discerned by the title of his chapter: "Of the forcible abduction and unlawful taking away of females; and of clandestine marriages." It also had a complex relationship with property: the male guardian's property rights in their child or ward, certainly; but also protection of property rights held by women who were heirs apparent or held property of their own. Some of these cases have few surviving documents yet allow us to see the contours of these acts and how they intersected with sexual assault. All shared the commonality of being applications of paternalistic laws designed to govern unmarried women.

While forcible removal of a female could implicate abduction as well as sexual assault, some cases involved neither. Complaints of abduction could include elopements of willing partners in the face of disapproving fathers in his role as paterfamilias.[160] Such was the prosecution of Joseph Guitard for having "forcibly and feloniously abducted and stolen an heiress" of sixteen years and "of having afterwards married and defiled her and … having unlawfully and feloniously conveyed and taken [her] away from the care and possession of her parents and against their will and consent."[161] The property aspect of the offence remains palpable: the "heiress" removed from the "care and possession of her parents." Other cases encompass what is now referred to as abduction by a non-custodial parent.[162]

More commonly and relevantly, however, abduction involved sex-based crimes. The close interplay between the two could result in occasional confusion, as illustrated by a newspaper that identified one rape prosecution in 1843 as "abduction" when the allegations in the file and other newspapers did not bear this out.[163] However, as shown in table 9.4, four of the six cases involving abduction clearly evince the symbiotic relationship between these crimes. The prosecution of Joseph Latulip in 1840 is one such case. The complainant, Julie Carpentier, attested she was in the woods with her mother and two young men when she was accosted by the defendant. She spurned his advances; he then seized her and carried her to a wagon, driving her (along with his brother) to their family's house. Alerted to the events, Carpentier's father went to a local justice of the peace, who together secured her release. The next day Latulip returned and told her father "that if he did not make deponent get up out of bead (sic) that he ... would blow out the candle and brake (sic) what there was in the house and drag deponent out of bead (sic) dressed or not dressed." She arose, after which he "made a spring at her ... and she sliped (sic) through his hands ... and was obliged to make her escape through the window."[164] These facts leave little doubt of the culprit's intent.

Examples were also found involving procuring of women for prostitution. Two of these cases appear related: few details are known about Zoe Seguin, the "old hag" and only female defendant found in this study, other than she failed to appear in court to answer to the charge of abduction in her role as a procuress of a young woman to a Montreal brothel.[165] She is, however, almost certainly one of the parties alleged to have been spirited away by François Xavier Beaudry as a means of stymying his prosecution. Beaudry was implicated in multiple offences related to abduction, being indicted in 1847 for two counts of obstructing justice through "abduction of witnesses" (curiously referring to abduction here not in the strict legal sense) prior to his eventual prosecution two years later.[166] As documented in one account, this "outrage" of abducting a young girl, the "daughter of a poor habitant at Boucherville, under circumstances which excited a strong feeling at the time (now some two years ago)" had also resulted in two other indictments against the defendant "for keeping back witnesses who had important evidence to give in the case." The paper went on to explain that Beaudry is "a man possessed of considerable property, and the crown officers had reason to suppose that unfair means had been used to get the witnesses out of the way," as an explanation for the lengthy delay in bringing him to justice.[167] As further detailed, the "principal witness now, was the keeper of a house of ill-fame, to which the little girl was conveyed, after she was brought to Montreal by a horrible old hag, who played the part of procuress, and who is one of the witnesses not forthcoming."[168] The testimony of this witness and that of her father led the jury to convict. Beaudry was sentenced to six months' incarceration, coupled with a hefty fine of £500; this amount doubtlessly influenced both by his being affluent as well as the pecuniary motive that drove the crime.[169] Thus we have here what looks very much like a mid-nineteenth-century human trafficking ring.

Table 9.4 | Abduction prosecutions

Year/Defendant	Charge	Disposition	Sentence
1830 Joseph Guitard	Abduction/rape.*	Arrested and bailed; writ of habeas corpus.	No record found.
1840 Joseph Latulip	Assault with intent to ravish/ abduction.	No record found.	No record found.
1841 Emile Blais	Abduction.	Writ of habeas corpus.	No record found.
1846 Zoe Seguin	Abduction/ seduction.	Defendant defaulted.	N/A
1849 François X. Beaudry	Abduction.	Convicted.	Six months' imprisonment, £500 fine.
1850 Michael Coleman	Abduction.	Convicted.	Three years' imprisonment.

*Appears to have been a case of elopement.

The archives also disclose an abduction case that raised a novel legal question: could a defendant be charged with abduction if he was also the victim's guardian? The 1850 case of Michael Coleman raised this question, as he was stepfather to Anne Murray, the young woman he was accused of having abducted. Apprehended while trying to take her across the US border, Coleman was tried for abduction of a girl under sixteen years of age. While the file has not survived, his case is amply documented in the period press, disclosing among other salient facts that he paid an acquaintance to help lure his stepdaughter away from home. Although calling no witnesses (common for defendants in sex-based crimes for this period), his attorneys offered a spirited defence, successfully disqualifying his wife from testifying based on spousal privilege but arguing unsuccessfully that the victim's age was not satisfactorily established. At trial there was ample evidence of his misdeeds, including testimony from six witnesses – unusually, this included testimony from Ann herself.

The main defence strategy was to argue that under the civil law the accused was vested with guardianship of the girl and accordingly could not be her abductor. The court reserved judgment on this novel point of law, ultimately holding that this would properly be a "motion to arrest the verdict" should he be convicted, which unhappily for Coleman he was after only five minutes' deliberation.[170] Two weeks later, the court reconvened to rule on the motion. Justice Rolland emphasized that Ann's stepfather had taken her "from the possession and custody" of her mother while the mother was "under the marital puissance [authority] of her husband." The mother had guardianship prior to the marriage under "the law of nature," and the "subsequent marriage did not take it altogether from her." Furthermore, he had not been formally appointed as guardian. The mother then held the right to guardianship conjointly with him. "The right of protutor with which he was invested by his acquisition of the *puissance maritale* did not entirely destroy the right of the mother; it rather invested the stepfather with the duties and responsibilities, then with the rights and powers of the *tutelle* [guardian]." Under UK law, which the court stated was much more expansive in terms of the husband's authority, the mother still held power of guardianship. As the court concluded, "the *puissance* of the husband, then, being greater than in Canada, who shall say that the mother, who is under that stricter system, even, left this power, has not with us this power of protection over the morals and safety of her child, in the absence of the father. If so, this would be most especially her right when the father, being absent, is the person endeavouring to debauch her daughter." He may have been her guardian, the court ruled, but that was no defence when he held it jointly with the girl's mother, and moreover was the person committing the crime – the word "debauch" making clear to us the intent behind the act. Accordingly, the court denied the motion to arrest the verdict.[171] Coleman was sentenced to three years in the provincial penitentiary.[172]

Abduction cases are therefore a logical adjunct to child sexual abuse cases, although commonly involving the woman-child over the age of twelve, and involving a range of acts. The interplay between sexual assault and abduction is made manifest by these examples, involving as they do kidnapping, forcible concubinage or prostitution, and the like.

CONCLUSION

Conceptions of childhood were slow to change, and it would not be until the late nineteenth century ebbed into the twentieth that the notion of childhood, as a distinct psychosocial and physical stage of development, took root. Legal adaptation was even slower, and children were accorded legal rights haltingly as the century progressed.

Many factors militated against child abuse being successfully prosecuted – the obstacles common to prosecution of sexual assault in general, coupled with the socio-legal dynamics unique to those below the age of majority. If a system of private prosecution founded on masculine authority and privilege was ill designed to provide redress for victims of sexual assault, as it was, this was more markedly so for its youngest victims. Without child victim advocates and social welfare agencies, an adult guardian's initiation of legal proceeding was a sine qua non for such cases, but even when cases were filed young children could not testify and often could not swear out depositions. Only older children had any degree of agency and were accorded a voice in the process, although not at the trial itself. Medical evidence was of little assistance, as it generally could not be tied to a specific defendant; and the panoply of reasons that diverted sexual assault prosecutions were often in full play here as well. The young women here were legally protected only insofar as their minority status was reflected in the categories of sexual assault the law recognized; otherwise age was an impediment. They were too young to be believed in court, but not too young to be shielded from men's sexual advances. The historical record also indicates the woman-child would not have fared much better as an adult victim-witness in period courts. Despite these age-based crimes, many manifestations of child sexual abuse did not comport with any category of offence at all. With its emphasis on penetrative acts, assault that were not fully consummated – common with young victims – could at best be prosecuted as attempts. Children were physically violated, traumatized, even grievously injured, but under the gendered legal system of the period, only a very few could be deemed to have been legally violated. In the absence of statutory provisions covering indecent assaults, acts of molestation did not fit within any cognizable category, seen more as caresses than crimes. For the woman-child, neither the law as written nor as applied provided justice for more than a small minority of victims.

NOTES

I am indebted to Blaine Baker, Angela Fernandez, Brian Young, Mary Anne Poutanen, Constance Backhouse, Donald Fyson, and Jim Phillips for insightful comments on earlier drafts.

1 *Montreal Gazette*, 21 August 1826 (citing *Montreal Herald*).

2 See, e.g., Constance Backhouse, *Carnal Crimes: Sexual Assault Law in Canada, 1900–1975* (Toronto: The Osgoode Society for Canadian Legal History, 2008), 1 and generally.

3 For discussion of how the legal system fitfully prosecuted cases of child abuse and neglect for this period, see Ian C. Pilarczyk, "'To Shudder at the Bare Recital of those Acts': Child Abuse, Family, and Montreal Courts in the Early Nineteenth Century," in *Essays in the History of Canadian Law, Volume XI: Quebec and the Canadas*, edited by G. Blaine Baker and Donald Fyson (Toronto: University of Toronto Press for the Osgoode Society for Canadian Legal History, 2013), 370–426.

4 This study therefore excludes sexual assaults against females over the age of twelve; assaults of males, including children; and the wider range of sexual-based offences that included seduction, buggery, infanticide, bigamy, and the like.

5 For representative examples for the US and UK see, e.g., Marybeth Hamilton Arnold, "'The Life of a Citizen in the Hands of a Woman': Sexual Assault in New York City, 1790–1820, in *Passion and Power: Sexuality in History*, edited by Kathy Peiss and Christine Simmons (Philadelphia: Temple University Press, 1989), 35–56; Anna Clark, *Women's Silence, Men's Violence: Sexual Assault in England, 1770–1845* (London: Pandora, 1987); Shani D'Cruze, *Crimes of Outrage: Sex, Violence, and Victorian Working Women* (Southern Illinois University Press: DeKalb, 1998); Merrill D. Smith, ed., *Sex Without Consent: Rape and Sexual Coercion in America* (New York University Press: NY, 2001).

6 These works include Constance B. Backhouse, *Carnal Crimes: Sexual Assault Law in Canada, 1900–1975* (Toronto: The Osgoode Society for Canadian Legal History, 2008); Backhouse, "The Sayer Street Outrage:

Gang Rape and Male Law in 19th Century Toronto," in *Glimpses of Canadian Legal History*, edited by Dale Gibson and Wesley Pue (Winnipeg: Legal Research Institute, University of Manitoba, 1991), 47; Backhouse, "Nineteenth-Century Canadian Rape Law, 1800–1892," in *Essays in the History of Canadian Law, Volume II*, edited by D.H. Flaherty (Toronto: University of Toronto Press, 1983), 200; Backhouse, "Rape," in *Petticoats and Prejudice: Women and Law in Nineteeth-Century Canada* (Toronto: The Osgoode Society by Women's Press, 1991), 81; Terry L. Chapman, "Sex Crimes in the West, 1890–1920, An Overview," in *Papers from the Canadian Law in History Conference, Volume II* (Ottawa: Carleton University, 1987); Patrick J. Connor, "'The Law Should Be Her Protector': The Criminal Prosecution of Rape in Upper Canada, 1791–1850," in *Sex without Consent: Rape and Sexual Coercion in America*, edited by Merril D. Smith (New York: New York University Press, 2001), 103; Karen Dubinsky, *Improper Advances: Rape and Heterosexual Conflict in Ontario, 1880–1929* (Chicago: University of Chicago Press, 1993); Leslie Erickson, *Westward Bound: Sex, Violence, the Law and the Making of a Settler Society* (Vancouver: UBC Press for the Osgoode Society for Canadian Legal History, 2011); Dubinsky and Adam Givertiz, "'It Was Only a Matter of Passion': Masculinity and Sexual Danger," in *Gendered Pasts; Historical Essays in Feminity and Masculinity in Canada*, edited by Kathryn McPherson et al. (Toronto: University of Toronto Press, 2003), 65–79; Dubinsky, "Sex and Shame: Some Thoughts on the Social and Historical Meaning of Rape," in *Rethinking Canada: The Promise of Women's History*, edited by Veronica Strong-Broy and Anita Clair Fellman (Toronto: Oxford University Press, 1997), 171–81 (focusing on rural and northern Ontario, 1880–1930); Ruth A. Olson, "Rape: An 'Un-Victorian' Aspect of Life in Upper Canada," *Ontario History* 68, no. 2 (June 1976): 75–9; Carolyn Strange, "Patriarchy Modified: The Criminal Prosecution of Rape in York County, Ontario, 1880–1930," in *Essays in the History of Canadian Law, Volume V*, edited by J. Phillips, T. Loo, and S. Lewthwaite (Toronto: University of Toronto Press, 1994), 207.

7 Backhouse, *Carnal Crimes*, 166. This was likewise true of prosecutions for such crimes. Ibid., 168.

8 Louise A. Jackson, *Child Sexual Abuse in Victorian England* (London; New York: Routledge, 2000).

9 Stephen Robertson, *Crimes Against Children: Sexual Violence and Legal Culture in New York City, 1880–1960* (Chapel Hill; London: The University of North Carolina Press, 2005).

10 See, e.g., Nancy Hathaway Steinburg, *Children and the Criminal Law in Connecticut, 1635–1855: Changing Perceptions of Childhood* (London; New York: Routledge, 2005), 161–82; Carol-Ann Hooper, "Child Sexual Abuse and the Regulation of Women: Variations on a Theme," in *Regulating Womanhood: Historical Essays on Marriage, Motherhood and Sexuality*, edited by Carol Smart (London; New York: Routledge, 1992), 53–77.

11 Bruce Curtis, "'Illicit' Sexuality and Public Education in Ontario, 1840–1907," *Historical Studies in Education* 1, no. 1 (Spring 1989): 73–94.

12 Terry L. Chapman, "'Inquiring Minds Want to Know': The Handling of Children in Sex Assault Cases in the Canadian West, 1890–1920," in *Dimensions of Childhood, Essays on the History of Children and Youth in Canada*, edited by Russell Smandych et al. (Winnipeg: Legal Research Institute of the University of Manitoba, 1991), 183–204; Joan Sangster, "Masking and Unmasking the Sexual Abuse of Children: Perceptions of Violence Against Children in 'The Badlands' of Ontario, 1916–1930," *Journal of Family History* 25, no. 4 (October 2000): 504–26.

13 Sandy Ramos, "'A Most Detestable Crime': Gender Identities and Sexual Violence in the District of Montreal, 1803–1843," *Journal of the Canadian Historical Association* 12, no. 1 (2001): 27–48. Tamara Myers' work studies the construction of female delinquency and intersects with some of these issues although for a later period. See, e.g., Tamara Myers, *Caught: Montreal's Modern Girls and the Law, 1869–1945* (Toronto: University of Toronto Press, 2006).

14 See, e.g., Marie-Aimèe Cliché, "Un secret bien gardé: l'inceste dans la société traditionelle Québécoise, 1858-1938," *Revue d'histoire de l'Amérique française* 50, no. 2 (Fall 1996): 201–26; Dorothy E. Chunn, "Secrets and Lies: The Criminalization of Incest and the (Re)formation of the 'Private' in British Columbia, 1890-1940" in *Regulating Lives: Historical Essays on the State, Society, the Individual and the Law*, edited by John McLaren, Robert Menzies, and Dorothy E. Chunn (Vancouver: UBC Press, 2002), 120; Joan Sangster, "Masking and Unmasking the Sexual Abuse of Children: Perceptions of Violence against Children in the Badlands of Ontario, 1916–30," *Journal of Family History* 25.4, no. 2 (2000): 504–26.

15 The records include: Records of the Montreal Gaol [MG]; Registers [KB(R)] and Files [KB(F)] of the Court of King's/Queen's Bench; and Registers [QS(R)] and Files [QS(F)] of the Court of Quarter Sessions (all found within the Bibliothèque et Archives nationales du Québec, Centre d'archives de Montréal, hereinafter BaNQ-M); and Applications for

Pardons and Montreal Gaol Calendars (found at the National Archives of Canada in Ottawa, hereinafter NAC).

16 For discussion of the methodological issues raised by the sources, see Pilarczyk, "'So Foul A Deed': Infanticide in Montreal, 1825–1850," *Law and History Review* 30, no. 1 (May 2012): 576–9.

17 *Montreal Weekly Pilot*, 9 February 1847 (case of Michael McClusky); see also *Montreal Gazette*, 7 August 1847 (case of François X. Brunelle, noting that "[d]elicacy prevents our giving the evidence in this case"); *L'Aurore de Canadas*, 6 March 1840 (case of James Horn); *Montreal Gazette*, 9 February 1848 (case of Godfroy Céré). Similar dynamics were found in other crimes such as infanticide. See, e.g., Pilarczyk, "So Foul a Deed," 577.

18 Relatively few rape trials were covered in any detail during this period, in contrast to later periods. See, e.g., Dubinsky, "Sex and Shame," 178–179.

19 *Montreal Gazette,* 8 August 1847 (case of Francois Z. Brunelle).

20 More specifically, they generally included the names of defendants and less frequently the names of victims or complainants, or both. I am sympathetic to the arguments in favour of not disclosing the names of the victims in these cases, of the alleged perpetrators, and even possibly those convicted. However, as this information can often be gleaned from contemporary periodicals as well as in documents of record, and as the parties are all long deceased, I believe these stories are best recreated by using the names of parties. Especially given the legal system's penchant for stifling children's voices in these cases, I see naming them as a step towards revering their stories and lives. For discussion of this question, see, e.g, Backhouse, *Carnal Crimes*, 4.

21 By "unconscious testimony" I refer to the unstated assumptions, social mores, and other related aspects of larger culture that are embedded in sources and provide insight into the period. For further discussion in the context of Montreal infanticide cases, see Pilarczyk, "So Foul A Deed," 578. With respect to the newspapers, they were often deeply partisan and represent a variety of socio-political, linguistic, ethnic, and other agendas, but shared the commonality of generally reflecting white and middle-class sensibilities. For discussion of Montreal newspapers of the period, see ibid.

22 See, e.g., Hooper, "Child Sexual Abuse and the Regulation of Women," 55 (child sexual assault).

23 See, e.g., Constance Backhouse, "Credibility, Corroboration, and Legal Betrayal of Rape Victims," 2 and n.3 (unpublished paper on file with author, cited with permission); Erickson, *Westward Bound*, 120.

24 Fernand Ouellet, *Economic and Social History of Quebec, 1760–1850: Structures and Conjunctures* (Toronto: Gage Pub. in association with the Institute of Canadian Studies, Carleton, 1980), 659; H. Clare Pentland and Paul Arthur Phillips, *Labour and Capital in Canada, 1650–1860* (Toronto: Lorimer, 1981), 64.

25 G. Blaine Baker et al., *Sources in the Law Library of McGill University for a Reconstruction of the Legal Culture of Quebec, 1760–1890* (Montreal: Faculty of Law and Montreal Business Project, 1987), 9; Mary Anne Poutanen, *Beyond Brutal Passions: Prostitution in Early Nineteenth-Century Montreal* (Montreal: McGill-Queen's University Press, 2015), 24–9; for an overview of Montreal, see, e.g., Dany Fougères and Roderick MacLeod, eds., *Montreal: The History of a North American City*, 2 vols., (Montreal: McGill-Queen's University Press, 2017); in particular Laurent Turcot, "Daily Life in Montreal during the Eighteenth Century," 258–90; Dany Fougères, "The Modern City, 1840–1890," 380–423; Annie-Claude Labreque and Dany Fougères, "The Montreal Economy during the Nineteenth Century," 474–525; Martin Petitclerc, "Labour and the Montreal Working Class in the Nineteenth Century," 526–60; and Danielle Gauvreau, "Population, Social Identities, and Daily Life," 638–69.

26 Jean-Claude Robert, *Atlas Historique de Montréal* (Montréal: Libre Expression, 1994), 79.

27 Baker, *Sources in the Law Library of McGill University*, 13. For Montreal's economic transformation, see, e.g., Gerald Tulchinsky, *The River Barons; Montreal Businessmen and the Growth of Industry and Transportation, 1837–1853* (Toronto: University of Toronto Press, 1977); Fernand Harvey, *Revolution Industrelle et Travailleurs, Une Enquête Sur Les Rapports Entre La Capital Et Le Travail Au Quebec à La Fin Du 19e Siècle* (Montréal: Boréal Express, 1978).

28 Baker, *Sources in the Law Library of McGill University*, 13–14; Donald Fyson, *Magistrates, Police and People: Everyday Criminal Justice in Quebec and Lower Canada* (Toronto: Osgoode Society for Canadian Legal History by the University of Toronto Press, 2006), 8.

29 Danielle Gavreau, "Population, Social Identities, and Daily Life," in *Montreal*, edited by Fougères and Macleod, 646.

30 Baker, *Sources in the Law Library of McGill University,* 17–18; Fyson, *Magistrates, Police, and People*, 8–10. The archival sources were considerably spottier for this period as well.

31 Donald Fyson et al., "The Court Structure of Quebec and Lower Canada, 1764 to 1860," (Montreal: Montreal History Group, 2016) at http://www.profs.hst.ulaval.ca/Dfyson/Courtstr/o&t.htm.

32 See, e.g., Laurent Turcot, "Daily Life in Montreal during the Eighteenth Century," in *Montreal,* edited by Fougères and MacLeod, 275–6; see generally Mary Anne Poutanen, "Regulating Public Space in Early Nineteenth-Century Montreal: Vagrancy Laws and Gender in a Colonial Context, *Histoire Sociale/Social History* 35, no. 69 (May 2002): 35–58.

33 Bruce A MacFarlane, "Historical Development of the Offence of Rape," in *100 Years of the Criminal Code in Canada: Essays Commemorating the Centenary of the Criminal Code in Canada*, edited by Richard Peck and Josiah Woods (Ottawa: Canadian Bar Association, 1993), 126–7. This remained the definition during this period; see, e.g., Jacques Crémazie, *Les lois criminelles anglaises, traduites et compilées de Blackstone, Chitty, Russel et autres* (Québec: Impr. De Fréchette & Cie, 1842), 82 ("signifies carnal and illegal knowledge of a girl or woman, by force and violence and against their will"; author's translation). Jurists were more divided on whether penetration was sufficient to constitute the offence, or whether proof of emission was also required, and this confusion was echoed in jurisprudence until the 1830s. Implicit in this is that rape could not be committed against a male, although forcible buggery or sodomy could.

34 See, e.g., Backhouse, "Nineteenth-Century Canadian Rape Law, 1800–1892," 202.

35 *Offences Against the Person Act*, 1828, 9 Geo. IV c 31, s. 18 (UK). See also MacFarlane, "Historical Development of the Offence of Rape," 151.

36 See, e.g., Backhouse, "Nineteenth-Century Canadian Rape Law, 1800–1892," 204.

37 *An Act for Consolidating and Amending the Statutes in this Province Relative to Offences Against the Person,* 1841, 4 and 5 Vict. c 27, s. 2 ("And be it enacted, That every person convicted of the crime of Rape, shall suffer death as a Felon."); see also Backhouse, "Nineteenth-Century Canadian Rape Law, 1800–1892," 204; see also W. C. Keele, *The Provincial Justice, or Magistrate's Manual, Being a Complete Digest of the Criminal Law of Canada, and a Compendious and General View of the Provincial Law of Upper Canada, with Practical Forms, for the Use of the Magistracy*, 2nd ed. (Toronto: H & W Rowsell: 1843), 117.

38 *An Act for Consolidating and Amending the Statutes in this Province Relative to Offences Against the Person,* 1841, 4 and 5 Vict. c 27, s. 18. See also Backhouse, "Nineteenth-Century Canadian Rape Law, 1800–1892," 205. English law appeared unsettled on this point. See, e.g., William Oldnall Russell, Daniel Davis, and Theron Metcalf, *A Treatise on Crimes and Indictable Misdemeanors*, vol. 1, 2nd ed. (London: Joseph

Butterworth and Son, 1826), 558–60; see, e.g., Crémazie, *Les lois criminelles anglaises*, 83.

39 *An Act for Better Proportioning the Punishment to the Offence, in Certain Cases, and for Other Purposes Therein Mentioned*, 1842, 6 Vict. c 5, s. 5. See also Keele, *The Provincial Justice, or Magistrate's Manual*, 108; Backhouse, "Nineteenth-Century Canadian Rape Law, 1800–1892," 206.

40 *An Act for Consolidating and Amending the Statutes in this Province Relative to Offences Against the Person*, 1841, 4 and 5 Vic. c 27, s. 25 (subjecting assaults with intent to commit felony to a term not greater than two years in prison, as well as fine and the provision of sureties to keep the peace, except for assault with intent to rape or buggery); see also Keele, *The Provincial Justice, or Magistrate's Manual*, 54.

41 *An Act for Consolidating and Amending the Statutes in this Province Relative to Offences Against the Person*, 1841, 4 and 5 Vic. c 27, s. 27; see also Keele, *The Provincial Justice, or Magistrate's Manual*, 55.

42 Macpherson William. "Treatise on the Law Relating to Infants," (London, A. Maxwell & Son, 1842).

43 Ibid., at 572. Minors could be emancipated earlier if orphaned, etc.; see, e.g., ibid., at 576 discussing such provisions under the French *Civil Code*.

44 Ibid., at 572. He further noted some restrictions still remained above those age limits.

45 Ibid., at 576–7.

46 Graham Parker, "The Legal Regulation of Sexual Activity and the Protection of Females," *Osgoode Hall Law Journal* 21, no.2 (September 1983): 211; see also Keele, *The Provincial Justice, or Magistrate's Manual*, 517.

47 In the UK, the age of consent was raised to thirteen in 1875, and to sixteen in 1885. Jackson, *Child Sexual Abuse*, 3. In Canada, it was twelve until 1890, when raised to fourteen. Backhouse, "Credibility," 5 and n.15.

48 *An Act for Consolidating and Amending the Statutes in this Province Relative to Offences Against the Person*, 1841, 4 and 5 Vict. c 27, s. 17. Like rape, these were crimes against females only. Interestingly, other jurisdictions inverted this sentencing regime; nineteenth-century Connecticut treated crimes against females over ten as capital (changed in 1830 to life in prison), while under ten was punishable by life (changed to seven to ten years' imprisonment). Nancy Hathaway Steenburg, *Children and the Criminal Law in Connecticut, 1635–1855: Changing Perceptions of Childhood* (New York: Routledge, 2005), 171.

49 Other than abduction, these offences generally fall outside the purview of this essay. Cases involving incest, and crimes related to child abuse and

neglect are examined in Pilarczyk, "Child Abuse," 370–426. For discussion of infanticide, see Pilarczyk, "So Foul a Deed," 575–634.

50 Jackson, *Child Sexual Abuse*, 5. For discussion of childhood, see, e.g., Phillipe Ariès, *Centuries of Childhood: A Social History of Family Life* (New York: Alfred A. Knopf, 1962); Hugh Cunningham, *Children and Childhood in Western Society Since 1500* (London; New York: Longman, 1995); Peter Coveney, *The Image of Childhood, The Individual and Society: A Study of the Theme in English Literature* (Baltimore: Penguin Books, 1967); Colin Heywood, *A History of Childhood: Children and Childhood in the West from Medieval to Modern Times* (Oxford: Polity Press, 2015).

51 Jackson, *Child Sexual Abuse,* 114. For discussion, see generally James R. Kincaid, *Child Loving: The Erotic Child and Victorian Culture* (New York: Routledge, Chapman & Hall, 1992).

52 Jackson, *Child Sexual Abuse*, 4–5; see also Hooper, "Child Sexual Abuse and the Regulation of Women," 56 (founding of NYSPCC).

53 See, e.g., Jackson, *Child Sexual Abuse,* 2; George Behlmer, *Child Abuse and Moral Reform in England, 1870–1908* (Stanford: Stanford University Press, 1982). The reluctance to consider incest within these movements was to remain the case until the early twentieth century. Sangster, "Masking and Unmasking the Sexual Abuse of Children," 505.

54 Jackson, *Child Sexual Abuse*, 2.

55 Ibid.

56 For discussion of the legal regime governing claims of physical abuse or neglect of children, see Pilarczyk, "Child Abuse"; for claims against employers by servants (including minors), see Pilarczyk, "'Too Well Used by His Master': Judicial Enforcement of Servants' Rights in Montreal, 1830–1845," *McGill Law Journal* 46 (2001): 491–529.

57 The "virgin cure" or "virgin cleansing" myth has spanned centuries and jurisdictions, and was prominent in the Victorian era in the UK. It continues to persist today. See, e.g., Hanne Blank, *Virgin: The Untouched History* (New York, NY: Bloomsbury USA, 2007); Roger Davidson, "'This pernicious delusion': Law, Medicine, and Child Sexual Abuse in Early Twentieth-Century Scotland," *J. of the History of Sexuality* vol. 10 no. 1 (2001): 62; Deborah Posel, "The Scandal of Manhood: 'Baby Rape' and the Politicization of Sexual Violence in Post-Apartheid South Africa," *Culture, Health, and Sexuality* (May 2005): 239–52.

58 See, e.g., Jackson, *Child Sexual Abuse*, 32.

59 Karen Dubinsky and Adam Givertz, "'It Was Only a Matter of Passion': Masculinity and Sexual Danger" in *Gendered Pasts; Historical Essays in*

Feminity and Masculinity in Canada, edited by Kathryn McPherson et al. (Toronto: University of Toronto Press, 2003), 69; see also Backhouse, *Carnal Crimes*, 9 (noting that early researchers depicted sexual assault as "anomalous individual acts").

60 Rob Shields, *Places on the Margin: Alternative Geographies of Modernity* (London: Routledge, 1991), 7.

61 Sangster, "Masking and Unmasking the Sexual Abuse of Children," 505.

62 Most likely meaning here "to stimulate to sympathetic feeling"; see *The Oxford English Dictionary*: https://www.oed.com.

63 *Montreal Gazette*, 3 March 1840.

64 See, e.g., *Montreal Herald*, 3 March 1840; *Montreal Transcript*, 3 March 1840; *L'Aurore de Canadas*, 6 March 1840 (case of James Horn).

65 Although relatively few such examples seem to have survived, this would likely not be unusual as private prosecutors were expected to help line-up witnesses and support the Crown's prosecution.

66 The Queen v. James Horn (KB 30 November 1839), *in* BaNQ-M, KB(F) (affidavit of Henry and Mary Hadley).

67 See *L'Aurore de Canadas*, 13 March 1840; *Montreal Gazette*, 17 March 1840; *Montreal Herald*, 17 March 1840.

68 It is also possible this was charged down as a lesser offence; however, this was counseled against by at least one contemporary jurist, who cautioned against charging for assault with intent if there was any likelihood the full charge would be proven, as (under English law at least) it might result in acquittal on the grounds that the misdemeanor was subsumed under the felony. Russell, *A Treatise on Crimes*, 564.

69 The Queen v. Godfroy Céré (KB 18 November 1847), *in* BaNQ-M, KB(F) (affidavit of Elailde Labour). Other details are not reclaimable from the document. As was typical, newspapers refused to discuss the evidence. See, e.g., *Montreal Gazette*, 9 February 1848 (trial).

70 *Montreal Transcript*, 17 February 1848 (account of conviction and sentence); see also *Montreal Gazette,* 16 February 1848.

71 *Montreal Transcript*, 17 February 1848. *Montreal Gazette,* 16 February 1848, remarked similarly that "[t]he prisoner seemed quite overwhelmed by his situation."

72 *La Minerve*, 27 March 1848 (account of commutation); MG(R), 18 November 1847 (noting his incarceration, and release on 24 April 1848 "by being sent to Penitentiary"). The pardon application was not found. For discussion of pardons see, e.g., Carolyn Strange, "Mercy and Parole in Anglo-American Criminal-Justice Systems from the Eighteenth Century to the Twenty-First Century," in *The Oxford Handbook of the*

History of Crime and Criminal Justice, edited by Paul Knepper and Anja Johansen (New York: Oxford University Press, 2016), 573–96.

73 The Queen v. Étienne Carrier (KB 25 February 1843), *in* BaNQ-M, KB(R).

74 The Queen v Étienne Carrier (KB 21 January 1843), *in* BaNQ-M, KB(F) (affidavit of Joseph Carron).

75 *Montreal Gazette*, 2 March 1843 (trial and verdict); see also *La Minerve*, 2 March 1843, ibid.

76 *La Minerve*, 2 March 1843 (author's translation). His acquittal was also noted in The Queen v Étienne Carrier (KB 28 February 1843), *in* BaNQ-M, KB(R).

77 *La Minerve,* 27 August 1829 (conviction); *La Minerve*, 31 August 1829; *Canadian Courant*, 2 September 1829 (sentence).

78 *Montreal Weekly Pilot*, 29 January 1847 (citing *Montreal Gazette*).

79 *La Minerve*, 8 February 1847.

80 See, e.g., *Montreal Gazette*, 21 January 1847; *Montreal Weekly Pilot*, 26 January 1847; and *Montreal Weekly Pilot*, 29 January 1847 (committed to trial); *Montreal Weekly Pilot*, 9 February 1847 (indictment, trial, and verdict); *La Minerve*, 8 February 1847 (verdict); *Montreal Weekly Pilot*, 19 February 1847; *Montreal Weekly Pilot*, 19 February 1847; *La Minerve*, 15 February 1847 (sentence).

81 The Queen v. Francoise Brunelle (KB 12 July 1846), *in* BaNQ-M, KB(F) (affidavit of Marie Belle). No other documents related to this case have survived.

82 See, e.g., *Montreal Gazette*, 7 August 1847; *Montreal Transcript*, 17 August 1847; see also *La Minerve*, 8 February 1847 (true bill).

83 See, e.g., *Montreal Gazette*, 7 August 1847 (trial and conviction); *La Minerve*, 16 August 1847; *Montreal Weekly Pilot*, 17 August 1847; *L'Aurore,* 17 August 1847; *Montreal Gazette*, 18 August 1847; *Montreal Transcript*, 18 August 1847 (sentence).

84 Christine Stansell, *City of Women, Sex and Class in New York, 1789–1860* (New York: Random House, 1986), 182–3.

85 See, e.g., Robertson, *Crimes Against Children*, 41.

86 Ibid., 161. Robertson notes that this offense, with its lesser evidentiary burden and lower sentences, effectively supplanted rape prosecutions after it was introduced in New York City in 1927. Ibid.,161–78.

87 DR v. Charles Cooper (QS 13 September 1826), *in* BaNQ-M, QS(F) (deposition of Mary Wright the younger).

88 Ibid.

89 DR v. Charles Cooper (QS 13 September 1826), *in* BaNQ-M, QS(F) (deposition of Mary Wright). She claimed she would have filed the

deposition earlier but her husband had been wounded by an axe in an unrelated incident.

90 DR v. Malcolm Fraser (QS 12 August 1833), *in* BaNQ-M, QS(F) (deposition of James Fraser).

91 See, e.g., Crémazie, *Les lois criminelles anglaises,* 82; Russell, *Treatise on Crimes*, 557.

92 The Queen v. Thomas Williamson (QS 13 July 1840), *in* BaNQ-M, QS(F) (deposition of Francis C.F. Arnoldi on claim of assault with intent to ravish).

93 Domina Regina v. Thomas Williamson (QS 13 July 1840), *in* BaNQ-M, QS(F) (ibid., on claim of "loose idle and disorderly" conduct). The records of the Police Court confirm "A warrant of Arrest was granted on the Affidavit of Francis C.F. Arnoldi on charge of an Assault with intent to Ravish, The Defendant was arrested, after Examination case discharged." Domina Regina v. Thomas Williamson (PC 12 July 1840), BaNQ-M, PC, 233. It is for this loose, idle and disorderly charge that his files may have ended up in those of the Court of Quarter Sessions.

94 Russell, *A Treatise on Crimes*, 560.

95 Dominus Rex v. Joseph Levère Clément (QS 17 January 1832), *in* BaNQ-M, QS(F) (complaint of Angelique Chartrand); ibid., (QS 19 January 1832), *in* BaNQ-M, QS(F) (true bill for aggravated assault and battery). This case was not counted herein.

96 *Montreal Gazette*, 23 October 1850 (case of Joachim Legault dit Desloriers). The judge admitted him to bail until decision was rendered at the end of term, although no information on the formal outcome was found. This case was not counted herein. I am aware of no period legal definition for caress, and its common meaning as a loving or gentle touch seems belied by the facts as alleged.

97 For discussion of indecent assaults in twentieth-century Canada, see, e.g., Backhouse, *Carnal Crimes*.

98 Mary Beth Hamilton Arnold, "'The Life of a Citizen in the Hands of a Woman': Sexual Assault in New York City, 1790–1820" in *Passion & Power: Sexuality in History*, edited by Kathy Peiss and Christina Simmons (with Robert A. Padgug) (Philadelphia: Temple University Press, 1989), 35–56.

99 See, e.g., Chapman, "Inquiring Minds Want to Know," 202; Ramos, "A Most Detestable Crime," 28.

100 See, e.g., Carolyn Conley, "Rape and Justice in Victorian England," *Victorian Studies* 29, no.4 (Summer 1986): 526–8.

101 As noted in Backhouse, "The Sayer Street Outrage," 48, in the context of later nineteenth-century Ontario:

> Most criminal proceedings were initiated by concerned citizens at this time. Fledgling police forces were simply unequipped to handle much more than preliminary investigation and arrests ... . The laying of charges was a fairly heavy responsibility for private citizens to bear, but ... also permitted considerable freedom for individuals to activate the criminal law.

102 For discussion, see generally Backhouse, *Carnal Crimes*.

103 NAC, 14 Appeal Petitions (AP), 0.5360-5362 (pardon application of François Reaume).

104 Domina Regina v. John Spooner (KB 7 May 1840), in BaNQ, KB(F) (affidavit of Julia Dunvar).

105 Jackson, *Child Sexual Abuse*, 8–9. Jackson's description of these documents albeit for a later period in the UK, are insightful:

> The historian is confronted with a sea of stories all claiming to be "truths," a series of contestations in courtroom or street, words of anger, bitterness, reproach, pain. However, although the sequence of "truths" may have been framed in line with certain pre-existing narrative structures and in relation to a wider cultural and symbolic framework, there is also blood, pain and tears which make it impossible to forget there is a "real" child, father, or mother involved.

106 Dominus Rex v. Luke Bowen (KB 30 September 1830), *in* BaNQ-M, KB(F) (affidavit of Melonie Poutré).

107 Domina Regina v. John Spooner (KB 7 May 1840), *in* BaNQ, KB(F) (affidavit of Julia Dunvar).

108 The Queen v. Jean Baptiste Rivais (KB 18 July 1843), *in* BaNQ-M, KB(F) (affidavit of Margaret Holmes). As she was above the age of twelve, this case is not counted.

109 Jackson, *Child Sexual Abuse,* 71; for discussion of medical testimony in child rape trials see generally ibid., 71–89.

110 See, e.g., T.R. and J.B. Beck, *Elements of Medical Jurisprudence* (Albany: Websters and Skinners, 1823); Thomas Percival, *Medical Ethics* (Manchester: S. Russel, 1803); Michael Ryan, *A Manual of Medical Jurisprudence: Compiled from the Best Medical and Legal Works* (Philadelphia: Cary and Lea, 1832); Alfred Swaine Taylor, *Elements of Medical Jurisprudence* (London: Deacon, 1844).

111 Dominus Rex v. Jean Baptiste Labelle the younger (KB 19 May 1825), *in* BaNQ-M, KB(F) (habeas corpus and arrest warrant). This could well be an

example of a man attempting the "virgin cure" as a supposed cure for sexually transmitted diseases.

112 *Montreal Gazette,* 7 September 1826; see also *Montreal Gazette,* 21 August 1826 (citing the *Herald*) (case of Joseph Massé).

113 The Queen v. Etienne Carrier (KB 21 January 1843), *in* BaNQ-M, KB(F) (affidavit of Theotiste Lavallé).

114 Ibid., (affidavit of Edward Walter Carter, JP, Surgeon); see also ibid., (affidavit of John Mignault, Surgeon).

115 *Montreal Gazette*, 28 February 1843 (true bill); *Montreal Gazette,* 2 March 1843 (trial and acquittal); *La Minerve*, 2 March 1843 (true bill; also trial and acquittal); KB February 1843–March 1843 in BaNQ-M, KB(R), 10, (true bill and plea), 22–3, (trial and acquittal) (KB 28 February 1843).

116 *La Minerve,* 2 March 1843. One wonders the reception such a defendant might have had in his community following such an event: did neighbours accept the outcome, or was he ostracized? The question must remain unanswered.

117 NAC, 14 Appeal Petitions (AP), 0.5360-5362 (pardon application of François Reaume, 23 October 1839). Unlike the usual flowery and obsequious petitions that attacked the fairness of their trials, excoriated Crown witnesses, claimed exculpatory evidence was wrongfully excluded, or earnestly protested their innocence, Reaume made none of these claims. While they frequently referenced family members facing penury and obloquy, as did he, his assertion he had never before faced charges was unusual. One is tempted to infer that he was hoping for a pardon on humanitarian grounds only.

118 Ibid. As she was eleven, she was considerably older than many of the other victims.

119 A situation that was to continue well into the twentieth century. See, e.g., Backhouse, *Carnal Crimes*, 173–174; Backhouse, "Credibility," 13–14.

120 Compare with Arnold, "The Life of a Citizen in the Hands of a Woman," 37 (detailing victims as young as six years old).

121 The Queen v. Francoise Brunelle (KB 12 July 1846), *in* BaNQ-M, KB(F) (affidavit of Marie Belle).

122 For the legal system's questioning of the reliability of child witnesses, see, e.g., Steenburg, *Children and the Criminal Law in Connecticut, 1635–1855*, 161–82; Backhouse, *Carnal Crimes*, 165–92.

123 Dominus Rex v. Charles Cooper (QS 13 September 1826), *in* BaNQ-M, QS(F) (deposition of Mary Wright the younger). For a similar example, see, e.g., The Queen v. Francoise Brunelle (KB 12 July 1846), *in* BaNQ-M,

KB(F) (affidavit of Marie Belle); Dubinsky, "Sex and Shame," 175; Robertson, *Crimes Against Children*, 42.

124 The Queen v. Francois X. Brunelle (KB 12 July 1846), *in* BaNQ-M, KB(F) (affidavit of Marie Belle). See also Robertson, *Crimes Against Children*, 42.

125 Robertson, *Crimes Against Children*, 42

126 See, e.g., *Montreal Gazette*, 8 March 1842 (case of William Smout), reporting that the "prosecutrix and other witnesses for the Crown not appearing to support their complaint, a jury was impanelled (sic) to acquit the defendant, who was accordingly acquitted and discharged."

127 See, e.g., Fyson, *Magistrates, Police and People,* especially 227–71.

128 See, e.g., Dominus Rex v. Jean Baptiste Labelle the younger (KB 19 May 1825), *in* BaNQ-M, KB(F); Domina Regina v. John Spooner (KB 7 May 1840), ibid.

129 For discussion of women utilizing the legal system, see Fyson, *Magistrates, Police, and People*; see also Mary Anne Poutanen, "Reflections of Montreal Prostitution in the Records of the Lower Courts, 1810-1842," in *Class, Gender, and the Law in Eighteenth and Nineteenth-Century Quebec: Sources and Perspectives*, edited by Donald Fyson, Colin Coates, and Kathryn Harvey (Montreal: Montreal History Group, 1993), 99–125; Kathryn Harvey, "Amazons and Victims: Resisting Wife-Abuse in Working-Class Montréal, 1869–1879," *Journal of the Canadian Historical Association* 2 (1991): 131–48.

130 For similar discussion around adult victims, see, e.g., Ramos, "A Most Detestable Crime," 30.

131 Seven out of fifteen defendants were identified as French-Canadian.

132 See note 107.

133 See, e g., Dubinsky, "Sex and Shame," 177; Ramos, "A Most Detestable Crime."

134 Philip Girard, Jim Phillips, and Blake Brown, *A History of Law in Canada, Volume One: Beginnings to 1866* (Toronto: University of Toronto Press, 2018), 580.

135 *Montreal Transcript*, 10 September 1842; see also *Montreal Gazette*, 3 September 1842 (case of Ambroise Leseige). This case was not included in this study. It was a well-known legal truism that prostitutes were incapable of being raped, even if the common law supposedly held to the contrary. See, e.g., Russell, *A Treatise on Crimes*, 563; Crémazie, *Les Lois Criminelles Anglaises*, 83. Both noted this would go to the witnesses' credibility, however.

136 This mirrors what others have found; see, e.g., Chapman, "Inquiring Minds Want to Know," 200–2; Arnold, "The Life of a Citizen in the Hands of a Woman," 37.

137 *Montreal Gazette*, 2 March 1843 (trial of Etienne Carrier).
138 Pilarczyk, "So Foul a Deed," 175; Pilarczyk, "'Acts of the Most Sanguinary Rage': Spousal Murder in Montreal, 1825–1850," *American Journal of Legal History* 57, no. 3 (2017): 338.
139 *Montreal Gazette*, 7 September 1826.
140 *Times and Daily Commercial Advertiser*, 2 February 1844 (citing the *Examiner*).
141 A similar point was made by other commentators. See, e.g., Arnold, "The Life of a Citizen in the Hands of a Woman," 39; Robertson, *Crimes Against Children*, 38.
142 This likely reflects that children were generally given tasks from very early childhood; as mentioned earlier, the construct of childhood as necessitating development and a need for recreation is a modern one.
143 *Montreal Gazette*, 29 October 1850 (trial and verdict for rape). See also *Montreal Weekly Pilot*, 17 January 1850 (true bill for assault with intent); *La Minerve*, 21 January 1850 (ibid.); *Montreal Gazette*, 29 March 1850 (ibid.); *Montreal Weekly Pilot*, 30 March 1850 (plea to assault with intent); *Montreal Gazette*, 17 July 1850 (true bill for rape); *Montreal Gazette*, 19 July 1850 (plea to charge of rape); *La Minerve*, 28 October 1850 (trial and verdict for rape); *La Minerve*, 31 October 1850 (ibid.); *Montreal Weekly Pilot*, 31 October 1850 (ibid.); *La Minerve*, 31 October 1850 (trial and verdict for assault with intent).
144 The Queen v. Étienne Carrier (KB 25 February 1843), *in* BaNQ-M, KB(R).
145 The Queen v. Francoise Brunelle (KB 12 July 1846), *in* BaNQ-M, KB(F) (affidavit of Marie Belle).
146 The Queen v. William Smout (KB 12 April 1841), *in* BaNQ-M KB(F) (affidavit of James Anderson); see also affidavit of Mary Anne Anderson (ibid.). It is unfortunate to note that Mary Anne could also face corporal punishment at her father's hands on top of the trauma she suffered; this is another example of the fear that overlay many such assaults.
147 See, e.g., DR v. Charles Cooper (QS 13 September 1826), *in* BaNQ-M, QS(F) (deposition of Mary Wright the younger); Domina Regina v. John Spooner (KB 7 May 1840), *in* BaNQ, KB(F) (affidavit of Julia Dunvar); NAC, 14 Appeal Petitions (AP), 0.5360-5362 (pardon application of François Reaume, 23 October 1839).
148 Similarly to Backhouse, *Carnal Crimes*, 168; Robertson, *Crimes Against Children*, 38.
149 *Montreal Weekly Pilot*, 6 November 1846 (citing *Three Rivers Gazette*). This case was not counted herein as taking place outside of the Judicial District of Montreal.

150 See, e.g., Steenburg, *Children and the Criminal Law in Connecticut,* 178.

151 Ibid.

152 In the UK (excluding Scotland) until 1908. See, e.g., Hooper, "Child Sexual Abuse and the Regulation of Women," 57; Steenburg, *Children and the Criminal Law in Connecticut,* 178. Other jurisdictions had outlawed it much earlier. Ibid., 178.

153 I use the term "shadow evidence" to refer to the phenomenon of acts surfacing within judicial records but in a secondary context to the one being examined: for example, a domestic abuse complaint that mentions incest in the narrative, but for which that act is not related to the legal cause of action; or in which a term (such as incest) is used to describe an allegation or charge that does not comport with accepted legal categories of the period. For period examples, see Pilarczyk, "To Shudder at the Bare Recital," 393–394.

154 *Montreal Gazette,* 21 August 1826 (committed to gaol); *Montreal Gazette,* 7 September 1826 (true bill, trial, and verdict); *Canadian Courant,* 9 September 1826 (ibid.). The file was not found. For an example of a case charging the father of a fifteen year old (and accordingly not included herein) with "assault with intent to ravish his daughter," see The Queen v. Joseph Cavallier (KB 6 December 1847), *in* BaNQ-M, KB(F).

155 Queen v. James Horn (KB 30 November 1839, *in* BaNQ-M, KB(F) (letter to Attorney General by Henry Headley).

156 NAC, 14 Appeal Petitions (AP), 0.5360-5362 (pardon application of François Reaume, 23 October 1829). The notation "not referred the case appearing so bad" was written on his petition.

157 For alcoholism as accelerant in family violence during this period, see, e.g., Kathryn Harvey, "'To Love, honour, and obey': Wife-Battery in Working Class Montreal, 1869–1879," *Urban History Review* 19, no. 2 (June 1990): 128; Pilarczyk, "'Justice in the Premises': Family Violence and the Law in Montreal, 1825–1850" (DCL thesis McGill University, 2003), 214–361 (spousal violence); ibid., 362–445 (spousal murder). It often provided mitigation for the murderous husband and provocation on the part of the deceased spouse. See Pilarczyk, "Acts of the Most Sanguinary Rage," 330–1. For alcoholism and child abuse, see Pilarczyk, "Child Abuse," 388–9.

158 *Black's Law Dictionary*, 6th ed. (St Paul: West Publishing, 1991), 3.

159 Russell, *Treatise on Crimes*, 569–81.

160 See, e.g., Samuel X. Radbill, "A History of Child Abuse and Infanticide," in *Violence in the Family*, edited by Suzanne K Steinmetz and Murray A. Straus (New York: Harper & Row, 1974), 173–9.

161 Dominus Rex v. Joseph Guitard (KB 18 June 1830), *in* BaNQ-M, KB(F) (notice of commitment to Montreal Gaol based on arrest warrant). The documents show that the couple left voluntarily and against her father's permission for purposes of being married. Ibid., (KB 1 July 1830) (affidavit of Noël Joannet); ibid., (affidavits of Antoine Lavallée and his wife).

162 See, e.g, The Queen v. Emile Blais et al. (KB 23 July 1841) *in* BaNQ-M, KB(F) (petition by Sister Scholastique for habeas corpus alleging abduction); ibid. (KB 20 July 1841) (petition by William N. Crawford for habeas corpus for abduction).

163 *La Minerve*, 7 September 1843 (trial of Jean Baptiste Rivais); The Queen v. Jean Baptiste Rivais (KB 18 July 1843), *in* BaNQ-M, KB (F). See also *Montreal Gazette*, 5 September 1843; *Times and Commercial Advertiser*, 7 September 1843.

164 Dominus Rex v. Joseph Latillip et al. (KB 1 September 1840) *in* BaNQ, KB(F) (affidavit of Julia Carpentier). Her father's affidavit also alleged that Joseph and his father fought with neighbours and himself after they intervened. Ibid., (affidavit of Laurent Carpentier). The justice of the peace who transcribed these affidavits appeared responsible for much of the confusion, between often-illegible handwriting, indifferent spelling, lack of punctuation, and inconsistencies in how he spelled the parties' names.

165 *Montreal Gazette*, 19 August 1846; see also (MG 17 June 1848) *in* BaNQ, MG(R) (bailed 8 July 1848).

166 *Montreal Transcript*, 23 February 1847 (indictment of François Xavier Beaudry for abduction of witnesses).

167 *Montreal Weekly Pilot*, 9 February 1849.

168 Ibid.

169 Ibid., 19 February 1849; *La Minerve*, 15 February 1849; *Montreal Gazette*, 15 February 1849. His affluence is further shown by affidavits filed on his behalf by neighbours. (MG 6 January 1849) *in* BaNQ, MG(R).

170 See, e.g., *Montreal Gazette*, 18 March 1850; *Montreal Weekly Pilot*, 16 March 1850 (true bill); *Montreal Gazette*, 20 March 1850; *Montreal Weekly Pilot*, 23 March 1850; *La Minerve*, 21 March 1850 (trial). For further discussion of this case in the context of incest or abduction, or both, see Pilarczyk, "Child Abuse," 395–7.

171 *Montreal Gazette*, 1 April 1850 (italics mine); The Queen v. Michael Coleman (KB March 1850-October 1856) *in* BaNQ, KB(R), 59 (motion denied), ibid., (KB 26 March 1850).

172 *Montreal Gazette*, 1 April 1850; *La Minerve*, 1 April 1850; *Montreal Weekly Pilot*, 3 April 1850; The Queen v. Michael Coleman *in* BaNQ, KB(R), 66–7 (sentence).

When I started at McGill University's Faculty of Law as an assistant professor, Blaine was already a legend and his teaching the gold standard for the Faculty. Though I never had the opportunity of being taught by him, I felt like I was continuously learning from him. In that respect, he was a great, and kind, teacher to me. His polymath interest in all aspects of law extended even to my area of intellectual property law, where he had taught the course a number of times at McGill, before the field could even be called one. His attention to detail and brilliant grasp of legal doctrine in context meant that he was ideal in thinking through the logistics of a novel discipline. He taught the course several times and even supervised two published student papers on biotechnology patent law and price control of patented medicines in Canada.

When I took over the Canadian Legal History course in 2008 he shared all his materials with me. The course was rigorous and profound. But I knew immediately upon looking at the materials that I couldn't teach Blaine's course. Like everything he did, the course was so idiosyncratically him, and such a pure expression of his character that I knew it would end up as parody in my hands. Even in writing this piece for this collection and reviewing his works on law-practice history that have influenced me it is amazing how clear his voice is in his writing, how fluid and elegantly, almost effortlessly, he expressed himself. In teaching my own Legal History course I relied on the central conceits of his approach to teaching, and those have remained the backbone of the course: what is legal history? What is legal historiography? When does it work and why or why not? In addition, the importance of big ideas and micro histories, honesty, integrity, and rigor in the expression of ideas and in viewing one's work, and most importantly, as anyone can tell from his biography, the core duty to mentor and support the writing of others, particularly students. Thank you, Blaine, for giving me so much to which to aspire.

Tina Piper

10

The Making of Canada's First Technology Transfer Office (1916–1939)

S. Tina Piper

INTRODUCTION

The National Research Council gradually established the first Canadian technology transfer office from the late 1920s to the early 1930s. A technology transfer office commercializes technologies that have been developed by the university or scientific research institute that houses it. Its operations straddle science, business, and law. This type of commercialization happens when an institution obtains a patent over the invention through the relevant administrative process and then either sells that patent to a manufacturer or concludes a licensing agreement that permits a manufacturer to develop the technology. Technology transfer offices are the primary means through which research innovations become available to the general public and are a critical, but often ignored, piece in the history of science and innovation. The catalogue of inventions brokered through these offices is a tour of scientific invention of the twentieth and twenty-first centuries.[1] Their operations have been of great interest to researchers, administrators, and politicians because of the potential for huge windfalls, so-called home run inventions that can make millions and even billions of dollars for institutions.[2] The luck and alchemy involved in finding and selling those inventions adds to the intrigue surrounding technology transfer offices. Historically and to the present, the promise of potential patent income is a valuable incentive for recruiting researchers, and office revenue is a proxy for assessing the "effectiveness," "relevance," and "importance" and of the associated institutions and their researchers.[3] The pursuit of profit through commodification of publicly funded research, however, has always stood in awkward tension with the public interest mandate of these institutions.

The technology transfer office at the National Research Council was an institution determined to reduce the large proportionate share of foreign (mostly US) patents and inventions in the Canadian market. During this period few patents were being applied for by Canadian inventors and almost none with the ambition of using the patent to make the technology more (not less) available. It is worth noting in respect to this latter point that from the earliest beginnings of the organized patent system in Canada, patents were largely obtained by US based inventors to protect US inventions in order to market or manufacture them in Canada.[4] For example, taking 1916 as a representative year, out of the 6,644 patents issued and recorded by the Canadian Intellectual Property Office's database that year,[5] only 1,259 (17 per cent) were issued to Canadian inventors, while 5,562 (76 per cent) went to US inventors.[6] This had the effect of skewing patent law and agent practices to protecting the interests of foreign inventors in Canada, a tide the National Research Council sought to turn. It did so through its creative technology transfer practices. When constituted in 1916 for the purpose of advancing scientific and industrial research for the benefit of the public, the council's founders believed its patenting policies had to serve the "public interest." Then as now, it was not obvious what it meant to serve the public interest through patenting. The patent system had traditionally been used to secure monopoly reward for individual inventions, so much so that some professions (e.g., medicine and the military) restricted, or even forbade, their members from patenting innovations. In these professions, this monopoly protection was seen to compromise the public interest bona fides of its members, enclosing for a protected period drugs and innovations that could potentially help many more people if they were freely accessible.[7] Thus the council sought to exercise exclusive property rights over its own inventions in a way that still left them available for broad use. This essay will show how precisely the council did this by applying open (or non-exclusive) licensing strategies to limit the extent of monopoly control of its innovations, using its patents to generate income that helped fund its public science operations.[8] More broadly, this chapter will also consider the emergence of an office that moved technology from research laboratories at Canada's National Research Council to the public. Inspired by research into office practices and particularly Blaine's research, this essay uses letters, notes, diaries, and other primary sources to piece together the story of Canada's first technology transfer office.[9] A close examination of evidence of the National Research Council's patenting, licensing, and dissemination practices supports a number of conclusions about the office's contribution to the building of unique Canadian norms of innovation post-WWI during an important time when what characterized Canada as its own nation was just emerging.[10] Using a method that Blaine Baker would have appreciated,[11] this essay also focuses on the patenting of the National Research Council's CN 6400 locomotive in 1932 in the public interest as an illustrative example. Very little has been written on the history of technology transfer offices in Canada, particularly for the period I examine,[12] and nothing that considers it a part of legal history.[13] Focusing on the National Research Council's technology transfer office is significant because it also went on to become the template for Canadian technology transfer organizations throughout much of the twentieth century.[14] It led directly to the creation of the Canadian Patents and Development Limited at the National Research Council, the government-led technology transfer agency until the 1990s.[15]

This essay proceeds chronologically in three parts. Part I recounts the early history of the National Research Council, focusing on the centrality of patent policy in its founding. Part II explores the period of growth and formalization of patent policy at the National Research Council during its second president's term. And, finally, Part III considers the commercialization and licensing practices that arose from this period of growth (in the latter half of the 1930s).

PART I: EARLY BEGINNINGS OF THE NATIONAL RESEARCH COUNCIL[16]

What started as a British imperial project in a colonial nation quickly became the foundation for a nation-building scheme.[17] While some parts of colonial Canada had been initially linked by railways such as the Grand Trunk in the 1850s, the first transcontinental railway was only completed in the late nineteenth century, symbolizing the "realization of the national dream, that is, the creation and consolidation of a northern transcontinental nation."[18] The railway both rapidly settled the federation and sowed the seed of an emerging sense of nationhood that loosened Canada's ties with Great Britain, as the country was no longer divided by harsh terrain which left the pacific coast isolated. This emergence of transportation technologies spurred economic growth and development, aiding in the development of metropolitan centres.

With this emerging national identity stemming in part from technological innovation, Prime Minister Borden officially created the National Research Council in 1916 at the urging of the British Government, after it had created its own Department of Scientific and Industrial Research (DSIR).[19] The organizing committee for the DSIR had concluded that similar organizations should be set up with overseas governments willing to cooperate; they envisioned collaboration between the organizations across the Empire for its express benefit.[20] The National Research Council actively modeled itself on similar institutions in other countries, such as the UK's DSIR,[21] the US Mellon Institute,[22] and the US Bureau of Standards.[23]

The "Honorary Advisory Council for Scientific and Industrial Research," as the NRC was first known, concluded at its first meeting from 4–6 December 1916 that "the results of any research supported by the Government should be national" and profits from any inventions should go back to supporting research, even though at the time the council had no inventions to speak of.[24] In those early days, scientific research was nascent; the universities received limited government funding to conduct research and were themselves not supporting much research. A study conducted in 1918 concluded that fewer than twelve PhD degrees in pure science had ever been granted in Canada and that there were only about fifty "pure" researchers in total in Canada.[25] Some rudimentary research was being conducted in government departments such as Mines (established in 1907), Marine and Fisheries (established in 1867), and the Forest Products Laboratories of Canada (established in 1913).[26] The private sector was not more active – only thirty-seven firms in Canada had research laboratories, most with only one employee.

Canada's means of supporting and encouraging innovation in this period were similarly rudimentary.[27] The legal infrastructure of patent law consisted primarily of the Patent Office, officially affiliated with the Department of Agriculture, which was governed by the provisions of the Patent Act.[28] Canada's patent bar started to formally organize in 1925 when Alexander MacRae (who was to become patent agent for the National Research Council) chaired the first meeting of the newly created Intellectual Property Institute of Canada.[29] In the early twentieth century, Canadian universities and government research divisions had no official policy regarding the patenting of research results, and the first Research Offices only developed in the late 1970s. Formal technology transfer offices did not appear until the early to mid-1980s.[30] Despite the dearth of scientific infrastructure and capacity, the immense potential of science to improve people's lives and promote national interests was starting to be appreciated and the National Research Council saw itself playing a key role in this regard in the future as research expertise and institutional capacity grew.

An initial technology transfer infrastructure had to be set up at the National Research Council to govern innovations emanating from their researchers. Specifically, the National Research Council had to ensure some return revenues from the technology while also ensuring its use in the public interest. An early obstacle to this was that the Advisory Research Council in January 1919 had passed a unanimous resolution recommending that: "experts in the Government service be allowed to patent in their own name their discoveries and inventions, provided they assign half of their patent rights in Canada to the Government of Canada, to be devoted to scientific research – the rights outside of Canada to be retained by the patentee."[31] The first president of the National Research Council, H.M. Tory did much to amend this employee-owned policy and develop office practices to raise revenue for the council and ensure the use of technologies in the public interest. Nominated as a council member on 21 February 1923, Tory went on to become temporary chairman that year, and on 1 June 1928 was appointed as the first president of the council.[32] Tory laid the foundation for the National Research Council's operations during his time with the council from 1923 to 1935. He was particularly concerned that Canada not end up as, as he put it, "a nation of peasants and traders," with its natural resource wealth going "to swell the coffers of people having greater initiative than we apparently possess."[33] He noted that 66 per cent of Canadian patents sold went to American manufacturers and only 24 per cent of Canadian patents were licensed to Canadian firms.[34]

Tory had spent his formidable career negotiating the boundaries between public and private interests. According to his biographers, Tory had "absorbed a strong dose of that loose middle-class reformist ideology known as progressivism" which was characterized by "an attachment to the employment of modern scientific and social scientific means in order to encourage reform."[35] As a career university administrator and academic (he had attained the rank of associate professor of mathematics at McGill) he had founded or been first president of several notable Canadian universities, including the University of Alberta (1908–1929), and the McGill University College, later part of the University of British Columbia (1906). He was the first chairman and founder of the Alberta Council of Scientific and Industrial Research (1919) while he was president of the University of Alberta. The same movement that produced the National Research Council had also spurred the support and organization of scientific and industrial research in the provinces leading to the creation of Alberta's Research Council, the Ontario Research Foundation in 1928, and others.[36] During his time in Alberta, he had been in charge of researching and developing the capacity to exploit the tar sands.[37] He had fielded numerous aggressive and hyperbolic solicitations from eager inventors of oil exploitation technologies and he repelled these with ease.[38] Through his varied career, Tory had developed the skills required to plan, initiate, dream, and network to create the technology transfer office he imagined at the National Research Council, particularly through modifying legislation and recruiting eminent advisers.[39] He was in a position to establish the infrastructure for a technology transfer office that could bring together the seemingly conflicting positions of patenting and the public interest.

Tory spent many of his early days at the council developing a policy to govern patents held by National Research Council employees over the inventions that the National Research Council would eventually commercialize. The unique circumstances prevailing at the time the National Research Council was created greatly influenced his deliberations. Organized group scientific research was nascent.[40] The National Research Council was neither clearly public nor private. As a research institution it would develop inventions that should be disseminated for widespread use but not compete directly with commercial partners.[41] Researchers at institutions, if not properly remunerated and recognized, had plenty of opportunities to seek their fortune through independent patent commercialization.[42] The importance of civilian inventive contributions to the war effort during WWI and compensation for those inventions by the UK government had led to a sense that invention for the purposes of the state should be remunerated above and beyond a salary. All these conditions influenced the direction of the National Research Council.

The perspective of the National Research Council on employee patents was also influenced by the policies of similar types of institutions. The UK's DSIR, a government agency that performed research intended for use by industry, required employees to assign all rights to inventions made in the course of their duties.[43] These patents were held by the Imperial Trust and licensed out on a non-exclusive basis at a low royalty rate.[44] The US-based Mellon Institute, while nonprofit and affiliated with the University of Pittsburgh, styled itself as a research service group for companies and it comprised fellows funded by a particular industry.[45] Inventions in that institution belonged to the donor who could decide whether to obtain a patent, or could even keep the research secret.[46] The US National Bureau of Standards was a federally-funded research institute for other branches of government and industry, and its patent policy held that generally patents should not be obtained, but if they were any such patents "should naturally be dedicated for free unrestricted use by the public."[47]

The options for regulating employees' inventions at the National Research Council boiled down to the following: (i) allowing employees to patent their research in their own names and pursue patents independently; (ii) patenting in the institution's name and rewarding the employee by promotion or other incentives; and (iii) not patenting at all and dedicating the innovation to the public. Tory and his secretary, S.P. Eagleson, favoured the second option as it would give the council the freedom to commercialize its selected technologies for both monetary and non-monetary purposes while allowing employee contributions to be recognized. They were buoyed in this conclusion by the DSIR's own policy along these lines, as well as by the cautionary tale of the US National Bureau of Standards, discussed below.[48]

The broader landscape of technology transfer practices in Canada and in its two closest partners, the US and UK, at the time was diverse and without consistent norms and varied by type of invention. The established eastern universities (e.g., Dalhousie, Toronto, McGill) had neither technology transfer offices nor official patenting policies. The commercialization of any technologies developed by researchers at those institutions tended to be improvised after the researcher presented the university with an invention to manage.[49] One well-known example of this, in 1921, was the discovery of insulin at the University of Toronto.[50] The desire to manufacture and sell insulin on a large scale led its inventors to create a sui generis technology transfer arrangement. The researchers assigned all rights to the university which applied for a patent explicitly to protect the manufacture from being blocked by third parties, set up a third-party Insulin Committee to manage the patent rights and enlisted a commercial partner (Eli Lilly) to manufacture and sell insulin.[51] Any profits from the sale of insulin went to fund further research.[52] Tory was well aware of this arrangement as he had solicited information from his friend J.B. Collip, one of the researcher-inventors, in 1922.[53] The insulin arrangement was complicated by the ethical injunctions by the US, UK, and Canadian Medical Associations against physicians patenting their inventions for profit, issued in 1847, 1903,[54] and 1928[55] respectively.

Canadian practices were informed by those in the UK and the US. While UK universities did not seem to have a uniform set of practices or policies, US academic inventors were much more experimental in developing innovative business models to manufacture and sell their inventions.[56] In another work, my co-author and I explore in more detail the six primary models of academic research commercialization that emerged between 1910 and 1935 in the US.[57] These included establishing an independent non-profit research foundation in 1912, electing a special patent-managing committee for the invention of tethelin in 1915 and thyroxin in 1916, and forming an external foundation to manage synthetic vitamin D in 1924.[58] Other strategies surveyed in this period up to 1935 included encouraging researchers to patent their own inventions or dedicate the rights to the public.Patent dedication meant that a patent was obtained, but then instead of being sold or licensed to a manufacturer it was left open to anyone who wished to use the patent (or "dedicated to the public," in the language of the times). This meant that the invention was available to anyone who wanted to use it and avoided ongoing patent management costs, which could be significant. It was a strategy adopted in the early twentieth century by institutions as diverse as the US War Department, Harvard University,[59] the National Bureau of Standards, and the US National Research Council that toyed with it for years.[60] However, if a manufacturer adopted the invention, made some minor changes, and then patented those innovations they might be able to block the use of the original invention without a license from them. Manufacturers were also reluctant to invest in bringing a product to market without a guarantee of some degree of exclusivity. Both scenarios had played out at the National Bureau of Standards.[61] Both Tory and Eagleson seemed quite influenced by the National Bureau of Standards' experience through communications with US colleagues at that institution and wished to avoid its plight.[62]

The National Research Council employee-owned patent policy only stood for five years, and in that period no inventions were patented by National Research Council researchers. In 1925, Tory introduced a more detailed patenting policy through legislation which took a different approach, providing that the National Research Council, instead of the researcher, retained full ownership of all inventions and discoveries made by its employees.[63] This change made, Tory and his council began to develop processes for obtaining and then commercializing patents, the core work of a technology transfer office.

In the early days, the records suggest that the main processes they put in place for obtaining patents were discovering what was patentable within the research units of the National Research Council and then recording and monitoring what was eventually patented. The decision to get a patent was made through a hub-and-spoke model of administration, where the hub was the Associate Committee on Patents and Awards who were advised and informed by a six-member subcommittee from each laboratory division.[64] In practice, in the ten years the Associate Committee operated (1928–1938), it existed in name only; it never met and made no decisions.[65] Its work was performed entirely by the secretary to the Associate Committee, Frank Lathe, and the subcommittees, who met on a regular basis. Lathe was the first full-time research scientist on staff at the council and was a prolific patentee in the period before 1940. He was responsible for much of the early patent commercialization efforts at the National Research Council, whereas the subcommittees decided whether and where patents should be applied for, obtaining "competent advice" if necessary.[66]

The birth of a more formal technology transfer office can be traced to a note written by Lathe to Tory on 10 January 1934. In it, Lathe wrote that he was "not at all satisfied with our present practice in regard to patents" and "that the time has arrived when we should consider some arrangement which may be more satisfactory and of a more permanent character." The research required to obtain patents and their commercialization required a full-time employee.[67] His proposal was to make Arthur C. Halferdahl, a research chemist, responsible for patents under Lathe's ultimate supervision.[68] Halferdahl would devote "whatever time is necessary" to patent questions and his other duties would be reduced as necessary, thus making him the National Research Council's first patents officer.[69] Lathe also suggested that certain changes should be made to organize patents correspondence and filing systems, that is, that files should have up-to-date information of the actions taken in respect of a particular patent and that correspondence should come from one person.[70] Thus was the beginning of the office and its procedures.

The National Research Council's technology transfer office grew organically out of an organization itself tasked with developing science and technology in the service of the nascent Canadian public interest. It is worth noting that in the beginning, it was unclear whether the public interest would be better served by encouraging researchers through the grant of patent rights, or by providing institutional support and employment for researchers, or some combination thereof. The second view prevailed and this makes sense historically given that Canada had neither a particularly active scientific community nor the markets, agents, or culture of patenting countries like the US and UK had to support researchers patenting their own innovations. Vesting patents in the institution also allowed for the development of organized technology transfer, the subject of the next part of this essay.

PART II: MCNAUGHTON AND THE BUILDING OF A NATIONAL IDENTITY

McNaughton's Contribution to Office Procedures

Despite the organizational changes detailed above, the National Research Council's patent-related activities remained disorganized. Tory was succeeded by General A.G.L. McNaughton who took over as president of the National Research Council in 1935.[71] McNaughton's training and inventing acumen gave him unique insight into managing and developing a successful technology transfer office. It was thought that because of his experience he had "the ability to judge a situation on its merits, regardless of any personal interests that may be at play."[72] Typically, military men believed in the rule of law, accepted the nation state as the highest form of political organization, and were trained to be responsible to a higher interest. A characteristic value imparted by military training was a strong belief in authority, as well as a reliance on precedent or historical example to develop principles to be used in the future.[73] These mental attributes positioned McNaughton well to help build the National Research Council's technology transfer office.McNaughton was the son of a successful frontier general store owner in Saskatchewan and had trained as an engineer at McGill University, obtaining his MSc in 1912 and enlisting in the Canadian militia in 1909. He was himself a prolific inventor and held the National Research Council's second official patent. His scientific advances in artillery technology are credited with helping the Canadians win at Vimy Ridge in WWI and contributed to his promotion to lieutenant colonel of the Canadian Corps artillery. When he returned to Canada in 1920, he enlisted in the regular army[74] and was appointed chief of the general staff in 1929, a role he occupied until being appointed National Research Council president in 1935. He later acted as the president of the UN Security Council following WWII.

McNaughton recounts that "[w]hen I came to look at the labs I, frankly, was very distressed at the conditions which I found ... a condition that literally verged on despair."[75] Perhaps motivated by this, once McNaughton took over the helm of the National Research Council, patents and research commercialization became a priority.[76] The formalism and elaborate structure of the Tory years yielded to the rugged practicality and efficiency that were hallmarks of McNaughton's management style. In a note to file, McNaughton writes that he had decided "that for the moment it is advisable to deal with particular [cases] rather than to try to establish a general policy in regards [to] patents."[77] This case-by-case outlook seemed to typify his approach to the issue of patents at the National Research Council: where Tory had been more concerned to establish broader policy, probably prematurely in terms of what existed on the ground, McNaughton was interested in the nuts and bolts of the operation, developing policy as needed. Thus decisions about what was best for the public interest were also made on a case-by-case basis. McNaughton formally disbanded the moribund Associate Committee in 1938 and the departmental subcommittees became the principal patent committees.[78] Under McNaughton's leadership,

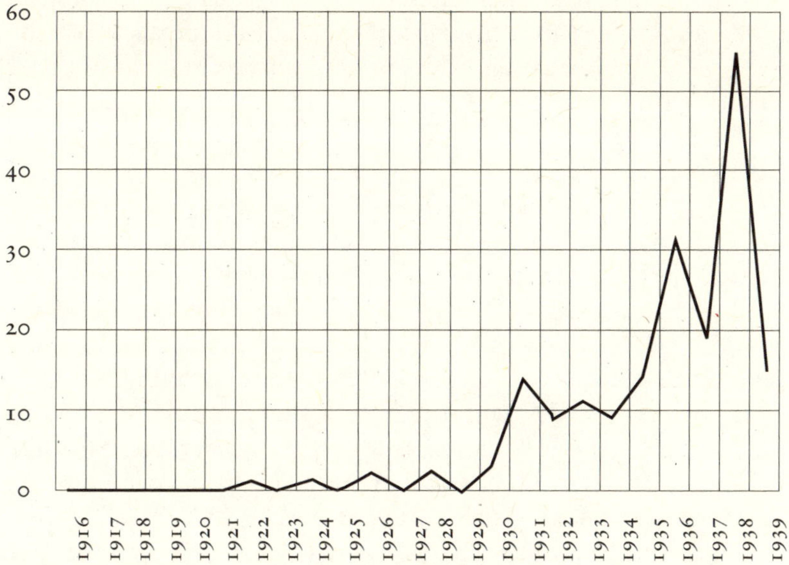

Figure 10.1 | Patents filed from 1916 to 1939 show that they grew rapidly during McNaughton's term.

the pursuit of patents acquired a sense of purpose and direction. During Tory's years, as Figure 10.1 demonstrates, the number of patents applied for in any given year never exceeded fifteen. A 19 April 1933 report records that only eleven National Research Council patents had been granted (both in Canada and internationally) from the twenty-five applications that had been made (for eight inventions in Canada and internationally).[79] Once McNaughton took over, applications rose rapidly to a high of fifty-five patents in 1938, only to drop off during WWII as war concerns consumed much of the National Research Council's energy. Of the 145 patents filed during McNaughton's tenure fifty-eight were granted.[80] Some of this growth in patent applications could be attributed to the fact that more applied research was being done at the National Research Council during McNaughton's tenure. Perhaps the increase in numbers was also influenced by the growth of a culture of invention at the council, as more researchers became aware of peers whose work had been patented. However, generating invention disclosures from researchers that lead to patent applications is challenging. It requires a combination of organizational strategies and competencies on the part of the agents managing this process that technology transfer offices have been trying to understand and perfect since their inception.[81] In part this is because finding patentable technologies requires specialized communication with researchers by well-informed officers.[82] Patents are also expensive and arduous to draft, thus a technology has to have a reasonable prospect of success for a patent to be filed; understanding in advance which patents can succeed, and which will not, is a skill.[83] Thus the fact that the number of patents filed during McNaughton's term rose so sharply is notable and can reasonably be associated with his leadership and direction.[84]

After the Associate Committee was disbanded, the decision to obtain a Canadian or US patent, or both, was generally left to the discretion of the researcher familiar with the field and the result of a patents search by the National Research Council patent agent, Alexander MacRae. His role was to determine whether the invention met the legal criteria of novelty and non-obviousness. In almost all the files, researchers' opinions guided the process to determine in which countries to apply for patents and which companies and individuals to solicit when trying to market the patents (so much so that sometimes the file was titled with the name of the researcher rather than the invention).[85] American and British patents were, unsurprisingly, the second and third most popular patents obtained, after Canadian patents, and in most cases a US patent was sought contemporaneously with the Canadian one. Each departmental subcommittee also had an annual budget for applying for patents; this presumably encouraged them to select patents wisely.[86] The files document that the bulk of the work after applying for the patent was considering which countries other than Canada or the US to get patents. Once the patent was obtained, the work shifted to shepherding the correspondence with companies who might be interested in making "offers for any patent rights in any of the above patents, either by outright sale or on a royalty basis."[87] Where industrial partners were present, they provided guidance as to where international (non-US) patents should be sought. Research into the industries in those countries would be conducted, which would sometimes be quite basic. For example, for the rubber patents named "Reanite," the process consisted of merely listing crude rubber purchases by manufacturing industries

Table 10.1 | Income and expenses related to patents from 1918–1948 at the NRC

Year	Amount spent on patents	Patent royalties
1936	$3809.15	$1384.39
1937	$1371.00	$4677.72
1938	No data	$9508.77
1939	No data	$3867.94
1940	No data	No data
1941	No data	No data
1942	$1059.00	$20,231.21
1943	$1721.71	$20,749.01
1944	$3414.13	$59,503.68
1945	$8114.97	$42,836.51
1946	$7036.25	$32,833.38
1947	$5893.51	$25,935.62
1948	$5114.59	$33,062.51

in a range of countries. This blunt measure was complemented by a more detailed discussion of political conditions (e.g., "we feel that it is a great gamble to keep up a patent in Czecho-Slovakia"),[88] the size of the market, and whether patent rights were respected within those countries. International patent applications, that is, other than for the US, were suspended at the outbreak of WWII.[89]

This case-by-case approach allowed for decentralized decision-making and flexibility in considering a range of factors, including what was in the public good. Developing a patent policy had been a priority of Tory's tenure but the success of McNaughton's approach is perhaps best evidenced by the annual reports, which only start reporting patent royalties after he became president in 1935. Royalties climbed from an initial amount of $1,384.39 in 1936 to peak revenue of $59,503.68 in 1944, falling slightly after WWII to $33,062.51, with an average annual royalty stream of $23,144.61 per year between 1936 and 1948.

This peak amount would have represented over $400,000 per year in current dollars, a significant amount of money for a public research institute.[90] This amount approached what was received as laboratory fees ($97,428.03) the same year and is significant because laboratory fees were the mainstay of the National Research Council's self-generated income.[91] As C.J. MacKenzie commented in 1946: "it is greatly to [McNaughton's] credit that every project initiated at that time subsequently developed into a major contribution."[92] By the time McNaughton left the National Research Council in 1939 to lead the First Canadian Infantry Division in WWII, he had built up a technology transfer operation that through patent income would contribute to the National Research Council's ability to innovate in the public good and to make important contributions to the war effort. Indeed, the National Research Council's contribution included, among other inventions, the proximity fuse,[93] atomic energy, dried eggs, Canadian bacon, Pykerete,[94] and radar. The patent for this latter invention was in fact held jointly by McNaughton and Lieutenant-Colonel William Arthur Steel; they formally assigned it to the National Research Council in 1936.[95] In addition to its wartime contributions the National Research Council also developed more aspirational, nationalistic projects. One example is the CN 6400 streamliner, to be discussed in the next section, an aesthetically appealing and highly functional locomotive.

McNaughton's prioritization of patents and their commercialization allowed Canada's public research council to be partially sustained through patent royalties on innovations. These patenting activities likely also served the non-pecuniary purposes of enhancing the organization's reputation, promoting Canadian inventiveness and ingenuity abroad, and contributing to the war effort. Ironically McNaughton's case-by-case policy that eschewed broad statements of policy and "the public interest" had allowed for a greater flexibility to make decisions that, at least in retrospect, seemed to be more in the public interest than the policies of his predecessor Tory. The weakness of McNaughton's policy, however, was that it relied a great deal on the person in charge – him.

Expertise

McNaughton and his peers were adept at instrumentalizing patents to achieve their own ends. But where had they gained this expertise with commercialization? McNaughton's work experience was largely with the military and the National Research Council itself was the first institution of its kind in Canada. As it happens, in the late nineteenth to early twentieth century there flourished an active industry and abundant literature of advice and self-help manuals aimed at inventors which the evidence suggests consolidated, and aided in the transmission and acquisition of this expertise, promoting a culture of invention.[96] Successful independent inventors like Thomas Edison (1847–1931), Nikola Tesla (1857–1943), and the Wright brothers spurred a public fascination with invention, and its possibilities for great wealth and fame. This led to numerous how-to manuals aimed at the ambitious inventor, two of the most popular of which were Simonds' *Practical Suggestions on the Sale of Patents* and Cresee's *Practical Pointers for Patentees, Containing Valuable Information and Advice on the Sale of Patents*.[97] In Canada, these works were complemented over a century later, in 1927, when Harold G. Fox, a litigator, scholar, and eventually managing director of the Lightning Fastener Company,[98] published the first organized digest of Canadian patent cases.[99] A year earlier, F.B. Fetherstonhaugh and Fox's magisterial, 734-page *Law and Practice of Letters Patent of Invention in Canada* had also been published.[100] These treatises were supplemented by Canadian pamphlets and booklets aimed at inventors, imitating the style of the US inventor help manuals, publications like Donald Ridout's *Inventor's Pocket Companion*,[101] William C. Linton's *Inventor's Adviser and Manufacturer's Handbook to Patents, Trade marks, Designs, Copyrights, Prints and Labels*[102] and F.B. Fetherstonhaugh's alliterative *The Abc of Patents; Plain Practical Pointers*.[103]

Some or all of these sources were likely relied on by McNaughton, Halferdahl, and others given the extent to which they followed the approaches mentioned in those manuals, although I could not find any documents that cited a particular text.[104] But given the similarities between the way National Research Council officials implemented their commercialization strategies and the instructions given in these manuals it can be inferred that NRC officials were aware of them. For instance, the texts encourage inventors to advertise their invention in newspapers (although "[c]ontinuous advertising in every issue of a daily or weekly newspaper, is a great waste of money"),[105] use patent brokers or selling agents, set up companies, and find a promoter. Simonds' step-by-step instructions on how to sell an invention describes precisely the procedure the National Research Council in fact followed in selling its inventions, including creating a pamphlet that describes the invention containing:

> [A] concise but very careful description of the invention and its operation, setting forth its advantage over the common article, or process, on which it is an improvement. It should contain a careful statement of the actual first cost of the article or process, supported by facts and figures, and offers of responsible parties, if any have been made, to manufacture at such prices […] It should further show, by actual statistics, taken from reliable sources, how extensive a market is offered to the invention, taking into account the average life of the article, whole duration of the patent, and from this should be computed the whole sum to be realized, if the whole market is supplied […] It is probably not best to put into the circular the terms upon which the patent, or rights under it, will be sold. That can be better set forth in a letter to accompany the circular. [106]

The National Research Council staff would likely have heard about or gained access to these resources from a range of sources including the local patent bar and through their subscriptions to trade magazines. It seems likely that a great deal of borrowing was going on between the different publications, perhaps under-acknowledged given the ephemeral nature of many of these forms of legal literature.

Another source of information and expertise on obtaining patents was the local patent bar. The National Research Council worked with Alexander MacRae, a lawyer who initiated virtually all the patent filings for the National Research Council in the period before WWII. MacRae was a former engineer who was instrumental in creating the Canadian Institute of Patent Solicitors in 1926.[107] He was eventually elected president and served from 1941–1943.[108] MacRae first started working for the National Research Council while managing the Ottawa branch of the UK firm Marks & Clerk, processing their patent applications. In 1932, he founded his own practice in Ottawa, MacRae & Co., that continues as a law firm to the present day.[109] By 8 June 1932, Tory had stated that "due to the extremely satisfactory service given by Mr MacRae" all patent applications would go through him until further notice.[110] And so they did for the period under consideration in this chapter.

In addition to the inventor manuals, a range of magazines and trade journals were founded or expanded in the mid-nineteenth century.

These played a key role in constituting a culture of invention that celebrated inventors and entrepreneurs, "placing them in the pantheon of national heroes."[111] US publications available to Canadians included *Scientific American, American Artisan, American Inventor*, and the *Patent Rights Gazette*. These supplemented the US Patent Office's printed lists of patents issued, sale of specifications, articles about important new inventions, and forum for those who might want to sell their patent rights.[112] In Canada, during the 1910s, the *Star* took on the role of informing the public of new inventions, patents for sale, interesting inventors, and peculiar inventions.[113]

Tory, McNaughton, and the other officials of the National Research Council were immersed in this culture of inventions, patents, promotion, and advertising. These publications played a law-creating role in producing practices of technology transfer that guided Canadian institutions until the 1980s.[114] Notably, while technology transfer offices are in the business of "knowledge translation," it is interesting that in creating the Technology Transfer Office itself its founders were translating knowledge from US and Canadian publications into practice. The technology transfer office itself was a technology, and in the case of the National Research Council, particularly adapted to its purpose even if it got off to a slow start.

The next and last section considers the particular practices that McNaughton and his deputies adopted in translating commercialization norms and the procedures they suggested to serve their understanding of the office's public interest mandate.

PART III: COMMERCIALIZATION AND LICENSING PRACTICES

Commercialization and Licensing Practices at the National Research Council

In order to document the National Research Council's licensing practices, I reviewed and organized the approaches evident in the files pertaining to particular inventions, drawing out broader themes.[115] The earliest file that stores and documents formal attempts to commercialize an innovation appears in 1932, during commercialization of the so-called "magnesite patents," a patent over an asbestos product.[116] In the period under consideration from 1932–1939, officials seem to have attempted to sell or license the patent for nine projects, ranging from maple products to a protective coating for preventing the carbonization of alloy steels.[117]

From these files emerge consistent patenting and licensing practices. First, inventions were patented in the employee's name (rather than in the name of the National Research Council) and assignments were not recorded at the Patent Office. While on its face the practice of using employee names seems to contradict the policy of government ownership of inventions, doing so was a strategic decision. In a letter from the National Research Council's patent agent MacRae to Lathe, MacRae explained that this practice had been adopted to "avoid the suggestion" that the National Research Council was "competing with industrial companies."[118] The patent was then assigned to the National Research Council, thus ensuring the patent would not violate the employee patent policy that vested ownership in the council. While debates over who owned inventions were common before inventions began to be patented, once they were patented, it seems that these inquietudes disappeared. Researchers generally played a key role in guiding the research commercialization through committee structures. This kept them at the centre of the process.

Colloquially, the activity of technology transfer was referred to as "disposal,"[119] although the reality is that rarely were these rights fully disposed of, or transferred, either by sale or exclusive license. Indeed, Lathe had flagged that the council was accumulating patents but needed "a method of procedure ... by which patents owned by the Council can be made available to the public both in Canada and in foreign countries," a process that only developed once McNaughton was president.[120] The council under Tory relied on informal word of mouth and personal connections to dispose of patents, which was not as effective a strategy when there were more patents involved.

The council had decided in several instances to patent defensively to protect the council's research and invention. This was the approach taken towards the magnesite, maple products, and plant hormones patents, to name a few. Defensive patenting meant the patent would be available for free use in Canada, perhaps with royalties in the future should the invention prove profitable, and the council would "collect royalties in the United States."[121] If in the infrequent case a private company had funded an investigation at the council, the National Research Council might only ask for some portion of royalties on the patent.[122] In the case of patents without an obvious research partner, or with a diverse market of possible Canadian businesses that might generate reasonable royalties, or both, the council solicited licensees broadly. Throughout, the council sought to avoid real and potential conflicts of interest as it sat awkwardly, straddling the worlds of commerce and science. Its scientists conducted research with the objective of finding commercial applications in the "public interest" that might then generate revenue streams for the organization or improve the fortunes of commercial partners.[123]

A key question that followed from getting a patent and then finding someone who wanted to license it was on what terms it would be licensed. An exclusive licence over the patent would lock up the invention and allow a monopoly. Businesses preferred this option as it allowed them greater profits and to take more risks investing in manufacturing and distributing the product. Broad non-exclusive licencing terms could allow for greater competition, particularly other companies attempting to manufacture and sell the product at a lower and more accessible price. It also risked, however, that no one would attempt to commercialize the product as the potential for reward was unpredictable and was lower than the amounts invested. Non-exclusive licencing also allowed the patent holder greater control over who and how the patent was commercialized, and importantly for the National Research Council's mandate, allowed price controls by permitting the patent holder to license to competitors if prices got too high.

Unsurprisingly, each technology raised unique concerns, such as whether the interested firms were "responsible," whether enough product could be produced to allow Canada to stop importing it, and whether one key firm or many should be approached to implement the process.[124] Thus, McNaughton's style of licencing resembled how he decided which inventions to patent – there was no overarching policy. Instead, decisions were made on a case-by-case basis by the associate committees, imbuing the National Research Council with the ability to flexibly take into account public interest considerations. McNaughton and his staff appreciated the potential for licencing, however, and took a principled position to generally favour non-exclusive licencing to make products as available to the public as possible. As Eagleson wrote to Pitt in 1939, "under the provisions of the Research Council Act these patent rights are vested in the Council and are made available to the public under conditions determined by the Council."[125]

Although the council's letters invariably specified that inventions were licensed non-exclusively in Canada to Canadian companies and could be licensed exclusively elsewhere, the files show that this practice was not followed rigorously and could be altered as needed. Sometimes Canadian rights were exclusively licensed to Canadian companies, particularly in situations when National Research Council officials felt that the public interest so determined. The public good outlook that animated the National Research Council's licencing policy was further elaborated by the licensing practices that surrounded the CN 6400 locomotive patent.[126]

Licensing of the CN *6400 Locomotive*

In 1931 Canadian National Railways (CNR) asked the National Research Council for help in overcoming problems resulting from their locomotive smokestacks. The CNR was an ideal research partner for the National Research Council as it united the institution's priorities of scientific progress and economic development in Canada. The CNR was a national railway, incorporated in 1919 as a Crown corporation that by 1923 comprised the bankrupt Grand Trunk Pacific Railway, the Canadian Northern Railway lines, lines the government already held and other small lines that had also folded.[127] As locomotives had gradually begun to increase in size and power, smokestacks, while not shrinking, had become proportionately smaller to the body of the train itself and smoke was dangerously obscuring the vision of the drivers.[128] CNR probably approached the National Research Council for help as the council had recently built the first wind tunnel in Canada and its scientists were well suited to undertake this research problem. To clear the obstructing steam, J.J. Green and J.H. Parkin in the National Research Council's Division of Mechanical Engineering (Aeronautics Section), in close cooperation with two scientists at CNR, undertook research in the wind tunnel to improve airflow around railcars moving quickly.[129] The final product, the CN 6400 locomotive, reduced air resistance by 35 per cent, allowing the impeding steam to dissipate more effectively. Important to understanding the CN 6400 licensing negotiations is that the process of streamlining had resulted in a uniquely visually-appealing train embodying an optimistic modernism whose design was a "confluence of science and style," and involved Canadians in the "Streamline Moderne"[130] trend emerging in the US (see Figure 10.2).[131]

The Canadian patent on the CN 6400 locomotive was applied for in 1932 and issued in 1933. Additionally, a patent was issued in France that same year, and UK, US, and Switzerland patents were issued in 1934. Surviving correspondence suggests that while the underlying principle of non-exclusive licencing for the benefit of the Canadian public remained sound, the contractual details were specific to the parties involved. In correspondence with Brooks, Green notes that patents had been taken out defensively on the CN 6400 to "protect the Canadian Public."[132] With patent protection in hand, the new locomotive design was subsequently publicized widely in periodicals as diverse as *Railway Age*[133] and the *Christian Science Monitor*.[134] The council, through Tory, decided that the patents would be offered to CNR and Canadian Pacific Railways (CPR) "free of charge" but "should either railroad build locomotives of this form for export, then some financial arrangement will be made at the time with the Research Council who will receive some return for their contribution to the locomotive development."[135] At this time, CNR and CPR were the two major competing railroads in Canada; Tory's strategy was likely to rely on mutual competition and the possibility that either might develop the patented technology in a manner that would generate royalties down the road.

Giving the patent to the railroads was not an act of pure generosity; Parkin observed that the companies "will not be in a position to purchase or pay royalties on this patent" for many years as they were struggling owing to the Great Depression. But he concluded that "the advertising value to the Council in disposing of the patent in foreign countries, if it were adopted on Canadian locomotives, would be very great."[136] Tory translated this for his government superiors: the "two railways should be permitted to use them without charge as it would be of advantage to Canada."[137] The National Research Council apparently tried to entice CPR to build the locomotive because Parkin had heard, through "gossip," that CPR had gone to the US to find "designs or the brains to produce the designs" of a streamlined locomotive, which he characterized as "odd, but unfortunately typical of Canadian practice." Nevertheless, the general outlook was one of optimism. Defensive patenting would not only make the innovation more beneficial to the public, the dedication would also highlight the National Research Council's role in contributing to the Canadian economy by creating jobs and would link the National Research Council to the emerging notions of modernism and optimism through technology and innovation.

When McNaughton inherited the file, it appeared nothing had been done to sell the foreign rights, which was how the National Research Council expected to profit from this invention. McNaughton attempted to sell the US rights to CNR.[138] However, CNR was not interested in buying them as they decided that the principles of streamlining "have found expression in a large number of designs developed in the United States and elsewhere" and are "so broad as to make it difficult to turn to financial advantage the features embodied in the Parkin-Green patent."[139] In deciding whether to act on this, perhaps by trying to get licencing fees from US companies, McNaughton noted that National Research Council experience to date had shown that "it is practically impossible for the Council to deal with the question of obtaining the remuneration which is desirable from foreign builders and users."[140]

Ultimately, CNR built five CN 6400 locomotives at the Montreal Locomotive Works factory in 1936.[141] CPR later built a less visually-striking but functional version.[142] Two years later, the president of CNR, Hungerford, offered to buy the US patent outright for $600 with the proviso that all royalties collected from US manufacturers after $600 would be remitted to the NRC, up to $2,400. The National Research Council had clearly been hoping for at least $3,000, and had offered the patent to other US buyers earlier for $5,000.[143] The passage of time and lack of success evidently softened their negotiating position, although not to the point where they were willing to accede to Hungerford's initial request to pay no royalties at all.[144]

To complete the story of the CN 6400 locomotive, when King George VI and Queen Elizabeth came to visit on the Royal Tour of 1939, the CN 6400 was chosen to carry the royals across the country and later it was sent across Canada like a "mechanical celebrity" to make special appearances in Canadian cities.[145] When the age of steam ended in the late 1940s most steam locomotives were destroyed but CNR spared a CN 6400 because of its technical and symbolic importance. It is now housed in the National Museum of Science and Technology in Ottawa.[146]

The licencing surrounding the CN 6400 can be viewed as an illustration of the defensive patenting and public interest dedication policies that the National Research Council actively implemented. Patent dedication was even more compelling when coupled with the potential for advertising or publicity for the National Research Council. The documents suggest that patenting in the public interest

Figure 10.2 | A picture of CN's 6400.

was a way of making the National Research Council relevant and of service to Canadians by highlighting their role in encouraging the creation of Canadian jobs and supporting the Canadian economy. Patent dedication, as an active strategy, or rationalization after the fact, made particular sense in a case like the CN6400 where the patent was otherwise hard to dispose of.

CONCLUSION

Canada's first technology transfer organization was an invention itself. Its creation was envisioned by Tory, realized by McNaughton, and pursued by the secretaries acting out its daily routines. The National Research Council's role in commercial research developed over the years from the initial Advisory Council to managing its own facilities with permanent research staff numbering 251 people in 1940.[147] Not only did the National Research Council's technology transfer office go on to become the model for Canadian technology transfer offices throughout much of the twentieth century, the National Research Council built an organization that devised its own version of operating relatively successfully in the public interest when Canada's own identity as a federation was newly emerging.

The office's challenges were indicative of issues that would arise in the formalization of professional technology transfer as it developed over the twentieth century in Canada – issues that contemporary technology transfer offices still grapple with. This essay explored some of these, particularly understanding how a government-funded organization could profit from the innovation of its researchers; how it could collaborate with Canadian businesses for mutual benefit; to what extent the technology transfer office should continue to assert and market patent rights; when patent rights should be sought and licensed out; and when to secure credit, income, or settle with goodwill in order to help Canadian scientists participate in an international scientific community.

The CN 6400 is an illustration of the National Research Council's approach to patenting in the public interest. Patenting in the public interest was a way of making the National Research Council relevant and of service to Canadians by highlighting its role in encouraging the creation of Canadian jobs and supporting the Canadian economy. Defensive patenting and dedication to the public interest were policies that the National Research Council actively implemented. These, combined with the other law-creating practices the National Research Council undertook, served to lay the foundation for Canada's first technology transfer offices. The office's practices were both routines that became a template for running a Canadian technology transfer office, and norms that elaborated patent law. Through these office practices, the National Research Council was able to marry the seemingly contradictory notions of using the patent system, traditionally associated with private gain, and the promotion of Canadian interests through technology.

NOTES

I am grateful for the comments on earlier drafts by Angela Fernandez, Ian C. Pilarczyk, Brian Young, Laura Murray, and two anonymous reviewers, and to my research assistants Meghan Pearson, Andrea Salguero-Florian, and Logan Stack. All remaining errors are my own.

1 See generally, for the US, D.C. Mowery, R.R. Nelson, B.N. Sampat and A.A. Ziedonis, *Ivory Tower and Industrial Innovation: University Industry Technology Transfer Before and After the Bayh-Dole Act* (Stanford: Stanford University Press, 2015), especially chapter 3; H. Etzkowitz, *The Triple Helix: University-Industry-Government Innovation in Action* (Routledge: 2008).

2 See report of the Standing Committee on Industry, Science, and Technology, *Intellectual Property and Technology Transfer: Promoting Best Practices*, 42nd Parliament, 1st Session (Ottawa: House of Commons, 2017); Samuel Trosow, Michael B. McNally, Laura E. Briggs, Cameron Hoffman, Cassandra D. Ball, Adam Jacobs, and Bridget Moran, "Technology Transfer and Innovation Policy at Canadian Universities: Opportunities and Social Costs," FIMS Publications no. 23 (2012), https://ir.lib.uwo.ca/fimspub/23.

3 G.A. Van Norman and R. Eisenkot, "Technology Transfer: From the Research Bench to Commercialization: Part 2: The Commercialization Process," *JACC: Basic to Translational Science*, no. 2 (2017): 197–208, https://doi.org/10.1016/j.jacbts.2017.03.004.

4 While Upper and Lower Canada had previously had their own patent acts, Canada's *Patent Act* came into force in 1869.

5 The first year of this study.

6 "Canadian Patents Database," Canadian Intellectual Property Office, accessed 9 August 2020, https://www.ic.gc.ca/opic-cipo/cpd/eng/introduction.html. These numbers are representative of other adjacent years for which data are available, e.g., 1912 (15 per cent Canadian/67 per cent US); 1913 (17 per cent Canadian/60 per cent US); 1914 (19 per cent Canadian/66 per cent US); 1915 (17 per cent Canadian/71 per cent US); 1917 (14 per cent Canadian/78 per cent US); 1918 (15 per cent Canadian/76 per cent US); 1919 (16 per cent Canadian/72 per cent US); 1920 (no data). The first so-named Canadian patent was in fact granted to an American inventor, Samuel Hopkins, for a method of making potash and pearl ash: Wikipedia, s.v. "Samuel Hopkins (Inventor)," last modified 28 September 2019, https://en.wikipedia.org/wiki/Samuel_Hopkins_(inventor)#:~:text=Hopkins%20also%20received%20the%20first,and%20soap%20from%20wood%20ash.%22.

7 See generally T. Piper, "War Creates Commons," in *Governing Knowledge Commons*, edited by Brett M. Frischmann, Michael J. Madison, and Katherine Jo Strandburg (Oxford: Oxford University Press, 2014).

8 Technology can be licensed either exclusively or non-exclusively; the choice between the two is important. Exclusive licensing ties-up inventions but increases royalties, while non-exclusive licensing generally reduces royalties but leaves the technology widely available.

9 G. Blaine Baker, "Ordering the Urban Canadian Law Office and its Entrepreneurial Hinterland, 1825 to 1875," *University of Toronto Law Journal* 48, no. 2 (Spring 1998): 175–251; G. Blaine Baker, "Law Practice and Statecraft in Mid-Nineteenth-Century Montreal: The Torrance-Morris Firm, 1848 to 1868," in *Essays in the History of Canadian Law, Volume IV: Beyond the Law: Lawyers and Business in Canada, 1830–1930*, edited by C. Wilton (Toronto: Butterworths Canada, 1990). See also A. Fernandez and B. Tice, "Bertha Wilson's Practice Years (1958–1975): Establishing a Research Practice and Founding a Research Department in Canada," in *One Woman's Difference: The Contributions of Justice Bertha Wilson*, edited by Kim Brooks (Vancouver: University of British Columbia Press, 2009), 15–38.

10 Canada emerged from WWI with an awakened national consciousness, which inspired publications and organizations dedicated to expressing a unique Canadian identity and viewpoint: Jonathan F. Vance, *Death so Noble: Memory, Meaning, and the First World War* (Vancouver: University of British Columbia Press, 1997), 229.

11 See, e.g., a piece Blaine supervised: W.E.B. Code, "The Salt Men of Goderich in Ontario's Court of Chancery: *Ontario Salt Co. v. Merchant's Salt Co.* and the Judicial Enforcement of Combinations," *McGill Law Journal* 38 (1993): 518–68.

12 Andrew Kretz, "Inventions for Industry. Canadian Patents and Development Limited and the Commercialization of University Research in Canada," *Scientia Canadensis* 36, no. 2 (2013): 1– 36, https://doi.org/10.7202/1027020ar; Donald J. C. Phillipson, "The Steacie Myth and the Institutions of Industrial Research," *HSTC Bulletin: Journal of the History of Canadian Science, Technology, and Medicine* 7, no. 3 (1983): 117–34.

13 The historiography exploring technology transfer tends to focus more on the following: scandals and scams, e.g., Eric S. Hintz, '"A Swindling Concern': The National Institute of Inventors, 1914–1925," *Proceedings of the 2009 IEEE Conference on the History of Technical Societies*, (2009); non-institutional intermediaries like lawyers, patent agents, and invention

marketers, e.g., Naomi R. Lamoreaux and Kenneth L. Sokoloff, "Intermediaries in the US Market for Technology, 1870–1920," *National Bureau of Economic Research Working Paper* No. 9017, 2012, http://www.nber.org/papers/w9017; Naomi R. Lamoreaux and Kenneth L. Sokoloff, "Long-Term Change in the Organization of Inventive Activity," *PNAS* 93, no. 23 (1996): 12686–92, https://doi.org/10.1073/pnas.93.23.12686; Naomi R. Lamoreaux, Kenneth L. Sokoloff, and Dhanoos Sutthiphisal, "Patent Alchemy: The Market for Technology in US History," *The Business History Review* 87, no. 1 (2013): 3–38, https://doi.org/10.1017/S0007680513000123; K. Swanson, "The Emergence of the Professional Patent Practitioner," *Technology and Culture* 50, no. 3 (2009): 519–48; legislative or policy reform, e.g., D.C. Mowery, R.R. Nelson, B.N. Sampat, and A.A. Ziedonis, *Ivory Tower and Industrial Innovation: University Industry Technology Transfer Before and After the Bayh-Dole Act* (Stanford: Stanford University Press, 2015); or effective strategies and practices for technology transfer offices as part of the business and industrial organization literature, e.g., G. George, "Learning to be Capable: Patenting and Licensing at the Wisconsin Alumni Research Foundation 1925–2002," *Industrial and Corporate Change* 14, no. 1 (2005): 119–51, https://doi.org/10.1093/icc/dth046; R. Henderson, A. Jaffe, and M. Trajtenberg, "Universities as a Source of Commercial Technology: A Detailed Analysis of University Patenting, 1956–1998," *Review of Economics and Statistics* 80, no. 1 (1998): 119–27.

14 See generally Kretz, "Inventions for Industry."

15 Ibid.

16 Two comprehensive histories of the National Research Council provided the context for and illustrated the significance of the documents I was seeing: M.W. Thistle, *The Inner Ring: the Early History of the National Research Council of Canada* (Toronto: University of Toronto Press, 1966) and W. Eggleston, *National Research in Canada: The NRC, 1916–1966* (Toronto: Irwin Clarke, 1978). The NRC website was also an important source of information, see "History," National Research Council Canada, last modified 4 March 2019, https://nrc.canada.ca/en/corporate/history.

17 A. A. den Otter, *The Philosophy of Railways: The Transcontinental Railway Idea in British North America* (Toronto: University of Toronto Press, 1997), 97. See also J. A. Eagle, *The Canadian Pacific Railway and the Development of Western Canada, 1896–1914* (Montreal: McGill-Queen's University Press, 1989); R. B. Fleming, *The Railway King of Canada: Sir William Mackenzie, 1849–1923* (Vancouver: University of British Columbia Press, 1991); T. Murray, *Rails Across Canada The*

History of Canadian Pacific and Canadian National Railways (Beverly, MA: Voyageur Press, 2011).

18 den Otter, *The Philosophy of Railways*, 208.

19 W. Eggleston, *National Research in Canada: The* NRC, *1916–1966* (Toronto: Irwin Clarke, 1978), 2.

20 Eggleston, *National Research in Canada*, 3.

21 Honorary Advisory Council for Scientific and Industrial Research, Ottawa, 4–6 December 1916. The first morning's agenda included a list of twenty-three files, reports, pamphlets, and books concerning "Scientific and Industrial research." These materials were of British origin except for one item from Canada's Department of Trade and Commerce. See RG 77, vol. 94, Library and Archives Canada [LAC].

22 Mention of the Mellon Institute is common in the early meetings of the committee, e.g., "Third Meeting at Ottawa, February 15th 1917," RG 77, vol. 94, LAC; see also M.W. Thistle, "Letter to Hume Cornyn from H.M. Tory, Edmonton (26 Sept. 1927)," in *The Inner Ring: the Early History of the National Research Council of Canada* (Toronto: University of Toronto Press, 1966), 240.

23 Thistle, *Inner Ring*, 240. See also Thistle, *Inner Ring*, 256 (letter to the Hon. Howard Ferguson from H.M. Tory, Ottawa 21 Nov. 1927). In fact the permanent establishment of the NRC was referred to as a "Bureau of Standards": Eggleston, *National Research in Canada*, 11.

24 Honorary Advisory Council for Scientific and Industrial Research, RG 77, vol. 94, LAC.

25 "Pure" meaning researchers who were not researching with or for industry: Thistle, *Inner Ring*, 36, 29.

26 Clayton Keith, "Canadian Accomplishments in Forest Products Research," *The Forestry Chronicle*, (April 1990): 148–55, https://pubs.cif-ifc.org/doi/pdf/10.5558/tfc66148-2.

27 See generally V. Marier and T. Piper, "Early Twentieth-Century Canadian Medical Patent Law in Practice: JB Collip and the Discovery of Emmenin," *University of Toronto Law Journal* 60, no. 3 (2010): 855–91.

28 M. Coleman, "The Canadian Patent Office from Its Beginnings to 1900," *Bulletin of the Association for Preservation Technology* 8, no. 3 (1976): 56–63. Accessed 24 August 2021. doi:10.2307/1493571.

29 Gareth E. Maybee and Robert E. Mitchell, *History of the Patent and Trade Mark Profession in Canada* (Ottawa: Intellectual Property Institute of Canada, 1985).

30 D. Fisher and J. Atkinson-Grosjean, "Brokers on the Boundary: Academy-Industry Liaison in Canadian Universities," *Higher Education* 44 (2002):

449; P. Enros and M. Farley, *University Offices for Technology Transfer: Toward the Service University* (Ottawa: Science Council of Canada, 1986).

31 Policy re Patents Government Employees in memorandum to the Hon. A.K. Maclean, acting minister of Trade and Commerce Ottawa from Dr A.B. Macallum, 3 January 1919, RG121, vol. 110, L14-0-10, LAC.

32 R.W. Boyle, "Henry Marshall Tory," University of Alberta Alumni Association last accessed 6 August 2020, https://sites.ualberta.ca/ALUMNI/history/peoplep-z/47OctTory.htm. See generally Eggleston, *National Research in Canada*.

33 Thistle, *Inner Ring*, 209.

34 "Disposal of Patent on Maple Products 'Our Special Canadian Patent Proposition' from the Guaranteed Patent Protection Company," 11 June 1934, RG 121, vol. 109, L14-0-3, Library and Archives Canada, Ottawa, Canada. The remaining 10 per cent likely were not sold or otherwise licensed as no one wished to commercialize the invention or it had no real market.

35 E.A. Corbett, *Henry Marshall Tory: A Biography* (Toronto: Ryerson Press, 1954), xv.

36 *The Canadian Encyclopedia*, s.v. P. C. Enros, "Scientific Research and Development," accessed 6 August 2020, https://thecanadianencyclopedia.ca/en/article/scientific-research-and-development. The founding of UBC and the University of Alberta has been attributed to the tremendous growth and expansion that had occurred in Western Canada between 1891 and 1911. A university was an inducement to settlement and an anchor for a community, unlike eastern universities that had principally been developed for religious reasons: Corbett, *Henry Marshall Tory,* xii (foreword by Doug Owram). As Owram says, "[A university] was an educational, political, social and business investment all in one."

37 H.M. Tory fonds 1908–1927, accession #68-9, Box 37, items 450–61, University of Alberta Archives, Edmonton, Alberta.

38 H.M. Tory fonds 1908–1927.

39 Boyle, *Henry Marshall Tory Biography.*

40 US Department of Justice, "Patent Policies and Practices of the Department of Commerce Concerning Inventions of its Employees and Contractors," in *Investigation of Patent Practices and Policies – Report and Recommendations of the Attorney General to the President* (Washington: US Government Printing Office, 1947b), 102.

41 "I feel that if the time ever comes when it is recognized that Bureau employees may freely take patents along the line of their work in the

Bureau and have a monopoly in the disposal of such patent rights that the reputation of the Bureau will suffer, that the confidence of industry in the work of the Bureau and the usefulness of the Bureau to industry will be seriously impaired; and that there *is* [emphasis in original] danger that the wholehearted cooperation with industry which the Bureau has always enjoyed in remarkable measure will suffer." Memorandum, 4 October 1928 by Director Burgess in US Department of Justice, "Patent Policies and Practices of the Department of Commerce Concerning Inventions of its Employees and Contractors," 101.

42 US Department of Justice, "Patent Policies and Practices of the Department of Commerce Concerning Inventions of its Employees and Contractors," 101.

43 Ibid., 99.

44 Ibid., 101.

45 "While it is informally allied with the University of Pittsburgh, the Institute's research and patent program is independent of the University, and the Institute considers it advantageous to be able to determine its patent policy without reference to the factors that may influence an educational institution supported by public funds." See US Department of Justice, "Patent Policies and Practices of Educational and other Nonprofit Organizations," in *Investigation of Patent Practices and Policies – Report and Recommendations of the Attorney General to the President* (Washington: US Government Printing Office, 1947), 4.

46 US Department of Justice, "Patent Policies and Practices of Foreign Governments Concerning Inventions of their Employees and Contractors," 4.

47 Ibid., 83.

48 Ibid., 100.

49 Marier and Piper, "Early Twentieth-Century Canadian Medical Patent Law in Practice," 874.

50 See generally Michael Bliss, *The Discovery of Insulin* (Toronto: University of Toronto Press, 2000), 119.

51 Statement read by J.J.R. Macleod to the Insulin Committee meeting regarding patents and royalties, 28 April 1924, A1982-0001, Box 6, Folder 1, University of Toronto Archives, Toronto, Ontario, Canada online: The Discovery and Early Development of Insulin, http://link.library.utoronto.ca/insulin/.

52 J.J.R. Macleod, "Insulin and the Steps Taken to Secure an Effective Preparation," *Canadian Medical Association Journal* 12, no. 12 (1922): 899.

53 Correspondence from Dr Collip to Dr Tory, 25 January 1922, MS. COLL. 269 (Collip), Box 37, Folder 2, University of Toronto Archives, Toronto, Ontario, Canada, online: The Discovery and Early Development of Insulin, http://link.library.utoronto.ca/insulin/.

54 Conference on Medical Patents, 20 April 1932, "Professional Opinion and Practice in Relation to Medical Research and the Patent Law," British Medical Association Central Ethical Committee minutes 1931–32, index 16, 2, The National Archives, Kew, Richmond, UK; Report of Departmental Committee on the Patents and Designs Acts and Practice of the Patent Office, Board of Trade, Cmnd 3829 1931, Her Majesty's Stationery Office, The National Archives, Kew, Richmond, UK.

55 Section 4 Canadian Medical Association's 1928 *Code of Ethics*, Box MG28 I343 vol. 5, LAC.

56 Marier and Piper, "Early Twentieth-Century Canadian Medical Patent Law in Practice," 871.

57 Ibid., 871.

58 Ibid., 873.

59 In the words of the president, "We have declared it our general policy that (1) we as a University would not take out a patent unless it was to be dedicated to the public, and (2) that except in unusual cases we should not expect any individual or private concern to be a beneficiary of a patent." Correspondence from Harvard president to Principal Douglas, 4 April 1939, R.G. 0002, Box 0098, Folder "Patents Policy" file 02500, McGill University Archives, Montreal, Quebec, Canada.

60 Jane E. Robbins, "Solving the Patent Problem: Cognition, Communication, and the National Academy of Sciences in the Evolution of University Patent Policy, 1917–1966," (unpublished PhD diss., University of Pennsylvania, 2004), 203–4.

61 US Department of Justice, "Patent Policies and Practices of the Department of Commerce Concerning Inventions of its Employees and Contractors," 106.

62 Ibid., 106: correspondence from Director Burgess of the National Standards Bureau to F.E. Lathe of the National Research Council, 29 March 1928.

63 Following upon the revision of the constituting Act by the *Research Council Act [Honorary Advisory Council for Scientific and Industrial Research]*, 1924 (UK), 14-15 Geo. V, c 64, s 11(1): "All discoveries, inventions and improvements in processes, apparatus or machines, made by a member or any number of members of the technical staff of the Council shall be vested in the Council and shall be made available to the

public under such conditions and payment of fees or royalties or otherwise as the Council may determine subject to the approval of the Governor in Council."

64 Associate Committee on Patents and Awards, RG77, 1988-89049, Box 7, file 4-P4-7, LAC.

65 Associate Committee on Patents and Awards, 31 March 1934, RG77, 1988-89049, Box 7, file 4-P4-7, LAC.

66 Associate Committee on Patents and Awards, page 3, RG77, 1988-89049, Box 7, file 4-P4-7, LAC.

67 Correspondence from Frank Lathe to Newton, 18 March 1934, RG77, 1988-89049, Box 7, file 4-P4-7, LAC.

68 Correspondence from Frank Lathe to Newton, 18 March 1934.

69 Correspondence from Frank Lathe to Henry Marshall Tory, 10 January 1934, RG77, 1988-89049, Box 7, file 4-P4-7, LAC.

70 Correspondence from Frank Lathe to Henry Marshall Tory, 10 January 1934.

71 "McNaughton Center at McGill," *Institute of Electrical and Electronics Engineers (IEEE) Student Branch* accessed 7 August 2020, http://www.sb-ieee.ece.mcgill.ca/McNaughton.html. His archives reside at McGill University: "McNaughton, Andrew G.L. 1887-1966," *Archives McGill*, accessed 7 August 2020, http://www.archives.mcgill.ca/resources/guide/vol2_3/gen06.htm#McNAUGHTON,%20ANDREW%20G.L.

72 Vance, *Death So Noble*, 232.

73 Samuel P. Huntington, *The Soldier and the State: The Theory and Politics of Civil-Military Relations* (Cambridge: Belknap-Harvard University Press, 1957), 64.

74 Note that that during the war, the regular army and Canadian Expeditionary Force (CEF) were distinct organizational entities. The CEF was the army raised by Canada for service overseas.

75 Eggleston, *National Research in Canada*, 95.

76 Correspondence from Frank Lathe to Andrew McNaughton, 21 October 1935, MG 30 E-133 Series II, vol. 125, LAC.

77 McNaughton note to file, undated, MG 30 E-133 Series II, vol. 125, LAC.

78 Letter from McNaughton to S.J. Cook, 20 August 1938, RG77, 1988-89049, Box 7, file 4-P4-7, LAC.

79 Associate Committee on Patents and Awards, 19 April 1933, RG77, 1988-89049, Box 7, file 4-P4-7, LAC.

80 Kretz, "Inventions for Industry," 4. This was about the same success rate (40 per cent vs. 44 per cent) of patent applications prior to McNaughton's term.

81 This research continues to this day and is embodied by the work conducted and sponsored by AUTM which is a North-American

association of technology transfer professionals. See "About us," AUTM, accessed 6 August 2020, https://autm.net/.

82 See e.g., J. Owen-Smith and W.W. Powell, "To Patent or Not: Faculty Decisions and Institutional Success at Technology Transfer," *Journal of Technology Transfer* 26 (2001): 99–114.

83 McNaughton gauged his chances of success by holding advance meetings with members of the Patent Office to assess whether it was worth filing a patent: S.T. Piper, "Growing a Patent Culture: Plant Hormones Research and the National Research Council," in *Putting Intellectual Property in its Place*, edited by L. J. Murray, S. T. Piper, and K. Robertson (Oxford: Oxford University Press, 2014).

84 Note that patent data compiled for the same period from the Canadian Patents Database suggests that during the same period (1916–1939) patents filed by Canadian individuals and corporations decreased from a high of 19 per cent (1916) of all patent applications to 1.5 per cent (1939) of all patent applications: Canadian Patents Database, https://www.ic.gc.ca/opic-cipo/cpd/eng/search/basic.html.

85 E.g., "Efforts to Dispose of Dr Cambron's Patents," RG 121, vol. 11, File L14-0-15, LAC.

86 Magnesite Patents Generally, RG 121, vol. 110, File L-14-0-13, LAC.

87 "Efforts to Dispose of Dr Cambron's Patents," RG121, vol. 11, File L14-0-15, LAC.

88 Rubber Patents Correspondence from H.C. Evans to R.J. Reaney, 22 January 1940, RG 121, vol. 111, File L14-0-22, LAC.

89 Ibid., Rubber Patents. See generally correspondence from H.C. Reaney to R.J. Evans, 17 June 1940, RG 121, vol. 111, File L14-0-22, LAC.

90 A review of the annual reports of the National Research Council's peer organizations (the US National Research Council, the DSIR, the Mellon Institute) yielded no comparable information on patent royalties which could suggest a number of things: that they were not tracking patent royalties, that patent royalties were too low merit reporting, that patent royalties were accruing largely to inventors rather than the institution (perhaps the case with the Mellon Institute).

91 NRC *Annual Report Fiscal Year 1943–44*, RG77 1988-89/049, file 4-P8-2 (FA77-1), LAC.

92 Eggleston, *National Research in Canada*, 118.

93 The proximity fuse (aka fuze) was a British idea developed in collaboration with American and Canadian scientists. It is a fuse designed to detonate an artillery shell once the specified distance to the target is covered or when a specified plane is achieved. The National Research Council

collaborated with researchers at the University of Toronto to develop a dependable power supply for the radio transmitter: Martin L. Friedland, *The University of Toronto: A History* (1st ed.) (Toronto: University of Toronto Press, 2002), 354–455.

94 A floating aircraft carrier made out of sawdust and ice for landing planes.

95 Note that while the invention of radar has been widely credited to the British scientist, Sir Robert Watson-Watt, there is substantial evidence to show that other scientists and principally McNaughton may have in fact had the basic idea for radar earlier. McNaughton had assigned this patent to the National Research Council for $1 in 1936 as "it would not be proper for me to press this development [the development of a prototype cathode ray radio compass by the NRC and the work of the Radio Committee constituted in 1931] so long as I had even any remote financial interest in the matter apart from my capacity as President of the Council": Memorandum by AGL McNaughton "Personal Inventions. Cathode Ray Direction Finder & Plotter/24 v. II," 8 December 1936, MG 30 E133, vol. 303, AGL McNaughton Fonds, LAC.

96 Piper, "War Creates Commons," 403–7.

97 W. M. Edgar Simonds, *Practical Suggestions on the Sale of Patents* (Hartford, Conn.: privately printed, 1871), http://www.archive.org/stream/practicalsuggestoosimo#page/n3/mode/2up; Cresee, *Practical Pointers for Patentees, Containing Valuable Information and Advice on the Sale of Patents* (New York: Munn & Co., 1907). Scientific American also published *Hints to Inventors,* and *United States Patent Law,* short, small, cheap, even free publications: Swanson, "The Emergence of the Professional Patent Practitioner," 542. See also Hutchinson and Criswell, *Patents and How to Make Money Out of Them* (New York: D. Van Nostrand, 1899). See also, G.M. Hopkins, *Inventor's Manual, How to Work a Patent To Make It Pay*, Rev. ed. (New York: Norman W. Henly & Co., 1901), https://catalog.hathitrust.org/Record/100488949

98 A zipper company: J. Tumbridge, "A Short History of Harold G. Fox," http://www.thefoxfund.com/harold.htm.

99 H. G. Fox, *Digest of Canadian Cases Relating to Patents, Trade Names, Passing Off and Designs* (Toronto: Carswell, 1927).

100 F. B. Fetherstonhaugh and Fox, *Law and Practice of Letters Patent of Invention in Canada* (Toronto: Carswell, 1926).

101 D. C. Ridout, *The Inventor's Pocket Companion: Containing the Canadian Patent Act of 1872: a Synopsis of the Patent Laws in All Other Countries and Giving Instruction How to Apply for Home and Foreign Patents: Also the Population of Canada in Provinces, and of the United States in States,*

with Many Useful Notes and Comments (Ottawa: Taylor, [1872]), (date unknown, attributed to 1872). See also Charles H. Riches, *Hand Book on Patent and Trade Mark Law of Canada and United States* (Toronto: Riches, 1895); G. E. Maybee, *Patent and Trade Mark Problems of Manufacturers in Canada* (Toronto : Ridout & Maybee, [1929]); E. J. Fetherstonhaugh, *The Prospective Patentee : a Synopsis of the Patent Laws and Rules of Practice of Canada and the United States of America: Containing Abridged Information Relating to Other Countries / Prepared Exclusively for the Benefit of Inventors and Those Interested in Patent Matters* ([Montreal: Desbarats], c1909); Marion and Marion, *The Inventor's Help*, 5th ed. (Montréal: Marion & Marion, c1898); Marion and Marion, *The Inventor's Adviser and Manufacturer's Hand Book to Patents, Trade Marks and Designs* (Montréal: Marion & Marion, c1904).

102 William C. Linton, successor to Marion & Marion. See William C. Linton, *Inventor's Adviser and Manufacturer's Handbook to Patents, Trade marks, Designs, Copyrights, Prints and Labels* (Montreal: n.p., c1919)

103 F. B. Fetherstonhaugh, *The Abc of Patents; Plain Practical Pointers* (Toronto: Carswell, 1906). Blaine Baker was particularly interested in the legal treatise, most recently B. Baker, "Story'd Paradigms for the Nineteenth-Century Display of Anglo-American Legal Doctrine," in *Law Books in Action: Essays on the Anglo-American Legal Treatise*, edited by A. Fernandez and M. Dubber (Oxford: Oxford Hart, 2012). Baker also addressed the ephemeral nature of how-to manuals for the practitioner, and how that meant they were often not preserved: B. Baker, "The Reconstitution of Upper Canadian Legal Thought in the Late-Victorian Empire," *Law & History Review* 3 (1985): 219–92.

104 E.S. Hintz, "The Post-Heroic Generation: American Independent Inventors, 1900–1950," (PhD diss., University of Pennsylvania, 2010), 119.

105 W. M. Edgar Simonds, *Practical Suggestions on the Sale of Patents*, 37, http://www.archive.org/stream/practicalsuggestoosimo#page/n3/mode/2up .

106 Simonds, *Practical Suggestions*, 19–20.

107 G.E. Maybee and R.E. Mitchell, *History of the Patent and Trade Mark Profession in Canada* (Ottawa: Patent and Trademark Institute of Canada, 1985), 25.

108 Maybee and Mitchell, *History of the Patent and Trademark Profession in Canada*, 27.

109 Magnesite Patents Generally, RG 121, vol. 110, File L-14-0-13, LAC.

110 Memorandum from Tory to Lathe, 8 June 1932, RG 121, vol. 1, File L-14-0-13, LAC.

111 R.V. Jenkins, "Words, Images, Artifacts, and Sound: Documents for the History of Technology," *The British Journal for the History of Science* 20, no. 1 (1987): 43.

112 Lamoreaux and Sokoloff, "Intermediaries in the US Market for Technology, 1870–1920," http://www.nber.org/papers/w9017: 8–9.

113 See e.g., *Toronto Daily Star*, 1 September 1910, 12; *Toronto Daily Star*, 2 October 1913, 14; *Toronto Daily Star*, 22 September 1910, 13; *Toronto Daily Star*, 17 November 1910, 8.

114 The formal office, officially constituted in October 1947 as Canadian Patents Development Limited, was wound up by ministerial order in 1990 as part of a governmental effort to reduce the size of government.

115 The LAC files for the National Research Council are organized by invention.

116 Magnesite Patents Generally, RG 121, vol. 110, File L-14-0-13, LAC.

117 Files with only a few relevant documents are not considered in this study including the Stedman distillation column, RG 121, vol. 100, file L14-0-4, LAC; Efforts to Dispose of Polymerization Products Patent, RG 121, vol. 100, file L14-0-14, LAC; General Correspondence – Carbon Black, RG 121, vol. 100, file L14-0-17, LAC.

118 Correspondence from Alexander MacRae to Frank Lathe, 9 May 1932, RG 121, vol. 110, File L-14-0-13, LAC.

119 Disposal of Indole Acetic Patents, RG 121, vol. 110, File L14-0-11, LAC, Ottawa Canada; Disposal of Patents etc., RG 121, vol. 110, File L14-0-20, LAC.

120 Correspondence from Frank Lathe to the members of the Associate Committee on Patents and Awards, National Research Council, 24 August 1933, RG 77, 1988-89048, Box 7, File 4-P4-7, LAC.

121 Frank Lathe to the members of the Associate Committee on Patents and Awards, 24 August 1933, RG 77, 1988-89048, Box 7, File 4-P4-7, LAC.

122 In the years considered for this study for which data are available in the National Research Council annual reports (1926–1939), industry financial contributions to research average 5 per cent of gross revenues, thus constituting a very small portion of revenues for the institution.

123 In an earlier work I explore the complicated networks of collaboration, competition, and exchange within which the National Research Council was embedded for the development of plant hormone technology during the period covered by this paper. This network included other research institutions, corporate partners, and government actors like the Canadian Patent Office, whose interests, purposes and understandings of the public interest varied widely: S.T. Piper, "Growing a Patent Culture: Plant

Hormones Research and the National Research Council," in L. Murray, T. Piper, and K. Robertson, *Putting Intellectual Property in its Place: Rights Discourses, Creative Labor and the Everyday* (Oxford: OUP 2014).

124 Patent on the "Utilization of Asbestos Rock," by G.S. Whitby, 14 July 1933, RG 77, 1988-89048, Box 7, File 4-P4-7, LAC.

125 Correspondence from S.P. Eagleson to Pitt, 7 September 1939, RG 121, vol. 110, File L-14-0-13, LAC.

126 The actual title of the patent is "Locomotive," CA 337225 and it can be found at "Patent 337225 Summary," Canadian Intellectual Property Office – Canadian Patents Database, accessed 6 August 2020, http://brevets-patents.ic.gc.ca/opic-cipo/cpd/eng/patent/337225/summary.html.

127 Daniel Francis, *Selling Canada: Three Propaganda Campaigns that Shaped the Nation* (Vancouver: Stanton & Dosil, 2011), 144–53.

128 G. Wilson, "Designing Meaning: Streamlining, National Identity and the Case of Locomotive CN6400," *Journal of Design History* 21, no. 3 (2008): 240.

129 Eggleston, *National Research in Canada*, 53; Wilson, "Designing Meaning," 253.

130 An international style of Art Deco design that emphasized long horizontal lines and curving forms to give the impression of sleekness and modernity: Wikipedia, s.v. "Streamline Moderne," last modified 29 July 2020, https://en.m.wikipedia.org/wiki/Streamline_Moderne.

131 The Depression of the 1930s had given rise to a social movement that placed "special value on the idea of the modern and derived hope from the promise of a better future through scientific and technological improvements," a similar spirit to that which had animated the founding of the National Research Council: Wilson, "Designing Meaning," 242, 245.

132 Correspondence from J.J. Green to C.E. Brooks, chief of Motive Power, Operation Dept., Canadian National Railways, 6 March 1933, RG 77, vol. 147, file 17-7L-1, LAC.

133 Correspondence from Chicago and Northwestern Railway Company, Law Department Baker to J.J. Green, 7 June 1933, RG 77, vol. 147, file 17-7L-1, LAC.

134 Correspondence from J.H. Parkin to C. Shaw esq., general manager, A Wander Ltd. Peterborough, Ontario, 27 April 1934, RG 77, vol. 147, file 17-7L-1, LAC.

135 Correspondence from J.J. Green to E. Winfield, editor Canadian Railway and Marine World Magazine Toronto, Ontario, 2 February 1935, RG 77, vol. 147, file 17-7L-1, LAC. This condition appears to have been insisted upon by Hon. Stevens, chairman of the Committee of the Privy Council on

Scientific and Industrial Research, letter from J.H. Parkin to H.M. Tory 8 January 1935, RG 77, vol. 147, file 17-7L-1, LAC.

136 Correspondence from J.H. Parkin to H.M. Tory, 12 February 1934, RG 121, vol. 109, file L14-0-1, LAC.

137 Correspondence from H.M. Tory to Hon. Stevens, chairman of the Committee of the Privy Council on Scientific and Industrial Research, 20 October 1934, RG 121, vol. 109, file L14-0-1, LAC.

138 Disposal of patents on steam locomotives, letter from J.H. Parkin to H.M. Tory, 12 Feb 1934, RG 121, vol. 109, L14-0-1, LAC.

139 Correspondence from Hungerford (president of CNR) to C.D. Howe, minister of Transport, 10 December 1936, RG 121, vol. 109, file L14-0-1, LAC.

140 Disposal of patents on steam locomotives correspondence from A.G.L. McNaughton to L.D. Wilgress, director, Commercial Intelligence Service, Dept of Trade and Commerce, 29 April 1936, RG 121, vol. 109, file L14-0-1, LAC.

141 "CN 6400," *Ingenium Channel*, 10 April 2015, https://ingeniumcanada.org/innovation/story/cn-6400.

142 Wilson, "Designing Meaning," 245.

143 Correspondence from MGN to chair of Committee of the Privy Council, 5 July 1938, RG 121, vol. 109, file L14-0-1, LAC.

144 Correspondence from Hungerford to president of NRC, 17 January 1938, RG 121, vol. 109, file L14-0-1, LAC.

145 Ibid., 248.

146 Ingenium Channel, "CN 6400." See "Canadian National Railways 'CN6400/U4A' Locomotive," Ingenium Collection and Research, accessed 6 August 2020, https://ingeniumcanada.org/artifact/Canadian-national-railways-6400u4a-locomotive.

147 US Department of Justice, "Patent Policies and Practices of Foreign Governments Concerning Inventions of their Employees and Contractors," 81.

Surprisingly, I did not know Blaine even though we were both writing legal history at McGill University. Perhaps this was because he did not frequent any of the activities or dinners of the Montreal History Group, a collective based in the History Department and a hub in the writing of Quebec legal history. We met only once in a law seminar at McGill in which Ian C. Pilarczyk had invited me to discuss my research on vagrant women. Although our exchange was very fruitful, our paths never crossed again: this speaks to the academic silos that existed at the time between those who did legal history in law faculties and in history departments. Nevertheless, we shared a mutual fascination with the history of criminal justice, with the ways in which Montreal residents learned about the law in daily life, in the strategies they employed to navigate the criminal justice system to make complaints and to meet some of their subsistence needs, and with popular-class resistance and resilience. I am honoured to make this contribution to a book celebrating Blaine Baker.

Mary Anne Poutanen

11

Petty Theft in the City: Women and Everyday Justice in the Montreal Archives, 1768–1841

Mary Anne Poutanen

INTRODUCTION

Around suppertime in late November 1835, baker John Tassie left his bread cart unattended on Craig Street in Montreal while he made a delivery. Upon returning, he discovered that ten loaves were missing from the cart and observed a woman running away. Tassie immediately dashed after her and when he caught up to the presumed thief, she had three of the loaves in her arms; another woman had made off with the other seven.[1] He took his larceny complaint to the Peace Office at the courthouse where a clerk recorded his version of the incident in a deposition; a magistrate issued warrants of arrest against Adélaide St-André and Betsy Lafranchise; he later charged them with petty larceny. It is plausible that their alleged theft of bread from Tassie's cart was happenstance, a simple act executed to split the proceeds of their crime. To reduce the likelihood of both being caught, they chose to flee in different directions should Tassie appear before they could vanish from the scene. Being homeless sex workers, it is equally credible that St-André and Lafranchise were hungry and stole the ten loaves for nourishment and given the quantity of bread perhaps to share with others who lived on the streets with them.

The gendered experiences of plebeian women accused of petty larceny, like those of Adélaide St-André and Betsy Lafranchise, and whose cases ended up in the city's Court of Quarter Sessions of the Peace are at the heart of this contribution. While much research on larceny rates in nineteenth-century British North America, the United States, Europe, and Australia has demonstrated that men were overrepresented in the statistics and that criminal acts were differentiated according to gender, other studies have established that women as well as men perpetrated property offences although in smaller numbers.[2] With whom they committed these criminal acts has been open to debate. Peter Lawson, for example, argues in his examination of female criminality in early modern Hertfordshire that most of the women committed larceny with accomplices: nearly a third involved other women and almost half comprised men. These features, he has suggested, speak to the phenomenon of patriarchy, which shaped women's dependent criminal behaviour.[3] This study takes issue with the view that women were largely dependent criminals directed by men, arguing instead that women's experiences in the commission of property crime were far more diverse and complex.[4] Garthine Walker's analysis of female thieves in Cheshire challenges this binary model of sexual difference in which women are regarded as passive and men as assertive. She found that nearly two-thirds of female thieves worked mostly with other women and were bound up in a female culture of illicit activity.[5] In her study of a similar underworld of criminal activity in late eighteenth and early nineteenth-century Philadelphia, Susan Branson contends that the precariousness of women's lives fostered mutual dependence in a world absent of patriarchal constraints, which "altered or eliminated female dependence on men."[6] Moreover, Peter King has suggested that the prosecution of female larcenists was linked to anxieties about, and control of, young women many of whom were single, often living away from their families, and hence outside their fathers' supervision and discipline.[7] Therefore, taking into consideration Walker, Branson, and King's findings, this study pays close attention to the circumstances around which women stole, with whom they committed petty larceny, their marital status, and their immigration as well as migration history.

In Montreal, women stole an assortment of goods often related to their situation as unmarried female indigent residents of the city or to their responsibilities as wives, mothers, sisters, and daughters, in a variety of public, semipublic, and private spaces. The evidence suggests that some were motivated by revenge, intimidation (either self-initiated or under threat by a male partner), vanity, envy, and love. Most women stole on their own; those who committed larceny with accomplices did so usually with other women. Donald Fyson's investigation of criminal justice in Montreal and Quebec City, which shows that petty cases or low law composed everyday justice and affected the greatest number of people, supports another key theme in this study namely the role that reciprocity played in the day-to-day lives of women engaged in petty criminal acts.[8] My analysis of the subsistence strategies initiated by homeless women in Montreal reveals that many formed female bonds of mutual dependency critical to their survival. In the face of challenging life circumstances and without the support of men, they lived, worked, drank, stole, and went to court and prison together.[9] Paula J. Byrne's examination of criminal justice in early nineteenth-century New South Wales establishes that most of the women who police arrested for theft had stolen from those with whom they had close personal relations: neighbours, friends, or someone "they had been drinking, sleeping or living with."[10] Women took from people they knew because, as Lynn MacKay reasons, "the geographic boundaries of quotidian life were more circumscribed for women than for men."[11]

Feminist scholars have also argued that popular-class women participated in makeshift economies that were temporary and flexible, establishing bonds of mutuality with women they knew through informal borrowing networks in the neighbourhoods where they lived.[12] These networks, intended to solve immediate subsistence problems through lending and borrowing, were precarious, predicated on complex interactions, potential misunderstandings, cooperation, and conflict. Moreover, definitions of private property were fluid and women used the material possessions of others sometimes without permission especially when money was tight.[13] In point of fact, they borrowed items to make ends meet. Thus, misinterpretations related to these informal arrangements left women vulnerable to accusations of theft both as perpetrators and victims.[14]

This exploration of petty larceny builds upon my continued research interest, which considers the types of licit and illicit subsistence strategies that popular-class women implemented as well as upon previous research on sex work, vagrancy, and the sale and consumption of alcohol by women.[15] The study is based on 555 extant lower-court records (depositions and indictments) of the Court of Quarter Sessions of the Peace, which included at least one woman and covered the period 1768 to 1841. Women who avoided detection or who had entered into informal negotiations with victims of property crime are not included for obvious reasons. Those who were accused of grand larceny would have had their cases tried in the Court of King's or Queen's Bench, or both, and therefore are omitted.[16] For the purposes of this study, petty larceny involved offences relating to the theft of goods and money as well as women who were accused of receiving stolen goods. Other historical sources consist of police records, prison registers, newspapers, and genealogical resources. Altogether, these documents provide a window onto the circumstances under which women committed petty larceny, as well as complicated issues regarding their legal agency. My study examines women and the items they stole, the disposition of those stolen goods, the plaintiffs who made accusations of theft against these women, and the legal outcome where available. In addition to contributing to the quantification of acts of larceny, this essay also identifies the breadth of roles that women played in the judicial process as both defendants and plaintiffs. The study highlights the authority women claimed, an authority derived from their intimate knowledge of the legal system, the larceny laws in the period, and changing views of punishment.

The discussion begins with a review of the laws governing larceny and of the dominant discourse around theft. Next, I consider the women who were accused of theft, if they acted alone or committed property crimes with others, and with whom they acted if not alone. Finally, the essay explores what women stole, why they did so, the circumstances around which the alleged crimes occurred, how women disposed of the goods they obtained, and the outcome of their cases in court, as well as any punishment they received.

LAWS GOVERNING PETTY LARCENY

Larceny laws changed very little over the period under study (1768–1841). From 1768, marking the first court record I located of a woman accused of larceny, there was a fine-tuning of some of the more serious offences increasingly moving categories of larceny from capital to non-capital crimes.[17] In 1789, for example, the death penalty ended for simple larceny under twenty shillings; it then became petty larceny.[18] By 1824, the death penalty was abolished for different types of larceny and replaced by banishment or imprisonment.[19] As Fyson reminds us, in light of the lawmaking stasis borne of the growing conflict between the legislative assembly and the executive council, the subsequent rebellions of 1837 and 1838, and creation of the Special Council (1839–1840) any attempt at reforming the law in those decades failed.[20] In 1841, the Legislative Assembly of the Province of Canada adopted the *Act for consolidating and amending the Laws in this Province, relative to Larceny and other Offences connected therewith*.[21] This Act came into force as of 1 January 1842.

To appraise larceny laws, I turn to Richard Burn's 1764 edition *The Justice of the Peace and Parish Officer*, which was used in Montreal throughout the period under study.[22] Burn defined larceny as the felonious stealing and carrying away of another person's property. Since it had to be accompanied by criminal intent, taking goods belonging to another by accident was not included.[23] According to Burn, a felony was "an offence of a high nature, yet it is not limited to capital offences only, but still retaineth somewhat of this larger acceptation; for petit larceny is felony, although it is not capital."[24] A misdemeanour was "all those crimes and offences, for which the law has not provided a particular name; and they may be punished according to the degree of the offence, by fine, or imprisonment, or both."[25] Theft over the value of 12d or 1 shilling constituted grand larceny, which was a capital offence. Burn noted however that such severe punishment was rarely handed down given the rate of inflation, which had essentially cheapened the value placed on human life.[26] By contrast, petty larceny was any theft under the value of 12d or 1 shilling. As already stated, in 1789, petty larceny was changed to theft under the value of 20 shillings rather than 12d or 1 shilling.[27] It is rather disheartening to note that twenty-five years had seen the value of a human life rise by just 11 shillings. According to Burn, there could be no accessories to this offence "before or after": "for the accessories *before* are in the same degree as principals; and accessories *after*, by receiving the offenders, cannot be in law under any penalties as accessories, unless the acts of Parliament that induce those penalties do expressly extend to receivers or comforters, as some do."[28]

The circumstances around an act of theft demarcated which of the larceny-related charges would be applied to the accused. For example, a person could be prosecuted for larceny from the person or from the house (in which case, it constituted burglary). Burglary also included theft from outbuildings or from a shop if the shopkeeper lodged in the building but only larceny if that was not the case.[29] Force was considered essential; however, a charge of stealing privately could be laid in situations where no force was used. Should the theft involve breaking into a dwelling house, and not entering by an open door, with the intention to steal at the same time causing residents to be fearful then it was housebreaking even if nothing was taken.[30] The charge of robbery was reserved for anyone who placed his or her victim in a state of fear while taking from the person money or other goods.[31] If someone knowingly bought or received stolen goods, received, harboured, or concealed a felon or thief, or pawned stolen items, he or she could be charged with receiving or buying stolen goods and considered an accessory after the fact.[32]

Once a magistrate levied such a charge, a series of legal steps followed. The process involved in prosecuting an accused meant that he or she would not be tried until the next court session; in the meantime, the defendant could be imprisoned or released on bail. Bail could be granted to anyone charged with petit larceny as long as he or she had no previous offences or where the accused had not committed the felony in the open.[33] No justice of the peace could punish an offender at his discretion. The rules pertaining to evidence meant that the confession of the larcenist was better than the testimony of witnesses.[34] A poor person who entered into a recognizance to appear in court to give evidence could be compensated financially for his time.[35] As Byrne points out, to ensure restitution at court, it was critical that the stolen objects be found; without them as evidence, the grand jury would not allow the trial to proceed. Thus, those caught with stolen property in their possession were easier to prosecute.[36]

The court could apply a range of punishments singularly or in combination to those found guilty of theft and included forfeiture of goods, transportation, whipping, and other forms of corporal punishment.[37] In cases involving grand larceny, down charging – reducing the value of the stolen goods so as to constitute a lesser offence – was a common practice to avoid the death penalty. Those convicted of petty larceny could not suffer the loss of life or land but only of goods and chattel.[38] Retribution might also include fines and transportation beyond the seas in addition to prison sentences.

ELITE DISCOURSES ON THEFT

By the 1830s, Montreal elites, namely French and English-speaking justices of the peace, physicians, lawyers, philanthropists, businessmen, landowners, clergy, and newspaper editors, became alarmed by what they perceived as growing rates of larceny as well as sites of licit and illicit alcohol consumption. It was also a decade of unrest marked by rising migration from the countryside, overseas immigration, cholera epidemics that claimed thousands of lives, and by violent confrontations – such as the 1832 by-election riots and the rebellions of 1837 and 1838 – between civil society, the colonial state, and the military. This turmoil was met by a more vigorous policing of both men and women. Not only did city notables worry that people conspired against the state in taverns, but they also decried public houses, beer shops, small groceries, brothels, and pawnshops as sites of larceny frequented by thieves, pickpockets, and vagrants, as well as serving as destinations for stolen goods. These establishments, it was argued, promoted crime because of their links to a culture of illicit activities and insofar as they encouraged intemperance and immorality.[39] Elites were notably not writing about the taverns, inns, or houses of prostitution they frequented. While grand jurors usually constructed theft as a male crime, by 1825 they began to express their patriarchal unease over what they perceived as women's growing role in larceny, allegedly under the direction of men: "In present circumstances even women are emboldened to associate with the leading thieves; and having first cheered them forward to the general plunder of the Country, they next play the part of receivers of stolen goods and the procurers of false witnesses."[40] Given that women were expected to act as the moral compass of the family, female larcenists carried the double burden of not only being branded as a criminal but also as deviant or morally bankrupt.[41]

City elites proposed, as an early first line of defence against property crime, better street lighting and more effective policing of public space. Since criminals were seemingly hard at work under the cover of darkness, both a system of street lighting and a vigilant night watch were critical "to secure the repose and preserve the property of the citizens."[42] The bourgeoisie was essentially looking after its own interests. By 1815, St Paul Street, where Montreal elites had established their commercial enterprises, was illuminated with whale oil lamps; and, by 1818 similar street lighting began to appear on Notre Dame Street where these same elites resided. Twenty years later, the Montreal Gas Light Company sought permission from the municipal government to take over the operation of existing lights (including their conversion to coal oil, maintenance, and lighting), a network composed of at least 150 lamps in the city's centre.[43] Montreal's lighting practices followed those of nineteenth and twentieth-century North American and

European cities. Streetlights were first established in elite commercial and residential areas before moving slowly across the urban landscape until the poorest neighbourhoods were eventually illuminated.[44] Montreal's suburbs would have to wait for street lighting and routine police patrols. Since it was the responsibility of the newly-formed watchmen to light and extinguish the lamps each evening and morning, regular policing occurred in the town. It would seem that they served its clientele well. Magistrate David Ross, in his charge to the 1829 grand jury, stated: "Since the last Quarter Sessions, by means of the Watch, the pilfering thieves who infested this city, have been nearly all taken up and confined in prison, and prevented from committing their usual depredations."[45]

The following decade, elite discourse underscored a perceived burgeoning rate of crime, which was linked, as they saw it, to an increasingly inadequate system of policing.[46] Public censure of law enforcement had replaced Magistrate Ross's endorsement of the Watch as an 1836 letter to the editor of the *Montreal Gazette* reveals: "On the entire continent of America, there is probably no city, where person and property are more exposed to danger, than, at this moment, in Montreal. Without police – without a lamp in our streets, and with a magistracy almost inefficient for want of funds – a field is opened for the perpetration of crime, as wide and undisputed, as the most lawless could desire."[47]

As a second line of defence, elites turned to temperance as a means to reduce criminal activity especially with respect to safeguarding private property. According to this strategy, crime prevention had to "destroy the cause by which it is committed," that is to say through more rigorous regulation of drinking establishments frequented by the popular classes such as "low tap rooms licensed either as taverns, beer shops, or small groceries which serve as places of resort for thieves, pickpockets and vagrants of every denomination."[48] From their perspective, better control over taverns could be introduced by reducing their number and by granting licences only to respectable residents of the city. Elites also viewed pawnbrokers, especially those with businesses on the main street of the St Lawrence suburb, as corrupt because they encouraged larceny by being intermediaries for thieves to dispose of their stolen goods.[49] Grand jurors demanded that only licenced pawnbrokers of the best character be allowed to open shops.[50] Their regulatory gaze converged equally on city brothels. Given that the police were unable to abolish residential prostitution, elites argued that it was incumbent upon authorities to govern illicit activities in brothels around alcohol consumption, disorderly behaviour, sex, and fencing: "*Il arrive aussi souvent que ces maisons recèlent les objets volés, et mettent ainsi les voleurs à l'abri de toute poursuite*."[51] Notwithstanding the discourse of a few privileged city residents that blamed society's ills on drink or alcohol abuse, grand jurors also linked poverty with criminality and recognized that without employment or assistance, those discharged from prison had few options other than larceny or starvation.[52]

Elites reiterated a need to categorize prisoners in the common gaol so as to separate those who were perceived as hardened female criminals (usually the homeless or sex workers) from those who were viewed as novices and to introduce a work program similar to that in the House of Correction. In 1836, when a new prison for the district was opened at Longue Pointe elites optimistically proclaimed that there would finally be a proper system of classification and prisoners would be kept in solitary confinement at night.[53] It was not to be. Work, some argued, would also serve dual purposes as a proper form of punishment and as a means to rehabilitate offenders. Others looked to science to determine a person's likelihood for criminal activity. American phrenologist, Dr Jonathan Barber, visited Montreal to deliver a series of lectures and to demonstrate phrenology's relevance at the new gaol by examining the physical contours on skulls of forty prisoners, women as well as men. He impressed even the skeptics of phrenology according to the *Montreal Gazette*. In the majority of cases, Barbour "distinguished between the bold and determined offender, and the novice in crime – the ruffian, and the man of gentle disposition – the abandoned wretch, destitute of all religious principles, and he who maintains his belief in Christian revelation."[54]

To warn city residents about local larcenists, newspapers such as the *Montreal Gazette* routinely printed the names of women and men who were charged, acquitted, or found guilty of property crimes. Certain cases were highlighted in some detail cautioning the reading public about servants who stole from their masters or mistresses or about disreputable women who pilfered from soldiers even suggesting that these men ought to be more discriminate about the company they kept. Such advice was directed at the lower ranks of the military and not officers who frequented city brothels without restraint or censure. In March 1840, the *Montreal Transcript* featured two stories involving larceny by women: the first, Caroline Greenwood's theft of money from Joseph Simpson, a recently discharged soldier of the King's Dragoon Guards; and the second, servant Catherine O'Neil's pilfering of a watch and wearing apparel from John Clarke.[55]

As a third line of defence, elites demanded changes to the way justice was administered in order to hasten the disposition of cases involving a range of misdemeanours and petty larceny. In April 1830, the grand jury brought attention to those prisoners who had been charged with theft and had already been detained in prison for a long time without yet having gone to trial: "they will have been confined about a year before it shall be ascertained whether they are guilty of the offence for which they have been deprived of their liberty; the Grand Jury present this as an abuse in the administration of the laws, and as ... [an] unnecessary encroachment on the liberty of the subject (sic)."[56] In point of fact, these prisoners were incarcerated for a longer period than any sentence the magistrates would have handed down for petty larceny if they had been found guilty. There were many reasons for delays in court cases as my study of sex work in the same period shows: they were postponed from one term to another when complainants and even defendants out on bail failed to appear at court. While authorities could and did resort on occasion to the Court of Oyer and Terminer to deal with a backlog of cases, especially following the rebellions of 1837 and 1838, as early as January 1837, grand jurors were recommending that a police court be established "wherein cases, like the great majority of those which now come before the Quarter Sessions would be summarily determined" and thus justice would be "much more effectively and expeditiously attained."[57] By 1840, the chorus grew louder as grand juries repeatedly endorsed a police court to deal with a range of offences that included keeping a disorderly house, petty assault, and petty larceny, which had tied up the Court of Quarter Sessions because of a prisoner's right to a trial by jury.[58]

THE WOMEN ACCUSED OF THEFT

When Adélaide St-André and Betsy Lafranchise allegedly stole bread from John Tassie's cart, they shared common traits with other women accused of larceny. Both St-André and Lafranchise were unmarried Canadians. With respect to ethnicity, at least 286 or 44 per cent of the 655 accused were Canadian, a tenth of them (10.8 per cent) being male accomplices. Of the remaining 365 who represented other ethnicities and racialized people, less than a tenth (7 per cent) were men but a large number were Irish women; those of African descent and Indigenous constituted a minuscule percentage.[59] Although marital status was not recorded in every instance, 77 per cent were single, 11 per cent were married, and 12 per cent were widows. That nearly a quarter were either married to or widows of tradesmen, soldiers, and labourers supports my assertion that many of the thefts were likely acts related to subsistence strategies implemented in popular-class households, some of which were linked to the borrowing networks women had established in the neighbourhoods where they lived. That a significant proportion of women were accused of perpetrating property crimes without accomplices suggest more diverse reasons that include among others, indigence, revenge, envy, and vanity. How do we understand Maria Campbell's alleged theft of a merino cloak that had been a half-hour loan? Margaret Atchison, who was married to George Richardson, had offered Campbell the cloak while she retrieved her trunk. A short distance from the Richardson house, Campbell leaped off the cart she was riding in and disappeared with the cloak.[60] Although it is an example of borrowing gone awry, Campbell might have been motivated for other reasons, for example she may have wanted the cloak for herself. In another case of borrowing but clearly with ulterior objectives, thirty-four-year-old Marie-Angélique Blanchard, wife of Michel Camus, used the pretext of asking for salt from her neighbour Jane McDonald to scrutinize the details of the house's interior and objects. She returned later in the day when McDonald was absent from the house, and took a petticoat and glass decanter.[61]

Table 11.1 shows that of the 655 accused in the 555 cases involving larceny, nearly three-quarters (466) of the women stole on their own which suggests that most of the thefts were opportunistic. Of those who were denounced for committing acts of larceny with others, more than two-thirds did so with other women. There is no evidence to suggest that any of the women established larceny networks to prey on others. Male accomplices represented less than a third. Only ten women were accused of committing property crimes with their husbands,[62] as was the case of Marie Miron and Gilbert Bernon who, along with Pierre Millet, were charged with stealing three lemons and a pound of butter from Toussaint Labelle.[63] While I do not know why

Table 11.1 | Distribution of larceny acts alone or with accomplices, 1768–1841

Category	#	%	With Women	With Men	Other Information
Alone	466	71.14			
with 1 other	119	18.16	91 (76.5%)	28 (24%)	
with 2 others	33	5.03	14 (42%)	18 (55%)	1 unknown
with 3 others	25	3.8	17 (68%)	8 (32%)	1 case all women
with 5 or more others	12	1.83	7 (58%)	5 (42%)	
Total	655	100	129	59	1

Marie Miron participated in this theft of food, there are a number of possible reasons that can explain it. She may have been motivated by hunger, by her husband's intimidation, or by her affection for him.

Table 11.2 reveals that the majority of larceny cases involving accomplices took place between 1825 and 1841. It coincided with growing prosecution of female larcenists as demonstrated in Table 11.3. This was a period when, as Fyson has pointed out, everyday criminal justice was undergoing profound changes with respect to state formation and social regulation.[64] Thus, a more vigorous policing of women – especially those who were unmarried and newcomers seemingly outside the supervision of responsible men – was a consequence of growing immigration, migration from the countryside, and social and political unrest.

Table 11.2 | Distribution over time of larceny cases involving accomplices, 1768–1841

Accomplices	Period 1* (1768–1789)	Period 2 (1790–1824)	Period 3 (1825–1841)
Alone	17	86	374
1 other	119	12	47
2 others	33	2	9
3 others	25	2	4
5 or more others	12		2
Total	17	102	436

* Periodization was determined by changes in the law reducing the types of larceny that could result in the death penalty. Thus, the first period, 1768 to 1789, ends when 29 George III c.3 s.7 abolishes the death penalty for simple larceny under twenty shillings; simple larceny becomes petty larceny. By the end of the second period, 1790 to 1824, 4 George IV c.4-5-6 reduces the number of different types of larceny that could lead to the death penalty replacing it with banishment or imprisonment. The third period, 1825 to 1841, ends with 4 & 5 Victoria c.25 which changed larceny laws significantly: the division between petty and grand larceny was abolished; all larceny was considered as grand larceny; larceny as well as larceny-related charges such as robbery, stealing from the person, and break and enter was punishable by incarceration at hard labour in the penitentiary for not more than seven years (in simple larceny) and fourteen years to life (for robbery and burglary) or elsewhere for not more than two years. Robbery involving injury was punishable by death.

Table 11.3 | Distribution of larceny cases, 1768–1841

Period	Number	Percentage
1. (1768–1789)	17	3
2. (1790–1824)	102	18.5
3. (1825–1841)	436	79
Total	555	100

WHAT WOMEN STOLE

Most of the items women were accused of stealing resonated with their daily lives – those to which they had ready access as well as those associated with domestic activities – and included clothing, footwear, food, bedding and linens, fabric and sewing materials, as well as a variety of other household commodities such as wood and money. They came across these goods in diverse places within a circumscribed area related to their day-to-day excursions. Women stole out of back yards, courtyards, and military facilities, on the streets, at markets, in taverns and shops, in public spaces such as the Champs-de-Mars and along the Lachine canal, as well as in dwelling houses. As Byrne and MacKay have argued, women ordinarily pilfered from those they knew and that the geographic boundaries of women's daily lives were both limited and scrutinized.[65] Take the example of Mary Goldsmith who, when confronted by labourer Benjamin Tindall, admitted to stealing various articles of wearing apparel from his house. Tindall told the clerk writing up his deposition that "from circumstances and information which deponent (Tindall) has received verily believes that the articles were stolen by Mary Goldsmith who has for a week boarded in the deponent's family and that Mary Goldsmith has acknowledged to have stolen articles."[66] Feminist research has also established that Montreal women, as elsewhere, lived large parts of their lives in public under the watchful eyes of neighbours where they performed household chores, gossiped and socialized, retrieved water from communal taps, babysat each others' children, and eked out a living through licit and illicit means.[67]

While close quarters and watchful eyes surely prevented many people from stealing objects they otherwise might have, some women threw caution to the wind and took advantage of opportunities to steal, choreographing these thefts by hiding small items in their clothing, splitting up the goods (as in the case of St-André and Lafranchise) to make it difficult for the victim to retrieve all of the stolen articles, or moving an object from one person to another. Sophie Dupéré, Sophie Proulx, and Joseph Dollar's system of theft may have served them well until their encounter with innkeeper Bartholomew O'Brien. While he was visiting a cellar at the St Ann's Market, Proulx took his purse, containing six American half dollars, twelve quarters, and change, that he had left unattended on a table, passed it to Dupéré, who in turn slipped it to her son Joseph Dollar.[68] Given that the market cellars were reputed sites of sex commerce and that both Sophie Dupéré and Sophie Proulx were known streetwalkers, O'Brien's reasons for being in the cellar were highly suspect. Notwithstanding the cellars' reputation and perhaps his own vigilance, O'Brien was not deterred from initiating a prosecution of the three would-be thieves once he noticed that the purse was missing.

Table 11.4 reveals that wearing apparel was a common target of thieves, representing nearly a third (31 per cent) of the goods identified in court records; they were valuable and easy to pawn or sell door-to-door. Wearing apparel, as Adrienne Hood has observed, also played a key role in reflecting individual identities and the expense of new clothing made the theft of used wearing apparel tempting.[69] According to Garthine Walker, with respect to aggregate sums spent on necessities within the household economy, clothing in Cheshire was the most expensive item to purchase after food.[70] In Montreal, fuel would have been a very costly item to procure for any household; the cost of wood rose in winter when it was most needed.[71] The extra clothing required in intemperate weather with poor indoor heating would have followed. Maria Campbell's theft of garments belonging to Marie-Françoise Champagne also reinforces Byrne's assertion that the accused often knew the plaintiffs as demonstrated by the following example. One evening in 1792, Jean-Baptiste Léonard gave Maria Campbell shelter in his home. Sometime during the night, she absconded with Champagne's petticoat, cape, cap, ribbon, and soap. When the two women ran into each other at the port, Champagne recognized the cap Campbell was wearing and confronted the would-be thief about the objects she had stolen; Campbell retorted that Champagne could "try to find them but they were in a safe place!"[72] Given Campbell's admission that she had stolen the goods and hid them from Champagne, her motivation for this illicit act suggests that Campbell had done so for malicious purposes possibly as an act of revenge or of jealousy given that the stolen objects related to grooming.

Closely related to clothing was its production. In an era when female apparel was made by hand, fabric was certainly in high demand and represented 15 per cent of the known goods stolen. Women shoplifted (as well as pilfered from neighbours) pieces of textiles and sewing materials such as dress patterns, buttons, and ribbon. Shopkeepers accused women of stealing these items whilst

Table 11.4 | Types of goods stolen (where known)

Objects of Theft	Number	Percentage
Wearing Apparel	139	31
Fabric and Sewing Materials	69	15
Miscellaneous Goods	45	10
Food	44	9
Household Goods and Furniture	44	9
Money	30	7
Linens and Bedding	22	5
Footwear	16	4
Wood	13	3
Watches	13	3
Jewellery	11	2
Tools	7	2
Total	453	100

in their places of business on another pretext. Robert Campbell, for example, denounced Marie Lebeau and Betsey Jackson to the justice of the peace for taking eleven yards of calico fabric from his store. According to his rendering of events, while Jackson distracted his store clerk who was showing her various articles, Marie Lebeau hid the fabric under her gown. As Jackson and Lebeau were about to leave the store, Campbell grabbed Lebeau and in the ensuing struggle, the calico material fell to the floor.[73]

Women also took household commodities (which represented 9 per cent of the known items stolen) comprising furniture, dishes, teapots, and cutlery – silver spoons were especially popular – as well as pots and pans. If one includes bedding and linens, then nearly a fifth (14 per cent) of the stolen goods composed an array of household objects. They stole bedding and linens stored in trunks inside houses or hung out to dry on back yard lines. Some of these thefts were seemingly opportunistic crimes. Such was the case for Mary Warren and Charlotte Hamelin, who took children's clothing, baby linens, and household linens belonging to François Mathurin off the clothesline. Mathurin told the clerk writing up his deposition that "*le lendemain une partie des articles, savoir, une petite robe de coton, une tablier de coton et deux petits draps ont été trouvés en la possession de Mary Warren et de Charlotte Hamelin.*" He also claimed that Warren and Hamelin were "debauched" women who were in the habit of loitering on the bank behind his yard at night perhaps either to solicit or to socialize.[74]

Most of the stolen objects were close at hand, familiar, of known value, and effortless to sell. There also appears to be very little seasonal variation in patterns of theft or in the types of items targeted.[75] How easy they were obtained is impossible to gauge given the level of surveillance in neighbourhoods, even if doors were left unlocked, which certainly provided some degree of security. While the evidence demonstrates that brothel-keepers locked the doors to their establishments at night and that elites secured their homes and businesses with locks, it is unclear if the popular classes safeguarded their places with locks as well. Women also targeted an assortment of goods not usually associated with their role in the household economy: iron weights, glass, hair, harness and bridle, carriage cushions, lining, and curtains, and tools including a carpenter's plough as in the case of widow Maria Chambers who stole the item from Antoine Lindsay.[76] That some women pilfered goods not commonly related to their varied roles add another layer to the complexities of women and larceny. They were likely stolen for the benefit of male partners or in order to sell for quick cash.

Food theft exemplified, more than anything else, a struggle to subsist and represented nearly a tenth (9 per cent) of the goods stolen by Montreal women. Items such as poultry, fish, butter, oats, flour, sugar, maple sugar, and bread were part of the basic household diet amongst the popular classes. Fyson's examination of eating patterns in early nineteenth-century Montreal shows that bread comprised the most important food staple.[77] Keeping in mind that the city was undergoing tremendous turmoil and transformation in its social, economic, political, and demographic fabric accompanied by social dislocation in the countryside, the decline of the fur trade, epidemics, and growing immigration, daily life was precarious for many. People faced seasonal unemployment or underemployment, inadequate wages, and the constant struggle to provide food and shelter at ever-rising costs. Food theft would have been a strategy to ameliorate growing misery.

THE REASONS WOMEN STOLE

There was no single compelling reason why women committed larceny. While need was an important factor in theft, the motives were often far more multifaceted. Some women who faced economic crisis in the light of a husband's unemployment, illness, desertion, or death initiated illicit subsistence strategies that included selling liquor without a licence, sex work, and larceny. The women appearing before London courts who MacKay so carefully studied, offered commonplace explanations when charged with theft, including claims that they had purchased, found, or borrowed the objects.[78] The accused had to be prudent, however, in constructing plausible accounts given that guilty verdicts resulted in harsh punishment. The same was true for Montreal women who put forward a miscellany of similar accounts including, among others, that the items in question had been given, loaned, bought, borrowed, or found. Charlotte Prudhomme's convoluted explanation as to why she was wearing a coat belonging to John Mactier's wife when Mactier confronted her at the market is but one of many examples. Prudhomme claimed that while she was at Longue Pointe with her brother, they met a woman named Marguerite (no last name given) who offered the coat for sale for which her brother paid a dollar and a half. She further elaborated in her voluntary examination that she had accompanied George Barron, likely John Mactier's servant, to Mactier's house where she had spent the night with him in the garret where the coat in question had been stored. Again she denied having stolen it. Baron then claimed that Prudhomme must have stolen the coat while he was asleep. Both were charged with petty larceny.[79]

Women larcenists furnished other explanations as well. Marguerite Martin blamed shoplifting a shawl on being eight months pregnant;[80] and, Mary Diller attributed her theft of a cotton sheet from George Wyatt's yard to a state of intoxication.[81] Mary Fundy made a similar excuse when she sold a man's black hat belonging to John Powell to Hugh Grant, which she had lifted from his house where she lived. Grant's description of his encounter with Fundy in the marketplace also showcases her poverty. Carrying the hat in one hand and a butter basket in the other, Fundy presented the hat to Grant for half a dollar. Grant offered her two shillings and three pence and a dram. When he asked her where she got the hat, Fundy claimed that she "came by it honestly"; he paid for the hat and because Fundy was so poor, gave her two extra coppers. Three days later, Mary Fundy arrived at the residence where Grant was a servant accompanied by John Powell to ask for the hat back. She admitted to having stolen it while drunk; Powell reimbursed Grant the amount he had paid Fundy; and Fundy and Powell left with the hat.[82] Although Powell had promised Fundy that no harm would come to her if she returned the hat, she was charged with petty larceny following his private prosecution of her. When a search warrant turned up James Scullin's bed spread and clothing in Emilie Gauthier's wooden box, she denied any responsibility for being in possession of stolen goods, maintaining that she had purchased them "*d'un garçon qu'elle ne connait pas de nom et qu'elle lui a payé un écu pour le tout.*"[83] Widow Elizabeth Benoit *dite* St-Charles offered another reason for having watchmaker George Northgraves' double-cased silver watch in her possession, claiming that he had given it to her for sex: "*J'ai couché avec lui, il m'a sollicité pendant longtemps et en conséquence de mon consentement il m'a donné la montre.*"[84] Similarly, when sex workers were accused of property crime, some declared that they had received the alleged stolen goods from clients who had paid them for sex. Olive Marcotte maintained that Isaac Davies had offered her a muff and boa "*pour l'usage de ma personne après l'invitation du dit Davis.*" She accused him of maliciously prosecuting her after having refused Davis "*ma personne et mon lit.*"[85]

Homeless women turned to property crime as one of a patchwork of subsistence strategies they employed to counter hunger, malnutrition, hypothermia, illness, and the dangers associated with living rough on the streets. They purloined items such as food, firewood, blankets, and alcohol to help them get through a day, a week, or a month. Adélaide St-André and Betsy Lafranchise's encounter with John Tassie's alluring and abandoned bread cart demonstrates that some of these thefts were seemingly random and opportunistic acts as part of their "improvisational, hand-to-mouth subsistence."[86] Women's propensity to commit petty larceny underscores, what Lawson has pointed out: that "petty theft can be seen as a natural expression of their subsistence identity."[87] This was certainly the case for Bridget Howe who lived "rough" and accumulated several larceny charges over the period under study. She had a history of lifting small objects such as silver spoons and attempting to deflect blame onto young boys as the culprits. Thomas King, principal waiter at the mess of the 71st Regiment and responsible for its silver and plate, accused Howe of stealing a silver spoon from the dining hall. Howe claimed that a boy had given it to her; this small but valuable object could be easily turned into cash or used to purchase food and drink.[88] Four months later, Howe was once again in trouble with the law having been charged with stealing two silver spoons, which she claimed she had purchased from "a little boy in the new market."[89]

The link between poverty and larceny (however much disparaged) was not lost on one of the judges of the Court of King's Bench, who in a charge to the grand jury stated: "Several of the offences charged in the Calendar of the Gaol, consist of Larcenies, committed in and about the city – but this may be in some measure accounted for, from the crowd of idle and indigent persons we see constantly hovering about in our streets, nor ought we to be surprised, that recourse should be had by some of these, to acts of depredation to supply their wants."[90] Larceny served as the means by which some homeless women sought imprisonment for shelter, food, and medical and (in very sad situations) palliative care during inclement weather. Two female prisoners admitted to members of a grand jury during its quarterly inspection of the city's correctional facilities that despite the wretched conditions they encountered while incarcerated, they had perpetrated property offences as a survival strategy to escape the severity of winter in prison, thereby thwarting the purposes of incarceration, which elites had hoped it would serve.[91]

But necessity alone does not explain all acts of larceny. There are numerous examples of servants who stole items from their employers even though they received food and lodging as part of their meagre wages. In the course of working as domestics, they confronted temptations and tensions that underscored their relationships with employers. Mary Riley, for instance, was a domestic in the household of Hugh and Margaret McKay when she was accused of stealing her mistress' merino gown. Apparently, Riley informed neighbour Eliza Dobbin that while she would not wear the dress, McKay had to make an effort to find it.[92] It appears that Riley was angry with her mistress and stole the gown out of revenge. Another servant, Melanie Delisle, allegedly stole baby bonnets from David

Handlow's household at the instigation, she asserted, of Marie Imbault *dite* Matha. Over the course of a month and a half, Delisle passed her the bonnets for which she received 10 sols.[93] Others, likely lured by temptation, pilfered articles before leaving service or after being terminated. Grocer Michael Wymes accused Hannah Murray a servant of John Johnston, of stealing a watch belonging to Patrick Connolly before she left service. He asked for a warrant to search the Dublin Tavern where he believed it was concealed.[94] Accusations of larceny against a servant might also border on the malicious. Take for example, shoemaker Duncan Fisher who claimed that his servant Nancy Harris had in her possession two pieces of China ribbon, which he believed were stolen. He then accused her of pilfering a number of other items – shawls, linens, and money – which had mysteriously disappeared from his shop. In her defence, Harris argued she had purchased the ribbon from Mrs McClements and had never taken anything from her employer. She was charged with theft of the ribbon.[95]

My study of sex work shows that women inhabited an illicit culture where they stole items such as money, clothing, jewellery, and watches all of which were linked to their relationships with and proximity to clients, co-workers, and brothel-keepers. They are well represented in larceny prosecutions. The women took small, valuable, but easily concealed objects from clients who were distracted, intoxicated, or asleep. When Magdeleine McDonald came across Joseph Dodds lying on a wharf inebriated and asleep, she used the cover of darkness to slip her hands into his pockets and remove bank notes and a silver watch.[96] Equally, thefts in brothels were commonplace. James Johnson accused Ellen Morris and Susan Waters of stealing his pocketbook containing £15 in banknotes and coins while he was visiting Morris' house of prostitution. He found the pocketbook and its contents buried in the basement.[97] The theft of clothing and jewellery were typical objects. Take for example Julie Mathurin and Scholastique Lavictoire who resided in Joseph Perrault's house of prostitution. Mathurin denounced Lavictoire for illicitly removing a black veil from a suitcase to a justice of the peace and demanded a warrant to search the house of Lavictoire's mother where it was apparently hidden.[98] Brothel-keepers also accused sex workers of stealing clothing from them. Rosalie Laprise complained to a justice of the peace that Marie Diller stole her *robe d'Indienne*[99] and that Caroline Locas took a shift, gown, and ribbon from her house and hid the articles in Angèle Belanger's house.[100] The economic and social relationships between brothel-keepers and sex workers were often characterized by tensions and discord. Diller and Locas may have felt entitled to these items given that brothel-keepers kept a sizeable portion of the proceeds derived from prostitution. Conflict bordering on intimidation also boiled over outside of the establishments, as was the case involving the well-known sex worker Maria Jordan. As she passed in front of Ellen Turner's brothel on St Mary Street, the madam, Mary Ann Cunningham, William McKay, and Alexandre Bonnier snatched her shawl, bonnet, boa, gold ring, and purse.[101] This theft illustrates well the violence perpetrated by fellow practitioners of the trade upon each other. By stealing these items, Turner, Cunningham, McKay, and Bonnier took the trappings of her economic success and the clothing she used to attract clients.

While necessity played an important role in many acts of female larceny, court depositions present a more complex and nuanced picture of the motivations behind property crime. Women took goods from neighbours as part of an informal borrowing network, domestic servants pinched items from their masters and mistresses, and sex workers and vagrants inhabited and participated in what Garthine Walker has referred to as a female culture of dishonest activity pilfering items left, right, and centre.[102] To dispose of stolen goods, they moved between the criminal underworld and everyday life, making the criminal part of the everyday.

DISPOSING OF STOLEN GOODS

Studies show that women knew the value of the items they stole, which in turn influenced the choices they made.[103] In other words, they took objects about which they were knowledgeable and of which they could dispose handily. Since women typically had access to many of these goods, being seen in public with them would not have drawn much attention. Notwithstanding food (taken by the hungry to be consumed) or even some clothing appropriated illegally to replace tattered apparel, stolen goods had to be converted into cash.[104] That women were not stealing clothing to wear but to sell, helps to explain why clothing thefts did not increase during the winter. In Montreal, female larcenists sold them in the streets and door-to-door, or brought them to fences and pawnshops for much-needed cash. The charge of receiving stolen goods was a serious one and thus risky, however. When Mary Ann Fitzgerald admitted to stealing clothing from Arthur Samuels, she claimed that Mary Gordon consented to keeping the items at her house. Gordon's son, Francis Lalahan, who was also charged with the theft, told authorities that when the stolen goods were brought to his mother's house, he immediately threw them out of the window. He was resolute in protecting his mother, insisting that she had neither participated in the theft nor should be charged with receiving stolen goods.[105]

Many in popular-class neighbourhoods frequented pawnshops as a short-term subsistence strategy, the pawnshop serving as a sort of "poor man's bank."[106] When necessary, people pawned their own items to make ends meet. As we saw above, grand jury members were uneasy about the proliferation of pawnshops and condemned them as "convenient receptacle[s] to thieves for the disposal of their plunder" and recommended that they be placed under police control or abolished.[107] City constables were certainly familiar with these businesses.[108] Others resorted to fences working out of taverns and homes. Take for example the case of Margaret Perigord and Eliza Robinson who robbed Catherine Ryan and Sarah Singleton while they were on the stroll in front of the Bonsecours Church. Robinson sold Ryan's large red shawl for thirty sol to Monsieur L'Esperance, a tavern-keeper, who lived at the foot of the current; three of the black feathers making up a plume also worn by Catherine Ryan "were sold by an Irish woman to some Irish people in the Recollet Suburbs."[109] In this way, Montreal women moved between a criminal underworld – made up of a network of pawnshops, lodging houses, brothels, taverns, and other public buildings – and everyday street life.

Women also acted as fences. When police served a search warrant on Mary Ann Hetherington as a receiver of stolen goods, they unearthed a cache of household goods composed of a variety of linens, towels, books, wearing apparel, and purses.[110] The Marcottes were a particularly notorious family seemingly connected to this criminal underworld and reputed to be fences. Matriarch and brothel-keeper Elisabeth Deganne, her daughters, and cousins the Moses brothers, garnered numerous arrests but few convictions for operating a disorderly house and being receivers of stolen goods. Elisabeth Deganne's daughter Elisabeth Marcotte and cousin Joseph Moses (who was eventually transported to Bermuda with his brother Augustin for stealing in 1828) were both charged and found guilty of theft and receiving stolen property.[111] On another occasion, James Benny accused Elisabeth Deganne of stealing two boxes of window glass from his courtyard. Upon discovering that the items were missing, Benny visited local stores specializing in the product to determine if any of the merchants had recently been offered glass for sale. Oilman Rosco Corse informed him that a "woman of bad fame" had tried to sell him glass but he had refused to buy it. Benny and Corse went together to the store of W.S. Phillips and discovered Elisabeth Deganne and Louise Briand in the act of delivering glass to the storekeeper. In her defence, Deganne claimed that her late husband had purchased the glass at an auction sale held at Cuvillier's.[112]

Other women preferred to sell stolen items themselves, hawking them in the streets or going door to door. Since female participation in the second-hand trade as hucksters and basket women was well known, the street provided an important venue in which to dispose of stolen goods. At the same time, peddling purloined objects this way exposed would-be thieves to police scrutiny. By way of example, Constable George Wells became suspicious of Julie Deschamps when she tried to sell a large brown cotton sheet to a group of carters. Because she was unable to provide a believable account as to how she acquired the sheet, he arrested her.[113] By contrast, Biddy Handley and Jane Hicks were more discrete when they went door to door to sell clothing they had stolen from Martin Duval. Handley offered a cloth jacket for sale;[114] Jane Hicks tendered a dress. She told Josephte McFarlane that she needed money to buy food for herself and her children. McFarlane acted as a pawnbroker and agreed to loan her fifteen sols for the dress but when Hicks did not return to reclaim the dress, McFarlane accused her of selling her stolen property.[115]

PROSECUTING LARCENY

Historians have argued that resorting to the criminal justice system was part of an armamentarium of strategies used by communities to resolve conflicts when extra-legal means proved ineffective.[116] King's study of property crime in Essex shows that underreported larceny cases were common; the vast majority of those accused of theft escaped prosecution by paying off would-be plaintiffs.[117] We know little about extra-legal or rough justice in Montreal. Court records do show that ordinary city residents, women and men alike, policed their neighbourhoods and dispensed personal and community injunctions against wayward members through gossip, the charivari, riots, public ridicule, and threats and blows.[118] There are also individual cases, which provide the occasional glimpse into aspects of rough justice. The beating Maria Jordan received at the hands of John Hart and James Burrell for having allegedly perpetrated a theft against one of them is a case in point.[119] In all likelihood, some, perhaps many, of the larceny cases connected to borrowing networks were settled between the parties without having to resort to the courts.

The victims' legal pursuit of would-be larcenists suggests a popular knowledge of the criminal justice system, its purposes and practices, as well as a willingness to engage in a process on their own terms, which could result in financial outlay. It also underscores an important interaction between the purveyors of justice and the public who sought legal redress.[120] Clare Lyons has argued that such initiatives also reflected public opinion since it was the responsibility of individuals to privately prosecute wrongdoers.[121] All larceny victims – including twenty-year-old John Tassie in his quest for justice against the bread-stealing Adélaide St-André and Betsey Lafranchise – would have had much to consider before initiating a private prosecution. Peter King has identified at least three features of the judicial process that deterred many potential prosecutors from laying formal complaints before a justice of the peace. First, legal redress was expensive for most; following the cost of the initial deposition, plaintiffs had to disburse additional monies at every step as their complaints wound through the judicial system. Second, it was time-consuming because over the course of each court session, prosecutors did not receive a specific time when their cases would be heard. Thus, they had to wait, sometimes days at a time, at the courthouse before being called to appear. Some defendants deliberately did not show up in order to defer verdicts being rendered against them. Consequently, magistrates usually postponed the court cases until the sitting of the next session and plaintiffs were obliged to return to the courthouse under the same circumstances and possibly have their prosecution of complaints delayed yet again. Third, the process was complex since plaintiffs were responsible for gathering the evidence and organizing the arrests of offenders albeit with the assistance of a justice of the peace, they risked reprisals from the accused, and the outcome was uncertain. All of the necessary documents had to be filled out correctly and the evidence sufficient or compelling. Be that as it may, plaintiffs still had a great deal of discretionary power which allowed them to not only influence the outcome but abandon the court procedure at any point without penalty before a verdict was handed down.[122] The exercise of discretionary powers also resulted in down charging since property crimes involving housebreaking, shoplifting, and grand larceny were capital offences.

Nonetheless, John Tassie was not deterred. Perhaps pushed by his employer Walter Benny who may have been willing to cover the costs, Tassie pursued the alleged bread thieves at court. Arrest warrants were issued which the police served. Adélaide St-André and Betsey Lafranchise appeared before the justice of the peace to answer to the charge. Convinced that there was enough evidence to continue, the grand jury wrote up the indictment. Since all parties appeared at the Court of Quarter Sessions, the case was processed quickly. Defendants were entitled to counsel – benches were reserved for lawyers in Quarter Sessions – and there is evidence that some made use of this privilege.[123] The accused initiated other strategies as well as offering up an assortment of reasons in her defence from casting doubt onto the accuracy of the prosecution and the reputation of the complainant, declaring innocence, providing extenuating circumstances to excuse the act (pregnancy and drunkenness), claiming to be a casualty of circumstances, testifying that the item had been purchased from a stranger (Bridget Howe's claim of buying silver spoons from a boy at the market is a case in point), and flat out failing to appear on their court-appointed day and thereby delaying the court case.

The grand jurors deemed the charge against St-André and Lafranchise a true bill (in other words, agreeing the evidence supported the bill of indictment). The two defendants entered not guilty pleas. The petit jury acquitted the women – likely without having left the jury box – even though John Tassie, Walter Benny, and High Constable Benjamin Delisle had served as Crown witnesses. Why the jurors handed down such a verdict in John Tassie's pursuit of St-André and Lafranchise is unknown since it is rare to find notes explaining the verdict. However, Table V reveals that the petit jury rendered a decision in 41 per cent of the larceny cases involving 273 accused of which a little more than a quarter (27 per cent) were guilty verdicts. Hence, three-quarters of the time, the petty acts were going unpunished, perhaps because they were perceived by

Table 11.5 | Outcome of larceny cases for individuals, 1768–1841 (where recorded)

Outcome	Number	Percentage
Deposition only	104	16
No Bill/Ignoramus	198	30
Discharge	5	1
True Bill	77	12
Not Guilty	96	14
Guilty	177	27
Total	655	100

jurors as not serious enough to warrant punishment or the plaintiff was perceived as being vindictive or overly punitive in pursuing the prosecution. In such cases of jury nullification, even though members of the jury may have recognized that the defendant had violated the law, they returned a not guilty verdict nevertheless. Indeed, by refusing to apply the law or by rejecting the evidence, jurors were exercising agency in their own right.

Plaintiffs, both women and men, had other goals in mind when they initiated private prosecutions, which underscore their exercise of discretionary power. The criminal justice system served as an important venue to discipline neighbours as borne out by the third of the accused (16 per cent) whose complaints against them were abandoned after the deposition. Plaintiffs instituted another strategy of not appearing at court even after the grand jury deemed the indictment a true bill. While plaintiffs were willing to pay the initial fee accorded to swearing out a complaint, most were not prepared to take their participation in the justice system as far as Tassie did. An 1841 editorial in the *Montreal Transcript* blamed the poor conviction rate on the ignorance of the juries and on witnesses who simply lied when testifying.[124] Low conviction rates suggest that some sort of settlement may have been reached before the parties appeared at court. As Fyson has pointed out, the arrest of an accused proved to be enough of an intervention for many plaintiffs and perhaps enough of a punishment for a relatively minor crime to deter them from stealing again. Moreover, they had nothing to gain from the state's punishment of the accused for which they bore much of the expense.[125]

PUNISHMENT FOR THEFT

Most convicted female larcenists, when sentences were recorded, received jail terms. Table 11.6 shows that between 1768 and 1789, seven women, who were found guilty of larceny, had to submit to corporal and "shaming" punishments, consisting of lashes or whippings, carting, and the pillory or stocks.[126] Clearly, such forms of punishment were rare. Nonetheless, they served to publically identify female thieves, to allow local residents to participate in retribution, and to convey a forceful message to everyone about the consequences of breaking the law. Two of the five women were subjected to especially harsh public punishment. Justices of the peace condemned Ann Lancford, who was found guilty of petty larceny, to a public lashing: the "prisoner shall go to the place from whence she came and there remain till Fryday (sic) next the 28th instant when she is to be tyed (sic) to a cart's tail and conducted naked to the weist (sic) to Quebec Gate where she is to receive five lashes at the Old Chapelle, five lashes at the Chateau, five lashes at Landrivières corner, ten lashes at the market place, and five lashes at the corner of the courthouse, and then she is to be discharged on paying her fees."[127] In the second case, Thérèse Carplette who had asked for clemency "being big with child," was all the same sentenced to spend one week in prison, then one hour in the stocks between 10 and 11 o'clock "with a paper on her breast expressing her crime."[128] The act of watching someone in the pillory was understood to express a censure of socially untoward acts. Subsequently, spectators were given an effective moral lesson about the importance of criminal justice and the consequences of criminality. It was easy to draw a crowd to participate in these shaming punishments.[129] Being subjected to the pillory likely resulted in diminished future employment possibilities. The only other time that a female larcenist faced public humiliation was in 1815. Cécile Mercier, her head uncovered, was paraded through St-Paul and Notre Dame streets wearing a sign with the words "*voleuse* / thief" written on it.[130]

Public shaming rituals fell out of favour as magistrates abandoned this form of punishment for prison sentences. This change followed similar trends elsewhere; in parts of Europe and the United States the public spectacle of punishment was gradually coming to an end by the turn of the nineteenth century. Michel Foucault has argued that in time punitive practices changed from being a public event to the most secretive part of the penal process: "reform of the mind over corporeal punishment of the flesh." Punishment shifted to the suspension of civil rights by a "system of constraints and privations, obligations and prohibitions," which replaced punishment based on physical pain.[131] Prison terms (sometimes at hard labour) were common in 95 per cent of sentencing overall. Table 11.6 shows that outside of the single case involving Cécile Mercier, by 1810, all convicted women larcenists were sentenced to imprisonment. Incarceration was meant to punish the perpetrators, to inculcate thieving women with a respect for the law and hard work, and to promote self-discipline and decency. Even when punishment was administered privately, local newspapers sporadically published the names of those accused, acquitted, or found guilty of property offences, such as Catherine O'Neil and Caroline Greenwood whose names appeared in the *Montreal Transcript* for theft.

The thirty-six women sentenced to the House of Correction encountered a rigid system designed to punish through shame, deprivation, strict enforcement of rules, and hard labour. Opening for the first time in 1807 in the basement of the prison, inmates wore a uniform of coarse material distinguished as prison wear which was meant to both humiliate them as well as serving to more easily identify those who succeeded in escaping. Each prisoner was expected to work every day (work that was divided into three categories: light, moderate, and severe) except Sundays and religious holidays.[132] By contrast, women sentenced to the common gaol wore their own clothing and did not have to work.

Table 11.6 demonstrates that nearly three-quarters of the women (where information was given) who were judged guilty of petty larceny were given lengthy prison sentences in the common gaol; fewer women were placed in the house of correction, which was generally reserved for vagrant women and sex workers. Moreover, the house of correction did not operate continuously over the period under study: it functioned between 1802–1810; 1811–1816; 1817–1827; 1829 to 1835; and, from 1839 onward.[133] Several were sentenced to only

Table 11.6 | Types of punishment, 1768–1841 (where recorded)

Period	Sentence	Number	Length of Imprisonment
1. (1768–1789)	Imprisonment	8	Common Gaol = 8 (2 imprisoned for less than 1 month; 2 for 1 month; 3 for 6 months; and 1 unknown)
	Pillory/Stocks	4	
	Whipping	1	
	Fine or Fees	2	
2. (1790–1824)	Imprisonment	56	Common Gaol = 41 (13 imprisoned for less than 1month; 12 for 1 month; 4 for 2 months; 10 for 3 months; and 2 for 6 months) House of Correction = 15 (2 imprisoned for less than 1 month; 2 for 1 month; 3 for 3 months; 7 for 6 months; and 1 for 7 months)
	Public Humiliation	87	Common Gaol = 67 (34 imprisoned for less than 1 month; 12 for 1 month; 8 for 2 months; 9 for 3 months; 1 for 4 months; 2 for 6 months; 1 for 12 months) House of Correction = 21 (5 imprisoned for less than 1 month; 7 for 1 month; 4 for 2 months; 4 for 3 months; and 1 for 4 months)
3. (1825–1841)	Imprisonment	100	
Total		159	

Of the five cases, which were discharged, one concerned Mary Ann Ball who was so young that the court and jury decided to discharge the accused to the care of her mother. (DR v. Mary Anne Ball (QS October 1837), *in* BaNQ-VM, QS(F).

twenty-four hours of imprisonment, as was the case for Mary Howe. The necessity of classifying prisoners – separating the hardened from the novice – was brought home when twelve-year-old Mary Howe and her mother were arrested for larceny and held until trial in the Common Gaol. At court, Mary entered a plea of guilty. The justices of the peace sentenced her to twenty-four hours of incarceration, "deeming it better for the girl to be abroad, then within the walls of the prison" where she was exposed to "the very dredges of the female population of the city." The *Montreal Gazette* wrote up Mary's story as a poignant reminder of the need for prison reform by way of a house of refuge and a penitentiary.[134] By the third period, magistrates sentences women to shorter periods of incarceration.

CONCLUSION

When John Tassie denounced Adélaide St-André and Betsy Lafranchise as bread thieves to a magistrate in late November 1835, the three of them began a journey that started at the police office and ended in the courtroom of the Quarter Sessions of the Peace. The two would-be larcenists were part of a cohort of 555 cases of property crimes perpetrated by 606 women and fifty-nine men between 1768 and 1841. This study shows that women played diverse and complex roles with respect to larceny usually acting alone but sometimes with other women and less so with male accomplices. They were often accused of pinching and pilfering goods such as wearing apparel, footwear, household objects, fabrics, and food associated with household economies and borrowing networks. Others stole an assortment of items such as tools, planks of wood, window glass, and hair, not typically connected to women, work, and household. By studying the records of the Court of Quarter Sessions of the Peace, the petty or low crimes that made up everyday justice provide a window onto acts of stealing of which so many women were accused. For many of them, theft served as a subsistence strategy to cope with homelessness and fragile household economies. But necessity does not explain all acts of larceny. Servants, for example, were tempted by the belongings of their mistresses and masters out of envy or revenge, sex workers inhabited an illicit culture where theft associated with clients, co-workers, and brothel-keepers were commonplace, wives stole with husbands because of intimidation or love, and individual women pilfered goods out of vanity.

While John Tassie doggedly pursued his accusation against Adélaide St-André and Betsy Lafranchise to a verdict and lost, the majority of plaintiffs, with their own established objectives, which often times conflicted with those of legal authorities, exercised their discretionary powers by abandoning or opting out at different stages of the court process. Plaintiffs sought to discipline alleged thieves, perhaps even to pressure them to reach a settlement before going to court. Notwithstanding the laws governing larceny, which allowed for harsh sentences in the form of corporal and shaming punishments, transportation across the seas, and lengthy prison terms, magistrates chose incarceration over public retribution. Across the period, most female larcenists received prison sentences of shorter duration. This study begins to uncover the impact that larceny laws and their application had on the women in Montreal who were charged with this felony and the diverse reasons they committed this felony. Although understanding the intricacies of the laws governing petit larceny is important, so too are the experiences of the women to whom the laws were applied. While my research findings resonate with publications on female larceny elsewhere in England, Australia, and the United States, it is clear that we need more criminal justice studies which situate gender at their heart in order to appreciate the complexities of illicit acts, the authority women claimed derived from their knowledge of the legal system, the goals of plaintiffs who privately prosecuted wrongdoers, and to avoid broad and doubtful conclusions about gender-based criminal activity.

NOTES

This project on women who committed petty larceny was made possible by a postdoctoral fellowship (Montreal History Group) 2005–2006 and a FRQSC grant (2008–2012), "La Modernité à Montréal, 1790–1970: Autorités et vulnérabilités," McGill University, Denyse Baillargeon (principal investigator), Montreal History Group (co-applicants). I would also like to thank research assistant Valerie Minnett for her valuable work and Daniel Palacios for helping me analyze the data.

1 DR v. Adélaide St-André and Betsy Lafranchise (QS 27 November 1835), in Bibliothèque et Archives Nationales du Québec à Ville de Montréal [hereafter BAnQ-VM], QS(F) (deposition of John Tassie).

2 There are many studies on women, criminality, and property crime. See for example, John Beattie, "The Criminality of Women in

Eighteenth-Century England," *Journal of Social History* 8, no.4 (Summer 1975): 80–116; Jane B. Price, "'Raised in Rockhead, Died in the Poor House': Female Petty Criminals in Halifax, 1864–1890," in *Essays in the History of Canadian Law, Voliume III: Nova Scotia*, edited by Philip Girard and Jim Phillips (Toronto: University of Toronto Press, 1990), 200–31; Garthine Walker, "Women, Theft and the World of Stolen Goods," in *Women, Crime and the Courts in Early Modern England*, edited by Jenny Kermode and Garthine Walker (London: Routledge, 1994), 81–105; John Beattie, "Women, Crime and Inequality in Eighteenth-Century London," in *Crime and Inequality*, edited by J. Hagan and R.D. Peterson (Stanford: Stanford University Press, 1995), 116–39; Peter Lawson, "Patriarchy, Crime, and the Courts: The Criminality of Women in Late Tudor and Early Stuart England," in *Criminal Justice in the Old World and the New: Essays in Honour of J.M. Beattie*, edited by Greg T. Smith, Allyson N. May and Simon Devereaux (Toronto: University of Toronto Press, 1998), 16–57; Lynn MacKay, "Why They Stole: Women in the Old Bailey, 1779–1789," *Journal of Social History* 32, no. 3 (March 1999): 623–39; Jim Phillips and Allyson N. May, "Female Criminality in 18th-Century Halifax," *Acadiensis* 31, no.2 (Spring 2002): 71–96.

3 Lawson, "Patriarchy, Crime, and the Courts," 17–18, 25.

4 See Walker, "Women, Theft and the World of Stolen Goods," 83.

5 Ibid., 82–5.

6 Susan Branson, "Beyond Respectability: The Female World of Love and Crime in Late Eighteenth and Early Nineteenth-Century Philadelphia," *Studies in Eighteenth-Century Culture* 25, no.1 (1996): 246. See also Judith Fingard, "Jailbirds in Mid-Victorian Halifax," *Dalhousie Law Journal* 8, no.3 (1984): 81–102.

7 Peter King, *Crime, Justice, and Discretion in England 1740–1820* (Oxford: Oxford University Press, 2000), 196–207.

8 Donald Fyson, *Magistrates, Police, and People: Everyday Criminal Justice in Quebec and Lower Canada, 1764–1837* (Toronto: University of Toronto Press, 2006). Joanne Turner, in a study of female petty offenders, has made a similar argument: "Summary Justice for Women: Stafford Borough, 1880–1905," *Crime, Histories & Societies* 16, no.2 (2012): 55–77.

9 Mary Anne Poutanen, "Bonds of Friendship, Kinship, and Community: Gender, Homelessness, and Mutual Aid in Early-Nineteenth-Century Montreal," in *Negotiating Identities in 19th and 20th Century Montreal*, edited by Bettina Bradbury and Tamara Myers (Vancouver: University of British Columbia Press, 2005), 36. Elsewhere, see Maria Luddy, "An

Outcast Community: The 'Wrens of the Curragh,'" *Women's History Review* 1, no.3 (1992): 341–55.

10 Paula J. Byrne, *Criminal Law and Colonial Subject: New South Wales 1810–1830* (Cambridge: Cambridge University Press, 1993), 74.

11 MacKay, "Why They Stole," 629.

12 See for example, Olwen Hufton, *The Poor of Eighteenth-Century France, 1750–1789* (Oxford: Clarendon Press, 1974); Christine Stansell, *City of Women: Sex and Class in New York, 1789–1860* (New York: Knopf, 1986); Ruth L. Smith and Deborah M. Valenze, "Mutuality and Marginality: Liberal Moral Theory and Working-Class Women in Nineteenth-Century England," *Signs* 13, no. 2 (Winter 1988): 277–98; Ellen Ross, *Love and Toil: Motherhood in Outcast London, 1870–1918* (New York: Oxford University Press, 1993); Bettina Bradbury, *Working Families: Age, Gender, and Daily Survival in Industrializing Montreal* (Toronto: McClelland & Stewart Inc., 1993); Anna Clark, *The Struggle for the Breeches: Gender and the Making of the British Working Class* (Berkeley: University of California Press, 1995).

13 Lynn MacKay explores the relationship between fragile household economies and larceny in her article, "Why They Stole," 627. Other important studies include: Stansell, *City of Women*; Smith and Valenze, "Mutuality and Marginality"; Ross, *Love and Toil*; and Clark, *The Struggle for the Breeches*. See also Rosemary A. Peters, who shows that in France, the concept of property rights evolved over the eighteen and nineteenth centuries wrought by political changes and by industrialization ("Codes for Honest People," in her book, *Stealing Things: Theft and the Author in Nineteenth-Century France* (Lanham, MD: Lexington Books, 2013)).

14 MacKay, "Why They Stole," 627–8.

15 See for example, Mary Anne Poutanen, "Due Attention Has Been Paid to All Rules: Women, Tavern Licences, and Social Regulation in Montreal, 1840–1860," *Histoire Sociale/Social History* 50, no. 101 (May 2017): 43–68; Mary Anne Poutanen, *Beyond Brutal Passions: Prostitution in Early Nineteenth-Century Montreal* (Montreal: McGill-Queen's University Press, 2015); Mary Anne Poutanen, "Bonds of Friendship, Kinship, and Community" in *Negotiating Identities in 19th and 20th Century Montreal*, edited by Bettina Bradbury and Tamara Myers (Vancouver: University of British Colombia Press), 2–14; Mary Anne Poutanen, "Regulating Public Space in Early Nineteenth-Century Montreal: Vagrancy Laws and Gender in a Colonial Context," *Histoire Sociale/Social History* 35, no. 69 (May 2002): 35–58; Mary Anne Poutanen, "The Homeless, The Whore, The Drunkard, and the Disorderly: Contours of Female Vagrancy in the Montreal Courts,

1810–1842," in *Gendered Pasts: Historical Essays in Femininity and Masculinity in Canada*, edited by Kathryn McPherson, Cecilia Morgan, and Nancy Forestell (Don Mills, Ont.: Oxford University Press, 2003), 29–47.

16 Richard Burn defined grand larceny as "a felonious and fraudulent taking, carrying away, by any person, of the mere personal goods of another, above the value of 12 d.1." Petty larceny constituted a theft less than that, *The Justice of the Peace and Parish Officer* Vol. 2 (London, 1764), 59.

17 Fyson, *Magistrates, Police, and People*, 22.

18 *29 George III c.3 s.7*, 1789.

19 *4 George IV c.4-5-6*, 1824.

20 Fyson, *Magistrates, Police, and People*, 34.

21 The 1841 *Act of the Legislative Assembly* for the Province of Canada changed the laws governing larceny in significant ways for both Upper and Lower Canada. First, the division between petty and grand larceny was abolished, "the value of the property stolen, shall be deemed to be of the same nature." Second, all larceny was considered as grand larceny had been before the act's implementation. Third, larceny as well as larceny-related charges such as robbery, stealing from the person, and break and enter was now punishable by incarceration and hard labour in the penitentiary for not more than seven years (in simple larceny) and fourteen years to life (for robbery and burglary) or elsewhere for not more than two years. Robbery involving injury was punishable by death. Receivers of stolen goods, knowing that they were illegally taken, could be convicted as an accessory after the fact and be imprisoned no less than seven and not more than fourteen years in the penitentiary or elsewhere not exceeding two years. And last, abettors in larceny cases were punishable on summary conviction (*4 & 5 Victoria c. 25*, 1841).

22 In 1789, Quebec City clerk of the peace and protonotary Joseph-François Perrault translated sections of the 1764 Burn's edition into French; decades later, he published a guide for law students explaining the fundamentals of Lower Canada's criminal law. See *Le juge à paix et officier de paroisse, pour la province de Québec: extrait de Richard Burn*; trans. José F. Perrault (Montréal: Fleury Mesplet, imprimeur, 1789); Joseph-François Perrault, *Questions et réponses sur le droit criminel du Bas Canada: dédiés aux étudiants en droit* (Quebec: [s.l. : n.p.], 1810).

23 Burn, *The Justice of the Peace, Vol.* 2, 59.

24 Burn, *The Justice of the Peace, Vol. 1*, 467.

25 Burn, *The Justice of the Peace, Vol.* 2, 155.

26 Ibid., 63.

27 *17 George III c.3*, 1789.

28 Burn, *The Justice of the Peace, Vol. 1*, 1.
29 Burn, *The Justice of the Peace, Vol. 2*, 177.
30 Ibid., 64–5.
31 Burn, *The Justice of the Peace, Vol. 2*, 385.
32 Ibid., 69.
33 Ibid., 63.
34 Burn, *The Justice of the Peace, Vol. 1*, xix.
35 Burn, *The Justice of the Peace, Vol. 2*, 73.
36 Byrne, *Criminal Law and Colonial Subject*, 160.
37 Burn, *The Justice of the Peace, Vol. 2*, 64.
38 Ibid., 59, 64.
39 See Poutanen, *Beyond Brutal Passions.*
40 Grand Jury Presentment (QS 2 October 1825), in BaNQ-VM, QS(F).
41 Jim Phillips, "Women, Crime, and Criminal Justice in Early Halifax, 1750–1800," in *Essays in the History of Canadian Law, Volume V: Crime and Criminal Justice, edited by* Jim Phillips, Tina Loo, and Susan Lewthwaite (Toronto: University of Toronto Press, 1994), 184–5.
42 Grand Jury Presentment (QS 19 January 1818), in BaNQ-VM, QS(F).
43 Carole Simard, *L'éclairage des rues montréalaises de 1818 à 1850 : Du système d'éclairage à l'huile à l'émergence de l'industrie gazifière* (unpublished History of Montreal seminar, McGill University, March 1981), 18.
44 See for example, Mark J. Bouman, "Luxury and Control: The Urbanity of Street Lighting in Nineteenth-Century Cities," *Journal of Urban History* 14, no.1 (November 1987): 28; Peter C. Baldwin, "'Nocturnal Habits and Dark Wisdom': The American Response to Children in the Streets at Night, 1880-1930," *Journal of Social History* 35, no. 3 (2002): 593–611; Peter C. Baldwin, "In the Heart of Darkness: Blackouts and the Social Geography of Lighting in the Gaslight Era," *Journal of Urban History* 30, no. 5 (July 2004): 752; Poutanen, *Beyond Brutal Passions*, 46–7; Nicolas Kenny, "City Glow: Streetlights, Emotions, and Nocturnal Life, 1880s–1910s," *Journal of Urban History* 43, no.1 (2017): 102.
45 *Montreal Gazette*, 10 January 1829.
46 On the history of policing in Montreal, see generally Allan Greer, "The Birth of the Police in Canada" in *Colonial Leviathan: State Formation in Mid-Nineteenth-Century Canada*, edited by Allan Greer and Ian Radforth (Toronto: University of Toronto Press, 1992), 17–49; Daniel Diciare, "Police et société à Montréal au milieu du XIXe siècle" (master's thesis, Université du Québec à Montréal, 1999); Fyson, *Magistrates, Police, and People*, 137–41; Poutanen, "Policing Prostitution: Police Officers, Prostitutes, and Ambiguity" in *Beyond Brutal Passions*, 209–48.

47 *Montreal Gazette*, 27 October 1836.

48 Grand Jury Presentment (QS 30 April 1836), in BaNQ-VM, QS(F).

49 Grand Jury Presentment (QS 19 July 1838), in BaNQ-VM, QS(F).

50 Grand Jury Presentment (QS 18 January 1840) in BaNQ-VM, QS(F).

51 Grand Jury Presentment (QS 30 October 1837) in BaNQ-VM, QS(F). "It also happens often that these houses hide the stolen objects, and thus the thieves are protected from prosecution," my translation.

52 Grand Jury Presentment (QS 19 July 1836) in BaNQ-VM, QS(F). For more on an exploration of this link between poverty and crime, see the following publications by Jean-Marie Fecteau: *Un nouvel ordre des choses: la pauvreté, le crime, l'État au Québec, de la fin du XVIIIe siècle à 1840* (Montréal: VLB, 1989); Jean-Marie Fecteau, "Between the Old Order and Modern Times: Poverty, Criminality, and Power in Quebec, 1791–1840," in *Essays in the History of Canadian Law,* edited by Phillips, Loo, and Lewthwaite (Toronto: University of Toronto Press, Osgoode Society for Canadian Legal History, 1994), 293–323; Jean-Marie Fecteau, *La Liberté du pauvre: sur la régulation du crime et de la pauvreté au XIXe siècle québécois* (Montréal: VLB, 2004).

53 *Montreal Gazette*, 3 September 1836.

54 *Montreal Gazette*, 6 September 1836.

55 *Montreal Transcript*, 3 March 1840. Who John Clarke was remains unclear.

56 Grand Jury Presentment (QS 30 April 1830), in BaNQ-VM, QS(F).

57 Grand Jury Presentment (QS 19 January 1837), in BaNQ-VM, QS(F). The Court of Oyer and Terminer was held at the behest of the governor when the Court of King's/Queen's Bench could not deal with the number of pending criminal cases. It had the same criminal jurisdiction. (Donald Fyson, with the assistance of Evelyn Kolish and Virginia Schweitzer, *The Court Structure of Quebec and Lower Canada, 1764–1860, Revised Version 1996–2016* (Montreal: Montreal History Group / Groupe d'histoire de Montréal, 1994, 1997, 2016).

58 Grand Jury Presentment (QS 30 October 1840), in BaNQ-VM, QS(F). See also Fyson, *Magistrates, Police, and People*; Poutanen, *Beyond Brutal Passions*.

59 Four could not be identified.

60 DR v. Maria Campbell (QS 20 April 1835), in BaNQ-VM, QS(F) (deposition of Margaret Atchison).

61 DR v. Marie-Angélique Blanchard (QS 3 September 1813), in BaNQ-VM, QS(F) (deposition of Jane McDonald).

62 In theory, married women, as *femes coverts*, were understood to be subservient to men and marriage made them invisible; thus, married women were exempt from conviction if they were acting under the direction of their husbands. In practice, the court held married couples equally responsible for their criminal activities. G.S. Rowe's study of *feme coverte* in Pennsylvania shows that in criminal prosecutions involving married couples, wives and husbands were treated the same. The criminal courts paid little attention to coverture and less so over time. Rowe has proposed that the reason for a lack of compassion shown toward married women is that they were judged according to the paradigm of the household economy. Since a woman was intimately partnered to her husband in establishing and maintaining the family economy, so too were they bound together when involved in the commission of a crime. (GS Rowe, "*Femes Covert* and Criminal Prosecution in Eighteenth-Century Pennsylvania," *American Journal of Legal History* 32, no. 2 (1988): 151–4. Furthermore, Fyson has argued in his seminal study of everyday criminal justice that even given Lower Canada's two systems of justice, married women not only initiated private prosecutions but few of them claimed to be authorized by their husbands to do so following the requirements of the *Coutume de Paris*, nor did they act as mere accessories to male plaintiffs (Fyson, *Magistrates, Police, and People*, 299).

63 DR v. Marie Miron, Pierre Millette, and Gilbert Bernon (QS 11 June 1833), in BaNQ-VM, QS(F).

64 Fyson, *Magistrates Police, and People*, 356-7; see generally Poutanen, *Beyond Brutal Passions*.

65 Byrne, *Criminal Law and Colonial Subject*; MacKay, "Why They Stole," 626.

66 DR v. Mary Goldsmith (29 July 1821), in BaNQ-VM, QS(F) (deposition of Benjamin Tindall).

67 For Montreal, see generally Bradbury, *Working Families* and Poutanen, *Beyond Brutal Passions*. Elsewhere, consider the work of Stansell, *City of Women*; Elizabeth Blackmar, *Manhattan for Rent, 1785–1850* (Ithaca: Cornell University Press, 1989); Judith Fingard, *The Dark Side of Life in Victorian Halifax* (Porters Lake, NS: Pottersfield Press, 1989); Penelope Corfield, "Walking the City Streets: The Urban Odyssey in Eighteenth-Century England," *Journal of Urban History* 16, no.2 (February 1990): 132–74.

68 DR v. Sophie Dupéré, Sophie Proulx, and Joseph Dollar (QS 7 April 1835), in BaNQ-VM, QS(F) (deposition of Bartholomew O'Brien).

69 See Adrienne Hood, *The Weaver's Craft: Cloth, Commerce, and Industry in Early Pennsylvania* (Pittsburgh: University of Pennsylvania Press, 2011), 2.

70 Walker, "Women, Theft and the World," 89.

71 For more on the cost of wood, see Robert Sweeny, *Les relations ville-campagne: le cas du bois de chauffage* (Montréal: Éditions du MBHP, 1988).

72 DR v. Maria Campbell (QS 10 October 1792), *in* BaNQ-VM, QS(F) (deposition of Marie-Françoise Campagne).

73 DR v. Marie Lebeau and Betsey Jackson (QS 22 July 1837), in BaNQ-VM, QS(F) (deposition of Robert Campbell).

74 DR v. Mary Warren and Charlotte Hamelin (QS 4 July 1808), in BaNQ-VM, QS(F) (deposition of François Mathurin). "The following day a part of the articles, namely, a little cotton dress, a cotton apron and two small sheets were found in the possession of Mary Warren and Charlotte Hamelin," my translation.

75 An examination of 240 depositions involving petty larceny shows the following seasonal variations: 23.75 per cent in winter; 21.25 per cent in spring; 27.5 per cent in summer; and 27.5 per cent in autumn.

76 DR v. Maria Chambers (QS 4 April 1835), in BaNQ-VM, QS(F) (deposition of Antoine Lindsay).

77 Donald Fyson, "Eating in the City: Diet and Provisioning in Early Nineteenth-Century Montreal" (MA thesis, McGill University, 1989), 88.

78 MacKay, "Why They Stole," 624–5.

79 DR v. Charlotte Prudhomme (QS 24 July 1793), *in* BaNQ-VM, QS(F) (deposition of John Mactier; voluntary examination of Charlotte Prudhomme; and voluntary examination of George Baron).

80 DR v. Marguerite Martin (QS 23 April 1839), in BaNQ-VM, QS(F) (voluntary examination of Marguerite Martin).

81 DR v. Mary Diller (QS 15 February 1839), in BaNQ-VM, QS(F) (voluntary examination of Mary Diller).

82 DR v. Mary Fundy (QS 21 February 1795), in BaNQ-VM, QS(F) (deposition of John Powell; deposition of Hugh Grant; and voluntary examination of Mary Fundy).

83 DR v. Emilie Gauthier (QS 7 February 1828), in BaNQ-VM, QS(F) (voluntary examination of Emilie Gauthier), "of a boy whom she does not know by name and whom she paid him a crown for all," my translation.

84 DR v. Elizabeth Benoit (QS 14 November 1827), in BaNQ-VM, QS(F) (voluntary examination of Elizabeth Benoit (St-Charles), "I slept with him,

he asked me to sleep with him for a long time and as a result of my consent he gave me the watch," my translation.

85 DR v. Olive Marcotte (QS 1 December 1841), in BaNQ-VM, QS(F) (voluntary examination of Olive Marcotte), "... for the use of my person after the invitation of said Davis ... my person and my bed," my translation.

86 Linda Woodbridge, *Vagrancy, Homelessness, and English Renaissance Literature* (Chicago: University of Illinois Press, 2001), 6.

87 Lawson, "Patriarchy, Crime, and the Courts," 52.

88 DR v. Bridget Howe (QS 16 July 1838), in BaNQ-VM, QS(F) (deposition of Thomas King; voluntary examination of Bridget Howe).

89 DR v. Bridget Howe (QS 14 November 1838), in BaNQ-VM, QS(F) (deposition of Olivier Dubois; voluntary examination of Bridget Howe).

90 *Montreal Gazette*, 5 March 1829.

91 Grand Jury Presentment (QS 19 January 1843), in BaNQ-VM, QS(F). Such uses of the prison for refuge parallels my own study on the city's sex trade and that of Fyson. See Fyson, *Magistrates Police, and People*; and Poutanen, *Beyond Brutal Passions*. Appalling jail conditions greeted the women who were confined and awaiting trial, as well as those who were convicted of larceny. Neglect and inadequate resources meant that both the House of Correction and Common Gaol were overcrowded, vermin-ridden, filthy, and foul smelling at any time during the year. In summer, the building was suffocating owing to poor ventilation and in winter frigid due to deficient heat. Inadequately dressed prisoners suffered especially from the cold and snow, which penetrated prison wards through broken windowpanes. Some inmates slept on the floor, others on straw beds with only thin blankets for cover. The stoves were located too far from the cells, so, to stay warm, women huddled together in small rooms. Prisoners subsisted on bread and water during the week; meat was added to a watery broth on Sundays and holidays. (Poutanen, *Beyond Brutal Passions*, 285–7).

92 DR v. Mary Riley (QS 1 June 1835), in BaNQ-VM, QS(F) (deposition of Eliza Dobbin).

93 DR v. Melanie Delisle (QS 11 November 1839), in BaNQ-VM, QS(F) (voluntary examination of Melanie Delisle).

94 DR v. Hannah Murray (QS 7 November 1835), in BaNQ-VM, QS(F) (deposition of Michael Wymes).

95 DR v. Nancy Harris (QS 20 December 1791), in BaNQ-VM, QS(F) (deposition of Duncan Fisher, 1 December 1791; voluntary examination of Nancy Harris, 20 December 1791).

96 DR v. Magdeleine McDonald (QS 13 September 1839), in BaNQ-VM, QS(F) (deposition of Joseph Dodds).
97 DR v. Ellen Morris and Susan Waters (QS 23 August 1825), in BaNQ-M, QS(F) (deposition of James Johnson).
98 DR v. Scholastique Lavictoire (QS 1 February 1816), in BaNQ-VM, QS(F) (deposition of Julie Mathurin).
99 DR v. Marie Diller (QS 1 July 1839), in BaNQ-VM, QS(F) (deposition of Rosalie Laprise).
100 DR v. Caroline Locas (QS 3 May 1833), in BaNQ-VM, QS(F) (deposition of Rosalie Laprise).
101 DR v. Ellen Turner, Mary Ann Cunningham, William McKay, and Alexandre Bonnier (QS 10 January 1838), in BaNQ-VM, QS(F).
102 Walker, "Women, Theft and the World," 82–5.
103 See for example, Walker, "Women, Theft and the World," 90, 99; and MacKay, "Why They Stole," 624.
104 Michael Macilee, "Burglary and Property Theft," in his book, *The Liverpool Underworld: Crime in the City, 1750–1900* (Liverpool: Liverpool University Press, 2011), 175.
105 DR v. Mary Ann Fitzgerald and Francis Lalahan (QS 2 May 1838), in BaNQ-VM, QS(F) (deposition of Sarah Kinster; voluntary examination of Mary Ann Fitzgerald; and voluntary examination of Francis Lalahan).
106 Macilee, "Burglary and Property Theft," 175–6.
107 Grand Jury Presentment (QS 30 April 1836), in BaNQ-VM, QS(F).
108 Although the following case falls outside the period under study by three months, it is indicative of the familiarity policemen had with pawnshops. When widow Julie Perrault reported the theft of her brown cloth cloak, the chief constable, Hypolite Jérémie, visited pawnbroker Frederick Neuty's establishment. The clerk produced the cloak for which he had paid 5 shillings and 6 pence. Jérémie returned to the pawnshop with Marguerite Bourgoyne but the clerk denied that it was Bourgoyne who had pawned the wearing apparel. Perrault pled guilty and was sentenced to two months in the House of Correction (DR v. Julie Perrault (QS 28 March 1842) in BaNQ-VM, QS(F) (deposition of Hypolite Jérémie)).
109 DR v. Margaret Perigord and Eliza Robinson (QS 16 February 1827), in BaNQ-VM, QS(F) (deposition of Catharine Ryan).
110 *Montreal Transcript*, 26 May 1840. There are several instances in my cohort of women, such as Mary Ann Hetherington, being charged with receiving stolen goods. It is likely that the numbers are higher but searching for cases in other historical sources is beyond the scope of this study.
111 *Montreal Herald*, 21 April 1824.

112 DR v. Elisabeth Deganne (QS 24 February 1827), in BaNQ-VM, QS(F) (deposition of James Benny, 14 October 1825; and indictment 24 February 1827).

113 DR v. Julie Deschamps (QS 5 December 1839), in BaNQ-VM, QS(F) (deposition of George Wells).

114 DR v. Biddy Handley and Jane Hicks (QS 5 January 1831), in BAnQ-VM, QS(F) (deposition of Jacob Abdella).

115 DR v. Biddy Handley and Jane Hicks (QS 30 December 1830), in BaNQ-VM, QS(F) (deposition of Josephte McFarlane).

116 See for example, Susan Dawson Lewthwaite, "Law and Authority in Upper Canada: The Justices of the Peace in the Newcastle District, 1803–1840," (PhD Thesis, University of Toronto, 2001).

117 King, *Criminal Justice and Discretion*, 5.

118 On rough justice, a subject that interested Blaine Baker, see for example, Bryan Palmer, "Discordant Music: Charivaris and Whitecapping in Nineteenth-Century North America," *Labour/Le Travail* 5 (1978): 5–62; Dan Horner, "'Like a Thread of Gold': Tracing Alfred Perry's Lifelong Engagement with Montreal's Politics of Ethnic Confrontation," in *Engaging with Diversity: Multidisciplinary Reflections on Plurality from Quebec*, edited by Stephan Gervais, Raffaele Iacovino, and Mary Anne Poutanen (Bruxelles: Peter Lang Publishing, 2018), 327–46; Dan Horner, "Shame upon you as men!: Competing Visions of Masculine Authority in the Aftermath of Montreal's Gavazzi Riot," *Social History / Histoire Sociale*, 44, no.1 (2011): 29–52; Dan Horner, "Solemn Processions and Terrifying Violence: Spectacle, Authority and Citizenship during the Lachine Canal Strike of 1843," *Urban History Review/ Revue d'histoire Urbaine,* 38, no.2 (2010): 36–47; and Poutanen, *Beyond Brutal Passions*, 127.

119 DR v. Maria Jordan (QS 24 December 1838), in BaNQ-VM, QS(F) (deposition of Pierre Portras).

120 This familiarity with justice has been noted by Jennine Hurl-Eamon about eighteenth-century Londoners: "It would have been difficult to move about on London's streets without receiving some sort of informal education on the workings of the criminal justice system." (Jennine Hurl-Eamon, *Gender and Petty Violence in London, 1680–1720* (Columbus: The Ohio State University Press, 2005), 17.) Popular knowledge and use of justice underscores a normative function of law. (Byrne, *Criminal Law and Colonial Subject*, 209.)

121 Clare A. Lyons, *Sex among the Rabble: An Intimate History of Gender & Power in the Age of Revolution, Philadelphia, 1730–1830* (Chapel Hill:

North Carolina Press, 2006), 198. See also Fyson, *Magistrates, Police, and People*; and Poutanen, *Beyond Brutal Passions*.

122 King, *Crime, Justice, and Discretion*, 17–31.

123 Mr Monk, for instance, acted as counsel for the accused Selina Robinson who was too ill to appear at court (DR v. Selina Robinson (QS January 1841), in BaNQ-VM, QS(F)). Fyson's examination of Quarter Sessions registers shows that lawyers were involved in a quarter of indictable cases usually acting for plaintiffs. (Fyson, *Magistrates, Police, and People*, 246.)

124 *Montreal Transcript*, 14 September 1841.

125 Fyson, *Magistrates, Police, and People*, 258–61.

126 One of the anonymous readers asked quite rightly about a gendered discretion in the application of punishment: were female prisoners subjected to shaming sentences more than their male counterparts? Although a potentially intriguing line of inquiry, it is unfortunately outside the scope of this study. That said, my examination of sex work in the same period shows that women were more likely to receive longer periods of incarceration for keeping a disorderly house or being disorderly than for property crime and even for those against the person.

127 DR v. Ann Lancford (QS October 1768), in BaNQ-VM, QS(F).

128 DR v. Thérèse Carplette (QS November 1786), in BaNQ-VM, QS(F).

129 See for example, John C. Weaver, *Crimes, Constables, and Courts: Order and Transgression in a Canadian City, 1816–1970* (Montreal: McGill-Queen's University Press, 1995), 23.

130 DR v. Cécile Mercier (QS 19 July 1815), in BaNQ-VM, QS(F).

131 Michel Foucault, *Discipline and Punish: The Birth of the Prison* (New York: Vintage Books, 1979), 8–11.

132 These regulations were reprinted in the *Montreal Gazette*, 23 September 1811.

133 Poutanen, *Beyond Brutal Passions*, 284.

134 *Montreal Gazette*, 14 January 1836.

Blaine Baker was a legal historian, of course, but he was also the one who introduced me to the idea of law and society when I was a law student at McGill, even though I don't remember him using those words, and I didn't realize until later that was what he was doing. He took care in his courses always to link law to the places, the people, and especially the times that produced it. As a first year law student in 1999 I took his Contracts course, which I feared would mean reading endless boilerplate. But as Blaine taught it, it was instead a look at how law structured society through agreements of all kinds. Later, in his Canadian Legal History course in my last year, the historical aspects of law and society – present but implicit in the Contracts course – came to the front, as he took us on a tour of different corners of Canadian history to show how law shaped society and vice versa. Blaine's legal history always impressed me for that breadth of scope. And I was a tough judge, having gone into law with a doctorate in history already in hand. Legal history to Blaine was never doctrinal elucidation within a legal bubble, nor was it a presentist story of how we got to now. Sensitive to the details in the sources, yet engaged with wider questions, he gave law a humanist dimension that continues to inform my own teaching in law and society.

Eric H. Reiter

12

The Case of the Theologizing Blacksmith: Liberalism, Conservative Catholicism, and Defamation in 1870s Quebec

Eric H. Reiter

INTRODUCTION

The early 1870s in Quebec were marked by heightened tensions between secular liberals and conservative Roman Catholics over the proper ordering of church and state.[1] Each side ranged across various viewpoints, but tended to see their adversaries as existential threats to society and used often stark language to argue their points. According to the Programme catholique manifesto of 1871, for instance, "the separation of Church and State is an absurd and ungodly doctrine."[2] Liberal polemicist Louis-Antoine Dessaulles was equally strong on the opposite side: "Reactionaries have declared war on modern society, on human thought, on moral free will, on many of the most important conquests of civilization, and no one is allowed any longer to think except as they do, even within the temporal sphere!"[3]

This conflict over the orientation of law and society was fought out among Quebec's leading intellectual figures, both ecclesiastical and secular, but it also had a grassroots dimension, which will be our subject here. During the 1870s, cases began to be brought to court in which individuals sued Catholic priests for having slandered them from the pulpit. The specifics varied: some priests accused individuals of illicit liquor trade, others of sexual improprieties, still others of general dishonesty. The priest typically urged his faithful to shun

Figure 12.1 | Louis-Cléophas Renaud dit Blanchard, about 1873.

or boycott the alleged miscreants, though in some cases he went further and threatened non-compliant parishioners with denial of the sacraments. All of these cases generated considerable controversy in the courtroom and the press alike.

One of the earliest such affairs was our case of the theologizing blacksmith. Louis-Cléophas Renaud *dit* Blanchard (see Figure 9.1), curate of the rural parish of Saint-Ephrem-d'Upton, near Saint-Hyacinthe, objected to the theological opinions voiced publicly by a formally-educated blacksmith, Damase Richer, and urged his flock to drive the man from the village by boycotting his shop.[4] The blacksmith sued for injury to his reputation, and the resulting litigation, shaped by the plaintiff's lawyers who were closely connected to liberal interests, quickly expanded to embrace wider issues of fundamental rights and liberties in Quebec.[5] The apparently petty quarrel between the blacksmith and the *curé* reveals the local side of broader issues of law, politics, and society at a formative time for both Quebec's civil law and Canada's constitutional order.[6]

CONSERVATIVE CATHOLICS AND LIBERALS

The wider struggle of which *Richer v. Renaud dit Blanchard* was a small part had a long history in Europe but was fought with particular vehemence in Quebec.[7] Related to more general tensions over modernity and its opponents, the most contested issues in Quebec were those over the ordering of church and state and the balancing of secularism and the Catholic church's spiritual authority.

On the ecclesiastical side, Quebec's conservative Catholics held a range of viewpoints about the appropriate degree of compromise and cooperation between church and state over modern developments like liberal democracy, fundamental rights, and science. Most hostile to compromise was Ignace Bourget, bishop of Montreal and Quebec's most prominent proponent of ultramontanism, the idea that the single true centre of the Catholic church was the papacy in Rome and that there was no place for local or national ecclesiastical independence such as claimed by the Gallican church in France.[8] Under Bourget's leadership, Quebec's ultramontanes advocated a stark rejection of secular modernity along the lines set out in Pope Pius IX's *Syllabus of Errors* of 1864, which condemned "the principal errors of our time," chief among them liberalism. Bourget likened "these damnable errors" to "venomous serpents slithering among the children of the Holy Church, poisoning their spirits and corrupting their hearts."[9]

Archbishop Elzéar-Alexandre Taschereau of Quebec City took a different and more moderate position within the Quebec Catholic hierarchy.[10] Though some ultramontane critics branded him a "liberal Catholic," Taschereau was very much a conservative in matters of doctrine, devotion, and politics, though of a less confrontational and uncompromising stripe than Bourget. For our purposes, in politics and constitutional ordering Taschereau espoused separate spheres, in contrast to the ultramontanes' hierarchical view of the primacy of the spiritual over secular matters.

The diocese of Saint-Hyacinthe, where our story takes place, fell somewhere between those two positions. While both Bishop Charles La Rocque (episcopacy 1866–75) and his vicar-general (and later successor) Louis-Zéphirin Moreau (bishop from 1875–1901) had spent much of their formative years in the ultramontane milieu of Bourget's entourage in Montreal, in Saint-Hyacinthe both were more moderate and pragmatic, and carefully avoided alienating their superior Archbishop Taschereau.[11] The bishops were not the whole story, however, and the Séminaire de Saint-Hyacinthe had since the 1830s itself been an influential centre of ultramontane thought in the diocese and indeed across Quebec, and was a potent force in the conflict with liberals through much of the century.[12]

Though Archbishop Taschereau was the titular head of the Catholic church in Quebec, Bourget's forceful personality meant that his influence was considerable, and he was supported by strong allies like Bishop Louis-François Laflèche of Trois-Rivières. And though Saint-Hyacinthe was a sister bishopric to Montreal and not its subordinate (as it would be from 1886 when Montreal was elevated to an archdiocese), newspapers, pamphlets, and books forcefully and widely promoted ultramontane ideas in the diocese and so shaped local discussions despite the positions of its bishop. In sum, while the Catholic position was more diverse than ultramontanism alone, the ultramontane position came to symbolize the conflict, particularly in the eyes of liberals and their allies.

Liberals returned fire from across the ideological divide, though they too were far from a homogenous group, with Protestant and Catholic liberals in particular often having different viewpoints and agendas.[13] For Catholic liberals, faced with spiritual censure or excommunication, the outcome of the struggle over the orientation of the Catholic church was personally as well as socially important. Some, particularly members of the Institut Canadien like Dessaulles and Joseph Doutre, were especially vocal in their resistance to the exclusionary definition of the church promoted by the ultramontanes.[14] Dessaulles's speech on tolerance to the Institut in December 1868, quoted above, was typical of the liberal position regarding politics, economy, law, and social and intellectual life in general. Reprinted in the Institut's *Annuaire* of 1868, it earned that publication a place on the Catholic church's *Index of Prohibited Books*, and the Institut itself a formal interdiction from Bishop Bourget.[15] Like their adversaries, liberals too had their newspapers, pamphlets, and institutions to publicize their position.

What was new around 1870 was that strict ultramontanes seemed to be gaining the upper hand, at least in certain parts of Quebec, and so were emboldened to push their positions more radically.[16] Also new around 1870 was that liberals were bringing more and more of those confrontations before the civil courts, forcing judges to adjudicate the respective jurisdictions of church and state and the rights and obligations of individuals within that emerging order. The most notorious example was the long Guibord affair, beginning in 1869, in which Bishop Bourget refused to bury the remains of Joseph Guibord, a member of the interdicted Institut Canadien.[17] Other contentious issues included priests "unduly influencing" their parishioners to vote a certain way (generally Conservative) under threat of denial of the sacraments, contestations over tithes and school taxes following change of religious affiliation, and, our subject here, cases of priests defaming individuals from the pulpit.[18]

APOSTASY IN UPTON

The trigger of the dispute between the blacksmith and the *curé* was a revolt within their parish of Saint-Ephrem-d'Upton, a recently formed township east of Saint-Hyacinthe.[19] Compared to its surrounding region, Upton had significantly higher percentages of non-French inhabitants (in 1871, 8.9 against 1.5 per cent) and of non-Catholics (6 against 1.2 per cent).[20] This reflects its liminal position, linked both to the seigneurial zone around Saint-Hyacinthe and the newer townships to the south and east.[21] This area had also long been fertile ground for Protestant missionaries, and Upton's non-Catholics were a mixture of anglophones and francophone converts.[22]

The revolt began in early 1870, when the heads of twenty-six families – all but one francophone, and mostly groups of neighbours, some with family connections – formally abjured the Roman Catholic faith.[23] The instigator was a Grand Trunk Railway worker named Pierre Pilon, who on 23 May 1870 recorded a formal abjuration before notary Michel-Esdras Bernier in Saint-Hyacinthe.[24] This official act underscored the seriousness of the decision, but more crucially provided proof of change of status for tithes, school taxes, and other obligations, such as paying for church construction and maintenance.[25] Twenty-five other men followed Pilon two days later, most farmers or labourers, but a few of them prominent members of the community.[26] The notary formally served the twenty-six abjurations on *curé* Blanchard, and battle was joined.

Mass conversions like this were not unusual, and more often reflected political or practical reasons than spiritual ones. In the case of the Upton twenty-six, their dissatisfaction with the Catholic church seems mostly to have been disagreement over the location of the new, permanent parish church. Siting of churches had long been a source of friction across Quebec, given the economic and other benefits of proximity.[27] In February 1870, the Upton *fabrique* had sought the bishop's permission to replace the old chapel with a new church and presbytery within the town centre.[28] They made the final decision to acquire the land (and assume significant debt) on 15 May, which launched a wave of opposition and, the following week, the abjurations.[29]

The diocese of Saint-Hyacinthe had seen similar resistance several times before, most recently in 1866, when ten families just south of Upton in Saint-Valérien-de-Milton had left the Catholic church.[30] Blanchard's strategy in Upton was to put the new church on hold (it would not be dedicated until 1875) and seek the advice of his bishop about the rebels. Louis-Zéphirin Moreau, diocesan vicar-general and administrator, sent a stern pastoral letter on 28 May 1870 to be read during Sunday mass. Addressed to those remaining within the church, the letter made clear that their relatives and neighbours had by their abjurations "put themselves entirely and forever in the hands of the Devil, accepted him as their master, and set themselves up as his slaves." The apostates' wives would regret the day they married those men, since when their husbands died they would have to suffer seeing the men's bodies "thrown into a field where filthy animals would trample them underfoot." The letter ordered three consecutive Sundays of public prayers "to sway God's anger" and to re-establish peace and unity within the parish.[31] The language was deliberately provocative: excommunicates buried by the Catholic church were of course interred in unconsecrated ground, not thrown into open fields, but Moreau's point was clear. The still-unresolved Guibord affair taking place in nearby Montreal put the theology and politics of burial on people's minds, so Moreau's imagery was calculated to scare as many as possible into returning. In that it seems to have worked.

As often happened with protest conversions, once the point was made, the converts gradually made their way back. Already in June, some of the abjurers were having second thoughts,[32] and in October the vicar-general's dire predictions had unforeseen help from the grisly fate of ringleader Pierre Pilon, crushed to death while working on the Grand Trunk line. Blanchard reported to his superiors that Pilon's death had terrified the other apostates, and the Catholic press spelled things out still more clearly, reporting that Pilon had been "struck by the hand of an outraged and irritated God."[33] Not all were swayed by God's wrath, however. In the 1871 census for Upton (taken in April), two of the men were still holding out, each identified as "Protestant" (without further specification) at the head of a family of Catholics.[34]

Also among Upton's Protestants was blacksmith Damase Richer, an anomaly in several respects. He was not one of the abjurers, but seems previously to have converted.[35] More unusually, he was a formally-educated blacksmith, having attended the Séminaire de Saint-Hyacinthe beginning in 1846. He overlapped for some of his studies with Blanchard, who had begun there two years later, and indeed, as we will see, the litigation between the two became something of a Séminaire reunion, since the judge and most of the lawyers were likewise graduates.[36] The Séminaire was a *collège classique*, one of the best in Quebec at the time, and students studied a broad curriculum over seven or eight years, including French, Latin, Greek, English, religion, rhetoric, philosophy, mathematics, history, and geography.[37] The Séminaire was also at the time a centre of ultramontanism under its successive leaders Jean-Charles Prince, later first bishop of Saint-Hyacinthe, and Joseph-Sabin Raymond.[38] Later

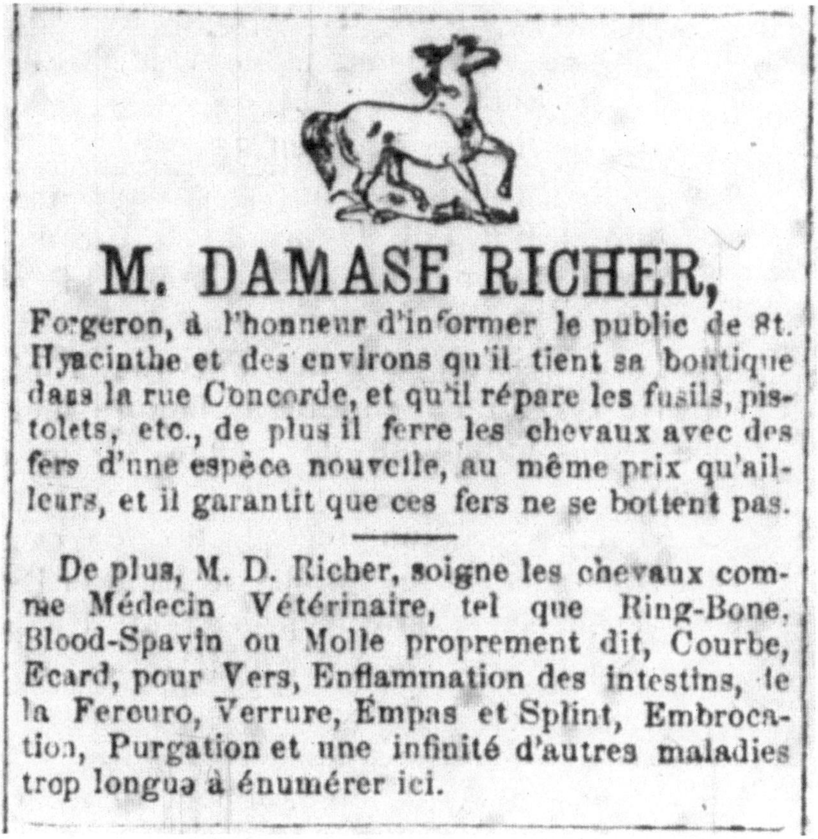

Figure 12.2 | Advertisement for Damase Richer's first blacksmith shop in Saint-Hyacinthe, which ran from late 1862 into 1863. In addition to shoeing horses, Richer repaired firearms and practised veterinary medicine.

events would suggest that both Blanchard and Richer were affected by these intellectual currents in their formative years, though with strikingly different results.

The Séminaire drew the sons of families from a wide socio-economic background. Richer's father was a teacher and later a bailiff in Saint-Hyacinthe, and Damase's education may have been undertaken with an eye towards a similar career.[39] After his time at school, however, Richer took a highly unusual path for an educated man: opening a small-town smithy (see Figure 9.2).[40] His older brother as well as some more distant relatives were blacksmiths, so he must have acquired sufficient knowledge at some point. Richer was one of two blacksmiths in town, and information in the 1871 census suggests his trade was considerably larger.[41] Like any small business owner, however, the loyalty of clientele was crucial, and Richer was vulnerable to anything that might diminish it. That would be a factor in the litigation.

Richer's conversion, whenever it took place, was permanent. From early in his time at Upton, his connection to the Catholic church – and perhaps organized religion in general – was slight. Upon arrival in Upton in the mid-1860s, he purchased a pew in the parish church, but reportedly only his wife and children ever used it, and by 1870 he had given it up.[42] He was alone in leaving the Catholic church, however. His first wife, Célina Lavoie, was buried as a Catholic in 1877, and when he remarried a mere four months later, it was at the Montreal Roman Catholic cathedral with special dispensation for mixed religions. He identified as an Anglican until his death at age fifty-three in 1886, and was buried in the Anglican cemetery at Acton Vale. His seven surviving children, all from the first marriage, remained Catholic except for his youngest son, noted physician Arthur-Joseph Richer, who became Anglican in adulthood.[43]

Richer may have played some informal role in the religious disturbances in Upton in 1870, though details are lacking. Afterwards, however, he was a provocateur amidst the ongoing religious tensions. As the liberal *Montreal Witness* put it, "He seems to have been a sort of village oracle – a scintillation of free thought shining across the dim ecclesiasticism in which the Bishop of St. Hyacinthe keeps his diocese so diligently wrapped."[44] Though we know nothing certain about Richer's politics, his religious contrarianism suggests liberal leanings.[45] Blanchard told a story that once when the bishop of Saint-Hyacinthe visited the parish, Richer had refused to remove his hat when they met.[46]

More worrisome from the *curé*'s perspective was that Richer's shop – across the street from the Anglican church – was where some of the men of the town gathered to talk religion, and where Richer put his academic training to use by holding forth on purgatory, votive masses, and other classic topics of disagreement between Catholics and Protestants. He often used a joking tone: one time Richer had fun mocking Blanchard's warning from the pulpit that "if the farmers don't have masses said, the wheat ears will be short."[47] With open rebellion in his parish, Blanchard was not about to tolerate his freethinking former schoolmate, and matters quickly came to a head.

RICHER V. RENAUD DIT BLANCHARD

During Sunday mass on 13 November 1870, Blanchard addressed the issue of the theologizing blacksmith from the pulpit. Witnesses were mostly consistent about the general gist of his remarks. Blanchard began by noting that though some of the apostates had returned to the fold, the danger remained. He mentioned Protestant proselytizers selling anti-Catholic pamphlets in the area, but a more immediate peril lurked within the village. Octave Brissette, one of Blanchard's witnesses, gave a representative version of the priest's words:

> There are certain shops in the village where bad things are said against religion and its ministers. It seems to me that there are enough respectable shops where you can be well served that you don't have to go to those others. I'm not preventing you from going there today, but if it continues, especially those who like to listen to people spouting off against religion, I will refuse them the sacraments. It's not enough to have hung around the benches at college for seven or eight years to be competent to explain religion.[48]

All agreed that Blanchard had threatened to withhold the sacraments from any who continued to frequent the informal religious discussions. Witnesses disagreed mainly about how specific Blanchard had been, a key element of a defamation action. No one testified that Blanchard had identified Richer by name, but most witnesses knew right away that Richer was his target. As Brissette said, he knew it was Richer, "because I didn't know anyone else in the parish who said such bad things against religion."[49] But what clinched it was the reference to college: the educated shopkeeper was Richer, as everyone knew.

Denunciations of individuals from the pulpit were common enough at the time, and the Richer-Blanchard case was in many ways typical of such affairs. Where it differed was that Blanchard denounced Richer not for a vice like intemperance or sexual immorality, the condemnation of which enjoyed broad social support, but for holding and expressing nonconforming religious beliefs. That broadened the resulting litigation beyond a simple damages claim for reputational injury.

Richer filed an action against Blanchard in January 1871 in Saint-Hyacinthe Circuit Court for damage to his reputation and a resulting loss of business. As an editorial in a Catholic newspaper coyly put it, Richer had been ready to let the matter drop due to lack of funds to pursue it, when "a certain party, always first in for the kill when it came to persecuting the clergy," provided the needed funds.[50] The reference seems to be to Richer's lawyer, Raphaël-Ernest Fontaine, recently called to the bar and like the two parties in the case, a product of the Séminaire de Saint-Hyacinthe.[51] More to the point, he had a growing reputation as a free thinker and opponent of clerical pretensions. As the same paper put it a few years later, "those who have grudges against a member of the clergy and vengeances to pursue, are certain to find refuge with Mr Fontaine."[52] Fontaine clearly saw the blacksmith's case as just the sort of thing liberal activists were looking for to challenge the expansive jurisdictional claims being made by the Catholic hierarchy: it was an interference with a basic individual liberty, and its circumstances could attract news coverage.

More than a hundred of Blanchard's parishioners – including the mayor, a justice of the peace, two churchwardens, and a physician – saw the political import as well, but from the other side. They published a petition signalling their support of the *curé* and their outrage with Richer: "We see in this act nothing but malice and hatred by certain sectarians against the Catholic religion and its ministers. We see in it an assault on the freedom of the Catholic religion and on the rights of the priest to warn his flock against erroneous doctrines."[53]

Whatever Richer's talents, he was not legally trained, so it was Fontaine who initially framed the action. In the declaration outlining the case, Richer alleged that Blanchard's words, spoken "in hatred" and with a view to driving him out of the village, depicted him "as a man unworthy of public confidence, a dishonest man, without principles, without religion, without honour, a bad Catholic and a bad Christian and citizen."[54] (Interestingly, Richer did not identify himself as a Protestant, as he would three months later to the census enumerator. This was likely strategic, to neutralize a justification argument from the defence.) Further, Richer alleged that Blanchard had condemned him not just from the pulpit on that one Sunday, but also in private conversations with parishioners throughout the year, persistently threatening to refuse the sacraments to anyone who spoke to the blacksmith. All this, he said, caused him to suffer damages of more than $1000, but "to avoid excessive costs" (a typical formula), he reduced his demand to $190. This both avoided antagonizing the judge with an unreasonably inflated demand, and also kept the matter within the Circuit Court's jurisdiction, where costs were lower than at the Superior Court.[55]

The action then sat idle for an entire year before Blanchard produced a defence. The file is silent on why the case moved so slowly. Since Richer did not seek to foreclose Blanchard from pleading, either the parties were discussing retraction or settlement, or else Richer was determined to bring the matter to court.[56] In any event, the case revived in January 1872, when Blanchard changed his lawyer (to Hubert-Wilfrid Chagnon, yet another Séminaire graduate) and filed his defence.[57] His arguments were typical for defamation actions: he denied any intent to injure Richer or that Richer had suffered any damage; he denied referring to Richer by name or implication; he denied counselling anyone to boycott Richer; he claimed privilege for any private conversations on religious matters. He also raised a much broader argument: as a priest, "he had a right to make such remarks from the high pulpit, and that he is answerable to no civil tribunal for them." Apostasy was a serious pastoral issue, so he had the right to deal with it by putting his parishioners "on guard against the doctrines and religious propaganda of the said apostates and other persons of religious denominations linked to Protestantism."[58] This connected the case to the hot issue of the constitutional relationship between church and state, framing it as a matter of clerical rights and duties. Such a response was what Richer and his lawyer were hoping for, and Blanchard did not disappoint.

With the issues joined, the leisurely pace continued, as the two sides deposed their witnesses (ten for Richer, including several of the former abjurers, six for Blanchard) on various days scattered between January 1872 and March 1873, with the case continued nineteen times over that period.[59] The rules at the time barred parties from testifying on their own behalf, so the views of Richer and Blanchard were not directly recorded.[60] Testimony focused mainly on what Blanchard had said and whether his listeners would have interpreted his words as referring to Richer. Witnesses also addressed the effects of Blanchard's remarks on Richer's business, but the results were equivocal, and even some of Richer's own witnesses testified they saw no effect whatsoever.[61]

The hearing was finally held on 24 October 1873 before Justice Louis-Victor Sicotte, who heard the parties' arguments and considered the written depositions. Sicotte, himself a graduate of the Séminaire de Saint-Hyacinthe from the 1820s, was involved in a number of prominent religious liberty cases, and his reported judgments were in general rather liberal, reflecting his background as a young Patriote who had moved towards the centre later in life.[62] Already in 1865, just a few years into his judicial career, he was voicing strong support in a school tax case for "the absolute right inherent in each citizen to the free exercise of his faith and religion."[63] In an 1872 case about whether a priest could collect unpaid tithes from a parishioner who claimed to have left the Roman Catholic church, Sicotte dismissed the priest's action in terms that would have heartened Richer and his team: "In this country, freedom of conscience is the basis of society."[64]

On the merits of Richer's case, Sicotte found that the priest's remarks had targeted Richer's business only, and not his reputation or character. Furthermore, Blanchard had spoken from strictly religious motives, without malice or intent to offend. If Blanchard was guilty of anything, it was harshness against Richer in his private remarks to individual parishioners, made while exercising his pastoral duty of counsel. In the absence of any proof of material loss, Richer had suffered no injury, and without injury, there was no defamation. That effectively disposed of the case.[65]

Sicotte went further, however, and addressed Blanchard's rights claims. The question was one of "liberty of preaching, of religious independence," and whether Blanchard had remained within "his right of religious censure." The case boiled down to a conflict between opposed holders of the same, more fundamental, right, "the right to contradict." Richer was within his rights to ridicule a priest for recommending masses as an agricultural stimulant, and for that Blanchard would have no action against him. By the same token, Blanchard was within his rights to tell people not to go listen to a blacksmith's theological musings, and Richer similarly had no recourse against that.

Sicotte carefully avoided the constitutional issue of church and state, though by ruling on the case he implicitly rejected Blanchard's assertion of blanket priestly immunity from the civil courts. He did, however, make clear that he viewed a priest's right to teach – as long as he stayed on the religious side of the line, wherever that line might be – as something in which "justice has no right to intervene." To assert the contrary would be tantamount to "the way of proceeding of all tyrannies, the system of all persecutions; force versus freedom; constraint versus tolerance." If the priest's advice went too far or was misguided, correction would come from the marketplace of ideas, not the civil courts.

Sicotte dismissed the case three days after the hearing; four days after that Richer inscribed it for review by the Superior Court. By this time, Richer had changed lawyers, to the Montreal firm of Doutre, Doutre, and Hutchinson, led by liberal standard-bearer Joseph Doutre, who was at that moment preparing to take the Guibord case to the Privy Council.[66] Blanchard too changed his team (Chagnon had been named to the bench), moving to the strongly conservative (and Conservative) firm of Mousseau, Chapleau, and Archambault.[67] The lawyers on each side had extensive journalistic experience, reflected in the presentation of the arguments, which were garnished with frequent exclamation points, rhetorical asides, and literary flourishes.[68] Clearly each side was trying to speak beyond the judges in front of them, and although coverage of the case had been limited so far, that was about to change.

At the Court of Review, where the hearing "was argued with considerable warmth," the mundane questions of defamation took a back seat to the issues of the powers, rights, and duties of a priest, which had been hinted at but not fully engaged at trial.[69] Richer (via Joseph Doutre) stressed that the case raised social and not just theological issues, and the tenor of Justice Sicotte's trial judgment mystified him: "One wonders in what time and in what country we are living! Either there are some atmospheric currents that unbeknownst to us are disturbing judicial equilibrium, or up above in the darkness, communications more or less acknowledged are being made in a direction that threatens our society with the most abject enslavement."[70] (Blanchard quoted this passage in his own factum, suggesting sarcastically that yes, Justice Sicotte "dared render a judgment by the dictation of the Jesuits or of Rome."[71]) Comparing himself to political prisoners in ancient Rome who were denied food and fire, and invoking the severity with which the Catholic church treated Indigenous peoples who missed mass in Quebec's early days, Richer stressed Blanchard's (and by extension, the ultramontane church's) malice. He argued that parish priest and church hierarchy together worked under the pretext of religion "to destroy a man who displeases, to serve an incompatibility of humour and to organize against this poor blacksmith the most formidable persecution, the kind that counts on the starvation of the enemy."[72]

The case was much more than a private vendetta, however, and Richer's central argument made clear the links to contemporary liberalism and its struggle against the theocratic ambitions of some in the Catholic church: "The laity have rights that the priest cannot violate with impunity."[73] What were those rights? Chief among them was freedom of expression, and Richer argued that he had "the right to speak with his friends about whatever passes through his head. ... A priest or minister does not have the right to single out a private citizen to speak ill of him."[74] Denying Blanchard's right like this was the usual and essential way to demonstrate fault, since at the time doing what one had a right to do could not be a fault.[75] Less common before the twentieth century was Richer's strong articulation of a countervailing fundamental liberty (of expression) that was constrained only by the limits of law, not by morality or religion. Religion might be "the moral law of our age and of our land," but Richer's claimed right to express ideas, even religious ideas, operated within – and could only be judged by – a secular legal world.[76]

Blanchard (that is, his lawyers) responded to Richer's rhetorical gauntlet, calling the latter's factum a "parody of the most unwholesome productions of Victor Hugo." He competed in kind, using his own colourful language and exclamation points: "a man can always save himself. If he's offered the alternative of being burned at the stake or of dying of hunger and thirst, he can avoid these unhappy alternatives by crossing the 45th parallel!!!"[77] More substantively, he made clear that the idea that priests did not know how to preach and needed to be instructed by a lowly blacksmith was absurd, even sinister: "Bismarck thinks like this; this is also the opinion of Victor Emmanuel, Mazzini and Garibaldi, as well as a crowd of others."[78] This was classic ultramontane fare, evoking the familiar contemporary issues of the church's loss of the Papal States and the German *Kulturkampf*.[79] Describing Richer as "our village free thinker" and his arguments as the ravings "of a delirious brain, of a sick imagination," Blanchard for the most part kept things simple: Richer had proved no damage, whether material or moral, and if he had left

Upton (by this time he had relocated to nearby Acton Vale), it was because he was tired of shoeing horses and not because of anything the priest had done or said.[80]

The broader issue, of course, was whether an attack on religious beliefs could be the basis for a civil suit, and in closing, Blanchard came back to the point about rights and duties he had raised at trial. Because of the perilous situation in the parish in 1870, it had been "his right and his duty" to preach about false teachings in his November sermon.[81] He made no mention of competing rights; indeed he gave no indication that Richer held any rights at all. Nor did he acknowledge any limits to his own rights, such as a duty to refrain from exercising that right when it might injure another socially or economically. Instead, his factum presents the image of a dedicated pastor guarding his flock in the face of an imminent danger: "What could be more simple, more natural, more legal?"[82]

The majority of the Court of Review reversed Sicotte's decision on 31 March 1875, awarding Richer $100 plus costs in both courts.[83] The main judgment was by Justice Charles Mondelet, a liberal and a highly polarizing figure on the bench.[84] Like Sicotte, he had been a radical during the Rebellion; later he married an anglophone in an Anglican ceremony, though he himself remained a Catholic.[85] In May 1870, his judgment at first instance in the Guibord affair was hailed by liberals but universally attacked in the Catholic press for ordering the burial to proceed, and he took part in several other priestly defamation cases.[86]

Much of Mondelet's decision in *Richer* was a long lesson for Blanchard on how to be a good priest and the importance of charity and moderation in pastoral care. This lecture from the bench must have irked Blanchard even more than Richer's amateur theologizing. Threats and force, Mondelet began, are "directly contrary to the natural right of man, a right that he holds from God Himself." In rural communities especially, where religiosity (and, he suggested, credulity) are more marked, threats to withhold the sacraments become powerful indeed, and can cause irreparable damage to individuals unless the courts step in to restore order. He concluded on a strongly liberal note, arguing for a reason-based view of truth and the primacy of individual will: "Whether one has been to college for seven or eight years or less matters little; the essential is to have the truth, and light should be everywhere. One should not put it under a bushel, any more than one should be permitted to put an embargo on man's will and thoughts."[87]

Mondelet's definition of truth was clearly broader than Blanchard's, and embraced the products of both human reason and divine revelation. In the end, he found that Richer had proved his case, while Blanchard had not justified his defence. Justice Frederick William Torrance agreed, finding that Blanchard had abused his influence, and so must be liable by "the law of the land, to which all must bow."[88] Justice Joseph-Amable Berthelot dissented on the formal ground that the trial judge was best placed to appreciate the evidence. He did however note that a parish priest had the right to warn his flock "against keeping bad company."[89]

This time Blanchard appealed, and both sides reprised their arguments from the Court of Review. On 22 March 1876, the majority of the Court of Queen's Bench reversed again, dismissing the action on the narrow grounds that neither slander nor damage had been proved. The court divided on whether priests enjoyed immunity in commenting on religious matters. Justice Samuel Cornwallis Monk held they did as long as they stuck to their role as spiritual advisers; Chief Justice Antoine-Aimé Dorion and Justice John Sewall Sanborn were just as emphatic that they did not. Justice Thomas Kennedy Ramsay suggested they might, but felt a definitive resolution should await a clearer case, while Justice Ulric-Joseph Tessier expressed no opinion one way or the other.[90]

With that the case ended. By that time Blanchard had been transferred to another parish, nearby Sainte-Angèle-de-Monnoir; he died in 1894.[91] His pet project, the new Upton church, would be overseen by his successor. Upton became increasingly Catholic following the brief schism of 1870, and by the 1881 census, the few Protestant families all had English or Scottish names. As for Richer, after the move to Acton Vale he had begun identifying as a trader (*commerçant*) rather than a blacksmith, but his new business affairs went badly, and creditors circled. In October 1875, his wife petitioned the Superior Court for *séparation de biens*, in what might have been a ploy to insulate his assets, but which was more likely a sign of marital discord.[92] Her suit, which was granted, alleged that his chronic drunkenness, mounting debts, and fraudulent business dealings jeopardized the assets to which she was entitled by law and by the couple's marriage contract.[93] Richer, as we saw, identified as Anglican for the rest of his life. Ironically, in 1877 his eldest son Louis Damase married a relative of Blanchard – one wonders whether the old schoolmates encountered each other again at the wedding.[94]

RIGHTS AND LIBERTIES IN *RICHER* AND BEYOND

Though *Richer* began as a defamation action, its arguments and the reactions it provoked quickly expanded into the broader conflict over separation of church and state. On the one side were freedom of religion and demands for the recognition by the state and the civil legal system of the liberties and prerogatives of the clergy. On the other were freedoms of conscience, of expression, and of the press. Those values were deployed fluidly: both sides, for instance, claimed freedom of expression, with secular liberals asserting a right to critique, while Catholic priests relied on freedom of preaching or teaching in the face of defamation suits from parishioners. These broader themes linked obscure small-town conflicts between clergy and laity with key questions about constitutional ordering in the post-Confederation period, and religious freedom and its limits became an important early site for the development of rights discourse in Quebec society.

While *Richer* meandered through the system, another similar case overtook it in the courts and eventually far overshadowed it in the press. Like the *Richer* appeals, *Derouin v. Archambault* also brought forward the issue of fundamental rights and liberties. In that case, a local priest used the pulpit to try to chase a local merchant seeking a liquor licence out of Saint-Barthélemy, near Sorel.[95] At trial, Justice Adolphe-Basile Routhier, the most overt ultramontane on the bench, as expected held that since a priest's power to educate derived directly from God, not from any civil authority, civil judges were powerless to limit it.[96] The law conferring that "right" on the priesthood "was promulgated nineteen centuries ago now, on the mount in Galilee, and since then it has been the law of the whole world. It is written in express terms in the Code *par excellence*, which we call the Gospel, a Code superior to all the codes of nations."[97] Routhier dismissed the case, holding that even if the priest's words had caused some injury to the plaintiff, the required fault was absent since the priest was within his rights in speaking them. The Court of Review, with Charles Mondelet leading the way, reversed Routhier's ruling in September 1874, six months before they would hear *Richer*. The majority pointedly stated that the trial judgment rested on a flawed premise: "priests, bishops, and all ministers of religion are and must be subject to the law, and must respect the rights of citizens."[98] The press, of course, split neatly between Catholic papers praising Routhier's trial judgment and liberals congratulating Mondelet for keeping theocracy at bay.[99]

Derouin was only the most prominent of a number of similar defamation cases pursued around this time.[100] Unlike Damase Richer, the slandered parishioners in the later cases tended to prevail, a sign of the shifting balance towards the liberals, particularly after Bishop Bourget's retirement in 1876 and Wilfrid Laurier's efforts to define a liberalism aligned with Quebec society.[101] Eventually, the question of clerical influence in elections came to dominate the debate over religious liberties, particularly the challenge to a Charlevoix by-election that ended up as one of the first cases of the new Supreme Court of Canada, in which the justices strongly rejected the idea of clerical immunity from the civil courts and secular law.[102]

The rights implications of these cases were debated equally vigorously (though more polemically) in the press as in the courts.[103] The debate on the liberal side was particularly interesting, because it quickly expanded beyond Quebec and Canada. Indeed, the rights aspect of the question of religious liberties allowed the Quebec cases to resonate with readers in English Canada and beyond, which in turn brought a strong rhetorical dose of British liberties back into the Quebec debate, thereby constitutionalizing a private-law matter.

Richer itself was presented from its earliest news coverage in terms of fundamental rights. The letter in the Catholic *Courrier de St-Hyacinthe* condemning Richer's newly-instituted action, for example, described the case as "an attack on the freedom of the Catholic religion and on the rights of the priest to warn his flock about bad teachings."[104] The liberal press was slower to pick up on the case, but by the time it reached the Court of Review editorials began using it to critique conservative Catholics' expansive jurisdictional claims. A week after the review hearing, the Montreal *Daily Witness* underscored what it saw as the danger of leaving the trial judgment in place. While the paper acknowledged that "all men have an undoubted right to withdraw their patronage if they choose" from anyone they disagree with, more than just individual interests were at stake. "The question is whether it is competent for an officer of a Church supported by the State to use its public services and its sacraments as engines for the damage of citizens."[105] Once the review judgment was handed down, the same paper spelled out the problem still more clearly: "Living under the British flag and entitled in the fullest measure to all the privileges of a free people, they [Roman Catholics] are nevertheless robbed of freedom of conscience, freedom of speech, a free press, a free soil, and other inestimable privileges enjoyed by other nations, by a power that dares them to think otherwise than it thinks, to read what it says they shall not, to be educated elsewhere than under its eye – to believe what it declares they must not, or, in general to call their characters, property or lands their own."[106]

Such assertions of fundamental rights in peril were nourished from outside Quebec as well, as the debate crossed borders and linguistic lines. The English liberal press outside Quebec eagerly picked up on the clerical defamation cases, seeing in them public rights of citizenship standing against their threatened suppression by the Catholic church. The Toronto *Nation*, in a long condemnation of Justice Routhier's trial judgment in *Derouin*, condemned Catholic pretensions to unlimited jurisdiction in the strongest terms, ending with the pointed remark that when judges like Routhier put faith before law, "a little extract of Bismarck would prove a valuable disinfectant in the Superior Court of Quebec."[107] The following week, the Ottawa *Times* reprinted excerpts from the piece in the *Nation*, adding spicy editorial commentary of its own:

> Who is Judge Routhier, that he should set himself up against the spirit of the law, the precedents of the Quebec Courts, themselves, and the rights and feelings of British subjects in Canada? Does he think that in this free, constitutional land we are going to return to the system of the middle ages, and acknowledge the audacious claims of a school of ecclesiastics which have been rejected by the Government of every Catholic country in Europe? One would expect more sense and breadth of mind in the parish beadle than is shewn by this learned Judge of a British Court.[108]

This waving of the standard of individual rights was picked up in American and British papers as well. The *New-York Times* praised the Court of Review's ruling in *Richer* for showing "a higher regard for the law, and more respect for the rights of the subject" than the *curé*, who sought "to protect young men from the sin of having ideas of their own."[109] Various English papers similarly trumpeted the "goodly victory over priestly tyranny" and its "blind and narrow despotism."[110]

CONCLUSION

Both sides used these clerical defamation cases to make constitutional points, which reveals some of the intermingling of private and public law in Quebec in the years immediately following codification and Confederation. That fluidity in part reflected how the relatively neat division of federal and provincial powers in the *British North America Act, 1867* was at odds on some points with certain provisions in the *Civil Code of Lower Canada* of 1866, notably on citizenship and its rights, which straddled that division.[111]

In considering cases like *Richer* and *Derouin*, conservative Catholics saw the question of church and state as a constitutional matter that had been decided at least since the Conquest in favour of the separate and entire jurisdiction of the church in spiritual matters. In contrast to moderates like Taschereau, ultramontanes adopted an expansive understanding of ecclesiastical jurisdiction, rejecting cooperation between the two spheres and advocating something close to theocracy. To ultramontane writers like Siméon Pagnuelo, Canada's constitutional order rested of necessity on the broadest possible scope for "spiritual matters," which, buttressed by old ideas of natural law, overrode whatever secular individual rights citizens might claim to have.[112] Liberals, by contrast, saw the constitutional arrangement as creating a broad zone for secular individual rights, guaranteed by law and protected against abuses by the secular courts. An ecclesiastical jurisdiction, limited to purely spiritual matters, was carved out of that secular legal order, but the spiritual realm had to be strictly defined and rigidly contained. That meant, for example, that a secular court could order the burial of a member of the Institut Canadien, even if it was powerless to order that the burial plot remain consecrated ground.

Damase Richer's legal confrontation with his former classmate is an entertaining story about a serious issue. Richer, his lawyers, and the press turned his personal conflict with his *curé* into a broader challenge to the antiliberal ambitions of the Catholic clergy in 1870s Quebec. As such, the case was argued not just in terms of individual moral injury, as all defamation cases of the time were, but also in the language of fundamental rights and liberties. *Richer* was not a turning point in thinking about rights: its influence was limited, and it was overshadowed by more prominent cases like the Guibord affair and *Derouin*. Still, the case of the theologizing blacksmith is a good illustration of the symbolic power of the contested language of fundamental rights during the formative years of Canada's constitutional order.

NOTES

For helpful comments and critiques, I thank the editors of this volume, the participants at the pre-publication workshop in Toronto, and Peter Gossage and Shannon McSheffrey. Unless otherwise noted, all quotations from primary sources are my own translations of French originals.

1 Yvan Lamonde, *Histoire sociale des idées au Québec (1760–1896)* (Saint-Laurent, Qc.: Fides, 2000), 359–81; Philippe Sylvain and Nive Voisine, Les XVIIIe et XIXe siècles, tome 2: Réveil et consolidation (1840–1898), Histoire du catholicisme québécois, vol. 2, ed. Nive Voisine ([Montreal]: Boréal, 1991), 365–96.

2 "Programme catholique," *Journal des Trois-Rivières* (20 April 1871), 2; Nadia Fahmy-Eid, "Les ultramontains et le *Programme catholique*," in Nive Voisine and Jean Hamelin, eds., *Les Ultramontains canadiens-français* (Montreal: Boréal Express, 1985), 161–81.

3 Louis-Antoine Dessaulles, Speech on Tolerance, in *Annuaire de l'Institut-Canadien pour 1868* (Montreal, 1868), 14; Jean-Paul Bernard and Yvan Lamonde, "Dessaulles, Louis-Antoine," *Dictionary of Canadian Biography*, vol. 12, http://www.biographi.ca [DCB]; Yvan Lamonde, *Louis-Antoine Dessaulles: un seigneur libéral et anticlérical* ([Saint-Laurent, Qc.]: Fides, 1994), 223–35.

4 Details of Richer's life will be given below; unfortunately I have not located a photograph of him. On Blanchard, see A. Denis, *Album photo-biographique du clergé catholique du diocèse de St. Hyacinthe* (Saint-Hyacinthe : n.p., c. 1873), unpaginated (with a roughly contemporary photograph); Cyprien Tanguay, *Répertoire général du clergé canadien* (Montreal, 1893), 329; J.-B.-A. Allaire, *Dictionnaire biographique du clergé canadien-français*, vol. 1: *Les anciens* (Montreal : Imprimerie de l'École catholique des sourds-muets, 1910), 57 (with a later photograph).

5 *Richer v. Renaud dit Blanchard*, 20 L.C.J. 146, which prints the judgments of the Circuit Court (Saint-Hyacinthe, 1873), the Superior Court in Review (1875), and the Court of Queen's Bench (1876); these will be cited as *Richer* with parenthetical indication of the court. Further information comes from the archival case file of the Queen's Bench appeal: Bibliothèque et Archives nationales du Québec, Centre Vieux-Montréal [BAnQ-VM], TP9, S2, SS5, SSS1, cont. 2009-02-001/125 (no. 17 of 1876)

[*Richer* case file]. The Circuit Court file contains only a few subpœnas and a draft judgment: BAnQ-VM, TP10, S21, SS4, SSS1, cont. 1983-09-067/1761 (no. 1529 of 1871). I have not located the review court file.

6 See Joseph Kary, "The Constitutionalization of Quebec Libel Law, 1848–2004," *Osgoode Hall Law Journal* 42 (2004): 229–70, though Kary does not discuss these ecclesiastical slander cases. On nineteenth-century rights discourse, see E.A. Heaman, "Rights Talk and the Liberal Order Framework," in Jean-François Constant and Michel Ducharme, eds., *Liberalism and Hegemony: Debating the Canadian Liberal Revolution* (Toronto: University of Toronto Press, 2009), 147–75, esp. 162–3; Richard Risk and Robert C. Vipond, "Rights Talk in Canada in the Late Nineteenth Century: 'The Good Sense and Right Feeling of the People,'" *Law and History Review* 14 (1996): 1–32.

7 For Quebec, see the literature cited in note 2 above. For Europe, see Robert Aubert, Johannes Beckmann, Patrick J. Corish, and Rudolf Lill, *The Church in the Age of Liberalism*, trans. Peter Becker, vol. 8, *History of the Church*, ed. Hubert Jedin and John Dolan (London: Burns & Oates, 1981), 304–34.

8 "Ultramontane" originally referred to Catholics in France who rejected the liberties and independence of the local Gallican church and looked instead over the Alps to Rome as the central ecclesiastical authority.

9 "Mandement de Monseigneur l'Évêque de Montréal, publiant l'Encyclique de N.S.P. le Pape, Pie IX, du 8 décembre 1864, et le résumé renfermant les principales erreurs de notre temps," in *Mandements, lettres pastorales, circulaires et autres documents publiés dans le diocèse de Montréal depuis son érection* (Montreal, 1887), 5: 42–54, quotation at 42 [*Mandements* (Montreal)].

10 What follows is based on Brian Young, *Patrician Families and the Making of Quebec: The Taschereaus and McCords* (Montreal and Kingston: McGill-Queen's University Press, 2014), 264–5, 277–80, and Young, "Legal Clericalism and Teaching Legal Culture in the Archdiocese of Quebec, 1852–98," in Michel Doyon, ed., *Avocats, société et politique au Québec, 1763–1867* (Montreal: Yvon Blais, 2018), 149–72.

11 Philippe Sylvain, "La Rocque (Larocque), Charles," *DCB*, vol. 10; Nive Voisine, "Moreau, Louis-Zéphirin," *DCB*, vol. 13.

12 Jean-Paul Bernard, "Les fonctions intellectuelles de Saint-Hyacinthe à la veille de la Confédération," *Sessions d'étude – Société d'histoire de l'Église catholique* 47 (1980): 5–17.

13 James M. Forbes, "Protestant Liberty: Religion and the Making of Canadian Liberalism, 1828–1878" (Ph.D. thesis, University of Calgary, 2019).

14 Yvan Lamonde, *Gens de parole: conférences publiques, essais et débats à l'Institut Canadien de Montréal 1845–1871* ([Montreal]: Boréal, 1990); Philippe Sylvain, "Doutre, Joseph," DCB, vol. 11.

15 "Decretum feria II. die 12 Julii 1869" and "Annonce à faire au prône," *Mandements* (Montreal), 6:23–4 and 46–9.

16 Lamonde, *Louis-Antoine Dessaulles*, 223–4.

17 Lamonde, *Histoire sociale des idées*, 363–6. Studies of the affair tend to be strongly partisan, e.g., Adrien Thério, *Joseph Guibord victime expiatoire de l'évêque Bourget: l'Institut canadien et l'affaire Guibord revisités* (Montreal: XYZ, 2000).

18 E.g., on undue influence, Charles Lindsey, *Rome in Canada: The Ultramontane Struggle for Supremacy over the Civil Authority* (Toronto, 1877); on tithes and school taxes, *School Commissioners of St Bernard de Lacolle v. Bowman* (1865), 16 L.C. Rep. 204, 10 L.C.J. 103 (Sup. Ct, Sicotte J.) [*Bowman* cited to L.C. Rep.]; *Soly v. Brunelle* (1872), 9 R.L. 319, 16 L.C.J. 101 (Sup. Ct, Sicotte J.) [*Soly* cited to R.L.].

19 Léonard Laflamme, "Bribes d'histoire religieuse de la paroisse Saint-Ephrem d'Upton," in *Album souvenir centenaire de Saint-Ephrem d'Upton 1856–1956* ([Upton: n.p., 1956]), unpaginated; *Les Six Cantons: Bulletin de la Société d'histoire de la région d'Acton* (December 2009), vol. 15, no. 2, https://75a2f6d0-857d-45f6-9e58-3ca5ad3b51c2.filesusr.com/ugd/a0ad4d_60f9c5b42eea481cadab05ee78bbbf12.pdf.

20 Statistics from Christine Hudon, *Prêtres et fidèles dans le diocèse de Saint-Hyacinthe 1820–1875* (Sillery, Qc.: Septentrion, 1996), 451 and 456. In 1831 Saint-Ephrem-d'Upton had been entirely Roman Catholic (ibid., 455). See also J.I. Little, "The Catholic Church and French-Canadian Colonization of the Eastern Townships," *University of Ottawa Quarterly* 52 (1982): 142–65; Hudon, "Le prêtre, le ministre et l'apostat: les stratégies pastorales face au protestantisme canadien-français au XIXe siècle," Études d'histoire religieuse 61 (1995): 81–99; Hudon, "Family Fortunes and Religious Identity: The French-Canadian Protestants of South Ely, Quebec, 1850–1901," in Nancy Christie, ed., *Households of Faith: Family, Gender, and Community in Canada, 1760–1969* (Montreal and Kingston: McGill-Queen's University Press, 2002), 138–66.

21 I am grateful to Peter Gossage for suggesting this point.

22 On missionaries and conversions, see Hudon, "Le prêtre"; René Hardy, *Contrôle social et mutation de la culture religieuse au Québec 1830–1930* (Montreal: Boréal, 1999), 17–66; Richard Lougheed, "Clashes in Worldview: French Protestants and Roman Catholics in the 19th

Century," in Jason Zuidema, ed., *French-Speaking Protestants in Canada: Historical Essays* (Leiden: Brill, 2011), 99–117.

23 Hudon discusses the schism in "Le prêtre," 86, 97–8; *Prêtres et fidèles*, 77, 387; "Family Fortunes," 146. Several Catholic-aligned newspapers covered the abjurations (as "sad news"): *Courrier de St-Hyacinthe* (28 May 1870), 2; *L'Ordre* (30 May 1870), 2; "Des gens à la foi robuste!" *Journal des Trois-Rivières* (2 June 1870), 3.

24 Bernier's chronological register is available online, BNnQ, CN602, S85.

25 Hector L. Langevin, *Droit administratif ou Manuel des paroisses et fabriques*, 2nd ed. (Quebec City, 1878), 28–9 (on construction of churches) and 117–18 (on tithes, and citing judgments that held that such a notarial act was not required).

26 Antoine McEvila was a saw-mill owner of Irish or Scottish origin and part of Upton's founding family; Joseph Pilon was later mayor of Upton and an occasionally successful candidate for provincial and federal office.

27 Allan Greer, *The Patriots and the People: The Rebellion of 1837 in Rural Lower Canada* (Toronto: University of Toronto Press, 1993), 58–62.

28 The details that follow are from Hudon, *Prêtres et fidèles*, 72–9; Laflamme, "Bribes d'histoire religieuse." Today the location of the original chapel is marked by a roadside cross outside the town: http://www.patrimoineduquebec.com/ajouts/upton/.

29 The debt was $2000 by around 1878: Hudon, *Prêtres et fidèles*, 119.

30 Hudon, "Le prêtre," 85–6; Hudon, "Family Fortunes," 146.

31 "Lettre pastorale aux fidèles de St-Ephrem-d'Upton au sujet de l'apostasie de 26 d'entre eux," in *Mandements, lettres pastorales et circulaires des Évêques de St-Hyacinthe* (Montreal, 1889), 3: 303–11.

32 *Courrier de St-Hyacinthe* (14 June 1870), 2, reprinted in *Journal des Trois-Rivières* (17 June 1870), 2 and *L'Ordre* (18 June 1870), 1.

33 Letter from Blanchard to Joseph La Rocque, bishop of Saint-Hyacinthe (26 October 1870), quoted in Hudon, *Prêtres et fidèles*, 387; "Un exemple," *Nouveau monde* (11 November 1870), 4 (quotation); "Un exemple," *Union des Cantons de l'Est* (24 November 1870), 3.

34 Census of 1871 (Saint-Ephrem-d'Upton), Antoine McEvila (p. 22) and Alexandre Filiatrault (p. 24). Isaac Giard (p. 9) was not among the abjurers, but appears as a French "Protestant" with all other family members Catholic. In the 1881 census all three were listed as Roman Catholic.

35 In the 1861 census (for Milton, p. 144) he was listed as Catholic, but as "Protestant" in 1871 (for Saint-Ephrem-d'Upton, p. 11). In 1871 he also listed his origin as German (he had one German great-grandparent).

36 C.-P. Choquette, *Histoire du Séminaire de Saint-Hyacinthe depuis sa fondation jusqu'à nos jours*, vol. 2 (Montreal: Imprimerie de l'Institution des sourds-muets, 1912), 367; *Catalogue des élèves du Séminaire de St. Hyacinthe depuis 1818* (Saint-Hyacinthe, 1875), 78.

37 Hudon, *Prêtres et fidèles*, 169–74; Claude Galarneau, *Les collèges classiques au Canada français (1620–1970)* (Montreal: Fides, 1978); Louise Bienvenue, Ollivier Hubert, and Christine Hudon, *Le collège classique pour garçons: études historiques sur une institution québécoise disparue* (Montreal: Fides, 2014).

38 Nadia Fahmy-Eid, "Prince, Jean-Charles," *DCB*, vol. 8; Yvan Lamonde, "Raymond (Raimond), Joseph-Sabin," *DCB*, vol. 11; Bernard, "Les fonctions intellectuelles."

39 Here and throughout, biographical information about Richer and his family comes from documents on Ancestry.ca.

40 He had a shop in Saint-Hyacinthe already in early 1863: see the advertisement in *Courrier de St-Hyacinthe* (20 February 1863), 4, col. 5.

41 Census of 1871 (Saint-Ephrem-d'Upton), table 6, pp. 1–2. Richer listed three male employees under age sixteen and annual revenue of $1560; Thomas Durand's shop listed one male employee under age sixteen and revenue of $600.

42 *Richer* case file, depositions of Étienne Bissonnet for defendant (25 January 1873), 4, and Louis Lebœuf for defendant (25 January 1873), 3.

43 Georges Desrosiers, Benoît Gaumer, and Othmar Keel, "Richer, Arthur-Joseph," *DCB*, vol. 15. The entry does not mention his religion, but in the 1891 census for St Ann Ward, Montreal, his religion is listed as Church of England.

44 "Another Ecclesiastical Slander Case," *Montreal Witness* (*Tri-Weekly Edition*) (3 April 1875), 2 (English original).

45 In 1877, Richer was involved in an election brawl in Acton Vale, but the political alignments are unclear: "Bagarre à Acton-Vale," *Courrier de St-Hyacinthe* (11 January 1877), 2; "Elections municipales," *Gazette de Sorel* (16 January 1877), 2; "Les émeutiers d'Acton," *Gazette de Sorel* (27 January 1877), 2; *Courrier de St-Hyacinthe* (1 February 1877), 2.

46 *Richer* case file, deposition of Joseph Pilon for plaintiff (24 October 1872), 13.

47 *Richer* case file, deposition of Benjamin Ouimet for plaintiff (24 January 1872), 9.

48 *Richer* case file, deposition of Octave Brissette for defendant (12 November 1872), 1.

49 Ibid.

50 Editorial, *Courrier de St-Hyacinthe* (2 February 1871), 2.

51 Fontaine's junior partners at the time were a young Honoré Mercier and Paul de Cazes. Fontaine had a long and distinguished career, and was named to the bench in 1901, shortly before his death. Pierre-Georges Roy, *Les juges de la Province de Québec* (Quebec City: Rédempti Paradis, 1933), 213.

52 "Les principes de M. Fontaine exprimés par lui-même," *Courrier de St-Hyacinthe* (24 June 1876), 2, an attack published when he was candidate in a provincial by-election. See also Frank Myron Guttman, *The Devil from Saint-Hyacinthe: A Tragic Hero: Senator Télesphore-Damien Bouchard* (New York: iUniverse, 2013), 65.

53 Published as part of an editorial, *Courrier de St-Hyacinthe* (2 February 1871), 2. Brief notes about the pending action also appeared in *L'Ordre* (3 February 1871), 3, and *Union des Cantons de l'Est* (9 February 1871), 2.

54 Included in *Richer* case file, Requête en appel (filed 11 June 1875), 2–6, quotations at 2–3; it was originally filed 30 January 1871.

55 The Circuit Court's jurisdictional ceiling was $200: *Code of Civil Procedure* (Ottawa, 1867), art. 1054 [CCP].

56 By art. 1070 CCP, the defence could be foreclosed once the plaintiff filed a demand to plead, which Richer did on 7 February 1871. On the filings, see *Richer* case file, Record (filed 16 August 1875).

57 His original lawyers were Chicoine and Bernier, about whom I have found no details. On Chagnon, see Roy, *Les juges*, 107. Chagnon's former law partner was Louis-Victor Sicotte, the judge hearing the case; his current partner in 1872 was Sicotte's son Victor-Benjamin. Either of these would be certain grounds for recusal in a later era, but at the time such rules were less restrictive. See arts. 176–91 CCP, and Philip Girard, Jim Phillips, and R. Blake Brown, *A History of Law in Canada, Volume One: Beginnings to 1866* (Toronto: University of Toronto Press for Osgoode Society for Canadian Legal History, 2018), 435.

58 The defence (originally filed 18 January 1872) is included in *Richer* case file, Requête en appel (filed 11 June 1875), 6–10, quotations at 7–8.

59 As was usual, witnesses were deposed *en enquête*, in writing and out of court, before a judge sitting for that purpose: arts. 263–99 CCP. The written depositions then became part of the case file.

60 Thomas McCord, ed., *Civil Code of Lower Canada*, 2nd ed. (Montreal, 1870), art. 1232 [CCLC] (the rule was not changed until the 1890s).

61 E.g., *Richer* case file, depositions of Pierre Lavina Larose for plaintiff (27 January 1872), 11, and François Paquette for plaintiff (24 January 1872), 10.

62 Andrée Désilets, "Sicotte, Louis-Victor," DCB, vol. 11; Roy, *Les juges*, 503.
63 *Bowman*, 205. On this case, see Anonymous, "The Right of Non-Residents to Become Dissentients – Judge Sicotte's Decision," *Journal of Education for Lower Canada* 9:12 (December 1865): 161–4; David Fraser, *"Honorary Protestants": The Jewish School Question in Montreal, 1867–1997* (Toronto: University of Toronto Press for Osgoode Society for Canadian Legal History, 2015), 275–6.
64 *Soly*, 320.
65 *Richer* (Circ. Ct), 146–8. The judgment was also printed in full in *Courrier de St-Hyacinthe* (15 November 1873), 1–2.
66 Sylvain, "Doutre, Joseph." Joseph was educated in Montreal, but his brother and partner Gonzalve attended the Séminaire de Saint-Hyacinthe.
67 Joseph-Adolphe Chapleau and Joseph-Louis Archambault had both studied at the Séminaire de Saint-Hyacinthe. On Mousseau see: Andrée Désilets, "Mousseau, Joseph-Alfred," DCB, vol. 11; Roy, *Les juges*, 391. On Chapleau see: Andrée Désilets, "Chapleau, Sir Joseph-Adolphe," DCB, vol. 12. On Archambault see: John Douglas Borthwick, *History and Biographical Gazetteer of Montreal to the Year 1892* (Montreal, 1892), 297–8.
68 The Court of Review case file is missing, but the factums seem to have been substantially identical to those later submitted to the Court of Queen's Bench.
69 "The Courts," *Daily Witness* (2 March 1875), 2 (English original).
70 Quoted in *Richer* case file, Factum de l'intimé (filed 17 December 1875), 5.
71 *Richer* case file, Factum de l'appelant (filed 11 December 1875), 2.
72 *Richer* case file, Factum de l'intimé (filed 17 December 1875), 5.
73 Ibid., 6.
74 Ibid.
75 Eric H. Reiter, *Wounded Feelings: Litigating Emotions in Quebec, 1870–1950* (Toronto: University of Toronto Press for Osgoode Society for Canadian Legal History, 2019), 46–7.
76 *Richer* case file, Factum de l'intimé (filed 17 December 1875), 6.
77 *Richer* case file, Factum de l'appelant (filed 11 December 1875), 3.
78 Ibid., 2.
79 *Church in the Age of Liberalism*, 250–62 (Italy), 272–83 (German-speaking regions).
80 *Richer* case file, Factum de l'appelant (filed 11 December 1875), 3–4, 7.
81 Ibid., 8.
82 Ibid.

83 *Richer* (Sup. Ct Rev.) prints excerpts of the opinions; more complete versions are in "La diffamation cléricale encore punie," *Daily Witness* (2 April 1875), 1, and "Jugement de l'hon. juge Mondelet," *Daily Witness* (3 April 1875), 1.

84 Elizabeth Nish, "Mondelet, Charles-Elzéar," DCB, vol. 10; Roy, *Les juges*, 379; Jonathan Swainger, "A Bench in Disarray: The Quebec Judiciary and the Federal Department of Justice, 1867–1878," *Cahiers de droit* 34 (1993): 59–91.

85 Mondelet's death was recorded in the register of Notre Dame Basilica in Montreal, and he was buried in the Catholic Notre-Dame-des-Neiges cemetery (documents available on Ancestry.ca).

86 On Guibord, see *L'Ordre* (3 May 1870), 1; "Affaire-Guibord," *Nouveau Monde* (5 May 1870), 2. Mondelet was part of the Court of Review in *Derouin v. Archambault* (30 September 1874), discussed below.

87 Quotations from "Jugement de l'hon. juge Mondelet," *Daily Witness* (3 April 1875), 1.

88 *Richer* (Sup. Ct Rev.), 150 (English original). On Torrance, see G. Blaine Baker, "Law Practice and Statecraft in Mid-Nineteenth-Century Montreal: The Torrance-Morris Firm, 1848 to 1868," in Carol Wilton, ed., *Essays in the History of Canadian Law, Volume IV: Beyond the Law: Lawyers and Business in Canada, 1830 to 1930* (Toronto: Osgoode Society, 1990), 45–91; Roy, *Les juges*, 549.

89 *Richer* (Sup. Ct Rev.), 149; "Legal Intelligence," *Montreal Herald* (1 April 1875), 1 (quotation, English original); "Clerical Denunciation," *Montreal Witness (Tri-Weekly Edition)* (3 April 1875), 3.

90 *Richer* (QB).

91 "Nouvelles religieuses," *Journal de Québec* (23 September 1874), 2.

92 On judicial separation, see art. 1311 CCLC. The action was often suspected of covering collusion or fraud: Gonzalve Doutre, *Les lois de la procédure civile*, vol. 2 (Montreal, 1869), 366.

93 *Lavoie v. Richer* (unreported; Sup. Ct, Saint-Hyacinthe, 4 February 1876), case file BAnQ-VM, TP11, S21, SS2, SSS1, cont. 1995-09-001/1303 (no. 1684 of 1875). In an action undertaken against him in 1872 by his former lawyer Raphaël Fontaine, who had (apparently coincidentally) acquired Richer's promissory note arising from a failed business dealing, Richer had signed the note "Damascus Richey," not a strong endorsement of his probity in business matters. *Fontaine v. Richey* (unreported; Sup. Ct, Saint-Hyacinthe, 3 April 1876), case file (no. 1688 of 1875) in the same box as *Lavoie v. Richer*.

94 The bride was Victoria Renaud *dit* Blanchard; her relationship to Louis-Cléophas Renaud *dit* Blanchard was not particularly close, but I have not been able to pin it down.

95 *Derouin v. Archambault* (1874), 5 RL 308 (Sup. Ct), reversed (1874), 19 LCJ 157 (Sup. Ct Rev.) [*Derouin*].

96 On Routhier, see Yves Hébert, "Routhier, Sir Adolphe-Basile," *DCB*, vol. 14; Roy, *Les juges*, 477.

97 *Derouin* (Sup. Ct), 312.

98 *Derouin v. Archambault* (Sup. Ct Rev.), 158 (C. Mondelet J.).

99 Catholic papers: "Affaire Drouin [*sic*] vs Archambault," *Courrier du Canada* (12 October 1874), 2; "Le jugement de l'honorable juge Routhier," *Courrier du Canada* (9, 11, 13 November 1874), 2; "Revue de la semaine," *Gazette des campagnes* (18 February 1875), 130–1. Liberal papers: "Judge Routhier's Famous Judgment," *Daily Witness* (1 October 1874), 2; "The Routhier Judgement," *(Quebec) Saturday Budget* (10 October 1874), 3.

100 *Brossoit v. Turcotte* (1873), 20 LCJ 141 (Sup. Ct, Beaudry J.), damages increased (1875), ibid. (QB); *Vigneux v. Noiseux* (1877), 21 LCJ 89 (Sup. Ct, Sicotte J.); *Leblanc v. Bédard*, unreported (6 September 1875, Circ. Ct, L'Assomption, Olivier J.), details in "Dépêches télégraphiques," *Gazette de Joliette* (7 September 1875), 2. An unusually late example is *Lefebvre v. Jobin* (1917), RJQ 52 C.S. 492, 23 R. de J. 534; "L'Action du maire Lefebvre," *La Presse* (27 June 1917), 7, 13.

101 Wilfrid Laurier, "Political Liberalism: Definition of the Liberal Idea," in Ulric Barthe, ed., *Wilfrid Laurier on the Platform* (Quebec City, 1890), 51–80. See generally Yvan Lamonde, "Le libéralisme et le passage dans le XXe siècle," in Yvan Lamonde, ed., *Combats libéraux au tournant du XXe siècle* (Montreal: Fides, 1995), 9–38.

102 *Brassard et al. v. Langevin* (1877), 1 SCR 145, esp. 220 (Ritchie J.). See [Louis-François Laflèche], *L'influence spirituelle indue devant la liberté religieuse et civile (Extraits du Journal des Trois Rivières)* (Trois-Rivières, 1881); Jus [Gustave Lamothe], "Les droits du clergé dans les élections," *Revue canadienne* 17 (1881): 23–34, 92–101, 194–207.

103 Beyond the press, scholarly contributions were published as well. On the Catholic side: Siméon Pagnuelo, Études historiques et légales sur la liberté religieuse en Canada (Montreal, 1872) (formally approved by Bishop Bourget, *Mandements* [Montreal], 6: 235–9, 8: 446); Désiré Girouard, "Constitutional Law. Church and State," *Revue critique de législation et de jurisprudence du Canada* 1 (1871): 431–56 and 2 (1872): 1–32,

113–46. On the liberal side: Alexander T. Galt, *Civil Liberty in Lower Canada* (Montreal, 1876); Galt, *Church and State* (Montreal, 1876); Lindsey, *Rome in Canada*.

104 Editorial, *Courrier de St-Hyacinthe* (2 February 1871), 2.

105 "The Courts," *Daily Witness* (2 March 1875), 2 (English original).

106 "Another Ecclesiastical Slander Case," *Montreal Witness (Tri-Weekly Edition)* (3 April 1875), 2 (English original).

107 "Judicial Ultramontanism in Quebec," *(Toronto) Nation* (25 June 1874), 154 (English original).

108 "Judge Routhier's Law," *(Ottawa) Times* (1 July 1874), 2 (English original). See also "Arbitrary Ecclesiastics," *(Toronto) Daily Globe* (5 April 1875), 2.

109 "The Village Blacksmith," *New-York Times* (11 April 1875), 6 (English original). See also "A Novel Lawsuit," *Valley Falls (Kansas) New Era* (1 May 1875), 2, and reprinted elsewhere.

110 "Blacksmith Defeating the Priests," *York (UK) Herald* (5 May 1875), 6 (English original), and reprinted elsewhere.

111 *British North America Act, 1867*, ss. 91(25) and 92(13); arts. 18–38 CCLC ("Title First. Of the Enjoyment and Loss of Civil Rights").

112 Pagnuelo, Études historiques; cf. also Girouard, "Constitutional Law," who makes a version of this argument.

My first introduction to Blaine Baker was as a student in first year Constitutional Law at McGill, when he served as a guest lecture for two classes, discussing the context around Privy Council federalism decisions of the early twentieth century. I remember his compendious knowledge, his stream-of-consciousness lecturing, which transported the question-asker to another dimension. I later took Administrative Process; my clearest memory is walking through the *Ontario Human Rights Act*, line by line, to discern the purpose of the legislature and infer the operations of the agency, from his famous "worm's eye view." In Canadian Legal History, the following year, I feasted on his distinctive style again.

I spoke at Blaine's retirement party in a downtown Toronto firm. I recalled the time he had judged my practice mooting session for the Laskin competition. He hadn't pulled his punches; I recounted his liberal use of adjectives such as "pedantic" and "unpersuasive" to describe my earnest and overly prepared presentation. The story brought the house down: it was as though everyone in the room, there to celebrate the man, could imagine his frankness, delivered after the signature pregnant pause. The shared laughter felt at once tender and cathartic.

We reunited at the University of Toronto Faculty of Law, him a post-retirement adjunct lecturer, me a new doctoral student. For a brief period we each had an office in the same hall of a satellite location during a renovation. I would drop by and he would drop off envelopes of his old syllabi, articles, and notes. In that musty, out-of-the-way hallway, his door was always open. Entering into his office was like going home. Throughout my doctorate, he silently helped me, reading each chapter of the dissertation and providing compendious comments and citations to explore. He nominated me for an award, silently again, and after I graduated hosted me for liberal afternoons in his new, sunlight-filled, temperature-disregulated office in an out-of-the way corner of Flavelle House. He shared the unspoken history of his own alma mater and my new place of work. He delighted in his new phase of life: he lived retirement as the discovery of new opportunities and the synthesis of his life's work. This was true of his final essays and his unrealized plans for teaching Legal Process at the University of Toronto – the subject of this paper. The last thing I remember him telling me was that he approached every article by reading the footnotes first.

David Sandomierski

13

The Limits of Adjudication in the First-Year Curriculum: The Recurring History of Legal Process at the University of Toronto Faculty of Law

David Sandomierski

INTRODUCTION

In the early to mid-1940s, a movement was brewing at Harvard Law School. Its core premise was that social legislation's rise, spurred by the New Deal, illustrated an important social and civic role for lawyers. As Kunal Parker has written, with the New Deal, "the country's entrenched common lawyerly judiciary was compelled to cede ground to, and otherwise to accommodate, an explosion of democratically- and administratively-generated law."[1] This shift in the relative importance of judicial, legislative, and administrative legal processes soon impacted law schools, where proponents started to question the implicit predominance of the judicial process reflected in the signature case method of studying law pioneered by Harvard Law School Dean Christopher Columbus Langdell in 1870.Under the Langdellian case method, which between 1895 and 1915 spread to over a third of all US law schools and gradually came to predominate North American legal education, students learned primarily to scrutinize judicial decisions as a way of distilling legal rules "inductively," modeled on the natural sciences, and to develop analogical reasoning skills.[2] A standard core curriculum predominated throughout Canada and the United States, consisting of almost uniformly similar course offerings of Contracts, Torts,

Property, and Criminal Law, taught primarily using appellate cases.[3] In these courses, the emphasis was squarely on adjudication, the legal process concerned with resolving disputes, usually by members of the judiciary, the independent branch of government.

This focus on adjudication helped to cultivate a distinctively legal way of thinking; thinking like a lawyer would soon grow to become the paradigmatic objective of legal education, while the Socratic method of teaching – the process of professors iteratively questioning students about judicial reasoning (popularized by films such as *The Paper Chase*) – would become to be considered the signature pedagogy of legal education.[4]

As transformative as the Langdellian innovation was – it eventually almost completely replaced the teaching of law through didactic lectures and would influence both medical and business education across the United States[5] – its limitations were being acutely felt with the rise of social legislation enacted during the New Deal period. This essay begins with an account of the ferment in law schools in the early 1940s brought about by an emphasis on processes other than adjudication.[6] The emblem of the movement was a set of mimeographed Legal Process teaching materials produced by Harvard Law School professors, Henry Hart and Albert Sacks. These materials circulated widely for around forty years[7] and played an important role in encouraging law students to view different legal processes as appropriate to addressing different types of social problems.[8] The Legal Process materials were a pedagogical manifestation of a concern with, as Lon Fuller famously put it, "the forms and limits of adjudication." They reflected a desire to prepare law students to contribute to the increasingly important responsibilities that lawyers (including elite law school law professors) were taking on to regulate the national economy through labour and other kinds of important administrative boards.[9]

This essay then goes on to chart the migration of these Legal Process ideas and their implications for legal education at one Canadian law faculty, the University of Toronto Faculty of Law.[10] Like many law schools of the period, the Faculty was populated by a large number of Harvard graduates. This essay will ask to what extent these graduates imported or "proselytiz[ed]"[11] the Legal Process ideas of the Harvard iconoclasts, and the extent to which these ideas took root. This essay is as much a study of how ideas travel via the medium of law teaching and mentorship as it is an illustration of the inherent conservatism of pedagogical and curricular development in law schools. It might seem intuitive to non-lawyers that different fora and processes (such as legislatures, courts, administrative bodies, and alternative mechanisms such as negotiation and mediation) are differently suited to tackling different problems, that they all involve law, and thus that law school would naturally expose students to a menu of all these processes and their related skills. However, the more singular aims of the Langdellian case method, with its emphasis on thinking like a lawyer and adjudication, have been remarkably tenacious and hegemonic.[12] Curricular developments and debates at the University of Toronto Faculty of Law in the postwar period illustrate the perennial problem of how to define, model, and teach the distinctive contributions that future lawyers are to make in society. This story is one instance of a more widespread tension between those who wish to incorporate multiple legal processes and problem-solving modes into the legal curriculum, and those who prefer to concentrate on conventional appellate judicial decisions.

For those who believe that the legally educated have a great deal to contribute to society – or, correlatively, that society has much to benefit from having versatile, critical legal-problem solvers – the stakes are high. The debates about curriculum and pedagogy serve as proxies for debates about what is important and relevant to becoming a lawyer, and for what society needs from its legally educated citizens. The aspiration to expose students to multiple legal processes – and the concomitant desire to expand the law student's toolkit to include negotiation, drafting, policy, law reform, and planning skills – seeks to broaden the ambit and reach of legal education. While some may have given up on the world-changing potential of legal education, yet others continually re-affirm it.[13] In any event, perennial debates about curricular reform, infused with the implicit idea that legal curricular reform matters for society, appear to be a persistent and recurring feature of the North American legal academy. For this reason, if nothing else, this study is instructive.

This essay participates in the tradition of internalist legal history,[14] examining a relatively understudied class of "insider" persons within the law: Canadian law professors. Professors' decisions about what to teach in their classes and what to approve as part of the curriculum contribute to the transmission of legal consciousness, affecting what substantive content students are exposed to and conveying higher order messages of what is relevant to becoming a lawyer. Debates over curricular development represent one of the rare instances where these meta decisions are rendered explicit, advocated for, and contested. As Rod Macdonald has written, "thoughtful curricular reform is a law school's primary heuristic device."[15] By detailing the process of curricular reform debate at the University of Toronto, this essay conducts a sort of archaeology of legal education – one that seeks to "make visible and personal"[16] the process of deciding what messages law students (and future lawyers) will be exposed to at formative moments in their intellectual and professional development.

Along the way, I also explore various pedagogical choices, including course titles, syllabi, and evaluation methods. Such an inquiry extends the catalogue of "mandarin legal materials" with which the historian of legal thought is concerned.[17] While many professors will not author treatises or edit casebooks, all command a position of authority in their classrooms. If not mandarins tout court, they are certainly mini-mandarins of their classrooms, authorities for the students they teach over the years. The ways that these educators frame their courses and evaluate convey important messages about the privileged content of law, its conceptual apparatus, and the core professional competency of thinking like a lawyer.[18] A scrutiny of these materials, in the tradition of critical legal history, helps us understand "the power that legal forms hold over our minds" and how the conceptual apparatus passed along by law professors seeps into the "marrow" of lawyers' bones.[19]

This piece is written with the scholarship, teaching, service, and spirit of Blaine Baker in mind. Baker's own scholarship sought to "get as close to the ground … as possible, by shunning reified sources of historical knowledge like appellate judicial decisions."[20] Baker also took a scholarly interest in the development of legal thought at the University of Toronto.[21] At McGill, Baker played an active role in both formal and informal curricular development, as Richard Janda reminds us in his contribution to this volume.[22] His teaching "emphasized the 'worm's-eye' rather than 'bird's-eye' views of state action," seeking to expose students to a diversity of modes of legal ordering through both his Administrative Process course at McGill and teaching Legal Process at the University of Toronto.[23] In his classroom, Baker often spoke about the pathological nature of the litigated case and warned against learning from this dysfunctional and unrepresentative artifact that could obfuscate the parties and their original concerns. He would point out that many of the leading cases did not actually contain the legal principles they were taken to stand for. As a historian, he would warn about the dangers of only relying on reported cases when so many went unreported. Baker was keenly aware of the tendency of Canadian law teachers to perpetuate a traditional approach to teaching law despite scholarly inclinations to the contrary.[24]

With many of these connections and lessons in mind, it is in his honour that I attempt to reconstruct the story of attempts to decentre adjudication at the University of Toronto Faculty of Law.

HARVARD LAW SCHOOL AND THE POSTWAR FERMENT IN LEGAL EDUCATION

In the wake of New Deal legislation and in the optimism of the immediate postwar period, the 1940s and 1950s experienced a proliferation of presentations and publications on the social purpose of legal education. These highlighted the need for lawyers to solve problems, participate in public policy, integrate law with social sciences, and to develop skills in diverse legal processes so as to contribute as citizens to all aspects of the regulatory state.[25] During this time, the sustained (if marginalized) experiment in education for diverse legal processes was being undertaken at Harvard, originating in the late 1930s and culminating in the 1958 "tentative" edition of Hart and Sacks' teaching materials, which eventually became *The Legal Process: Basic Problems in the Making and Application of Law*.[26]

These ideas made their way into more programmatic curricular debates, at Harvard Law School at least, in 1957, through the preliminary statement of the Committee on Legal Education. Chaired by Lon Fuller, the report argued that law teaching "centers on the process by which appellate cases are decided rather than on the problems of planning and strategy with which lawyers are chiefly concerned in practice," that it "does not sufficiently emphasize problems of draftsmanship," that "law school places a disproportionate emphasis on private law, to the neglect of administrative and public law," and that legal education "treats law in isolation from the related social sciences" and "does not give the student a philosophic and historical grounding in the law."[27]

Several months after delivering this report, Fuller attended a meeting of the American Association of Law Schools whose proceedings portray the widely felt "ferment in the law schools." This included an increasing emphasis on the "economic and social matrix of problems[,] ... drafting legal instruments ... [and] alerting students to their responsibilities as citizens and potential civic leaders," as well as a move to install legislation, "long neglected, ... in the programs of a substantial number of schools."[28] The next year, in a paper published in the first volume of the *Journal of Legal Education*, Fuller argued that the "[o]bject of legal education is to convey an understanding of the processes in which the lawyer participates," emphasizing the currently unmet need to provide equal emphasis to legislative and adjudicative processes.[29]

EARLY 1960S: MULTIPLE LEGAL PROCESSES IN LEGAL EDUCATION: AN INITIALLY SLOW MIGRATION TO TORONTO

Around the same period, a different sort of ferment in legal education was happening north of the border. In dramatic act of resistance against the provincial-law society in Ontario, which through the 1940s had asserted an unopposed monopoly over legal education in the province, Caesar Wright led several leading law teachers in 1949 to leave the provincially-controlled law school, Osgoode Hall School, and begin teaching at the University of Toronto. After almost a decade of battle with the law society, in 1957 Wright eventually secured the ability of the University of Toronto graduates to qualify for admission to the law society.[30]

During this early fledgling period and in the two decades of institutional growth that followed it, Wright populated his faculty heavily with graduates from Harvard. By 1962, Wright boasted in a letter that ten out of the fourteen members of the faculty had Harvard training,[31] a remarkable figure given the historically predominant influence of Oxford and Cambridge on other University of Toronto faculties.[32] Two more Harvard graduates, Dick Risk (LLM, 1962) and Arnold Weinrib (LLM, 1966), would soon join. Of these twelve Harvard-educated professors, a good number were influenced by Hart, Sacks, and Fuller, and at least half appear to have played some role in proposed, imagined, successful, or abortive attempts to decentre adjudication in law teaching or through legal scholarship. Despite this initial interest, however, the early 1960s saw only unrealized initiatives. Sometimes abandoned, sometimes suppressed, attempts by individual professors to avoid an "excessive court orientation"[33] flourished only in isolation and were largely rejected by the institutional bodies of the law faculty.

An early proponent, James Milner, who studied with Fuller from 1949 to 1950 and joined the University of Toronto in 1950, was influenced by Fuller's article, and spent the better part of two decades proselytizing Fuller's ideas through his casebook writing, scholarship, and leadership of the Association of Canadian Law Teachers. Nevertheless, these efforts largely did not penetrate into the mainstream during his lifetime.[34] For example, Milner proposed (but never wrote) a book with Bora Laskin on an "Introduction to the Study of Canadian Law." In Milner's words, it would have included "the judicial process, legislative process, the administrative process and the organization of the legal profession [and] some idea of the institutions and their function."[35]

John Willis's commitment to the theme appears to be more sustained, in a way that Wright himself perhaps anticipated. Announcing Willis's return to Toronto after a seven-year hiatus at the University of British Columbia, Wright wrote, "I am hoping that Professor Willis' ability in the public law field may be put to use by the introduction of a new course ... [which] will in some way be related to the legislative process."[36] Just over a year later, Willis presented on a panel on administrative law that was framed by the panel's chair, Walter Gelhorn, as concerned with the "functional limits of adjudication."[37] The conference at which the presentation was made was a US, UK, and Canadian tripartite conference on legal education, attended by Laskin, Wright, Milner, and Albert Abel, and organized by Lon Fuller.[38]

In January 1962, a few months after the conference, Willis and Milner picked up the theme of decentring adjudication, proposing a system of first-year small-group tutorials. Their proposed subject was "legislation – the first-year curriculum places too much emphasis on what courts do – and the topics to be studied (a) interpretation (b) the legislative process (c) drafting. The method of study should be by assigning problems to which the students have to give written answers."[39] The proposal was, however, "unfavourably received." The chief reason for this appears to be reluctance to disrupt the established system of first-year legal instruction: "Abel thought the first year was alright as it stands and LaBrie thought that it was a waste of effort to put more time on the first year students because 'a first year is a first year is a first year.' The consensus was that nothing should be done about this proposal at present. It is mentioned here in order to keep a proposal that will be made again by Willis and

Milner before the eyes of the Faculty."[40] Francis LaBrie's comments not only emblemize a conservative attitude toward the first-year curriculum, but portray a fairly unambitious vision of the law school's role in preparing students for diverse forms of social contribution. It illustrates the attitude of resistance that Willis and Milner might have encountered.

At the same meeting, Bernard Green, a recently hired Harvard graduate (about whom Wright had corresponded with Fuller in March 1960)[41] proposed a new course "with the concurrence of Willis." Green suggested that the second-year course would be "similar to that done by Hart at Harvard" and would "examine over the whole range of legal life, the characteristics and limits of legislative, judicial, administrative and 'free contract' processes as a means of resolving disputes ... [T]he present law school curriculum tends to be fragmented into little bits with the student lacking in the overall picture of what law is about."[42] This proposal, too, was "received without any particular enthusiasm." The author of the minutes (presumably Wright) can almost be heard to sigh as he writes, "It is repeated here because the proposal will be brought up again."[43]

Such reticence is emblematic of the attitudes toward Legal Process ideas of the faculty in the early 1960s. While a number of individuals (Milner, Willis, possibly Laskin, Green, and Bruce Dunlop[44]) seem to have been committed to decentring adjudication, the written record suggests that there was minimal institutional buy-in. By the mid-1960s, however, the tide was starting to turn.

MID-1960S: LEGAL PROCESS IDEAS GAINING PURCHASE

Beginning in the mid-1960s, a greater chorus of professors refers to Legal Process ideas in their proposals to the Committee on Curriculum and Calendar Revision. In a memorandum dated 30 November 1965, Dick Risk proposed a Canadian Legal History course (he had proposed an earlier version in 1963),[45] and in doing so signaled that Legal Process ideas were in the air:

> I think one of my functions in giving this course is to try to tempt the students to think about law somewhat generally. Yet, when I have discussed this question with some of my colleagues, I have been surprised to be told that what I am really teaching

> is "jurisprudence," or "the legal process," or "social legislation," or "modern legislative problems." My own naivety shocks me. I thought that all I was trying to do was to teach legal history properly. I still do.[46]

Risk's course description discloses a concern with multiple legal processes – it emphasizes "the growth and functions of our major legal institutions: the legislatures, the courts, the administrative tribunals, and the legal profession."[47]

The rise of the Legal History course signals an increasing concern with distinctively academic (as opposed to professional) courses being taught at the Faculty. For example, John Willis, around the time of Risk's memorandum, offered some thoughts on these "civilizing," "University" courses:

> I view all 3 options – jurisprudence, comparative law and legal history as trying to do the same thing – viz. to look at law in a wider context. Jurisprudence – how the pretty little pictures in our heads about what we think life is all about affect the law. Comparative Law – how different countries, having different ideas from us of what life and so law, is about – set about reflecting those ideas in institutions that are different from ours. Legal History – how our law, always in the process of becoming, becomes, in the world of "what actually happens" the law we have now and why.[48]

These sentiments reflect almost verbatim comments made by Milner in a 1958 presidential address to the Association of Canadian Law Teachers, when he tied them explicitly to multiple legal processes: "If we are really conscientious ... every course we teach becomes in one sense a course in jurisprudence, legal history, and comparative law. The examination and re-examination of problems in the judicial and legislative processes receive lasting and recurrent attention."[49]

In December 1966, almost five years after his unsuccessful proposal for a first-year Legislation course with Willis, Milner came back to the Curriculum and Calendar Revision Committee, proposing yet again a full first-year course in Legislation. Though not proposing to teach it himself,[50] Milner's proposal recalls Fuller's 1948 essay and his own Fuller-esque comments in his 1963 casebook on contracts:[51]

> The First Year is the most impressionable or formative year of the three and I think we should try to induce some special feeling for the legislative process at this stage, so that our students accept statute law and the legislative process on a footing with the judicial process. […]
>
> The course in Legislation, as I envisage it, would require three hours a week and should introduce the student to the legislative process from the political beginnings through to judicial interpretation and back again.[52]

Milner's proposal was not taken up,[53] though it did not receive the same hostility as his and Willis's proposal did in January 1962. Moreover, as discussed below, it may have played a role in catalyzing a more thoroughgoing investigation into the possibility of such a course a few years later.

If the faculty was not ready for Milner's first-year Legislation course in December 1966, it felt quite differently about a proposed second-year course. In a memorandum to committee chair, John Willis, Stanley Schiff described his part of a cotaught Jurisprudence course as discussing "legal institutions using Hart & Sacks, *The Legal Process* (1958)."[54] Schiff proposed that his part of the course "should be extended into a full-year two-hour course labelled 'The Legal Process' which would "emphasize the interlocking relationships of the institutions and the nature and techniques of decision-making appropriate to each."[55] The second-year Legal Process course appears in the Faculty of Law course calendar in 1967–68, with a somewhat abbreviated version of the description that Schiff had proposed to the committee.[56] By 1969, the course description had expanded to include more functional and problem-solving elements.[57] Schiff would continue to teach the second-year course until the late 1980s.[58]

LATE 1960S: INCURSIONS INTO THE FIRST-YEAR CURRICULUM

Although Milner's December 1966 proposal was unsuccessful, it may have paved the way for future developments. In November 1967, the Curriculum Committee of the Faculty of Law was formed. The committee, composed of Edmund Alexander, Bruce Dunlop, Frank Iacobucci, and Stanley Schiff, and chaired by Dick Risk, undertook a major revisioning of the curriculum, with a special emphasis on the first year.[59] In September 1968, the committee began work on a report ultimately published in May 1969 (it would become known as the Risk Report). The report is a magisterial reflection on the nature and objectives of the law school, the essence of professional education, and the needs to reform its curriculum to attain its goals, which, Risk writes, are captured by Llewellyn's argument in "The Study of Law as a Liberal Art" that "law government is a service institution: in service lies its soul – service for client or cause or class, or for some dream which embraces all classes and even a world."[60]

In summarizing the more granular objectives of the law school, Risk placed ideas relating to multiple legal processes front and centre. The report's first listed objective was to cultivate an "understanding of the functions and relations of legal institutions," including how different processes expressed social values.[61] Students would develop "the ability to isolate and unravel problems ... into forms appropriate for decision according to the terms of the legal institutions or processes."[62] The introduction to judicial, legislative, and administrative processes would include an introduction to the "form, functions, and work-products of the institutions."[63]

As a result, perhaps, of the objectives being articulated this way, Risk proposed that the first year should include a mandatory, three-credit course entitled An Introduction to the Legislative and Administrative Processes. Recalling Milner and Fuller, and echoing the earlier efforts of Willis, Risk wrote:

> The present curriculum for First Year is distorted by the emphasis on cases, the common law, and the adjudicative process. The purpose of this course is obvious: to remedy this distortion by introducing the legislative and administrative processes ... Legislatures and legislation should be dominant. Some of the possible topics are the structure, procedure, products and functions of legislatures, and statutory interpretation. The administrative process and judicial control of administrative tribunals should be introduced only briefly.[64]

The main recommendation of the first-year introductory course was accepted.[65] Milner and Willis's proposal from 1962, to institute seminars on Legislation, reprised again by Milner in 1966 with an explicit aim to correct excessive court orientation, had finally made its way into the first-year curriculum – although Milner would never live to see it: he died suddenly in June 1969 of a heart attack on a plane flying between Toronto and Ottawa.

1970s: RISE AND FALL OF THE INTRODUCTORY COURSE

The introductory course in the legislative and administrative processes proposed by the Risk Report was taught seven times, from 1970–71 to 1976–77. In all but the first year, when it was cotaught by Angela Swan and Desmond Morton, Dick Risk delivered it.[66] The course appears to have experienced three separate iterations – at least as reflected in its title – before it was discontinued in 1977. In the 1980s, a related course – Public Law – was taught by Risk and Hudson Janisch.

In its first iteration, the introductory course was named as anticipated. The course description of Introduction to Legislative and Administrative Processes was somewhat sparse, but reflected a functional orientation and a concern with multiple legal processes. The course offered "introductory materials designed to illustrate the problems of legislation as a means of achieving any desired goal; the context in which the legislative process operates; the relation between the legislature, the courts and administrative bodies and some problems of drafting and interpretation."[67] It was a full-year course, two hours per week per semester, in contrast with Contracts, Property, and Torts, which were also full-year courses but with three hours per week per semester.

In its second iteration, 1973–74 and 1974–75, the course title changed to The Development of Canadian Law and Legal Institutions. The course description removed the purposive function of understanding legislation "as a means to achieving any desired goal" and shifted towards a somewhat more descriptive account of the "characteristic structures and functions of these institutions, and the process of creation and change." Emphasis, nevertheless, remained "on legislation and public authorities," and on the development and context of Canadian law and legal institutions. The course was shortened to one semester, three hours a week.[68]

Two years later, in 1975–76, Risk renamed the course once again, to An Introduction to Statutes and Administrative Law. In the course description there is a whisper of an allusion to Fullerian inquiries into the "usual forms, functions and limits" of statutes and administrative agencies, and it also includes the context of "their expansion during the twentieth century." For the first time, both statutory interpretation and "the control of administrative agencies by courts" are mentioned.[69] This course was offered for two years.

The course descriptions move from the functional – a concern with how legislation can achieve goals – to the more descriptive, and finally to a more granular analysis of the relationship between courts and other legal processes. The course materials reflect this progression: chapter titles in the first iteration foregrounded the legal processes, such as "The Power of the Legislature"; "The Common Law and Legislation"; and "An Introduction to the Administrative Process."[70] By the end, in 1976, the course began with four chapters reflecting substantive and historical examples before moving into explicit consideration of legislation and its relationship to the courts, including themes of statutory interpretation and judicial control of administrative action.[71] The 1976 materials contain a one-page introduction to the course that almost directly channels the 1969 Risk Report and the critiques of legal education voiced by Milner, Fuller, Willis, and others:

> The major purpose of this course is to introduce statutes and administrative law. The reason for giving it is simply that *statutes and administrative agencies are a large element of the contemporary legal order and the work of lawyers*. This reason, and *the lengthy failure of law schools to respond*, are elaborated in the four readings. […]
>
> The emphasis will be … [on] the distinctive functions and limits of statutes contrasted to the common law, the effect of extensive legislation on the functions of the common law and courts, the interpretation of statutes by courts, and the control by courts of administrative agencies. *This emphasis reflects the ways in which most lawyers usually deal with statutes … while demonstrating that common law and courts are not the only kind of law and legal institution*.[72]

In this passage, Risk not only signals to students the shortcomings of conventional legal education – its overemphasis on the common law system, and its failure to reflect what lawyers actually do (engagement with statute law and drafting of planning documents) – but also tells students that they will be getting something very different.

While this theme seems particularly well developed by the 1976 course, there are indications from the examinations of the courses from across the years that Risk was trying to cultivate this different approach throughout the course's multiple iterations. Risk examined students on their understanding of the relationship between courts, the legislatures, and administrative agencies, deploying related fact patterns with an increasing emphasis on history and strategies of statutory interpretation. The examinations reflect Risk's evolving interest in legal history (Risk was greatly influenced by Willard Hurst at Wisconsin, on whose class he sat in and with whom he dined weekly during his sabbatical in 1969–70)[73] and a heightened emphasis on context and critical reflection on the interrelation of statutes, courts, and administrative agencies.[74]

Despite Risk's evident investment in the course and its ideas, the course was discontinued after 1976–77. Today, Risk refers to the course as a "failure": the students were not engaged, and Risk felt that the materials did not fully work.[75] Perhaps it was just too different from the dominant case-based approach followed in the rest of the first-year curriculum.

A few years later, in 1980–81, when Hudson Janisch arrived on faculty, and owing probably to Janisch's own interests, a different version of the course was instituted: Public Law. In its early years, Bora Laskin and Katherine Swinton taught it alongside Risk and Janisch; Risk and Janisch taught it for four years, and it was offered for the last time in 1984–85 by Risk, Janisch, and Alan Brudner. Following a recommendation by a curriculum committee chaired by Katherine Swinton, it was replaced by Constitutional Law in 1985–86.[76] Schiff continued to teach the upper-year Legal Process course, based substantially on the Hart and Sacks materials, until the 1989–90 academic year.

Regarding the first-year introductory course, the sense of it being a failure appears to have been shared. For example, as Risk related to me, a colleague amenable to the project forecasted that the course would not last, saying to Risk at the time that Contracts, Property, and Torts courses would "bury you alive." The successive retitling of the course and its downgrading from a four-credit, two-semester course to a three-credit, one-semester course might indicate attempts to accommodate the course to an unreceptive audience. Even the attempt to revitalize the course's ideas, through the Public Law course, seem somewhat doomed to failure. Writing years later, the dean of law, Ron Daniels, outlining an "exceedingly ambitious" mandate to design a "cutting-edge curriculum for the next millennium," wrote, "I recognize that there is likely to be little excitement about a resurrection of the old public law course, but I worry nonetheless that the factors which led to the introduction of the public law course in the first place (excessive attention in the first year programme on private law and appellate cases, the need to concentrate on the role of the regulatory state) are equally valid, if not more so, today."[77]

Daniels' words seem to suggest that the Public Law course (and perhaps, its antecedent introductory courses) was not remembered favourably throughout the law faculty. They also suggest that the premonition that Contracts, Property, and Torts would "bury alive" the introductory course appears largely borne out. Not only does Daniels cite the overemphasis on appellate case law and under emphasis on the regulatory state, but as a factual matter, from 1985 until the early 2000s, the standard first-year curriculum was, without fail, composed entirely of these three core private law courses, supplemented with courses in Criminal Law, Constitutional Law, Civil Procedure, and a course that covered perspectives on law, all taught as part of the short module Bridges program.[78] The felt need to correct the overemphasis on appellate adjudication, identified in the 1969 Risk Report, persisted throughout this period. A curriculum committee report in 1986 recommended that "the Dean strike a Committee to explore possible opportunities for student involvement in the processes of the legislative branch of government."[79] What followed was a two-decades-long preoccupation with the theme, as revealed in curriculum committee reports of 1991, 1996, 1999, 2001, and 2009.

LEGAL PROCESS FOR A NEW CENTURY: CIVIL PROCEDURE AND ADMINISTRATIVE LAW

Throughout the 1970s, when Risk was teaching the introductory course, the first-year curriculum also included Civil Procedure. Civil Procedure taught students the content of rules governing the litigation process, and so Risk's course, emphasizing legislative and administrative processes (which includes how rules are enacted, interpreted, and applied), could have been complementary. Once the introductory course disappeared from the curriculum, Civil Procedure began to develop into "a broader, more policy-oriented course, on the procedures of litigation."[80] In 1991, a special committee on the first-year curriculum, chaired by Hudson Janisch, recommended further broadening to "include an examination of administrative and legislative procedures and non-adjudicative modes of dispute resolution."[81] Subsequently, instructors in Civil Procedure made "significant changes" to the course, including "comparing and contrasting different conceptions of procedure and various dispute resolution processes, including adjudication, mediation, negotiation, and mixed models."[82] The committee's other recommendation – to augment the focus on legislation and administrative law – was comparatively underemphasized.

In 1996, the Curriculum Committee chaired by Patrick Macklem addressed the Civil Procedure course in its compendious response to Dean Daniels's mandate letter. The Macklem Report summarized past broadening of Civil Procedure and recommended further broadening in content and course title, suggesting "that the course be renamed, 'Legal Process,' to emphasis its differences from the traditional rules-oriented Civil Procedure Course." Emphasis was placed on a conceptual deepening of judicial processes and their relationship to professional ethics and responsibility, as well as alternative dispute mechanisms. A concern with subjects more aligned with the Risk course – "statutory interpretation, and analyses of legal structuring of democratic and political processes" – was present, but secondary.[83]

It took until 2002–03 for the Civil Procedure course to be renamed Legal Process. The delay in part might be due to a preoccupation by the Curriculum Committee on largely upper-year issues for a couple of years.[84] In November 1999, Dean Daniels tasked Kent Roach, chair of the First Year Curriculum Committee, with a review of the first-year curriculum, in light of the sense that "the promise of reform set out in the Macklem Report remain[ed] unfulfilled." The committee was specifically asked to reconsider the basket of courses in light of "the effect that globalization, technological innovation, growth of the administrative state, and decline of the professional ideal have had on the nature of law and legal institutions."[85] In a later document distributed to faculty, Daniels reiterated the gap left in the curriculum by the disappearance of the Janisch-Risk course from years ago, again alluding to the causes for its disappearance and describing the continued need for "rigorous examination of public law and its supporting institutions." He noted that "recently some students have expressed concern about the need for an introductory course to public institutions and public law (including statutory interpretation) that would loosely track the content of the old public law course."[86]

The report by the committee chaired by Kent Roach – who himself had published a significant article on the Legal Process as recently as 1997[87] – was thorough, including an appendix that outlined the history of curriculum committees at the Faculty of Law going back to the 1969 Risk Report.[88] The Roach Report reiterated the recommendation of the Macklem Report that the course be retitled Legal Process.[89] The course would expose students to the procedures surrounding litigation, but also to alternative processes like negotiation and mediation. The new approach would enable students to evaluate the strengths and weaknesses of adversarial litigation and avoid portraying "a simplistic view of the role of lawyers" as solely concerned with that process.[90]

While this represented a broadening of the existing Civil Procedure course, and a de-emphasis on teaching rules for their own sake,[91] it also afforded a relatively marginal place to legislative and administrative processes. While administrative agencies and legislatures were mentioned,[92] the emphasis remained squarely on the litigation process and its alternatives. This paradigm, no doubt, invited a broader outlook on the subject than what had previously existed,[93] but the emphasis was clearly on alternative dispute resolution, rather than a survey of alternative non-adjudicative processes for solving diverse legal problems. The conventional rules of civil procedure continued to figure prominently.[94] The impression given by the Roach Report is that the concerns dating to the 1991 Janisch Report, as well as a novel transnational preoccupation, were the primary considerations.[95] Within a year, however, the ambitions of the Roach Report were deemed somewhat unworkable, and a 2001 report by Associate Dean Mayo Moran (she would succeed Daniels as dean in 2006) recommended reducing the course in length with a "narrower focus on the structure of adjudication and its alternatives."[96]

For the six years, beginning in 2002–03, during which that iteration of Legal Process was offered as a first-year course, it was taught by a wide variety of instructors. It was offered in the first semester for just one semester, unlike the other mandatory first-year courses, which were full-year and could be easily identified as either public or private law. As a result, Legal Process was the only first-year course in which the December test was a final grade rather than "to assist only" (i.e., the grade would only count if it helped the student in the final grade calculation in April and was therefore "fail safe"). Angela Fernandez, who taught the course in 2005 and 2007, recalls that the focus on the one "real" grade created quite a lot of distracting anxiety.[97] According to Fernandez, its different content and organization marked it out as "separate but unequal," as there was a perception that while it was the only course with a grade that "really counted," its content was perceived as less serious and challenging than the other core courses, only deserving one semester of study and lacking a core doctrinal focus.[98]

From 2002–03 to 2008–09, there were a total of sixteen sections of the Legal Process course (two sections a year for the first two years, three sections thereafter), taught by no less than nine different instructors (Ayelet Shachar, Jennifer Schulz, Lorne Sossin, Kenneth Jull, Trevor Farrow, Angela Fernandez, Albert Yoon, Adam Dodek, and Simon Stern). Not surprisingly with such a large group of instructors, there was a range of approaches, with the examinations for the period ranging between an emphasis on the rules of civil procedure, to broader, more creative approaches.[99] Judging from the examinations of the period, the reports of various curriculum committees made recommendations to concentrate on alternative dispute resolution measures, and transnational concerns were followed to some extent. The theme of institutional competence continued to appear – although proportionately much less frequently than it had in the earlier, Risk days of the course. Nevertheless, the overwhelming emphasis remained on the examination of the rules of civil procedure, albeit with a decidedly critical bent in many cases.[100]

Following an influential Curriculum Committee report chaired by Sujit Choudhry in 2009,[101] the course was renamed Legal Process, Professionalism, and Ethics (LPPE) in 2009–10. The main purpose of doing so was to integrate the evaluation of the material in what had previously been a bridge week in professionalism and ethics, although the two parts of the course were imagined to be taught separately.[102] As with the Roach Report, it was anticipated that the LPPE course would de-emphasize the teaching of the rules of civil procedure – these rules "could be studied in an upper year elective course" while the first-year course would "emphasize the foundations of the legal system, dispute resolution, and access to justice."[103]

More interestingly, perhaps, for our purposes, are the comments in the Choudhry Report on Administrative Law, which Choudhry proposed to make a mandatory first-year course. There is a lively discussion of many of the themes and objectives dating to the Risk Report. For example, Administrative Law is said to involve "the rule of law and the separation of powers, procedural justice and the duty of fairness, bias and independence, standard of review, discretion, rulemaking and regulatory regimes, tribunals, and statutory interpretation."[104] These pedagogical goals reflect the older concerns with the legislative and administrative processes and their relationship to courts and the broader constitutional order. This connection is even more evident from an excerpted letter in the report from "a majority of the Administrative Law group":

> There is a broad agreement that we need a public law course in first year that addresses the nature of the regulatory state and its place in the constitutional order (i.e., separation of powers – legislature/executive/judiciary), the rule of law, statutory interpretation. However, the old public law course failed to serve this need; that is, delivering an understanding of what we will refer to as "public law" issues […]
>
> [A]dministrative law should not be used as a vehicle for teaching these issues – it *is* these issues.[105]

The Administrative Law course seemed to be an attempt to solve the perennial problem of the overexposure to the adjudicative processes and its corrupting effects. Dean Moran's mandate letter to Choudhury made an oblique reference to these longstanding concerns with adjudication. She wrote, "Our first year curriculum is modelled after the core program of predominantly private law courses devised by Dean Langdell of Harvard more than a century ago. Although our program has evolved over time, the Langdellian structure remains central."[106] The Choudhry Report's goal of encouraging students to understand "the sense of the institutions of their role in the constitutional order and of their relationship to other institutions" could have just as easily animated Risk's earlier courses. Introduction to Legislative and Administrative Processes, Public Law, and Administrative Law can be seen as analogous attempts to pluralize the legal processes to which law students are exposed, to help students better understand their interrelation, and to disrupt the conventional emphasis on appellate cases and doctrine in the putatively core courses.

The report was also transparent in its strategy for achieving the success of the first-year Administrative Law course. Dean Moran referred to the "fail[ure] of the old public law course,"[107] and the appendix to the Choudhry Report explained why it rejected the idea of requiring a course in public law similar to the Risk and Janisch course in the following terms: it "would likely lack coherence, internally and across sections, would be difficult to staff, could be devalued by students compared to other courses, and would likely not have faculty support."[108] Instead, Administrative Law was forecasted as succeeding in part because it "is a long-standing course with a coherent and well-defined legal core, and would likely not suffer from status degradation in terms of student perception," and would have "faculty leaders" – the majority of the Administrative Law Group in support of the proposal.[109] In these considerations, we can infer a more complete articulation of the reasons why Risk's course was considered a "failure." The emphasis on an established doctrinal core with faculty champions are elements offered almost as prophylactics against the Administrative Law course being "buried alive" by the well-established core courses in the first-year curriculum.[110]

For five years, from 2009–10 to 2014–15, Administrative Law was a mandatory first-year course at the University of Toronto taught in second semester, and Legal Process, Professionalism, and Ethics was taught in the first term. Judging roughly from the limited set of examinations available for the five out of seven professors who taught LPPE during that period,[111] it appears that the proportion of broader themes decreased, while the proportion of questions on the rules and principles of civil procedure increased.[112] As for Administrative Law, to the extent that it was taught as the judicial review of administrative action with its preoccupations with reviewing standards, it would have been almost completely case oriented and so likely would have done little or nothing to further the goal of decentring adjudication. In any event, first-year Administrative Law at the University of Toronto did not prove as enduring as the Choudhry Report had anticipated. In 2015–16, it was removed from the first-year curriculum and returned to the upper-year program.[113] LPPE remained for one year, and thereafter reverted to the title Legal Process. In recent years, the trend of an emphasis on civil procedure continues.[114]

It appears that neither Administrative Law nor Legal Process have completely addressed the perennial concerns of the overemphasis of appellate cases and the predominance of the private law curriculum. Blaine Baker himself tried once (in 2013–14),[115] and had he lived longer, he might have made greater strides. His anticipated 2018–19 Legal Process syllabus was compendious in its pluralistic embrace of multiple legal processes. The readings reflect a life's work dedicated to decentring adjudication and replacing it with the facilitative, purposive, and constitutive elements of multiple legal processes, in all their minutiae.[116] Perhaps more impactfully from a student perspective, Baker anticipated evaluating the course in part through an in-term research paper and a twelve-hour take-home examination, devices arguably more amenable to reflection and engagement with theoretical themes than the standard in-person three-hour examination. Sadly, Baker never lived to teach that iteration of the course, a fact that may be emblematic of the perennially unrealized aspirations of diversifying legal processes in first-year teaching at the University of Toronto Faculty of Law.

CONCLUSION

The ghosts of Harvard continue to haunt the first-year curriculum at Toronto. These include not only the primary ghosts of Langdell and Holmes – the former, expressed through the vestigial dominance of appellate cases, doctrinal cores, and the "triumphant"[117] categories of Contracts, Property, and Torts; the latter, the echoes of the faculty's realist and pragmatist origins.[118] The Harvard iconoclasts – Fuller, Hart, and Sacks – also rattle around. The influence of these secondary ghosts are reflected in the continually revived aspiration to decentre adjudication in its many guises: the Fullerian social architect ideal; the Legal Process movement; and a commitment to "public law," with its concern for statutes, administrative agencies, and judicial review – the three branches of government for which legal processes are either analogues or avatars.

What Milner, Dunlop, Schiff, Green, and others brought from Harvard in the 1950s and 1960s has motivated successive generations of curricular architects at the Faculty, from Risk to Macklem to Roach to Choudhry (many of whom are themselves graduates of Harvard Law School.)[119] Through these curriculum committee reports, one can hear and see the influence of a prior generation – Milner and Willis, who were denied their early chances to innovate, and even Lon Fuller, whose prescient 1947 Preliminary Report on Legal Education and campaign for the "lawyer as social architect" never flourished in his lifetime.[120] To the extent that curricular debate is the law school's "primary heuristic device,"[121] the aspirational pronouncements in the curriculum committee reports express what might be a more commonly felt disquiet with the Holmesian and Langdellian juggernauts and the many challenges in escaping them. The secondary ghosts of Harvard animate the continual impetus by deans, committee chairs and members, and faculty members at large to refresh and reimagine how legal education can cultivate legal thought, professionalism, and citizenship.

Yet even these voices become obscured over time: Introduction to Legislative and Administrative Processes is renamed, reissued, and eventually revived as Public Law, only to become transmuted into Constitutional Law, which becomes canonized – now a persistent, "core" feature of the curriculum, a rare enduring success of curricular reform – just as its antecedent becomes the emblem for failure. The signature innovations of the twenty-first century either prove not as resilient as hoped – Administrative Law's conspicuous disappearance from the first-year curriculum after just five years – or to only partially resist the enchantment of doctrinal legal education (Legal Process's continued preoccupation with the rules of civil procedure, or Administrative Law's emphasis on judicial review of administrative action).

In more ways than one, the premonition of Risk's colleague around the release of the Risk Report was accurate: Contracts, Property, and Torts by far outlasted Risk's introductory course. Not only did Public Law become the metonym for curricular failure, but the salient characteristics of the dominant first-year private law offerings – "long-standing course[s] with a coherent and well-defined legal core" – became the standards against which to appraise the likelihood of future success. Despite the successive attempts to learn from past failures, the aspiration to place the other legal processes on an equal footing with adjudication remain unrealized. The "objectives of Contracts, Property and Torts," as Risk wrote in 1969 – "the skills traditionally associated with the case system, the doctrine and problems distinctive to each, and an introduction to the judicial process"[122] – continue to weigh down the insurrection. Yet one suspects, as surely as Wright must have felt when the first stirrings arose, that it may never truly go away.

NOTES

I am grateful to the editors for organizing the symposium and the collection, and for their written comments on the paper, especially those by Angela Fernandez. I would like to thank Tyler Mäkinen, Sara Badawi, Madeleine Douglas, and Talya Bertler (all JD students at Western University) for their research and editorial support. I am very grateful to Dick Risk for illuminating conversations and a careful read of an earlier draft.

1 Kunal M. Parker, "Writing Legal History Then and Now: A Brief Reflection," *American Journal of Legal History* 56, no. 1 (2016): 170–1.

2 Bruce A. Kimball, "The Proliferation and Transformation of Harvard's Case Method in the United States, 1870s–1990s," in Susan Bartie and David Sandomierski, eds., *American Legal Education Abroad* (New York University Press, 2021), 1–13.

3 See Alfred Z. Reed, *Present-Day Law Schools in the United States and Canada*, Carnegie Foundation Bulletin 21 (Boston: Merrymount Press, 1928), 256.

4 See William M. Sullivan et al., *Educating Lawyers: Preparation for the Profession of Law* (San Francisco: Jossey-Bass, 2007); Elizabeth Mertz, *The Language of Law School: Learning to "Think Like a Lawyer"* (New York: Oxford University Press, 2007).

5 Kimball, "The Proliferation and Transformation."

6 See William N. Eskridge Jr and Philip P Frickey, "An Historical and Critical Introduction to *The Legal Process*," in Henry M Hart Jr and Albert M Sacks, *The Legal Process: Basic Problems in the Making and Application of Law* (Westbury, NY: Foundation Press, 1994), lii, lxxix (Hart encouraged his students to become "expert in the arts and science of ordering human affairs"). See also Kent Roach, "What's New and Old about the Legal Process," *University of Toronto Law Journal* 47, no. 3 (1997): 368 ("[t]he most striking feature of *The Legal Process* is its breadth and expansive understanding of the different skills that lawyers will require to serve their public and private clients").

7 The materials were produced in mimeographed form beginning in the early 1950s, receiving constant editing between 1955 and 1958. The 1958 version circulated widely as a "tentative edition." That tentative edition was reprinted with a substantial introduction by Eskridge and Frickey. See Henry M. Hart, Jr and Albert M. Sacks, *The Legal Process: Basic Problems in the Making and Application of Law*, tentative edition (Cambridge: s.n, 1958). The Bora Laskin Law Library at the University of

Toronto has copies of both the earlier and later publications. On the history of publication, see William N. Eskridge Jr and Philip P. Frickey, "The Making of *The Legal Process*," *Harvard Law Review* 107, no. 8 (1994): 2041–5.

8 Neil Duxbury, "Faith in Reason: The Process Tradition in American Jurisprudence," *Cardozo Law Review* 15, no. 3 (1993): 658. See also Charles L. Barzun, "The Forgotten Foundations of Hart and Sacks," *Virginia Law Review* 99, no. 1 (2013): 9; Roach, "What's New and Old," 366, 372.

9 Lon L. Fuller, "The Forms and Limits of Adjudication," *Harvard Law Review* 92, no. 2 (1978): 353. One of Fuller's concerns was the inappropriate resort to adjudication for "polycentric" problems, including economic problems, which he felt were better dealt with by managerial discretion or contract. On the role of lawyers and law professors in administrative boards, see Robert W. Gordon, "Professors and Policymakers: Yale Law School Faculty in the New Deal and After," in Anthony T. Kronman, ed., *History of the Yale Law School* (New Haven, CT: Yale University Press, 2004), 85, 104; Jerold S. Auerbach, *Unequal Justice: Lawyers and Social Change in Modern America* (New York: Oxford University Press, 1976), 217–9.

10 Other studies have explored the export of Legal Process ideas to other jurisdictions. See e.g., Susan Bartie, *Free Hands and Minds: Pioneering Australian Legal Scholars* (Oxford: Hart, 2019) (postwar Australia); William N. Eskridge Jr, "Nino's Nightmare: Legal Process Theory as a Jurisprudence of Toggling between Facts and Norms," *Saint Louis University Law Journal* 57, no. 4 (2013): 905 (Israel); Anna Spain, "Using International Dispute Resolution to Address the Compliance Question in International Law," *Georgetown Journal of International Law* 40, no. 3 (2009): 811 (United Nations international dispute resolution in North Korea).

11 Kimball, "The Proliferation and Transformation," 21.

12 See Grey, "Langdell's Orthodoxy," *University of Pittsburgh Law Review* 45, no. 1 (1983): 1; Duncan Kennedy, "Toward an Historical Understanding of Legal Consciousness: The Case of Classical Legal Thought in America, 1850–1940," *Research in Law and Sociology* 3 (1980): 3. For an in-depth look at one protagonist in this story, James Milner, and his relationship to Lon Fuller, see David Sandomierski, "Catalytic Agents? Lon Fuller, James Milner, and the Lawyer as Social Architect, 1950–1969," *University of Toronto Law Journal* 71, no. 1 (2021): 91–125.

13 Compare Harry Arthurs, *Connecting the Dots: the Life of an Academic Lawyer* (Montreal; Kingston: McGill-Queen's University Press, 2019), 136 ("The agenda of liberal legal education ... probably never did achieve the transformation of legal thought, culture, practice, and institutions that we all hoped for."); Roderick A. Macdonald, "Curricular Development in the 1980s: A Perspective," *Journal of Legal Education* 32, no. 4 (1982): 590 ("a concerted effort [of curricular renewal] ... will lead ... to a continual and creative rediscovery of ourselves. In the end, can there be a higher mission for legal education?").

14 See generally Angela Fernandez, "Legal History as the History of Legal Texts," in Markus D. Dubber and Christopher Tomlins, eds., *The Oxford Handbook of Legal History* (Oxford University Press, 2018).

15 Macdonald, "Curricular Development," 569.

16 Fernandez, "Legal History as the History of Legal Texts," 13.

17 Robert W. Gordon, "Critical Legal Histories," *Stanford Law Review* 36, no. 1 (1984): 120–3; Susanna L. Blumenthal, "Of Mandarins, Legal Consciousness, and the Cultural Turn in US Legal History: Robert W. Gordon –1984." Critical Legal Histories. *Stanford Law Review* 36: 57–125; *Law & Social Inquiry* 37, no. 1: 167.

18 See Mertz, *The Language of Law School*; David Sandomierski, *Aspiration and Reality in Legal Education* (Toronto: University of Toronto Press, 2020).

19 Gordon, "Critical Legal Histories," 124. See also Robert W. Gordon, "The Case for (and Against) Harvard," review of *Logic and Experience: The Origin of Modern American Legal Education*, by William P. LaPiana, *Michigan Law Review* 93, no. 6 (1995): 1244.

20 G. Blaine Baker, "Ordering the Urban Canadian Law Office and Its Entrepreneurial Hinterland, 1825 to 1875," *University of Toronto Law Journal* 48, no. 2 (1998): 175.

21 G. Blaine Baker and Jim Philips, "Introduction," in *A History of Canadian Legal Thought: Collected Essays of R.C.B. Risk*, edited by G. Blaine Baker and Jim Philips (Toronto: Osgoode Society for Canadian Legal History, 2006), 14–18.

22 Richard Janda, "Traces of Blaine Baker upon McGill's Faculty of Law," infra, 83–115.

23 G. Blaine Baker, "Character-Building at Multiple Sites of Justice: Administration and Teaching as Text, Scholarship as Ethical and Political Action," in *The Unbounded Level of the Mind: Rod Macdonald's Legal Imagination*, edited by Richard Janda, Rosalie Jukier, and Daniel Jutras (Montreal; Kingston, ON: McGill-Queen's Press, 2015), 217–8

(Administrative Process "emphasizes the interactive relations of bureaucrats with each other and with their regulatees, the range of hard, soft, and implicit forms in which administrative norms can be expressed, and especially inter-and transsystemic comparisons among delegated governments-in-miniature or sites of bureaucratic justice. I did something similar in course development with a 'legal process' class in the 2013–14 academic year").

24 Baker contributed this insight to me through email correspondence and in-person meetings throughout my doctoral dissertation, alerting me to John Willis's own reflections on such tensions. See John Willis, "Canadian Administrative Law in Retrospect," *University of Toronto Law Journal* 24, no. 3 (1974): 227. See Sandomierski, *Aspiration and Reality in Legal Education*, 317 (n 789).

25 Esther Lucille Brown, *Lawyers, Law Schools and The Public Service* (New York: Russel Sage Foundation, 1948), 5; Harold D. Lasswell and Myres S. McDougal, "Legal Education and Public Policy," *Yale Law Journal* 52, no. 2 (1943): 203; Albert James Harno and Reginald Heber Smith, *Legal Education in the United States* (San Francisco: Bancroft-Whitney, 1953), 181–2; Walter Gellhorn, "The Law School's Responsibility for Training Public Servants," *University of Chicago Law Review* 9, no. 3 (1942): 474.

26 Eskridge and Frickey, "The Making of," 2041–5.

27 Preliminary Statement of the Committee on Legal Education of the Harvard Law School, 1 March 1947, Lon Fuller, chair (on file with author), iv–v. Robert Summers discusses the report briefly in his intellectual biography of Fuller. See Robert S. Summers, *Lon L. Fuller* (Stanford: Stanford University Press, 1984), 137.

28 Harno and Smith, *Legal Education in the United States*, 181–2. See also "Proceedings of the Annual Meeting of the Association," *Association of American Law Schools Proceedings of the Annual Meeting* 7 (1947): 7 (indicating the date as 28–30 December 1947).

29 Lon L. Fuller, "What the Law Schools Can Contribute to the Making of Lawyers," *Journal of Legal Education* 1, no. 2 (1948): 192.

30 See generally C. Ian Kyer and Jerome E. Bickenbach, *The Fiercest Debate: Cecil A. Wright, the Benchers, and Legal Education in Ontario, 1923–1957* (Toronto: University of Toronto Press, 1987).

31 Letter from Wright to Claude Bissell, president of the University of Toronto, 14 November 1962, Accession A82/0041, box 032, School Correspondence 1962–63(4), University of Toronto Archives (University of Toronto Faculty of Law Records), Toronto. These included Wright

himself (SJD, 1927), John Willis (who studied as a "special student" with Felix Frankfurter in 1932, obtaining no degree), Bora Laskin (LLM, 1937), Albert Abel (LLM, 1937, SJD 1943), Stanley Edwards (LLM, 1947), James Milner (LLM, 1950), Ronald St John Macdonald (LLM, 1955), Bruce Dunlop (LLM, 1957), Bernard Green (LLM, 1958), and Stanley Schiff (LLM, 1961). See Harvard Law School, *Alumni Directory of the Harvard Law School* 1973 (Cambridge, MA: Harvard Law School, 1973), 518–21.

32 See Martin L. Friedland, *The University of Toronto: A History* (Toronto: University of Toronto Press, 2002), 302–5, 326, 414.

33 James B. Milner, "One Canadian View of the Case Methods," *Journal of the Society of Public Teachers of Law (new series)* 3, no. 1 (1955): 32.

34 See Sandomierski, "Catalytic Agents?"

35 Letter from James Milner to Lon Fuller, 3 March 1959, Clara Thomas Archive (Milner Papers, 1992–014/005 (149)), Toronto.

36 Letter from Cecil A. Wright (no recipient), 21 April 1959, Accession A82/0041, box 027, "Faculty – Memos 2," University of Toronto Archives (University of Toronto Faculty of Law Records), Toronto.

37 Walter Gellhorn, "Summary of Colloquy on Administrative Law," *Journal of the Society of Public Teachers of Law (new series)* 6, no. 1 (1961): 73–4. See also Nathanial L. Nathanson, "American Administrative Law," *Journal of Legal Education* 14, no. 1 (1961): 45 ("The Judicialization of the Administrative Process"); John Willis, "Canadian Administrative Law," *Journal of Legal Education* 14, no. 1 (1961): 59 ("Extent to Which Administrative Process Judicialized"); Harry Street, "English Administrative Law," *Journal of Legal Education* 14, no. 1 (1961): 66 ("Legislative and Judicial Aspects of Administrative Action").

38 At the conference, Fuller mentioned the concept of the "lawyer as social architect" and the interaction of means and ends. See *Journal of Legal Education* 14 (1961): 116, 167.

39 Committee on Curriculum and Calendar Revision, Faculty of Law, University of Toronto, "Matters For Consideration – 1962," Accession A82/0041, box 030, "Law School 1961–62 (5)" University of Toronto Archives (University of Toronto Faculty of Law Records), Toronto, 1.

40 Ibid.

41 Wright's letter displays what Eric Adams has called the "casual" antisemitism of the period: "I am curious to know why, if there be any reason, Green has not been lined up for some teaching post either in Canada or the United States. I have a very high regard for his capabilities and, indeed, I have asked him to come up and see me some time in the next two weeks. My only reason for having any hesitancy about him was due to the fact

that I was a little cautious about obtaining an undue proportion of our own graduates, as well as the fear of an undue proportion of persons with, shall I say, the same *ethnic background*." Letter from Wright to Fuller, 14 March 1960, Caesar Wright Papers, B1982-0028, box 003, University of Toronto Archives, Toronto [emphasis added]. Fuller's response on 16 March also indicates that "the ethnic issue may also be a minor factor" in Green being unable to find a suitable academic position in the US." Letter from Fuller to Wright, 16 March 1960, Caesar Wright Papers, Accession B1982-0028, box 003, University of Toronto Archives, Toronto. On "casual and prevalent" antisemitism, see Eric M. Adams, "The Dean Who Went to Law School: Crossing Borders and Searching for Purpose in North American Legal Education, 1930–1950," *Alberta Law Review* 54, no. 2 (2016): 1.

42 Committee on Curriculum and Calendar Revision, Faculty of Law, University of Toronto, "Matters For Consideration – 1962," Accession A82/0041, box 030, "Law School 1961–62 (5)" University of Toronto Archives (University of Toronto Faculty of Law Records), Toronto, 2.

43 Ibid. The resistance to the legislation seminar and the Legal Process course does not seem to flow from a resistance to any curricular innovation. At the same meeting, a proposal for a course in Civil Liberties by Laskin was accepted. Faculty of Law, University of Toronto, "Report of Committee on Curriculum and Calendar Revision" (n.d), Accession A82/0041, box 030, "Law School 1961–62," University of Toronto Archives (University of Toronto Faculty of Law Records), Toronto. This document appears in the same folder as "Matters for Consideration – 1962" so is presumably a report following the discussion of those matters.

44 Another proposal at the level of the individual course was made by Bruce Dunlop – who was a student at Harvard during the 1956–57 academic year, when a highly influential "Legal Philosophy Discussion Group" was held, out of which emerged a number of Legal Process classics (Eskridge and Frickey, " The Making of," 2048–9). He wrote to Wright with a proposal to change the teaching of Evidence so as to "reduce the amount of time spent in reading and analyzing cases," emphasizing that "[o]ne of the main aims of law-teaching is to bring the student into contact with the type of problem a lawyer has to solve." Memorandum from Bruce Dunlop to Caesar Wright, 7 September 1961, Accession A82/0041, box 030, University of Toronto Archives (University of Toronto Faculty of Law Records), Toronto.

45 Committee on Curriculum and Calendar Revision, Faculty of Law, University of Toronto, "Matters for Consideration 1963," Accession A82/0041, box 032, "Law School 1962–63 (9)," University of Toronto Archives (University of Toronto Faculty of Law Records), Toronto.

46 Memorandum from R.C.B. Risk to Curriculum Committee, 30 November 1965, Accession A82-0041, box 036, "CAW (To Be Answered)," University of Toronto Archives (University of Toronto Faculty of Law Records), Toronto.

47 Ibid.

48 John Willis, "Comparative Law" (handwritten memorandum) (n.d., but in apparent response to a memorandum dated 8 October 1965 by Edward McWhinney), Accession A82/0041, box 018, "Memos To and From Faculty," University of Toronto Archives (University of Toronto Faculty of Law Records), Toronto. This sense of the importance of jurisprudence lay in contrast to Wright's disdain of the course. As Wright wrote to his mentor while at Harvard, torts scholar F.H. Bolen, a year after graduating, "This year, Jurisprudence – Thank God – is gone – in fact, I like to think that perhaps I killed it" (quoted in Kyer and Bickenbach, *The Fiercest Debate*, 101, 90).

49 Milner, "Fact and Fancy in the Idea of a University Law Faculty," *University of Toronto Law Journal* 13, no. 1 (1949): 40.

50 "First Year – Proposed Course on Legislation – Extract from a letter from Jim Milner," enclosure to John Willis, memorandum to the Committee on Curriculum and Calendar Revision, 1 December 1966, Accession A82/0041, box 034, "Law School Correspondence 1966–67," University of Toronto Archives (University of Toronto Faculty of Law Records), Toronto ("probably we should look for a bright young man who would work at it over the next two or three years").

51 See J.B. Milner, ed., *Cases and Materials on Contracts* (Toronto: University of Toronto Press, 1983), xvii ("All of these [lawyerly] activities are in a sense legislative, rather than adjudicative, and they justify, in my view, an even greater emphasis on the legislative area than our legal education presently offers"); Fuller, "What the Law Schools Can Contribute," 193 ("legal education in this country has almost totally neglected the legislative process, and has dealt with only one aspect of the adjudicative process, that of our appellate courts").

52 "First Year – Proposed Course on Legislation – Extract from a letter from Jim Milner," enclosure to John Willis, memorandum to the Committee on Curriculum and Calendar Revision, 1 December 1966, Accession

A82/0041, box 034, "Law School Correspondence 1966–67," University of Toronto Archives (University of Toronto Faculty of Law Records), Toronto.

53 The 1967 calendar lists Agency, Civil Procedure, Contracts, Criminal Law and Procedure, Land Law, Introduction to Legal Research, Personal Property, and Torts as the first-year courses. Faculty of Law, University of Toronto, *Calendar 1967–68*, 16–17.

54 The inclusion of legal process in a jurisprudence course recalls Milner's observations about Hart's Legislation seminar, that he "thought [he] was back in Jurisprudence for five weeks." Letter from Milner to Wright, 4 May 1950, Clara Thomas Archive (Milner Papers, 1992-014, box 005, file 161), Toronto.

55 Memorandum from Stanley Schiff to John Willis (n.d.) (enclosed with memorandum from John Willis to the Committee on Curriculum and Calendar Revision, 1 December 1966), Accession A84/0041, box 034, "Law School Correspondence 1966–67," University of Toronto Archives (University of Toronto Faculty of Law Records), Toronto. Swan, though not a Harvard graduate, demonstrated her own partiality for Legal Process ideas when she included Lon Fuller, Henry Hart, and Walter Gellhorn in a list of suggestions to Wright for centenary professorships. John Swan, memorandum to Dean Wright, n.d., but appearing immediately after Milner's memorandum about a proposed course on legislation circulated by Willis along to the Committee on Calendar Revisions, 1 December 1966, Accession A84/0041, box 034, "Law School Correspondence 1966–67," University of Toronto Archives (University of Toronto Faculty of Law Records), Toronto.

Along with Desmond Morton, Swan taught the first iteration of the first-year Introduction to the Legislative and Administrative Process course in 1970–71 and would go on to develop a casebook on contracts in the late 1970s, inspired by Fuller and Ian Macneil, that deployed a problem-oriented approach to studying contracts, relying on the realistic "reasonable expectations of the parties" theory and eventually developing into a full-blown "solicitor's approach" to the subject matter. See John Swan and Barry J. Reiter, *Contracts: Cases, Notes, and Materials* (Toronto: Butterworths, 1978). For a detailed discussion of Swan's casebook and its intellectual influences, see Sandomierski, *Aspiration and Reality in Legal Education*, chapter 3.

56 See University of Toronto Faculty of Law, Academic Calendar, 1967–68, 19; memorandum from Stanley Schiff to John Willis (n.d.) (enclosed with memorandum from John Willis to the Committee on Curriculum and

Calendar Revision, 1 December 1966), Accession A84/0041, box 034, "Law School Correspondence 1966–67," University of Toronto Archives (University of Toronto Faculty of Law Records), Toronto.

57 University of Toronto Faculty of Law, *Academic Calendar, 1969–70*, 19–20 ("In the examination of the working of each institution, concrete fact-situations illustrate the nature of the problems of community living to which the appropriate technique of decision-making of the particular institution may best be applied, the limitations of the techniques of that institution in terms of the nature of the problems, and the necessary inter-relationships of one institution with all others"). The course description remains largely the same through the early 1970s.

58 The course appears to have been largely Schiff's, although other professors, such as Barry Reiter, taught a section of it from time to time. In the final few years of the course, it was very poorly subscribed. Course evaluations from 1986–87 to 1989–90 record there being five, three, two, and two students respectively in the course; 1989–90 appears to be the final year in which Schiff offered it. See Course Calendars, University of Toronto, 1969–1979 (available at University of Toronto Archives); Course Evaluations, 1984–1994 (on reserve at the Bora Laskin Law Library, Faculty of Law, University of Toronto).

59 Risk writes in the report that his Curriculum Committee is a successor to a "Special Committee on Long Range Planning" established in 1963 and that it "seems to have acquired" the jurisdiction of previous Committee on Curriculum and Calendar Revision. *Report of the Curriculum Committee Faculty of Law, University of Toronto*, May, 1969 (R.C.B. Risk, chair), Halifax, Dalhousie Archives, Ronald St John Macdonald fonds, subseries 36.10, "University of Toronto – Report of the Curriculum Committee," 2 [Risk Report].

60 Karl Llewellyn, "The Study of Law as a Liberal Art," in *Jurisprudence: Realism in Theory and Practice* (Chicago: University of Chicago Press, 1962), 391, quoted in Risk Report, 12.

61 Risk Report, 13–14.

62 Ibid., 19–20.

63 Ibid., 21.

64 Ibid.

65 Stanley Schiff recorded a dissent, the reasons for which are worth discovering. Schiff had, of course, been instrumental in introducing the upper-year Legal Process course, which the 1969 report expressly retains. Did Schiff disagree with including such ideas in first year? If so, why? Did he perceive it as a challenge to his own upper year course?

66 Angela Swan formerly went by the first name John.

67 Course Calendars, 1970–71, 1971–72, and 1972–73. The descriptions are substantially similar.

68 Course Calendars, 1973–74, 1974–75.

69 Course Calendars, 1975–76, 1976–77.

70 Richard C. B. Risk, *Materials for an Introduction to the Legislative and Administrative Processes*, Bora Laskin Law Library, University of Toronto, online: https://ia800703.us.archive.org/5/items/materialsforintroorisk_0/materialsforintroorisk_0.pdf.

71 Chapter titles include: (1) The Beginning of Individual Equality: The Property of Married Women; (2) The Beginning of the Welfare State: Compensation for Industrial Accidents; (3) The Beginnings of Consumer Protection: The Purity of Milk; (4) The Railroads: The Beginnings of Economic Regulation; (5) The Attitudes of Lawyers: A Footnote to the First Four Chapters; (6) Delegated Legislation: Introduction and Controls; (7) Statutes and Courts: The Supremacy of Parliament; (8) Statutes and Courts: An Introduction to Statutory Interpretation: An Easy Case and Some Readings; (9) Statutes and Courts: Statutory Interpretation: A Harder Case; (10) Statutes and Courts: Statutory Interpretation: The Planning Act; (11) Statutes and Courts: Codification; (12) Judicial Control of Administrative Action. R.C.B. Risk, *Materials for an Introduction to Statutes and Administrative Law*, 1976, Bora Laskin Law Library, University of Toronto, online: https://ia802906.us.archive.org/35/items/materialsforintroorisk/materialsforintroorisk.pdf.

72 Ibid. Emphasis added.

73 Conversation with author, 4 March 2020. Hurst was known by his peers as a strong advocate for exposing students to a variety of lawmaking agencies and their social functions, as well as to the connection between social research and legal practice. See Robert W. Gordon, "Introduction: J. Willard Hurst and the Common Law Tradition in American Legal Historiography," *Law and Society Review* 10, no. 1 (1975): 44–5, 49. Hurst also had a keen focus on retraining young recruits away from the bad habits they learned in law school. See Robert W. Gordon, "Willard Hurst as a Colleague," *Wisconsin Law Review*, no. 6 (1980): 1123. Hurst's *Law and the Conditions of the Freedom in the Nineteenth Century United States* largely concentrated on how statute law (as opposed to reported cases) is a tool that can be used to shape the social environment (Madison, WI: University of Wisconsin Press, 1956). Hurst's master-work, *Law and Economic Growth: The Legal History of the Lumber Industry in Wisconsin, 1836–1915* (Cambridge: Harvard

University Press, 1964) explored how legal ideas and institutions allocated decision-making power and ordered social change as well as the impact legal processes have on politics, history, and cultural values. Legislation figures as a prominent legal process in this work as well.

74 See R.C.B. Risk, Introduction to Legislation Christmas Tests, 1971, University of Toronto Faculty of Law; R.C.B. Risk, Introduction to Legislation Annual Examination, 1972–73, question 5; R.C.B. Risk, Development of Canadian Law and Legal Institutions, Supplemental Examination, 1974–75, Part A, questions 1, 2, 3, 4, 5, 6, 6.1, Part B, questions 1, 2; R.C.B. Risk, Introduction to Statutes, Annual Examination, 1975–76, questions 1(a), 1(d), 2, 3. Examinations are on file at the Bora Laskin Law Library at the University of Toronto.

75 Conversation with author, 4 March 2020.

76 "The Recent History of Curriculum Reform Reports," appendix A, *First Year Curriculum Committee Report*, 30 March 2000 (Kent Roach, chair) [Roach Report], 31 ("On December 10, 1984, the First Year Curriculum Report ... recommended that Public Law be replaced with Constitutional Law that would include not only federalism, the *Charter of Rights and Freedoms* but also parliamentary sovereignty, the rule of law and statutory interpretation"). Risk began teaching Constitutional Law in 1987–88 and continued on throughout the 1990s.

77 Ron Daniels, memorandum to the Curriculum Committee, 4 November 1995, 3, reproduced in appendix A to the *Report of the Curriculum Committee*, 8 April 1996 (Patrick Macklem, chair), 1, 9, 85 [Macklem Report].

78 See the course calendars of the respective years.

79 Faculty of Law, University of Toronto, *Curriculum Committee Report*, March 1986 (Brian Langille, chair), 48, 23 ("Our discussions of these recommendations led the Committee to a discussion of our lack of contact with the legislative branch of government. It is our view that development of opportunities for our students to become involved in the work of the legislature or its committees is well worth pursuing").

80 Special Committee on the First Year Curriculum Report (Hudson Janisch, chair) [Janisch Report], 5, cited in Macklem Report, 41.

81 Roach Report, 31. See also Macklem Report, 41 ("The Special Committee outlined two possible means of broadening Civil Procedure: to offer a course on procedures that takes into account administrative and legislative processes; to undertake a more systematic look at alternative modes of dispute resolution").

82 Macklem Report, 41.

83 Macklem Report, 41–2 ("the rules of civil procedure should ... form part of a richer inquiry into the nature of legal processes, ethics, access to justice, lawyering roles and responsibilities, and the strengths and weaknesses of alternative dispute resolution mechanisms. We also encourage instructors to address public law matters in the course, perhaps by case studies involving statutory interpretation, and analyses of legal structuring of democratic and political processes").

84 See Curriculum Committee report, 13 March 1997 (Brian Langille, chair), 1 (responding to the mandate letter by the Dean Daniels to Brian Langille, focusing on "course weighting and alternative modes of evaluation") [Langille Report 1997]; report of the Special Committee on Implementation of the 1996–97 Curriculum Committee Report Recommendations (April, 1998) (Denise Reaume, chair) (focusing on diversification in the upper year curriculum, criteria for determining seminar course weighting, the perspective course requirement, and the compulsory moot).

85 Draft letter from Ron Daniels (unsigned, but context suggests this authorship) to Kent Roach, (1 November 1999).

86 Ibid.

87 See Roach, "What's New and Old," 368.

88 Final report on the Committee to Review the First Year Curriculum (Kent Roach, chair) (n.d., but distributed to Faculty on 30 March 2000 by Dean Daniels), appendix A. An earlier history of curriculum committee reports can also be found in the March 1986 Curriculum Committee Report (Brian Langille, chair) at 2ff (detailing curriculum efforts prior to 1949, the Risk Report, and others).

89 Roach Report, 18.

90 Ibid., 18–19.

91 Ibid., 20 ("The course would not aim to teach the rules per se, but rather to use the rules to illustrate a particular conception of dispute resolution and particular circumstances of what fairness, justice and truth-seeking require").

92 Ibid., 25 ("public law topics could be expanded through an examination of the legislature and administrative agencies").

93 Ibid., 21 ("One main goal might be to examine the concept and 'value' of process, including the relationship between substance and process; the relation of process to concepts of justice, truth, fairness; *the plurality of processes for resolving disputes and the values underpinning the different processes*" [emphasis added]). See also appendix D, 36, listing one of the central learning objectives as "the concept and 'value' of process,"

including "the relationship between substance and process; the relationship of process to concepts of justice, truth, fairness, and "the values underpinning [the] different processes."

94 Roach Report, 20 (the "first year process course, even one with the ambition of providing an overview of the entire legal process, would most *likely examine the stages of the civil litigation such as commencement of proceedings, pleadings, costs rules, discovery, estoppel, standing rules etc. This would give the course a doctrinal core* like other first year classes" [emphasis added]).

95 Transnational concerns were raised by Daniels in mandate letters to Macklem and Roach. See memorandum from Daniels to Curriculum Committee, 4 November 1995, 6ff (discussion of globalization); letter from Daniels to Roach, 1 November 1999 (referring to the "effect that globalization ... [has] had on the nature of law and legal institutions"). The Roach Report considers the transnational point in detail at 14ff. One recommended "central learning objective" of the course related to "globalization and re-locating decision-making powers" (appendix D, 37). See Roach Report, 23 (the proposal "reflects the fundamental importance of process in legal education and the reality that processes for resolving disputes are diverse and not confined to national borders").

96 Susan L. Gratton, "Educating Tomorrow's Lawyers: Designing a First Year Law Curriculum for the 21st Century," 5 February 2008 (report prepared for the Choudhry Committee in preparation of the Choudhry Report), on file with author ("The expanded Legal Process course proposed by the Roach Committee had proved impossible to staff and students continued to be highly dissatisfied with the course").

97 Angela Fernandez, comments on an earlier draft, 13 July 2020.

98 Fernandez recalls one student course evaluation to the effect "smart teacher; too smart to be teaching this course." While perhaps a backhanded compliment, it brought home vividly to her how the course was perceived by students, at least at that time. The course has since been moved to second semester. And since the rest of the first-year curriculum has been semesterized (with the exception of small groups), the one-semester stigma has been reduced if not eliminated (editorial comments to author, 13 July 2020).

99 For an example of a creative approach, see e.g., question 6 of the 2005–06 final examination for Legal Process, which was identical for the sections of Angela Fernandez, Kenneth Jull, and Lorne Sossin ("The victims of 'The Good Ship Science' have been approached by a young lawyer turned writer who wants to write a novel about their encounter with

the judicial system and there is even talk of a movie. How do you think the story should be told? Specifically, do you think it should tell a triumphant tale or a more pessimistic one, in comparison to the way in which 'A Civil Action' was told? Be sure to make explicit which model of legal process you think the story should be based on").

100 A total of twenty examinations from this period have been reviewed and the questions catalogued according to the principal themes they appear to cover. Acknowledging the imprecision of this activity, it nevertheless provides a snapshot of the relative emphasis of the themes examined in the courses. In total, eleven broad themes were identified, with the frequency indicated in parentheses: rules of civil procedure (17); critiques of civil procedure (7); access to justice (7); confidentiality (5); judicial bias (4); institutional competence (4); globalization/jurisdiction (3); alternative dispute resolution (3); professional ethics (2); standing (2); rule of law (1).

101 2008–2009 Standing Curriculum Committee, Faculty of Law, University of Toronto, *Final Report to Faculty Council* (April 2009) (Sujit Choudhry, chair) [Choudhry Report]. At the time of writing, the report could be accessed online using the internet archive: https://web.archive.org/web/20090830073017/https://www.law.utoronto.ca/documents/general/CurriculumCommittee_FinalReport_2009.pdf.

102 Choudhry Report, 7.

103 Ibid., 12, 11.

104 Ibid., 12.

105 Ibid., 7–8 (emphasis in original). The report continues: "[I]f one reads the Supreme Court's decision in CUPE in the light of the Court of Appeal's and the Board's decision one gets a remarkable snapshot of the ways in which different approaches to statutory interpretation, both the extent and the nature of the exercise, turn on the sense of institutions of their role in the constitutional order and of their relationship to other institutions." The case reference is to *C.U.P.E. v. N.B. Liquor Corporation*, [1979] 2 S.C.R. 227 (privative clauses should be upheld unless the interpretation of the Act is patently unreasonable such that it could not be rationally supported by relevant legislation).

106 Dean's mandate letter from Mayo Moran to Sujit Choudhry (12 November 2007) in Choudhry Report, 19–23. In its report, the committee explains why it preferred a first-year Administrative Law course to making it mandatory in second year: it helps "ameliorate the imbalance between private law versus public law concepts in the current first year program."

107 Choudhry Report, 7. This is a striking parallel to Dean Daniel's mandate letter to Patrick Macklem.

108 Ibid., 30. The committee also emphasis that a new Public Law course would "create new demands for staffing and could create staffing problems for the upper year program" (31).

109 Ibid., 12. A lack of staffing had also been a concern with earlier course proposals. See James Milner, "First Year – Proposed Course on Legislation – Extract from a Letter from Jim Milner," enclosure to John Willis, memorandum to the Committee on Curriculum and Calendar Revision, 1 December 1966, Accession A82/0041, box 034, "Law School Correspondence 1966–67," University of Toronto Archives (University of Toronto Faculty of Law Records), Toronto ("I concede that the real difficulty is finding a man to give it ... probably we should look for a bright young man who would work at it over the next two or three years" [ellipsis in original]). One also suspects that Risk taught Introduction to Legislative and Administrative Processes because there were few others available to do so. The Risk Report, 28 acknowledges the work involved in developing the course ("This course must be created, and the job of creation will be an immense one").

110 The committee make a significant effort to portray Administrative Law on an equal footing with Property, Contracts, Torts, Constitutional Law, and Criminal Law, which it describes as "conceptual building blocks for the study of law and the legal order, and [which] function as *de facto* prerequisites for many of our upper year offerings." For example, it asks "whether there are other areas of law that are similarly presupposed by the upper year program" (9), and writes, "While Administrative Law will require our students to grapple with complex legal issues, we feel that the same can be said of the other first year courses" (12).

111 Examinations are available from Professors Stern, Sossin, Shachar, Morgan, Baker, and Yoon. They are missing for Professors Semple (2012–13), Stern (2012–13, 2014–15), Shachar (2012–13, 2013–14), and Chiao (2014–15).

112 The representative themes, deploying the imperfect methodology of identifying each question with a principal theme, are: civil procedure (8), critique of civil procedure (2), standing (2), alternative dispute resolution (1), judicial bias (1), globalizaton/ jurisdiction (1), ethics (1), access to justice (1), class actions (1), institutional competence (1).

113 It seems likely that those who taught the course in those years would have different things to say about the challenges it posed for first-year students and why the course failed and the project was ultimately abandoned. It also seems likely that many who taught it were not even aware of the pluralizing-legal-process agenda whence it came. It is ironic that it did not

succeed at the University of Toronto, when arguably Baker created a successful version of it at an earlier time at McGill. When Baker developed and taught the Administrative Procedure course at McGill, he probably went the furthest of the many experiments of realizing the imagined goal of decentring adjudication in the law student's understanding of the legal process. Fernandez took the course in the late 1990s and recalls Baker emphasizing the importance of learning how to read a statute (without falling asleep), parsing the definition from the other sections, thinking about what the title means, and so on. Baker had the students in the group read the empowering statutes for various administrative agencies with an emphasis on parsing and understanding the privative clauses legislatures built into those statutes in order to prevent courts from reversing the expertise of such tribunals (e.g., the Human Rights Tribunal of Ontario). This was the "worm's-eye view." The courts were also the "camel's nose in the tent," to reference the cartoon in Cory Verbauwhede's essay in this collection. As Fernandez recollects, Baker was explicit about the course not being a course in the judicial review of administrative action, so much so that she thought she ought to take a different course on that topic the following year with another instructor and it was, indeed, a completely different course. Fernandez, editorial comments on this paper, 13 June 2020.

114 From 2015–16 to 2018–19, the themes explored in the examinations included civil procedure (6), standing (1), confidentiality (1), administrative law (1), jurisdiction (1) and privilege (1).

115 Baker's examination for 2013–14 is distinctively pluralistic, offering students choice to write about issues including cost awards, instrument choice, the lawyer-client relationship, persuasive legal authority, sites of justice, standing to sue and intervene, class actions, the economics of dispute settlement, arbitration, and the public accountability of decision-makers in alternative dispute resolution processes, but there was a sense in which Baker was unsatisfied with that course, leading him to completely revamp it several years later. See Blaine Baker, annual examinations, Legal Process, Professionalism, and Ethics, Faculty of Law, University of Toronto, April 2014; Blaine Baker, email correspondence with author, 2 May 2018 ("the first and second time I taught the course, I merely pulled existing local course packs off the shelf – which did not work very well").

116 For Baker's 2019 course outline and reading list, see Appendix.

117 See Thomas C. Grey, "Langdell's Orthodoxy," *University of Pittsburgh Law Review* 45, no. 1 (1983): 47.

118 See Martin L. Friedland, *Searching for WPM Kennedy: The Biography of an Enigma* (Toronto: University of Toronto Press, 2020), 165–8.
119 Risk, Macklem, and Choudhry all have degrees from Harvard Law School. Roach completed his graduate studies in law at Yale.
120 Sandomierski, "Catalytic Agents?"
121 Macdonald, "Curricular Development," 569.
122 Risk Report, 23.

In the corner of the above photograph sits Blaine Baker at the end of the last lecture in the last course he ever taught at the McGill Faculty of Law, on 29 November 2016. It is a fortuitous shot of him insofar as the student who took it had actually been intending to photograph the conceptual map that Blaine had hastily drawn on the blackboard at the beginning of the class. To me, that map captured Blaine's *weltanschauung* perhaps better than anything he ever published. It is, therefore, fitting to include it in this volume of essays in his honour and, specifically, in this essay, which focuses on one aspect of that worldview. Blaine drew the map in response to my urging that he for once – and at long last – sketch out the broader vision at which he often hinted but which he had never fully committed to in his published work. It schematized Blaine's conception of four coherent historical systems of social regulation since about the middle of the eighteenth century, the three approximate pivotal dates being 1830, 1930, and 2000. My contribution to this volume attempts to reconstitute, and extrapolate from, some of Blaine's key insights which have fascinated me ever since I was first his student in 2004.

Cory Verbauwhede

Figure 14.1 | Blaine Baker at the end of the last lecture in the last course he ever taught at the McGill Faculty of Law, on 29 November 2016.

14

The Camel's Nose in the Constitutional Tent: Extrapolating from G. Blaine Baker's Thoughts on Late Nineteenth-Century Legal Liberalism and Elite Lawyer Resistance to the Canadian Welfare State

Cory Verbauwhede

This essay is meant both as a tribute to Blaine Baker and as an attempt to salvage some of his important hypotheses about the liberal safeguards that lawyer-politicians worked into the constitution in response to the growth of social movements in Canada. Baker was loath to officially commit himself to macroscopic history, preferring "at this stage in the writing of Canadian legal history to continue 'sinking deep fence posts' in that field of inquiry [...] while leaving the 'stringing of wire' between those posts [...] for the future."[1] His untimely death prevented him from playing a larger part in the stringing of that wire, though he had much to contribute. This is especially true for the question of the implementation of the welfare state. Given the unfinished nature of his *œuvre*, my archival search has included unpublished papers, research and class notes (both my own and others'), syllabi, letters, and email correspondence.[2]

Large swaths of Canada's federal welfare state – including unemployment insurance, universal family allowances and pensions, and Medicare – were instituted between the mid-1930s and the mid-1960s.[3] This momentous shift, away from a society in which welfare was organized around discretionary relationships based on kinship and charity to one in which major social needs were increasingly provided for by the state as of right, generally only gets passing notice in the legal literature on the historical significance of the *British North America Act*.[4] This is surprising for two reasons. The most obvious one is that, during those thirty years, federal-provincial relations were the hotly-contested battleground on which proponents and detractors of an enhanced social role for the state clashed and that clash left neither the state nor the constitution unchanged.[5] The second reason is more subtle, and it ties into the central topic of the present essay. It relates to how the BNA *Act* became such a formidable obstacle to welfare-state building in the first place. This failure to explicitly link the development of the BNA *Act* with the fate of claims for increased social welfare is even more striking if one accounts for the well-established fact that, at least in democratic systems, decentralized constitutions present immense challenges to the implementation of the welfare state.[6] Canada was no exception to that rule, and it faced two considerable added difficulties. The first was that the BNA *Act* effectively entrenched classical liberalism by giving what were at that time considered to be "public" functions to the federal government while leaving the "private" sphere to the provinces.[7] The second was that, to put it schematically, the federal government largely represented the anglophone Protestant majority, whereas the francophone Catholic minority was gradually forced to retrench to the province of Quebec. This growing chasm became a potential abyss for anyone who proposed a greater role for public law, whose natural locus at the time was the federal government, since it had greater taxation powers, economic clout, and geographic reach.[8] In Quebec in the 1930s, increasing cultural rivalries broadened the scope of the resistance to federal welfare programs that had already been staged by the larger provinces in earlier decades.[9] Indeed, given these obstacles, it can be justifiably said that Canada constructed its welfare state despite its federal constitution and foundational cultural divide.

During the course of his career, Baker identified important gaps in Canadian legal history which, if filled, would greatly help to understand the hurdles to state support presented by the constitution and its interpretation. His only published work to directly address this topic is his 1995 book review of Robert Vipond's *Liberty and Community: Canadian Federalism and the Failure of the Constitution*.[10] While praising Vipond's study of the "cultural constraints on our ability to imagine other political futures, and [...]

the linguistically given structure of sovereignty arguments common to federalists, provincialists, and libertarians alike,"[11] Baker made several "hortatory comments" for further research. He took issue with the fact that, to Vipond, the "provincial-rights movement was essentially a constitutional event."[12] In his view, "[the assessment that] Canadian constitutional law was and is much more than mere rhetoric or partisan politics [...] is so underappreciated in contemporary literature that it warrants exhaustive and uncompromising demonstration."[13] Though he thought Vipond's work was an excellent start, Baker called upon legal historians to pay more attention to the broader cultural and social themes which formed the context of constitutional battles and influenced their outcomes. These crucial links were being ignored because of law's insularity and its tendency to conceal real issues behind technical jargon, even from its own practitioners and analysts.[14]

Following the lead of other legal historians such as Robert W. Gordon and David Sugarman, Baker urged his colleagues to account for the "deadly serious attempt to rationalize the ground rules of interactive life in liberal society" as more than just political expediency by opportunistic provincial-rights movements.[15] According to this analysis, much of North Atlantic constitutional change at the end of the nineteenth century was part of a vast project to "keep the state in check."[16] Baker argued that, though mid-nineteenth-century judicial activism was transparent about the law's adaptability to evolving ends, that movement abruptly subsided just a few decades later.[17] In the Canadas, codification and other law-reform movements of the post-rebellion period were unabashedly instrumental and Baker revealingly labelled such efforts "strategic Benthamism."[18] Indeed, he thought that the BNA *Act* itself "can be viewed as a kind of finale to [an] era of fast-paced utilitarianism."[19] Something changed, however, in the decades straddling the turn of the century.[20]

Baker's colleagues abroad had found that, in order to withhold legal instrumentalism from the masses in the face of the broadening of democracy and its accompanying social movements, which were demanding their own instrumental legal changes, elites started to beat a retreat by developing a "legal ideology" with a "Diceyan" or "modern" version of the "rule of law" as their shield.[21] Baker hypothesized that the defensive legal liberalism that was being developed in other North Atlantic jurisdictions was also influential in the Canadian context.[22] In the process, he saw both Ontario's and

Quebec's legal circles as having experienced a widespread closing of the mind, as they abandoned instrumental "polyjurality" and "legal pantheism" and instead sought refuge in "formalistic," "positivist," and "unimaginative," non-instrumental theories and approaches to law.[23] Through mechanisms that will be explored in this essay, the upshot of this transformation was the appearance of a new kind of legal nationalism – Baker would have said "legal nativism" – which was suspicious of state expansionism.[24] This was an international trend, but it became especially powerful in Quebec owing to the existence of its own *Civil Code of Lower Canada*, whose pedigree could be persuasively argued to go all the way back to the *Quebec Act*, which to French Canadians symbolized historical defiance of the British invaders.[25]

The three related gaps in the historiography of the constitution identified by Baker and to which we now turn are, first, the underappreciation of key cultural changes brought about by lawyer-politicians who "reconceived governance in legislative and adjudicative terms"; second, the lack of recognition of the powerful provincial-rights movement in Quebec that paralleled its Ontario counterpart in importance and effect, albeit through private-law advocacy; and third, the interaction between those movements and the "promotion of cultural nationalism through law" in both central-Canadian provinces.[26] Together, they paint a picture that suggests that the links between patriotism, federalism, and the liberal imperative of keeping the private and the public spheres separate have been underemphasized in general understandings of the shaping and the application of the BNA *Act*. Understanding these links helps to explain why the Canadian constitution became such a daunting barrier to the establishment of the welfare state.

THE CLOSING OF THE CENTRAL-CANADIAN LEGAL MIND AT THE END OF THE NINETEENTH CENTURY

The first historiographical gap that Baker identified was the "as-yet incompletely understood paradigm shift in local conceptions of judicial agency and legal knowledge that seems to have occurred gradually between Confederation and 1900."[27] To him, this was the key episode of a century-long transformation that he saw as having taken place. Indeed, to Baker, the nineteenth century saw a "transition of 'ideal types' of provincial legal practice from legal work structured around the 'rule of bureaucracy' during the pre-rebellion period, to an embrace by lawyers of the 'rule of legislation' at mid-century, to the adoption of the 'rule of judge-made law' in the decades straddling the turn of the twentieth century."[28] Baker elaborated: "In stark contrast to the local bar of the 1820s and 1830s," he wrote, "central-Canadian lawyers of the first decades of the twentieth century are notable for their comparative lack of interest in official nation-building processes, their absence from what had come to be known as the civil service, and for their overt hostility towards non-judicial public administration."[29] It was this rise in importance of the judiciary at the expense of the executive and legislative branches which interested Baker with respect to the end of the nineteenth century.

The most revealing manifestations of this cultural shift were the provincial-rights movements, whose exploration as regards the "Ontarian version of that late nineteenth-century constitutional episode" was pioneered by Vipond and R.C.B. (or "Dick") Risk.[30] These movements, Baker told his students, were "screaming for further engagement by contemporary constitutional writers."[31] Much like Vipond, Baker saw the Ontarian provincial-rights movement as having successfully "privatizated public law" through the elaboration of a rhetoric in which "an artificial political construct like a province has exactly the same kind of autonomy and sovereignty as individuals" and through the invention of "judicial review in constitutional court, [even in the absence of that] concept in the BNA *Act*."[32] Indeed, Baker pointed out that, despite the existence of "at least three written 'constitutions of Canada'" prior to Confederation, "[p]erceptions about the appropriateness of recurrence to one or another of these forums [had not previously been] structured by an exclusive text [... nor had such choices been] reviewed judicially."[33]

However, as noted above, Baker, unlike Vipond, did not think that the transformations he described were primarily constitutional events. To Baker, provincial autonomists did not just happen to be liberals as well; rather, provincialism was the particular shape that liberalism took in the Canadian context. After all, the same "rights-discourse" was developing in highly centralized states such as Great Britain, outside of contexts of debates surrounding decentralization, and a new liberalism – one which was to varying degrees "haunted by socialism" – was everywhere ascendant across the North Atlantic at the turn of the century.[34] Both Baker and Vipond, however, agreed that fundamental cultural changes occurred, with broad implications up to the present, and that this transformation led to an impoverishment of democratic discourse and a corresponding hobbling of governmental power, in a context in which, in Vipond's words, "the most controversial issues [were treated] as if they raised only jurisdictional questions that could be discussed and resolved in terms of rights."[35]

Vipond had identified and explained the process whereby the BNA *Act*'s powers of federal disallowance and reservation of provincial statutes fell into disuse through instrumentally-minded provincial-rights advocates, but Baker thought that this explanation did not capture the full scope or meaning of these changes. In his review, he pointed to several related developments that indicated a more fundamental transformation:

> There are suggestive signals in the historical record that divisions of constitutional power for which sections 91 and 92 of the BNA *Act* provided were regarded by many federally oriented "Fathers of Confederation" as temporary ones, the most that could be achieved in intercolonial conferences of the 1860s. There are further indications that some elected representatives, routinely sitting simultaneously in post-Confederation provincial and federal parliaments under abortive provisions for dual representation, intended to continue club-like constitutional negotiations in those legislatures with a view to gradual consolidation of federal power through section 94 unification of private law and consequent piecemeal abandonment by the provinces of section 92 jurisdictions.[36]

For Baker, what had happened was not just that the federal government had been stripped of its superior status, but that the constitution itself had become ossified and deprived of its flexible nature. This loss of flexibility went hand in hand with the shift in focus from parliamentary to judicial power. Baker did not pursue these questions further in his published work, though they underlie his research and publications covering that period. His papers do, however, contain the "rough draft" of an introduction that he presented publicly on at least two occasions, as well as the associated research folders.[37] The article seems to have been meant to be a companion to his 1985 *Law and History Review* article "The Reconstitution of Upper Canadian Legal Thought in the Late-Victorian Empire."[38] It suggests how Baker would have continued his exploration of such topics:

> The […] shift in the culture of institutional comparison wrought by elite lawyers' early interaction with the text of the BNA *Act* provides this essay's focus. […] More precisely, how have adjudicative disputes about the comparative merits of provincial or federal action phrased in Confederation's division-of-powers language participated in the generation or the marginalization, over time, of […] other statal vocabularies of Canadian institutional comparison [such] as those of federal disallowance of provincial legislation, Dominion-provincial conferences, coloured papers, or referenda?[39]

To Baker, such change could not be fully accounted for by pointing to structural features of the BNA *Act* like the presence of articles 91 ("Powers of the Parliament") and 92 ("Exclusive Powers of Provincial Legislatures"). Far from constituting part of the explanation, the overemphasis on the formal division of powers that came to define the constitution for many years lay, instead, at the core of the phenomena that cried out for analysis, namely, why some powers were given to the federal government and others to the provinces; why Canadian federalism became so uncooperative; and why jurisdictional boundaries became so unyielding.[40]

To illustrate this movement away from "co-ordinated federalism" and "normative diversity," Baker proposed to make an "inquiry into the cultural conditions for affirmation of a particular professional conception and vocabulary of institutional comparison."[41] He was interested in how the legal subculture which eventually prevailed had come to replace other ways of governing federal institutions. As he noted, "[a]uthority, justification, and responsibility are large concepts. By contrast, the BNA *Act*'s vocabulary of divisions of state power is a limited, casuistic and abstract one, even when the texts of sections 91 and 92 are fleshed out by admitting the doctrines of statutory interpretation, the rules of judicial precedent, and the arts of constitutional rhetoric."[42] How, Baker wondered, had a strict and literal reading of the constitution crowded out a more diverse set of governance practices? Baker's introductory thoughts were only meant to be the first fragments of a bigger picture, but they do leave the unsettling feeling that there are important pieces missing from existing analyses.

As in the review of Vipond's article, Baker concentrated on the "Fathers of Confederation [prioritizing the] sharing and debating [of] conceptions, sources and vocabularies of public validity [,first,] in the process of drafting the BNA *Act,*" and then again, seven years later, when federal legislation was passed in 1872 to prevent members of Parliament from sitting in provincial legislatures.[43] The research summaries and endnote comments indicate that Baker's interest in the contrast between the earlier and later periods stemmed from its implication that the paths of the Dominion and the provinces were diverging to such an extent that further constitutional renegotiations were becoming all but impossible.[44] Indeed, the mere fact that the BNA *Act* initially permitted dual representation calls out for further analysis.[45]

Baker's other notable topic in that text was the promotion, by the Canadian Bar Association's Committee on Uniform Laws, of private law consolidation based on section 94 of the BNA *Act*. He pointed out that, by its very existence, albeit hamstrung by a provincial veto, "[s]ection 94 anticipates the gradual achievement of a negotiated legislative union, and a corelative shrinking of provincial autonomy."[46] Indeed, Baker noted that, before disappearing into oblivion, the consolidation of Canadian private law was actively discussed in the first decades of the twentieth century, and that it even formed the background to McGill University's law faculty's National Programme of integrated civil, common, and public law between 1916 and 1927.[47] "One of [Baker's] working assumptions" was "that the uniform laws movement was the principal early Canadian opposition to the apparent belief of the majority of English Privy councillors and central-Canadian constitutional lawyers that the essential British North American state was a set of formal rules managed by technically-adept barristers and appellate adjudications."[48]

Although "the definitive history on section 94 is waiting to be written," Baker noted elsewhere that "traces abound in primary and secondary sources of that constitutional provision's significance as an arena for federal-provincial confrontation, and for the responsive construction of provincial-rights theory."[49] Likewise, in his aforementioned companion article on late nineteenth-century Ontario legal culture, Baker had already remarked that opposition to the "rise of formalistic Anglophilia [...] in common law Canada [...] found its prime expression in a third unification and codification of laws initiative" and that "[t]he proponents of this project seem to have been motivated by a desire to reassert legal principle and parliamentary sovereignty, and thus to take the control of law out of the hands of increasingly tired, hypertechnical, anglophilic courts and lawyers."[50]

Ultimately, Baker's insights centred on elements that call into question our inherited fixation on textual division-of-powers arguments and the anachronisms to which they give rise. As a legal historian, Baker was interested not only in what a given forum's normative environment was, but, crucially, how questions of forum- and instrument-choice influenced substantive rules, and how "public sentiment was cultivated in support of economic policy or (more profoundly) what cultural assumptions underlay preference for particular instruments or goals."[51] In the process, he came to an understanding that no one so far has adequately explored: that provincial-rights movements in Ontario and Quebec were two sides of the same classical liberal coin, and that they fed into increasing patriotism in both provinces.[52]

PROVINCIAL RIGHTS, "PROPERTY AND CIVIL RIGHTS," AND LEGAL PATRIOTISM IN ONTARIO AND QUEBEC

A great deal has been written about the Ontarian provincial-rights movement and its principal leader, Oliver Mowat.[53] The phenomenon of turn-of-the-century *Civil Code* nationalism in Quebec, exemplified by the writings of Pierre-Basile Mignault, is also well known.[54] However, what is relatively unexplored in the literature is Baker's hypothesis that the two were linked through their common furtherance of legal liberalism.[55] Baker pointed out that analogous movements extended far beyond central Canada, as "[t]he promotion of cultural nationalism through law was an increasingly common late nineteenth- and early twentieth-century phenomenon throughout the North Atlantic world."[56] Moreover, patriotism was just one of the characteristics that they shared. They also emerged at a time of increasing religious proselytism, fervent moralism, and rampant xenophobia.[57] These cross-cultural parallels have been largely ignored by constitutional scholars, as has the fact that they coincided with class-based defensive action against such democratic reforms as universal male suffrage and the political recognition of workers' unions.[58]

For Baker, it was "important to label Quebec provincialism as a species of Canadian provincial-rights thought" and to question "the assertion that the late nineteenth-century Canadian provincial-rights movement was headquartered in Ontario."[59] Indeed, in his view, Ontario's and Quebec's provincial-rights movements functioned as a constitutional tag team: while the former gained acceptance for watertight jurisdictional compartments within an increasingly unamendable constitution, the latter ensured, through strategic use of the 1866 *Civil Code of Lower Canada*, that the expression "property and civil rights" be understood in the broadest possible way. Though others – notably Paul Romney – see this alliance as stemming from an original "compact" between nations whose essence remained the same from the *Constitutional Act* of 1791 through the virulent reaction to the *Act of Union* of 1840 and up to the BNA *Act*.[60] However, Baker attributed provincialism in both of its incarnations to the rise of legal liberalism in the decades following Confederation. This disagreement as to theoretical perspective and historical periodization is important to the understanding of Baker's project.

Far from being centred on cultural continuity, Baker's theoretical foundation was the dramatically changing political economy at the end of the nineteenth century.[61] Baker thus wrote that analyses of provincialism in Quebec "[have] been compelled to deal directly with Vipond's themes such as shared sovereignty, the relationship between individual and provincial autonomy, and the rule of law, largely by virtue of the unique presence in Quebec's political experience of the quasi-constitutional *Civil Code of Lower Canada*."[62] He saw the new rule-of-law ideal that the *Code* embodied as having done "triple duty": "[i]t defined and preserved the autonomy of individuals vis-à-vis each other and the provincial state, and it was explicitly relied upon to circumscribe the sovereignty of the federal state as against the province."[63] This "triple-duty" refers to three types of relationships that were transformed by the adoption of the *Code*: between individuals, between individuals and the state, and between the provincial and federal governments.

Baker summed up the nature of those transformations in a 2009 handwritten letter in response to Eric Adams' thesis on constitutional rights in Canada.[64] First, between individuals, "the *Code* entrenched and is structured around "human rights" like freedom of contract, the inviolability of the person, freedom of land-ownership, and freedom of willing. The Codal entrenchment of those values in 1866 marked a significant departure from the antecedent, pre-liberal regime, and the *Code* that was structured around them was left more-or-less untouched for a century and a quarter."[65] Second, regarding individuals' interaction with the state, "the quasi-constitutional entrenchment of [the aforementioned liberal] values not only redefined judicial personhood in Quebec but also was thought to limit the provincial state's ability to impinge on them through conventional (non-codal) legislation."[66] Finally, between the federal and provincial governments, "the *Code* was thought to be one big 'definition section' for the term-of-art 'property and civil rights' from the *Quebec Act* that was brought forward in section 92 of the BNA *Act*. [… T]he enacted portions of the *Code* were thought to occupy and thus define the field of property and civil rights, and therefore define the constitutional boundary between federal and provincial spheres of power."[67] In sum, Baker saw the *Civil Code* as being a classical liberal bulwark against the state, be it federal or provincial.

Both Romney and Baker noted the pivotal importance of the 1880s, but they drew sharply divergent inferences from the nationalistic turn of Quebec politics at that time. Romney took his cue from Thomas-Jean-Jacques Loranger, a constitutionalist whom he credited with being the first to "[tie] the cause of provincial rights to earlier struggles against legislative union" at the end of 1883.[68] Romney saw those struggles as evidence that the BNA *Act* was a pact between equals rather than a centralizing document: "[a]s a compact of provinces, [the federal compact] established provincial governments that were equal to each other in constitutional status. As a compact of founding peoples, however, it assigned to the government of Quebec a special function – the conservation of French-Canadian culture in its historic homeland."[69] This double-aspect theory was his key to explaining cross-party cultural tensions that had always been there. To Romney, it was the centralizing John A. Macdonald who had diverted the constitution, and in the 1880s the tables were turning on him.[70]

Baker, on the other hand, saw the important takeaway from the same period as being its clear caesura with the cross-cultural collaboration rooted in the reform movements of both Canadas, which had been seeking to establish responsible government since the

1820s.[71] Indeed, where Romney saw an unholy cross-cultural alliance between Ontario Reformers and Québécois *Bleus* to further the cause of autonomy, Baker thought that the liberal provincial-rights movements increasingly fed into the centripetal cultural forces of Ontarian Anglophilia and Quebec nationalism:

> In Quebec, where the idea of the sovereignty of parliamentary law achieved comparatively pure expression in the 1866 *Civil Code of Lower Canada*'s comprehensive codification of private law, [the] emergent pre-occupation with the modern Rule of Law was represented primarily by disparagement of unlegislated common law intrusions, near deification of the cartesian logic of codified civil law, and by nationalistic association of the province's enacted private law with [*Québécois*] culture. In Ontario, perceptions of the mutual supremacy of legislations and adjudication seem to have been buttressed by exaggerating the independence of these realms of juridical activity, and by redefining mandarin lawyers as custodians or expert interpreters of normative statal texts in the courts.[72]

Baker thought that this "exaggerated" judicial independence in Ontario had accompanied the "interruption of a venerable ethos and the development [of] rampant amnesia" in the Ontarian bar between 1890 and 1920.[73] He linked this to the rise over that time period of mutual "xenophobia" in Ontario and Quebec.[74] One of Baker's most intriguing hypotheses was that, though there had been "substantial professional intercourse between the legal communities of Upper and Lower Canada until approximately 1885," it then abruptly stopped.[75] In Ontario, that sudden shift coincided with a swift and widespread "migration" – in large part to the United States – of eclectic Upper-Canadian law libraries, as the shift of focus towards the British Empire rendered such eclecticism unattractive for a variety of reasons.[76] At about the same time, according to social historian Jean-Marie Fecteau, Quebec legal culture also turned in on itself. Fecteau thought that "the *malaise* of the elites vis-à-vis the state [had] an exact parallel in the legal realm. Indeed, the period that spans from 1885 to 1929 was [...] dominated by civil law scholars. It is during that time that the province's most eminent jurists developed a veritable cult of '*notre Code civil*' ['our *Civil Code*']."

However, upon closer examination, this contrived reverence is clearly defensive: it bears witness to the relentless resistance to any form of interference with the sacred canon of civil regulation."[77] To Baker, as with Ontario's provincial-rights champions, Quebec's legal nationalists were the vanguard of antistatism. After all, the *Civil Code* was, as Brian Young has shown, originally a liberal, not a nationalistic document, and Baker noted that "commentary of the Confederation era tended to fix upon codal promotion of the concept of free will, rather than links to continental European legal culture, as its ideological coup."[78] It was this liberal "coup" embodied by the *Civil Code* which was such a powerful antidote to increased state reach. Nationalism was just a way of protecting the territory gained when classical liberalism started to fall out of favour.

David Howes' study of the contrasting worldviews of two leading Quebec legal scholars on each end of this timeline – roughly 1875 and 1929 – substantiates Baker's point. Howes identified a similarly momentous sea change in Quebec legal culture which occurred at about the same time as the one Baker had described for Ontario. He illustrated his findings by comparing the "polyjurality" of Henri-Elzéar Taschereau – Supreme Court justice from 1878–1906 and its Chief Justice as of 1902 – to the "monojurality" of Pierre-Basile Mignault – also a Supreme Court justice, from 1918 to 1929. According to Howes:

> [T]he conceptual world of Taschereau is practically unthinkable to us – educated, as we are, on the other side of the Mignault divide. [...] What is meant by the term "polyjurality" is a tendency to regard other legal traditions (or cultures) as presenting "alternatives *for* us" as opposed to "alternatives *to* us." The latter disposition, with all the exclusivity it implies, is more characteristic of Mignault, given his emphasis on preserving intact "*la pureté de notre droit*" ["the pureness of our law"].[79]

The fundamental difference lay in Taschereau's openness to source eclecticism, normative diversity and universal concepts, as against Mignault's exclusive and hermetic interest in the specific place, time, and rules embodied in the CCLC.

Mignault was a central figure in the history of Quebec provincial rights. According to Robert Yalden, he "would eventually rise to a position of unquestioned authority in Quebec's legal community,

[... and] quickly became known as an ardent advocate of the importance of preventing common law from infecting the integrity of the *Code civil*."[80] In line with Baker's hypothesis concerning the *Civil Code* being both a liberal and a provincialist document, Mignault "stressed that private law, the *Code*, and property and civil rights were all one thing, while public law was another."[81] With respect to the constitution, furthermore, as Baker noted, to advocate for a broad reading of the *Civil Code* was ipso facto to do likewise for section 92(13) of the BNA *Act* on "property and civil rights." Hence, it is paradoxically the very anachronism inherent in liberalism's positivistic insistence on universal rules that served Quebec provincial nationalists so well in their efforts to particularize them to a specific ethnic group.[82] That anachronism enabled them to all but erase the *Code*'s liberal roots and replace them with nationalistic ones.[83] As a result, rewriting of history effectively fuelled artificial amalgamations of private, provincial, Catholic, and French-Canadian law as against its public, federal, Protestant, and English-Canadian opponent. These amalgamations were to have dramatic effects with respect to the federal government's burgeoning public-law powers. The change explains why, in Quebec, federalist socialists, as of the early 1930s, found themselves fighting against provincial nationalists, without immediately grasping why, nor how big an obstacle they faced.[84]

SOCIAL LEGISLATION, THE *CIVIL CODE*, AND THE CONSTITUTION IN THE 1930S

As was the case in other North-Atlantic jurisdictions, debate raged in Canada and Quebec during the interwar period over what to do about the "social question," that is, the increasingly organized working classes. Just two days after the Winnipeg General Strike came to an abrupt close at the end of June 1919, the International Labour Office was set up in Europe as part of the Versailles peace treaty in a bid to counter revolutionary movements through piecemeal legislation in matters of workers' compensation and social insurance.[85] Unlike elsewhere, however, in Canada, the constitution came to overdetermine the result of that debate, in no small part owing to the successful rebranding of the *Civil Code of Lower Canada* as a cultural artifact. In a brilliant sleight of hand, its classical liberal vision of the respective roles of the state, the Church, and the family were purported by cultural nationalists to be an essential feature of French-Canadian society rather than an essential feature of the laissez-faire society which much of Canada shared. In other words, during the Great Depression, when social questions became urgent, the *Civil Code* continued to do double duty as a government regulation inhibitor writ large and as a nationalist bastion against federal incursions into Quebec's social ordering. As a result, 1930s federalist social welfare advocates were on a collision course with Quebec nationalists, and social legislation came to be entangled in constitutional relations with that province for decades to come.[86]

According to legal sociologist Jean-Guy Belley, the specificity of the modern history of legal processes is their takeover by the state.[87] For his part, Fecteau considered that it was only in the 1930s that one saw the beginning of the "destruction of the old model based on charity in favour of the promotion of *social rights*, understood as legitimate manifestations of fundamental needs that are attached to the person as a member of the social body."[88] To Belley, it was not just that the state gained in strength, but that it won the battle to define the very content of the law.[89] Before the advent of the welfare state, public authority controlled a conglomerate of territorial jurisdictions, while leaving mostly intact the power of private economic, religious, or associational authorities.[90] It is only by placing the constitutional debates of the 1930s into the context of such fundamental shifts that one can fully understand them, as well as the fierce opposition that was mounted in favour of the status quo. Given the federal structure of the Canadian state, the constitution was a battleground for antiregulation movements.

Baker's insights into the classical liberal roots shared by the Ontario and Quebec provincial-rights movements, and the role that the *Civil Code* played in furtively carrying on that intellectual framework, go a long way towards explaining how the province of Quebec became the leading opponent to the Canadian welfare state until the late 1950s. This requires explanation, since such opposition was by no means limited to Quebec.[91] Indeed, that the *Civil Code* played any role at all in the debate about the place of government in society needs to be investigated, since the "night-watchman state" liberalism it embodied was broadly shared in common law provinces, which of course had no such document. The influence of the Catholic Church in Quebec is certainly part of the explanation, though its counterparts in English Canada were traditionally no less averse to state intervention in welfare work.[92] As Baker explained, the *Civil Code* presented itself as a cultural artifact, but the mission it accomplished with respect to the role of the state was economic and political: it tied a certain conception of the state to an essentialized version of Quebec culture. As Jean-Marie Fecteau noted, "this tendency took the shape of a veritable cult surrounding the *Civil Code*, which was seen as not only the safeguard of language and mores, but also of liberty and of justice vis-à-vis the state."[93]

The main constitutional story to be told about the 1930s in Canada, then, is not one of Dominion-provincial relations, though admittedly they provide the unavoidable backdrop to some of the most important policy events of the decade. The primary plot is in fact the unprecedented move toward government intervention and the fierce and partially successful opposition thereto, notably by lawyers and judges who successfully used legal liberalism, in the guise of provincial rights, against the state.[94] Baker reminded us that, "[s]ince [classical] liberalism entails maximizing the freedom of self-regarding individuals, legal liberalism is devoted to specifying the boundaries between one right holder and another, and the boundaries between public power and private rights."[95] The late nineteenth-century legal liberalism that socialists confronted in the 1930s was one which had "involved formalizing and systematizing legal theory, and thus trivializing comparative jurisprudence by recasting it as a mere study of analytical differences among discrete systems of positive law."[96] As Maurice Tancelin has put it: "Democracy is not just a matter of public law. The distinction between private and public law is not a break; the two are inseparable, like the substance of civil law and the rules of procedure."[97] What constitutionalists too readily omit is the struggle that took place over where to redraw the line between public and private law in the face of the widespread and profound discrediting of the liberal framework.[98] This omission is understandable, but it should be addressed, in view of the notorious difficulties scholars face when broaching such specialized topics.[99]

When Frank Scott, a socialist law professor, and his colleagues at the League for Social Reconstruction, started advocating for strong federal social programs in the early 1930s, they were destined to hit the culturalist wall that Mignault and others had patiently been building. Scott's socialism was not just incidental to his constitutional views in the 1930s, it was their very basis.[100] Furthermore, as we have seen, Mignault's use of the *Civil Code* was in part in its capacity to serve as a public-law inhibitor. Their opposition, however, took place on the constitutional battlefield: Scott forcefully argued for federal jurisdiction under "Peace, Order and Good Government" (s. 91) and treaty (s. 134) powers, whereas Mignault and other nationalists in Quebec defended an expansive understanding of private-provincial law by way of the sanctification of the provincial *Civil Code* as a cultural artifact.[101]

From Baker's perspective, to be able to adequately understand the history of "legal looking things," one needed to take into account not only the fact that "law is a relatively discrete 'cultural field,'" but also that its practitioners comprise a "'semi-autonomous social sphere' or a 'local culture.'"[102] On a higher theoretical level, he saw the positivistic stance he denounced as being itself historically situated. In line with that theory, Scott's and Mignault's opposing constitutional strategies commanded radically different approaches to legal interpretation: while Scott had to overcome formalistic interpretations of the BNA *Act* by the Judicial Committee of the Privy Council, the anachronism inherent in positivism served Mignault well.[103] Though, as Baker remarked, law can be autonomous, and probably often is on minor points, the extent of its autonomy is variable, especially when the stakes are high.[104] Unlike the US, Canada had no power over its highest court, much to the chagrin of federalist socialists like Scott who aspired to, at the very minimum, FDR-type social reform. In the 1930s, Scott and his allies attempted without success to re-instrumentalize what had become a formalistic and staid interpretation of the constitution.[105] It is no coincidence that one of Scott's first speeches on the question, written in 1929 or 1930, lamented the irony of the fact that, while "[t]he American federal government, though faced with the historical handicap of interstate rivalries and the constitutional handicap of state residuary powers [...] has largely overcome the doctrine of state rights [... in] Canada the development [...] has taken the opposite course."[106]

Indeed, Scott effectively anticipated Baker's thesis by half a century, and Baker probably owed at least some of his understanding to his discussions with Scott at the McGill Faculty of Law.[107] Testifying in front of the Special Committee on the *British North America Act* in March 1935, Scott denounced the fact that business leaders and their lawyers, posing as champions of provincial rights, had highjacked the debate about the place of government in the social sphere:

> Within the past decade or so I think there has been a movement in Canada towards the idea that there must be greater state regulation of industry. [...] I think it fair to say that the larger business interests oppose the idea of regulation. Hence the large economic interests in Canada are instinctively on the side of provincial rights, since regulation of business by provinces would necessarily be less effective and less extensive than regulation by the Dominion. We may note that Canada's two most highly industrialized provinces; namely, Quebec and Ontario, have been the strongest upholders of the doctrine of provincial rights in recent years. The fact that an essentially English-speaking province like Ontario has backed the provincial-rights theory shows that there is much more in it than can be explained in terms of race, and I suggest that considerable support for it comes from economic groups that are thinking of their personal freedom from state interference rather than of any constitutional right.[108]

Though Scott certainly abhorred what he considered to be a "fascist" turn in then contemporary Quebec politics, what annoyed him more fundamentally was what he saw as the dressing up of Quebec provincial-rights rhetoric with the clothes of French-Canadian or Catholic cultural nationalism, or both.[109] To him such framing was a red herring: in bringing to the fore cultural and religious principles, antisocial forces in Quebec were distracting francophones from the economic foundation of social problems, which transcended both culture and religion.

According to Baker, Scott "disparaged [the provinces'] ability in resolve or resources to build the welfare state of which he dreamed, and he thought that it was too easy for morally-challenged people like Maurice Duplessis to become big fish in those small ponds."[110] In a later text, Scott summed up the problem he apprehended with the following quotation by economist Burton S. Keirstead, to whom "Quebec [could not] maintain its cultural values intact by attempting to maintain a separate economy and distinct political entity, for the provincial area [was] inadequate for proper economic controls and the Quebec economy would continue to reflect the exploitation and instability of the national economy."[111] Scott's chief worry was that provinces as entities were too small in the vast North-American economy to be able to regulate economic forces in any meaningful way.[112] This is what explains his insistence on the separation of the concept of provincial rights from that of minority rights: he believed that the latter, including those of francophone, Catholic Quebecers, would be better protected by a strong central government.[113]

As Sean Mills has explained, however, neither Scott nor his socialist colleagues fully grasped why, despite this apparent convergence of interests, there was so little support for their positions in Quebec.[114] Had Scott and his allies been more attuned to the cultural realities of French Canadians, perhaps they would have been better able to influence the fallout of the 1937 Privy Council decisions, which effectively saw five provincial *Union nationale* governments successfully stonewalling federal efforts in the field of social security up until 1960, though admittedly with considerable help from similarly conservative governments in other provinces, especially that of Ontario.[115] As regards the second half of the 1930s, such efforts coincided with the Quebec government's denunciation of the Special Committee's mandate, as well as that of the Rowell-Sirois Commission that followed it, on the grounds that centralization was their hidden agenda.[116] In a letter communicating Quebec's refusal to participate in the work of the commission, its spokesperson stated that "[d]espite the very skilful choice of terms used in the appointment order, it is clear that the Government of Canada intends to use your report, if your conclusions are appropriate, to introduce a measure to amend the constitution, in the direction of greater centralization. This goal becomes even clearer when referring to the deliberations of the Special Committee [of 1935]."[117] Similarly arguing in the sense of decentralization, the influential text written for the Rowell-Sirois Commission by Esdras Minville, a prominent French-Canadian intellectual, concludes with the statement that Quebec laws "are inspired by the social doctrine of the Roman Catholic Church and are based on the *Civil Code*," and that "this system of laws proves the particularist spirit of the province of Quebec and its attachment to a particular and traditional conception of social relations and their order."[118]

A little over ten years later, Scott saw the wall against which his and others' 1930s aspirations had been dashed. In a 1951 article in which he looked back upon the constitutional events of the two preceding decades, he identified two "political factor[s] in the problem of centralization," namely "the power relations existing between Quebec and Ottawa [... and] the power relationship between business and government."[119] Though he pointed out that these need not be necessarily related, in the context in which he was writing, he saw them to be formidable political allies.

Of the three guarantees granted French Canadians by the BNA *Act* that Scott identified – "language, denominational schools and the civil law" – it was the *Civil Code* which "seem[ed] to be most affected by centralization."[120] However, according to Scott, appearances were deceptive. He maintained that the real cause of the retreat of the civil law lay elsewhere, namely in the rise of government intervention, be it federal or provincial. He observed that between 1867 and the time at which he was writing, "the legislature of Quebec in the exercise of its autonomy […] adopted a truly formidable list of statutes which […] superimposed upon the civil law a body of new rules affecting or restraining its application. […] What is happening, and what nothing can prevent, is the emergence of new aspects of property and civil rights, which have to be dealt with on new principles not found in either the civil or the common law."[121] Behind cultural arguments, then, Scott saw this government regulation to be the autonomists' real target. Indeed, federal regulation was to him but a variation on the same kind of measures that had been gaining ground in provincial legislatures, for subjects "which clearly are of national scope and importance […] notably in relation to economic regulation, insurance against calculable risks of modern society such as old age and ill health, and international obligations."[122] In other words, to Scott, it was the emerging welfare state which was threatened by provincial autonomy.

The very next article in the *Canadian Bar Review* was by Louis-Philippe Pigeon, a provincial autonomist who had been the law clerk of the Quebec legislature under Liberal Premier Adélard Godbout and would later be appointed to the Supreme Court of Canada. His primarily technical arguments were nonetheless draped in cultural garb. To him:

> [L]aws have a cultural aspect; hence due consideration should be given in framing them to the character, condition and beliefs of those for whom they are made. Autonomy is designed for the very purpose of meeting this requirement. The French-speaking population of the province of Quebec is obviously the group of Canadian citizens specially interested in it. For them autonomy is linked up with the preservation of their way of life.[123]

What was principally being preserved in constitutional debates from the 1930s to the late 1950s was the autonomy to avoid state intervention in the field of social protection. According to social historian Martin Petitclerc, between 1921 and 1960, in Quebec, "the defence of the [taxpayer financed but privately operated] public assistance system became an essential condition for any party that aspired to power, and the conservatives who had a few years earlier denounced this 'intolerable' state intervention in the affairs of the Church became its strongest supporter."[124] This is the convoluted way in which the questions of social legislation in Canada and Quebec became embroiled in cultural and constitutional arguments.[125]

CONCLUSION

Baker liked to use the metaphor of the camel's nose in the tent – conveying the idea that once its nose is in, it is impossible to prevent the whole camel from following – and the cartoon below was taken from a question in one of his examinations regarding the "tory touch" hypothesis in Canadian politics, according to which the increased presence of the state in Canada as opposed to the United States is attributable to Canada's "Red Tory" heritage.[126] The phrase "tory touch" was coined by Louis Hartz as shorthand for the hypothesis that "while the United States is the perfect bourgeois fragment, the 'archetype' of monolithic liberalism unsullied by tory or socialist deviations, English Canada is a bourgeois fragment marred by non-liberal 'imperfections' – a tory 'touch,' and therefore a socialist 'touch.'"[127] The image of the government representing the camel in the business tent is particularly apt in communicating how Baker saw the transition from the utilitarian embrace of targeted government intervention in the middle of the nineteenth century to the defensive antiregulation liberalism at its end. As we have seen, the BNA *Act* played a crucial role in this opposition. Far from revealing a "Tory touch," the constitution's instrumentalization in social matters is indicative of a strong and enduring opposition by conservative forces to the rise of the welfare state, an opposition that paralleled the hostility in the United States against the New Deal.[128] Indeed, until the 1940s and perhaps as late as 1950, the United States was well ahead of Canada with respect to social legislation.[129] Socialists such as Frank Scott and his "agrarian socialist" CCF allies – and not "Red Tories" – were

/4

Mail political cartoon is intended to provide encouragement for persons contemplating this question.

Question 5 (33 1/3%)

British North American periodicals of the early-nineteenth century reflect great interest in, if not preoccupation with, the provision of public works. One letter-writer to the *Quebec Gazette* complained in 1817, that:

...5

Figure 14.2 | Satirical cartoon excerpted from Blaine Baker's 1983 fall legal history exam, by Edward L. Franklin in the *Globe and Mail*.

instrumental in making sure that the welfare state did not go the same way as it did south of the border, notwithstanding their multiple defeats.[130]

To Baker, from about the time of Confederation, business interests were starting to get nervous about the government's nose in their tent. He argued that the shift in "cultures of authority" of the late nineteenth century was intimately related to the intensification of the regulatory state in Canada. During this time, the judiciary as a whole saw its previously held power partially amputated through the rise of the executive branch's new administrative agencies and the non-judicial tribunals in which their decisions were upheld and enforced. Like the American "Commonwealth historians"[131] which he held in high regard, Baker spent an important part of his career attempting to pierce the veil of these new "statal" forms, to which his development of a completely original course at McGill University's Faculty of Law on the "administrative processes" of myriad public agencies attests.[132] He understood that it is only with such a "worm's-eye view" that one could truly grasp the fundamental shifts that had occurred in the government age. This is how he came to link democracy, "Rule of Law" ideology, elite lawyers, provincial rights, Quebec's *Civil Code*, and the welfare state. This kind of "lateral thinking" – a term he often used – is what made him thrive.

Baker identified the provincial-rights movements as being, at their core, defensive battles fought by the legal profession – and its wealthy business backers – against rising democratic demands and the new government institutions to which they gave shape. This "bird's-eye" view allowed him to see deep analogies between apparently unrelated movements in Ontario, Quebec, and beyond which few have attempted to analyze together. Just as scholarship on provincial rights in Ontario and *Civil Code* nationalism in Quebec have been kept artificially apart, so it has been for such constitutional debates as a whole and those pertaining to the size and role of the state, especially as regards social legislation. In unitary states, 1930s opposition to classical liberalism took the form of debate between, inter alia, socialism, Keynesianism, and social Catholicism.[133] In the case of Quebec and Canada, the most influential proponents of these ideas were principally identified by reference to where they stood on the federal-provincial divide, and the text of the BNA *Act* has loomed so large in constitutional historiography that it has overshadowed the substantive disagreements that fueled its divergent readings. To fully understand what was going on, one must be able to appreciate both the role that the rising welfare state played in the changing nature of constitutional arguments and the ways in which the constitution impeded the establishment of social rights.

NOTES

I am grateful to the editors for a close re-reading of this text and for having made this volume possible. I would particularly like to thank Brian Young and Dick Risk for their guidance throughout the many versions of this text over a long period of time. Thank you also to Rosemarie Bernard for allowing me to use her photograph of Baker and to Sammy Cheaib and the two external reviewers for helpful edits.

1 G. Blaine Baker, "Introduction. Quebec and the Canadas, 1760 to 1867: A Legal Historiography," in *Essays in the History of Canadian Law: Quebec and the Canadas*, edited by G. Blaine Baker and Donald Fyson (Toronto: University of Toronto Press, 2013), 3–95, 3.

2 Baker's academic archives, found both in his office at McGill and sent along from his home by his executor, were scanned in the spring of 2019 with the help of Genevieve Westgate, under the supervision of Ian C. Pilarczyk and Brian Young. Richard Janda organized access to the archives. Other sources are my own class notes and emails as well as those of colleagues who were kind enough to share them with me. These sources can be made available upon request.

3 The meaning of the "welfare state" is notoriously elusive. My working definition is centred on the state taking on a role in social matters which goes beyond charity. It is intimately connected to the development of "social rights," which in turn connote notions such as universalism and citizenship and which Baker would have said are "status-based." See Jean-Marie Fecteau, "Du droit d'association au droit social: Essai sur la crise du droit libéral et l'émergence d'une alternative pluraliste à la norme étatique, 1850–1930," *Canadian Journal of Law & Society* 12, no. 2 (1997): 143–57, especially 156n37. For early welfare measures, see Elisabeth Wallace, "The Origin of the Social Welfare State in Canada, 1867–1900," *The Canadian Journal of Economics and Political Science* 16, no. 3 (1950): 383–93.

4 See, e.g., Peter W. Hogg and Wade K. Wright, "Canadian Federalism, the Privy Council and the Supreme Court: Reflections on the Debate about Canadian Federalism," UBC *Law Review* 38, no. 2 (2005): 329–52: they briefly mention the Canadian New Deal and Medicare, as well as the

"benefits" of provincial "experimentation" in such matters, but the deeper links between the constitution and increased state involvement in social welfare are not pointed to. For its part, the historical literature dealing with the welfare state cannot ignore the BNA *Act*. See Elsbeth A. Heaman, *A Short History of the State in Canada* (Toronto: University of Toronto Press, 2015) and Doug Owram, *The Government Generation: Canadian Intellectuals and the State 1900–1945* (Toronto: University of Toronto Press, 1986).

5 For example, two landmark parliamentary commissions on the constitution – the 1937 federal Rowell-Sirois commission and the 1953 Tremblay commission in Quebec – dealt extensively with social welfare matters during that time and the BNA *Act* was amended several times on social matters (in 1940, 1951, and 1964).

6 Daniel Wincott, "Social Policy and Social Citizenship: Britain's Welfare States," *Publius: The Journal of Federalism* 36, no. 1 (2006): 169–88, 169.

7 Jean-Marie Fecteau, "Prolégomènes à une études historique des rapports entre l'État et le droit dans la société québécoise, de la fin du XVIIIe siècle à la crise de 1929," *Sociologie et sociétés* 18, no. 1 (1986): 129–38, 135.

8 To this day, constitutional historiography follows this cultural divide, with only a few exceptions. See Hogg and Wright, "Canadian Federalism," 330.

9 For studies on the role of business in the implementation of "facilitative local legislation in expansively interpreted provincial jurisdictions," see G. Blaine Baker, "The Province of Post-Confederation Rights," *University of Toronto Law Journal* 45, no. 1 (1995): 77–100, 87n21. See also James R. Mallory, *Social Credit and the Federal Power in Canada* (Toronto: University of Toronto Press, 1954).

10 Baker, "Province."

11 Ibid., 98.

12 Baker cites Vipond: "[I]n attempting to account for one of the pivotal constitutional episodes in Canadian political history, most historians and political scientists have resorted to some extra-constitutional standard of explanation […] It must be emphasized that the provincial-rights movement was at base a constitutional movement. Its advocates realized that the thing they wanted […] depended on expressly constitutional reforms" (Baker, "Province," 86).

13 Baker, "Province," 92.

14 Like Baker, Jean-Marie Fecteau saw the increasing "insertion of law into society" from the middle of the nineteenth century as an ideological aspect of law in the government age that hindered historical knowledge. See Jean-Marie Fecteau, "Savoir historique et mutations normatives: Les défis

d'une nécessaire convergence entre droit et histoire," in *In the Eye of the Beholder*, edited by Pierre Noreau (Montréal: Thémis, 2007), 35–56, 47. See also G. Blaine Baker, "'So Elegant a Web': Providential Order and the Rule of Secular Law in Early Nineteenth-Century Upper Canada," *University of Toronto Law Journal* 38, no. 2 (1988): 184–205, 186–7 and "Professional Empires," (this unpublished paper is described below at note 37), 20n74. See also Robert W. Gordon, "Historicism in Legal Scholarship," *Yale Law Journal* 90, no. 5 (1981): 1017–56.

15 The quotation is from Robert W. Gordon, review of *Tort Law in America: An Intellectual History*, by G. Edward White, *Harvard Law Review* 94, no. 4 (1981): 903–18, 915. See also David Sugarman, "The Legal Boundaries of Liberty: Dicey, Liberalism and Legal Science," *Modern Law Review* 46, no. 1 (1983): 102–11.

16 Gordon, ibid.

17 On the question of American-style court-facilitated "judicial subsidization" of industrial development, Baker's unpublished LLM thesis explored how its paucity was more than compensated in the Canadian context by lawyer-heavy legislatures. See G. Blaine Baker, "Government Involvement in Economic Growth: Promotion to Regulation in Upper Canada, 1791-1875" (unpublished master's thesis, Columbia University, 1980). See also Baker, "Quebec and the Canadas," 23.

18 G. Blaine Baker, "Strategic Benthamism: Rehabilitating United Canada's Bar Through Criminal Law Codification, 1847–54," in *Essays in the History of Canadian Law, Volume X: A Tribute to Peter N. Oliver*, edited by Jim Phillips, R. Roy McMurtry, and John T. Saywell (Toronto: University of Toronto Press, 2008), 257–319. To Baker, such strategies had been devised to restore the respectability of legal institutions through the superficial emulation of the increasingly prestigious natural sciences. On respectability and its decline, see Baker, "So Elegant a Web."

19 Baker, "Quebec and the Canadas," 10.

20 Baker sets the transformation as having occurred between 1890 and 1920. See G. Blaine Baker, "The Reconstitution of Upper Canadian Legal Thought in the Late-Victorian Empire," *Law and History Review* 3, no. 2 (1985): 219–92, 221. David Howes writes of a slightly longer timeframe, from 1875 to 1929. See David Howes, "From Polyjurality to Monojurality: The Transformation of Quebec Law, 1875–1929," *McGill Law Journal* 32, no. 3 (1987): 523–58. For his part, Fecteau establishes the transition period as 1885–1929. See "Prolégomènes," 139. It is no coincidence that this corresponds to what Vipond has termed the "*laissez-faire* era [in the United States], that is roughly 1880–1930." See Robert C.

Vipond, "Alternative Pasts: Legal Liberalism and the Demise of the Disallowance Power," UNB *Law Journal* 39 (1990): 126–157, 141.

21 See Sugarman, "The Legal Boundaries of Liberty," 105. See also Fecteau who, writing with Europe in mind, stated that "[t]he 1860s, 1870s and 1880s saw the rapid development of a new, deeply undemocratic liberalism, which was suspicious of the state and the mechanisms of representation that had once been at the heart of the bourgeoisie's conquest of power. [...] Especially from the 1860s on, the formation of a *legal ideology*, often with scientific pretensions and always with an objectivist basis, aimed at transcending politics and compensating for its possible slippages" in "Du droit d'association au droit social," 149 and 156, my translation and emphasis. Baker uses the expression "modern Rule of Law" in Baker, "Professional Empires," 11.

22 See Baker, "Reconstitution," 222n9.

23 Baker, "Reconstitution," respectively 239, 285, 233, 277, 286. Howes links the Quebec and Ontario experiences: see Howes, "Polyjurality to Monojurality," 525n3. The deleterious formalism, introversion, and mutual suspicion that accompanied such a retreat were, in Baker's opinion, at the heart of the development of Canada's two "legal solitudes," which ultimately led to the sometimes-grave, never-deeply-buried constitutional conflict that has been a mainstay of Canadian politics ever since (Baker, ibid., 263–4). Robert Yalden argues that the powerful tradition of thought in Quebec which is bound up in the liberalism which generated the very *Civil Code* to which nationalists attempted to give a different meaning helps to explain why the separatist movement never succeeded in getting more traction: Robert Yalden, "Unité et Différence: The Structure of Legal Thought in Late Nineteenth-Century Quebec," *University of Toronto Faculty of Law Review* 46, no. 2 (1988): 365–89.

24 Baker, "Strategic Benthamism," 284: "Nativism became a powerful force across the North Atlantic world in the decades straddling the turn of the twentieth century, and made deep inroads into legal culture that should provide an organizing theme for social and intellectual histories of that later period."

25 Baker's "Canadian Legal History" syllabus contained a section on "legal nativism." The unit's supplemental reading list included international titles such as Richard A. Cosgrove, *Our Lady the Common Law: An Anglo-American Legal Community, 1870–1930* (New York: New York University Press, 1987); Hector MacQueen, "Legal Nationalism: Lord Cooper, Legal History and Comparative Law," *Edinburgh Law Review* 9, no. 3 (2005): 395–406; and Stephen Jacobson, "Law and Nationalism in

Nineteenth-Century Europe: The Case of Catalonia in Comparative Perspective," *Law and History Review* 20, no. 2 (2002): 307–47. It should be noted here that the very name *Civil Code of Lower Canada*, adopted twenty-five years after the abolition of the entity called "Lower Canada," speaks to the complex cultural positioning of that document from the start.

26 See Baker, "Professional Empires," 10 and "Quebec and the Canadas," 13.

27 G. Blaine Baker, "R.C.B. Risk's Canadian Legal History," in *Essays in the History of Canadian Law: In Honour of R.C.B. Risk*, edited by G. Blaine Baker and Philip Girard (Toronto: University of Toronto Press, 1981), 17–60, 34.

28 Baker, "Strategic Benthamism," 289. Baker's counter-intuitive use of the word "bureaucracy" here can be explained by the following citation regarding Upper Canada's system of government: "Since neither land ownership nor commerce could provide a sufficient basis for power or gentility, a provincial bureaucracy supplied and supported by the legal profession was widely affirmed on material as well as ideological and spiritual grounds as the most suitable keystone for the province's social pyramid" ("So Elegant a Web," 190).

29 Baker, "Professional Empires," 10–11.

30 See Baker, "Province," 79n7–8. We will turn to the Quebec version of this phenomenon in the next section.

31 Course notes, "Comparative Modern Legal History," McGill University, 5 October 2005.

32 Course notes, ibid. Compare Vipond, "Alternative Pasts," 139–47. Vipond describes how judicial review waxed at the same time as federal disallowance of provincial legislations waned, thanks to the establishment of the Supreme Court in 1875 and the strengthening of the reference case procedure, at the behest of provincial autonomists, in 1891. This amendment allowed judges to hear argument and required them to give detailed reasons for their decisions. See Charles Feldman, *Parliament and Supreme Court of Canada Reference Cases* (Ottawa: Library of Parliament, 2015).

33 Baker, "Professional Empires," 13.

34 Fecteau, "Du droit d'association au droit social," 149. See also Sugarman, "The Legal Boundaries of Liberty," 109–10: "For Dicey [...] the reconceptualisation of the law became imperative as [his] fear of Socialism and the breakdown of ordered government increased in the final decades of the nineteenth century." Dicey sought to form "conservative democracies," and to give constitutions based on popular sovereignty the "stability and permanence which [had] hitherto been found only in monarchical or

aristocratic states." He admired America for its referendums and legalistic spirit (the "Rule of Law") and wrote of "the consummation of the boundary theory of the common law." Fecteau notes that in Quebec, "this trend takes the form of a veritable *Civil Code* cult, which sees the *Code* as the guardian not only of language and mores, but also of freedom and justice against the state" (Fecteau, ibid., 149n17, my translation).

35 Vipond, "Alternative Pasts," 155.

36 Baker, "Province," 88–9.

37 The article's full title is "Professional Empires of Comparison and Authority: Élite-Building Conceptions of Central-Canadian Federalism." Baker mentions that "portions of this paper were presented to Duke University's Department of History and to the 1988 meeting of the Canadian Association of Law Teachers." He also states that research assistance was offered by Frank Denton and that he had received financial assistance from McGill's Faculty of Law. The introduction, which is a mere twenty-four pages of double-spaced typed text, nonetheless contains almost eighty extensive footnotes covering in themselves another twenty pages. In a 3 March 1988 letter to Patrick Glenn, Baker mentions that "[a]lthough the body of the essay is in various stages of incompletion and incoherence, the introduction does set out the themes I am developing and the methodology I think I am deploying, and also attempts to situate the study in relevant secondary literature." Throughout this article, page numbers refer to the only extant copy of the introduction, which was found in Baker's archives in his office, along with two accompanying folders of related research. Unfortunately, I was unable to find drafts of the other parts of the essay.

38 Baker, "Reconstitution." At about the same time, Baker had been working on G. Blaine Baker, Kathleen E. Fisher, Vince Masciotra, and Brian Young, *Sources in the Law Library of McGill University for a Reconstruction of the Legal Culture of Quebec, 1760–1890* (Montreal: Faculty of Law and Montreal Business History Project, 1987).

39 Baker, "Professional Empires," 11, 19–20. Baker provides supporting citations to "literature which treats these other arenas of conflict, but which rarely conceives of the processes of choosing among them as cultures of authority alternate to those of textual exegesis managed by élite lawyers" (Baker, ibid., 20n73).

40 It is worth comparing that approach with today's cooperative federalism. For a revealing plea for Canada to revert to "watertight" constitutional powers, see Asher Honickman, "Watertight Compartments: Getting Back to the Constitutional Division of Powers," *Alberta Law Review* 55, no. 1 (2017): 225–52.

41 Ibid., 12, 18.

42 Ibid.

43 Baker, "Professional Empires," 12–13. Similar laws were passed in the provinces.

44 For a detailed exploration of the divergent approaches to such questions in Parliament, I am indebted to one of the external reviewers for pointing me to Jonathan Swainger, *The Canadian Department of Justice and the Completion of Confederation, 1867–78* (Vancouver, UBC Press, 2000).

45 It is telling that Hogg and Wright, "Canadian Federalism" – which was written by two authors who are regularly cited by the Supreme Court on constitutional interpretation and history – does not even consider this question. Regarding Vipond's treatment of the issue, Baker thought that he "probably should have said more about the abolition […] of the practice of dual electoral representation" (Baker, "Province," 90).

46 Baker, "Professional Empires," 17. For an article that canvasses the various attempts to use section 94, including the one by the Canadian Bar Association, see L. R. MacTavish, "Uniformity of Legislation in Canada – An Outline," *Canadian Bar Review* 25, no. 1 (1947): 36–52. MacTavish notes that one of the five objects of the CBA upon its founding in 1891 was "to promote […] uniformity of legislation throughout Canada" (46).

47 Baker, ibid., 17. See Roderick Macdonald, "The National Law Programme at McGill: Origins, Evolution, Prospects," *Dalhousie Law Journal* 13, no. 1 (1990): 211–363.

48 Baker, ibid., 18.

49 Baker, "Province," 89. On the notion of the *Code* serving as "a prototype for federal uniformity under section 94 of the British North America Act," see "Reconstitution," 226–7 and 241–2. See also Howes, "Polyjurality to Monojurality," 528. For a typical example of the kind of text Baker was referring to, see Frank R. Scott, "Section 94 of the British North America Act," *Canadian Bar Review* 20 (1942): 525–44.

50 Baker, "Reconstitution," 272.

51 Baker to Verbauwhede, 18 December 2012.

52 Ontario patriotism is perhaps less well-known, though a recentring at the end of the nineteenth century on the British Empire is widely acknowledged. As an extreme example of patriotism, Baker points to the development of the "Canada First" movement, whose aims were to suppress Old World formalities and to promote self-government and anti-Americanism: see "Reconstitution," 270–2.

53 Baker noted however that what he considered to be its "nativist" context has been underemphasized. See Baker, "Province," 93.

54 See Brian Young, "Overlapping Identities: The Quebec *Civil Code* of 1866, Its Reception and Interpretation," in *Le Code Napoléon, un ancêtre vénéré? Mélanges offerts à Jacques Vanderlinden*, edited by Régine Beauthier and Isabelle Rorive (Brussels: Bruylant, 2004), 259–84; Jean-Gabriel Castel, "Le juge Mignault défenseur de l'intégrité du droit civil québécois," *Canadian Bar Review* 53, no. 3 (1975): 544–57; Sylvio Normand, "Un thème dominant de la pensée juridique traditionnelle au Québec: la sauvegarde de l'intégrité du droit civil," *McGill Law Journal* 32, no. 3 (1987): 559–601; Jean-Guy Belley, "Une croisade intégriste chez les avocats du Québec: La Revue du droit (1922–1939)," *Les Cahiers de droit* 34, no. 1 (1993): 183–217.

55 David Howes shared Baker's analysis of a late nineteenth-century transformation in both provinces: see "Polyjurality to Monojurality," 525n3. Paul Romney, a contemporary proponent of the provincial compact theory, saw the two movements as linked, but for very different reasons. See below.

56 Baker, "Quebec and the Canadas," 13.

57 See Mariana Valverde, *The Age of Light, Soap, and Water: Moral Reform in English Canada, 1885–1925* (Toronto: University of Toronto Press, 2008); Carolyn Strange and Tina M. Loo, *Making Good: Law and Moral Regulation in Canada, 1867–1939* (Toronto: University of Toronto Press, 1997); and Jean-Marie Fecteau, *The Pauper's Freedom: Crime and Poverty in Nineteenth-century Quebec* (Montreal: McGill-Queen's University Press, 2017).

58 One exception is Michael Mandel, who has noted that the "democratic critique of judicial review goes back a long time": Michael Mandel, "Against Constitutional Law (Populist or Otherwise)," *University of Richmond Law Review* 34, no. 2 (2000): 443–60, 444–5.

59 Baker, "Province," 95–6.

60 Paul Romney, *Getting It Wrong: How Canadians Forgot Their Past and Imperilled Confederation* (Toronto: University of Toronto Press, 1999), 136–143. Romney attacks the "Baker-Howes school" in "Very Late Loyalist Fantasies: Nostalgic Tory History and the Rule of Law in Upper Canada," in *Canadian Perspectives on Law and Society: Issues in Legal History*, edited by W.W. Pue and B. Wright (Ottawa: Carleton University Press, 1988). See also the writings of the French-Canadian academics cited in Hogg and Wright, "Canadian Federalism," 330n8.

61 Thus Romney for example cites the 1956 Tremblay Report on constitutional questions as another instantiation of the French-Canadian compact theory ("Provincial Equality" at 24). Following Baker, I would more

readily emphasize its anti-Keynesianism. As Quebec Premier Maurice Duplessis himself affirmed in 1946, "the issues […] are not racial issues; they are national issues; it is bureaucracy against democracy" (cited in Owram, *Government Generation*, 323). See note 5 above and the next section below.

62 Baker, "Province," 93. I am indebted to one of the external reviewers for pointing me to a stimulating discussion of similar themes in the French context: see Rémy Cabrillac, "Le Code Civil est-il la véritable constitution de la France?" *Revue juridique Thémis* 39 (2005): 245–59.

63 Baker, "Province," 95.

64 Excerpt from a letter by Baker to Eric Adams commenting on the latter's unpublished thesis: Eric M. Adams, "The Idea of Constitutional Rights and the Transformation of Canadian Constitutional Law, 1930–1960" (PhD diss., University of Toronto, 2009). As Brian Young has noted in his chapter in this collection, Baker devoted enormous amounts of time and energy to mentoring his students and giving advice to colleagues. The letter excerpted here – and indeed this entire essay – is a testimony to that otherwise invisible legacy. It is reproduced with permission from Dr Adams.

65 Ibid. It must be noted here that the change was more gradual than this citation suggests. See, in the context of employment law, Thierry Nootens, "Droit civil, condition ouvrière et transition au capitalisme industriel au Québec," *Canadian Journal of Law and Society*, no. 31 (2016): 47–64.

66 Ibid.

67 Ibid. One external reviewer noted that Baker mistakenly affirmed in his handwritten letter that "The final book of the draft *Code*, which dealt with commercial matters like banking, maritime matters and bills of exchange, was not enacted in 1866 because it had by then become clear that they would become federal prerogatives under the proposed BNA *Act*." However, the correction provided makes Baker's deeper point even more intriguing: "Actually, Book IV was enacted and came into force with the rest of the *Code*, but many sections were repealed in the 1870s by Canadian statutes on Maritime Law or by the *Bills of Exchange Act, 1890*."

68 Paul Romney, "Provincial Equality, Special Status, and the Compact Theory of Canadian Confederation," *Canadian Journal of Political Science* 32, no. 1 (1999): 21–39, 31; see 27: "while Loranger made no claims pertaining to francophone minorities outside Quebec, his language makes it clear that he visualized the provincial compact in national terms." The text cited is the translation of Thomas-Jean-Jacques Loranger, *Lettres sur*

l'interprétation de la constitution fédérale, dite l'Acte de l'Amérique britannique du nord, 1867 (Quebec, A. Coté et cie., 1883), first letter.

69 Romney, "Provincial Equality," 38.

70 Romney, *Getting it Wrong*, 137.

71 See Baker, "Province," 85.

72 Baker, "Professional Empires," 11.

73 Baker, "Reconstitution," 221.

74 Ibid., 263. See note 52 above on what Baker saw as the accompanying "Anglophilia" that took hold of the Ontarian bar.

75 Ibid., 241.

76 Ibid.

77 Fecteau, "Prolégomènes," 136, my translation.

78 Brian Young, *The Politics of Codification: The Lower Canadian Civil Code of 1866* (Montreal: McGill-Queen's University Press, 1994). See also John E.C. Brierley, "Quebec's Civil Law Codification, Viewed and Reviewed," *McGill Law Journal* 14, no. 4 (1968): 521–89. Baker, "Province," 94.

79 Ibid., 525, italics in the original.

80 Yalden, "Structure of Legal Thought," 383. See the citation in Howes, "Polyjurality to Monojurality," 551.

81 Yalden, "Structure of Legal Thought," 382n59.

82 Normand makes this point about anachronism in the conclusion to Sylvio Normand, "Le droit civil canadien de Pierre-Basile Mignault ou la fabrication d'un palimpseste," in *Le Faux en droit privé*, edited by Nicolas Kasirer (Montreal: Thémis, 2000), 133–54. See also Normand, "Un thème dominant"; Belley, "Croisade intégriste."

83 But see Yalden, "Structure of Legal Thought," on the surviving liberal streak in Quebec.

84 This is not to deny the role of the Catholic Church in Quebec and its vehement antisocialism. However, the compatibility of the Church's role with classical liberalism has been underestimated. See Jean-Marie Fecteau, "La dynamique sociale du catholicisme québécois au XIXe siècle : éléments pour une réflexion sur les frontières et les conditions historiques de possibilité du 'social,'" *Social History* 35, no. 70 (2002): 495–515. See also, in the Ontarian setting, with respect to Protestantism, Baker, "Province," 91: "one looks in vain [in the literature] for references to Ontarian moral fervour, evangelism, nativism, or the social gospel. That kind of integration would be helpful for purposes of reconciling moral regulation with the provincialists' commitment to private autonomy, and to reconfigure the idea of a minimal state with sectarian notions of social justice."

85 Sandrine Kott, "ILO, Social Justice and Communist Worlds: Competitions, Rivalries and Convergences," *Le Mouvement Social* 263, no. 2 (2018): 139–151.

86 This dynamic completely changed with the advent of the Quiet Revolution, as it had already done under Liberal Adélard Godbout from 1939–44, during which time article 91 of the BNA *Act* was amended to give the federal government jurisdiction over unemployment insurance. Other notable changes during that term were women's right to vote on the provincial level, free elementary education, and the creation of Hydro Quebec.

87 Jean-Guy Belley, interview, 17 June 2015. See also Jean-Guy Belley, "Le 'romantisme juridique': la réception du droit social dans la pensée juridique traditionnelle en France et au Québec," in *Droits, liberté, démocratie*, edited by Jocelyne Lamoureux (Montreal: ACFAS, 1991), 33–43; Canada, Royal Commission on Economic Union and Development Prospects for Canada, *The Evolution of the State since the Great Depression of 1929 and the Role of Law*, by Jean-Marie Fecteau and Guy Rocher, Study no. 36 (Ottawa: Macdonald Commission, 1984).

88 Jean-Marie Fecteau, "L'émergence d'un réseau public d'établissements : régulation monopoliste et contraintes locales," in *Pour une approche critique du droit de la santé. Droit et matérialisation des politiques sociales*, edited by Andrée Lajoie and Patrick A. Molinari (Montreal : Presses de l'Université de Montréal, 1987), 103–53, 103–4, my translation; italics in the original.

89 Belley, "Romantisme juridique."

90 Ibid. The 1921 Public Assistance law in Quebec is a good example. The change related to how the system was financed: charitable institutions would henceforth be two-thirds funded by public bodies, yet private control remained intact.

91 See Owram, *Government Generation*, 322.

92 See Wallace, "Origin of the Social Welfare State," 389.

93 Fecteau, "Droit d'association au droit social," 149n17.

94 On the role of the Catholic Church, see note 84 above.

95 Baker, "Reconstitution," 263n137.

96 Ibid.

97 Maurice A. Tancelin, *Des obligations en droit mixte du Québec* (Montreal : Wilson & Lafleur, 2009), 1034.

98 This is the implicit ideological issue in the 1937 JCPC decisions: was unemployment insurance actually "insurance" or something entirely new?

Had labour law become a national concern rather than an individual contract between employer and employee? Etc.

99 On this issue, see Donald Fyson, "Les historiens du Québec face au droit," *Revue juridique Thémis* 34 (2000) : 295–328. On the lack of acknowledgment of the growth of the state in legal history, see Cory Verbauwhede, "Jean-Marie Fecteau et l'histoire du droit en 3D," *Bulletin d'histoire politique* 25, no. 1 (2016): 25–38. But see Normand, "Un thème dominant"; Richard C. B. Risk, "Lawyers, Courts, and the Rise of the Regulatory State," *Dalhousie Law Journal* 9, no. 1 (1984): 31–54, 31.

100 That is not to say, however, that one should regard them as merely instrumental, as historian Michiel Horn came close to doing: Michiel Horn, "Frank Scott, The League for Social Reconstruction, and the Canadian Constitution," in *Canadian Constitutionalism: 1791–1991*, edited by Janet Ajzenstat (Ottawa: Canadian Study of Parliament Group, 1992), 213–23. See also Michiel Horn, *The League for Social Reconstruction: Intellectual Origins of the Democratic Left in Canada 1930–1942* (Toronto: University of Toronto Press, 1980); Sandra Djwa, *The Politics of the Imagination: A Life of F.R. Scott* (Toronto: McClelland and Stewart, 1987).

101 For Scott, see Frank R. Scott, *Social Reconstruction and the BNA Act* (Toronto: Thomas Nelson & Sons 1934) and Baker, "Province," 88–90; for Mignault, see Normand, "Un thème dominant" and Belley, "Croisade intégriste."

102 Baker, "Professional Empires," 20. Baker cites Sally Falk Moore, *Law as Process: An Anthropological Approach* (London: Routledge & Kegan Paul, 1978), 59–65 and Clifford Geertz, *Local Knowledge: Further Essays in Interpretive Anthropology* (New York: Basic Books, 1983).

103 See note 82 above.

104 A stark example of just how little autonomy it can have is the jurisprudential about-face of the American Supreme Court following Franklin D. Roosevelt's 1937 "court-packing" bill that had been designed to break that court's staunch opposition to his New Deal policies.

105 See also John T. Saywell, *The Lawmakers: Judicial Power and the Shaping of Canadian Federalism* (Toronto: University of Toronto Press, 2002), 187–237. On formalism and the Constitution, see Patrick J. Monahan, "At Doctrine's Twilight: The Structure of Canadian Federalism," *University of Toronto Law Journal* 34, no. 1 (1984): 47–99.

106 Frank R. Scott, "Political and Judicial Institutions of Canada and the US" (National Archives of Canada, Francis Reginald Scott Fonds, MG 30,

D211, Vol. 1, Articles 1930), 8. A hand-written note on the document indicates that the speech may have been given in 1929.

107 See Baker, "Province," 88.

108 Canada, Special Committee on the BNA *Act*, *Proceedings, Evidence, and Report* (Ottawa: The Special Committee, 1935), 82. Scott was testifying on the invitation of CCF MP J.S. Woodsworth: see 45. Scott is by no means unique in having linked provincial-rights movements with oligopolistic capitalism, though he may have been the first. See James R. Mallory, "The Five Faces of Federalism," in *The Future of Canadian Federalism*, Paul-André Crépeau and Crawford B. Macpherson (Toronto: University of Toronto Press, 1965), 3–15.

109 On Scott's views on "fascism" in Quebec, see Sean Mills, "When Democratic Socialists Discovered Democracy: The League for Social Reconstruction Confronts the 'Quebec Problem,'" *Canadian Historical Review* 86, no. 1 (205): 53–81. Scott's use of that term was not limited to Quebec politicians, as he used similar language in 1939 to denounce Ontario's leaders when they attacked LSR member Frank Underhill. See Frank R. Scott, "Fascism in Ontario" (National Archives of Canada, Francis Reginald Scott Fonds, MG 30, D211, Vol. 1, Academic Freedom: Correspondence 1938-1950).

110 Baker to Adams, see note 64 above.

111 Quoted in Frank R. Scott, "Centralization and Decentralization in Canadian Federalism," *Canadian Bar Review* 29, no. 10 (1951): 1095–1125.

112 Socialists like Scott were not the only ones to make this kind of argument. W.P. Kennedy also feared that the powers and the independence of the provinces could be exploited by "vast economic interests." See Richard C.B. Risk, "Canadian Law Teachers in the 1930s: When the World Was Turned Upside Down," *Dalhousie Law Journal* 27, no. 1 (2004): 1–54, 28.

113 See his testimony to the 1935 Special Committee on the BNA *Act*. See also Scott, "Centralization and Decentralization."

114 Mills, "Democratic Socialists."

115 Owram, *Government Generation*, 322–3. The five terms were 1936–1939; 1944–1948; 1948–1952; 1952–1956; 1956–1960. On how Prime Minister Mackenzie King used the Quebec-Ontario opposition to the post-war welfare state to further his own liberal agenda, see Alvin Finkel, "Paradise Postponed: A Re-Examination of the Green Book Proposals of 1945," *Journal of the Canadian Historical Association* 4, no. 1 (1993): 120–42.

116 See René Durocher, "Maurice Duplessis et sa conception de l'autonomie provinciale au début de sa carrière politique," *Revue d'histoire de l'Amérique française* 23, no. 1 (1969) : 13–34. It is worth noting that the 1939 Royal Commission, like the Special Committee, was also set up further to a CCF-Woodsworth initiative. See Grace MacInnis, *J.S. Woodsworth: A Man to Remember* (Toronto: The Macmillan Company of Canada, 1953), 183.

117 Louis-Émery Beaulieu, "Déclaration du gouvernement du Québec," 3 (National Archives of Quebec, 1960-01-483 \ 687), my translation.

118 Canada, Royal Commission on Dominion-Provincial Relations, *La législation ouvrière et le régime social dans la province de Québec*, by Esdras Minville, appendix V of the report (Ottawa: Rowell-Sirois Commission, 1939), 5. According to Martin Petitclerc, "the National Union government [...] presented the public assistance system as a nationalist identity referent until the very end of the 1950s. [...] In this regard, the essential document is Esdras Minville's brief to the Rowell-Sirois Commission in the late 1930s." See Martin Petitclerc, "'Je ne serais ni Bleu ni Rouge, je serais de la Commission des Assurances Sociales ...': L'impartialité de la commission Montpetit à l'épreuve de la partisanerie politique dans le Québec des années 1930," *Bulletin d'histoire politique* 23, no. 3 (2015): 38–59, 41; 50n56, my translation.

119 Scott, "Centralization and Decentralization," 1122.

120 Ibid., 1123–4.

121 Ibid.

122 Ibid.

123 Ibid., 1134.

124 Petitclerc, "Ni Bleu ni Rouge," 41, my translation.

125 In Quebec, the Quiet Revolution of the 1960s changed the underlying political logic dramatically and inaugurated a period in which nationalism and generous social programs went hand in hand. This created the opposite constitutional dynamic, in which the federal and Quebec governments, for a time, vied to provide the highest level of social protection.

126 The term "Tory touch" was coined in Louis Hartz, *The Founding of New Societies: Studies in the History of the United States, Latin America, South Africa, Canada, and Australia* (New York: Harcourt, Brace and World, 1964).

127 Gad Horowitz, "Conservatism, Liberalism, and Socialism in Canada: An Interpretation," *The Canadian Journal of Economics and Political Science* 32, no. 2 (1966): 143–71, 148.

128 See Jennifer Klein, *For All These Rights: Business, Labor, and the Shaping of America's Public-Private Welfare State* (Princeton: Princeton University Press, 2003).

129 See Bruno Théret, *Protection sociale et fédéralisme: l'Europe dans le miroir de l'Amérique du Nord* (Montreal: Presses de l'Université de Montréal, 2002), 144–54. See also Antonia Maioni, *Parting at the Crossroads: The Emergence of Health Insurance in the United States and Canada* (Princeton: Princeton University Press, 1998).

130 See Seymour Martin Lipset, *Agrarian Socialism: The Cooperative Commonwealth Federation in Saskatchewan: A Study in Political Sociology* (Berkeley: University of California Press, 1950), which argues that there was a similarly strong movement in the northwestern American states. Owing in part to the inability of third-parties to gain any leverage at the national level, contrary to Canada, that movement was never able to influence policy in a significant way.

131 See, e.g., Milton S. Heath, *Constructive Liberalism: The Role of the State in Economic Development in Georgia to 1860* (Cambridge: Harvard University Press, 1954); Louis Hartz, *Economic Policy and Democratic Thought: Pennsylvania, 1776–1860* (Cambridge: Harvard University Press, 1948); Oscar Handlin and Mary Flug Handlin, *Commonwealth: A Study of the Role of Government in the American Economy: Massachusetts, 1774–1861* (New York: New York University Press, 1947). Baker understood these scholars as former New-Deal administrators and academics who had become disillusioned by the conservative turn of US politics in the late 1940s and beyond, and who were seeking to influence public policy by arguing that the nineteenth century was not the heyday of liberalism that the neoliberals were arguing it had been.

132 The course named "The Administrative Process" (PUB-2 400) was last taught at McGill University in the winter session of 2018, and as far as I know it is the only course of its kind taught in Canadian law faculties. It radically differs from its sister course, "Judicial Review of Administrative Action" (PUB-2 401), in that it takes the administrative agency's perspective rather than that of the court whose task it is to review the agency's decisions.

133 See Fecteau, "Du droit d'association au droit social," 156.

APPENDIX

University of Toronto Faculty of Law
Legal Process (LAW100HIS – Four Credits)
First Year – Winter 2019

Professor Blaine Baker

1. SYNOPSIS

This course is an introduction to normative thinking, dispute pre-emption and resolution, and processes of civil litigation. It begins with a look at interfaces among informal, facilitative, state, and stateless law. It then turns to lawyers' roles in conflict management, especially the ethical and financial constraints on those roles. It will then consider, as a large case-study of dispute management, the regulations, statutes, and common-law doctrines that govern the grounds on which parties and claims can be heard in or excluded from courts (the law of standing, justiciability, intervention, limitation periods, and re-litigation). That discussion will lead to consideration of strategic behavior in civil litigation (around issues of jurisdiction, preliminary relief, discovery, confidentiality, and summary judgment). The material on civil procedure concludes with a look at class actions, a relatively new way of addressing harms for which conventional litigation may not be suitable or in respect of which political lobbying has failed. The course then turns to select topics in "alternative" dispute resolution, including power balancing by facilitators and decision-makers, collaborative law practice, and restorative justice.

II. CLASS MEETINGS

Class meetings will be held [blank]. No detailed syllabus, other than this outline and the class-by-class reading lists of required and supplemental material contained in it, will be distributed for the course. The order and rate at which material will be discussed in class is negotiable, and specific articles or primary legal sources will be identified from the reading list for consideration on a class-by-class basis, a week or two in advance of the session in which they will be taken up. It is important that students do their best to attend classes and prepare reading assignments in advance of them. It should generally be adequate for each student to prepare the "required" readings for each class, and to contribute appropriate commentary to group discussion. I also undertake to prepare assignments in advance of class, and to offer suitable commentary. In the event that a student is unable to be prepared for class, which will happen from time to time, I would appreciate having that situation brought to my attention in confidence before the outset of the relevant class session.

III. INSTRUCTOR CONTACT

My University of Toronto Faculty of Law office is Room 207 of Falconer Hall at 84 Queen's Park. I will generally be there on Tuesdays, Thursdays, and Saturdays in the winter term of the 2018-19 academic year (otherwise, I will be there by chance), and students are welcome in the office at those times without appointments. I can be reached in that office by telephone at 416-946-3755 (leaving phone-mail messages if necessary), or by e-mail at <blaine.baker@mcgill.ca>. I will also put aside time after each of the appointed class sessions for informal, small-group, or one-on-one conversations.

IV. EVALUATION

Evaluation in this course will be by way of an in-term research paper written from secondary sources (about 1,800 words), elaborating beyond the required readings on one or another of the twenty-four topics covered in class and worth one-third of each student's final grade. I will provide suitable, individually-oriented guidance for those projects, if that guidance is sought. Those in-term papers must be submitted by the due-date for written work in the second term of the 2018-19 academic year. A twelve-hour, take-home examination (about 3,600 words), worth two-thirds of each student's final grade, will be administered any time between the first day of the examination period and the due date for written work in the second term of the 2018-19 academic year (see 'University of Toronto Faculty of Law Take-Home Policy' for details). My practice is to provide four questions, and ask that students answer any two of them. A couple older exams I have given in this course can be found on Bora Laskin Law Library Reserve.

V. TEACHING/LEARNING MATERIALS

The 900-page (!!!) prototype for teaching/learning materials in courses like this one is C.A. Auerbach, *The Legal Process: An Introduction to Decision-Making by Judicial, Legislative, Executive, and Administrative Agencies* (San Francisco, CA: Chandler Publishing, 1961). Because that course-pack has not been updated recently, and because there has never been a Canadian version of it, a list of (mostly) electronically-available "required" and (sometimes) electronically-available "supplemental" readings for this course, broken down on a theme-by-theme basis, is contained in this outline. And, although there are no assigned reference materials for the course, G. Furlong, *The Conflict Resolution Toolbox: Models and_Maps for Analyzing, Diagnosing, and Resolving Conflict* (Mississauga, ON: J. Wiley, 2005)*, R.N.M. Graham, *Legal Ethics: Theories, Cases, and Professional Regulation* (Toronto: Emond-Montgomery, 3rd ed., 2014), J. Macfarlane, *Dispute Resolution: Readings and Case Studies* (Toronto: Emond-Montgomery, 4th ed., 2016), P.M. Perrell and J.W. Morden, *The Law of Civil Procedure in Ontario* (Markham, ON: LexisNexis, 3rd ed., 2017), J. Walker, *et al., The Civil Litigation Process: Cases and Materials* (Toronto: Emond-Montgomery, 8th ed., 2016), J. Walker, *et al., Class Actions in Canada: Cases, Notes, and Materials* (Toronto: Emond-Montgomery, 2014), and J.B. White, *The Legal Imagination: Studies in the Nature of Legal Thought and Expression* (Chicago: University of Chicago Press, 1985) are widely-deployed teaching tools that can be used as reference sources and guides. The *Advocates' Quarterly* is the main local legal periodical that deals with legal process issues. The last section of the reading materials in this outline also contains a list of monographic and article-length bibliographies of general relevance to the course.

VI. CLASS-BY-CLASS READING ASSIGNMENTS (ASTERISKS MARK ELECTRONICALLY-AVAILABLE SOURCES)

1.) INFORMAL LAW – REQUIRED READING:

D. Jutras, "The Legal Dimensions of Everyday Life" (2001), 16 *Can. J. L. & Soc'y.* 45–64*.

S. Macaulay, "Non-Contractual Relations in Business" (1963), 28 *Am. Soc. Rev.* 55–67*.

1.) INFORMAL LAW – SUPPLEMENTAL READING:

L.L. Fuller, "Two Principles of Human Association" in J.R. Pennock and J.W. Chapman, eds., *Voluntary Associations (Nomos 11)* (New York: Athlone Press, 1969).

M. Galanter, "Justice in Many Rooms: Courts, Private Ordering, and Indigenous Law" (1981), 19 *J. Legal Pluralism & Unofficial L.* 1–48*.

A. Kaufman and L. Zacharias, "From Trust to Contract: The Legal Language of Managerial Ideology, 1920–1980" (1992), 66 *Bus. Hist. Rev.* 523–572*.

W.M. Reisman, *Law in Brief Encounters* (New Haven, CT: Yale University Press, 1999) *passim.*

2.) FACILITATIVE LAW – REQUIRED READING:

J. Lurie, "Private Associations, Internal Regulation, and Progressivism: The Chicago Board of Trade as a Case Study" (1972), 16 *Am. J. Legal Hist.* 215–238*.

C. Provis, "Honesty in Negotiation" (2000), 9 *Bus. Ethics* 3–12*.

2.) FACILITATIVE LAW – SUPPLEMENTAL READING:

W.E.B. Code, "The Salt Men of Goderich in Ontario's Court of Chancery: *Ontario Salt* v. *Merchant's Salt* and the Judicial Enforcement of Combinations" (1993), 38 *McGill L.J.* 517–624*.

C.M. Hanycz, *et al., The Theory and Practice of Representative Negotiation* (Toronto: Emond-Montgomery, 2008) *passim.*

J. Nyden, *et al., Getting to We: Negotiating Agreements for Highly Collaborative Relationships* (New York: Palgrave, Macmillan, 2013) *passim.*

N. Reynolds, "The New Neighbor Principle: Reasonable Expectations, Relationality, and Good Faith in Pre-Contractual Negotiations" (2017), 60 *Can. Bus. L. J.* 94–123*.

3.) "LOW" STATE LAW – REQUIRED READING:
C.A. Reich, "The New Property" (1964), 73 *Yale L. J.* 733–787*.
P.C. Weiler, "The Administrative Tribunal: A View from the Inside" (1976), 26 *U. Toronto L. J.* 193–214*.

3.) "LOW" STATE LAW – SUPPLEMENTAL READING:
J.A. Conley, "Doing it by the Book: Justice of the Peace Manuals and English Law" (1985), 6 *J. Legal Hist.* 257–298*.
P. Craven, *Petty Justice: Low Law and the Sessions System in Charlotte County, New Brunswick* (Toronto: University of Toronto Press, 2014) *passim**.
C.M. Flood and L. Sossin, eds., *Administrative Law in Context* (Toronto: Emond Publishing, 3rd ed., 2018) *passim.*
M. Gammage and M. Bay, "Settlement Conferences in the Ontario Small Claims Court" (2017), 46 *Advoc. Q.* 374–401*.

4.) "HIGH" STATE LAW – REQUIRED READING:
D. Sugarman, "The Legal Boundaries of Liberty: Dicey, Liberalism, and Legal Science" (1983), 46 *Mod. L. Rev.* 102–111*.
S.M. Waddams, *Introduction to the Study of Law* (Toronto: Carswell, 7th ed., 2013) 37–42, 59–69, 79–90, 97–106*.

4.) "HIGH" STATE LAW – SUPPLEMENTAL READING:
J.M. Brisson, *La formation d'un droit mixte: l'evolution de la procedure civile* (Montreal: Themis, 1986) *passim.*
N. Duxbury, *The Nature and Authority of Precedent* (Cambridge, UK: Cambridge University Press, 2008) *passim**.
P.W. Kahn, *Making the Case: The Art of the Judicial Opinion* (New Haven, CT: Yale University Press, 2016) *passim**.
M.J. McNamara, *From Tavern to Courthouse: Architecture and Ritual in American Law* (Baltimore, MD: Johns Hopkins University Press, 2004) 125–139.

5.) STATELESS LAW – REQUIRED READING:
J.P. Braithwaite, "Standard Form Contracts as Transnational Law" (2012), 75 *Mod. L. Rev.* 779–805*.
R. Michaels, "What is Non–State Law: A Primer" in M.A. Helfand, ed., *Negotiating State and Non-State Law: The Challenge of Global and Local Legal Pluralism* (New York: Cambridge University Press, 2015) 41–58*.

5.) STATELESS LAW – SUPPLEMENTAL READING:
H. Dedek and S. Van Praagh, eds., *Stateless Law: Evolving Boundaries of a Discipline* (Farnham, UK: Ashgate, 2015) *passim**.
"Symposium on Third-Party Funding" (2014), 55 *Can. Bus. L. J.* 1–196*.
T. Shultz, *Transnational Legality: Stateless Law and International Arbitration* (Oxford, UK: Oxford University Press, 2014) *passim**.
A.M. Slaughter, "Judges: Constructing a Global Legal System" in A.M. Slaughter, ed., *A New World Order* (Princeton, NJ: Princeton University Press, 2004) 65–103*.

6.) RECONCILING INFORMAL, SELF-MADE, ASSOCIATIONAL, STATE, AND STATELESS LAW – REQUIRED READING:
Highwood Congregation of Jehovah's Witnesses v. *Wall*, SCC 2018.
G. Marquis, "Doing Justice to British Justice: Law, Ideology and Canadian Historiography" in W.W. Pue and B. Wright, eds., *Canadian Perspectives on Law and Society* (Ottawa: Carleton University Press, 1988) 43–78*.

6.) RECONCILING INFORMAL, SELF-MADE, ASSOCIATIONAL, STATE, AND STATELESS LAW – SUPPLEMENTAL READING:
S.G. Drummond, *Incorporating the Familiar: An Investigation into Legal Sensibilities in Nunavik* (Montreal: McGill-Queen's University Press, 1997) *passim**.
A.J. Esau, *The Courts and the Colonies: The Litigation of Hutterite Church Disputes* (Vancouver: University of British Columbia Press, 2004) *passim**.
J. Macfarlane, *Islamic Divorce in North America: A Shari'a Path in a Secular Society* (Oxford: Oxford University Press, 2012) *passim**.
V.V. Palmer, *Mixed Jurisdictions Worldwide: The Third Legal Family* (Cambridge, UK: Cambridge University Press, 2001) *passim*.

7.) POPULAR CONFLICT MANAGEMENT – REQUIRED READING:
J. Kary, "Judgments of Peace: Montreal's Jewish Arbitration Courts, 1914–1976" (2016), 56 *Am. J. Legal Hist.* 436–489*.
B.D. Palmer, "Discordant Music: Charivaries and Whitecapping " (1978), 3 *Labour/Le Travail* 5, at 9–39*.

7.) POPULAR CONFLICT MANAGEMENT – SUPPLEMENTAL READING:
R.C. Ellickson, *Order Without Law: How Neighbors Settle Disputes* (Cambridge, MA: Harvard University Press, 1991) *passim**.

M. Morin, *et al., Les tribunaux et l'arbitrage en nouvelle France et au Quebec* (Montreal: Themis, 2012) *passim.*
W.E. Nelson, *Dispute and Conflict Resolution in Plymouth County, Massachusetts* (Chapel Hill: University of North Carolina Press, 1981) *passim.*
W.O. Weyrauch, ed., *Gypsy Law and Romani Legal Traditions* (Cambridge, UK: Cambridge University Press, 2001) *passim.*

8.) LAWYERS' CONFLICT MANAGEMENT – REQUIRED READING:

A.M. Dodek, "Regulating Law Firms in Canada" (2012), 90 *Can. B. Rev.* 383–440*.
M. Galanter and W. Henderson, "The Elastic Tournament: A Second Transformation of the Big Law Firm" (2008), 60 *Stan. L. Rev.* 1867–1929*.

8.) LAWYERS' CONFLICT MANAGEMENT – SUPPLEMENTAL READING:

J.P. Heinz, *et al., Urban Lawyers: The New Social Structure of the Bar* (Chicago, IL: University of Chicago Press, 2005) *passim.*
E.M. Iacobucci and M.J. Trebilcock, "An Economic Analysis of Alternative Business Structures for the Practice of Law" (2014), 92 *Can. B. Rev.* 57–104*.
D. Sugarman, "Simple Images and Complex Realities: English Lawyers and their Relationship to Business and Politics" (1993), 11 *Law & Hist. Rev.* 257–301*.
C. Wilton, "Introduction" in C. Wilton, ed., *Inside the Law: Canadian Law Firms in Historical Perspective* (Toronto: University of Toronto Press, 1996) 3–56.

9.) ETHICAL CONSTRAINTS ON LAWYERS' CONFLICT MANAGEMENT – REQUIRED READING:

R. Moorhead and V. Hinchly, "Professional Minimalism: The Ethical Consciousness of Commercial Lawyers" (2015), 42 *J. L. & Soc'y.* 389–412*.
M.A. Wilkinson, *et al.*, "Do Codes of Ethics Actually Shape Legal Practice?" (2000), 45 *McGill L. J.* 645–680*.

9.) ETHICAL CONSTRAINTS ON LAWYERS' CONFLICT MANAGEMENT – SUPPLEMENTAL READING:

J.S. Auerbach, *Unequal Justice: Lawyers and Social Change in Modern America* (New York: Oxford University Press, 1977) *passim**.

A.M. Dodek and A. Wooley, eds., *In Search of the Ethical Lawyer: Stories from the Canadian Legal Profession* (Vancouver: University of British Columbia Press, 2016) *passim**.
P.M. Sibenik, "The Black Sheep: The Disciplining of Territorial and Alberta Lawyers" (1988), 3 *Can. J. L. & Soc'y*. 109–139*.
R.A. Willie, "A Proper Ideal During Action: Fraternity, Leadership, and Lifestyle in Winnipeg Lawyers' Professional Culture" (1992), 27 *J. Can. Stud.* 58–72*.

10.) FINANCIAL CONSTRAINTS ON LAWYERS' CONFLICT MANAGEMENT – REQUIRED READING:
McIntyre Estate v. *Ontario (Attorney General)* (2002), 61 OR (3d) 257 (CA)*.
H.M. Kritzer, "Contingent Fee Lawyers and their Clients: Settlement Expectations, Settlement Realities, and Issues of Control in the Lawyer-Client Relationship" (1998), 2 *Law & Soc. Inq.* 795–821*.

10.) FINANCIAL CONSTRAINTS ON LAWYERS' CONFLICT MANAGEMENT – SUPPLEMENTAL READING:
C.E. Abela and N. Khan, "The Impact of Alternative Fee Structures on Settlement" (2017), 47 *Advoc. Q.* 26–37*.
F. Batlan, *Women and Justice for the Poor: A History of Legal Aid* (Cambridge, UK: Cambridge University Press, 2015) *passim*.
R. Engler, "Opportunities and Challenges: Non-Lawyer Forms of Assistance in Providing Access to Justice for Middle-Income Earners" in M.J. Trebilcock, *et al.*, eds., *Middle Income Access to Justice* (Toronto: University of Toronto Press, 2012) 145–154, 169–172*.
E.S. Knutsen and J. Walker, "What is the Cost of Litigating in Canada" in C. Hodges, *et al.*, *The Costs and Funding of Civil Litigation: A Comparative Perspective* (Oxford, UK: Hart, 2010) 239–260.

11.) DISPUTE SETTLEMENT – CHOICE OF LAW – REQUIRED READING:
C. Burke Robertson, "The Impact of Third-Party Financing on Transnational Litigation" (2011), 44 *Case West. Reserve Int'l. L. J.* 159–181*.

A. Eckhart, *et al.,* "Environmental Liability in Trans-border Harms: Law and Forum Choice" (2008), 24 *J. L. Econ. & Org.* 434–457*.

11.) DISPUTE SETTLEMENT – CHOICE OF LAW – SUPPLEMENTAL READING:

L. Collins, *Dicey and Morris on the Conflict of Laws* (London, UK: Sweet and Maxwell, 15th ed., 2012) *passim.*
R. Mortensen, "Homing Devices in Choice of Tort Law: Australian, British, and Canadian Approaches" (2006), 55 *Int'l. & Comp. L. Q.* 839–878*.
P.Nygh, *Choice of Forum and Laws in International Commercial Arbitration* (Boston, MA: Kluwer Law, 1997) *passim.*

12.) DISPUTE SETTLEMENT – CHOICE OF FORUM – REQUIRED READING:

M. Pavlovic, "Contracting out of Access to Justice: Enforcement of Forum-Selection Clauses in Consumer Contracts" (2017), 62 *McGill L. J.* 389–440*.
R.C. Vipond, "Alternative Pasts: Legal Liberalism and the Demise of Disallowance" (1990), 39 *U. New Brunswick L. J.* 126–157*.

12.) DISPUTE SETTLEMENT – CHOICE OF FORUM – SUPPLEMENTAL READING:

R.K. Agarwal and D. Fenton, "Litigation Funding Agreements Outside the Class Action Context" (2017), 59 *Can. Bus. L. J.* 1–30*.
G.B. Born, *International Arbitration and Forum Selection Agreements: Drafting and Enforcing* (The Hague: Kluwer Law, 5th ed., 2016) *passim.*
G. Saumier and J. Bagg, "Forum Selection Clauses Before Canadian Courts" (2013), 46 *U. Brit. Colum. L. Rev.* 439–487*.

13.) DISPUTE SETTLEMENT – STANDING TO SUE – REQUIRED READING:

J. Walker and L. Sossin, *Civil Litigation* (Toronto: Irwin Law, 2010) 54–63*.
Canadian Council of Churches v. *The Queen*, [1992] 1 SCR 236*.

13.) DISPUTE SETTLEMENT – STANDING TO SUE – SUPPLEMENTAL READING:

B.R.D. Alarie and A.J. Green, "Interventions at the Supreme Court of Canada: Accuracy, Affiliation, and Acceptance" (2010), 48 *Osgoode Hall L. J.* 381–410*.

G.B. Baker, "Legal Identity from Maine and Durkheim to Graveson, Tribe, and Vining" (1981), 19 *West. Ont. L. Rev.* 307–341*.

T.A. Cromwell, *Locus Standi: A Commentary on the Law of Standing in Canada* (Toronto: Carswell, 1986) *passim.*

W. Kymlicka, "Social Membership: Animal Law Beyond the Property/Personhood Impasse" (2017), 40 *Dalhousie L. J.* 123–156*.

14.) DISPUTE SETTLEMENT – GEOGRAPHIC VENUES IN WHICH TO SUE – REQUIRED READING:

A. Brighenti, "On Territory as Relationship and Law as Territory" (2006), 21 *Can. J. L. & Soc'y.* 65–86*.

Morguard Investments Ltd. v. *De Savoye*, [1990] 3 SCR 1077*.

14.) DISPUTE SETTLEMENT – GEOGRAPHIC VENUES IN WHICH TO SUE – SUPPLEMENTAL READING:

R.A. Brand and S.R. Jablowski, *Forum Non Conveniens: History, Global Practice, and Future under the Hague Convention on Choice of Court* (New York: Oxford University Press, 2007) *passim**.

T.C.W. Farrow, "Globalization, International Human Rights, and Civil Procedure" (2003), 41 *Alta. L. Rev.* 671–712*.

C. Kearney, "Case Comment: International Human Rights – Corporate Liability – Claims not Actionable under Alien Tort Statute – *Kiobel* v. *Royal Dutch Petroleum Co.*" (2011), 34 *Suffolk Trans. L. Rev.* 263–272*.

T.J. Monestier, "Jurisdiction and the Enforcement of Foreign Judgments" (2013), 42 *Advoc. Q.* 107–143*.

15.) DISPUTE SETTLEMENT – WHEN TO SUE – REQUIRED READING:

Consumers' Glass v. *Foundation Co. of Canada Ltd.* (1983), 51 OR (2d) 385 (CA)*

Novak v. *Bond*, [1999] 1 SCR 808*.

15.) DISPUTE SETTLEMENT – WHEN TO SUE – SUPPLEMENTAL READING:

Limitations Act, 2002, SO 2002, c. 24, Schedule B*.

B. Hovius, "Limitation Periods in Property Claims" (2015), 34 *Can. Fam. L. Q.* 281–302*.

G. Mew, *The Law of Limitations* (Toronto: LexisNexis, 2016) *passim.*

S.G.A. Pitell and J.M. Corbell, "Commencing Proceedings Just After the Limitation Period" (2008), 35 *Advoc. Q.* 265–283*.

16.) DISPUTE SETTLEMENT – PRE-LITIGATION DISCOVERY – REQUIRED READING:

Grossman v. *Toronto General Hospital* (1983), 146 DLR (3d) 280 (Ont. Gen. Div.)*.

J. Harr, *A Civil Action* (New York: Random House, 1995) 150–193 (three copies on Law Library course reserve).

16.) DISPUTE SETTLEMENT – PRE-LITIGATION DISCOVERY – SUPPLEMENTAL READING:

T.L. Archibald, *et al., Discovery in Canadian Common Law: Practice, Techniques, and Strategies* (Toronto: LexisNexis, 2017) *passim.*

J. Hollander, *Discovery Techniques: A Practical Guide to the Discovery Process in Civil Actions* (Toronto: Irwin Law, 2013) *passim.*

Rules of Civil Procedure, RRO 1990, Reg. 194, as amended, r. 30*.

S. Wortzman, ed., *E-Discovery in Canada* (Toronto: LexisNexis, 3rd. ed., 2017) *passim.*

17.) DISPUTE SETTLEMENT – PRIVILEGE AND CONFIDENTIALITY – REQUIRED READING:

E.S. Knutsen, "Keeping Settlements Secret" (2010), 37 *Florida State U. L. Rev.* 945–980*.

Ontario (Ministry of the Environment) v. *McCarthy, Tetrault* (1992), 9 CELR (NS) 12 (Ont. Prov. Ct.)*.

17.) DISPUTE SETTLEMENT – PRIVILEGE AND CONFIDENTIALITY – SUPPLEMENTAL READING:

A.M. Dodek, *Solicitor-Client Privilege* (Toronto: LexisNexis, 2014) *passim.*

P. Stanley, *The Law of Confidentiality: A Restatement* (Oxford, UK: Hart, 2008) *passim*.
G.D. Watson and F. Au, "Solicitor-Client Privilege and Litigation Privilege in Civil Litigation" (1998), 77 *Can. B. Rev.* 315–353*.

18.) A THEORY OF CLASS ACTIONS – REQUIRED READING:
P. Hayes, "Exploring the Viability of Class Actions Arising from Environmental Toxic Torts" (2009), 19 *J. Environ. L. & Prac.* 189–224*.
S. Issacharoff, "Class Actions and State Authority" (2013), 44 *Loyola U. Chi. L. Rev.* 369–390*.

18.) A THEORY OF CLASS ACTIONS – SUPPLEMENTAL READING:
S. Chiodo, *The Class Actions Controversy: The Origins and Development of Ontario's Class Proceedings Act* (Toronto: Irwin Law: 2018) *passim*.
H.P. Glenn, "Class Actions in Ontario and Quebec" (1984), 62 *Can. B. Rev.* 247–330*.
C. Jones, *Theory of Class Actions* (Toronto: Irwin Law, 2003) *passim**.
V. Scott, "Access to Justice and Choice of Law Issues in Multi-Jurisdictional Class Actions in Canada" (2012), 43 *Ottawa L. Rev.* 233–266*.

19.) CLASS ACTION MANAGEMENT – REQUIRED READING:
Cloud v. *Canada (Attorney General)* (2004), 247 DLR (4th) 667 (Ont. CA)*.
J. Walker, "Coordinating Multijurisdictional Class Actions Through Existing Certification Processes" (2005), 41 *Can. Bus. L. J.* 112–122*.

19.) CLASS ACTION MANAGEMENT – SUPPLEMENTAL READING:
J. Cassels and C. Jones, *The Law of Large-Scale Claims: Product Liability, Mass Torts, and Complex Litigation in Canada* (Toronto: Irwin Law, 2005) *passim**.
Class Proceedings Act, 1992, SO 1992, c.6*.
S. Ellman, "Client-Centeredness Multiplied" in G. Watson, *et al.*, eds., *The Civil Litigation Process* (Toronto: Emond-Montgomery, 5th ed., 1999).
Hollick v. *Toronto*, [2001] 3 SCR 158*.

20.) "ALTERNATIVE" DISPUTE RESOLUTION – REQUIRED READING:

O. Fiss, "Against Settlement" (1984), 98 *Yale L. J.* 1073, at 1075–1090*.
J. Macfarlane, "Why do People Settle?" (2001), 46 *McGill L. J.* 663–712*.

20.) "ALTERNATIVE" DISPUTE RESOLUTION – SUPPLEMENTAL READING:

P. Brooker, *Mediation Law: Journey through Institutionalism to Juridification* (Oxford, UK: Routledge, 2013) *passim**.
D.A. Hoffman and R.N. Wolman, "The Psychology of Mediation" (2013), 14 *Cardozo J. Conflict Res.* 759–806*.
T. McMorrow, "Learning to Mediate Through Teaching Mediation" in A. Rochette, ed., [2015] *Can. Legal Educ. Ann. Rev.* 49–70.
J. Webber, "Compelling Compromise: Canada Chooses Conciliation over Arbitration" (1991), 28 *Labour/Le Travail* 15–57*.

21.) CURRENT ISSUES – COLLABORATIVE LAW – REQUIRED READING:

S. Abney, "Moving Collaborative Law Beyond Family Disputes" (2014), 38 *J. Legal Prof.* 277–301*.
M. Keet, *et al.*, "Client Engagement Inside Collaborative Law" (2008), 24 *Can. J. Fam. L.* 145–171*.

21.) CURRENT ISSUES – COLLABORATIVE LAW – SUPPLEMENTAL READING:

C. Healy, *Collaborative Practice: An International Perspective* (New York: Routledge, 2018) *passim**.
S.R. Peppet, "The Ethics of Collaborative Law" (2008), 3 *J. Dispute Res.* 131–162*.
R.W. Shields, *et al.*, *Collaborative Family Law* (Scarborough, ON: Carswell, 2003) *passim*.
"Uniform Collaborative Law Rules and Uniform Collaborative Law Standards" (2014), 48 *Fam. L. Q.* 55–177*.

22.) CURRENT ISSUES – RESTORATIVE JUSTICE – REQUIRED READING:

J. Christe, "The Origins of Modern Restorative Justice: Five

Examples from the English-Speaking World" (2013), 46 *U. Brit. Colum. L. Rev.* 33–80*.
K. Stanton, "Canada's Truth and Reconciliation Commission: Settling the Past" (2011), 2(3) *Int'l. Indigenous Policy J.* art. 2 (20 pp.)*.

22.) CURRENT ISSUES – RESTORATIVE JUSTICE – SUPPLEMENTAL READING:
M.J. Klarman, *Brown v. Board of Education and the Civil Rights Movement* (New York: Oxford University Press, 2007) *passim**.
M. Liebman, *Restorative Justice* (London, UK: Jessica Kingsley, 2007) *passim*.
J.R. Miller, *Residential Schools and Reconciliation: Canada Confronts its History* (Toronto: University of Toronto Press, 2017) *passim*.
L. Mulcahy, "Telling Tales about Relational Contracts: How do Judges Learn about the Lived World of Contracts?" in D. Campbell, *et al.*, eds., *Changing Concepts of Contracts: Essays in Honour of Ian R. McNeil* (Bassingstoke, UK: Palgrave, Macmillan, 2013) ch. 7.

23.) CURRENT ISSUES – SUBSTANTIVE VS. JURIDICIAL EQUALITY – REQUIRED READING:
J. Leitch, "Coming off the Bench: Self-Represented Litigants, Judges, and the Adversarial Process" (2017), 47 *Advoc. Q.* 309–343*.
B. Miller, *et al.*, "Levelling the Odds: The Effect of Quality Legal Representation in Cases of Asymmetrical Capacity" (2015), 49 *Law & Soc'y. Rev.* 209–239*.

23.) CURRENT ISSUES – SUBSTANTIVE VS. JURIDICIAL EQUALITY – SUPPLEMENTAL READING:
M. Flaherty, "Self-Represented Litigants, Active Adjudication, and the Perception of Bias: Issues in Administrative Law" (2015), 38 *Dalhousie L. J.* 119–146*.
D. Flynn, "The Social Worker as Family Mediator: Balancing Power in Cases Involving Family Violence" (2005), 58 *Aust. Soc. Work* 407–418*.
O. Gazal Ayal, "Imbalances of Power in ADR: The Impact of Representation and Dispute-Resolution Method on Case Outcomes" (2014), 34 *Law & Soc. Inq.* 791–823*.

L. Ma, *et al.*, "National Survey of Tribunal Responsiveness to Self-Represented Parties" (2016), 29 *Can. J. Admin. L. & Prac.* 165–185*.

24.) OVERVIEW OF THE LEGAL PROCESS – REQUIRED READING:
D.M. Engel, *The Myth of the Litigious Society: Why We Don't Sue* (Chicago, IL: University of Chicago Press, 2016) chs. 8 and 10*.
W.B. Wendel, "The Limits of Positivist Legal Ethics" (2017), 30 *Can. J. L. & Jur.* 443–465*.

24.) OVERVIEW OF THE LEGAL PROCESS – SUPPLEMENTAL READING:
H.W. Arthurs, "Why Canadian Law Schools do not Teach Legal Ethics" in K. Economedes, ed., *Ethical Challenges to Legal Education and Conduct* (Oxford, UK: Hart Publishing, 1998) 105–118.
D. Bamford, *et al.*, "Learning the 'How' of the Law: Teaching Procedure and Legal Education" (2013), 51 *Osgoode Hall L. J.* 93–155*.
A.M. Dodek, "Canadian Legal Ethics: A Subject in Search of Scholarship" (2000), 50 *U. Toronto L. J.* 115–135*.
J. Macfarlane, *The New Lawyer: How Clients Are Transforming the Practice of Law* (Vancouver: University of British Columbia Press, 2nd ed., 2017) 191–242*.

25.) BIBLIOGRAPHIES OF LEGAL PROCESS SOURCES – SUPPLEMENTAL READING:
T.C.W. Farrow, "Dispute Resolution and Legal Education: A Bibliography" (2005), 7 *Cardozo J. Conflict Res.* 119–138*.
H. Smit, *Commercial Arbitration: An International Bibliography* (London, UK: Sweet, 1999) *passim.*
C. Spiegel, *Book by Book: An Annotated Guide to Young Peoples' Literature with Peace-Making and Conflict-Resolution Themes* (Cambridge, MA: Educators for Social Responsibility, 2010) *passim.*

Blaine Baker, 6 May 2018

Bibliography: Works by G. Blaine Baker, 1979–2019

Tracings of Gerald Le Dain's Life in the Law, with R. Janda, 3rd ed. Montreal: McGill-Queen's University Press, 2019.

"Musings and Silences of Chief Justice William Osgoode: Digest Marginalia about the Reception of Imperial Law." *Osgoode Hall Law Journal* 54, no. 3 (2017).

"Testamentary Archeology in Late-Victorian Ontario: William Martin's Little, Posthumous Legal System." *Canadian Journal of Law and Society* 30: no. 3 (2015): 345–64.

"Character-Building at Multiple Sites of Justice: Administration and Teaching as Texts, Scholarship as Ethical and Political Action." In *The Unbounded Level of the Mind: Rod Macdonald's Legal Imagination,* edited by 214–22. Montreal: McGill-Queen's University Press, 2015.

"Quebec and the Canadas, 1760–1867: A Legal Historiography." In *Essays in the History of Canadian Law: Quebec and the Canadas*, edited by 3–95.Toronto: University of Toronto Press, 2013.

Essays in the History of Canadian Law: Quebec and the Canadas, with D. Fyson, eds. Toronto: University of Toronto Press, 2013.

"Popularizing the Rule of Law: Sheldon Amos and the International Scientific Series, 1874 to 1909." *Journal of Legal History* 33, no. 1 (2012):151–84.

"Story'd Paradigms for the Nineteenth-Century Display of Anglo-American Legal Doctrine." In *Law Books in Action: Essays on the Anglo-American Legal Treatise*, edited by 2–107. Oxford: Hart Publishing, 2012.

"Strategic Benthamism: Rehabilitating United Canada's Bar Through Criminal Law Codification, 1847–54." In *Essays in the History of*

Canadian Law: A Tribute to Peter N. Oliver, edited by 257–319. Toronto: University of Toronto Press, 2008.

"Introduction: Canadian Legal Thought." In *A History of Canadian Legal Thought: Collected Essays*, edited by 3–29.Toronto: University of Toronto Press, 2006.

A History of Canadian Legal Thought: Collected Essays, with J. Phillips, eds. Toronto: University of Toronto Press, 2006.

"Willis on Cultured Public Authorities." *University of Toronto Law Journal* 55, no. 3 (2005): 335–60.

"R.C.B. Risk's Canadian Legal History." In *Essays in the History of Canadian Law: In Honour of R.C.B. Risk*, edited by 17–60. Toronto: University of Toronto Press, 1999.

Essays in the History of Canadian Law: In Honour of R.C.B. Risk, with J. Phillips, eds. Toronto: University of Toronto Press, 1999.

"Ordering the Urban Canadian Law Office and its Entrepreneurial Hinterland, 1825 to 1875." *University of Toronto Law Journal* 48, no. 2 (1998): 175–251.

A Noble Roster: One Hundred and Fifty Years of Law at McGill, with I. Pilarczyk (editorial committee: J.E.C. Brierley, N. Kasirer, and S.J. Toope). Montreal: Gelfand-Martineau, 1999.

"Public Frivolity and Patrician Confidence: Lower Canada's 'Brothers-in-Law,' 1827 to 1833." In *Mélanges Paul-André Crépeau*, edited by 43–73. Cowansville, PQ: Blais, 1997.

"William Proudfoot" and "William Albert Reeve." In *Dictionary of Canadian Biography*, vols. 12 and 13, edited by 848–50; 887–8. Toronto: University of Toronto Press, 1990–1994.

"The Province of Post-Confederation Rights" *University of Toronto Law Journal* 45 (1994): 77–100.

"Civil Law – The French Colonies" and "Legal Professions – The French Colonies." In *Encyclopedia of the North American Colonies*, vol. 1, edited by J.E. Cooke, 430–2, 443–5. New York: Charles Scribner, 1993.

"Interstate Choice of Law and Early-American Constitutional Nationalism." *McGill Law Journal* 38, no.2 (1993): 454–511.

"Law Practice and Statecraft in Mid-Nineteenth-Century Montreal: The Torrance-Morris Firm, 1848 to 1868." In *Beyond the Law: Lawyers and Business in Canada 1830 to 1930*, edited by 45–91. Toronto: Butterworth, 1990.

Review of P. Baskerville. *The Bank of Upper Canada: A Collection of Documents*. Ottawa: Champlain Society, 1987. *Ontario History* 81 (1989): 69–75.

"So Elegant a Web: Providential Order and the Rule of Secular Law in Early-Nineteenth-Century Upper Canada." *University of Toronto Law Journal* 38, no. 2 (1988): 184–205.

Sources in the Law Library of McGill University for a Reconstruction of the Legal Culture of Quebec, 1760-1890, with K.E. Fisher, V. Masciotra, and B. Young. Montreal: McGill University and Montreal History Project, 1987.

"The Juvenile Advocate Society, 1821 to 1826: Self-Proclaimed Schoolroom for Upper Canada's Governing Class." *Historical Papers of the Canadian Historical Association* 20 (1985): 74–101.

"The Reconstitution of Upper Canadian Legal Thought in the Late-Victorian Empire." *Law and History Review* 3, no. 2 (1985): 219–92.

"Bibliographic Reconstruction of Canadian Legal Culture." *Bibliographical Society of Canada* 25 (1985): 11–20.

"William Warren Baldwin," "Jonathan Belcher," "William Hume Blake," "William Henry Draper," "Joseph-Francois Lafitau," "Augustus Henry Frazer Lefroy," "Hellen Emma MacGill," "David Mills," "Sir William Mulock," "Emily Cowan Murphy," "William Smith," "Louis-Guillaume Verrier," "Richard Chapman Weldon," and "Solomon White." In *Biographical Dictionary of the Common Law*, edited by A.W.B. Simpson, 30–1, 40–1, 61–2, 156, 300, 310, 334, 377–8, 479, 480, 519–20, 527, 530. London: Butterworth, 1984.

"Legal Education in Upper Canada, 1785 to 1889: The Law Society as Educator." In *Essays in the History of Canadian Law*, edited by D.H. Flaherty, 49–142. Toronto: University of Toronto Press, 1983.

"Legal Identity: From Maine and Durkheim to Graveson, Tribe, and Vining." *Western Ontario Law Review* 19, no. 2 (1981): 307–41.

Reports of Family Law Reprint Series (1824–1970), with J.G. McLeod and G.P. Rodrigues, eds. Toronto: Carswell, 1979–81.

Contracts in the Family, with J.G. McLeod. Toronto: Butterworth, 1979.

Contributors

CONSTANCE BACKHOUSE is a member of the Faculty of Law at the University of Ottawa. She has published a number of prize winning books: *Petticoats and Prejudice: Women and Law in Nineteenth-Century Canada*; *Challenging Times: The Women's Movement in Canada and the United States; Colour-Coded: A Legal History of Racism in Canada, 1900–1950*; *The Heiress vs the Establishment: Mrs Campbell's Campaign for Legal Justice*; *Carnal Crimes: Sexual Assault Law in Canada, 1900–1975*. Her latest books, *Claire L'Heureux-Dubé: A Life,* and *Two Firsts: Bertha Wilson and Claire L'Heureux-Dubé at the Supreme Court of Canada* were released in 2017 and 2019. She was made a fellow of the Royal Society of Canada in 2004 and named to the Order of Canada in 2008.

TOM COLLINS is an associate at Gowling WLG in Toronto. In 2020, he graduated from the Faculty of Law, University of Toronto, and he received the Patricia Julia Myhal Scholarship for Excellence in Legal Writing. Tom is the author of "Common Intentions: The Standard of Review for Standard Form Wills," *Estates Trusts & Pensions Journal*, 39:2 (2020).

ANGELA FERNANDEZ is Professor of Law at the Faculty of Law, University of Toronto, where she is cross-appointed to the Department of History. Her scholarly works include co-editing a collection of essays on the legal treatise, *Law Books in Action: Essays on the Anglo-American Legal Treatise* (Oxford: Hart Publishing, 2012) and her book about the fox in the (in)famous property law case *Pierson v. Post, The Hunt for the Fox: Law and Professionalization in American Legal Culture* (Cambridge: Cambridge University Press, 2018). She is a regular contributor to the legal history section of *Jotwell* (the Journal of Things We Like (Lots)) and is Associate Editor of Book Reviews (Americas) for *Law and History Review*. She is also a fellow with the Oxford Centre for Animal Ethics and has been a member of BASAN (the Brooks Animal Studies Academic Network) with the Brooks Institute for Animal Rights, Law and Policy since 2019.

KATHY FISHER is a Montreal-born, Edmonton-based documentarian and multidisciplinary artist. A graduate of the Faculty of Law, McGill University and member of the Barreau du Québec and Law Society of Alberta (now retired), she practised predominantly as a research lawyer and taught legal research. An oral historian for over four decades, Fisher interviewed legal scholars, judges, and senior lawyers, specializing in legal and women's history. She currently works in film providing visual and archival research for documentary productions, including her own. A performance poet, she regularly produces words and music events. Her poems have been published in traditional and on-line literary journals. Current projects include a poetry manuscript, *below the belt,* and a WWI documentary on her pilot grandfather, *Strange Friend*.

PHILIP GIRARD is Professor of Law at Osgoode Hall Law School, York University, Toronto. His scholarly works include *Bora Laskin: Bringing Law to Life* (2005), *Lawyers and Legal Culture in British North America: Beamish Murdoch of Halifax* (2011), and (with Jim Phillips and R. Blake Brown) *A History of Law in Canada, Volume One: Beginnings to 1866* (2018), and (with Jim Phillips) *A History of Law in Canada, Volume Two: Law for A New Dominion, 1867–1914* (2022). Professor Girard is Associate Editor of the Osgoode Society for Canadian Legal History, was named an honorary fellow of the American Society for Legal History in 2011, and was elected a fellow of the Royal Society of Canada in 2021.

RICHARD JANDA is Associate Professor at the Faculty of Law, McGill University and an associate member of the Bieler School of Environment. He is currently leading the Myko project (www.myko.org), which explores how to connect everyone to the environmental footprint of their choices in real time. He has written, among other things, on corporate social responsibility, digital law, and theories of justice. He is a member of International Observatory on the Societal Impacts of AI and Digital Technology, a research collaborator at the Centre de recherche en droit publique and a former member of the Quebec Commission des droits de la personne et droits de la jeunesse.

NICHOLAS KASIRER is a research scholar at the Paul-André Crépeau Centre for Private and Comparative Law, McGill University and Justice of the Supreme Court of Canada. He was James McGill Professor at McGill where he taught for over twenty years and was Dean of the Faculty of

Law from 2003 to 2009, and served on the Quebec Court of Appeals from 2009 to 2019.

JIM PHILLIPS is Professor of Law at the University of Toronto, cross-appointed to the Department of History and the Centre for Criminology and Socio-Legal Studies. He is also Editor-in-Chief of the Osgoode Society for Canadian Legal History. He was formerly law clerk to Madam Justice Bertha Wilson at the Supreme Court of Canada, and in 2013 won the Mundell Medal awarded by the attorney general for Ontario for "a distinguished contribution to law and letters." He teaches property, trusts, and legal history. He has co-edited four volumes of the Osgoode Society for Canadian Legal History and University of Toronto Press's *Essays in the History of Canadian Law* and, with Philip Girard, a history of Canada's oldest surviving superior common law court, *The Supreme Court of Nova Scotia 1754–2004: From Imperial Bastion to Provincial Oracle*. He is also the author, with Rosemary Gartner, of *Murdering Holiness: The Trials of Franz Creffield and George Mitchell* (UBC Press, 2003). He has published over sixty articles and book chapters on British imperial history and eighteenth-century India, on property and charities law, US legal history, and, principally, Canadian legal history. He is currently writing, with Philip Girard and Blake Brown, a history of law in Canada. The first of two volumes of this history, *A History of Law in Canada, Volume One: Beginnings to 1866*, was published in 2018. The second, *A History of Law in Canada, Volume Two: Law for a New Dominion, 1867–1914*, with Philip Girard, will be published in 2022.

IAN C. PILARCZYK is a lecturer at Tufts University, Visiting Seminar Coach at NuVu Cambridge, and a small business owner in Boston. He was formerly a lecturer, director of Executive, Online, and Special Initiatives, and founding director of the Executive LLM in International Business Law and the Legal English Certificate Program at Boston University School of Law. Prior to that he was the founding associate director of the Fletcher School of Law and Diplomacy's LLM in International Law.

TINA PIPER is Associate Professor at the Faculty of Law, McGill University where she has taught since 2006. She teaches and researches in the areas of intellectual property law, property law, and Canadian legal history. Most recently she co-authored *Putting Intellectual Property in its Place: Creative Labour and the Everyday* (Oxford University Press), with Laura Murray and Kirsty Robertson, that considered the legal history of early patent law and technology practices in Canada. She is currently working on a project concerned with the decolonization of property law stemming from her experiences teaching property law from three traditions (common law, civil law and Indigenous legal traditions).

MARY ANNE POUTANEN teaches interdisciplinary studies at McGill University and history at Concordia University. She is a member of the Montreal History Group and of the Centre for Interdisciplinary Research on Montreal at McGill. She is also the author of the award-winning book, *Beyond Brutal Passions: Prostitution in Early Nineteenth-Century Montreal*. Her current research focuses on women's work in hospitality in mid-nineteenth-century Montreal.

ERIC H. REITER is Professor of History at Concordia University, where he teaches legal history and law and society. He is also a retired member of the Barreau du Québec, and a member of the Centre interuniversitaire d'études québécoises. His research focuses on the history of Quebec civil law in the nineteenth and twentieth centuries. His book *Wounded Feelings: Litigating Emotions in Quebec, 1870–1950* (Osgoode Society and University of Toronto Press, 2019), was awarded the Canadian Historical Association's Best Scholarly Book in Canadian History Prize for 2020.

DAVID SANDOMIERSKI is Assistant Professor at the Faculty of Law, Western University, Ontario. He holds an SJD from the Faculty of Law, University of Toronto where his dissertation received the Governor General's Academic Gold Medal. Sandomierski has received the Peter Oliver Prize from the Osgoode Society for Canadian Legal History, as well as the Scholarship of Teaching and Learning Award from the Canadian Association of Law Teachers. He is a founding co-director of the Collaborative Research Network on Legal Education of the US Law and Society Association. His recent book, *Aspiration and Reality in Legal Education* (University of Toronto Press, 2020) explores the relationship between realist and formalist ideas in Canadian law teaching.

CORY VERBAUWHEDE is a lawyer and a doctoral student in history at Université du Québec à Montréal. He is a member of the Centre d'histoire des régulations sociales. He teaches health and social services law at the École nationale d'administration publique.

BRIAN YOUNG is James McGill Professor (Emeritus) of Canadian History at McGill University. He is author of *The Politics of Codification: The Lower Canadian Civil Code of 1866* and his most recent book is *Patrician Families and the Making of Quebec: The Taschereaus and the McCords* (2014). His broad interest in Quebec legal history and culture includes biographies of influential legal personalities like George-Etienne Cartier and the study of canon law as a neglected source of legal authority.

Index

Note: Page numbers in *italics* denote figures, and the following terms have been abbreviated when they appear in sub-headings:

The Consolidated Statutes for Lower Canada (CSLC)
The Consolidated Statutes for Upper Canada (CSUP)
The Consolidated Statutes of Canada Being the Public General Statutes Which Apply to the Whole Province (CS Canada)